TREES AND SHRUBS OF MINNESOTA

TREES AND SHRUBS OF MINNESOTA

WELBY R. SMITH

UNIVERSITY OF MINNESOTA PRESS

Minneapolis

London

The University of Minnesota Press gratefully acknowledges financial assistance provided for this book by the Minnesota Department of Natural Resources.

Published by the University of Minnesota Press
111 Third Avenue South, Suite 290
Minneapolis, MN 55401-2520
http://www.upress.umn.edu

Library of Congress Cataloging-in-Publication Data

Smith, Welby R. (Welby Richmond)
    Trees and shrubs of Minnesota : the complete guide to species identification / Welby R. Smith.
        p. cm.
    Includes bibliographical references and index.
    ISBN 978-0-8166-4065-2 (hc : alk. paper)
    ISBN 978-0-8166-4066-9 (pb : alk. paper)
    1. Trees—Minnesota—Identification. 2. Shrubs—Minnesota—Identification. I. Title.
    QK168.S65 2008
    582.1609776—dc22

                                                                2008014329

Printed in Canada on acid-free paper

The University of Minnesota is an equal-opportunity educator and employer.

22 21 20 19 18 17 16   10 9 8 7 6 5 4 3

Contents

Acknowledgments

Thanks are owed to many people who assisted during the preparation of this book. First among them are scientists of the Department of Natural Resources (DNR) who freely shared their knowledge and data, including Karen Myhre, Chel Anderson, Bruce Carlson, Lynden Gerdes, Fred Harris, Mike Lee, Tim Whitfeld, Robert Dana, Nancy Sather, Erika Rowe, and Roger Lake. I also thank Dick Oehlenschlager of the Science Museum of Minnesota, St. Paul.

Technical assistance was provided by Shannon Flynn, whose mastery of Geographic Information Systems (GIS) is responsible for the maps in the introduction to this book. Rolf Dahle designed the database and mapping software that created the Minnesota distribution maps that accompany each species account, and Hal Watson provided me with the technical capabilities to create digital files of the North American range maps. Morgan Graham, Norman Aaseng, and Al Epp also contributed to the production of the maps. Vera Wong prepared all of the line drawings.

Among the many taxonomic specialists who were consulted, a few provided major assistance. This includes Dr. Mark P. Widrlechner of the North Central Regional Plant Introduction Station, Iowa State University, Ames, Iowa. Mark is one of the few modern scientists to take on the taxonomy of blackberries (*Rubus*), and he does so with clear thinking and a critical eye. He examined all the blackberry specimens that I collected and served as the final authority on the taxonomy of the genus *Rubus* used in this book. He also supplied valuable information on cultivated species in a wide variety of genera.

Dr. James B. Phipps, University of Western Ontario, London, Ontario, who by all accounts is the world's leading authority on hawthorns (*Crataegus*), traveled with me throughout Minnesota in the pursuit of hawthorns, and examined and provided insight into the identification of about six hundred hawthorn specimens that I collected. These specimens and Jim's annotations form the basis of the hawthorn treatment in this book.

Dr. George W. Argus, Merrickville, Ontario, the preeminent authority on willows (*Salix*), patiently guided me through my study of the willows of Minnesota and conscientiously examined more than seven hundred willow specimens that I collected during field trips throughout the state. George never hesitated to share his knowledge and data.

Financial assistance was generously provided by the Elmer L. and Eleanor J. Andersen Foundation and the James Ford Bell Foundation.

Others who provided assistance include Esther McLaughlin (who read the entire manuscript and provided critical comments), Jan Wolff, Tom Kroll Bonita Eliason, Carmen Converse, Adele Smith, and Deborah Lewis.

Preface

Trees and Shrubs of Minnesota was created to serve a broad purpose and appeal to a broad audience, particularly those seeking information on the identification, distribution, and natural history of Minnesota's trees and shrubs (including woody vines). Although these are technical subjects, special training, for the most part, is not needed to find the answers.

This book is limited to woody species that are native or naturalized in Minnesota. Within the context of this book, the term *native* is defined as a species that was present as a reproducing population within the geographic boundaries of what is now Minnesota at the onset of continuous settlement by European-American settlers (c. 1850). *Naturalized* is defined as a species not native to Minnesota but currently (c. 2000) established and reproducing in natural or seminatural habitats without the direct aid of humans. Those species occurring only as a direct result of cultivation, no matter how hardy or persistent, are excluded. The choice of which species to include and which to exclude is sometimes a matter of judgment, for which the author accepts full responsibility.

Whether a particular species is categorized as a tree or a shrub is largely academic, and debating the subject can waste a good deal of time. However, using the somewhat arbitrary definitions found in the glossary, a brief summary shows there are 92 native tree species in Minnesota (of these, 37 may only reach the stature of a shrub under certain circumstances), 131 species of native shrubs (which excludes the 37 that can sometimes reach tree status), and 12 species of native woody vines. There are another 15 naturalized species, which include 9 trees, 5 shrubs, and 1 vine. This makes a total of 250 native and naturalized species.

Maps

The North American range maps that accompany each species were created primarily from published sources, mostly monographs and state floras. The state distribution maps are based entirely on herbarium specimens that have been collected by the author or seen and verified by the author or by a collaborator. In an effort to be as thorough as possible, every county in the state was visited repeatedly. Yet, without question, some species have been missed in nearly all of the counties.

Keys

The keys are strictly dichotomous, meaning that at each point two choices are offered. One choice should better describe the specimen in hand and will lead to another dichotomy and another choice. Taking a specimen successfully through the key will require patience, attention to fine detail, and a literal interpretation of the choices offered. Every effort has been made to create clear and unambiguous keys; unfortunately, not much can be done to make species in difficult genera easy to identify. This is especially true of blackberries (*Rubus*) and willows (*Salix* spp.).

Descriptions

The purpose of the descriptions is to describe the normal range of variability of each species as they exist in native populations in Minnesota. The data were taken directly from normal, mature individuals growing in native habitats in Minnesota. Be aware that populations of the same species growing in other states may differ somewhat. This is especially true of certain growth characteristics and phenology.

Natural History

Detailed natural history studies of trees and shrubs are relatively few, far fewer than might be thought. Where published studies have been found, they are cited in the text, but much of what is presented here is based on the author's experience and observations during 25 years as state botanist.

Names

Few topics elicit as much debate as the "correct" name for a tree. Botanists argue about the correct Latin name (for which there are rules and some hope for ultimate agreement); everyone else argues about the common name (for which there are no rules and very little hope for agreement). Latin names used in this book are furnished with synonyms where it was thought useful, but no attempt was made to account for all possible common names. As an example of the problems associated with common names, the small tree universally known as *Carpinus caroliniana* is called blue beech in Minnesota, hornbeam in New England, and ironwood in the Carolinas.

Photographs

The photographs were taken by the author using a 35mm Nikon camera, Kodachrome film, available light, and no post-processing. Although perhaps crude by modern digital standards the photos represent the authors best attempt to master 20th century technology.

Minnesota County Map

Introduction:
Trees and Shrubs in Minnesota

The Biotic Environment

The patterns of vegetation that existed in Minnesota at the time of settlement developed over thousands of years through the complex interactions of geological forces, climate, and fire. Although remnants of these presettlement patterns can still be seen today, they are no longer predominant; they have gradually been supplanted by the human-created landscape. However, these patterns are key to understanding why trees occur where they do.

Fortunately for Minnesotans, these patterns have been reconstructed in a map created by Francis J. Marschner (1882–1966) titled "The Original Vegetation of Minnesota" (Marschner 1974) (Map I.1). *Original vegetation* in this case means the vegetation that was present in Minnesota at the time settlers first arrived, as interpreted from the notes of the Public Land Survey (PLS) from the period 1847–1908. The map was created in 1930 but was not published until 1974.

The man who created the map is as intriguing as the map itself. Marschner, an Austrian immigrant, was a research assistant in the USDA Bureau of Agricultural Economics in Washington, DC. He was trained neither as an ecologist nor a cartographer and reportedly never set foot in Minnesota (Brady 2003).

It is even unclear why Marschner created the map. Whatever his reasons, the map has found many uses. Foremost among these is its role as a benchmark by which to measure changes in the vegetation that have resulted from human settlement. These changes can be documented at any scale, from statewide to a single acre (1/2 hectare).

Another use has been found by vegetation egologists who, taking these patterns as a starting point, have created an ecological land classification for Minnesota (Map I.2). The classification is hierarchical. The highest level is the province, which is defined using major climate zones, native vegetation, and plant biomes such as prairies, deciduous forests, and mixed deciduous/coniferous forests. There are four provinces in Minnesota.

The provinces are subdivided into 10 sections. Sections are defined by the origin of glacial deposits, regional elevation, distribution of plants, and regional climate. The sections are subdivided into 26 subsections, which are defined by glacial deposition processes, surface bedrock formations, local climate, topographical relief, and the distribution of plants, especially trees.

The Abiotic Environment

Climate

Because of its location in the interior of a large landmass, Minnesota has what is called a continental climate, which is characterized by cold winters with frequent incursions of cold air from the Arctic, and warm summers with periods of prolonged heat caused by warm air pushing northward from the south. Mean annual temperature ranges from 36°F (2°C) in the far north to 49°F (8°C) in the south (Map I.3), and historic temperature extremes range from 114°F (45°C) to −60°F (−51°C). Few places on the continent experience a greater range of temperature extremes.

The soil normally freezes about the first week in December and thaws about mid-April. The average maximum depth of frost ranges from 3–4 feet (92–123 cm) in the south, and from 5–6 feet (153–185 cm) in the north. In forested regions the depth is usually much less.

Mean annual precipitation is 34 inches (86 cm) in extreme southeast Minnesota, gradually decreasing to 19 inches (48 cm) in the northwest (Map I.4). Approximately two-thirds of the annual precipitation falls as rain during the five-month

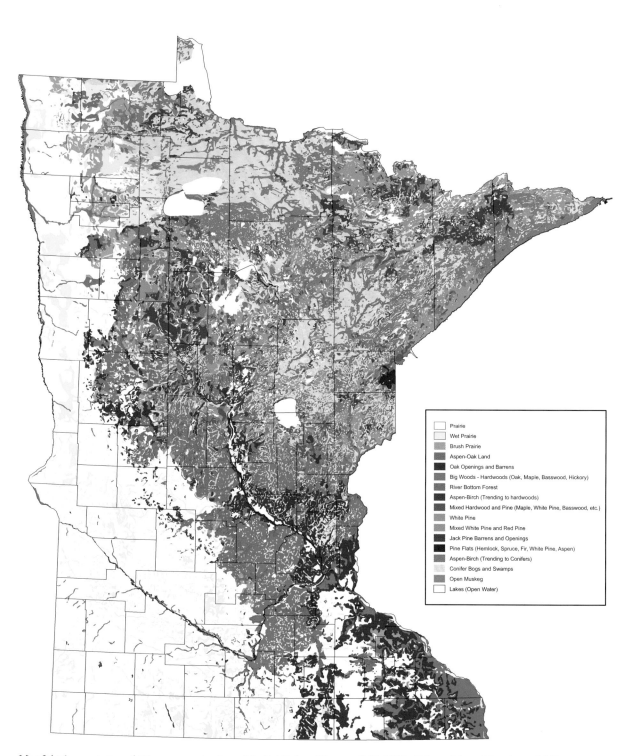

	Prairie
	Wet Prairie
	Brush Prairie
	Aspen-Oak Land
	Oak Openings and Barrens
	Big Woods - Hardwoods (Oak, Maple, Basswood, Hickory)
	River Bottom Forest
	Aspen-Birch (Trending to hardwoods)
	Mixed Hardwood and Pine (Maple, White Pine, Basswood, etc.)
	White Pine
	Mixed White Pine and Red Pine
	Jack Pine Barrens and Openings
	Pine Flats (Hemlock, Spruce, Fir, White Pine, Aspen)
	Aspen-Birch (Trending to Conifers)
	Conifer Bogs and Swamps
	Open Muskeg
	Lakes (Open Water)

Map I.1 The vegetation of Minnesota at the time of the Public Land Survey, 1847–1907. (Adapted from Marschner, 1974)

Upper Three Levels of ECS for Minnesota

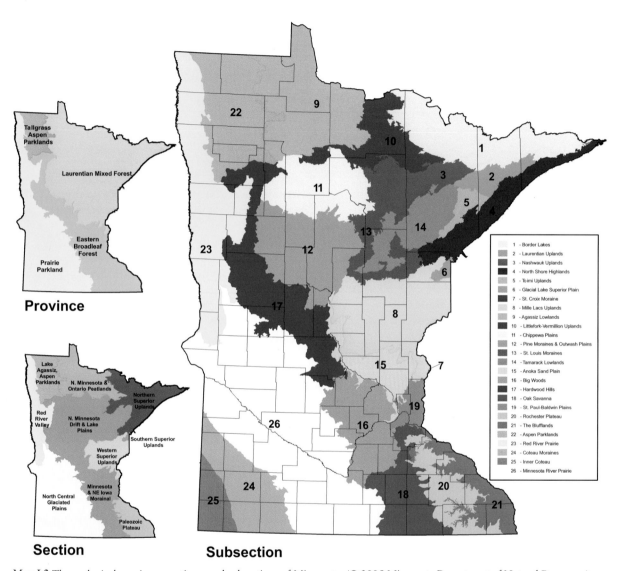

Province

Tallgrass Aspen Parklands

Laurentian Mixed Forest

Eastern Broadleaf Forest

Prairie Parkland

Section

Lake Agassiz, Aspen Parklands

N. Minnesota & Ontario Peatlands

Northern Superior Uplands

Red River Valley

N. Minnesota Drift & Lake Plains

Southern Superior Uplands

Western Superior Uplands

North Central Glaciated Plains

Minnesota & NE Iowa Moranial

Paleozoic Plateau

Subsection

1 - Border Lakes
2 - Laurentian Uplands
3 - Nashwauk Uplands
4 - North Shore Highlands
5 - Toimi Uplands
6 - Glacial Lake Superior Plain
7 - St. Croix Moraine
8 - Mille Lacs Uplands
9 - Agassiz Lowlands
10 - Littlefork-Vermillion Uplands
11 - Chippewa Plains
12 - Pine Moraines & Outwash Plains
13 - St. Louis Moraines
14 - Tamarack Lowlands
15 - Anoka Sand Plain
16 - Big Woods
17 - Hardwood Hills
18 - Oak Savanna
19 - St. Paul-Baldwin Plains
20 - Rochester Plateau
21 - The Bluflands
22 - Aspen Parklands
23 - Red River Prairie
24 - Coteau Moraines
25 - Inner Coteau
26 - Minnesota River Prairie

Map I.2 The ecological provinces, sections, and subsections of Minnesota. (© 2005 Minnesota Department of Natural Resources)

growing season from May to September. Historically, conditions of severe drought have occurred, on average once every 10 years in southwest and west central Minnesota, once every 25 years in eastern Minnesota, and once every 50 years in northeast Minnesota.

Seasonal snowfall averages near 70 inches (178 cm) in the highlands along the north shore of Lake Superior in northeast Minnesota, and gradually decreases to 40 inches (102 cm) along the southern and western borders of the state. Snow cover of 1 inch (2.5 cm) or more ranges on average from 85 days in the south to 140 days in the north. Hail, thunderstorms, tornadoes, floods, freezing rain, and ice storms complete the "Minnesota experience."

Soils

The term *soil* as used in this book is broadly defined as any solid material in which plants root. At the risk of oversimplifying an important topic,

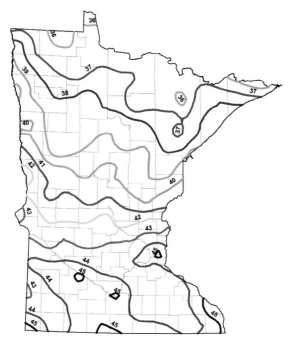

Map I.3 Mean annual temperature from 1961–1990. (Minnesota Department of Natural Resources, State Climatology Office)

dead leaves and twigs that fall to the soil surface, and a fraction within the soil that is derived from the partially decomposed remains of dead roots and soil organisms. The soil organic material does not contribute directly to plant nutrition until it undergoes a process of "mineralization" where, through a long process of decomposition, the mineral elements and molecules are released to the soil and become available to the plants again. Mineralization is especially critical for potassium and phosphorus, which are important plant nutrients and often in short supply in soils with high organic content. Beyond the role as an intermediate step in the cycling of plant nutrients, soil organic matter is essential to maintaining the whole soil environment and is one of the most important aspects of "soil fertility."

When a soil is composed entirely of organic material, it is called peat. Peat develops in wet areas where the decomposition of organic matter is slower than the rate of deposition so that peat accumulates over time. In peat, the process of mineralization happens very slowly; that is, nearly all of the minerals are tied up in organic compounds and not available as plant nutrients,

soils can be said to consist of two components: an organic component and an inorganic component. The inorganic component is composed of various minerals derived from weathering of the parent material (rock). This weathering is taking place all the time, yet most of the inorganic material found in Minnesota soils is ancient, and it was transported to where it is now by wind, water, or glaciers.

These mineral particles vary in size starting with gravel, the largest, and decreasing in size through sand, silt, and clay. The different sizes have different properties. The larger particles are primarily silica and are essentially inert. The smaller particles, especially the clay, are more variable in their mineral composition and are chemically very active. This is important because all plant nutrients are absorbed through the roots as mineral ions, which come primarily from the surface of clay particles. Soils that contain a mixture of different particle sizes are called loams (Map I.5). Loams are glacial tills, meaning that they were carried to where they are by the action of glaciers. They are considered the most fertile soils.

The organic component of soil includes a layer on top of the soil, called humus, that is derived from

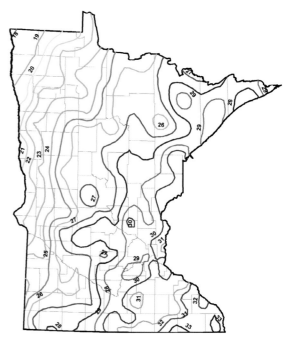

Map I.4 Mean annual precipitation from 1961–1990. (Minnesota Department of Natural Resources, State Climatology Office)

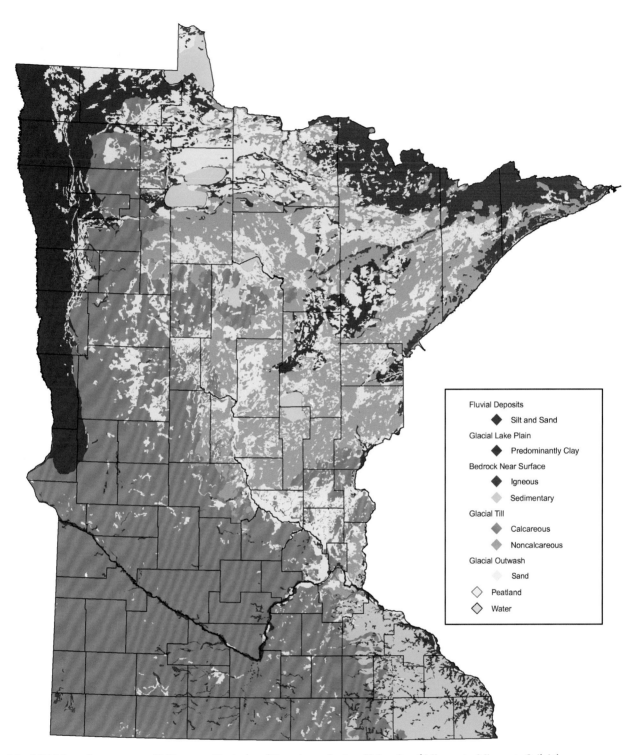

Map I.5 Major substrate types of Minnesota. (Agricultural Experiment Station, University of Minnesota, Minnesota Soil Atlas Project, 1969–1981)

Fluvial Deposits
◆ Silt and Sand
Glacial Lake Plain
◆ Predominantly Clay
Bedrock Near Surface
◆ Igneous
◇ Sedimentary
Glacial Till
◆ Calcareous
◆ Noncalcareous
Glacial Outwash
◇ Sand
◇ Peatland
◇ Water

which presents obvious problems for plants growing in this environment.

Peat can exist in several stages of decomposition; the more decomposed the peat, the greater the availability of nutrients. Fibric peat is the first stage; it still retains identifiable plant remains. When decomposition has progressed to the point where no identifiable plant parts remain, it is called hemic peat. In the ultimate stage of decomposition the material is called sapric peat, or just muck; this is the final stage in mineralization.

Fire

Of all the natural forces that shaped patterns of the presettlement vegetation in Minnesota, wildfire is among the most important. Patterns of vegetation are shaped by the location of fires on the landscape and how often they recurred. Fires typically originated from lightning strikes, usually during dry electrical storms in drought years. We know that Native Americans deliberately set fires, and by some accounts these fires also contributed to the shaping of vegetation patterns.

There is ample evidence that fire, more than any other factor, is responsible for the natural development of prairies and forests in Minnesota (Heinselman 1973; McAndrews 1965). The evidence comes from historical reconstructions aided by notes from surveyors of the PLS era, cores taken from fire-scarred trees, charcoal strata found in soils, and pollen analysis of cores taken from lake sediments.

The precise effect of fire on vegetation is hard to predict, but in general if the average fire frequency is less than perhaps 8–10 years, trees do not have enough time to get established, and a prairie will develop. If the average frequency is any longer than 10 years, trees will take hold, and a "forest" of one type or another will develop, given the latitude, climate, and soils of Minnesota (Map I.6).

It is important to understand that forests in Minnesota have evolved with fire over millennia. During that time, they have become not only adapted to fire but in some cases actually dependent on fire. This idea of fire-dependent forests is central to the study of forest ecology, but it is not intuitive. Clearly, individual trees are not dependent on fire; in fact, they are usually killed by fire, but the forest, as a biotic community, survives. By most biological measures the forest survives

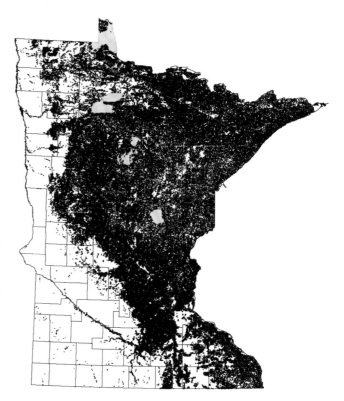

Map I.6 The distribution of all bearing trees recorded by the Public Land Survey, 1847–1907—a total of 352,259 records. This depicts a reasonable interpretation of the forest cover of Minnesota at the time of settlement.

even when everything aboveground has been killed. It has just returned to an early successional stage and begun a cycle of renewal. The condition of a forest following a fire is not much different than a forest emerging from winter; it is part of a cycle of renewal.

Fire-dependent Forests

Typically, forests that are dominated by early successional tree species such as pines (*Pinus* spp.), oaks (*Quercus* spp.), or aspens (*Populus* spp.) are fire-dependent, meaning that without fire the next generation of trees will be composed of different species. This happens because in most situations pines, oaks, and aspens cannot produce a second generation of trees on the site of the first generation. They may produce seeds, and those seeds may fall to the ground and even germinate beneath the parent tree, yet they will not survive to replace the aging parents because there is simply too little light beneath the canopy. They require a fire to kill the canopy trees, thereby allowing enough light for the progeny to survive. This is called a stand-replacing fire.

Without fire the seedlings of shade-tolerant species such as sugar maple (*Acer saccharum*), basswood (*Tilia americana*), and balsam fir (*Abies balsamea*) may get established. These species can survive in very low light and will eventually replace the current canopy species. This chain of events will bring the forest to the next, and perhaps ultimate, successional stage. So, strictly speaking, the forest itself is not dependent on fire, but the perpetuation of a particular successional stage is.

For fire-dependent forests in Minnesota, the period between intense, stand-replacing fire ranges from about 80–220 years (Minnesota Department of Natural Resources 2003). Jack pine (*Pinus banksiana*) woodlands and oak savannas have the shortest rotation time (80 years between stand-replacing fires), and forests of white pine (*Pinus strobus*) have perhaps the longest (195–220 years between stand-replacing fires).

Fire-sensitive Forests (Fire-excluded Forests)

Once a forest in Minnesota has been free from fire for a period of perhaps 400 years, it has reached the ultimate, or climax, stage. Maintaining the forest at this successional stage is dependent on *excluding* fire. Forests of this type are dominated by long-lived species that are typically shade tolerant; this enables them to continually replace themselves in the canopy without the need for fire to first remove the canopy trees. When a fire-excluded forest does burn (apparently inevitable under presettlement conditions), it will begin over again at the earliest stage.

Fire-excluded forests that are found in upland habitats are often dominated by sugar maple, basswood, American elm (*Ulmus americana*), or northern red oak (*Quercus rubra*). These are often called mesic forests because the soils are typically mesic (moist but not wet) and the minerals in the organic matter are continually recycled by gradual decomposition rather than by fire.

Fire-excluded forests, or more properly fire-excluded stages in forest succession, also occur in lowlands where the soil is wet. Examples include swamps dominated by northern white cedar (*Thuja occidentalis*), and floodplains dominated by plains

cottonwood (*Populus deltoides* subsp. *monilifera*) or silver maple (*Acer saccharinum*).

It is important to keep in mind that these scenarios have been pieced together from historical evidence. Nowhere in Minnesota is there an intact ecosystem still experiencing a natural fire regime. This means that the structure and composition of future forests will not be the result of fire but will be directly attributable to the activities of humans.

Patterns of Tree Distribution

The vegetation map, and knowledge of the major abiotic factors controlling the distribution of trees in Minnesota, provide some basis to address the distribution patterns of individual tree species. Four sources of large-scale data can be drawn upon for this task: herbarium specimens, the Public Land Survey (bearing tree data), the Gap Analysis Program, and Forest Inventory and Analysis. The first two provide a historical benchmark, and the last two a modern comparison. There are, however, unique challenges inherent in the undertaking.

Historical Data

Herbarium Specimens

A herbarium specimen is, at its essence, a pressed and dried plant, or portion of a plant, mounted on a sheet of paper accompanied by a label and organized and stored in some way for future reference (a herbarium is the place where the specimens are stored). Herbarium specimens are largely the product (and tool) of professional botanists and plant ecologists. They are usually collected to be used in taxonomic or morphological studies or sometimes to document the geographic distribution of species or the floristic composition of plant communities. In fact, herbarium specimens are the basic unit of data for all floristic studies, including this book.

Herbarium specimens of one type or another have been used for perhaps three centuries, a fact that illustrates one of the great values of such specimens: with proper care they last indefinitely, they can be studied and verified decades or even centuries after they were collected, and they accumulate over time to form an archive of plant knowledge. Far from being arcane artifacts of nineteenth-century botany (as they are sometimes portrayed in this era of molecular botany), they provide the only permanent, physical record of plant phenotype and distribution that can be directly verified at a later time.

Yet the use of herbarium specimens has limitations. The collecting, labeling, and processing of high-quality specimens are very laborious (but a noble contribution to science), so relatively few specimens can be collected even in a lifetime of dedicated fieldwork. Herbarium specimens are also expensive to store and curate, and few institutions are able to make the long-term commitment necessary to maintain an active research herbarium.

Given these difficulties, the large number of specimens in existence is truly astounding. As of 1990, Index Herbariorum (Holmgren et al. 1990) listed 2,639 herbaria in 147 countries, containing 272,800,926 plant specimens (and increasing at the rate of 3,543,675 specimens per year). About 22 percent, or 60,421,964 specimens, reside in 628 American herbaria, mostly supported by universities and colleges, and to a lesser extent by government land management agencies.

For the purpose of this book, only those specimens collected from wild populations in Minnesota are of use. The actual number of such specimens is impossible to determine. There is no central database of plant specimens or even much sharing of data between herbaria, and only now are individual herbaria starting to create databases of their own collections. Still, a figure of 175,000 specimens is probably a reasonable estimate. Most of the specimens reside in the University of Minnesota's herbarium in St. Paul, but others are scattered in herbaria throughout the Midwest and East. Given that there are about 2,000 species of wild plants in Minnesota (Ownbey and Morley 1991), an average of about 88 specimens per species seems realistic. For most species this is not enough to reveal fine patterns of distribution.

There are other limitations when using data from herbarium specimens to determine the distribution of tree species. Since many botanists actively seek out rare or unusual species or species that are of particular interest to them or to their research, certain species will be overrepresented in herbarium collections. Other species are cryptic and remain undercollected or overlooked entirely. Also, herbarium specimens generally cannot be used to detect trends over time because they are irregularly distributed over time.

So herbarium collections represent neither a systematic nor a random sampling of all the species in an area as large and ecologically diverse as Minnesota. In spite of this, herbarium specimens work extremely well to show geographic range over a large area, although they work less well to show distribution or relative abundance within a range.

Bearing Tree Data from the Public Land Survey (PLS)

A somewhat unexpected source of data comes from the Public Land Survey (PLS) records. The PLS was a legal land reference system employing a standard methodology to facilitate the sale of public property. It began with the passage of "An Ordinance for Ascertaining the Mode of Disposing of Lands in the Western Territory" by Congress on May 20, 1785. It was implemented in Ohio soon after, and eventually in all states from Ohio westward. The PLS reached Minnesota in 1847 and was essentially completed by 1908. The survey created a statewide grid by delineating a series of square townships 6 miles on a side. Each township was further divided into 36 equal "sections," with each section being one mile on a side. In this way, the entire state of Minnesota was covered by a grid of 1-mile-square sections. The grid existed not just on a map, it was actually marked on the ground. This survey was one of the most remarkable but largely unheralded accomplishments of the era, and a century later it was an absolute boon to ecologists, for reasons that will become clear when the methodology is explained.

At the corners of each section and at the midpoint of each line between the corners, a wooden corner post or cornerstone was erected. To facilitate the relocation of the corner if the post or stone were lost or moved, nearby trees were selected as "bearing trees." Typically, each corner had four bearing trees, with one located in each of the four contiguous sections. Each half-section corner (designating the corners of each quarter section) had two bearing trees, one in each of the two adjoining sections. For each bearing tree, the surveyor recorded its species, the diameter of the trunk, distance to the corner, and its azimuth, or "bearing," from the corner (hence the phrase "bearing tree"). Each surveyor was required to record these data in field notebooks, which are archived by the Minnesota Historical Society. This information is now contained within the Minnesota Department of Natural Resource's Natural Heritage Information System (NHIS) Bearing Tree Database. A summary of the database shows that there are 2,674 townships in Minnesota, with 249,466 section and quarter-section corners, with a corresponding total of 352,896 bearing trees (many corners fall in treeless prairies or marshes).

Although the bearing tree data were only intended to allow the section corners to be relocated, they in fact represent, as close as possible, a systematic sampling of the distribution and relative abundance of certain tree species as they existed before large-scale alteration of the landscape by humans. These data can be used by ecologists to roughly reconstruct the "original" forest cover of particular areas and to determine the distribution of individual tree species.

The bearing tree database may seem to be the sought-after gold mine of information, but there are hidden problems. Although the data were collected systematically and under a similar set of guidelines, their usefulness is severely limited by bias, mistakes, and in a few reputed cases, fraud. For example, bias was introduced at the beginning when the surveyors selected the individual bearing trees. It is generally thought that they tended to select medium-size individuals of long-lived species, but they were also likely to have selected those species that are common, abundant on the landscape, easy to identify, and well known to nonbotanists of the period. And some surveyors were almost certainly more conscientious or more skilled at tree identification than others. There is also considerable confusion over the common names of the trees used by various surveyors, and some names simply remain undecipherable because of illegible handwriting. And although the original data still exist, it is not possible to directly verify the accuracy of the data.

In spite of the biases and mistakes, statewide maps made from the data for a few tree species do appear to show authentic patterns (Maps I.7–I.22).

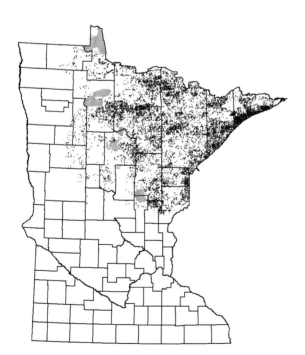

Map I.7 Balsam fir (*Abies balsamea*) bearing trees—13,773 records. (Public Land Survey, 1847–1907)

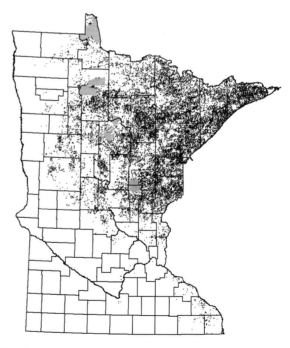

Map I.8 Paper birch (*Betula papyrifera*) bearing trees—26,797 records. (Public Land Survey, 1847–1907)

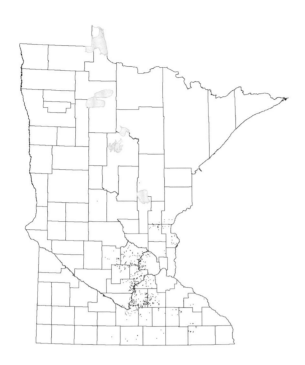

Map I.9 Bitternut hickory (*Carya cordiformis*) bearing trees—612 records. (Public Land Survey, 1847–1907)

Map I.10 Butternut (*Juglans cinerea*) bearing trees—521 records. (Public Land Survey, 1847–1907)

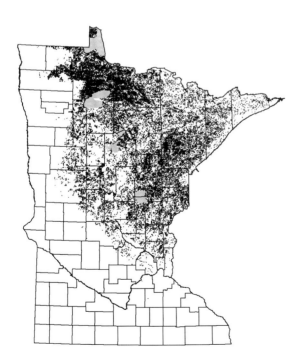

Map I.11 Tamarack (*Larix laricina*) bearing trees—59,614 records. (Public Land Survey, 1847–1907)

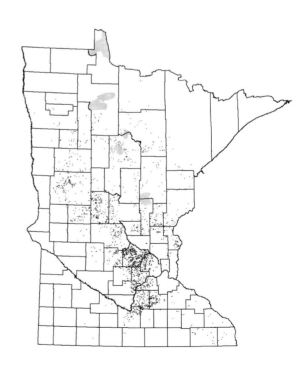

Map I.12 Ironwood (*Ostrya virginiana*) bearing trees—2,914 records. (Public Land Survey, 1847–1907)

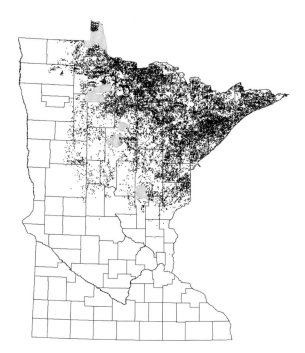

Map I.13 Spruce (*Picea glauca* and *P. mariana*) bearing trees—33,777 records. (Public Land Survey, 1847–1907)

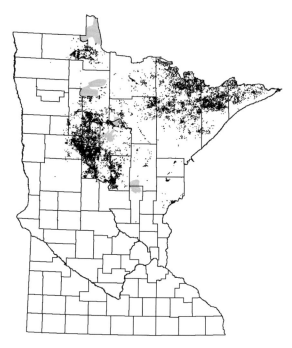

Map I.14 Jack pine (*Pinus banksiana*) bearing trees—19,199 records. (Public Land Survey, 1847–1907)

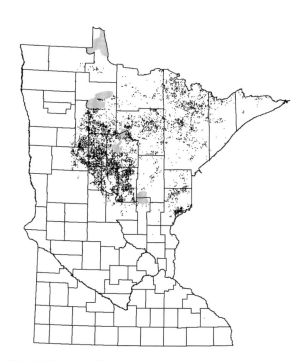

Map I.15 Red pine (*Pinus resinosa*) bearing trees—10,901 records. (Public Land Survey, 1847–1907)

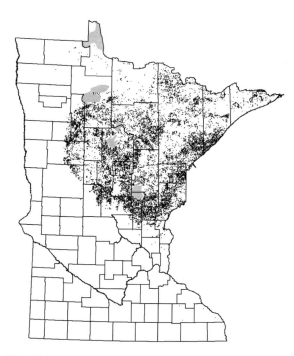

Map I.16 White pine (*Pinus strobus*) bearing trees—18,953 records. (Public Land Survey, 1847–1907)

Map I.17 Balsam poplar (*Populus balsamifera*) bearing trees—2,127 records. (Public Land Survey, 1847–1907)

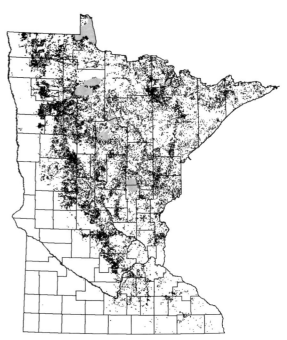

Map I.18 Trembling aspen (*Populus tremuloides*) bearing trees—45,636 records. (Public Land Survey, 1847–1907)

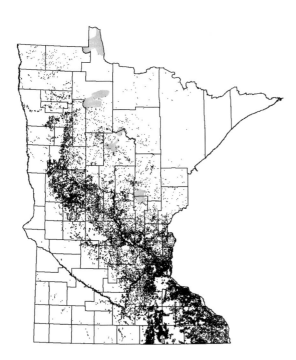

Map I.19 Bur oak (*Quercus macrocarpa*) bearing trees—44,191 records. (Public Land Survey, 1847–1907)

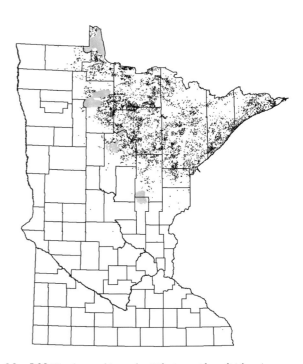

Map I.20 Northern white cedar (*Thuja occidentalis*) bearing trees—11,314 records. (Public Land Survey, 1847–1907)

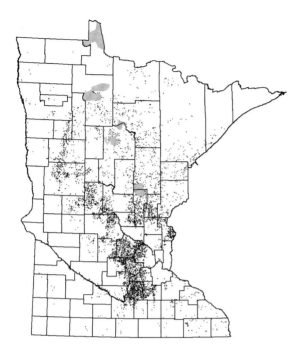

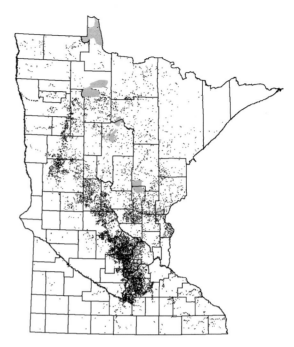

Map I.21 Basswood (*Tilia americana*) bearing trees—7,212 records. (Public Land Survey, 1847–1907)

Map I.22 American elm (*Ulmus americana*) bearing trees—13,378 records. (Public Land Survey, 1847–1907)

Contemporary Data

Piecing together presettlement tree distributions from historical data is fascinating but begs the question, how has the distribution of tree species and forests changed since presettlement times? Answering this question requires something resembling a current inventory of trees, by species, on a scale comparable to that of the PLS. Unfortunately, such an inventory does not exist and likely will never again be attempted.

Gap Analysis Program (GAP)

There is, however, a process developed by the U.S. Geological Survey and employed by the Minnesota Department of Natural Resources for evaluating vegetation by satellite imagery that holds some promise. The process, called the Gap Analysis Program (GAP), employs a method by which we can indirectly infer distribution patterns of certain tree species or certain "guilds" of similar species using satellite images taken from 1991–1993.

It must be emphasized that individual trees are not directly identifiable from satellite imagery; that capability does not yet exist. Instead, the "spectral

reflectance values" of 30 m × 30 m (about ¼ acre) plots of ground cover (vegetation) are interpreted to correspond to a particular tree species or group of similar-looking species. That is, certain colors and tones, and to a lesser extent spatial arrangement, of vegetation are assigned to certain species or groups of similar-looking species. Within this plot there may be several tree species, but the one species thought to be predominant is the one assigned to that unit. In every case the image must be interpreted based on a variety of characteristics. Although aerial photographs and inventory data were used to develop the spectral signature of the object, these interpretations were not always verified on the ground.

As it turns out, GAP seems to work adequately for determining the presence of tree cover, at least on a large scale (Map I.23), but not very well for identifying individual species or even groups of similar-looking species.

Forest Inventory and Analysis (FIA)

Another potential source of contemporary data comes from a project of the U.S. Department of

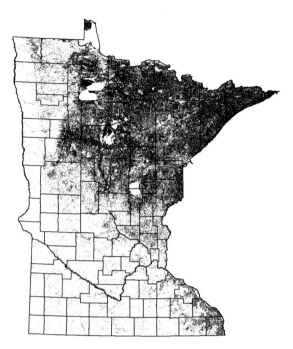

Map I.23 The current distribution of trees in Minnesota (c. 1991–1993) as interpreted from satellite imagery by the Gap Analysis Program.

Agriculture (USDA), Forest Service. It began as the Forest Survey Program in 1928 and is today known as Forest Inventory and Analysis (FIA). FIA is a national program that conducts and maintains comprehensive inventories of the forest resources in the United States. Its stated objective is to "determine the extent, condition and volume of timber growth and depletions of the Nation's forest land." In Minnesota, FIA is conducted by the Forest Service's North Central Research Station in St. Paul in association with the Minnesota Department of Natural Resources (Leatherberry et al. 1995).

The method used by FIA is to collect data from randomly selected permanent plots to determine current forest area, timber volume, tree growth, tree mortality, forest health, ownership classifications, and current land uses. Although the project generates large amounts of data, they are intended for purposes of timber management and have little direct application in floristic or ecological studies. For example, no distinction is made between native stands of trees and tree plantations, and critical distinctions between similar species are not consistently made.

Changes since Euro-American Settlement

Using data from Marschner's presettlement vegetation map as a historical benchmark, and using FIA plot data to estimate present conditions, we can make a useful assessment of changes in tree cover over time. The area of Minnesota is about 68 million acres, of which about 31.6 million acres, or 46 percent, was forested at the time large-scale Euro-American settlement began (see Map I.6). The remainder was prairie or brushland (40 percent), nonforested wetlands (10 percent), and open water (4 percent).

About 150 years later (2000), approximately 16.5 million acres, or 24 percent, of the land was covered by forest or woodlands of one type or another (Haugen and Mielke 2002). These figures indicate that nearly half of the original forests have been lost as a result of human settlement. Generally, the comparison shows that large tracts of unfragmented forest remain only in the northeast (see Map I.23), while the lands with better soils have been converted to agricultural uses, and those close to centers of commerce have been converted to urban and suburban uses.

This situation alone would be cause for concern, but a closer examination reveals an even greater problem. Most of the forests that survived have been degraded to the extent that they no longer bear a close resemblance to what they looked like before settlement. In other words, there have been fundamental changes in the nature of the surviving forests.

These changes have resulted primarily from logging and silvicultural practices and can be seen most easily in the structure and composition of surviving forests. For example, there has been a pronounced shift in the age structure of tree populations toward younger trees as the mature trees have been removed by logging. Also, there has been a reduction in diversity of tree species as certain species have been (and continue to be) selectively removed, either to be sold or to make room for more commercially valuable tree species. This leaves a smaller number of tree species left to grow in their place. In some cases this process is taken one step further: the complete conversion of sites from one dominant tree type to another, as from hardwood to conifer, for the purpose of hoped-for economic gains by the timber industry.

Other sources of degradation come from grazing of domestic livestock, noncompatible recreational use, the intentional or incidental exposure to herbicides, the invasion of nonnative species, alteration of drainage patterns, and the suppression of natural ecosystem processes such as fire, flooding, and erosion.

It is easy to demonstrate the effect these ecosystem changes have had at the species level. These are unintended effects that were not anticipated but are still the result of our conscious activities. Examples include the near total collapse of reproduction in populations of white pine (*Pinus strobus*) and northern white cedar (*Thuja occidentalis*), the vulnerability of elm (*Ulmus* spp.) and butternut (*Juglans cinerea*) populations to devastating waves of disease, the rapid disappearance of tamarack (*Larix laricina*) from upland habitats, the decline and near disappearance of savanna species, the disintegration of the symbiotic relationship between animals and plants, such as may have existed between bison and silver buffaloberry, and the disruptive effect of the nonnative common buckthorn (*Rhamnus cathartica*) on oak reproduction.

From an ecological perspective, these changes in the structure, composition, and function of the surviving forest communities are just as significant as the changes in acreage or geographic extent of the forests. This is because the changes have reduced the capacity of the remaining forests to perform certain important ecosystem functions. All this leads to impoverished forests that may not be able to provide the ecosystem services that people have come to depend on. In some ways, the continuing presence of trees and forests masks the real impact that these factors have on the forest ecosystem.

Key to Genera of Woody Plants in Minnesota

1. Leaves needlelike or scalelike, ≤ 3 mm wide.
    2. Leaves scalelike.
        3. A dwarf shrub with prostrate branches no more than 30 cm long and 3 mm in diameter; leaves and branchlets densely hairy; flowers with bright yellow petals . . . . *Hudsonia*
        3. An upright tree, or if a prostrate shrub (*Juniperus horizontalis*) branches often several meters long and up to 2 cm in diameter; leaves and branchlets glabrous; flowers lacking.
            4. Leafy twigs developing flat, fanlike sprays; cones brown, woody, with overlapping scales; bark gray, with long, thin, interlacing ridges . . . . *Thuja*
            4. Leafy twigs not developing flat sprays; cones bluish, fleshy, berrylike; bark brown, peeling or flaking, lacking discernable ridges . . . . *Juniperus*
    2. Leaves needlelike.
        5. Leaves borne singly.
            6. Leaves ≤ 5 mm long; a small, creeping, dwarf shrub with mat-forming stems . . . . *Empetrum*
            6. Leaves > 5 mm long; a tree or shrub but not a dwarf shrub.
                7. Leaves opposite or in whorls of 3; cones fleshy and berrylike . . . . *Juniperus*
                7. Leaves alternate or spirally arranged; cones ± woody with overlapping scales or with a fleshy, red, berrylike aril (*Taxus*).
                    8. Leaves attached flush to the branchlet.
                        9. An upright tree; leaf tip blunt or notched (at least those on lower branches); leaves spirally arranged; twigs with short, stiff hairs; bark with resin-filled blisters; seeds in an oblong cone 3–8 cm long . . . . *Abies*
                        9. A bushy shrub ≤ 2 m tall; leaf tip sharply pointed; leaves alternate; twigs glabrous; bark lacking resin-filled blisters; seed with a red, fleshy, cup-shaped aril 5–10 mm across . . . . *Taxus*
                    8. Leaves attached to a raised peglike base that persists on the branchlet after the leaf is removed.
                        10. Leaves 0.6–1.5 mm wide, ± 4-sided in cross section, rigid; cones usually > 2 cm long (range 1.5–6 cm); bark scaly . . . . *Picea*
                        10. Leaves 1.5–2 mm wide, 2-sided in cross section (flat), soft and flexible; cones ≤ 2 cm long; bark ridged and furrowed . . . . *Tsuga*
        5. Leaves borne in bundles of 2–35.
            11. Leaves in bundles of 15–35, deciduous; mature seed cones 1–2 cm long; leaves 1.2–3 cm long . . . . *Larix*
            11. Leaves in bundles of 2 or 5, evergreen; mature seed cones 3–20 cm long; leaves 2–20 cm long . . . . *Pinus*
1. Leaves not needlelike or scalelike, > 3 mm wide.
    12. Leaves compound.
        13. Leaves opposite.
            14. Leaflets entire or with a few shallow, irregular lobes or coarse serrations.
                15. A free-standing tree; leaflets 3–5, rarely 7; fruit a double samara with thin papery wings . . . . *Acer*
                15. A slender, climbing vine; leaflets 3; fruit a small, flattened achene with a long white plume . . . . *Clematis*
            14. Leaflets with fine serrations.
                16. Leaflets 3 . . . . *Staphylea*
                16. Leaflets 5–11.
                    17. A single-stemmed tree; flowers unisexual, small and inconspicuous, lacking petals; fruit a narrow samara . . . . *Fraxinus*
                    17. A multistemmed shrub; flowers bisexual, in large showy clusters, with white petals; fruit a small, globose berry . . . . *Sambucus*
        13. Leaves alternate.
            18. Leaflets with apices rounded, blunt, or obtuse.
                19. Leaflets with margins entire or with 3–5 teeth at apex.
                    20. Leaves pinnately compound; leaflets 9–49; a tree or shrub.
                        21. Branches with sharp, broad-based spines at the nodes; flowers white; pods 3–11 cm long; a tree several meters tall . . . . *Robinia*
                        21. Branches lacking spines; flowers blue or purple; pods < 1 cm long; a shrub ≤ 3 m tall . . *Amorpha*
                    20. Leaves palmately compound; leaflets 3; a subshrub < 30 cm tall . . . . *Sibbaldiopsis*
                19. Leaflets with margins serrate.
                    22. A shrub; stems bristly, at least on the lower portions; flowers large, pink or red . . . . *Rosa*

22. A tree; stems not bristly, but trunk may have long, sharp thorns; individual flowers tiny, yellowish green . . . . *Gleditsia*

18. Leaflets with apices acute or acuminate.

  23. Leaflets usually > 10 per leaf.

    24. A small shrub, ≤ 1 m tall; lower portion of stem bristly; flowers and fruits in erect umbels; fruit a blackish, berrylike drupe 4–8 mm in diameter . . . . *Aralia*

    24. A tree or large shrub, > 1 m tall; stem not bristly; flowers and fruits not in erect umbels; fruit not a blackish, berrylike drupe.

      25. A tall shrub with paired spines at the nodes; leaflet margins crenulate with a small gland at each notch . . . . *Zanthoxylum*

      25. A tree or tall shrub, spines absent; leaflet margins entire or serrate.

        26. Leaflets entire.

          27. A midsize tree; leaf bipinnately compound with 40+ leaflets; leaflets hairy on lower surface, bases rounded or obtuse; fruit a thick, heavy pod 8–15 cm long . . . . *Gymnocladus*

          27. A large shrub, stems not normally exceeding 5 cm in diameter; leaf pinnately compound with 9–13 leaflets; leaflets ± glabrous, bases acutely tapered; fruit a spherical drupe 4–5 mm across . . . . *Toxicodendron*

        26. Leaflets serrate.

          28. Leaflets 2.5–8 cm long, 0.7–2.5 cm wide; flowers bisexual, corolla white, 5–12 mm across; inflorescence a flat-topped cyme 4–14 cm across . . . . *Sorbus*

          28. Leaflets 6–14 cm long, 1.5–6 cm wide; flowers unisexual, yellowish green, ≤ 6 mm across; inflorescence a pyramidal-shaped panicle (*Rhus*) or a catkin (*Juglans*).

            29. A clonal shrub; first-year branchlets glabrous or with nonglandular hairs; pith of second-year branchlets solid, not chambered; fruit a cluster of red drupes, each ≤ 5 mm across . . . . *Rhus*

            29. A midsize to large tree; first-year branchlets with both glandular and nonglandular hairs; pith of second-year branchlets chambered; fruit a large nut 4.5–8 cm long . . . . *Juglans*

  23. Leaflets usually < 10 per leaf.

    30. A climbing vine.

      31. Leaflets 5 or occasionally 4 . . . . *Parthenocissus*

      31. Leaflets 3 . . . . *Toxicodendron*

    30. A self-supporting shrub or tree, or stems growing prostrate on the ground.

      32. A tall shrub with paired spines at the nodes; fruit a red, warty pod 4–6 mm in diameter . . . . *Zanthoxylum*

      32. A shrub or tree lacking spines at the nodes, although prickles or bristles may occur elsewhere on the stem (*Rubus*); fruit otherwise.

        33. A large tree with a single trunk; leaves pinnately compound with 5–9 leaflets . . . . *Carya*

        33. A large or small shrub, with single or multiple stems; leaves pinnately or palmately compound, leaflet number various.

          34. Leaves twice compound; flowers in umbels; stems bristly near base only . . . . *Aralia*

          34. Leaves once compound; flowers not in umbels; stems bristly or prickly throughout, or stems smooth.

            35. Stems (canes) biennial, usually with bristles or prickles, often arching or prostrate; stipules prominent . . . . *Rubus*

            35. Stems perennial, lacking bristles or prickles, not characteristically arching or prostrate; stipules absent or at least not prominent.

              36. Leaflets 0.5–3.5 cm long; flowers ≥ 1 cm across.

                37. A distinctly woody shrub up to 1 m tall; flowers yellow; leaflets usually 5, each with a pointed or blunt tip . . . . *Dasiphora*

                37. A nearly herbaceous subshrub rarely more than 20 cm tall; flowers white; leaflets 3, each with 3 teeth at the tip . . . . *Sibbaldiopsis*

              36. Leaflets 6–18 cm long; flowers < 1 cm across . . . . *Toxicodendron*

12. Leaves simple.

  38. Leaves alternate.

    39. Leaf margins serrate, toothed, crenate, wavy or lobed.

      40. A climbing vine.

        41. Stems climbing by twining entire stem around a support; tendrils absent.

          42. Fruit red; petals violet, reflexed; flowers with a bright yellow central column projecting forward; leaf margins often with 1–4 prominent lobes near base . . . . *Solanum*

42. Fruit black, orange, or yellow; petals whitish or greenish, not reflexed; flowers not as described above; leaf margins with 1–3 pairs of shallow lobes or entire.

    43. Leaves longer than wide, not lobed, margins serrate, leaf base tapered or rounded; apex acuminate; fruit orange or yellow . . . . *Celastrus*

    43. Leaves usually wider than long, with 1–3 pairs of shallow blunt lobes, margins not serrate, leaf base cordate; apex acute to obtuse or rounded; fruit blackish . . . . *Menispermum*

41. Stems climbing by slender tendrils produced at the nodes or base of the petioles.

    44. Stems covered with prickles; tendrils originating from the petioles; leaves not lobed; inflorescence an umbel . . . . *Smilax*

    44. Stems lacking prickles; tendrils originating from the stem (from nodes opposite a leaf); leaves 3–5 lobed; inflorescence a panicle . . . . *Vitis*

40. A self–supporting shrub or tree.

    45. Flowers borne in unisexual catkins, at least the male catkins elongated and pendulous with numerous tiny apetalous flowers; fruit a nut, nutlet, capsule or similar dry, nonfleshy structure (or a fleshy syncarp in *Morus*).

        46. A small shrub ≤ 1 m tall; leaves linear-lanceolate, about 5 times longer than wide, the margins with prominent rounded or rhombic-shaped lobes, the sinuses reaching nearly to the midvein . . . . *Comptonia*

        46. A shrub or tree; leaves proportionately broader, < 5 times as long as wide, margins various.

            47. A tree; leaf margins deeply lobed, the sinuses reaching at least halfway to the midvein.

                48. Leaf margins not serrate, lobes regular and ± symmetrical; fruit an acorn . . . . *Quercus*

                48. Leaf margins coarsely serrate; lobes irregular and asymmetrical; fruit a fleshy syncarp . . . . *Morus*

            47. A tree or shrub; leaf margins serrate or shallowly lobed, if lobed the sinuses reaching less than halfway to the midvein.

                49. Leaf blades usually < 6 cm long, widest at or above the middle, base tapered, apex obtuse or rounded.

                    50. Leaf surfaces dotted with minute yellow glands, margins with 1–5 pairs of teeth toward apex . . . . *Myrica*

                    50. Leaf surfaces lacking yellow glands, margins with numerous teeth along entire margin . . . . *Betula*

                49. Leaf blades usually ≥ 6 cm long, usually widest at or below the middle, base tapered, rounded, or cordate, apex acute or acuminate.

                    51. Fruit a dry capsule with numerous tiny seeds, each seed with a conspicuous tuft of long white hairs.

                        52. Lower surface of leaf blade often with blotchy copper-colored stains; leaf base rounded or occasionally cordate; buds large and coated with a sticky, yellow, aromatic resin . . . . *Populus*

                        52. Lower surface of leaf blades a uniform greenish or whitish color; leaf base various shapes; buds various sizes but not coated with a sticky, yellow, aromatic resin.

                            53. Petioles distinctly flattened in cross section, especially near the attachment with the blade, glabrous, 3–8 cm long; leaf blades no more than 1/3 longer than wide (l/w ≤ 1.3) . . . . *Populus*

                            53. Petioles roundish or channeled in cross section, glabrous or hairy, 0.2–3 cm long; leaf blades at least 1/2 longer than wide (l/w ≥ 1.5) . . . . *Salix*

                    51. Fruit not a capsule, seeds lacking a tuft of hairs.

                      54. A tree; leaf margins with 3–14 rounded or blunt lobes extending less than half the distance to the midvein; fruit an acorn . . . . *Quercus*

                      54. A tree or shrub; leaf margins with numerous sharp serrations but not lobed; fruit not an acorn.

                        55. A tall or midsize tree; bark peeling in papery strips . . . . *Betula*

                        55. A small tree or large shrub; bark not peeling.

                            56. Bark gray, smooth; lower surface of leaf blades with numerous tiny, dark brown glands (magnification needed); fruit a single-seeded nutlet 4–6 mm long attached to a leaflike bract 1.8–3.5 cm long . . *Carpinus*

                            56. Bark gray or brown, rough, scaly or furrowed; leaf blades lacking glands; fruit otherwise.

                              57. A small or midsize tree.

                                58. Fruit a small nutlet enclosed in an inflated, papery, pouchlike bract, the bracts arranged in a hopslike strobilus 3–5 cm long . . . . *Ostrya*

58. Fruit a fleshy structure (syncarp) 1–3 cm long, red, black, or occasionally white . . . . *Morus*

57. A large multistemmed shrub.

  59. Leaf tips acuminate; leaf base cordate or sometimes rounded; bark lacking lenticels; fruit a nut with a hard bony shell 1–1.5 cm across concealed within 2 foliaceous bracts . . . . . *Corylus*

  59. Leaf tips acute to obtuse; leaf base rounded or tapered; bark with conspicuous lenticels; fruit a tiny, flattened samara borne in a woody conelike structure . . . . *Alnus*

45. Flowers bisexual or unisexual but not borne in catkins, often with conspicuous, petaliferous flowers; fruit a fleshy pome, drupe, berry or berrylike structure, occasionally a dry capsule or winged samara.

  60. Petals fused (connate) to form the shape of an urn, only the tips of the petals separate (the free tip 0.5–2 mm long); leaves evergreen, thick and leathery, or if deciduous and thin, then < 4 cm long; a small shrub usually ≤ 1 m high.

    61. Leaves evergreen.

      62. A bog shrub to about 1 m tall; lower surface of leaf scaly; leaf blade < 1.3 cm wide; leaf margins crenulate; petioles 1–1.5 mm long; flowers in 1-sided racemes . . *Chamaedaphne*

      62. A shrub of dry, upland forests, no more than 15 cm tall; lower surface of leaf smooth; leaf blades > 1.5 cm wide; leaf margins with widely spaced bristle-tipped serrations; petioles 2–5 mm long; flowers single in axils of leaves . . . . *Gaultheria*

    61. Leaves deciduous . . . . *Vaccinium*

  60. Flowers not urn shaped, the petals separate their entire length, or in *Ribes* the lower portion fused to form a slender tube, or petals lacking; leaves deciduous and thin, the larger ones > 4 cm long; a tree or shrub.

    63. Leaf bases distinctly asymmetrical (the 2 halves different shapes, or 1 half offset from the other half at the point of attachment to the petiole); a tall tree or, in the case of *Hamamelis*, a large shrub.

      64. A large shrub; flowers with yellow, ribbonlike petals, appearing in fall; leaf margins wavy, leaf tips acute or rounded; leaf surfaces with stellate (branched) hairs . . . . . *Hamamelis*

      64. A large tree; flowers not as above, appearing in spring or summer; leaf margins serrate, leaf tips acuminate; leaf surfaces glabrous or with simple (unbranched) hairs.

        65. Fruit a flattened, winged samara ripening in spring; leaves with a single longitudinal nerve originating from the base and extending to the tip; leaves elliptical or occasionally obovate (widest at the middle or occasionally above the middle) . . . . *Ulmus*

        65. Fruit a spherical drupe ripening in autumn; leaves with 3–5 nerves originating from the base; leaves ovate (widest below the middle).

          66. Bark of young trees with narrow, wavy ridges and irregular, warty projections, eventually developing thickish, irregular scales that may loosen at the edges; flowers unisexual, petals lacking and sepals only 1.5–3 mm long; petioles 0.6–1.5 cm long; leaf tip long and drawn-out (attenuate); flowering in May; fruit a fleshy drupe . . . . *Celtis*

          66. Bark of young trees smooth, developing ridges and furrows in age; flowers bisexual, petals present, 6–9 mm long; petioles 3–7 cm long; leaf with a short abrupt tip (acuminate); flowering in July; fruit a hard, woody drupe . . . *Tilia*

    63. Leaf bases ± symmetrical; a small tree, shrub or climbing vine.

      67. A climbing vine; petals violet, reflexed; anthers bright yellow, converging into a prominent central column; leaves often with 1–4 (usually 2) prominent deep lobes near base . . . . *Solanum*

      67. A free-standing shrub or tree; petals and anthers not as described above; leaves lobed or unlobed.

        68. Flowers with ≥ 10 stamens each.

          69. Stem and/or branches with long, smooth thorns; stamens 6–20 . . . . *Crataegus*

          69. Stem and branches lacking long, smooth thorns (*Prunus* and *Malus* often have "stub" thorns at the tips of some branchlets); stamens often > 20 (6–50+).

            70. Petals 1–3.5 mm long; fruit a dry, papery follicle.

              71. Leaves 3-lobed; petioles 8–30 mm long; bark peeling in thin papery sheets; leaves with stellate (branched) hairs . . . . *Physocarpus*

              71. Leaves not lobed; petioles 1–5 mm long; bark smooth and firm; leaves with simple (unbranched) hairs . . . . *Spiraea*

            70. Petals 2.5–25 mm long; fruit a fleshy structure (e.g. apple, plum, cherry).

72. Stem ± herbaceous, ≤ 30 cm tall; with just 1–3 leaves and, at most, 1 flower; leaves wider than long (reniform) with a broadly cordate base . . . . *Rubus*

72. Stem distinctly woody, > 1 m tall; other features not as described above.

   73. Fruit an apple or plum 2–4 cm in diameter; some lateral branches ending in a sharp thorn; bark curling or peeling in strips.

     74. Petioles and lower surface of leaf blades densely woolly; leaves often with a pair of pronounced lobes near base; fruit a green apple (pome) 2.5–4 cm across; petals 1.3–2 cm long, white to pink . . . . *Malus*

     74. Petioles and lower surface of leaf blades not densely woolly; leaves not lobed; fruit a reddish or purplish plum (drupe) 2–3 cm across; petals 0.6–1.4 cm long, white . . . . . . *Prunus*

   73. Fruit smaller, 0.6–2 cm in diameter; branches lacking thorns; bark smooth or rough but not curling or peeling in strips.

     75. Stems (canes) biennial; leaf blades 5-lobed, 10–30 cm long and about as wide; petioles 6–18 cm long . . . . *Rubus*

     75. Stems perennial; leaf blades not lobed, ≤ 12 cm long and not nearly as wide; petioles < 6 cm long.

       76. Midvein on upper surface of leaf blade with small, dark, fingerlike glands (may require magnification); leaf bases acutely tapered; petals 4–6 mm long; fruit black . . . . *Aronia*

       76. Midvein lacking glands; leaf bases various; petals often > 6 mm long; fruit red or black.

         77. Petioles with 1–3 dark, sessile glands near attachment with blade . . . . *Prunus*

         77. Petioles lacking glands . . . . *Amelanchier*

68. Flowers with < 10 stamens each (stamens usually equal the number of petals).

   78. Stems and branches with sharp thorns at least 3 cm long; flowers ≥ 1.2 cm across; bark with flat, narrow, platelike scales . . . . *Crataegus*

   78. Thorns absent, or in *Ribes* nodal spines up to 2 cm long may be present; flowers < 1.2 cm across; bark not as described above.

     79. Leaves palmately 3–5 lobed; stems often bristly or prickly; flowers in racemes . . . . *Ribes*

     79. Leaves not lobed; stems not bristly or prickly; flowers not in racemes.

       80. Leaves with 3 longitudinal veins running roughly parallel from the base toward the apex (often called "triple-nerved"); a shrub ≤ 1.5 m tall . . . . *Ceanothus*

       80. Leaves with 1 longitudinal vein; a shrub or small tree, heights various.

         81. Leaves glabrous, widest at the middle or above, margins coarsely serrate with < 10 teeth per side, serrations confined to the upper half or 2/3 of leaf blade; flowers/fruit on long, slender stalks 1–3 cm long; fruit red . . . . *Nemopanthus*

         81. Leaves hairy, at least on lower surface, widest at the middle or below, margins finely serrate the entire length with ≥ 25 teeth per side; flowers/fruits on stalks < 1 cm long; fruit red or black.

           82. A large shrub > 1 m tall; veins impressed above, protruding below; fruit red; flowers white . . . . *Ilex*

           82. A small shrub usually < 1 m tall; veins not notably impressed above or protruding below; fruit black; flowers greenish yellow . . . . *Rhamnus*

39. Leaf margins entire and unlobed.

  83. A climbing vine.

    84. Climbing by twining entire stem around a support, tendrils absent; stems lacking prickles; inflorescence a panicle or cyme.

      85. Leaves usually wider than long; petioles 4–16 cm long; petals whitish, 1.3–1.8 mm long; fruits blackish . . . . *Menispermum*

      85. Leaves longer than wide; petioles 1.5–4 cm long; petals violet, 6–10 mm long; fruits red . . . . . *Solanum*

84. Climbing by slender tendrils originating from petioles; stems covered with prickles; inflorescence an umbel . . . . *Smilax*

83. An erect, self-supporting shrub or tree, or a dwarf shrub with vinelike stems creeping over the ground.

   86. A dwarf shrub with vinelike stems creeping over the ground.

      87. Leaves at least 2.5 cm long and 2 cm wide; leaf margin ciliate . . . . *Epigaea*

      87. Leaves no more than 1.6 cm long and 1 cm wide; leaf margin not ciliate.

         88. Branches, stems, and lower surface of leaves with closely appressed, bristlelike hairs (seen without magnification); fruit white . . . . *Gaultheria*

         88. Branches, stems and lower surface of leaves lacking bristlelike hairs; fruit red . . . . *Oxycoccus*

   86. An erect, self-supporting shrub or tree, or if the main stem prostrate, then with upright branches at least 10 cm tall.

      89. An evergreen shrub ≤ 1 m tall.

         90. A shrub 30–100 cm tall; leaves dull, not particularly thick or leathery.

            91. Leaves narrowly elliptical to linear, l/w = 6–20, with a sharply pointed tip; twigs glabrous . . . . *Andromeda*

            91. Leaves proportionally broader, l/w = 1.3–4.5, with a blunt or tapered tip; first-year twigs hairy (minutely so in *Chamaedaphne*).

               92. Corolla urn-shaped, < 7 mm across; flowers in a 1–sided terminal raceme; lower surface of leaf blade scaly . . . . *Chamaedaphne*

               92. Corolla spreading, 7–10 mm across; flowers in an umbel-like cluster; lower surface of leaf blade densely woolly . . . . *Rhododendron*

         90. A shrub 10–20 cm tall; leaves shiny, thick, and leathery.

            93. Lower surface of leaf blades with dark bristlelike glands (seen without magnification); leaf margins not hairy . . . . *Vaccinium*

            93. Lower surface of leaf blades glabrous or occasionally sparsely hairy, but not with dark bristlelike glands; leaf margins hairy . . . . *Arctostaphylos*

      89. A deciduous tree or shrub of various size.

         94. A shrub ≤ 1 m tall; petals fused (connate) to form the shape of a short cylinder or urn, only the tips of the petals free (the free portion 0.5–2 mm long); inflorescence a raceme.

            95. Leaf surfaces (especially lower surface) dotted with small, yellow, resinous glands . . . . *Gaylussacia*

            95. Leaves not dotted . . . . *Vaccinium*

         94. A shrub or small tree, size various; petals free their entire length or the lower portion fused to form a slender tube, or petals absent; inflorescence other than a raceme.

            96. Leaves covered with reflective silvery scales or occasionally stellate hairs; fruits drupelike and dry, covered with silvery scales . . . . *Elaeagnus*

            96. Leaves smooth or with simple hairs; fruits otherwise.

               97. Nodes conspicuously swollen; flowers yellow, appearing in early spring before the leaves . . . . *Dirca*

               97. Nodes not conspicuously swollen; flowers various.

                 98. Flowers borne in elongate catkins; fruit a nonfleshy capsule with numerous tiny seeds, each seed with a tuft of long, white hairs . . . . *Salix*

                 98. Flowers not in elongate catkins; fruit a fleshy drupe enclosing 1–5 seeds, seeds lacking a tuft of hairs.

                   99. Flowers white, 50–250 in a dense, flat-topped, terminal inflorescence; when the leaf blade is carefully pulled apart the lateral veins remain connected by delicate white threads . . . . *Cornus alternifolia*

                   99. Flowers yellowish or greenish, in clusters of 1–8 in leaf axils; when the leaf blade is pulled apart it breaks cleanly.

                     100. Leaf tip abruptly pointed; leaves ≥ 2.5 cm wide; lower surface of leaf blade usually hairy on main veins; fruit black; petioles hairy . . . . *Frangula alnus*

                     100. Leaf tip not abruptly pointed, but with a short mucro; leaves ≤ 2.5 cm wide; lower surface of leaf blade glabrous; fruit reddish or purple; petioles glabrous . . . . *Nemopanthus*

38. Leaves opposite or in whorls.

    101. Leaves toothed, serrate, or lobed.

        102. A dwarf, vinelike shrub with slender stems creeping along the ground; leaves evergreen, < 2 cm long ... *Linnaea*

        102. An upright tree, shrub or dwarf shrub, not vinelike or creeping; leaves evergreen or deciduous, > 2 cm long.

            103. A tree or in one case a tall shrub (*Acer spicatum*); fruit a winged samara 2–6 cm long .... *Acer*

            103. A shrub; fruit a capsule or drupe < 2 cm across.

                104. A low shrub < 25 cm tall; leaves evergreen, thick and shiny, in whorls of 3–8 .... *Chimaphila*

                104. A taller shrub; leaves deciduous, thin, shiny or dull, opposite in 2s.

                    105. Thorns often developing at the ends of the branchlets; fruit a black drupe ("berry"); leaves with 3–4 lateral veins per side and curving toward the apex; bark dark gray to blackish, often peeling in age; flowers greenish or yellowish green; large shrub or small tree 2–11 m tall .... *Rhamnus*

                    105. Thorns absent; fruit a red or whitish "berry," or not berrylike at all; veins various; bark not as described above; flowers not as described above; size various.

                        106. Flowers yellow; fruit a nonfleshy capsule with a long slender beak; leaf margins ciliate; a low shrub ≤ 1 m tall .... *Diervilla*

                        106. Flowers white, purple, or pinkish; fruit a fleshy berrylike structure or a leathery capsule; leaf margins not ciliate; a low or tall shrub.

                            107. Leaf margins not serrate; flowers sessile, white or pinkish .... *Symphoricarpos*

                            107. Leaf margins serrate; flowers on pedicels ≥ 5 mm long, white or purple.

                                108. Leaf margins with nonglandular serrations; petioles often with protruding glands at summit or sometimes with a flattened winglike margin; flowers white; fruit a spheroidal drupe ± circular in cross section .... *Viburnum*

                                108. Leaf margins with gland-tipped serrations; petioles lacking glands and winglike margins; flowers purple; fruit a 4–lobed leathery capsule; twigs somewhat 4–sided in cross section, the result of 4 longitudinal corky ridges or lines .... *Euonymus*

    101. Leaves entire.

        109. Dwarf, vinelike shrub with slender stems creeping along the ground; leaves evergreen, < 2 cm long .... *Linnaea*

        109. Upright shrub, small tree, or climbing vine; leaves deciduous or occasionally evergreen; usually > 2 cm long.

            110. Surface of leaves and petioles with sessile scales or silvery white, stellate hairs .... *Shepherdia*

            110. Surface of leaves and petioles glabrous or with simple (unbranched) hairs.

                111. A shrub ≤ 70 cm tall; leaves evergreen, usually ≤ 1 cm wide and at least 3 times longer than wide; flowers blue or purplish, 9–14 mm across, 5–merous .... *Kalmia*

                111. A shrub or climbing vine; leaves deciduous, > 1 cm wide and less than 3 times longer than wide; flowers various.

                    112. A climbing vine; the pair of leaves that occur just below the flowers perfoliate (fused at the base to form a single leaf with the stem passing through the middle) .... *Lonicera*

                  112. A free-standing shrub; leaves not perfoliate.

                      113. Petioles usually > 7 mm long; leaf tips acute to acuminate; flowers with 4 petals free to the base.

                        114. Leaves hairy on both surfaces; leaves always in 2s; flowers and fruits in an open cyme or panicle; fruit a fleshy, berrylike drupe; if the leaf blade is carefully pulled apart, the lateral veins remain connected by delicate white threads .... *Cornus*

                        114. Leaves glabrous, at least on upper surface; leaves occasionally in whorls of 3; flowers and fruit in a dense, spherical ball; fruit a dry nutlet; the leaf blade breaks cleanly if pulled apart .... *Cephalanthus*

                    113. Petioles < 7 mm long; leaf tips acute, obtuse, rounded or blunt; flowers with 5 petals, the lower portion fused into a tube.

                      115. Berries red, yellow, or orange; flowers in pairs, each ≥ 8 mm long (sometimes less in *L. villosa*) .... *Lonicera*

                    115. Berries whitish; flowers in clusters of 2–10, each < 8 mm long .... *Symphoricarpos*

TREES AND SHRUBS OF MINNESOTA

Abies, the firs

Pinaceae: Pine family

The genus *Abies* includes about 42 species, all evergreen trees, scattered throughout much of the northern hemisphere. There are approximately 11 species in North America, and 1 species in Minnesota. (*Abies* is the classical Latin name for the fir tree.)

Firs are widely cultivated, but other than the native balsam fir (*A. balsamea*), the only species commonly grown in Minnesota is white fir (*A. concolor*) from the western United States. It is larger than Minnesota's native fir and has long, bluish needles.

Abies balsamea (L.) Mill.

Balsam fir

Midsize to large **trees**, to 26 m tall and 48 cm dbh. **Bark** thin, gray, smooth, with numerous resin-filled blisters. **Branchlets** pale brown to pale greenish brown, with short, stiff hairs. **Leaves** needlelike or linear; borne singly; spirally arranged, but those on lower branches often twisted at the base giving the appearance of being two-ranked; evergreen, persisting 8–13 years; straight or curving upward, ± flattened; 1–3 cm long, 1–1.7 mm wide; apex notched or blunt, or those on upper branches sharply pointed; margins entire; upper surface shallowly grooved; lower surface with a prominent midrib or keel and whitish bands of stomata. Trees monoecious with separate male **cones** (strobili) and female cones on the same tree. Mature **male** (**pollen**) **cones** ovate to oblong; 6–10 mm long; borne from leaf axils of 2nd-year branchlets in the middle portions of the crown; pollen shed mid-May to early June. Mature **female** (**seed**) **cones** resinous; oblong to oblong-cylindrical; erect and often crowded; 3–8 cm long; on short, stout base 1–5 mm long or essentially sessile; borne on 2nd-year branchlets at the top of the crown; maturing in the autumn of the 1st year and fragmenting so the individual bracts, scales, and seeds are shed together, leaving only the bare spikelike axis, which may persist for a year; wind-pollinated. **Seeds** 3–6 mm long, with a thin, papery wing 8–14 mm long; wind- and gravity-dispersed. (*balsamea*: refers to the balsamic resin in the bark)

Identification

When comparing balsam fir to the spruces (*Picea* spp.), notice that the bark is smooth except for resin-filled blisters that burst when scraped with a fingernail. Also notice that the leaves (needles) are attached flush with the branchlet, while spruce leaves are attached to a raised, peglike base. In comparison with Canada yew (*Taxus canadensis*), the leaf tips are blunt or notched, at least those on the lower branches, and those of yew are pointed.

Natural History

Balsam fir is a common tree throughout the forested region of northern Minnesota with small outlying populations on cold slopes in southeast Minnesota and adjacent Iowa. The tallest firs are found on moist, loamy soil and may reach heights of 85 ft (26 m), which is shorter than most canopy species,

particularly the pines (*Pinus* spp.). Balsam fir also grows well in saturated peat. It can grow in pure stands or scattered with other forest trees, especially white spruce (*Picea glauca*) and northern white cedar (*Thuja occidentalis*).

Balsam fir is moderately short-lived, with a maximum age of perhaps 200 years (Heinselman 1973), which is less than the pines, spruces, and northern white cedar. But fir seedlings have the critical ability to become established and grow in the shade of other trees, even those of its own species. This allows it to perpetually replace itself in the canopy without large-scale disturbance. Only sugar maple (*Acer saccharum*) and eastern hemlock (*Tsuga canadensis*) are as shade tolerant. For this reason, balsam fir is the climax species in much of northern Minnesota, just as sugar maple is in the south.

Without some form of ecological intervention, balsam fir would undoubtedly dominate most of northern Minnesota, but intervention comes in many forms. Extensive stands are highly susceptible to spruce budworm (*Choristoneuro fumiferana* [Clemens]), which is a native insect capable of killing most of the fir over large areas during periodic outbreaks (Heinselman 1973). Balsam fir is also susceptible to fire and drought, and young fir are heavily browsed by deer and moose in the winter. They are shallowly rooted, even in deep soil, and blow over easily; those that survive natural forces are usually cut for pulp before reaching an age of 55.

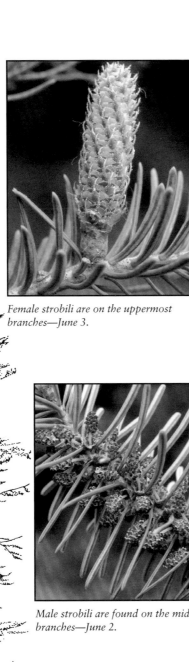

Female strobili are on the uppermost branches—June 3.

The erect seed cone is characteristic of all true firs—August 26.

Male strobili are found on the middle branches—June 2.

Bark is smooth except for resin-filled blisters—11" (28 cm) dbh.

A small grove of fir among birches.

Acer, the maples

Aceraceae: Maple family

The maples include somewhere between 110 and 200+ species of trees and shrubs; most are deciduous, but a few are apparently evergreen. They occur mostly in temperate regions of the Northern Hemisphere, particularly Asia. There are about 13 species native to North America, and 6 native to Minnesota. (*Acer* is the classical Latin name for the European maple.)

There are persistent rumors that striped maple (*A. pensylvanicum*) occurs in northeastern Minnesota, but there is no credible evidence to support the claim. It is a large shrub that occurs in forests just to the east of the state (Little 1977). It is similar to our native mountain maple (*A. spicatum*), but the bark has prominent pale stripes.

Selected clones of a naturally occurring hybrid between the native red maple (*A. rubrum*) and silver maple (*A. saccharinum*) are now quite popular as boulevard trees. There are also two nonnative maples often seen in cultivation. The first is Norway maple (*A. platanoides* L.), a European species that is commonly planted along streets and in parks for landscaping purposes. It is not yet naturalized in Minnesota, but in the eastern United States it has escaped to mesic forests, where it is displacing the native sugar maple and degrading wildlife habitat (Webb 2000).

The other nonnative is Amur maple (*A. ginnala* Maxim.), a large shrub or small tree brought from Asia as an ornamental. It persists long after cultivation and is beginning to spread to native habitats, especially in the Twin Cities area. It shows many of the characteristics of an ecologically harmful invasive species, and experience from the eastern states suggests it may not be safe to plant here.

Key to the Genus *Acer* in Minnesota

1. Leaves pinnately compound; twigs green in the summer .... *A. negundo*
1. Leaves simple; twigs brown or purplish.
   2. Leaf margins with 1–11 teeth per side; sinuses between teeth rounded at the bottom; sinus between the wings of the paired samaras U-shaped.
      3. Petioles with conspicuous stipules, at least the petioles subtending the terminal bud; buds completely or nearly hidden within the cup-shaped base of the subtending petioles; lower surface of leaf blade hairy across the entire surface (but more densely on main veins); hairs on lower surface between main veins wavy or upright and 0.2–0.5 mm long; leaf margins with 1–6 teeth per side, the smaller teeth reduced to rounded bumps; bark of mature trees dark gray to blackish with narrow ridges .... *A. nigrum*
      3. Petioles lacking stipules; buds fully or mostly exposed; lower surface of leaf blade often hairy only on main veins or in axils of main veins; hairs on surface between veins (if present) appressed or wavy, and 0.3–0.7 mm long; leaf margins with 5–11 teeth per side, usually pointed; bark of mature trees silvery gray with wide platelike ridges .... *A. saccharum*
   2. Leaf margins with 20 or more teeth per side; sinuses between the teeth sharply angled at the bottom; sinus between the wings of the paired samaras V-shaped.
      4. Leaves 3-lobed, the lobes triangular; petioles minutely hairy; branchlets hairy and lacking lenticels; flowers in long, erect panicles, appearing after mid-May when the leaves are fully expanded; a large multistemmed shrub .... *A. spicatum*
      4. Leaves 3–5-lobed, the apical lobe squarish at base (*A. rubrum*), or concavely tapered (*A. saccharinum*); petioles glabrous or hairy at the base only; branchlets glabrous and with conspicuous lenticels; flowers in dense umbel-like clusters, appearing before mid-May and before the leaves appear; a large tree.
         5. Apical lobe of leaf blade squarish, broad at base, and equaling about 1/2 the length of the entire blade; lower surface of leaf blade hairy only in axils of main veins and sometimes along the lower portion of main veins; petals 2–3 mm long; each seed plus wing 1.7–2.4 cm long .... *A. rubrum*
         5. Apical lobe of leaf blade concavely narrowed at base, and equaling about 3/4 the length of the entire blade; lower surface of leaf blade evenly and minutely hairy; petals absent; each seed plus wing 4–6 cm long .... *A. saccharinum*

Acer negundo L.

Boxelder

Large **trees**, to 35 m tall and 1.48 m dbh. **Bark** brown, or gray and brown, with short, thin, irregular ridges separated by shallow, narrow furrows. **Branchlets** summer green for 3–6 years or sometimes blue-glaucous, becoming purplish or reddish purple in winter; glabrous or occasionally densely short-hairy. **Leaves** pinnately compound, opposite, deciduous. **Petioles** 3.5–10 cm long, glabrous or occasionally short-hairy. **Petiolules** hairy, at least on the upper surface. **Leaflets** 3–5, rarely 7; ovate or the terminal leaflet elliptical to obovate; 5.5–10 cm long, 2–6 cm wide; base tapered or rounded; apex acute; margins entire or irregularly toothed to shallowly lobed; upper surface dark green, glabrous or hairy on main veins or along margins; lower surface pale green, hairy, especially on veins. **Inflorescence** a fascicle or raceme, borne from lateral buds on branchlets of the previous year. **Flowers** unisexual with each tree bearing either male flowers or female flowers, rarely bisexual. **Male flowers** in drooping, umbel-like fascicles of 10–20; peduncles hairy, 1–4.5 cm long, threadlike; sepals minute; petals none; stamens 2–5, exserted. **Female flowers** in drooping racemes of 6–12; pedicels hairy, about 1 cm long; sepals 3–5, elliptical, 1–2 mm long; petals none; stigmas 2; **anthesis** before or with the leaves, mid-April to late May; wind-pollinated. **Fruit** a double samara with thin, papery wings; each seed with its accompanying wing 3–5 cm long; maturing late August to late September, shed continuously until spring; wind-dispersed. (*negundo*: of uncertain derivation, possibly aboriginal)

Identification

Boxelder is potentially a large tree with a broad, irregular crown and bright green summer twigs (turning purple in the winter). It is the only North American maple with compound leaves. This can lead to confusion with the ashes (*Fraxinus*), except boxelder leaflets are usually notched on the margins, and the seeds are in pairs.
Note: The twigs and petioles are typically hairless, but in var. *interius* (Britt.) Sarg., which is occasionally seen in northern and central Minnesota, they are covered with short, dense hairs.

Natural History

Boxelder is seemingly ubiquitous statewide, particularly on floodplains and lakeshores, where it grows with plains cottonwood (*Populus deltoides* subsp. *monilifera*), peach-leaved willow (*Salix amygdaloides*), or green ash (*Fraxinus pennsylvanica*). It also occurs in upland sites, especially in young hardwood forests. It even manages to retain a presence in mid- and late-successional forests, at least in low spots or ecotones. Among the native trees boxelder is perhaps the most aggressive colonizer of old fields, fencerows, vacant lots, and roadsides, even in the driest, poorest soils and densest sods. In ideal habitats it can grow over 100 ft (30 m) tall and develop a thick trunk, massive limbs, and a broad crown. But the branches are brittle, so exposed trees usually have broken tops and crooked trunks, and it rarely survives more than 100 years (*fide* Burns and Honkala 1990).

In the past it was often planted for windbreaks in the prairie region. In fact, it was considered the perfect tree because it is easily transplanted and survives extremes in temperature and moisture conditions, including floods and droughts, and it sprouts prolifically from cut stumps (Maeglin and Ohmann 1973). It is now out of favor because of its irregular form and weather-beaten branches, and because the female trees attract large numbers of red and black boxelder bugs (*Leptocoris trivittatus* [Say]), which do no real damage to the trees but seem to alarm people.

Bark is typically brown, ridged, and furrowed—21" (53 cm) dbh.

Note the protruding stigmas of these female flowers—April 22.

Pollen from male flowers is carried by wind—April 25.

Fruits ripen in autumn and are released over the winter.

This is the only maple in Minnesota with compound leaves.

Acer nigrum Michx. f.

Black maple

Large **trees**, to 32 m tall and 70 cm dbh. **Bark** gray to blackish, with relatively deep furrows and short, narrow ridges. **Branchlets** brown or grayish, glabrous. **Leaves** simple, opposite, deciduous. **Petioles** 4–15 cm long, glabrous; stipules usually present, at least on petioles that subtend the terminal bud, often large and foliaceous. **Leaf blades** 9–17 cm long, 11–19 cm wide; base cordate; margins palmately 3- or 5-lobed, the apical lobe squarish below the acute apex, or somewhat triangular, and about half the length of the entire blade, the lateral lobes similar or slightly smaller, the basal lobes often reduced to mere undulations or occasionally lacking altogether; margins with 1–6 teeth per side, the teeth pointed or the smaller ones rounded; upper surface dark green, glabrous; lower surface pale green, hairy over the entire surface (but more densely on main veins and in axils of main veins), hairs between main veins upright or wavy, 0.2–0.5 mm long. **Inflorescence** a drooping, umbel-like corymb of 8–15 flowers, borne from terminal and uppermost lateral buds. **Flowers** unisexual or bisexual, both produced on the same tree but usually on separate branches; pedicels hairy, 3–6 cm long; calyx yellowish, irregularly 5-lobed; corolla lacking; stamens 6–9, exserted; **anthesis** mid-April to late May; wind- and insect-pollinated. **Fruit** a double samara with thin, papery wings; each seed with its accompanying wing 2.5–4 cm long; maturing early mid-September to mid-October; wind-dispersed. (*nigrum*: black, in reference to the bark)

Identification

Black maple is a large forest tree with blackish bark and a dense canopy of dark green leaves. It is very similar to sugar maple (*Acer saccharum*); in fact, the two species are known to hybridize. The best way to tell them apart is to look at the leaves growing closest to the end of the twig. Those of black maple will have conspicuous stipules at the base of the petioles; those of sugar maple will not.

The leaf shape of black maple is fairly consistent. There are relatively few teeth on the margins, and the teeth are more or less rounded, especially the smaller teeth, which are often reduced to small bumps or missing entirely. The leaf shape of sugar maple is much more variable, they usually have more teeth, and the teeth are usually more pointed. But sugar maple will sometimes have leaves that are shaped

nearly identical to those of black maple, especially the leaves on fruiting twigs. Also, notice that the leaves of black maple are less rigid than those of sugar maple; they tend to droop at the margins when hanging from the tree.

The distribution, length, and position of the hairs on the lower surface of the leaves are reliably different for the two species (see key), but these differences are so subtle that it may require careful comparison to known specimens to distinguish the two species on the basis of hairs alone.

Natural History

Black maple is a large canopy tree of late-successional forests. It is fairly common in the southeast, especially in Houston, Fillmore, Winona, and Wabasha counties, but it is absent or spotty elsewhere in the state. It is ecologically similar to sugar maple in a number of ways: it is equally tolerant of shade and has a similar phenology. In many forests the two species will even occur side by side, yet black maple seems to be more common on floodplains, especially in small- to medium-size valleys, where it may experience some short duration spring flooding and a limited amount of sedimentation. In contrast, sugar maple is very sensitive to flooding and is more likely to be found in uplands or on slopes.

Drooping margins are a consistent feature of black maple leaves.

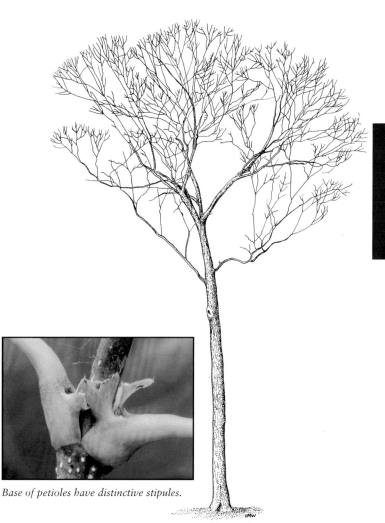

Fruits are very similar to those of sugar maple—August 22.

Base of petioles have distinctive stipules.

Black maple gets its name from its bark—27" (69 cm) dbh.

Drooping clusters of male flowers at mid-anthesis—May 4.

Maples 🌰 **11**

Acer rubrum L.

Red maple

Large **trees**, to 29 m tall and 64 cm dbh. **Bark** light gray and smooth when young, becoming dark gray and developing shallow furrows and narrow, platelike or scaly ridges. **Branchlets** brown to reddish brown, glabrous. **Leaves** simple, opposite, deciduous. **Petioles** 3–14 cm long, glabrous; stipules lacking. **Leaf blades** 7–14 cm long, 7–15 cm wide; base cordate to truncate or somewhat rounded; margins palmately 3- or 5-lobed, the apical lobe squarish below the acute apex and about half the length of the entire blade, the lateral lobes smaller and triangular, the basal lobes much reduced or absent; margins with 25+ pointed teeth per side; upper surface dark green, glabrous; lower surface pale green, hairy in the axils of the main veins, especially the basal veins, and sometimes along the lower portion of main veins. **Inflorescence** an umbel-like fascicle of 2–6 flowers, borne from lateral buds on branchlets of the previous year. **Flowers** 5-merous, unisexual with male flowers and female flowers on separate trees or rarely on different branches of the same tree, or flowers sometimes bisexual; male flowers yellowish or pink; female flowers red to magenta; peduncles glabrous, 4–8 mm long at anthesis, elongating to 6+ cm in fruit; sepals oblong, 1.7–2.7 mm long; petals oblong-linear, 2–3 mm long; stamens 5–7, exserted; **anthesis** well before the leaves appear, early April to mid-May; insect-pollinated. **Fruit** a double samara with thin, papery wings; each seed with its accompanying wing 1.7–2.4 cm long; maturing late mid-May to late June; wind-dispersed. (*rubrum*: red)

Identification

Red maple is a moderately large tree with bright red or pinkish flowers in the spring, and brilliant red foliage in the autumn. The leaf shape is similar to the other maples, but the leaf margins have more teeth than sugar maple (*A. saccharum*) and shallower lobes than silver maple (*A. saccharinum*).

Note: Red maple has been reported from southeastern Minnesota (Ownbey and Morley 1991) on the basis of a seedling that was collected on a 5-year-old dredge spoil island in the Mississippi River in Houston County. There is no other indication that a native population of red maple occurs in the southeastern part of the state.

Natural History

Red maple is relatively common in hardwood and conifer forests throughout most of central and northern Minnesota. There is even some evidence that its numbers have recently increased in proportion to those of other trees, presumably because of fire suppression. At the time of Euro-American settlement it was common only in fire-protected habitats such as lakeshores, pond margins, and hardwood swamps (U.S. Surveyor General 1847–1908), where it is still fairly common. But recently it has become more prominent in previously fire-prone upland forests, typically coming up under pioneering species such as oaks (*Quercus* spp.), aspens (*Populus* spp.), and birches (*Betula* spp.) and behaving as a climax or subclimax species.

Red maple is fast growing and relatively short-lived, rarely surviving more than 150 years (*fide* Burns and Honkala 1990). It can tolerate drought and seasonal flooding but not sedimentation, and the stumps will produce sprouts if the trunks are killed by fire or logging.

It flowers very early in the spring, well before the leaves appear, and by early summer the fruits are mature and released. The seeds appear to have few germination requirements; in fact, they will germinate in great numbers almost immediately upon reaching the ground. The seedlings are very tolerant of shade and often carpet the ground layer in hardwood forests.

The female flowers may be why it's called "red" maple—April 12.

Fruits ripen and fall by late June.

Male flowers can be yellow or pink—April 14.

Note the squarish terminal lobe and the numerous teeth.

Bark starts smooth, becomes furrowed in age—25"
(63 cm) dbh.

Acer saccharinum L.

Silver maple

Large **trees**, to 32 m tall and 1.53 m dbh. **Bark** thin, light gray; smooth when young, eventually developing long, thin plates that loosen from the edges and exfoliate. **Branchlets** brown to reddish brown, glabrous. **Leaves** simple, opposite, deciduous. **Petioles** 3–11 cm long, glabrous or hairy along the margins near the base; stipules lacking. **Leaf blades** 7–11 cm long, 8–13 cm wide; base cordate to truncate; margins palmately 5-lobed, the apical lobe concavely narrowed to the base, and about 3/4 the length of the entire blade, the lateral lobes similar, the basal lobes much reduced; margins with 20+ pointed teeth per side; upper surface dark green, glabrous; lower surface pale green, minutely hairy. **Inflorescence** an umbel-like fascicle of 3–6 flowers, borne from lateral buds on branchlets of the previous year. **Flowers** 5-merous, unisexual with male flowers and female flowers on separate trees, or on different branches of the same tree, or flowers occasionally bisexual; peduncles glabrous, elongating in fruit; sepals reduced to shallow lobes; petals lacking; stamens 3–7, exserted; **anthesis** well before the leaves appear, mid-March to late April; wind-pollinated. **Fruit** a samara with a thin, papery wing; loosely paired on the tree but falling separately; each seed with its accompanying wing 4–6 cm long; maturing as the leaves expand in early May to early June; wind-dispersed. (*saccharinum*: sugary)

Identification

Silver maple is a large tree with massive, spreading limbs, deeply lobed leaves, and shaggy bark. The leaf shape is most similar to red maple, but the lobes tend to be narrower and with concave margins, and the sinuses between the lobes are deeper.

Natural History

Silver maple is common in a variety of low, wet or moist habitats, especially on broad floodplains of large rivers. Here it can develop into a large canopy tree more than 100 ft (30 m) high, with a tall, straight trunk and broad crown. It can form pure stands, but more often it is mixed with plains cottonwood (*Populus deltoides* subsp. *monilifera*), peach-leaved willow (*Salix amygdaloides*), boxelder (*Acer negundo*), or sometimes American elm (*Ulmus americana*) or green ash (*Fraxinus pennsylvanica*).

Floodplains are inherently unstable habitats. They may experience frequent spring flooding accompanied by scouring and sediment deposition, often with force sufficient to uproot even large trees and bury smaller ones. Although silver maple manages to thrive under these conditions, its trunks are often scarred or broken by ice floes or undercut along eroding stream banks, where they eventually become snags or lean precariously over the water.

Silver maple is one of the first trees to flower in the spring, usually just after the snow has melted, which is well before the leaves appear. The fruits are mature about three weeks after pollination, and their release is timed to coincide with the receding spring meltwater. The freshly exposed sand and silt deposits provide an excellent seedbed, and the seeds can germinate almost immediately upon reaching the ground. But seedlings are only moderately if at all tolerant of shade, and those trapped beneath a closed canopy will usually not survive beyond the first year or two.

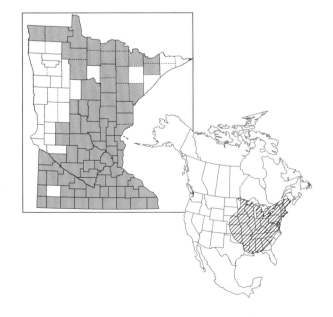

Female flowers are little more than red stigmas—April 9.

The fruits (samaras) develop in pairs but fall singly—May 6.

Bark is ash-gray and "shaggy"—22" (56 cm) dbh.

These male flowers have just shed their pollen—April 9.

Deep sinuses between the lobes and numerous teeth.

Maples 🍂 **15**

Acer saccharum Marsh.

Sugar maple

Large **trees**, to 33 m tall and 98 cm dbh. **Bark** brown or gray, with irregular furrows and ridges or sometimes narrow plates that may loosen and curl outward along the edges. **Branchlets** brown, glabrous. **Leaves** simple, opposite, deciduous. **Petioles** 3–13 cm long, glabrous or occasionally with a few long hairs near the base of the blade; stipules lacking. **Leaf blades** 8–15 cm long, 11–19 cm wide; base cordate; margins palmately 5-lobed, the apical lobe squarish below the acute apex, and about half the length of the entire blade, the lateral lobes similar or more triangular and slightly smaller, the basal lobes much reduced or occasionally indistinguishable; margins with 5–11 teeth per side, generally pointed or sometimes blunt; upper surface dark green, glabrous; lower surface pale green, hairy on the main veins or in axils of the main veins, sometimes also sparsely hairy on the surface between the main veins, these hairs (if present) tending to be appressed and 0.3–0.7 mm long. **Inflorescence** a drooping, umbel-like corymb of 8–15 flowers, borne from terminal and uppermost lateral buds. **Flowers** unisexual or bisexual, both produced on the same tree but usually on separate branches; pedicels hairy, 3–7 cm long; calyx yellowish, irregularly 5-lobed; corolla lacking; stamens 7–8, exserted; **anthesis** mid-April to early June; wind- and insect-pollinated. **Fruit** a double samara with thin, papery wings; each seed with its accompanying wing 2.5–4.5 cm long; maturing late August to early October; wind-dispersed. (*saccharum*: sugar)

Identification

Sugar maple is a large canopy tree with a thick trunk and dense crown. The leaves are broad and have 5 pointed lobes; they are dark green in the summer and brilliant red or yellow in the autumn. The shape of the leaves is very similar to those of black maple (*A. nigrum*), but the lobes are more pronounced and the teeth more numerous. The shape is also similar to Norway maple (*A. platanoides*), a native of Europe that is commonly planted along streets and in parks, but the leaves of Norway maple are somewhat broader.

Natural History

Sugar maple is common in late-successional mesic forests throughout much of Minnesota, especially southward. It prefers moist, well-drained, loamy soil, but it also grows on sandy soil over clay. It is very sensitive to flooding and does not occur on active floodplains or at the edges of lakes or marshes. It is also very sensitive to fire and rises to dominance only where fires have been excluded for perhaps 300 years or more (Minnesota Department of Natural Resources 2003). By nature it is a slow-growing, long-lived climax species, typically sharing the forest canopy with other climax species such as basswood (*Tilia americana*), red oak (*Quercus rubra*), and American elm (*Ulmus americana*).

Sugar maples flower in the spring just as the leaves are appearing. The seeds are mature by autumn and fall to the ground just before the leaves do. They germinate early the next spring at rates as high as 95% (*fide* Burns and Honkala 1990), and the seedlings produce their first leaves before the canopy trees do. Sugar maple seedlings are one of the few plants able to survive the deep shade that exists under a sugar maple canopy, and by early summer there may be more than 150,000 maple seedlings per acre (*fide* Burns and Honkala 1990) and very little else. Although the seedlings are extremely shade tolerant, most will die before the next batch of seeds is produced. But some will survive to become saplings, which can persist in the subcanopy for 120 years or longer, waiting to replace canopy trees when they die or are blown over (Canham 1985).

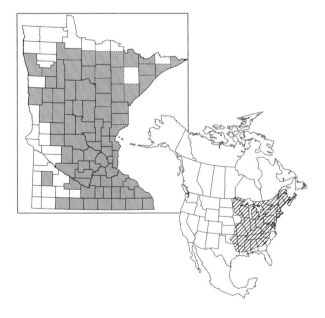

Stigmas of female flowers catch pollen on the wind—May 20.

Fruits are released in September and germinate the next spring—August 7.

The leaf margins have fewer teeth than red maple.

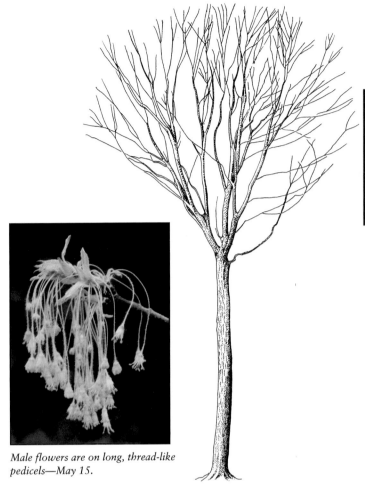

Male flowers are on long, thread-like pedicels—May 15.

Bark can be ridged or "platey"—this trunk is 25" (63 cm) dbh.

Acer spicatum Lam.

Mountain maple

Tall **shrubs** or small shrubby **trees**, with multiple upright **stems** to 7 m tall and 8 cm dbh; forming colonies by layering. **Bark** gray or mottled, smooth or somewhat rough. **Branchlets** reddish to reddish brown or purplish, hairy. **Leaves** simple, opposite, deciduous. **Petioles** 3–11 cm long, minutely hairy; stipules lacking. **Leaf blades** 7–14 cm long, 6–15 cm wide; base cordate; margins palmately 3-lobed, the apical lobe triangular, and about half or less the length of the entire blade, the lateral lobes similar or somewhat smaller, occasionally a pair of small basal lobes are barely discernable; margins serrate with 25+ teeth per side; upper surface dark green, glabrous; lower surface pale green, hairy. **Inflorescence** an erect, elongate, terminal panicle 4–8 cm long; bearing 50–200+ flowers. **Flowers** 5-merous, yellowish green, with unisexual and bisexual flowers produced on the same tree, and often in the same panicle; pedicels hairy; sepals ovate to oblong, 0.5–1.5 mm long; petals glabrous, narrowly oblanceolate, 1.5–4 mm long; stamens 7–8; **anthesis** after the leaves are fully developed, late mid-May to early July; insect-pollinated. **Fruit** a double samara with thin, papery wings; each seed with its accompanying wing 1.8–2.8 cm long; maturing late August to late September; wind-dispersed. (*spicatum*: in spikes, an inaccurate reference to the flowers)

Identification

Mountain maple is the only native maple that is a shrub—all the others are trees—and it is the only one with flowers on an erect stalk. The leaf shape is similar to red maple (*A. rubrum*), but the lobes are shallower, giving the leaf a more rounded appearance. The shape is also similar to high-bush cranberry (*Viburnum trilobum*), except the petiole is much longer (usually 5 cm or longer) and lacks glands where it joins the blade.

Natural History

Mountain maple is common in the understory of upland forests, both coniferous and hardwood, and occasionally swamp forests throughout most of northern Minnesota. It often shares the tall shrub strata with hazels (*Corylus* spp.), dogwoods (*Cornus* spp.), or viburnums (*Viburnum* spp.). Mountain maple is much less common, but still not rare, on the

Paleozoic Plateau in southeastern Minnesota, where it occurs primarily on cool, north and east-facing forested slopes, typically in the shade of sugar maple (*A. saccharum*), basswood (*Tilia americana*), or paper birch (*Betula papyrifera*).

It tends to favor moist, acidic soils, but it is adapted to a fairly broad range of forest conditions, including rocky slopes and gravelly lakeshores. Mountain maple is particularly well adapted to shady forest interiors. In fact, it regularly flowers and sets seed without the benefit of direct sunlight. Canopy trees, on the other hand, flower only after they have reached an opening in the canopy (Lei and Lechowicz 1990).

Where habitat conditions are ideal, mountain maple may form dense stands or patches. These patches are evidently clonal; that is, they develop by vegetative growth, not by seed. But exactly how the clones form is not clear; the mechanism has been reported as layering (Barnes and Wagner 1981) and as root suckering (Heinselman 1973). Mountain maple is also a prolific seed producer. The flowers appear in early summer after the leaves are full size, and develop into winged fruits by late summer. Most fruits are released in late autumn, starting about the time the leaves fall; the rest are released intermittently through the winter. The seeds remain dormant over the winter and germinate the following spring. Under normal forest conditions mountain maple grows slowly and lives a relatively short time, but it resprouts if top-killed by fire, cutting, or heavy browsing.

Erect panicles distinguish mountain maple—July 6.

Autumn foliage ranges from pink to red to maroon—Lake County.

The panicle droops as the fruits ripen—July 25.

Both male and female flowers can be seen in the same panicle.

Stems are typically multiple and tightly clustered.

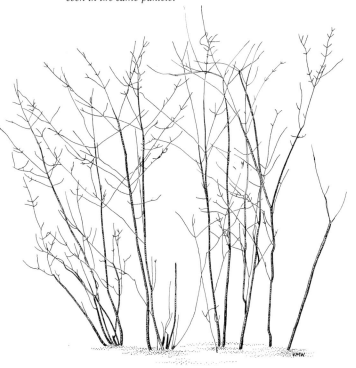

Alnus, the alders

Betulaceae: Birch family

The alders include about 25 species of deciduous trees and large shrubs distributed throughout the Northern Hemisphere and into South America. There are 8 species in North America, and 2 in Minnesota. (*Alnus* is the Latin name for a European alder.)

Key to the Genus Alnus *in Minnesota*

1. Leaf margins shallowly lobed (often interpreted as "double-serrate"), with sinuses about 3 mm deep; leaves with 10–13 lateral veins per side; male catkins on stalks 4–17 mm long; mature lateral female catkins (seen all year as small woody conelike structures) sessile .... **A. *incana* subsp. *rugosa***
1. Leaf margins not lobed ("single-serrate"); leaves with 6–9 lateral veins per side; male catkins essentially sessile; mature female catkins on stalks 8–30 mm long .... **A. *viridis* subsp. *crispa***

Alnus incana (L.) Moench subsp. *rugosa* (DuRoi) Clausen

Speckled alder
[*Alnus rugosa* (DuRoi) Spreng.]

Tall **shrubs** or small **trees**, with multiple upright or leaning **stems** to 8 m tall and 16 cm dbh; clonal by root suckering and layering. **Branchlets** brown to reddish brown or grayish, glabrous to glabrate or sometimes hairy. **Bark** thin, gray or brown, smooth except for pale, warty lenticels. **Leaves** simple, alternate, deciduous. **Petioles** 5–18 mm long, hairy. **Leaf blades** elliptical or sometimes ovate; 5–10 cm long, 3.5–6.5 cm wide; base rounded or tapered; apex acute to obtuse or occasionally somewhat acuminate; margins serrate and usually shallowly lobed with sinuses about 3 mm deep; upper surface dark green, dull, sparsely hairy to glabrate; lower surface pale green, dull, hairy, at least on midvein and in axils of lateral veins. **Inflorescence** unisexual, with male flowers and female flowers borne in separate catkins on the same branch. **Male catkins** reddish brown, slender, pendulous, 4.5–9 cm long at anthesis; borne on stalks 4–17 mm long, in racemose clusters of 2–6 at the ends of branchlets formed the previous year. **Female catkins** red, oblong, stiff, 2–5 mm long at anthesis; borne in racemose clusters of 1–4 (usually 3) just below the male catkins on branchlets of the previous year; developing into persistent woody, conelike structures 10–20 mm long, the lateral structures essentially sessile, the terminal one on stalk 4–8 mm long; **anthesis** late March to early May, before the leaves appear; wind-pollinated. **Fruit** a tiny, flattened samara with broad, lateral wings; 2.5–3.5 mm long; maturing late August to early October, released during winter; wind- and water-dispersed. (*incana*: grayish, hoary; *rugosa*: wrinkled)

Identification

Speckled alder is a large, coarse shrub with up to 20 stems coming from a single root crown. On occasion, it will produce only one stem, which may grow to a height of 20–26 ft (6–8 m) and take the form of a small tree. It is most similar to green alder (*A. viridis* subsp. *crispa*), a smaller shrub that favors upland habitats. Both alders have clusters of woody, conelike catkins at the tips of the branchlets, but the catkins are stalked in green alder, and sessile in speckled alder. *Note:* Worldwide, there are 4 subspecies of speckled alder: 2 occur in North America, but only 1 (subsp. *rugosa*) is found in Minnesota (Furlow 1979).

Natural History

Speckled alder is very common in wetlands throughout most of the forested region of Minnesota, especially in the north. It prefers moderately acidic conditions in direct sunlight or partial shade, particularly along the margins of swamps, marshes, streams, and lakes. It is also common in large wetland basins that support semipermanent shrub communities. Here it is usually mixed with willows (*Salix* spp.) or bog birch (*Betula pumila*), or it may form dense, monotypic stands that exclude all other woody species.

It establishes readily by seed on bare peat, wet sand, silt, and loam and spreads by root suckers and layering of lower branches. This makes it an excellent colonizer of unvegetated habitats formed by floods, breached beaver dams, or ice-scouring. It is also an aggressive colonizer of abandoned low-lying agricultural fields, hay meadows, and roadside ditches.

Individual stems are fast growing and relatively short-lived (normally 10–15 years, rarely more than 25 years), but they can resprout from the root crowns if they are damaged or killed. The root system is shallow and does well in saturated soils that are low in oxygen. They also have nodules that convert atmospheric nitrogen into a form useful to plants (Daly 1966).

Note the shallow lobes, then compare with green alder.

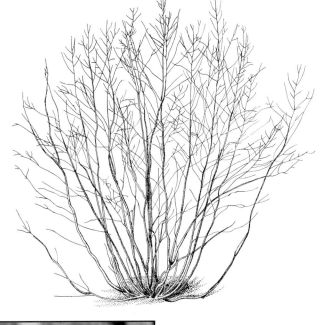

The red stigmas are all that show of the female flowers—April 12.

The seed "cones" ripen and shed their seeds in autumn—August 30.

Edge of a dense speckled alder thicket, 18' (5.5 m) tall—Lake County.

These male flowers have recently shed their pollen—April 21.

The bark is smooth except for pale, warty lenticels.

Alnus viridis (Vill.) DC. subsp. *crispa* (Ait.) Turrill

Green alder
[*Alnus crispa* (Ait.) Pursh]

Tall **shrubs**, with multiple upright **stems** to 4.3 m tall and 4.5 cm dbh; clonal by root suckering. **Branchlets** brown to reddish brown; glabrous or sparsely hairy the 1st year. **Bark** thin, gray, smooth except for pale, warty lenticels. **Leaves** simple, alternate, deciduous. **Petioles** 4–20 mm long, hairy. **Leaf blades** elliptical to ovate; 5–9 cm long, 3–6 cm wide; base rounded or tapered; apex acute to obtuse, or occasionally somewhat blunt; margins finely serrate, not lobed; upper surface dark green, dull, glabrous or glabrate; lower surface pale green, shiny, hairy, at least on midvein and in axils of lateral veins. **Inflorescence** unisexual, with male flowers and female flowers borne in separate catkins on the same branch. **Male catkins** bright yellow, slender, pendulous, 3.5–9 cm long at anthesis; sessile; in racemose clusters of 1–3 (usually 3) at the ends of branchlets formed the previous year. **Female catkins** narrowly cylindrical, stiff, 4–8 mm long at anthesis; borne in loose, racemose clusters of 2–5 on branchlets of the current year; developing into persistent, woody, conelike structures 8–19 mm long, on stalks 8–30 mm long; **anthesis** early May to early June, as the leaves appear; wind-pollinated. **Fruit** a tiny, flattened samara with broad, lateral wings; 2–4 mm long; maturing early September to early October, released during autumn and early winter; wind-dispersed. (*viridis*: green; *crispa*: curled or wavy, in reference to the leaf margins)

Identification
Green alder is a relatively large shrub, although it is generally smaller than speckled alder (*A. incana* subsp. *rugosa*). The leaves lack the shallow lobes of speckled alder, and they tend to have less acute tips and finer serrations on the margins. Also, the lower surface is shiny rather than dull. The leaves also resemble those of hazels (*Corylus* spp.), but the leaf tips are broader. *Note:* There are 4 subspecies of green alder: 1 occurs in Asia, and 3 in North America (Furlow 1979). The only subspecies in Minnesota is *crispa*.

Natural History
Green alder is locally common in the northern forest region of Minnesota, although it is somewhat sporadic and often goes unnoticed. It occurs most often as an understory shrub in stable upland forests with pines (*Pinus* spp.), paper birch (*Betula papyrifera*), white spruce (*Picea glauca*), or occasionally oaks (*Quercus* spp.). It seems to compete best in acidic, nutrient-poor soils, especially sandy or rocky soils. The soils are typically dry at the surface, although green alder is known to produce deep roots that may be able to reach a near-surface water table. The roots of green alder, like all the alders, form nodules that harbor symbiotic, nitrogen-fixing microorganisms (actinomcyetes) (Dalton and Naylor 1975). This enables them to convert atmospheric nitrogen into nitrate, which is a form useful to plants. Presumably, this gives green alder a competitive advantage in nitrogen-poor soils.

The habitats of green alder tend to be fire-prone, and if top-killed by fire, it resprouts vigorously from the roots (Heinselman 1973). Even in the absence of fire or other major disturbance, green alder will spread by root suckers, but it spreads relatively slowly and rarely forms large thickets like the hazels (*Corylus* spp.), dogwoods (*Cornus* spp.), and speckled alder (*A. incana* subsp. *rugosa*). Well-established populations seem to survive events such as logging, yet it does not aggressively colonize early successional forests or grossly disturbed habitats.

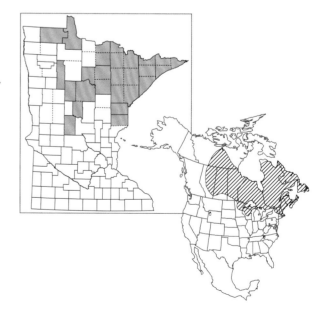

The stems are rarely more than 1.75"
(4.5 cm) in diameter.

The "cones" will open in autumn
and release winged seeds.

Female flowers are packed into
short, stiff catkins—May 3.

Loose, pendulous catkins bear the
male flowers—May 6.

A 12' (3.7 m) tall edge-grown specimen from Lake County.

The leaves have finely serrate margins but not lobes.

Amelanchier, the serviceberries

Rosaceae: Rose family

The serviceberries make up a large, complex genus of deciduous shrubs and small trees that are widely distributed in the Northern Hemisphere. There are about 25 to 35 species, with 18 to 25 in North America, and 8 in Minnesota. (*Amelanchier* is said to be derived from *amelanche*, the French common name for the European *Amelanchier ovalis* Medic.)

The serviceberries have a deserved reputation for being difficult to identify. To make it easier, the serviceberries that occur in Minnesota can be easily divided into three major morphological groups with relatively little complaint from taxonomists.

1. A single nonrhizomatous shrub, *A. bartramiana*, with 1–3 flowers per inflorescence, tapered leaf bases, and leaves not folded in bud. This is a distinct species that is relatively easy to identify.
2. A group of 3 tall, nonrhizomatous shrubs or small trees, with 5–12 flowers per inflorescence, proportionately narrow, pointed leaves with finely serrate margins. Represented in Minnesota by *A. arborea*, *A. laevis*, and, for convenience, *A. interior*, which is likely a hybrid between *A. laevis* and one or more species in the next group.
3. A group of perhaps 4 tall shrubs, mostly rhizomatous, with 6–13 flowers per inflorescence, easily distinguished by roundish leaves with coarsely serrate margins, containing an uncertain number of species, and a bewildering array of probable hybrids of undetermined origin, apomictically reproducing clones, polyploids, and ecotypes.

Each of the three groups can be easily recognized in the field as a coherent group, and the species in the first two groups can usually be keyed with confidence. It is the third group that causes much of the confusion—it must be admitted that the delineation of species in the third group is more or less speculative.

Nielsen (1939) took a somewhat radical approach to the third group and included 6 species: *A. mucronata*, *A. humilis*, *A. sanguinea*, *A. huronensis*, *A. alnifolia*, and *A. stolonifera* (*A. spicata*).

Morley (1969) took a pragmatic approach and placed members of this group into two "species complexes." He called one the "*A. sanguinea* complex," which included *A. sanguinea* and *A. huronensis*. He called the other the "*A. spicata* complex," which included *A. spicata*, *A. humilis*, *A. alnifolia*, and *A. muronata*.

The present treatment is a tentative compromise and includes four species in this group: *A. sanguinea* (treating *A. huronensis* as a synonym); *A. spicata* (treating *A. mucronata* as a synonym); *A. alnifolia*, and *A. humilis*. However, it is possible that none of these entities are stable biological species. When methods become available to truly understand the evolutionary relationships within this group of serviceberries, all these treatments will likely be abandoned.

Key to the Genus Amelanchier in Minnesota

1. Inflorescence with 1–3 flowers; young leaves essentially flat as they emerge from bud; petioles no more than 7 mm long at anthesis (may elongate to 10 mm by midsummer); base of leaf tapered with straight sides (cuneate); petals widest at the middle .... *A. bartramiana*
1. Inflorescence with 4–16 flowers; young leaves folded lengthwise as they emerge from bud; petioles 7 mm long or longer; base of leaf blades rounded, truncate, or cordate; petals generally widest above the middle.
   2. Summit of ovary glabrous, or with a few long hairs at the base of the style.
      3. The lower surface of the leaves covered with dense white hairs (becoming sparsely hairy by late season); fruits somewhat dry, mealy, and tasteless .... *A. arborea*
      3. The lower surface of the leaves glabrous, or young leaves with a few sparse hairs along the midvein; fruits sweet and juicy .... *A. laevis*
   2. Summit of ovary densely woolly, or at least evenly covered with hairs.
      4. Larger leaves with at least 27 teeth per side .... *A. interior*
      4. Leaves with fewer than 27 teeth per side.
         5. Stems nonrhizomatous (stems single or a few together in a tight clump; racemes drooping .... *A. sanguinea*
         5. Stems rhizomatous (stems more than one and spaced 10 cm or more apart); racemes stiff, usually erect or ascending.
            6. Leaf blades tending to be roundish or broadly elliptical; leaf apex and base truncate or broadly rounded; lateral veins conspicuous and remaining conspicuous even at the margin; terminal tooth usually shorter than the adjacent teeth, at most 0.5 mm longer .... *A. alnifolia*
            6. Leaf blades typically oblong, elliptical, or ovate; leaf apex angled, the base usually rounded but sometimes slightly heart-shaped; lateral veins anastomosing before reaching the margin; terminal tooth often exceeding adjacent teeth by more than 0.5 mm.
               7. The larger inflorescences 2.5–4 cm long, with 9–13 (16) flowers; sepals 1.5–3 mm long; leaves at anthesis with 4–6 teeth per cm (3–4 postanthesis) .... *A. humilis*
               7. The larger inflorescences 3.5–6 cm long, with 6–11 flowers; sepals 2.3–4.5 mm long; leaves at anthesis with 7–10 teeth per cm (4–6 postanthesis) .... *A. spicata*

Amelanchier alnifolia Nutt.

Saskatoon serviceberry

Tall **shrubs**, with multiple upright **stems** to 4 m tall and 4 cm basal diameter; forming rhizomatous colonies. **Branchlets** hairy and greenish the 1st year, becoming glabrous and brown to reddish brown the 2nd year. **Bark** thin, gray, smooth, becoming rough in age. **Leaves** simple, alternate, deciduous; half to three-quarters grown at anthesis; juvenile leaves green or bronze-tinged. **Petioles** hairy or glabrate, 1–2 cm long. **Leaf blades** broadly elliptical to roundish, or oblong to quadrangular; 2.5–4.5 cm long, 2–4 cm wide; base rounded to nearly truncate; apex rounded to nearly truncate; margins sharply serrate with 8–20 teeth per side; upper surface dark green, glabrous or glabrate; lower surface pale green to whitish green, densely hairy when young, becoming glabrous or glabrate at maturity. **Inflorescence** a terminal raceme, 2.5–4 cm long, with 6–12 flowers, erect or stiffly ascending. **Flowers** bisexual, 5-merous; pedicels hairy or glabrate, the lowermost 5–11 mm long; sepals triangular, 2–2.5 mm long; petals white, 5–11 mm long, obovate to spatulate; ovary densely woolly at summit; **anthesis** early May to early June; insect-pollinated. **Fruit** a berrylike pome; globose; 8–11 mm in diameter; dark purple to nearly black; maturing early July to early August; animal-dispersed. (*alnifolia*: with leaves like *Alnus*, the alders)

Identification

Saskatoon serviceberry is a midsize, clonal shrub usually 6–9 ft (2–3 m) tall, with smooth, gray bark and stiffly ascending branches. The leaves are small, roundish, or even squarish, with coarsely serrate margins. When the leaves are just unfolding, the undersides are covered with dense, woolly hairs giving them a whitish look. By summer the hairs are mostly gone, and the leaves look dark green. It is sometimes very difficult to tell Saskatoon serviceberry from the more common low serviceberry (*A. humilis*), which differs largely by characters of the leaf (see key). Since the leaves can be extremely variable, it is always helpful to examine leaves from several different branches.

Note: Saskatoon serviceberry is primarily a species of the Great Plains and western mountain region. It has been debated whether true Saskatoon serviceberry occurs as far east as Minnesota (Morley 1969), but by most interpretations it reaches at least the western third of the state (Nielsen 1939), and by at least one interpretation as far east as Quebec (McKay 1973). However, it is cryptic in the presence of similar-looking serviceberry species, so its true status is difficult to know. It is possible that Minnesota plants could all be the more easterly low serviceberry (*A. humilis*) or even spicate serviceberry (*A. spicata*). This is a group of very similar species (perhaps even a single species) characterized by roundish leaves with coarsely serrate margins. The debate goes deep to the heart of serviceberry biology and cannot be settled simply by a closer examination of Minnesota specimens.

Natural History

In Minnesota, Saskatoon serviceberry appears to favor open or brushy habitats within a prairie landscape, particularly coulees, meadows, stream banks, lakeshores, and the margins of bur oak (*Quercus macrocarpa*) or trembling aspen (*Populus tremuloides*) woods. It seems to prefer dry to moist soil, most often sandy, but also loamy, clayey, or even peaty. Periodic drought, spring flooding, and even fires are natural features of its habitat and are easily tolerated. However, it will not persist if the fire interval is as short as perhaps 3 or 4 years. Growth form is strongly rhizomatous, which can lead to large dense clones 25 ft (8 m) or more across. It does invade abandoned agricultural land, roadsides, and intermittent pastures but not aggressively and not beyond what is thought to be its original geographic range.

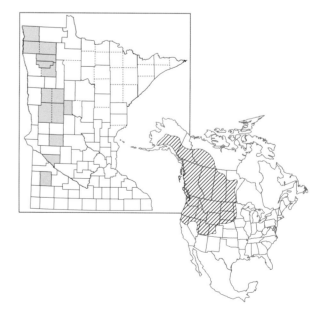

Unfolding leaves are covered with white, woolly hairs—May 18.

Stems are rarely more than 1.5" (4 cm) in diameter.

Fruits will ripen black or dark purple—August 11.

Amelanchier arborea (Michx. f.) Fern.

Downy serviceberry

Tall **shrubs** or small **trees** with multiple upright **stems** to 7.5 m tall and 8 cm dbh; nonrhizomatous. **Branchlets** slender, greenish, and usually hairy the 1st year, becoming brown to reddish brown and glabrate the 2nd year. **Bark** thin, gray, smooth. **Leaves** simple, alternate, deciduous; those on the flowering branchlets barely out of bud when the flowers open; juvenile leaves slightly to moderately bronze-tinged. **Petioles** hairy, especially early in the season, 1.5–3 cm long. **Leaf blades** ovate to elliptical, or slightly oblong to obovate; 4–8 cm long, 2.5–5 cm wide; base rounded or slightly cordate; apex acute to short-acuminate; margins sharply serrate, the larger blades with 25–45 teeth per side; upper surface dark green, glabrous or glabrate; lower surface pale green, densely white-hairy when young, retaining at least some hairs at maturity. **Inflorescence** a terminal raceme, 4–8 cm long, with 5–12 flowers. **Flowers** bisexual, 5-merous; pedicels hairy, the lowermost 0.5–2.5 cm long; sepals narrowly triangular to triangular-lanceolate, 3–5 mm long, hairy; petals white, narrowly obovate to narrowly oblong, 1.1–1.7 cm long; ovary glabrous at summit; **anthesis** late April to late May; insect-pollinated. **Fruit** a berrylike pome; ± globose; 8–12 mm in diameter; reddish purple to purple-black; maturing early July to early August; animal-dispersed. (*arborea*: treelike)

Identification

Downy serviceberry is a tall, multistemmed shrub or small tree, commonly reaching a height of 20 ft (6 m) and a stem diameter of 3 inches (8 cm). It is similar to smooth serviceberry (*A. laevis*) in that both species have finely serrate leaf margins and smooth ovaries. To see the ovary, look down through the top of the flower, or later in the year look at the small opening on the top of the fruit; there should be no hairs. Next check the leaves: those of downy serviceberry are hairy on the underside, and those of smooth serviceberry are without hairs. Be aware that the two species can hybridize and produce a plant with smooth ovaries like both parents and with leaf hairiness intermediate between the two parents.

Natural History

Downy serviceberry is common in much of eastern North America, although it barely reaches the eastern edge of Minnesota. The best habitats seem to be in the St. Croix River valley, where it thrives in forests of northern pin oak (*Quercus ellipsoidalis*), trembling aspen (*Populus tremuloides*), paper birch (*Betula papyrifera*), or pines (*Pinus* spp.). Soils are most often sandy or sandy loam, acidic and well-drained.

The shrub layer in these forests tends to be dominated by the hazels (*Corylus* spp.), but downy serviceberry easily overtops the hazels, nearly reaching the lower branches of the canopy trees. This "upper" shrub strata may also be occupied by pin cherry (*Prunus pensylvanica*) or round-leaved dogwood (*Cornus rugosa*), as well as smooth serviceberry (*A. laevis*) and inland serviceberry (*A. interior*). Interestingly, all three serviceberries are sometimes found growing side by side without one having an obvious competitive advantage over the others.

These forests are often early or midsuccessional communities that originate after fire or in more recent times after logging. Downy serviceberry responds to fire and cutting by resprouting from dormant buds at the base of the stem, thereby ensuring the maintenance of established populations. However, it is vulnerable to soil disturbances and herbicides, and it is not an effective colonizer of ruderal land or abandoned farmland.

Each raceme has 4–12 flowers—May 15.

Note finely serrate margins and acute tip.

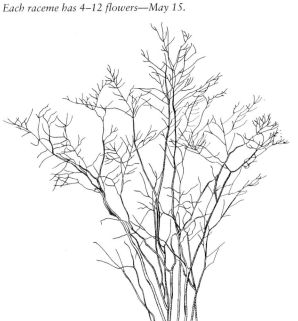

Fruits of downy serviceberry are dry and tasteless—July 15.

A 19' (6 m) tall, edge-grown specimen from Pine County.

Serviceberries 31

Amelanchier bartramiana (Tausch) Roemer

Mountain serviceberry

Midsize **shrubs**, with multiple upright **stems** to 2 m tall and 3 cm basal diameter; nonrhizomatous but sometimes layering. **Branchlets** glabrous, initially green becoming brown to reddish brown by the 2nd year. **Bark** gray, smooth to slightly rough. **Leaves** simple, alternate, deciduous; at least half-grown at anthesis; juvenile leaves slightly to moderately bronze-tinged. **Petioles** glabrous or glabrate, 3–10 mm long. **Leaf blades** elliptical to oblong-elliptical, or occasionally obovate; 3–5 cm long, 1.5–3 cm wide; base tapered; apex acute to obtuse, or somewhat rounded; margins sharply serrate with 27–48 serrations per side; upper surface dark green, glabrous; lower surface pale green, glabrous. **Inflorescence** usually a 2-flowered fascicle, occasionally a 3-flowered cymule or a solitary flower; borne laterally on 1st-year branchlet. **Flowers** bisexual, 5-merous; pedicels glabrous, 1.5–3 cm long; sepals narrowly triangular, 2.2–4 mm long; petals white, oblong-elliptical, 6–9 mm long; summit of ovary woolly; **anthesis** mid-May to early June; insect-pollinated. **Fruit** a berrylike pome; elongate-globose; 9–13 mm long; purplish black; maturing early mid-July to early August; animal-dispersed. (*bartramiana*: named for American botanist William Bartram, 1739–1823)

Identification

This is the smallest of the 8 serviceberries found in Minnesota, rarely over 6 ft (2 m) tall, and probably the most distinctive. The leaf bases are tapered, meaning they have straight sides that form an angle rather than being rounded or heart-shaped (cordate) like the other serviceberries, and it has no more than 3 flowers per inflorescence. Anything resembling mountain serviceberry but with more than 3 flowers and more than about 6 feet tall is likely a hybrid (which is not uncommon) between mountain serviceberry and any one of the other serviceberries.

Natural History

Mountain serviceberry is an understory shrub in a variety of forested habitats, most often in mixed conifer–hardwood forests and swamps, usually in moist or wet acidic soils. It is also found in brushy transition habitats as well as cliffs, rock outcrops, lakeshores, and stream banks. It does not compete well in sunny openings, where it is easily crowded out by more aggressive and faster-growing shrubs. It also does poorly in continuous shade, where the lack of light will suppress growth and reproduction. Intermittent shade seems to be preferred, but even in seemingly ideal habitat it is not particularly common. However, it is easily overlooked, perhaps because of its small size and inconspicuous form.

Mountain serviceberry does not form dense thickets as the hazels (*Corylus* spp.) or alders (*Alnus* spp.) sometimes do. Such thickets typically develop through the spread of underground stems called rhizomes, or through a process called root suckering, in which stems arise from long, invasive roots. Mountain serviceberry does not behave this way. Instead, its stems typically arise singly or in small clumps from a well-defined root crown that originated from a seed. There is an exception to this: under certain conditions it may spread by a process called layering, in which a stem becomes horizontal on the ground and takes root along its length, thereby establishing a series of interconnected root crowns. Each crown can then send up a new stem, which can result in the creation of a loose colony.

Flowers appear in clusters of 1–3—June 7, Cook County.

*Fruits can reach 1/2" (1.3 cm) in length—July 7,
Pine County.*

Amelanchier humilis Wieg.

Low serviceberry

Tall **shrubs**, with multiple upright **stems** to 4 m tall and 4 cm basal diameter; forming rhizomatous colonies (clones). **Branchlets** initially hairy and greenish, becoming glabrous and reddish brown by the 2nd year. **Bark** thin, gray, smooth or rough in age. **Leaves** simple, alternate, deciduous, one-third to two-thirds grown at anthesis. **Petioles** hairy, becoming glabrate, 1–2 cm long. **Leaf blades** oblong, elliptical, or ovate; 2.5–5 cm long, 2–4 cm wide; base rounded or slightly cordate; apex acute to blunt, or rounded, often mucronate; margins sharply serrate with 16–25 teeth per side; upper surface glabrous or glabrate; lower surface densely white-hairy when young, becoming glabrous or glabrate at maturity. **Inflorescence** a terminal raceme, 2.5–4 cm long, with 9–13 flowers. **Flowers** bisexual, 5-merous; pedicels hairy, becoming glabrate, the lowermost 9–11 mm long; sepals 1.5–3 mm long, triangular; petals white, 4.7–9.5 mm long, obovate to oblanceolate; summit of ovary densely woolly; **anthesis** early May to early June; insect-pollinated. **Fruit** a berrylike pome; ± globose; 7–11 mm in diameter; nearly black when ripe; maturing early July to early August; animal-dispersed. (*humilis*: low-growing, short)

Identification

Low serviceberry is one of the smaller serviceberries, often just 6 or 8 ft (2–2.5 m) tall, and it almost always has multiple stems. But rather than the stems all arising from a single base, they arise individually along a network of underground stems (rhizomes) at intervals of perhaps 4–12 inches (10–30 cm). This may result in a colony of ± evenly spaced stems covering many square yards (meters). This clonal growth form also occurs in Saskatoon serviceberry (*A. alnifolia*) and spicate serviceberry (*A. spicata*). All three species have similar leaf shapes and inflorescences, which can make it difficult to distinguish one from the other.
Note: The taxonomic relationship of the three species mentioned above is frequently debated and will likely be reinterpreted in the future. However, Nielson (1939) made a detailed study of low serviceberry in Minnesota and believed it to be a clearly defined species that could be readily separated from all others. He went so far as to describe three new varieties of low serviceberry, based largely on characteristics of the leaf, inflorescence, and bud

scales. Although his varieties seem inconsequential, his basic concept of the species is maintained here.

Natural History

Low serviceberry is common throughout most of Minnesota, particularly in open woods, around rock outcrops, moist meadows, unburned prairies, and lakeshores. In forested regions it is associated with both conifers and hardwoods, but it is usually found in an opening or along a margin where it gets direct sunlight for at least a portion of the day. Soils are usually sandy or loamy, occasionally clayey, peaty, or rocky; moisture conditions range from dryish to moist or even wet. It aggressively resprouts if top-killed by fire, cutting, or browsing and easily withstands drought and short-duration spring flooding, but it is sensitive to sedimentation.

In agricultural regions it often colonizes stable, grassy habitats, where it competes well with other shrubs, at least if given a head start. Unimpeded by competition it will form dense colonies (clones) up to 60 ft (20 m) across. There will be perhaps hundreds of stems spaced a foot (30 cm) or so apart, all connected underground by rhizomes. Even though the dense network of rhizomes makes these colonies quite resilient, they will eventually be overtopped by trees and shaded out.

Note the short, erect racemes—May 20.

The top of the ovary can be seen from this perspective—May 16.

Note leaves with coarse serrations and blunt tips—July 14.

Serviceberries   **35**

Amelanchier interior Nielsen

Inland serviceberry
[*A. wiegandii* Nielsen]

Tall **shrubs** or small **trees**, with single or multiple **stems** to 12 m tall and 14 cm dbh; infrequently rhizomatous. **Branchlets** glabrous; greenish the 1st year, brown or reddish brown the 2nd year. **Bark** thin, gray, smooth. **Leaves** simple, alternate, deciduous; one-third to two-thirds grown at anthesis; juvenile leaves slightly to moderately bronze-tinged. **Petioles** hairy when young, glabrous or glabrate at maturity, 1–2.5 cm long. **Leaf blades** ovate to elliptical or oblong; 4–6 cm long, 2.5–4 cm wide; base rounded or slightly cordate; apex obtuse to acute or abruptly short-acuminate; margins sharply serrate with 21–40 teeth per side; upper surface dark green, hairy when young, glabrous when full size; lower surface pale green, densely to sparsely hairy when young, glabrous or glabrate when full size. **Inflorescence** a terminal raceme, 4–7 cm long, with 7–12 flowers. **Flowers** bisexual, 5-merous; pedicels glabrous or glabrate, the lowermost 1–2 cm long; sepals triangular to narrowly triangular, 3–4.5 mm long; petals white, narrowly obovate to oblong-obovate, 0.8–1.7 cm long; ovary densely to sparsely hairy at summit; **anthesis** late April to early June; insect-pollinated. **Fruit** a berrylike pome; globose; 6–9 mm in diameter; dark purple when ripe; maturing early July to late August; animal-dispersed. (*interior*: inner or interior; in reference to its geographic range in the interior of the continent)

Identification

Inland serviceberry is usually a large, understory shrub with multiple stems rising from a single root crown. Occasionally it will take the form of a small, single-stemmed tree 20–30 ft (6–9 m) tall. The bark is gray and smooth, remaining smooth even in old age. The leaves are very difficult to tell from those of downy serviceberry (*A. arborea*); the shape is nearly identical, and both are hairy in the spring but nearly smooth by autumn. But inland serviceberry differs conclusively in that the top of the ovary is distinctly hairy, sometimes even woolly. It differs from smooth serviceberry (*A. laevis*) in the same way.
Note: It is likely that this entity, as it is described above, is actually a complex of fertile hybrids (and backcrosses) involving smooth serviceberry (*A. laevis*), low serviceberry (*A. humilis*), and/or roundleaf serviceberry (*A. sanguinea*). As a result,

what is being called inland serviceberry is quite variable in appearance, and yet it is relatively common and easily recognized.

Natural History

Inland serviceberry is fairly common within the forested region of Minnesota, especially in the north-central counties, where it is probably the most common species of serviceberry. It is an understory shrub or occasionally a subcanopy tree typically associated with oaks (*Quercus* spp.), trembling aspen (*Populus tremuloides*), paper birch (*Betula papyrifera*), or pines (*Pinus* spp.). It prefers dry to dry-mesic conditions, usually in sandy or sandy loam soils. It is moderately tolerant of shade, so it does occur in forest interiors, but it grows larger and produces more fruit along forest edges and in openings.

Although slow growing, individual stems occasionally reach 50 years of age, which is moderately long-lived compared to other small trees in similar habitats. It sometimes forms small clones, but it more often occurs as solitary clumps or isolated stems. It resprouts if the stems are damaged by heavy browsing or fire, allowing it to maintain a strong presence in fire-prone landscapes. It is not an aggressive colonizer of abandoned agricultural land or other ruderal habitats, but well-established, well-structured populations do persist through most logging operations, as long as the soil is not disturbed and herbicides are not used.

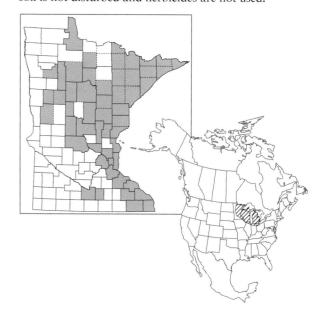

Fruits become dark purple at maturity—August 28.

Leaves are about half-grown when flowers appear—June 2.

Edge-grown specimen at peak anthesis on June 8—Cook County.

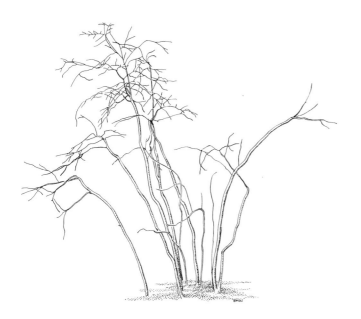

Bark remains thin, gray, and smooth.

Amelanchier laevis Wieg.

Smooth serviceberry

Tall **shrubs** or small **trees**, with single or multiple upright **stems** to 14 m tall and 18 cm dbh; nonrhizomatous. **Branchlets** slender, glabrous, greenish the 1st year, becoming brown to reddish brown the 2nd. **Bark** thin, mottled gray, smooth when young, developing thin, flat-topped ridges in age. **Leaves** simple, alternate, deciduous; those on the flowering branchlets about half-grown when the flowers open; juvenile leaves strongly bronze-tinged. **Petioles** glabrous, 1–2.5 cm long. **Leaf blades** ovate to elliptical or oblong; 4–7 cm long, 2.5–4 cm wide; base rounded or slightly cordate; apex acute to short-acuminate; margins sharply serrate, the larger blades with 25–40 teeth per side; upper surface dark green, glabrous; lower surface pale green, glabrous. **Inflorescence** a terminal raceme, 4–7 cm long, with 5–12 flowers. **Flowers** bisexual, 5-merous; pedicels glabrous, the lowermost 1.5–2.5 cm long in flower, 2.5–4 cm long in fruit; sepals narrowly triangular to triangular-lanceolate, 2.5–5 mm long; petals white, narrowly obovate to oblong-linear, 1–1.6 cm long; ovary glabrous at summit; **anthesis** late mid-April to late May; insect-pollinated. **Fruit** a berrylike pome; ± globose; 8–13 mm in diameter; deep red to blackish; maturing early mid-July to late mid-August; animal-dispersed. (*laevis*: smooth, lacking hairs)

Identification

Smooth serviceberry can be either a large, multistemmed shrub or a small, single-stemmed tree. As a tree it has a narrow crown of slender ascending branches and may reach a height of 45 ft (14 m) and a stem diameter of 7 inches (18 cm). The smooth gray bark seen on younger trees becomes ridged and furrowed like that of an ironwood (*Ostrya virginiana*) as the tree grows older. Inland serviceberry (*A. interior*) and downy serviceberry (*A. arborea*) are similar, but only smooth serviceberry lacks hairs on the leaves and the top of the ovary. *Note:* Many specimens found in Minnesota closely resemble smooth serviceberry except for the presence of hairs on the top of the ovary. This probably indicates some hybrid influence from low serviceberry (*A. humilis*) or roundleaf serviceberry (*A. sanguinea*). As a practical matter, these putative hybrids have been assigned to inland serviceberry (*A. interior*).

Natural History

Smooth serviceberry is fairly common in a few of the east-central counties; elsewhere it is occasional or infrequent. It seems to prefer well-drained sandy or sandy loam soils, usually where the surface is dry or slightly moist. It often appears as a large, multistemmed shrub in brushy habitats, yet its ultimate form is a single-stemmed understory tree in upland hardwood or mixed hardwood-conifer forests. It grows relatively slowly in forest interiors and may reach an age of 65 years, which is perhaps typical for an understory species this size. It is usually associated with early or mid-successional species of fire-prone habitats, particularly oaks (*Quercus* spp.), trembling aspen (*Populus tremuloides*), red maple (*Acer rubrum*), paper birch (*Betula papyrifera*), or pines (*Pinus* spp.).

Exactly how smooth serviceberry responds to fire has not been studied, but it can endure logging operations and live to resprout, at least if the roots are not damaged too badly. However, it does not readily invade cutover land if it was not there prior to logging, at least not until a new canopy forms. The same is true for abandoned farmland and other ruderal habitats.

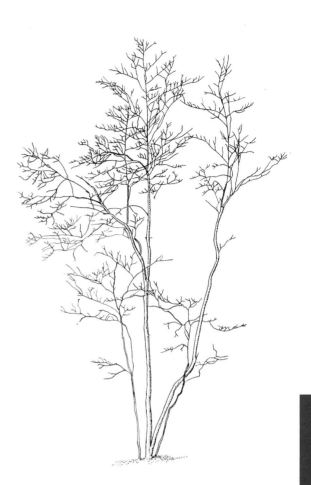

Flowering specimen at edge of steep ravine—Lake County, May 6.

Red fruits will ripen blackish in another 2–3 weeks—July 15.

Older stems become furrowed, this one is 4.5" (11 cm) diameter.

Immature leaves are strongly bronze-tinged—May 1.

Serviceberries 🌿 **39**

Amelanchier sanguinea (Pursh) DC.

Roundleaf serviceberry
[*A. huronensis* Wieg.]

Tall **shrubs** or small **trees**, with single or multiple upright **stems** to 8 m tall and 9 cm dbh; nonrhizomatous. **Branchlets** greenish and hairy or glabrate the 1st year, becoming reddish brown and glabrous the 2nd year. **Bark** thin, gray, smooth, or becoming rough in age. **Leaves** simple, alternate, deciduous, one-third to two-thirds grown at anthesis; juvenile leaves often bronze-tinged. **Petioles** initially hairy, becoming glabrous or glabrate, 1–2.5 cm long. **Leaf blades** elliptical to ovate or slightly oblong; 4–7 cm long, 2.5–4.5 cm wide; base rounded to slightly cordate; apex acute to obtuse or blunt; margins sharply serrate with 8–27 teeth per side; upper surface dark green, glabrous or glabrate; lower surface pale green, densely white-hairy when young, becoming glabrous or glabrate at maturity. **Inflorescence** a terminal raceme, 3–7.5 cm long, with 6–12 flowers. **Flowers** bisexual, 5-merous; pedicels initially hairy, becoming glabrous or glabrate, the lowermost 1–3 cm long; sepals 2.5–4 mm long, narrowly triangular to triangular-lanceolate; petals white, 7.5–13 mm long, obovate to oblanceolate; summit of ovary densely woolly; **anthesis** early May to early June; insect-pollinated. **Fruit** a berrylike pome; globose; 6–9 mm in diameter; dark purple or blackish; maturing late June to mid-August; animal-dispersed. (*sanguinea:* blood-red)

Identification

Roundleaf serviceberry can be either a small, single-stemmed tree or a large, multistemmed shrub. The leaves are sometimes roundish in outline, as the common name suggests, but they are more often elliptical or ovate, and the margins have fewer than 27 teeth per side. Also, there is a patch of dense, woolly hairs at the top of the ovary that is easily seen by looking downward through the top of the flower. These characters separate it from all but low serviceberry (*A. humilis*), spicate serviceberry (*A. spicata*), and Saskatoon serviceberry (*A. alnifolia*), from which it differs primarily by being nonrhizomatous. This means that all the stems come from a single root crown and are tightly clumped. Stems of rhizomatous species are more diffused; they tend to be spaced 4–12 inches (10–30 cm) apart.

Note: Trying to distinguish this species from the look-alikes mentioned previously can be frustrating and reflects genuine confusion over the evolutionary relationships among the various entities.

Natural History

Roundleaf serviceberry is adapted to a wide variety of habitats, including forest edges, open woodlands, rocky exposures, lakeshores, and river banks, often with oaks (*Quercus* spp.), aspens (*Populus* spp.), or pines (*Pinus* spp.). It is relatively fast growing but short-lived, and only moderately shade tolerant. It appears to be somewhat of an opportunist and will colonize abandoned agricultural land and cutover forest land, but not aggressively. The stems grow singly or in tight clumps; it does not form thickets or spreading clones.

Roundleaf serviceberry is not particularly common, although it can be found with some regularity in the north-central and northeastern counties. Wherever it is found, low serviceberry (*A. humilis*) and interior serviceberry (*A. interior*) will likely be nearby and more abundant. It is not unusual to find three or even four species of serviceberry growing together in the same area, sometimes even side by side.

The flowers can be up to 1" (2.5 cm) across—June 6.

In the presence of wildlife, ripe fruits disappear quickly—July 31.

The racemes of roundleaf serviceberry tend to droop—June 6.

All the serviceberries have smooth, gray bark when young.

Amelanchier spicata (Lam.) K. Koch.

Spicate serviceberry

[*A. stolonifera* Wieg.; *A. mucronata* Nielsen]

Large **shrubs**, with multiple upright **stems** to 4.5 m tall and 5 cm basal diameter; forming rhizomatous colonies. **Branchlets** hairy and greenish the 1st year, becoming glabrous and brown or reddish brown the 2nd year. **Bark** thin, gray, smooth. **Leaves** simple, alternate, deciduous; about half-grown at anthesis; juvenile leaves often bronze-tinged. **Petioles** hairy or glabrous, 1–2.5 cm long. **Leaf blades** ovate to elliptical or broadly elliptical; 3–6 cm long, 2–4 cm wide; base rounded to slightly cordate; apex acute to obtuse or rounded; margins sharply serrate or rarely entire, with 0–25 serrations per side; upper surface dark green, glabrous or glabrate; lower surface pale green, densely white-hairy when young, becoming glabrous or glabrate at maturity. **Inflorescence** a terminal raceme, 3.5–6 cm long, with 6–11 flowers, erect or ascending. **Flowers** bisexual, 5-merous; pedicels initially hairy, becoming glabrate, the lowermost 1–2 cm long; sepals narrowly triangular, 2.5–4.5 mm long; petals white, elliptical-obovate to oblong-obovate, 7–12 mm long; ovary woolly at summit; anthesis mid-May to early mid-June; insect-pollinated. **Fruit** a berrylike pome; globose; 7–9 mm in diameter; blackish; maturing early August to early September; animal-dispersed. (*spicata*: bearing a spike, an inaccurate description of the inflorescence).

Identification

Spicate serviceberry is a relatively large, multistemmed shrub reaching a height of 10–13 ft (3–4 m). It has smooth, gray bark and stiff, upright inflorescences. It is very similar (some would say identical) to roundleaf serviceberry (*A. sanguinea*), except it produces rhizomes. Rhizomes are horizontal stems that grow underground and sprout aerial stems at intervals of perhaps 6–12 inches (15–30 cm). This can result in a colony of more or less evenly spaced stems covering an area perhaps 3–10 ft (1–3 m) across. Nonrhizomatous species produce all their stems from a single root crown, resulting in a tight, compact cluster of stems. Spicate serviceberry is also very similar to Saskatoon serviceberry (*A. alnifolia*), but the leaves are somewhat more pointed and lack the conspicuous lateral veins.

Note: The entity described here as spicate serviceberry is one of the infamous "round-leaved" serviceberries

that seem to defy traditional taxonomy. Although it seems to be distinct in Minnesota, it is clearly different than what is called *A. spicata* in Michigan (Voss 1985). It is closer to published descriptions of *A. spicata* (*A. stolonifera*) from Ontario (Soper and Heimburger 1982) but still different. Perhaps the confusion can be resolved by a range-wide comparison of the relevant specimens, or perhaps it must wait for new techniques to reveal the underlying relationships among this difficult group of plants.

Natural History

Spicate serviceberry does not seem to tolerate shade and tends to favor open, exposed habitats, especially bedrock exposures, cliffs, rocky or sandy lakeshores, riverbanks, and open woodlands. It seems to occur only in the northeast, most commonly near the shore of Lake Superior, but it is not common. The most common serviceberry in the northeast appears to be inland serviceberry (*A. interior*).

The growth form of spicate serviceberry is strongly rhizomatous. When given room to spread it will form dense colonies, sometimes covering an area of several square yards (meters) with numerous closely spaced stems.

Fully ripe fruits on August 23—Lake County.

Erect racemes are characteristic of spicate serviceberry—June 15.

Leaves tend to be elliptical with a nearly blunt tip.

The stems are connected by underground rhizomes.

Amorpha, lead plant and false indigos

Fabaceae: Bean family

This North American genus includes about 15 species of shrubs, mostly in the southern states, with 3 in Minnesota. (*Amorpha* is from the Greek *amorphos*, without form, in reference to the flowers, which have only a single petal.)

Key to the Genus Amorpha *in Minnesota*

1. Leaflets 2.5–4.5 cm long; calyx lobes less than 1 mm long; mature pods 5–9 mm long; a shrub of lakeshores and riverbanks, often 2+ m tall .... *A. fruticosa*
1. Leaflets 0.6–1.5 cm long; calyx lobes greater than 1 mm long; mature pods 3.5–5.5 mm long; a shrub of open prairies, usually less than 1 m tall.
    2. Leaflets 0.6–1 cm long, the lower surface glabrous or with hairs only on midvein and along margins, and with numerous glandular dots usually visible to the unaided eye; inflorescence a single terminal raceme; calyx glabrous; mature pods 4–5.5 mm long, glabrous .... *A. nana*
    2. Leaflets 0.9–1.5 cm long, the lower surface with a uniform covering of dense woolly hairs, glands, if present, hidden beneath the hairs; inflorescence a cluster of 5–20 racemes; calyx densely hairy; mature pods 3.5–4.5 mm long, densely hairy ....*A. canescens*

Amorpha canescens Pursh

Lead plant

Midsize **shrubs** with multiple upright **stems** to 1.3 m tall and 1 cm basal diameter; clonal by root suckering. **Branchlets** of the current year densely canescent; 1-year-old branchlets glabrous or glabrate. **Bark** gray to brownish, somewhat rough. **Leaves** pinnately compound, alternate, deciduous; 4–10 cm long. **Petioles** to 2 mm long or lacking, canescent. **Leaflets** 19–49; ovate to oblong or elliptical; 9–15 mm long, 3–7 mm wide; base rounded to nearly truncate or subcordate; apex blunt to rounded, mucronate; margins entire; upper surface gray-green, densely to moderately hairy; lower surface pale gray-green, densely hairy, small pale sessile glands usually present but hidden beneath the hairs. **Inflorescence** a cluster of 5–20 erect racemes, each 4–17 cm long and 1–1.5 cm wide, borne on naked peduncles from the axils of the uppermost leaves. **Flowers** bisexual, 5-merous, blue; pedicels 0.5–1.2 mm long, moderately to densely hairy; calyx densely hairy, punctate-glandular, 2.5–4.5 mm long, the lobes lanceolate, 1.5–2 mm long; corolla reduced to a single petal enveloping the stamens and pistil, 4–5.5 mm long; **anthesis** late June to early August; insect-pollinated. **Fruit** a 1-seeded indehiscent pod 3.5–4.5 mm long; densely hairy and conspicuously punctate-glandular; maturing late August to early October; animal- and gravity-dispersed. (*canescens*: covered with fine, gray hairs; hoary)

Identification

Lead plant is a multistemmed prairie shrub, usually no more than waist high, with numerous small, soft, grayish (lead-colored) leaflets. What catches the eye are the numerous racemes of bright blue flowers clustered at the end of each branch. It is most similar to dwarf false indigo (*A. nana*), which is a smaller plant that has bright green foliage and a single raceme at the end of each branch.

Natural History

Lead plant is probably the most common and abundant shrub on open prairies. In fact, it is one of the few woody plants that can honestly be called a prairie specialist. In addition to prairies, it can be found in savannas and open woodlands, but only where there is direct sunlight. Savannas usually have widely spaced bur oak (*Quercus macrocarpa*) or jack pine (*Pinus banksiana*) and a ground cover of prairie grasses and forbs. Soil types range from sandy or gravelly to loamy, and from dry to mesic.

The roots of lead plant go very deep, easily to 10 ft (3 m), but it also produces shallow roots that spread horizontally just beneath the surface. These shallow roots (sometimes reported as rhizomes) can sprout aerial stems as far as 15 ft (5 m) from the parent plant (Weaver 1954). Over time, this can result in the creation of a loose colony but never a dense thicket.

Lead plant is relatively long-lived and generally slow growing. It is also very drought resistant and well adapted to repeated and frequent wildfire. When top-killed, it will resprout vigorously and flower the 1st year. In fact, it can resprout and flower every year for several successive years if necessary (Tester 1996). In this way it can function much as a herbaceous plant, but it will eventually decline if forced to continually resprout.

In the absence of fire lead plant will develop into a bushy although somewhat formless shrub, and produce few flowers or fruits. Still, it manages to persist in prairie remnants that have not burned in decades, at least where it has not been overgrown by trees or larger shrubs. Although it is persistent, it is slow to become established, and it does not invade roadsides or old fields.

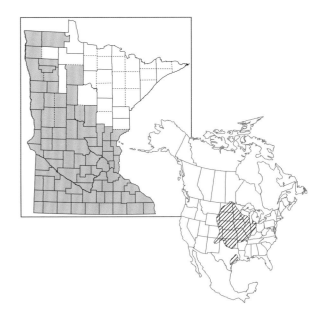

The individual leaflets are only about 1/2" (13 mm) long.

Note the densely hairy seed pods—September 20.

Showing "lead"-colored foliage on a Douglas County prairie—July 21.

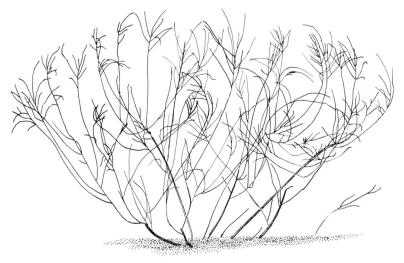

Flowers of Amorpha are unique; each has only 1 petal—July 18.

Amorpha fruticosa L.

False indigo

Large **shrubs**, with 1 to several upright or leaning **stems** to 3 m tall and 6 cm basal diameter; clonal by root suckering. **Branchlets** of the current year with short, white, appressed hairs; 1-year-old branchlets usually glabrate. **Bark** gray, roughened with short horizontal lenticels. **Leaves** pinnately compound, alternate, deciduous; 10–20 cm long. **Petioles** 1.5–3.5 cm long, with short, white, appressed hairs or occasionally glabrous. **Leaflets** 9–21; oblong to elliptical or occasionally ovate or obovate; 2.5–4.5 cm long, 0.9–2 cm wide; base tapered; apex blunt to rounded, occasionally slightly notched, mucronate; margins entire; upper surface dark green, minutely hairy to glabrate; lower surface pale green, with stiff, white, appressed hairs and often dotted with green sessile glands. **Inflorescence** a cluster of 1–4 (usually 3) erect racemes borne at the tips of leafy branchlets, each raceme 5–15 cm long and 1–2 cm wide. **Flowers** bisexual, 5-merous, blue or purplish; pedicels 1–2.2 mm long, sparsely to densely hairy; calyx sparsely hairy, punctate-glandular, 2.5–3.5 mm long, the lobes triangular-deltate, 0.5–0.8 mm long; corolla reduced to a single petal enveloping the stamens and pistil, 4.5–6.5 mm long; **anthesis** late May to early July; insect-pollinated. **Fruit** a 1-seeded indehiscent pod 5–9 mm long; glabrous or hairy; conspicuously pustulate-glandular; maturing mid-August to late September; animal- and gravity-dispersed. (*fruticosa*: shrubby)

Identification

False indigo is a relatively large, bushy shrub, often 6–9 ft (2–3 m) tall, with large compound leaves and showy racemes of small, blue or purplish flowers. Just looking at the leaves, it is more likely to be confused with black locust (*Robinia pseudoacacia*) than another species of *Amorpha*, but black locust is ultimately a tree rather than a shrub, and it has sharp spines at the nodes.

Natural History

False indigo is fairly common in the southern half of the state, especially on lakeshores and riverbanks where it will often arch over the water. In fact, this is one of the few shrubs that readily colonizes sandy beaches, ice-thrust ridges, and cut-banks. In doing so, it has the desirable effect of stabilizing this highly unstable zone, but it seems to take quite a beating in the process. It is often found with scarred stems, broken branches, or partially exposed roots, and yet it persists tenaciously.

Other habitats include alluvial meadows, shallow marshes, and swales, where it typically occurs in the company of willow shrubs (*Salix* spp.) and dogwoods (*Cornus* spp.). It is very tolerant of seasonal flooding, even sedimentation and erosion, but not shading or burning. It usually grows in wet soil or at least where its roots can reach the water table. It prefers basic (calcareous) or circumneutral soils, usually sand, silt, or occasionally shallow peat. It is generally absent from the more acidic wetlands and lakeshores that predominate in northeastern and north-central Minnesota.

False indigo can form fairly large colonies by root suckering, but it usually occurs in isolated clumps or in small, loose colonies. It is fast growing and short-lived, which allows it to function primarily as an opportunist that can rapidly colonize edges and ecotones. In time it is usually outcompeted by other shrubs or overtopped by trees; it is not a long-term member of any stable or homogeneous community.

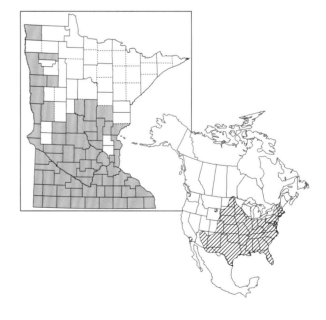

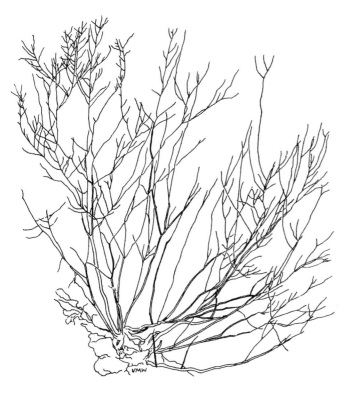

A 6' (2 m) specimen at the edge of a Freeborn County lake.

At peak anthesis on June 13 in Ramsey County.

The individual leaflets can be nearly an inch (2.5 cm) long.

The pods show typical legume structure—September 12.

Amorpha nana Nutt.

Dwarf false indigo

Midsize **shrubs**, with 1 or a few upright **stems** to 1 m tall and 7 mm basal diameter; clonal by root suckering or possibly rhizomes. **Branchlets** of the current year sparsely hairy to glabrate; 1-year-old branchlets glabrous. **Bark** gray to brownish, ± smooth. **Leaves** pinnately compound, alternate, deciduous; 3–9 cm long. **Petioles** 2–8 mm long, sparsely hairy. **Leaflets** 9–27; oblong to elliptical or obovate; 6–10 mm long, 3–5 mm wide; base rounded or tapered; apex blunt to rounded or notched, mucronate; margins entire or crenulate; upper surface dark green, glabrous; lower surface pale green, glabrous or more often sparsely hairy on midvein and at the margins, conspicuously dotted with numerous sessile glands (usually visible to the unaided eye). **Inflorescence** a solitary terminal raceme 2.5–8 cm long and 0.5–1.5 cm wide, borne at the end of a leafy branchlet. **Flowers** bisexual, 5-merous, blue; pedicels 1–2 mm long, moderately to densely hairy; calyx ± glabrous, punctate-glandular, 3–4.5 mm long, the lobes narrowly triangular with acuminate tips, 1.2–2 mm long; corolla reduced to a single petal enveloping the stamens and pistil, 4–6 mm long; **anthesis** early June to late June; insect-pollinated. **Fruit** a 1-seeded indehiscent pod 4–5.5 mm long; glabrous; conspicuously punctate-glandular; maturing late July to mid-September; animal- and gravity-dispersed. (*nana*: dwarf)

Identification

Dwarf false indigo is a compact, leafy shrub about knee high, usually small enough to be hidden in tall grass. It has deep blue flowers and small, compound leaves with numerous tiny leaflets. It is similar to the larger and more common lead plant (*A. canescens*), but the foliage is bright green and nearly hairless, which is subtly different from the hoary, gray-green leaves of lead plant. Also, each branch of dwarf false indigo ends in a single spikelike raceme, while each branch of lead plant ends in a cluster of 5–20 racemes.

Natural History

Dwarf false indigo is a rather uncommon plant found at scattered locations across the Great Plains, primarily in Minnesota and the Dakotas (Wilbur 1964). It is much less common than the familiar lead plant, although it does occur in similar prairie habitats. To those not familiar with the significance of prairies in the history of Minnesota, it should be known that most of western and southern Minnesota was prairie at the time of Euro-American settlement. A figure of 20 million acres (8 million hectares) is commonly used (Tester 1995). However, nearly all that has since been plowed under. A total of perhaps 150,000 acres (60,000 hectares) survives today, most in tiny fragments that are isolated from the ecological processes that originally sustained them.

Within prairies, dwarf false indigo is usually found in moist, loamy soil or occasionally on dryish hillsides. Reproduction by seed does occur yet seems rather limited. Most reproduction is clonal by suckering from roots (sometimes reported as rhizomes), but it does not spread aggressively. In fact, it rarely forms colonies of much size, and it is easily crowded out by larger shrubs. However, it does resprout after fire or browsing, and it easily withstands seasonal droughts.

In many ways it is less resilient than lead plant; it is easily extirpated by cattle grazing or annual mowing, and once it is gone, it returns very slowly if at all. And since it does not colonize pastures, brome fields, hay meadows, or roadsides, its presence is a reliable indicator of a relative lack of human disturbance. It is a species that will survive only with careful stewardship of surviving prairie remnants.

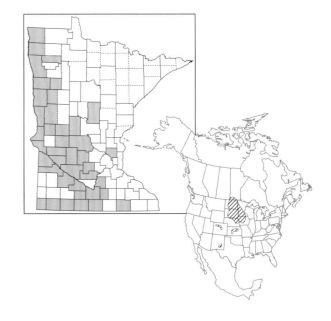

Flowers are in a terminal raceme—June 12.

Pods are similar to those of lead plant except hairless—August 18.

The entire shrub is only about knee high—June 21.

Andromeda, bog rosemary

Ericaceae: Heath family

The genus *Andromeda* consists of 2 closely related but apparently distinct species. *A. glaucophylla* Link is exclusively North American and is widespread in the coniferous forest region of Minnesota. *A. polifolia* L. is circumpolar and occurs only to the north of Minnesota. (*Andromeda* is a mythical Ethiopian princess.)

Andromeda glaucophylla Link

Bog rosemary

[*A. polifolia* L. var. *glaucophylla* (Link) DC.]

Low **shrubs**, with 1 or a few upright or ascending **stems** to 40 cm tall, often becoming decumbent and rooting at the nodes. **Branchlets** of the year brown, glabrous; becoming gray the 2nd year, eventually shedding the epidermal layer revealing a smooth red-brown or purplish surface. **Leaves** simple, alternate, evergreen; persisting until the 2nd season. **Petioles** barely distinct, 1–3 mm long. **Leaf blades** narrowly elliptical to linear or almost needlelike; 2.5–5 cm long, 2–8 mm wide, length/width 6–20; base acutely tapered; apex acutely tapered with a sharp point; margins entire, strongly revolute; upper surface dark green, glabrous, the mid-vein impressed; lower surface white or pale green, densely and minutely hairy, mid-vein prominently expressed; immature leaves often blue-glaucous. **Flowers** bisexual, 5-merous, whitish to pinkish; borne in terminal umbel-like clusters of 3–9, clusters drooping in flower but becoming erect in fruit; pedicels 3–10 mm long, glabrous; sepals triangular, 1–1.5 mm long; corolla urn-shaped, 4.5–6.5 mm long, the lobes less than 1 mm long and recurved; stamens 10, included; style shorter than the corolla, persistent in fruit; **anthesis** late mid-May to mid-June; insect-pollinated. **Fruit** a depressed-globular 5-valved capsule; often blue-glaucous; 3–5 mm across; maturing late June to early August; animal- and gravity-dispersed. **Seeds** numerous, light brown. (*glaucophylla*: with bluish green leaves)

Identification

Bog rosemary is a low-growing bog shrub rarely more than knee high with stiff, narrow, evergreen leaves (actually bluish when young). It produces small, drooping clusters of whitish flowers in late spring that become erect in fruit. When not in flower, it is most likely to be confused with bog laurel (*Kalmia polifolia*), but has alternate leaves and roundish twigs.

Natural History

Bog rosemary is common in peat bogs, swamps, and floating sedge mats, including the vast areas of muskeg in north-central Minnesota. These habitats are usually open or have widely spaced trees such as tamarack (*Larix laricina*) or black spruce (*Picea mariana*). The soils are permanently saturated and usually carpeted with *Sphagnum* moss. The moss is

capable of growing upward almost as fast as the stems of bog rosemary, so half or more of some stems may be buried in living moss. The buried stems can root adventitiously from the nodes, which allows bog rosemary to absorb water that is held between the *Sphagnum* plants rather than draw it from the peat below. This process is called layering and is common among peatland shrubs.

Bog rosemary competes well with mosses and sedges, but it is easily crowded out by larger, faster-growing shrubs. It is also sensitive to fire, drought, and prolonged flooding, and it is intolerant of shade and sedimentation. Given these limitations, it is perhaps not surprising that bog rosemary occurs only in stable habitats where the interval between large-scale disturbances is great. Under these conditions colonization by seed is uncommon; this is where layering becomes important. Once bog rosemary is established, it is able to persist by repeated layering of stems and branches. Yet, only the upper portions of the stems are actually living; the lower portions die from lack of aeration as they are buried by the gradual accumulation of peat. It is sometimes possible to trace the stems deep into the peat revealing well-preserved fragments that could be centuries old.

Although layering gives bog rosemary a limited capacity for clonal growth, it does not allow it to form large or dense clones like leatherleaf (*Chamaedaphne calyculata*), a common associate.

Flowers range from pale pink to ghostly white—June 5.

The flowers droop but the fruits stand erect—July 2.

Note the stiff, bluish green leaves.

Aralia, bristly sarsaparilla

Araliaceae: Ginseng family

Aralia is a genus of about 30 to 35 species occurring worldwide, mostly in southern and austral Asia. There are 7 species in North America, and 3 species in Minnesota. Of the 3 in Minnesota, 2 are entirely herbaceous: wild sarsaparilla (*A. nudicaulis* L.) and spikenard (*A. racemosa* L). (*Aralia's* derivation is obscure but is possibly from the French-Canadian word *aralie*.)

Aralia hispida Vent.

Bristly sarsaparilla

Low to midsize **shrubs** with a single upright **stem** to 80 cm tall, but only the lower 5 to 20 cm become woody (the remainder dying back each winter); armed with bristlelike prickles, especially near the base; clonal by root suckering. **Branches** lacking, or occasionally 1 or 2 near base. **Bark** brown to brownish gray. **Leaves** alternate, bipinnately compound, deciduous, 5–25 cm long. **Petioles** of lower leaves 4–10 cm long, sometimes bristly; upper leaves sessile or nearly so. **Leaflets** mostly sessile, ovate to lance-ovate or elliptical, 2–8 cm long, 0.8–4 cm wide; base acute to obtuse or rounded; apex acute to short-acuminate; margins sharply and irregularly serrate; upper surface dark green, glabrous or somewhat bristly on veins; lower surface pale green, otherwise similar. **Flowers** 5-merous, unisexual; borne in a loose, open, terminal inflorescence of a few to several long-peduncled, nearly spherical umbels each up to 4 cm in diameter; male flowers and female flowers in separate umbels on the same plant; petals whitish, about 2 mm long; **anthesis** late June to late August; insect-pollinated. **Fruit** a berrylike drupe; dark purple-black; dull; glabrous; ± spherical; 4–8 mm in diameter; with 1–5 stones; maturing early August to mid-September; animal-dispersed. (*hispida*: rough with firm, stiff hairs)

Identification

Bristly sarsaparilla is a small, leafy shrub rarely more than waist high, with a bristly base and twice-compound leaves. All but the lower 2–8 inches (5–20 cm) of the stem dies back each winter, so it is barely recognizable as a shrub. In fact, it is most likely to be mistaken for a herbaceous plant, probably its close relative wild sarsaparilla (*A. nudicaulis*). The bristly stem in winter might look something like that of a gooseberry (*Ribes* spp.), rose (*Rosa* spp.), or raspberry (*Rubus* spp.), except it is much shorter.

Natural History

Bristly sarsaparilla is fairly common in the forested region of northern Minnesota, but it is local and not usually abundant. There is also some evidence that populations can be transient and may not persist in any one place for more than a few years.

Bristly sarsaparilla typically occurs in direct sunlight or partial shade on rock outcrops and dry cliffs or in sandy or gravelly soil in forest openings. It is well adapted to these xeric habitats and easily withstands desiccation during droughts, yet it also occurs in swamps, where it grows in wet or moist peat or on rotting logs. Although it is capable of spreading clonally by producing offshoots from its roots, it does not typically form large patches or colonies in this way; seeds appear to be the primary means of reproduction.

It is sometimes found in pine forests where it is prominent only after a fire. The roots that survive a fire usually resprout vigorously and flower the 1st year, presumably taking advantage of released nutrients in the soil or increased light levels (Heinselman 1973). It is somewhat of an opportunist and will occasionally colonize grossly disturbed habitats such as abandoned gravel pits, railroad sidings, or log landings. But it is intolerant of shade and crowding, so it will not usually survive beyond the early stages of community succession.

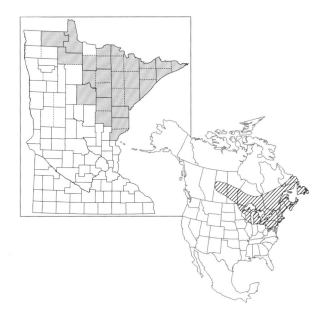

A male umbel at the onset of anthesis—August 4.

Leaves are twice-compound (bipinnate).

Fruits are arranged in a nearly spherical umbel—September 3.

The eponymous bristles are too weak to puncture skin.

On a bedrock outcrop in Cook County—July 22.

Bristly sarsaparilla 🌿 **59**

Arctostaphylos, bearberry

Ericaceae: Heath family

This genus contains about 50 species of evergreen shrubs, mostly in western North America and Central America. One species occurs in Minnesota. (*Arctostaphylos* is from the Greek *arktos*, a bear, and *staphyle*, a bunch of grapes.)

Arctostaphylos uva-ursi (L.) Spreng.

Bearberry

Low **shrubs,** with decumbent stems to 1 m long and with erect or ascending aerial **branches** to 20 cm tall; clonal by layering. **Branchlets** brown, covered with short or long hairs, often glandular. **Bark** brown, ultimately peeling or flaking. **Leaves** simple, alternate, evergreen; persisting 1 or 2 years. **Petioles** 2–5 mm long, hairy and often glandular. **Leaf blades** thick and leathery; obovate to spatulate; 1.2–2.5 cm long, 0.5–1 cm wide; base acutely tapered; apex rounded; margins entire, hairy; upper surface dark green, shiny, glabrous; lower surface pale green, dull, glabrous or occasionally sparsely hairy. **Inflorescence** a short, terminal raceme of 2–10 flowers. **Flowers** 5-merous, bisexual, white with pink tips; pedicels 2–3 mm long, glabrous; sepals ovate, 1–1.5 mm long, separate to the base; corolla urn-shaped, 4.5–6.5 mm long, the lobes rounded, < 1 mm long; stamens and style included; **anthesis** early May to early June; insect-pollinated. **Fruit** a red, spherical drupe; 6–12 mm in diameter; dry and mealy; maturing early August to late September and persisting into winter; animal-dispersed. (*uva-ursi:* grapes of the bear)

Identification

Bearberry is a low-growing, evergreen shrub with long, tough, vinelike stems that lay horizontally on the surface of the ground or just beneath the leaf litter. The stems produce short, upright branches with thick, shiny leaves. It is most likely to be confused with mountain cranberry (*Vaccinium vitis-idaea*) or possibly wintergreen (*Gaultheria procumbens*), but notice that the leaves of bearberry have short, white, crinkly hairs lining the margins (seen with magnification).

Note: For the better part of a century, botanists have attempted to segregate subspecific taxa of bearberry based on the nature of the hairs on the branchlets and petioles (Rosatti 1987; Packer and Denford 1974). The hairs may be short glandular, long glandular, short nonglandular, or long nonglandular and can occur in several combinations with little or no ecological correlation. The value of making formal distinctions based on hair type is not widely agreed upon.

Natural History

Bearberry is fairly common in the central and northern counties, where it is usually found in dry, sandy pine forests and in crevices of exposed bedrock. It is less common in the southeastern counties, where it typically occurs in sand barrens and on dunes. It is very resistant to drought; it will remain green and fresh when other plants have dried and turned brown. But it needs plenty of sunlight, so it usually grows in open, sparsely vegetated habitats where it is not crowded or overtopped by taller plants. This may also save it from ground fires, which are lethal to bearberry but are common in the dry landscape it inhabits. Since there is usually not enough fuel to carry a fire through bearberry microhabitats, fire often skips over or goes around.

The aerial branches of bearberry grow upright for 2 or 3 years, usually reaching a height of 4–8 inches (10–20 cm), then become decumbent. This means the branch becomes horizontal on the ground, but the tip continues to grow upright. In time, the horizontal portion may become covered with humus, then lose its leaves and take root, but the tip of the branch will continue to grow upright and produce new leaves. If the process continues, it can lead to the development of an extensive clone and create a matlike ground cover.

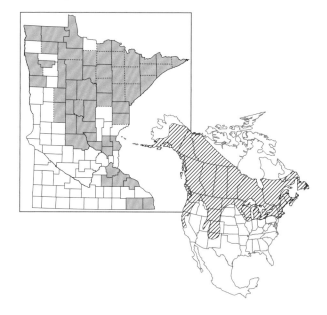

Fruits can be scarce even in a good year—August 27.

Urn-shaped flowers are common in the heath family—May 20.

The evergreen leaves can carpet the ground—Pine County.

Aronia, black chokeberry

Rosaceae: Rose family

Aronia is a small genus of two closely related species and their hybrid, all deciduous shrubs endemic to eastern North America. Only one of these species occurs in Minnesota. A recent revaluation has convinced most botanists to move *Aronia* to the genus *Photinia*, a genus of 45–60 trees and shrubs, mostly evergreen, and mostly from eastern Asia. (*Aronia:* taken from the European whitebeam tree, *Sorbus aria,* although the relationship is unclear)

Aronia melanocarpa (Michx.) Ell.

Black chokeberry

[*Photinia melanocarpa* (Michx.) Robertson & Phipps; *Pyrus melanocarpa* (Michx.) Willd.; *Pyrus arbutifolia* (L.) L. f. var. *nigra* Willd.; *Sorbus melanocarpa* (Michx.) Schneider]

Midsize to tall **shrubs,** with multiple erect or ascending **stems** to 2.5 m tall and 3 cm basal diameter; forming rhizomatous colonies. **Branchlets** initially greenish, becoming brown to reddish brown by the end of the 1st year; glabrous, glabrate, or hairy. **Bark** gray, smooth or somewhat rough. **Leaves** simple, alternate, deciduous. **Petioles** 2–9 mm long, glabrous. **Leaf blades** obovate to oblanceolate or elliptical, 3–7.5 cm long, 2–4 cm wide; base acute to somewhat attenuate; apex acute to short-acuminate; margins finely serrate with incurved gland-tipped teeth; upper surface dark green, glabrous, with a row of dark, slender glands along the midvein; lower surface pale green, glabrous or sometimes hairy. **Flowers** 7–18, bisexual, 5-merous, borne in compound cymes at the ends of leafy branchlets; pedicels 4–14 mm long, glabrous or hairy; sepals 1.3–2 mm long, triangular, sparingly glandular, the outer (lower) surface glabrous or occasionally hairy, the inner (upper) surface hairy; petals white, 4–6 mm long, glabrous; stamens numerous, shorter than the petals; styles 5; **anthesis** mid-May to early July; insect-pollinated. **Fruit** a black or blackish, spherical pome; 6–10 mm in diameter; maturing late August to early October; animal-dispersed. (*melanocarpa*: with black fruit)

Identification

Black chokeberry is a midsize shrub, usually 3–6 ft (1–2 m) tall, with pointed, serrate leaves. It produces clusters of white flowers in the spring when the leaves are about half-grown, and black fruits (pomes) in the fall. The leaves can be mistaken for those of choke-cherry (*Prunus virginiana*) or winterberry (*Ilex verticillata*), but a close examination of the upper surface of the leaf will reveal a row of small, dark, fingerlike glands on the midvein (may require a hand lens).
Note: Forms with particularly glossy leaves or unusually ornamental flowers have been bred in cultivation by the horticultural trade and are sold commercially.

Natural History

Black chokeberry is fairly widespread in the forested regions of northern and central Minnesota, but it is neither common nor abundant. A possible exception is the Anoka sandplain just north of the Twin Cities, where it can be found with some regularity in appropriate habitats. This usually involves peaty or sandy soil in acidic wetlands such as open-canopy tamarack (*Larix laricina*) swamps, shrub swamps, or shallow swales. Transitional habitats on rocky or sandy lakeshores occasionally serve as well. It appears to be fire-adapted since it resprouts from rhizomes if stems are damaged or killed by fire or browsing, but the rhizomes are sensitive to sedimentation and prolonged flooding.

Black chokeberry does not compete aggressively in dense, shrub-dominated communities; it simply does not grow as tall or as fast as the common willows (*Salix* spp.), dogwoods (*Cornus* spp.), or speckled alder (*Alnus incana* subsp. *rugosa*). What it does best is take advantage of large and small openings. This usually results in scattered individuals or small, rhizomatous colonies. Under ideal conditions, where competition is low and soil nutrients are high, it can develop large, dense colonies 60 ft (20 m) or more across.

The leaves are not more than 3 " (7.5 cm) long.

The dark, slender glands on midvein confirm black chokeberry.

Fruits look tempting but consider the common name—August 27.

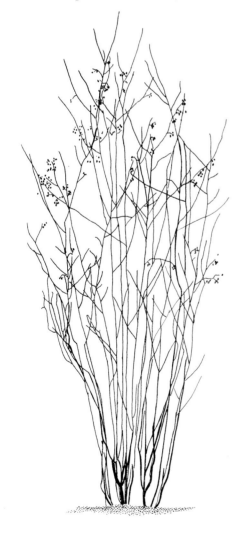

The flowers can be abundant—May 30.

Black chokeberry   🌿   **67**

Betula, the birches

Betulaceae: Birch family

The birches constitute a genus of about 35 species of deciduous trees and shrubs occurring throughout temperate and northern regions of the Northern Hemisphere. There are 18 species in North America and 5 in Minnesota. (*Betula* is the Latin name for the birch tree.)

All of the Minnesota species are known to hybridize freely wherever they occur together (Barnes, Dancik, and Sharik 1974; Clausen 1962; Dancik and Barnes 1972), but the only hybrid that seems to be common in Minnesota is Sandberg birch (*B.* ×*sandbergii* Britt.), which is the cross between paper birch (*B. papyrifera*) and bog birch (*B. pumila*).

Water birch (*B. occidentalis*) is a common western species most similar to bog birch (*B. pumila*). It comes very close to Minnesota's northwestern border, but to date has not been found in the state.

Key to the Genus Betula *in Minnesota*

1. Normal leaf blades 5–11 cm long, widest at or below the middle, tips acute or acuminate, margins with sharp serrations; a large or midsize tree with peeling bark.
    2. Leaf tips acuminate, bases tapered, rounded or heart-shaped (cordate), leaf margins shallowly double-serrate; 1st-year twigs sparsely if at all hairy.
        3. Twigs nonaromatic; mature (seed-bearing) female catkins pendulous, usually > 3 cm long, on stalks 7–23 mm long; bark white or less often grayish or pink-tinged.
            4. Leaf bases tapered, rounded or nearly truncate; mature female catkins 2–5 cm long, with bracts 4–5.5 mm long; fruit 1.3–3 mm long and 3–4.5 mm wide; bark white .. *B. papyrifera*
            4. Leaf bases heart-shaped (cordate); mature female catkins 4–6 cm long, with bracts 5.5–10 mm long; fruit 2.5–4.5 mm long and 4.2–6 mm wide; bark often grayish or pink-tinged .... *B. cordifolia*
        3. Twigs with strong scent of wintergreen when scraped or bruised; mature female catkins upright or ascending, often <3 cm long, sessile or on stalks to 3 mm long; bark pale metallic gold, yellowish brown, or gray in age .... *B. alleghaniensis*
    2. Leaf tips acute, bases tapered, leaf margins deeply double-serrate; 1st-year twigs densely hairy .... *B. nigra*
1. Normal leaf blades 2–3.5 cm long, widest at or above the middle, tips rounded or obtuse, margins with blunt serrations; a multistemmed shrub with nonpeeling bark .... *B. pumila*

Betula alleghaniensis Britt.

Yellow birch
[*B. lutea* Michx. f.]

Large **trees**, with a single upright **trunk** to 28 m tall and 120 cm dbh. **Branchlets** brown to reddish brown or purplish; sparsely hairy the 1st year, glabrous or glabrate the 2nd year; with the aroma of wintergreen when scraped. **Bark** pale metallic gold or yellow-brown, the thin outer layers peeling horizontally into papery strips; older trunks often becoming gray and developing large, thick, ragged-edged plates that often loosen or curl at the edges. **Leaves** simple, alternate, deciduous; borne in 2s from short lateral shoots and singly from elongate terminal shoots. **Petioles** 0.7–1.7 cm long, hairy. **Leaf blades** ovate to ovate-elliptical; 5–11 cm long, 3–6.5 cm wide; base rounded to somewhat cordate; apex acuminate; margins sharply double-serrate; upper surface dark green, sparsely hairy to glabrate; lower surface pale green, hairy on main veins and in axils of lateral veins. **Inflorescence** unisexual, with separate male catkins and female catkins on the same branch. Mature **male catkins** slender, pendulous, 6–12 cm long; borne in clusters of 1–3 from leafless terminal branchlets formed the previous year; bracts ovate, peltate. Mature (with seed) **female catkins** stout, erect or ascending, oblong, 2–4 cm long; borne singly from leafy lateral branchlets formed the current year; sessile or on stalks 1–3 mm long; bracts 3-lobed, 5.5–9 mm long, 5–7 mm wide; **anthesis** early May to early June; wind-pollinated. **Fruit** a winged nutlet (samara) 2.8–4 mm long, 2.5–3.5 mm wide; maturing mid-August to mid-September, released during autumn and winter; wind- and gravity-dispersed. (*alleghaniensis*: of the Alleghany Mountains)

Identification

Yellow birch is a large canopy tree, sometimes reaching 90 ft (28 m) in height, with a thick trunk, heavy ascending branches, a broad crown, and peeling bark. It can only be confused with another birch, either paper birch (*B. papyrifera*) or heart-leaved birch (*B. cordifolia*). But the leaf base is not heart shaped like heart-leaved birch, and the bark is usually some shade of yellow, not the pure white of paper birch. Also, yellow birch has a distinctive wintergreen aroma when the bark of a young twig is scraped.

Natural History

Yellow birch is fairly common in parts of Minnesota, particularly in the hardwood forests along the north shore of Lake Superior and in swamps in the east-central counties. It does well in rocky or bouldery soil and in shallow peat, yet it reaches its largest size when rooted in deep, well-drained loam. Pure stands of yellow birch are seldom, if ever, seen. Instead, individuals are usually integrated into diverse communities with other hardwood and conifer species.

Many of the attributes of yellow birch are indicative of a late-successional species, particularly its tolerance of shade, its relatively slow growth, and its longevity (it is reported to reach an age of 300+ years, *fide* Burns and Honkala 1990). Like most late-successional species, yellow birch is easily killed or damaged by fire, but it is a prolific seed producer, and seedlings do very well on the bare soil exposed by fire (Godman and Krefting 1960). However, bare soil is rarely found in undisturbed forests, which presents a problem in habitats where fire is rare. The solution is quite simple: seedlings of yellow birch have the ability to survive on moss-covered boulders and rotting logs, eventually sending their roots over the boulder or log into the ground (Harlow et al. 1991). When the log rots away, the sapling is left perched on "stilt" roots, which may be noticeable even in mature trees. It is also common to see mature trees with their roots wrapped around boulders.

Older trees develop thick, coarse bark—25" (63 cm) dbh.

Male flowers shortly after releasing pollen—May 11.

Twigs have a strong scent of wintergreen.

Seed-bearing catkins stand erect—September 18.

Female flowers at peak receptivity—May 10.

Young trees have thin, papery bark—9" (23 cm) dbh.

Betula cordifolia Regel

Heart-leaved birch

[*B. papyrifera* Marsh. var. *cordifolia* (Regel) Fern.]

Midsize or occasionally large **trees**, with a single **trunk** to 25 m tall and 77 cm dbh. **Branchlets** brown to reddish brown; sparsely hairy the 1st year, glabrous or glabrate the 2nd year; nonaromatic. **Bark** thin, smooth; white to pinkish white, silvery white or grayish, the thin outer layers peeling horizontally into large papery strips. **Leaves** simple, alternate, deciduous; borne in 3s or 2s from short lateral shoots and singly from elongate terminal shoots. **Petioles** 1–2.5 cm long, hairy. **Leaf blades** ovate; 5–11 cm long, 3–7 cm wide; base cordate; apex acuminate; margins sharply double-serrate; upper surface dark green, hairy to glabrate; lower surface pale green, usually hairy on main veins and in axils of lateral veins. **Inflorescence** unisexual, with separate male catkins and female catkins on the same branch. Mature **male catkins** slender, pendulous, 5–11 cm long; borne in clusters of 1–3 at the tips of leafless terminal branchlets formed the previous years; bracts ovate, peltate. Mature (with seed) **female catkins** stout, pendulous, cylindrical; 4–6 cm long; borne singly from leafy lateral branchlets formed the current year; on stalks 10–23 mm long; bracts 3-lobed, 5.5–10 mm long, 4.5–6 mm wide; **anthesis** early May to early June; wind-pollinated. **Fruit** a winged nutlet (samara) 2.5-4.5 mm long, 4.2-6 mm wide; maturing mid-August to mid-September, released during autumn and early winter; wind- and gravity-dispersed. (*cordifolia*: a reference to the heart-shaped leaves)

Identification

Heart-leaved birch is a midsize or sometimes large tree, occasionally reaching 80 ft (25 m) in height, with a wide crown and spreading branches. It is very similar to paper birch (*B. papyrifera*) but with heart-shaped leaves, larger bracts and seeds, and longer catkins. There are also subtle differences between the bark of the two species. The bark of paper birch starts out smooth, papery, and chalky white but eventually develops woody patches that turn dark gray or even black, especially near the base of older trees. The bark of heart-leaved birch is similar, but it is silvery gray rather than white, and it remains smooth and papery, even at the base of older trees. Hybrids between the two species are known, and hybrids between heart-leaved birch and yellow birch (*B. alleghaniensis*) are suspected.

Natural History

Heart-leaved birch is fairly common in parts of Lake and Cook counties, especially in mesic hardwood forests along the shore of Lake Superior, yet it is scarce elsewhere. In these counties, both heart-leaved birch and the more common paper birch act as pioneers after fire or logging, and along with trembling aspen (*Populus tremuloides*) tend to dominate early-successional forests. But because paper birch and trembling aspen are relatively short-lived and their seedlings are intolerant of shade, they will generally not persist past the first generation without another fire or similar stand-replacing disturbance to open habitat for their seedlings.

Heart-leaved birch, on the other hand, is longer lived, and the seedlings have the capacity to survive in moderate shade; they will even grow on "nurse logs" and produce "stilt" roots, like yellow birch does. These are adaptations that allow it to reproduce in undisturbed forests and persist into the late-successional or climax stage of forest development. In these latter stages heart-leaved birch typically occurs in the canopy with sugar maple (*Acer saccharum*), yellow birch, or occasionally northern white cedar (*Thuja occidentalis*), white spruce (*Picea glauca*), or white pine (*Pinus strobus*), sometimes in stands as old as 300 years.

Male catkins release their pollen, then shrivel and fall—May 20.

Female catkin as it appears just before pollination—May 20.

Heart-leaved birch takes its name from the shape of the leaf.

Seed catkins hang downward, and turn brown when ripe—August 23.

Bark tends to be grayish, not pure white—14" (36 cm) dbh.

Betula nigra L.

River birch

Tall or midsize **trees**, with a single or multiple upright **trunks** to 25 m tall and 57 cm dbh. **Branchlets** brown to reddish brown; densely hairy the 1st year, moderately hairy to glabrate the 2nd year; nonaromatic. **Bark** grayish, the thin outer layers of young trees peeling horizontally into papery strips, older trunks developing coarse scaly plates. **Leaves** simple, alternate, deciduous; borne in 2s or occasionally 3s from short lateral shoots and singly from elongate terminal shoots. **Petioles** 0.6–1.7 cm long, densely hairy. **Leaf blades** ovate to broadly lanceolate; 5–10 cm long, 3–7 cm wide; base obtusely angled; apex acute; margins sharply and deeply double-serrate; upper surface dark green, sparsely hairy to glabrate; lower surface pale green, usually hairy on main veins and occasionally in axils of lateral veins. **Inflorescence** unisexual, with separate male catkins and female catkins on the same branch. Mature **male catkins** slender, pendulous, 4–9 cm long; borne in clusters of 1–3 from leafless terminal branchlets formed the previous year; bracts ovate, peltate. Mature (with seed) **female catkins** stout, erect or ascending, oblong to short-cylindrical, 1.5–3.5 cm long; borne singly from leafy lateral branchlets formed the current year; on stalks 3–10 mm long; bracts 3-lobed, 6–10 mm long, 3.5–7 mm wide; **anthesis** late April to late May; wind-pollinated. **Fruit** a winged nutlet (samara) 3–5 mm long, 4–7 mm wide; maturing late mid-May to late mid-June; wind-, water-, and gravity-dispersed. (*nigra*: black)

Identification

River birch is a relatively tall, slender tree with long, ascending branches and a roundish crown. The leaves are triangular shaped with coarsely double-serrate margins. The bark of young trees is grayish or sometimes reddish and peels in thin, papery sheets like that of paper birch (*B. papyrifera*). The bark on the main trunk eventually develops into thick, gray scales, but the bark on the branches remains papery and peely.

Natural History

River birch was observed by the nineteenth-century botanist W. A. Wheeler (1899) to be "one of the most common trees on the islands of the Mississippi River" in Houston County. Although the islands Wheeler

spoke of have since been submerged behind dams, river birch is still fairly common along the Mississippi River, at least downstream from Lake City (Wabasha County). Away from the river, even a short distance, it disappears entirely. In Minnesota, river birch is strictly a floodplain species.

Conditions on floodplains often favor trees with pioneering abilities, that is, trees that can become established in the open on bare soil but remain for only one generation. In fact, floodplain habitat itself is transient in nature, constantly shifting because of erosion and sedimentation caused by regular spring flooding. River birch is particularly well adapted to these conditions. Unlike the other birches, it is very tolerant of flooding and sedimentation, and its seeds are released to coincide with the receding spring floodwater, thereby ensuring a favorable seedbed.

Although the seeds germinate almost immediately and the seedlings grow quickly (Koevenig 1976), most will eventually be overtaken and shaded out by plains cottonwood (*Populus deltoides* subsp. *monilifera*) or silver maple (*Acer saccharinum*), which employ an almost identical strategy but grow taller and generally live longer than river birch. Of course some river birch do reach maturity, usually those along a river's edge or slough margin where there is more sunlight. Edge habitats also bring greater exposure to wind, ice, and flood-borne debris. This may be why river birch, being a rather fragile tree to begin with, often develops broken limbs and leaning trunks.

*Male flowers are in long, slender catkins—
May 4.*

*Catkins release winged seeds in early summer—
June 8.*

*Mature trees develop coarse, scaly plates—
17" (43 cm) dbh.*

*Female flowers are in stout, erect catkins—
May 3.*

Note the double-serrate leaf margins.

Betula papyrifera Marsh.

Paper birch

Large **trees**, with a single or multiple upright **trunks** to 28 m tall and 54 cm dbh. **Branchlets** brown to reddish brown; hairy or glabrate the 1st year, glabrous or glabrate the 2nd year; nonaromatic. **Bark** thin, smooth, reddish brown on young stems, becoming chalky to creamy white at maturity, the thin outer layers peeling horizontally into papery strips, eventually becoming gray and deeply furrowed near base of older trunks. **Leaves** simple, alternate, deciduous; borne in 2s or sometimes 3s from short lateral shoots and singly from elongate terminal shoots. **Petioles** 1–2.5 cm long, glabrous or glabrate, or occasionally hairy. **Leaf blades** ovate; 5–9.5 cm long, 3–6 cm wide; base tapered, rounded or nearly truncate; apex acuminate; margins sharply double-serrate; upper surface dark green, sparsely hairy to glabrate; lower surface pale green, hairy on main veins and in axils of lateral veins. **Inflorescence** unisexual, with separate male catkins and female catkins on the same branch. Mature **male catkins** slender, pendulous, 5–10 cm long; borne in clusters of 1–3 at the tips of leafless terminal branchlets formed the previous year; bracts ovate, peltate. Mature (with seed) **female catkins** stout, pendulous, oblong to cylindrical; 2–5 cm long; borne singly from leafy lateral branchlets formed the current year; on stalks 7–17 mm long; bracts 3-lobed, 4–6 mm long, 3.5–5 mm wide; **anthesis** late April to early June; wind-pollinated. **Fruit** a winged nutlet (samara) 1.3–3 mm long, 3–4.5 mm wide; maturing mid-August to mid-September, released during autumn and early winter; wind- and gravity-dispersed. (*papyrifera:* paper-bearing, in reference to the bark)

Identification

Paper birch is a relatively tall tree with a small, narrow crown and chalky or creamy white bark that peels in thin papery strips. It is similar to yellow birch (*B. alleghaniensis*), but with white bark, not yellow or gray, and without a wintergreen fragrance. It is also similar to heart-leaved birch (*B. cordifolia*), but the leaves do not have a heart-shaped base.

Natural History

Paper birch is common throughout the forested region of Minnesota, especially northward. It is adapted to a wide variety of acidic soil types,

including sandy, rocky, or loamy soils and even shallow peat. Under favorable conditions it can grow rapidly and live to an age of 250 years (Heinselman 1973), although a maximum age of 140 years is probably more realistic (*fide* Burns and Honkala 1990).

Paper birch cannot reproduce in a closed forest; there is simply not enough light for the seedlings. So without some form of ecological intervention to set back succession, a stand of paper birch will last only one generation. It will typically be followed by more shade tolerant trees that are able to grow up through the birch canopy and assume dominance when the birches die. On mesic soils that is likely to be maples (*Acer* spp.), basswood (*Tilia americana*), or white spruce (*Picea glauca*); on wetter soils it might be balsam fir (*Abies balsamea*). Judging from the abundance of paper birch in northern Minnesota, intervention must be a frequent occurrence. In presettlement times the agent was fire, but now it is more likely to be clear-cutting.

The statewide drought of 1988–89 resulted in an estimated 450% increase in the annual mortality rate of paper birch in the 3 years following the drought, a greater increase than for any other tree species. As many as 20% of all paper birch trees in Minnesota, in all age classes, may have died from drought-related causes during that period (Minnesota Department of Natural Resources 1993).

The familiar bark of paper birch—7" (18 cm) dbh.

Shown are 100+ female flowers arranged spirally in an erect catkin—May 18.

Catkins will start releasing seeds in mid-August.

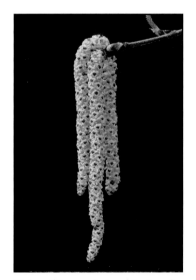

Male catkins are designed to spread pollen on the wind—May 18.

Multiple trunks are not unusual for open-grown paper birch.

Compare the leaf shape with heart-leaved birch.

Betula pumila L.

Bog birch

[*B. glandulifera* (Regel) Butler; *B. pumila* L. var. *glandulifera* Regel]

Tall **shrubs**, with multiple upright **stems** to 3.4 m tall and 3 cm basal diameter. **Branchlets** brown to reddish brown; hairy the 1st year, hairy or glabrate the 2nd year; nonaromatic. **Bark** thin, gray or brown to reddish brown, with pale horizontal lenticels, smooth or rough near the base of older stems, not peeling or peeling slightly on older stems. **Leaves** simple, alternate, deciduous; borne in 2s or occasionally 3s from short spurlike lateral shoots and singly from elongate terminal shoots. **Petioles** 1–7 mm long, hairy to glabrous. **Leaf blades** obovate or broadly elliptical to nearly circular; 2–3.5 cm long, 1.5–2.5 cm wide, those on fast-growing terminal shoots often larger; base acute to obtuse; apex rounded to obtuse; margins bluntly serrate or double-serrate; upper surface dark green, glabrous or glabrate; lower surface similar to upper but pale green. **Inflorescence** unisexual, with separate male catkins and female catkins on the same branch. Mature **male catkins** stout, ascending or erect, 5–15 mm long; borne singly from short, leafless, spurlike lateral shoots formed the previous year; bracts ovate, peltate. Mature (with seeds) **female catkins** stout, ascending, oblong to short-cylindrical; 9–18 mm long; borne singly from short, leafy, spurlike lateral shoots formed the current year; on stalks 3–9 mm long; bracts 3-lobed, 2.5–4.5 mm long, 2.5–4 mm wide; **anthesis** late mid-April to mid-May; wind-pollinated. **Fruit** a winged nutlet (samara) 1.5–2.2 mm long, 1.8–2.8 mm wide; maturing mid-August to late September, released during autumn and early winter; wind- and gravity-dispersed. (*pumila:* dwarf, in comparison to the other birches)

Identification

Bog birch is a large, multistemmed shrub usually 6–8 ft (2–2.5 m) tall, with slender, flexible branches and small, roundish leaves. Since this is the only birch in Minnesota that is strictly a shrub and the only one without peeling bark, it is not likely to be confused with another birch. However, it will hybridize freely with other species of birch growing nearby, especially paper birch (*B. papyrifera*). Hybrid populations may even contain backcrosses with either parent (Clausen 1962), resulting in a wide range of intermediate forms. Generally, any plant with characteristics of bog birch

but more than about 12 ft (3.5 m) tall and looking more like a small tree than a shrub is likely a hybrid.

Natural History

Bog birch is a common shrub throughout most of its range in Minnesota, especially northward. It occurs exclusively in wetlands, including fens, sedge meadows, and marshes. It is also common in thinly forested swamps where there are scattered tamarack (*Larix laricina*) or black spruce (*Picea mariana*), and it is a major component of many shrub swamps. But contrary to its common name, it does not occur in true bogs, which are too acidic and nutrient poor to support this species. It prefers a pH that ranges from somewhat basic (calcareous) to only moderately acidic.

Bog birch is nonclonal and reproduces only by seed, so it normally does not form dense thickets or pure stands. It is usually scattered in the vicinity of other shrubs such as willows (*Salix* spp.), dogwoods (*Cornus* spp.), or speckled alder (*Alnus incana* subsp. *rugosa*). It seems to do well in these situations unless it gets trapped in the shade of taller shrubs or overhanging trees. It also does well in habitats that experience limited spring flooding as long as the roots are not damaged by sedimentation or scouring. Damage to the stems and branches caused by fire or browsers such as moose or beaver is usually mitigated by rapid and vigorous resprouting.

A typical specimen from Marshall County measuring 6' (2 m) tall.

Stems are marked with pale, horizontal lenticels.

Male catkins are no more than 5/8" (1.5 cm) long—May 8.

Seed catkins still green in late July—note the tiny leaves.

Note the red stigmas of the female flowers—May 4.

Carpinus, blue beech

Betulaceae: Birch family

Carpinus forms a genus of about 25 to 30 species, mostly in north temperate regions of Europe and Asia. Two species occur in North America: 1 in Mexico and 1 in the United States. (*Carpinus* is the Latin name of the European hornbeam, *C. betulus*.)

Carpinus caroliniana Walt. subsp. *virginiana* (Marsh.) Furlow

Blue beech

Small **trees**, with 1 or a few **stems** to 10 m tall and 12 cm dbh, the surface irregularly fluted; clonal by root suckering. **Branchlets** slender, brown to reddish brown, hairy, becoming glabrous the 2nd or 3rd year. **Bark** thin, smooth, gray. **Leaves** simple, alternate, deciduous or marcescent. **Petioles** 0.5–1.5 cm long, hairy. **Leaf blades** ovate to ovate-elliptical, or ovate-oblong; 6–10 cm long, 2.5–5 cm wide; base rounded or slightly cordate; apex acuminate or occasionally acute; margins double- or single-serrate; upper surface dark green, sparsely hairy or glabrate; lower surface pale green, hairy, especially along veins, and with numerous tiny, dark brown glands. **Inflorescence** unisexual, separate male catkins and female catkins borne on the same branch. Mature **male catkins** slender, pendulous, 2–5 cm long; borne singly from short, leafless, spurlike lateral branchlets formed the previous year. **Female catkins** drooping, 1–3 cm long at anthesis, enlarging to 7 cm in fruit; borne singly from the tips of leafy terminal branchlets formed the current year; **anthesis** early May to late May; wind-pollinated. **Fruit** a single-seeded, ribbed nutlet; ovoid; 4–6 mm long; attached to the base of an asymmetrical, 3-lobed, leaflike bract 1.8–3.5 cm long; the bract and fruit shed together in autumn; wind- and animal-dispersed. (*caroliniana*: of Carolina)

Identification

Blue beech is an understory tree reaching a maximum height in Minnesota of about 32 ft (10 m) and a diameter of about 5 inches (12 cm). It has long, slender, horizontal branches and thin, smooth, grayish bark. The actual trunk, not just the bark, is irregularly fluted, evoking comparison to the sinew and muscle of a flexed arm. The trunk is sometimes crooked or leaning, but more often it grows straight with a form resembling ironwood (*Ostrya virginiana*). The leaves are also similar to those of ironwood and the elms (*Ulmus* spp.) but have tiny, dark, glandular dots scattered across the lower surface (seen with magnification).
Note: C. *caroliniana* is currently thought to consist of two subspecies, differing in characteristics of the leaf (Furlow 1987). Northern populations, including all Minnesota trees (as described here), are considered subsp. *virginiana* (Marsh.) Furlow. Southern and coastal plain populations are subsp. *caroliniana*. The ranges of both subspecies are combined on the accompanying North American map.

Natural History

Blue beech thrives in deep shade and is fairly common in the understory of late-successional hardwood forests. It is typically associated with maples (*Acer* spp.), basswood (*Tilia americana*), oaks (*Quercus* spp.), black cherry (*Prunus serotina*), or paper birch (*Betula papyrifera*). It is often found on river terraces but not in habitats that are subjected to frequent or prolonged flooding or sedimentation, and it does not colonize open fields, roadsides, or ruderal areas.

Although it typically occurs in the shade of larger trees, blue beech generally requires some light from at least a partial canopy gap to flower and set seed (an inevitable but episodic event even in forests not disturbed by human activities). Seedlings, however, do well in deep shade and can actually be damaged by direct sunlight. But most blue beech in a mature forest originate as root suckers, not as seedlings. These suckers sprout from long horizontal roots that spread just beneath the surface. This can lead to discernable colonies or clones with numerous scattered stems in several size and age classes, all connected underground by a common root system.

The leaves may seem nondescript, but the fruits are unique—August 18.

About a dozen female flowers are in this spiral catkin—May 3.

A male catkin just before the pollen is released—May 3.

Each fruit (nutlet) is attached to a 3-lobed bract—August 18.

Bark is thin, smooth, and gray; multiple stems are common.

Blue beech 🍃 **83**

Carya, the hickories

Juglandaceae: Walnut family

The hickories include 18 species of deciduous trees and shrubs, distributed in North America, Mexico, and eastern Asia. There are 11 species in the United States, and 2 in Minnesota. (*Carya* is from the Greek word for nut.)

Key to the Genus Carya *in Minnesota*

1. Buds sulfur yellow, or at least flecked with tiny yellow scales; leaf margins glabrous; branchlets of the current year essentially glabrous; leaflets 7 or 9; mature fruits 2–3 cm long, with a thin leathery husk; bark of mature trees with shallow ridges and furrows .... *C. cordiformis*
1. Buds brownish or grayish; leaf margins with small tufts of hairs; branchlets of the current year hairy; leaflets 5 or rarely 7; mature fruits 3–4.5 cm long, with a thick woody husk; bark of mature trees with large vertical plates that loosen and curl at the ends, appearing "shaggy" .... *C. ovata*

Carya cordiformis (Wangenh.) K. Koch

Bitternut hickory

Large **trees**, to 34 m tall and 50 cm dbh. First year **branchlets** relatively slender, brown, essentially glabrous; buds sulfur yellow. **Bark** thin, light gray, smooth when young, eventually developing flat interlacing ridges and narrow shallow furrows. **Leaves** pinnately compound, alternate, deciduous. **Petioles** 3–8 cm long; minutely hairy, less so near base. **Leaflets** 7–9; sessile or on short petiolules; narrowly elliptical to obovate; distal leaflets 7–15 cm long, 2–6 cm wide, medial and proximal leaflets progressively smaller; base acutely tapered or ultimately blunt, asymmetrical; apex narrowly acute or acuminate; margins serrate, glabrous; upper surface dark green, sometimes hairy on midvein otherwise ± glabrous; lower surface pale green, moderately hairy along midvein otherwise sparsely hairy or glabrate in age, with circular peltate scales. **Inflorescence** unisexual, with male flowers and female flowers borne in separate catkins on the same branch. **Male flowers** numerous, in slender, pendulous catkins 4–10 cm long; catkins borne in clusters of 3 from a common peduncle on lateral stublike branchlets formed the previous year, and occasionally from the base of branchlets of the current year. **Female flowers** 2–4; on a short spike borne from the apex of branchlets of the current year; **anthesis** early mid-May to mid-June; wind-pollinated. **Fruit** a nut enclosed in a thin leathery husk; compressed-spherical to broadly elliptical; 2–3 cm long; husk splitting in 4 segments from the apex to about the middle; seed very bitter; maturing mid-August to late September; animal- and gravity-dispersed. (*cordiformis*: heart-shaped, the reference not obvious)

Identification

Bitternut hickory is a tall, slender canopy tree with ascending branches and a narrow crown. The bark is light gray and initially smooth. When the trunk reaches perhaps 6–8 inches (15–20 cm) in diameter it begins to develop narrow, interlacing ridges that form a reticulate pattern that deepens with age. Each leaf has 7–9 leaflets that look most like those of shagbark hickory (*C. ovata*) and to a lesser extent those of butternut (*Juglans cinerea*), walnut (*J. nigra*), and the ashes (*Fraxinus* spp.). But only bitternut hickory has bright yellow buds, which has led to the common name "yellow-bud hickory." It is reported to hybridize with shagbark hickory (Stone 1997), but no hybrids have been reported from Minnesota to date.

Natural History

Bitternut hickory is fairly common in late-successional hardwood forests in the Big Woods region of southern Minnesota. It also occurs in hardwood forests as far north as Lake Winnibigoshish in Itasca County (Johnson 1927), but less commonly. It prefers deep, nutrient-rich, loamy soils, where it typically grows with sugar maple (*Acer saccharum*), basswood (*Tilia americana*), red oak (*Quercus rubra*), American elm (*Ulmus americana*), or green ash (*Fraxinus pennsylvanica*). Although fairly common, it is rarely if ever dominant; it does not define a community by its presence the way oak or maple might. It is slow growing beneath the canopy of a mature forest but fast growing in direct sunlight, and it can live 200+ years. It is moderately tolerant of floods and drought, but sensitive to fire.

The nuts are apparently too bitter to be eaten by animals (*fide* Burns and Honkala 1990), although by some accounts squirrels do eat them or at least disperse them around the forest. Although the process may not be clear, seedlings of bitternut hickory can become very abundant, even in forests with few mature hickory trees. They can survive several years with very little light, but they rarely survive to the sapling stage or beyond without a canopy gap to provide at least partial sunlight (Bray 1956).

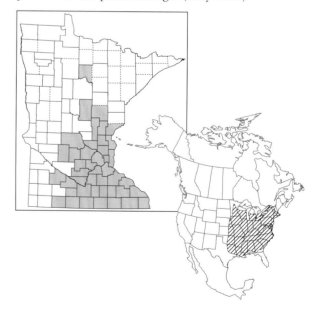

Each leaf has 5 or 7 serrate leaflets.

Young trunk beginning to develop mature bark—6" (15 cm) dbh.

Female flowers on June 9—note the broad, ruffled stigmas.

The nuts have a leathery husk that splits into 4 segments.

The male flowers are in long, drooping catkins—June 12.

Carya ovata (Mill.) K. Koch

Shagbark hickory

Large **trees**, to 30 m tall and 84 cm dbh. First-year **branchlets** stout, brown, hairy, becoming glabrate the 2nd year; buds brown or grayish. **Bark** relatively thin, ashy gray, developing coarse vertical plates that loosen at one or both ends and curl away from the trunk. **Leaves** pinnately compound, alternate, deciduous. **Petioles** 5–12 cm long; minutely hairy, more so near base. **Leaflets** 5 or rarely 7; sessile or on short petiolules; elliptical to narrowly elliptical or ovate-elliptical, terminal leaflet sometimes obovate; upper 3 leaflets 10–20 cm long, 3–9 cm wide, basal leaflets somewhat smaller; base tapered or ultimately blunt, asymmetrical; apex acuminate; margins serrate, with small tufts of hairs near summit of each tooth; upper surface dark green, glabrous; lower surface pale green, occasionally hairy along midvein otherwise ± glabrous but with minute peltate scales. **Inflorescence** unisexual, with male flowers and female flowers borne in separate catkins on the same branch. **Male flowers** numerous, in slender pendulous catkins 6–12 cm long; catkins borne in clusters of 3 from a common peduncle at the base of branchlets of the current year. **Female flowers** 2–4; on a short spike borne from the apex of branchlets of the current year; **anthesis** early May to early mid-June; wind-pollinated. **Fruit** a nut enclosed in a thick woody husk; compressed-spherical; 3–4.5 cm long; husk splitting into 4 segments from apex to base and releasing the nut; seed sweet; maturing mid-August to late September; gravity- and animal-dispersed. (*ovata*: ovate, the shape of an egg in outline)

Identification

Shagbark hickory is one of the most distinctive trees in southeastern Minnesota. The ash gray bark develops long, flat plates that tend to loosen and curl away from the trunk, giving it a "shaggy" appearance, much like the bark of silver maple (*Acer saccharinum*). The leaf can be confused with bitternut hickory (*C. cordiformis*) or possibly green ash (*Fraxinus pennsylvanica*), but only shagbark hickory has small tufts of hairs on the margins of the leaf blade (seen with magnification).

Natural History

Shagbark hickory is a fairly common forest tree but only in the stream-dissected terrain of the Paleozoic Plateau in the southeastern corner of the state. It typically occurs scattered with various species of oak (*Quercus* spp.) on dry, sandy or rocky soil, particularly on exposed ridgetops and south-facing slopes. It has a deep root system and is very drought resistant. It is also slow growing and long-lived, similar to the oaks (250–300 years, *fide* Harlow, et al. 1991). It is at least as shade tolerant as the oaks but more sensitive to fire, so it is not found in fire-maintained savannas.

On mesic, loamy soils it is usually an early or midsuccessional species. In time it is replaced by more shade tolerant species such as sugar maple (*Acer saccharum*) or basswood (*Tilia americana*), which grow up from the understory and shade out any hickory seedlings. But on droughty soil there are few species able to do this, which allows shagbark hickory, along with some oaks, to continually replace itself in the canopy, thereby functioning as an edaphic climax species.

The seed of shagbark hickory is sweet tasting and is the preferred source of the commercial hickory nut. However, there seems to be little tradition of gathering hickory nuts in Minnesota. The trees may be too scattered and good crops too infrequent to entice people to gather the nuts.

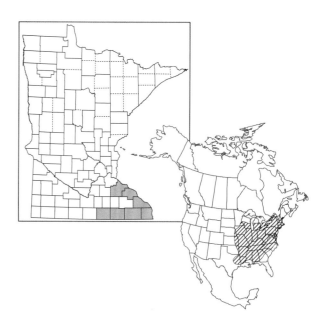

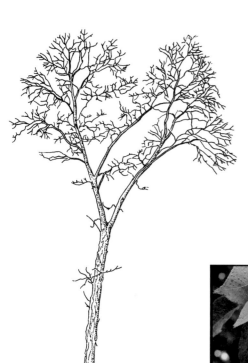

Male catkins are in clusters of 3—May 21.

Leaves have 5 leaflets, rarely 7.

"Shagbark" seems an appropriate name—20" (51 cm) dbh.

A thick, woody husk encloses the nut—August 22.

Look for female flowers at the tips of the branchlets—May 22.

The inner bud scales resemble flower petals.

Ceanothus, the New Jersey teas

Rhamnaceae: Buckthorn family

This is a genus of 45 to 60 species of shrubs and small trees endemic to North America. Most occur in mountainous and arid regions of the western United States and Mexico, with the greatest diversity in California. Two species are native to Minnesota; both are shrubs about 1 m tall, with triple-veined leaves and clusters of tiny white flowers. (*Ceanothus* is the ancient Greek name for an unknown plant.)

Key to the Genus Ceanothus *in Minnesota*

1. Leaf blades 2.5–4.5 cm wide, 1.5–2.1 times as long as wide (l/w = 1.5–2.1), with a broadly rounded base; flowers in clusters at the ends of long leafless stalks that arise from leaf axils .... *C. americanus*
1. Leaf blades 0.7–2 cm wide, 2.7–4 times as long as wide (l/w = 2.7–4), with a tapered base; flowers in clusters at the ends of normal leafy branchlets .... *C. herbaceus*

Ceanothus americanus L.

New Jersey tea

Midsize **shrubs**, with multiple upright **stems** to 1.5 m tall. 1st-year **branchlets** greenish to brownish, minutely hairy; 2nd-year branchlets brown, minutely hairy to glabrate. **Leaves** simple, alternate, deciduous. Petioles 3–12 mm long, hairy, with a few to several dark glands on upper surface. **Leaf blades** ovate; 4–8.5 cm long, 2.5–4.5 cm wide, length/width 1.5–2.1; base rounded or occasionally subcordate; apex acute to somewhat acuminate; margins with gland-tipped serrations; upper surface dark green, sparsely hairy; lower surface pale green, moderately hairy, especially on larger veins. **Flowers** bisexual, 5-merous, white; borne in dense umbel-like clusters at the ends of essentially leafless peduncles 3–12 cm long, the peduncles arising from leaf axils on branchlets of the current year; pedicels glabrous, 3–10 mm long, not elongating in fruit; sepals deltate with the tip curved inward, about 1 mm long; petals hooded, contracted to a slender claw, 1.5–2 mm long; stamens 5, about as long as the petals; **anthesis** early July to early August; insect-pollinated. **Fruit** a 3-lobed capsulelike drupe; blackish; depressed-globose; 3–5 mm across; maturing late mid-August to late mid-September; animal- and gravity-dispersed. (*americanus*: of America)

Identification

New Jersey tea is a bushy shrub, usually about waist high, with dense clusters of tiny white flowers. Only the lower portions of the stems are woody; most of the new growth remains herbaceous and dies back each winter. It is similar to narrow-leaved New Jersey tea (*C. herbaceus*), but the leaves are noticeably larger and broader and have a distinctly rounded base. The leaves of both species are notable for having three veins coming from the base rather than the usual one. Also note that the flower clusters of New Jersey tea are on long leafless stalks and appear in July. The flowers of narrow-leaved New Jersey tea are at the ends of normal leafy branchlets and appear in June.

Natural History

New Jersey tea is fairly common within its geographic range. However, it is somewhat spotty in distribution. It is best described as a prairie plant, but it also occurs in savannas, dunes, rocky bluffs, and open woodlands. In most cases these are open, sparsely vegetated native habitats, usually with dry or dryish sandy/gravelly soil. It will occasionally invade grassy roadsides or abandoned fields but not aggressively. It is generally more common than narrow-leaved New Jersey tea, and even though the two occur in similar habitats, they are rarely found together.

New Jersey tea takes several years to become established and even then it grows slowly. But in time it develops a large root system and becomes resistant to drought, fire, and browsing. If stems are damaged or killed, it will resprout from the root crown but not vigorously, and it will not usually flower the following year. Because it is nonclonal and reproduces only by seed, individuals are typically scattered rather than clustered, and it does not form dense colonies or thickets.

The common name dates from the Revolutionary War, when the leaves were supposedly used as a substitute for oriental tea. The taste is reportedly similar to oriental tea but it contains no caffeine. There is no record of pioneer use in Minnesota, although it is currently gaining favor as an ornamental shrub.

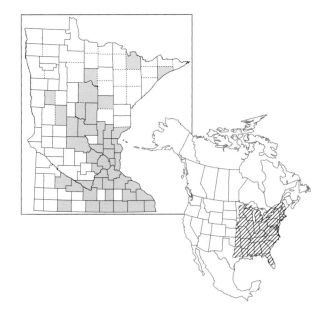

Flowers are in clusters at the ends of long stalks—July 18.

A typical specimen from Washington County—July 18.

Fruit is a 3-lobed, capsulelike drupe—August 30.

Leaves are "triple-veined" and relatively broad.

New Jersey teas 🌿 **93**

Ceanothus herbaceus Raf.

Narrow-leaved New Jersey tea
[*C. ovatus* Desf.]

Midsize **shrubs**, with a single or multiple upright **stems** to 1 m tall. 1st-year **branchlets** greenish to brownish green, minutely hairy; 2nd-year branchlets brown to purplish, minutely hairy. **Leaves** simple, alternate, deciduous. **Petioles** 3–7 mm long, hairy, usually lacking glands. **Leaf blades** elliptical or narrowly elliptical to lanceolate; 3–5.5 cm long, 0.7–2 cm wide, length/width 2.7–4; base tapered to an acute angle; apex acute or subobtuse to somewhat blunt; margins with gland-tipped serrations; upper surface dark green, sparsely hairy at least on main veins; lower surface similar to upper but somewhat paler. **Flowers** bisexual, 5-merous, white; borne in dense umbel-like clusters at the ends of leafy branchlets 7–20 cm long, the branchlets arising from nodes on branches of the previous season; pedicels glabrous, 3–10 mm long, becoming 7–18 mm long in fruit; sepals deltate with the tip curved inward, about 1 mm long; petals hooded, contracted to a slender claw, 1.5–2 mm long; stamens 5; **anthesis** early June to early July; insect-pollinated. **Fruit** a 3-lobed capsulelike drupe; blackish; depressed globose; 2.5–3.5 mm across; maturing early July to early mid-August; animal- and gravity-dispersed. (*herbaceus*: herbaceous, in reference to the branches)

Identification

Narrow-leaved New Jersey tea is a smallish, bushy shrub, usually about knee high. It tends to be inconspicuous until it comes into flower. It is sometimes confused with the more common New Jersey tea (*C. americanus*), which occurs in similar habitats. Both species have clusters of small, white flowers and share the unusual feature of triple-nerved leaves. But narrow-leaved New Jersey tea has smaller, proportionately narrower leaves that tend to be elliptical in outline rather than ovate, and they taper at the base. Also, the flower clusters occur at the ends of normal, leafy branchlets instead of long, naked stalks.

Natural History

Narrow-leaved New Jersey tea is somewhat uncommon and local in Minnesota. In the north-central counties it typically occurs in dry, sandy soil in thin-canopy forests with jack pine (*Pinus banksiana*),

bur oak (*Quercus macrocarpa*), or northern pin oak (*Q. ellipsoidalis*). In the southeast it is usually found in dry, sandy or gravelly hill prairies, barrens, dunes, and savannas.

It does not compete well in dense cover; it usually grows in the open where there is little competing vegetation. Even in good habitat, individuals often seem to be widely spaced or gathered into small, isolated groups. It certainly does not show any aggressiveness, even though it will tentatively colonize grassy roadsides and abandoned farmland if conditions are right.

It has an extensive root system and is very drought resistant. It also recovers well from fire or browsing by resprouting from dormant buds on the root crown. These sprouts, however, are not particularly robust; they usually require 2 or 3 years to regain vigor and produce flowers. The stems branch repeatedly and tend to spread along the ground producing dense clumps as much as 3 ft (1 m) across. These clumps are not a sign of vegetative reproduction. In fact, narrow-leaved New Jersey tea is nonclonal; it reproduces only by seed.

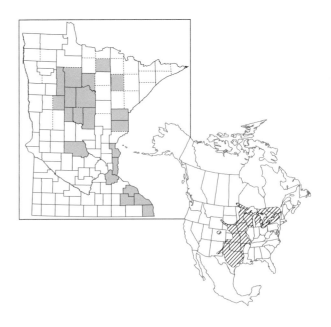

Fruits will turn black when fully ripe—July 21.

This specimen from Pine County is about knee high—June 27.

Leaves are similar to New Jersey tea but narrower.

Celastrus, American bittersweet

Celastraceae: Staff-tree family

This is a genus of about 30 species of woody vines, mostly in tropical and subtropical regions of eastern Asia, Madagascar, and the Americas. Only one species is native to the United States. (*Celastrus* is the ancient Greek name for an evergreen tree.)

Round-leaved or Oriental bittersweet (*Celastrus orbiculatus* Thunb.) was brought to North America from Asia in the late nineteenth century. It is superficially similar to the native American bittersweet, but the leaves are usually rounder, and the flowers are in axillary clusters of 2 or 3 rather than in terminal panicles of 5–60. Since its introduction, it has become naturalized in the eastern states and is spreading westward. It has not yet been found in Minnesota, although naturalized populations are known in Wisconsin and Iowa.

The primary vector is birds, which eat the fruit and spread the seeds in their droppings. There are also reports that it is sometimes substituted for the native American bittersweet (*Celastrus scandens*) in nursery stock. It is an aggressive woody vine that has the capacity to displace native species in forest habitats and is considered ecologically invasive. Another cause for concern is its ability to hybridize with the native American bittersweet (Pooler, Dix, and Feely 2002).

Celastrus scandens L.

American bittersweet

Climbing **vines** or occasionally sprawling **shrubs**, with dextrosely twining **stems** to 20 m tall and 7 cm diameter. 1st-year **branchlets** glabrous, green to greenish brown; becoming gray or brown the 2nd year. **Bark** thin, gray, rough, peeling or flaking on older stems. **Leaves** simple, alternate, deciduous. **Petioles** 1–2.5 cm long, glabrous. **Leaf blades** elliptical to ovate-elliptical or obovate; 5–11 cm long, 2.5–6 cm wide; base tapered or rounded; apex acuminate; margins with rounded or incurved gland-tipped serrations; surfaces glabrous, the lower surface somewhat paler than the upper. **Flowers** 5-merous, unisexual, each plant bearing either male flowers or female flowers; 5–60 borne in terminal panicles 2–6 cm long; pedicels 1–4 mm long, glabrous, jointed near the middle; sepals triangular to ovate-oblong, 1–2 mm long; petals white or greenish, 3–4 mm long; stamens 2.5–3.4 mm long; pistil 3–4 mm long, flask-shaped; **anthesis** mid-May to late mid-June; insect-pollinated. **Fruit** a somewhat spherical 3-valved capsule; 6–12 mm in diameter; orange to yellow; maturing early September to early October; animal-dispersed. **Seeds** 3–6; brown; elliptical; 4–6 mm long; each enclosed in a fleshy crimson aril. (*scandens*: climbing)

Identification

American bittersweet is a native vine of hardwood forests. It has neither tendrils nor aerial roots, instead it climbs by twining its entire stem around the trunk or branch of a tree. In Minnesota, the only other woody vines with alternate leaves that climb in this manner are moonseed (*Menispermum canadense*) and the naturalized European bittersweet (*Solanum dulcamara*). The honeysuckle vines (*Lonicera* spp.) also twine but have opposite leaves. The fruit of American bittersweet is a yellow or orange capsule that opens from the bottom (while still on the vine) to display 3–6 fleshy, crimson arils, each containing a single seed.

Natural History

American bittersweet is a fairly common vine in brushy thickets, woodland margins, and forest openings throughout most of the state. It is also found in forest interiors but less commonly. When growing in the open and without support, it becomes a formless, contorted, or mounded shrub about 3 ft (1 m) tall, which may eventually sprawl over rock piles, other shrubs, or herbaceous vegetation. Yet, when presented with the opportunity, it can twine on tree trunks that have a diameter as great as 18 inches (46 cm) and climb into the crown of mature trees, to a height of at least 65 ft (20 m).

American bittersweet is a dextrose climber, meaning it twines spirally upwards around the tree trunk from left to right, in this case at an angle of about 50 to 70 degrees (Putz and Mooney 1991). This mode of climbing has its advantages, but it does not accommodate radial growth of the tree trunk. As a result, growth of the tree eventually tightens the constriction of the vine, which inhibits the downward movement of carbohydrates from the leaves of the tree to the roots (Lutz 1943). When this happens, the radial growth of the tree trunk immediately above a constricting vine is greatly increased, and the growth immediately below is decreased. This will sometimes kill the tree, but more often the tree outlives the vine, which eventually dies and falls away, leaving the disfigured tree looking something like a corkscrew.

Wild populations are traditionally exploited for winter wreaths, which are commonly sold in nurseries and farmers' markets, and it is occasionally planted for ornament or commercial harvest.

Fruits as they appear in late summer and autumn.

Leaves have a narrow, pointed tip.

Vines are unisexual, these flowers are from a female vine—June 6.

Fruits open in winter to reveal crimson arils.

Flowers from a male vine, note the yellow anthers—June 13.

American bittersweet climbing a 6" (15 cm) dbh birch.

American bittersweet 99

Celtis, hackberry

Ulmaceae: Elm family

This is a genus of 60 to 70 species of mostly trees and a few shrubs. They occur in tropical and temperate regions worldwide, with 6 species in the United States and 1 in Minnesota. (*Celtis* is the ancient Latin name used by Pliny for an African species of lotus.)

Celtis occidentalis L.

Hackberry

Large **trees**, to 33 m tall and 93 cm dbh. **Bark** gray or brown, thin; initially with narrow wavy ridges and irregular warty projections, eventually developing blocky ridges or thickish irregular scales that may loosen at the edges. 1st-year **branchlets** greenish to brownish, becoming brown the 2nd year; glabrous or occasionally hairy. **Leaves** simple, alternate, deciduous. **Petioles** 6–15 mm long; hairy or glabrous. **Leaf blades** ovate to lanceolate or somewhat deltate; palmately 3-veined; 6–12 cm long, 3–7 cm wide; base cordate to rounded, or somewhat truncate, asymmetrical; apex attenuate; margins serrate; upper surface dark green, with short stiff hairs or essentially glabrous; lower surface similar to upper but pale green. **Flowers** unisexual with separate male flowers and female flowers borne on the same branchlet. **Male flowers** borne in small clusters near the base of 1st-year branchlets; pedicels 2–7 mm long, glabrous; sepals 5–6, greenish or yellowish, 2-3 mm long; petals absent; stamens 5–6, shorter than the sepals. **Female flowers** borne singly or in pairs in leaf axils on 1st-year branchlets; pedicels 0.3–1 cm long at anthesis, becoming 1–2 cm long in fruit; sepals 5–6, greenish or yellowish, 1.5–2.5 mm long; petals absent; stigmas 2, recurved, exceeding the sepals; **anthesis** late April to late May; wind-pollinated. **Fruit** a ± spherical, fleshy, drupe 7–12 mm in diameter; dull red-brown to red-purple; maturing late August to late September, remaining on the tree until eaten by birds; animal-dispersed. (*occidentalis*: western, of the New World)

Identification

Hackberry is a tall, slender forest tree with a broad, open crown. The rarely noticed flowers appear in the spring, just as the leaves are emerging. The fruit is a pea-size drupe, which is green all summer then turns a dark maroon in September. The bark of small- and medium-size hackberry have peculiar winglike ridges and warty projections. As the tree grows larger, the bark becomes scaly or blocky and looks quite different. When comparing the leaves of hackberry with those of the elms (*Ulmus* spp.), notice the 3 veins arising from the base, and the long, drawn-out tip.

Natural History

Hackberry is a common canopy tree in forests of southern and central Minnesota, especially on river terraces and floodplains. Although not a floodplain specialist, it ranks fairly high in tolerance of spring flooding and sedimentation. Well-drained, loamy soils seem to produce the largest trees, yet just about any nonacidic soil other than peat is accepted; this includes loams with high proportions of sand, gravel, silt, or clay.

Hackberry was said to "frequent the heaviest timber" in the original Big Woods (Winchell 1875). This would put it in the company of sugar maple (*Acer saccharum*), basswood (*Tilia americana*), and American elm (*Ulmus americana*), where it would function as a late-successional or climax species. But in direct competition for sunlight, hackberry seedlings usually lose out to sugar maple and basswood, so it rarely becomes a dominant species. Not surprisingly, the recent epidemic of Dutch elm disease appears to have benefited hackberry, which is one of the species successfully filling the gaps left by dying elms.

The seeds of hackberry are spread great distances in the droppings of birds, and they seem to germinate just about anywhere, even in a dense sod of prairie grasses. Hackberry is very drought resistant and exceptionally wind firm, probably aided by roots that reach as deep as 20 ft (6 m) (Parker 1969). It is not particularly fast growing, but it is relatively free from serious diseases, and it may live 200 years (*fide* Burns and Honkala 1990).

A 3-veined, asymmetrical base and long, drawn-out tip.

Female flowers are at the top, males at the bottom—May 1.

Fruits are green all summer, then turn maroon in September.

Note warty ridges on young trunk— 5" (13 cm) dbh.

The female flower is little more than a pair of stigmas—May 16.

Bark becomes scaly on older trunks— 29" (73 cm) dbh.

Cephalanthus, buttonbush

Rubiaceae: Madder family

This is a genus of about 17 species of shrubs and small trees, occurring in temperate and tropical regions of America, Asia, and Africa. Two species occur in North America, and 1 in Minnesota. (*Cephalanthus* is from the Greek *cephalus*, for head, and *anthos*, for flower.)

Cephalanthus occidentalis L.

Buttonbush

Tall **shrubs,** with multiple ascending, arching, or sometimes decumbent **stems** to 5 m tall and 10 cm dbh; clonal by layering. **Bark** gray or brown, rough, flaking in age. 1st-year **branchlets** glabrous, greenish or greenish brown; 2nd-year branchlets brown or gray-brown, with whitish, linear or narrowly rhombic lenticels. **Leaves** simple, opposite or occasionally in whorls of 3, deciduous. **Petioles** 0.5–2 cm long, glabrous. **Leaf blades** ovate to ovate-oblong or elliptical; 7–14 cm long, 3–7 cm wide; base tapered or rounded; apex acute to acuminate; margins entire, often minutely ciliate; upper surface dark green, glabrous, shiny; lower surface pale green, sparsely hairy on main veins. **Inflorescence** a tight spherical cluster of 100–200 flowers; each cluster 2–3 cm in diameter, borne singly at the ends of elongate leafless peduncles or peduncle branches that arise terminally or from axils of upper leaves. **Flowers** bisexual; 4-merous; sessile; calyx tubular, 2.5–4 mm long; corolla white or greenish, tubular, 8–12 mm long; anthers somewhat shorter than corolla; style long-exserted; **anthesis** late June to early August; insect-pollinated. **Fruit** a brown cone-shaped nutlet, 5–8 mm long, clustered into dense spherical heads; maturing early September to early October and persisting through the winter; animal- and water-dispersed. **Seeds** 4–5 mm long. (*occidentalis*: western, of the New World)

Identification

Buttonbush is a large, coarse shrub with numerous arching stems, smooth, shiny leaves, and ball-like clusters of small, whitish flowers. The general growth form and habitat might suggest silky dogwood (*Cornus amomum*), but the spherical flower clusters are genuinely unique. Also unique is the tendency of the leaves to occur in whorls of 3 rather than in 2s.

Natural History

Buttonbush has a wide geographic range to the south of Minnesota, but within Minnesota it is largely restricted to scattered wetlands on the floodplains of the Mississippi and St. Croix rivers. There are also two seemingly disjunct occurrences in Rice County. One is on the shore of Shields Lake, and the other is on an island in Cedar Lake, about 4 miles away.

Buttonbush is well adapted to floodplains and is very tolerant of flooding and sedimentation (Gill 1970). When its stems or branches are buried by flood-borne sediments, they can form adventitious roots and send up new shoots. This is a process called layering, which can lead to the formation of dense clonal thickets at the edge of open water or in bottomland marshes and sloughs.

Buttonbush is sometimes found colonizing newly formed islands in the Mississippi River, even in raw sand or silt on dredge-spoil islands. Buttonbush does very well in these early successional habitats, which are typically open or occupied by scattered tree saplings or shrubs. But because buttonbush is relatively intolerant of shade, it does not do well in a mature forest. So in typical floodplain forests of silver maple (*Acer saccharinum*), plains cottonwood (*Populus deltoides* subsp. *monilifera*), river birch (*Betula nigra*), or black willow (*Salix nigra*), buttonbush is usually limited to the narrow ecotone between the forest and open water, or to low spots within the forest where the canopy cover is thin.

Each spherical cluster contains 100–200 flowers—July 30.

Leaves are opposite or whorled, smooth-margined.

The bark is rough, sometimes flaky—this stem is 1.5 " (4 cm) diameter.

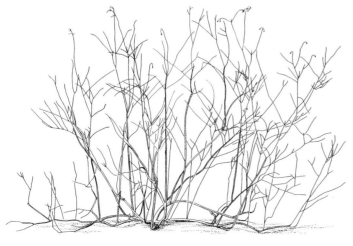

Tightly packed nutlets mature in September.

Chamaedaphne, leatherleaf

Ericaceae: Heath family

The leatherleaf genus consists of a single, circumboreal species occurring in North America, Europe, and Asia. (*Chamaedaphne* is from the Greek *chamae*, for on the ground, and *daphne*, laurel.)

Chamaedaphne calyculata (L.) Moench

Leatherleaf

Low to midsize **shrubs**, with erect or ascending **stems** to 1 m tall; clonal by growth of rhizomes and by layering. 1st-year **branchlets** brown, scaly, minutely hairy; the epidermal layer becoming gray the 2nd year and exfoliating to reveal a smooth purplish or brownish surface. **Leaves** simple; alternate; evergreen, shed the summer of the 2nd year after the new leaves reach full size. **Petioles** 1–1.5 mm long, glabrous or hairy. **Leaf blades** obovate to elliptical or oblong; those leaves below the inflorescence 1.8–3.4 cm long, 7–13 mm wide; those leaves within the inflorescence much reduced; base blunt; apex rounded, blunt, or tapered; margins crenulate, somewhat revolute; upper surface dark green, somewhat shiny, glabrous; lower surface pale green to rust-colored, dull, scaly. **Flowers** bisexual, 5-merous, whitish; borne singly from the axils of the reduced upper leaves, and forming a leafy 1-sided terminal raceme; pedicels 1–3 mm long, scaly; sepals triangular, scaly, 2–3 mm long; corolla 5–7 mm long, urn-shaped or cylindrical, the lobes 1–2 mm long and reflexed; style included or slightly exserted; **anthesis** early May to mid-June; insect-pollinated. **Fruit** a 5-celled capsule; depressed-globular; 2.5–4 mm across, with persistent style and sepals; maturing in autumn and shedding seeds through winter and the following spring; gravity- and water-dispersed. (*calyculata*: with an epicalyx, i.e., whorls of bracts below the calyx)

Identification

Leatherleaf is a medium-size bog shrub rarely more than waist high, with numerous short, wiry branches and leathery, evergreen leaves. It is one of four similar evergreen shrubs of the heath family that commonly occur in *Sphagnum* bogs; the other three are Labrador tea (*Rhododendron groenlandicum*), bog rosemary (*Andromeda glaucophylla*), and bog laurel (*Kalmia polifolia*).

Natural History

Leatherleaf is the most common and abundant shrub in Minnesota's peat bogs; its presence actually defines the plant community called "muskeg." It also occurs on boggy or rocky lakeshores and stream margins, and on floating sedge mats. Most of these habitats are carpeted with *Sphagnum* moss and away from dense tree cover, although there may be scattered black

spruce (*Picea mariana*) or tamarack (*Larix laricina*). The habitats are invariably acidic, nutrient-poor, and continually saturated. Leatherleaf is usually absent from nutrient-rich habitats, which are typically dominated by larger shrubs such as willows (*Salix* spp.), dogwoods (*Cornus* spp.), or speckled alder (*Alnus incana* subsp. *rugosa*).

Leatherleaf habitats are generally stable; they are not strongly influenced by droughts or floods, and they enjoy relatively long intervals between fire and other major disturbance. Under such conditions of apparent equilibrium, seedling establishment may be a rare event for leatherleaf, so reproduction is usually clonal. Clones of leatherleaf originate from a single individual that spreads radially by the growth of rhizomes and by layering. Rhizomes are simply underground stems that spread laterally; layering happens when aboveground stems or branches are overgrown by the living moss and respond by producing adventitious roots within the moss layer. These rooted branches can produce additional shoots, which may themselves go through the process of layering. In time, clonal reproduction that begins with a single individual can produce a dense thicket about waist high that can cover a large area. These clones may also fragment, creating smaller patches, or merge with other clones and create larger patches.

The flowers hang downward from a horizontal branch tip—May 17.

Growing at the edge of a bog pond in Pine County.

Note the closely spaced stems and small, stiff leaves.

Seed capsules are smaller than a pea, with long style—August 24.

Chimaphila, pipsissewa

Pyrolaceae: Shinleaf family

This is a genus of 4 to 8 species of evergreen shrubs, widely scattered in temperate and boreal regions of the Northern Hemisphere. Three species occur in the United States, and 1 in Minnesota. (*Chimaphila* is from the Greek *cheima*, winter, and *philein*, to love, in reference to its evergreen nature.)

Chimaphila umbellata (L.) Bart. subsp. *cisatlantica* (Blake) Hult.

Pipsissewa

Low **shrubs**, with 1 or a few upright **stems** to 23 cm tall; becoming decumbent and rooting at the nodes. **Branches** few, initially green becoming red-brown or purplish, glabrous, minutely roughened. **Leaves** simple; in whorl-like clusters of 3–8; evergreen, persisting 3–4 years. **Petioles** 2–7 mm long or barely distinguishable, glabrous. **Leaf blades** oblanceolate to narrowly obovate or occasionally elliptical; 3–5 cm long, 0.8–2 cm wide; base acutely tapered; apex obtuse to subacute; margins coarsely serrate, especially on the distal half; upper surface dark green, shiny, glabrous, veins impressed; lower surface pale green, dull, glabrous, midvein protruding. **Inflorescence** a terminal corymb of 3–7 flowers borne at the end of a minutely glandular peduncle 7–9 cm long that surpasses the uppermost leaves. **Flowers** bisexual, 5-merous, white to rose pink, saucer-shaped; pedicels 1–2.5 cm long, arching in flower, erect in fruit, minutely glandular; sepals ovate to deltate, minutely laciniate, 1–2 mm long; petals ovate to obovate or elliptical, minutely laciniate, 4–7 mm long; stamens 10; **anthesis** early to late July; insect-pollinated. **Fruit** a depressed globose capsule 5–7 mm across; maturing mid-August to mid-September, shedding seeds over winter and the following spring; wind- and gravity-dispersed. (*umbellata*: in umbels)

Identification

Pipsissewa is a small, evergreen subshrub (barely woody) about ankle high. The leaves are dark green, shiny, and attached in whorls of 3 or more. It is most likely to be confused with some of the evergreen members of the heath family (Ericaceae), especially bearberry (*Arctostaphylos uva-ursi*) and wintergreen (*Gaultheria procumbens*), but of these only pipsissewa has whorled leaves and flowers that are held on a stalk above the leaves.
Note: This is a species complex with circumpolar distribution and as many as 5 geographically distinct subspecies (Hultén 1971). The race that occurs in eastern North America (including Minnesota) has been named subsp. *cisatlantica* (Blake) Hult. West of the Great Plains are 2 or 3 related subspecies.

Natural History

Pipsissewa is fairly common in pine (*Pinus*) forests in the northern half of the state, occasionally becoming abundant enough to qualify as a ground cover. It is much less common in the south, where it typically occurs under oaks (*Quercus* spp.) and usually in rather small isolated patches. It generally prefers dry, sandy, nutrient-poor soil, especially where there is partial shade and sparse herbaceous vegetation.

Each aerial stem typically produces 2–4 short branches. Each year the branches elongate somewhat and produce a new whorl of leaves, retaining the whorls from the previous 3–4 years. From the center of each new whorl a long, leafless stalk is produced, which bears 3–7 flowers. After 5–8 years, a branch will have reached a height of about 8 inches (20 cm) and will recline (become decumbent), sending out roots where it contacts the ground. The reclined portion of the branch becomes bare of leaves and may become partially buried in the humus, but the tip of each branch continues to grow upright and add new whorls of leaves and occasionally new branches.

As the process is repeated, pipsissewa effectively creates small colonies with several aerial branches, all connected by the previous aerial branches, which are now lying on the ground and acting as stolons. In time, these colonies may fragment when one or more of the decumbent branches are severed, which may lead to the founding of a new colony.

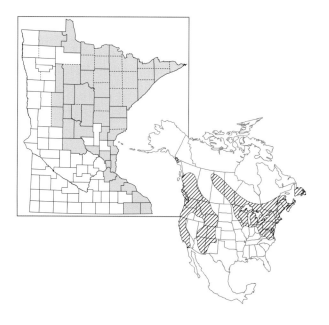

Leaves are evergreen and coarsely serrate—July 18.

The petals vary from white to rose-pink—July 18.

Colonies can be 10' (3 m) or more across.

The flowers arch over but the fruits stand erect—August 26.

Clematis, purple clematis and virgin's bower

Ranunculaceae: Crowfoot family

Clematis constitutes a genus of about 300 species of woody and semiwoody vines and herbaceous perennials occurring in temperate, subarctic, and tropical regions worldwide. About 25 species are native in the United States, and 2 are native in Minnesota. (*Clematis* is from the Greek *clema,* for a twig or branch; the reference is unclear.)

Many of the Old World species, and garden hybrids involving both Old and New World parents, are cultivated in Minnesota. Among the most common are the *C. jackmanii* hybrids and sweet autumn clematis (*C. ternifolia*). This last one can be very vigorous and often persists after cultivation, but none is known to be naturalized in Minnesota.

Key to the Genus Clematis *in Minnesota*

1. Flower blue or purplish, 3–6 cm long, solitary on a long peduncle, appearing in May or June when the leaves are about half-grown; lower surface of leaf with hairs on main veins, otherwise glabrous or nearly so .... *C. occidentalis*
1. Flowers whitish, 0.7–1.1 cm long, in clusters of 5–30, appearing in July or August when the leaves are fully grown; lower surface of leaf evenly hairy .... *C. virginiana*

Clematis occidentalis (Hornem.) DC.

Purple clematis
[*C. verticillaris* DC.]

Climbing or trailing **vines**, with slender flexible **stems** to 4 m long and 1 cm diameter. 1st-year **branchlets** yellowish brown, glabrous or occasionally sparsely hairy; 2nd-year branchlets brown to purple-brown, glabrous. **Leaves** ternately compound, opposite, deciduous. **Petioles** 5–9 cm long, sparsely hairy; may function as tendrils and twine on suitable support, in which case becoming lignified and persisting after the blades are shed and remaining on the stem for 2 or more years; petiolules 2–4 cm long. **Leaflets** ovate to lance-ovate, with 2–3 irregular lobes or unlobed; 4–9 cm long, 2–5 cm wide; base cordate to rounded; apex acute to somewhat acuminate; margins entire or more often with a few coarse irregular serrations or crenations; upper surface dark green, sparsely hairy to glabrate; lower surface similar to upper but somewhat paler. **Flowers** 4-merous, bisexual, blue to purplish, borne singly from axillary fascicles and subtended by 1 or 2 pairs of leaves; peduncle 2–6 cm long, sparsely hairy; sepals petaloid, elliptical to oblong or lance-oblong, 3–6 cm long, 1–1.8 cm wide, drooping; petals lacking; stamens numerous; **anthesis** early May to late mid-June, when leaves are about half-grown; insect-pollinated. **Fruit** a flattened achene; 3–4.5 mm long; brown; hairy, with persistent plumed style 4–7 cm long; numerous in large fluffy heads; maturing late June to early mid-September; wind-dispersed. (*occidentalis*: western, of the New World)

Identification

Purple clematis is a sprawling or weakly climbing vine occasionally reaching a height of 10–13 ft (3–4 m) but rarely much more. The compound leaves and general growth form are very similar to those of virgin's bower (*C. virginiana*). Also be aware that both species develop seed heads with dense tangles of long, downy plumes. The main difference is that virgin's bower has clusters of smallish white flowers, while purple clematis has a single, large, blue or purple flower that hangs downward like a bell.
Note: This species is divided into three geographic varieties, distinguishable by leaflet shape and flower color. The eastern range of the species (including Minnesota) is occupied solely by var. *occidentalis*, the western range by var. *dissecta* (C. L. Hitchc.) Pringle and var. *grosseserrata* (Rydb.) Pringle (Pringle 1997).

Natural History

Purple clematis is occasional in a variety of upland forest types, both deciduous and coniferous. Although it is most common in the northeast, it is never abundant; in fact, it usually occurs as scattered, transient individuals. It seems to prefer acidic, mesic or dry-mesic soil, often in rocky habitats. It will flower and set seed in the open or in moderate shade but apparently not in dense shade.

Purple clematis has no specialized structures for climbing; instead it uses the petioles of its leaves as tendrils to twine around small twigs. Although the leaves are shed each autumn, the petioles that have been used as tendrils turn woody and persist on the branch. In fact, they become very tough and typically outlast the branch, which usually lives only a few years.

Most branches produce only leaves the 1st year, with buds produced in the leaf axils. The 2nd year, the buds open, and each produces a fascicle (cluster) of two leaves and a flower, or often a lower bud will produce a new branch. The original branch will probably not produce leaves or flowers again and will soon die back to the point where a new branch begins (Pringle 1971).

The large, purple flowers hang downward, are bisexual—June 7.

Each leaf has 3 leaflets, and the petiole functions as a tendril.

A single seed head with perhaps 100 plumed seeds—September 13.

Clematis virginiana L.

Virgin's bower

Climbing or trailing **vines**, with slender flexible **stems** to 5 m long and 1 cm diameter. 1st-year **branchlets** brownish green, hairy; 2nd-year branchlets brown to reddish brown, moderately to sparsely hairy. **Leaves** ternately compound, opposite, deciduous. **Petioles** 4–10 cm long, moderately to sparsely hairy; may function as tendrils and twine on suitable support, becoming lignified and persisting after the blades are shed; petiolules 0.5–3 cm long. **Leaflets** ovate to lance-ovate, with 3 distinct or sometimes barely distinct lobes; 4–10 cm long, 2.5–8 cm wide; base cordate to rounded; apex acute to somewhat acuminate; margins with a few large coarse serrations; upper surface dark green, sparsely hairy to glabrate; lower surface pale green, moderately to sparsely hairy. **Flowers** 4-merous, unisexual, each plant bearing either male flowers or female flowers; whitish; borne in large open panicles of 5 to 30, from axils of leaves on elongate 1st-year branchlets; peduncles 2–8 cm long, hairy; sepals petaloid, elliptical to obovate or oblanceolate, 7–11 mm long, 2.5–5 mm wide; petals lacking; male flowers with fertile stamens only; female flowers with pistils and sterile stamens; **anthesis** mid-July to late August; insect-pollinated. **Fruit** a flattened achene 3–5 mm long; brown; hairy, with persistent plumed style 3–6 cm long; numerous in large fluffy heads; maturing late mid-August to late September; wind-dispersed. (*virginiana*: of Virginia)

Identification

Virgin's bower is a sprawling or weakly climbing vine usually 8–12 ft (2.5–4 m) long, with compound leaves and profuse clusters of small but showy white flowers. By late summer or autumn the flowers have developed into large, fluffy heads of long-plumed seeds. The leaves, seed heads, and growth form are quite similar to purple clematis (*C. occidentalis*). But instead of clusters of small, white flowers, purple clematis produces a single, large, blue or purple flower at the end of each peduncle.

Natural History

Virgin's bower is a common vine along the margins of mesic hardwood forests and in brushy thickets along streams. It is also seen sprawling over fences or low shrubs, or forming dense viney mats on rocks, beaches, and roadsides. It seems to prefer moist, loamy soil and full or partial sunlight, but it is occasionally found in forest interiors, where it may experience deep shade for much of the day. Virgin's bower is fast growing and short-lived, rarely persisting in any one place for more than a few years. During that short time it can produce large numbers of wind-borne seeds that are able to travel considerable distances. These dispersing seeds germinate quickly on a variety of substrates, allowing them to take advantage of brief opportunities provided by some localized gap or opening in the vegetation.

Although mostly a "scrambler," virgin's bower will sometimes climb to a vertical height as great as 16 ft (5 m), using its petioles as tendrils to twine around twigs of a supporting sapling or shrub. The petioles shed the blade portion of the leaf in autumn but remain attached to the branch. They then become somewhat woody and may persist on the branch for a 2nd year.

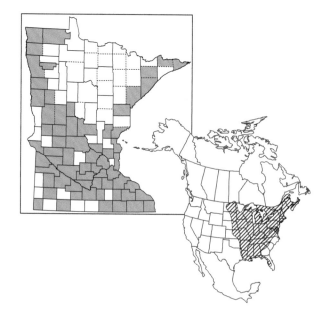

A female flower with cluster of pistils and ring of sterile stamens.

The male vine will contribute pollen but will not produce seeds.

A single leaf with 3 leaflets.

A cluster of seed heads from a female vine—September 18.

A female vine at peak anthesis on August 22.

Comptonia, sweet-fern

Myricaceae: Bayberry family

Comptonia is a monotypic genus endemic to eastern North America, closely related to sweet gale (*Myrica gale*). (*Comptonia* is named for Henry Compton, 1632–1713, amateur botanist and Bishop of London.)

Comptonia peregrina (L.) Coult.

Sweet-fern

Low to midsize **shrubs**, with erect or ascending **stems** to 1 m tall and 1 cm basal diameter; forming rhizomatous colonies. **Branchlets** coarse, brown to reddish brown or purplish, hairy. **Leaves** simple, alternate, deciduous or marcescent. **Petioles** lacking or up to 6 mm long, hairy; with lance-linear stipules. **Leaf blades** linear-lanceolate; 3–12 cm long, 0.5–2.5 cm wide; base acute; apex acute; margins with prominent rounded or rhombic-shaped lobes, the sinuses reaching nearly to the midvein (pinnatifid); upper surface dark green, hairy to glabrate, dotted with small yellow glands; lower surface pale green, hairy to glabrate. **Inflorescence** unisexual, male flowers and female flowers borne in separate catkins on the same or on different plants. **Male catkins** elongate, pendulous, 1.5–3 cm long; borne singly from leaf axils near the ends of 2nd-year branchlets. **Male flowers** 30–50, with 3–8 stamens; subtended by a single acuminate-tipped ciliate-margined bract about 2 mm long. **Female catkins** dense, spherical or ellipsoidal, 2–5 mm long; borne singly from leaf axils immediately below the male catkins, on 2nd-year branchlets. **Female flowers** 20–45; with 2 red stigmas; subtended by 1 short, broad primary bract and 7–9 lance-acicular secondary bracts that elongate in fruit; **anthesis** early May to early June before the leaves appear; wind-pollinated. **Infructescence** a burlike cluster 1–2 cm across, consisting of 8–15 1-seeded nutlike **fruits**, each fruit 5–6 mm long; elliptical-oblong or ovate; shiny; maturing in July; animal-dispersed. (*peregrina*: foreign, i.e., to Linnaeus, the original European author)

Identification

Sweet-fern is a small, bushy shrub usually about knee high, aptly named for its fernlike appearance and fragrant leaves. It is very distinctive and will not easily be mistaken for another shrub but could, at first glance, be mistaken for an herbaceous plant.

Natural History

Sweet-fern occurs sporadically in parts of northeastern and north-central Minnesota, most often in dry, sterile, sandy soil or in thin soil over bedrock. These sites are usually in the open or under a thin canopy of pines (*Pinus* spp.), oaks (*Quercus* spp.), or trembling aspen (*Populus tremuloides*). These habitats are invariably maintained by wildfire, and

indeed sweet-fern is strongly favored by periodic burning. In fire-suppressed habitats it may seem to disappear but will reappear quickly and vigorously within 5 years after a fire or, more likely these days, a clear-cut (Ahlgren 1970). This reappearance may be the result of new shoots sprouting from dormant buds on the surviving rhizomes, or from the germination of long-buried seeds, which can remain viable in the soil for decades (Del Tredici 1977).

When freed from competition for light and nutrients, sweet-fern cannot only make a reappearance, it can spread rapidly. The rhizomes can grow laterally more than 3 ft (1 m) per year (Hall, Aalders, and Everett 1976) and eventually create dense, tangled colonies about knee high. In fact, it is common to see distinct colonies 300 ft (110 m) or more across, which likely began from one seedling after a fire years before. It is even likely that some single colonies cover several square miles but have become fragmented and indistinct over time.

The burlike fruit clusters are apparently adapted for dispersal in the fur of mammals, which makes sweet-fern a successful colonizer. It becomes aggressive only when established colonies are released from competition, or in forestry jargon, "suppression." The roots reportedly form nodules that harbor nitrogen-fixing microorganisms (Bond 1967), a distinct advantage in the sandy, nitrogen-poor soils it typically inhabits.

Red stigmas reveal the female flowers—May 6.

Male flowers are in long catkins near tip of branch—May 6.

Each nutlike fruit is buried within a spiny bur—July 12.

The fragrant, fernlike leaves can be over 4" (10 cm) long.

A typical patch of sweet-fern from Pine County.

Sweet-fern

Cornus, the dogwoods

Cornaceae: Dogwood family

The dogwoods constitute a genus of about 65 species of deciduous trees and shrubs, rarely herbs. They are widespread but occur mostly in north temperate regions of Asia, North America, and the mountains of Central America. About 16 species occur in the United States, and 6 in Minnesota. One of the 6 Minnesota dogwoods, bunchberry (*C. canadensis*), is not included here because it produces only herbaceous shoots. (*Cornus* is from the Latin *cornu*, a horn, thought to be a reference to the hardness of the wood.)

Dogwoods, as a genus, are common and widespread in Minnesota. They can be recognized by their clusters of small, 4-petaled, white flowers, and leaves with arcuate lateral veins (veins that curve toward the tip of the leaf as they near the margin). If the leaf blade is carefully pulled apart, the lateral veins remain connected by delicate white threads (unraveled spiral thickenings in the vessel elements); this is usually a good test for dogwoods.

Key to the Genus Cornus in Minnesota

1. Leaves alternate; petioles often > 2.5 cm long; branchlets glabrous .... *C. alternifolia*
1. Leaves opposite; petioles < 2.5 cm long; branchlets usually hairy, at least the 1st year.
    2. Leaves roundish, 1–1.7 times longer than wide (length/width = 1–1.7), with 6–9 lateral veins per side (usually 7 or 8); branchlets of the current year with dark purple streaks .... *C. rugosa*
    2. Leaves proportionately narrower, 1.7–2.8 times longer than wide (length/width = 1.7–2.8), with 3–6 lateral veins per side; branchlets of the current year lacking noticeable streaks.
        3. Branchlets gray the 2nd year; leaves with 3–4 lateral veins per side (usually 4); inflorescence pyramid-shaped, nearly as tall as wide .... *C. racemosa*
        3. Branchlets greenish, reddish, or purplish the 2nd year; leaves with 4–6 lateral veins per side (usually 5 or 6); inflorescence flat-topped, distinctly wider than tall.
            4. Pith of twigs brown after the 1st year; sepals 0.7–1.5 mm long; petals 4.5–5.5 mm long; fruits ripening blue; bark gray .... *C. amomum*
            4. Pith white after the 1st year; sepals 0.2–0.7 mm long; petals 2.5–4 mm long; fruits ripening white; bark greenish or yellowish (or red in winter) .... *C. sericea*

Cornus alternifolia L. f.

Pagoda dogwood

Tall **shrubs** or ultimately small **trees**, with single or occasionally multiple **stems** to 7.5 m tall and 11 cm dbh; nonclonal, or juveniles sometimes clonal by layering. **Branches** of mature specimens characteristically horizontal, often in widely and evenly spaced whorls. 1st-year **branchlets** green (drying brown), glabrous; 2nd- and 3rd-year branchlets similar, pith white. **Bark** thin, gray to greenish gray, nearly smooth. **Leaves** simple, alternate, deciduous. **Petioles** 2–5 cm long, sparsely hairy or glabrate. **Leaf blades** elliptical to broadly elliptical or occasionally somewhat ovate or obovate; 5.5–11 cm long, 3–6 cm wide; base tapered or somewhat rounded; apex acuminate; margins essentially entire; lateral veins 5–6 per side (usually 6); upper surface dark green, glabrous or with a few scattered appressed hairs; lower surface pale green, with sharp stiff appressed hairs. **Inflorescence** a dense, ± flat-topped terminal cyme, 3–7 cm across, 1–3 cm high, with 50–250 flowers. **Flowers** bisexual, 4-merous; pedicels 1–4 mm long, hairy, jointed at summit, becoming red in fruit; sepals minute, about 0.2 mm long; petals creamy white, oblong to oblong-lanceolate, 2.5–3.5 mm long; stamens 4, much longer than the petals; **anthesis** late May to early July; insect-pollinated. **Fruit** a blue-black spherical drupe; 5–8 mm in diameter; maturing late July to late August; animal-dispersed. (*alternifolia*: alternate-leaved)

Identification

In some situations pagoda dogwood appears as a large shrub, but its ultimate form is a small tree with a maximum height in Minnesota of about 25 ft (7.5 m). It usually has a single stem that remains distinct nearly to the top, with horizontal branches in widely spaced tiers (pagoda-like). The flowers are small and creamy white and appear in dense clusters in early summer. Ripe fruits are dark blue-black and have bright red stalks. Pagoda dogwood is the only Minnesota dogwood with alternate leaves, but the leaves are often crowded together and may not appear alternate at first.

Natural History

Pagoda dogwood is a common understory tree in mesic hardwood forests, especially in the southern and central counties. It is found in loamy or sandy soils, usually under a canopy of oaks (*Quercus* spp.), aspens (*Populus* spp.), ashes (*Fraxinus* spp.), hickories (*Carya* spp.), basswood (*Tilia americana*), black cherry (*Prunus serotina*), or maples (*Acer* spp.). It is the most shade tolerant of Minnesota dogwoods and easily thrives in continual deep shade. However, specimens under a canopy gap or near a permanent edge do grow faster and produce more flowers and fruits. Birds relish the fruits and spread the seeds in their droppings, as they do for all dogwoods. Although the seeds are bound to end up in a variety of bird-preferred habitats, pagoda dogwood apparently succeeds only in forested habitats; it is never found in the open.

Juvenile plants less than about 3 ft (1 m) tall that occur in deep shade sometimes spread across the forest floor by layering. This process begins when a supple young stem becomes decumbent, that is, reclined on the ground. Whether the stems recline under their own power or are pressed to the ground by heavy snow or some other outside force is not clear. But once the stem is in contact with bare ground, it will remain horizontal and take root along its length. The tips of the branches will then turn upwards and grow vertically just like the original stem. This process, if repeated, can create a small colony 9–12 ft (3–4 m) across with a dozen or more upright stems (actually the tips of former branches). The colony can remain in this arrested state for a considerable time, but when a gap opens in the canopy above and more sunlight reaches the ground, the tallest stem will usually exert apical dominance and grow to maturity.

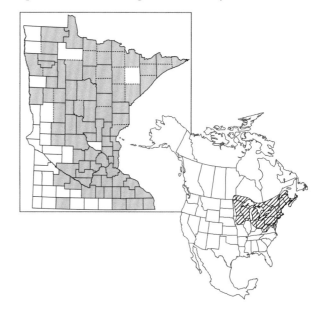

Blue fruits on red stalks—July 30.

At peak anthesis on May 26.

Bark is thin, gray, and nearly smooth—this stem is 4.5" (11 cm) diameter.

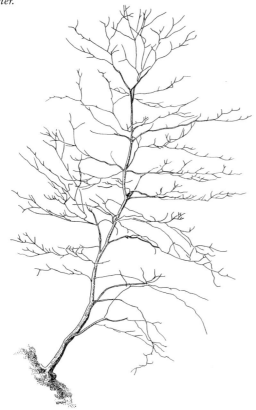

Each leaf has five or six lateral veins per side.

Dogwoods 🍃 **129**

Cornus amomum P. Mill.

Silky dogwood
[*C. obliqua* Raf.]

Tall **shrubs**, with multiple upright or arching **stems** to 4.5 m tall and 8 cm dbh, forming colonies by tip-rooting and layering of lower branches. 1st- and 2nd-year **branchlets** hairy, greenish purple to purplish or reddish purple, becoming gray the 3rd year; pith white the 1st year, brown thereafter. **Bark** gray, smoothish, becoming rough in age. **Leaves** simple, opposite, deciduous. **Petioles** 0.8–2 cm long, moderately to densely hairy. **Leaf blades** ovate to ovate-oblong or elliptical; 5–9 cm long, 2–5 cm wide; base rounded or tapered; apex acuminate; margins essentially entire; lateral veins 4–5 per side (usually 5); upper surface dark green, with stiff appressed white hairs; lower surface similar but pale green. **Inflorescence** a dense, ± flat-topped terminal cyme, 2.5–6 cm across, 1–3 cm high, with 35–175+ flowers. **Flowers** bisexual, 4-merous; pedicels 2.5–6 mm long, hairy, jointed at summit; sepals 0.7–1.5 mm long; petals creamy white, narrowly oblong-lanceolate, 4.5–5.5 mm long; stamens 4, about equaling the petals; **anthesis** mid-June to late mid-July; insect-pollinated. **Fruit** a blue or purplish spherical drupe; 6–10 mm in diameter; slightly fluted; maturing late July to mid-September; animal-dispersed. (*amomum*: Latin name of a shrub)

Identification

Silky dogwood is a large, bushy shrub, usually 6–13 ft (2–4 m) tall with multiple arching stems and a rounded silhouette. It looks a lot like red-osier dogwood (*C. sericea*), and the two often grow side by side, but silky dogwood has blue fruit, not white (seen in August and September), and twigs with brown pith, not white (seen all year).
Note: Minnesota specimens seem to fit descriptions of subspecies *obliqua* (Raf.) Wilson [var. *schuetzeana* (Meyer) Rickett], which compared to the typical subspecies is more northerly in distribution and has smaller and proportionately narrower leaves. Also, the leaves have tapered bases, fewer lateral veins, and mainly appressed, white hairs (Wilson 1964).

Natural History

Silky dogwood occurs throughout much of the hardwood forest region of central and southern Minnesota, but it is not particularly common or abundant. It grows almost exclusively in nonacidic wetlands; primarily in loams or rarely in sedge-derived peat. Suitable loams can be high in sand, silt or clay. It may be found in the partial shade of trees, but it is intolerant of deep shade and prefers the open. These conditions are often found in narrow transition zones around marshes and lakeshores and in swales, river bottoms, meadows, and seeps. These habitats are likely to support a mix of shrubs similar in size to silky dogwood, including red-osier dogwood (*C. sericea*), sand bar willow (*Salix interior*), and heart-leaved willow (*S. eriocephala*). Although silky dogwood is rare or absent in fire-prone habitats, it easily tolerates seasonal flooding and moderate levels of sedimentation, even moderate droughts.

Occasionally the tip of an otherwise normal branch will start to grow downward at an accelerated rate. When the tip reaches the ground, it will quickly take root, forming a loop. Then the tip will begin to grow upwards again. If the loop is broken, two individuals will have been created; each is genetically identical but autonomous. This is a specialized form of layering called tip-rooting, and if done repeatedly, it can result in the creation of numerous evenly spaced individuals, all clones, forming a small colony. The conditions initiating this phenomenon, as well as the conditions limiting it, are unknown.

Fruits are a distinctive blue-purple—August 27.

An 11' (3.4 m) tall specimen from Washington County.

Flowers are like those of red-osier dogwood except larger.

Multiple stems from a crowded base.

Cornus racemosa Lam.

Gray dogwood

[*C. foemina* P. Mill. subsp. *racemosa* (Lam.) J. S. Wilson]

Tall **shrubs**, with multiple upright **stems** to 5 m tall and 4 cm dbh; forming colonies by root suckering. 1st-year **branchlets** brown, sparsely hairy to glabrous; 2nd-year branchlets gray, glabrous, pith whitish or tan. **Bark** gray, smooth or somewhat rough. **Leaves** simple, opposite, deciduous. **Petioles** 0.5–1.5 cm long, minutely and sparsely hairy or essentially glabrous. **Leaf blades** elliptical to ovate; 5–9 cm long, 2–4.5 cm wide; base tapered; apex acuminate; margins essentially entire; lateral veins 3–4 per side (usually 4); upper surface dark green, with short stiff appressed hairs; lower surface similar to upper but pale green. **Inflorescence** a dense terminal panicle, pyramidal, 3–5 cm across, 2–4 cm high, with 20–75 flowers. **Flowers** bisexual, 4-merous; pedicels 2–6 mm long, hairy to sparsely hairy, jointed at summit, becoming red in fruit; sepals minute or lacking; petals creamy white, 2.5–4 mm long, lanceolate to ovate or oblong; stamens 4, equaling or slightly exceeding the petals; **anthesis** early June to early July; insect-pollinated. **Fruit** a whitish to pale blue spherical drupe; 5–8 mm in diameter; maturing early August to early September; animal-dispersed. (*racemosa*: in racemes, a reference to the flowers)

Identification

Gray dogwood is an upright shrub usually 6–9 ft (2–3 m) tall with numerous straight stems and rather short, ascending branches. The flower clusters are pyramid shaped, not flat topped like the other dogwoods. The fruit is whitish or pale blue when ripe, and the fruit stalks turn bright red. The leaves turn a dull maroon color in autumn and are shed later than those of most shrubs. It is most likely to be confused with red-osier dogwood (*C. sericea*), but gray dogwood is the only Minnesota dogwood with distinctly gray twigs and bark (actually, brown the first year, gray thereafter).

Natural History

Gray dogwood is basically a species of hardwood forest ecosystems. It typically occurs in mesic or somewhat dry sandy or loamy soil, often in the company of oaks (*Quercus* spp.), aspens (*Populus* spp.), black cherry (*Prunus serotina*), basswood (*Tilia americana*), elms (*Ulmus* spp.), or green ash (*Fraxinus pennsylvanica*). Although it is moderately tolerant of shade, it does not thrive or reproduce in continual deep shade. It prefers forests with thin canopies or openings under long-term canopy gaps, or a permanent forest edge. It is occasionally found in moist soil at the edge of wetlands, but it does not seem to withstand flooding or sedimentation.

By all indications, gray dogwood did not occur in the presettlement prairies or savannas, where the interval between wildfires was probably only 3 to 10 years. However, in postsettlement Minnesota, agriculture has supplanted prairies and savannas, and wildfires are largely a thing of the past. This has allowed gray dogwood to thrive where it could not before, especially in abandoned fields and pastures where, in the absence of competition, it may form large, dense clones by the growth of root suckers. Well-established clones can reach 65 ft (20 m) across with dense canopies as high as 16 ft (5 m), which create open understories. These clones can actually be dense enough to resist invasion of tree seedlings, thereby maintaining themselves for many decades (Dickinson, Putz, and Canham 1993). Individual stems within the clone, however, rarely survive beyond about 20 years. Replacement stems are appearing all the time, especially along the margin of the clone.

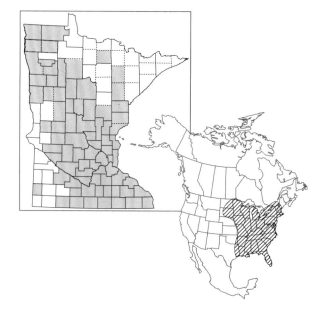

A dense clone at the edge of a forest—June 21.

Inflorescence is characteristically pyramid shaped.

Showing fall colors on September 22 in Hennepin County.

Older stems may develop rough bark.

Fruits are white or pale blue, on red stalks— August 30.

Dogwoods 🍃 **133**

Cornus rugosa Lam.

Round-leaved dogwood

Tall **shrubs**, with single or multiple upright **stems** to 5 m tall and 5 cm dbh; forming colonies by root suckering. 1st-year **branchlets** greenish with dark purple flecks or streaks, hairy; 2nd-year branchlets brown to reddish or purple-black, minutely hairy or glabrate, pith white. **Bark** gray or greenish, rough. **Leaves** simple, opposite, deciduous. **Petioles** 1–2 cm long, hairy. **Leaf blades** broadly ovate to broadly elliptical or nearly circular; 7.5–15 cm long, 5–10 cm wide; base rounded to nearly truncate or occasionally tapered; apex short-acuminate; margins essentially entire; lateral veins 6–9 per side (usually 7 or 8); upper surface dark green, with short stiff appressed hairs; lower surface pale green, with longish wavy hairs. **Inflorescence** a dense flat-topped or somewhat round-topped terminal cyme, 2–7 cm across, 1–4 cm high, with 30–150 flowers. **Flowers** bisexual, 4-merous; pedicels 1–5 mm long, hairy, jointed at summit; sepals minute, 0.2–0.5 mm long; petals creamy white, 3–4.5 mm long, ovate to lanceolate; stamens 4, exceeding the petals; **anthesis** early June to late July; insect-pollinated. **Fruit** a pale blue spherical drupe; 5–8 mm in diameter; maturing mid-August to late September; animal-dispersed. (*rugosa*: wrinkled)

Identification

Round-leaved dogwood is a large, graceful shrub with one or more slender, erect stems 7–13 ft (2.5–4 m) tall, sometimes taller. The flowers are in flat-topped clusters, and the fruits are pale blue when ripe. It is easily told from the other dogwoods by the large, roundish leaves. They tend to be widely spaced and held horizontal, and there are usually only 2 per branchlet. The dark purple streaks on the youngest twigs are also a unique character and most easily seen on fast-growing shoots.

Natural History

Round-leaved dogwood is common in the understory of upland forests throughout much of Minnesota. This includes landscapes that have a history of fire and those without. It is most often found in association with hardwoods, particularly oaks (*Quercus* spp.), aspens (*Populus* spp.), birches (*Betula* spp.), maples (*Acer* spp.), ashes (*Fraxinus* spp.), or elms (*Ulmus* spp.), but also with conifers, particularly the pines (*Pinus* spp.). It favors mesic to dry-mesic loamy or sandy soils, and often rocky slopes. It is rarely found in flood-prone habitats.

Round-leaved dogwood is moderately tolerant of shade, yet it does not favor the deepest shade. It is most abundant in forests with thin or open canopies and along forest borders where it gets direct sunlight for at least a portion of the day. In spite of being common over large areas, it is not an aggressive colonizer; it is rarely seen invading open land the way gray dogwood (*C. racemosa*) sometimes does. Still, it does sucker from the roots, and over time it can develop a sizeable "patch" or sometimes a small thicket, but more often it grows singly or with widely spaced stems. These stems may take the form of a small tree reaching as much as 16 ft (5 m) in height with the branches forming a dense crown near the top.

A single root crown showing multiple-aged stems.

Note the large, roundish leaves—June 18.

Four petals, 4 stamens, 1 carpel—standard issue for dogwoods.

Fruits turn pale blue when ripe—August 24.

At home in the understory of a northern forest—Carlton County.

Cornus sericea L.

Red-osier dogwood
[*C. stolonifera* Michx.]

Tall **shrubs**, with multiple upright or arching **stems**, to 4 m tall and 3 cm dbh; clonal by tip-rooting and layering. 1st-year **branchlets** greenish red to red, hairy; 2nd-year branchlets similar but usually glabrous, pith white. **Bark** greenish to yellowish or red (in fall and winter), smooth or rough. **Leaves** simple, opposite, deciduous. **Petioles** 1–2.5 cm long, hairy. **Leaf blades** ovate to elliptical, 5–11 cm long, 2.5–6 cm wide; base rounded or tapered; apex acuminate or occasionally acute; margins essentially entire; lateral veins 5–6 per side; upper surface dark green, with short stiff appressed hairs and/or somewhat longer, softer wavy hairs; lower surface similar but pale green. **Inflorescence** a dense flat-topped or somewhat round-topped terminal cyme, 2–5.5 cm across, 1.5–3 cm high, with 35–150 flowers. **Flowers** bisexual, 4-merous; pedicels 2–7 mm long, hairy, jointed at summit; sepals minute, 0.2–0.7 mm long; petals creamy white, 2.5–4 mm long, lanceolate to ovate; stamens 4, exceeding the petals; **anthesis** intermittent from mid-May to mid-August; insect-pollinated. **Fruit** a whitish spherical drupe; 5–8 mm in diameter; maturing early July to mid-September; animal-dispersed. (*sericea*: silky, with long, straight appressed hairs)

Identification

Red-osier dogwood is a fairly large, bushy shrub with numerous long, flexible stems and branches. It is usually 5–10 ft (1.5–3 m) tall with a rounded silhouette. The bark is typically some shade of green but turns red in the autumn, then green again the next spring. There is a more southerly species that has not yet been found in Minnesota called rough-leaved dogwood (*C. drummondii*); it is similar to red-osier dogwood except the leaves are rough and proportionately broader.
Note: Specimens with leaves that have wavy or curly hairs instead of the usual appressed straight hairs are not uncommon and have in the past been segregated as *C. baileyi* Coult. & Evans, or *C. stolonifera* Michx. var. *baileyi* (Coult. & Evans) Drescher.

Natural History

Red-osier dogwood is nearly ubiquitous in wetlands throughout most of the state; it is rare only in the southwest. Common habitats include swamps, marshes, fens, meadows, lakeshores, riverbanks, and ditch banks. Soil conditions are rarely an impediment and include sand, silt, clay, loam, and peat and range from continually saturated to seasonally saturated or barely moist. Red-osier dogwood even colonizes uplands, typically old fields and woodland edges, but it is not aggressive in uplands and rarely persists. Suitable sites have a pH value that ranges from highly basic (calcareous or alkaline) to moderately acidic. This range excludes only strongly acidic habitats such as the nutrient-poor bogs of the type often called "muskeg."

Red-osier dogwood may occur by itself or in highly structured shrub-dominated communities with various willows (*Salix* spp.), speckled alder (*Alnus incana* subsp. *rugosa*), or bog birch (*Betula pumila*). It is especially common in fire-prone habitats, and it does resprout vigorously after fire or heavy browsing. It can also tolerate spring flooding and a moderate amount of sedimentation, but it is generally intolerant of shade. Under normal conditions it will flower twice in a season; once from mid-May to early June, then again in July or August when fruit from the first flush is ripening. Rarely, a third flush may occur in September. Although seeds seem to be its primary mode of reproduction, it also spreads by layering.

Branches are green or yellowish in summer, red in winter.

Red-osier dogwood will flower in May, then again in July.

At the edge of Battle Creek in Ramsey County.

Fruit is a cream-colored drupe.

Corylus, the hazels

Betulaceae: Birch family

This is a genus of about 15 species of shrubs and trees, widespread in the north temperate regions of North America, Europe, and Asia. Three species occur in North America, and 2 in Minnesota. (*Corylus* is the classical Latin name for hazel, possibly derived from the Greek *corys*, a helmet, in reference to the husk that surrounds the nut.)

Hazels are unique in the birch family for producing clusters of nuts with hard, bony shells. The nut of the European *C. avellana* L. is the commercial filbert. It is cultivated in Europe and to a lesser extent in the United States, mostly in Oregon's Willamette Valley. The nuts of the native hazels are smaller and have a thicker shell but otherwise are considered equal to the European species. However, there is no commerce in native hazel nuts and little if any local tradition of gathering. But being so abundant, hazels are very important in the ecology of Minnesota forests. They provide much of the structure and function of the forest understory, and in the process provide wildlife habitat and influence succession of the canopy trees.

Key to the Genus Corylus in Minnesota

1. Petioles and 1st-year twigs with both nonglandular hairs and stalked glands; husk surrounding the nut broad, extending 0.5–2 cm beyond the nut; winter buds (seen August through April) rounded on top; the larger male catkins at least 4 cm long, and borne on a stalk 3–10 mm long .... *C. americana*
1. Petioles and 1st-year twigs usually with nonglandular hairs but without stalked glands; husk surrounding the nut forming a narrow tube-shaped beak extending 2–4 cm beyond the nut; winter buds acute; male catkins rarely more than 3.5 cm long, sessile .... *C. cornuta*

Corylus americana Walt.

American hazel

Tall **shrubs**, with numerous upright **stems** to 4.8 m tall and 3 cm dbh; forming extensive rhizomatous colonies. 1st-year **branchlets** brown to reddish brown or grayish; with stalked glands and nonglandular hairs; becoming glabrate the 2nd year. **Bark** thin, gray to gray-brown, smooth or somewhat rough. **Leaves** simple, alternate, deciduous. **Petioles** 7–20 mm long, with stalked glands and nonglandular hairs. **Leaf blades** ovate to elliptical or obovate; 6–12 cm long, 3.5–8 cm wide; base cordate or rounded; apex acuminate; margins irregularly double-serrate; upper surface dark green, sparsely hairy; lower surface pale green, hairy, especially on larger veins. **Inflorescence** unisexual, with male flowers and female flowers borne in separate catkins on the same branch. **Male catkins** slender, yellowish-brown, pendulous, 2.5–7 cm long; on stout peduncles 3–10 mm long, borne from leaf axils on twigs of the previous year. **Female catkins** much reduced and resembling leaf buds; borne from leaf axils on twigs of the previous year; **anthesis** late March to early May; wind-pollinated. **Fruit** a ± globose nut with a hard bony shell; 1–1.5 cm across; concealed within 2 broad foliaceous involucral bracts 2–3.5 cm long and 1.5–3 cm wide at the distal end, involucre covered with soft hairs and usually stalked glands; maturing late August to late September; animal-dispersed. (*americana*: of America)

Identification

American hazel is a relatively large shrub, typically 6–8 ft (2–2.5 m) tall, with numerous slender, erect stems. The leaves are essentially indistinguishable from those of beaked hazel (*C. cornuta*), and so are the nuts, but the shape of the husk that surrounds the nut is quite different. It forms a short, broad fringe at the end of the nut rather than the long, narrow tube of beaked hazel. Also, the petioles and 1st-year twigs have stalked glands (usually visible without magnification), which are absent on beaked hazel.

Natural History

American hazel probably runs a close second to beaked hazel (*C. cornuta*) as the most abundant understory shrub in Minnesota. It is ubiquitous in nearly all upland forest types, both hardwood and conifer, but it is most abundant under oaks (*Quercus* spp.), trembling aspen (*Populus tremuloides*), and to a lesser extent pines (*Pinus* spp.). It is uncommon in the north-central region and absent in the northeast, where its ecological role is taken over by beaked hazel. The range of the two hazels overlap in a broad swath through the middle of the state, and in this region they often occur mixed together. They seem quite compatible growing side by side, although American hazel appears to have a competitive advantage on the drier sites, and unlike beaked hazel it also occurs in prairie and savanna habitats.

The male catkins develop in late summer, and they overwinter with fully developed pollen. They open and shed their pollen very early the following spring, usually within two weeks of when the last snow melts. The nuts are mature by late summer, and those that survive the many seed predators will germinate the following spring.

Well-established plants produce large, horizontal rhizomes about 6 inches below the surface. These can sprout hundreds of stems, and if not constrained by competition, they can form large, dense clones as great as 30 ft (10 m) across. These rhizomes will vigorously replace existing stems that are killed by fire or cutting, but repeated short-interval fires can exhaust the rhizomes and kill the plant (Buckman 1964).

Typical suckering pattern of American hazel.

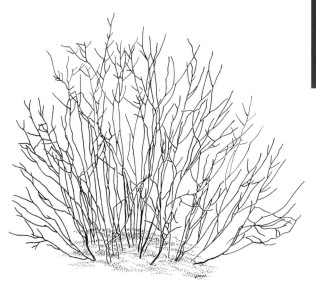

The petioles are covered with stalked glands.

Compare the shape of the husk with beaked hazel—August 20.

In the understory of a jack pine forest, Hubbard County.

Only the red stigmas give away the female flowers—April 11.

Male flowers are in long, pendulous catkins—April 11.

Corylus cornuta Marsh.

Beaked hazel
[*C. rostrata* Ait.]

Tall **shrubs**, with numerous upright **stems** to 4 m tall and 2 cm dbh; forming extensive rhizomatous colonies. 1st-year **branchlets** brown, hairy to glabrate, glands absent, becoming glabrous or glabrate the 2nd year. **Bark** thin, brown to gray-brown, smooth or somewhat rough. **Leaves** simple, alternate, deciduous. **Petioles** 7–18 mm long, hairy, glands lacking. **Leaf blades** ovate to elliptical or obovate; 6–11 cm long, 3.5–7.5 cm wide; base cordate to rounded; apex acuminate; margins irregularly double-serrate; upper surface dark green, sparsely hairy to glabrate; lower surface pale green, hairy, especially on larger veins. **Inflorescence** unisexual, with male flowers and female flowers borne in separate catkins on the same branch. **Male catkins** stout, yellowish, pendulous or curving, 1.5–3.5 cm long; sessile; borne from leaf axils on twigs of the previous year. **Female catkins** much reduced and resembling leaf buds; borne from leaf axils on twigs of the previous year; **anthesis** early April to early mid-May; wind-pollinated. **Fruit** a ± globose nut with a hard bony shell; 1–1.5 cm across; concealed within a single long, tubular, involucral bract 3.5–6 cm long, and 0.5–1 cm wide at the distal end, involucre densely covered with stiff bristly hairs, glands lacking; maturing late August to late September; animal-dispersed. (*cornuta*: horned, in reference to the long, slender beak on the fruit)

Identification
Beaked hazel is a fairly large shrub, usually about 6–8 ft (2–2.5 m) tall, with numerous slender, erect stems. The leaf shape and growth form are essentially indistinguishable from American hazel (*C. americana*), but the husk that covers the nut has a long, slender beak. Also, the twigs and petioles have no glandular hairs.
Note: The fruits should be handled with care. The stiff hairs on the husk can easily penetrate unprotected skin and cause a painful irritation.

Natural History
Beaked hazel is very common in the understory of upland forests throughout the central and northern counties. It is uncommon or rare in the southern forests and absent from prairie regions. It is most strongly associated with pines (*Pinus* spp.) and oaks (*Quercus* spp.), but it can also be abundant under aspens (*Populus* spp.), paper birch (*Betula papyrifera*), balsam fir (*Abies balsamea*), and most other tree species. In the north-central counties it often occurs side by side with American hazel, but beaked hazel tends to predominate on the moister sites, and American hazel on the drier sites.

At about 10 years of age beaked hazel begins to produce horizontal rhizomes that grow just beneath the soil surface. Over a 10- to 20-year period these rhizomes can sprout dozens of stems producing a dense clone 3–6 ft (1–2 m) across (Tappeiner 1971). These clones may eventually fragment and continue to expand or possibly merge with other clones, which may result in a dense and often pure understory of beaked hazel.

Beaked hazel occurs almost exclusively in fire-prone habitats, and it will normally resprout from buried rhizomes if top-killed by fire. However, if the fire is hot enough to consume the organic material in the soil, it may kill the rhizomes, which are usually within 6 inches of the surface (Buckman 1964).

Bark is rough but not coarse, this stem is 3/4" (2 cm) diameter.

Female catkins look like leaf buds with red stigmas—April 15.

Male catkins are stout and slightly curved— April 21.

The nut is round but the husk has a long beak—July 25.

A constant presence in northern forests—Cook County.

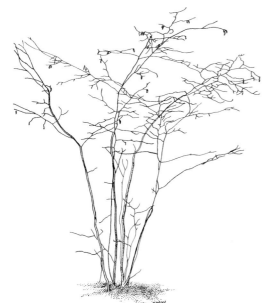

Petioles lack the stalked glands of American hazel.

Crataegus, the hawthorns

Rosaceae: rose family

The hawthorns comprise a very large and complex genus of about 200 species of deciduous shrubs and small trees. They are found primarily in eastern North America, but also in Asia, Europe, and Central America (Phipps et al. 1990). There are about 150 species in the United States, and 12 species in Minnesota. (*Crataegus* is the classical Greek name for hawthorn, from *kratos*, "strength," in reference to the wood.)

The 12 species of hawthorn that are considered native to Minnesota include 2 species that have not been seen in the state for over 100 years: *Crataegus coccinea* L. and *Crataegus scabrida* Sarg. Their discovery in Minnesota was adequately documented by authenticated herbarium specimens, so their status as original members of the native flora is not in dispute. However, repeated attempts to relocate them in the wild have failed, and they may now be gone from the state. Both are common eastern species that may have existed in Minnesota only as ephemeral or transient populations at the extreme northwestern edge of their range (Houston County in the southeastern corner of the state) and apparently have not persisted. They are regrettably left out of the present treatment only because the author has too little knowledge of them to present a meaningful treatment. All that is known to the author is summarized here:

Crataegus coccinea L.: Found once on July 15, 1899, by the botanist H. L. Lyon in section 28, Winnebago Valley, Houston County. Lyon noted "a couple of trees," but nothing more. A recent visit to the area found no hawthorns.

Crataegus scabrida Sarg.: Specimens were collected twice by botanist C. O. Rosendahl in June 1902. The first (#250) was on June 1 and recorded as "A single tree, in the forest, about 8 ft high, petals just shed. Near SW corner of sec 15 (Spring Grove Township, Houston County)." The second specimen (#336) was collected perhaps a half mile to the east on June 4: "in shaded woods, moist ravine. Single tree, about 14 ft high, 5 inches in diameter." A recent search of the specified area was inconclusive.

Another species of hawthorn was recently discovered at a single site in Big Stone County. Actually, it was discovered by the author in 1997 but thought, at the time, to be an unusual form of *C. chrysocarpa* (#26583 and #26877). A closer examination by Phipps in 2007 convinced him it was a previously overlooked Great Plains species, *Crataegus sheridana* A. Nels. Regrettably, this information did not arrive in time to prepare a full treatment for this book.

Biology

The complexity of hawthorn taxonomy can be traced to elaborate breeding behavior that until fairly recently was poorly understood (Campbell, Greene, and Dickinson 1991; Muniyamma and Phipps 1979a, 1979b, 1984, 1985). Fortunately, a technical knowledge of hawthorn biology is not needed to identify the species, but a brief nontechnical summary of the four general reproductive pathways employed by hawthorns may be useful.

1. Sexual diploids. These are apparently self-incompatible, meaning they are obligate outbreeders. They produce viable seeds only through cross-fertilization. These are the so-called pillar species from which the other species are presumed to have developed (Grant 1981). Examples from Minnesota include *C. punctata*, *C. mollis*, and likely *C. calpodendron* (Muniyamma and Phipps 1979b, 1984, 1985).
2. Sexual tetraploids. There is evidence that these species are self-compatible, meaning they can reproduce by outbreeding or inbreeding (self-fertilization). Some sexual tetraploids may also be facultative apomicts, which means they can produce viable seeds without any form of fertilization. This is accomplished through the nonsexual process of apomixis. In this process, the resulting seeds are genetically identical to the parent and are essentially clones. These hawthorns are normally fairly easy to identify, but the process of apomixis often results in the proliferation of local variants that are sometimes difficult to place in the correct species. Examples from Minnesota are believed to include *C. chrysocarpa*, *C. macracantha*, and *C. douglasii* (Dickinson et al. 1996; Muniyamma and Phipps 1985; Smith and Phipps 1988a, 1988b).
3. Apomictic triploids. These species produce viable seeds exclusively through the nonsexual process of apomixis. The only known Minnesota example is *C. succulenta*, which is assumed to have arisen from *C. macracantha* (a sexual species) through hybridization (Muniyamma and Phipps 1984).
4. Hybrids. A hawthorn employing any of the three previous reproductive pathways can potentially hybridize with a species employing the same or a different reproductive pathway. Although an apomict cannot hybridize with another apomict (since both are nonsexual), some apomicts do produce viable pollen, which can then pollinate a sexual plant. Although hybridization is often implicated in the difficulties of *Crataegus* taxonomy, nearly all good-quality Minnesota specimens can easily and confidently be assigned to a species. There is, in fact, little evidence of widespread hybridization occurring in Minnesota.

Natural History

In general, hawthorns require habitats with plenty of sun, little competition from fast-growing shrubs or tree saplings, protection from frequent or intense fire, and well-drained soils. Given this ecological profile, hawthorns on the presettlement landscape probably occupied the ecotones between forests and prairies, savannas, open-canopy woodlands, and brushy thickets. They would also have occurred where geological, topological, or erosional features created a suitable edge habitat such as along bedrock outcrops, in coulees, and on lakeshores and stream banks.

Hawthorn seeds usually take two years to germinate (Phipps, O'Kennon, and Lance 2003). Once established in a favorable habitat, they are notably slow growing, taking several years to reach maturity, but are relatively long-lived: 60-year-old specimens are not uncommon. Once mature, they normally flower annually and often produce abundant fruit. The fruits are consumed by a variety of animals such as insect larvae, rodents, bears, deer, and especially birds (Martin, Zim, and Nelson 1951), which are the primary agents for long-range seed dispersal.

Older hawthorn specimens are often surrounded by a younger generation produced by seeds falling directly from the parent tree and possibly by root suckering. The role of suckering in hawthorns' ecology is not clear, but observations by the author in Minnesota indicate that most hawthorn species do not sucker in the wild, or sucker weakly or infrequently. However, some of these same species are reported to sucker in cultivation (Phipps, O'Kennon, and Lance 2003).

Although slow to colonize, hawthorns can be very persistent once established. They often survive for decades after a forest canopy closes above them, and they are one of the few shrubs able to survive grazing by domestic livestock. However, if deprived of the important structural elements of their habitat, such as stable edges (ecotones), reproduction may cease, and the colony will eventually disappear. Today, hawthorns must find habitat in a landscape created largely by human activities and in the process have gained an undeserved reputation for being aggressive colonizers of ruderal habitats.

For whatever reason, hawthorns, as a genus, are generally uncommon in Minnesota. They usually occur as scattered individuals or in loosely knit "genus communities" with as many as five species intermingled in a small area. The origin and function of such communities are unknown but is likely related to the foraging behavior of birds, the primary dispersal agent of hawthorns.

Taxonomy

The hawthorns are a challenging genus and have never before been adequately studied in Minnesota. Previous treatments (Lakela 1965; Morley 1969; Ownbey and Morley 1991; Rosendahl 1955) were largely derived from a confusing and now outdated body of literature and a poor assemblage of herbarium specimens. The treatment presented here is based on a field study of over 300 hawthorn populations located throughout the state. Each population was visited repeatedly by the author over a period of 10 years to collect specimens and record observations. The results are documented by a series of about 600 herbarium specimens.

The present study has also taken advantage of recently published cytological and taxonomic research, and the generous assistance of Dr. J. B. Phipps, who has seen and verified all the specimens and provided guidance throughout the project. The taxonomic concept and nomenclatural conclusions followed here are those that have been developed by Phipps and his students over the past 25 years.

Identification

Trying to identify an unknown hawthorn can be frustrating. There is a large amount of variability, not all of which can be accounted for in the keys and descriptions. Rarely will a specimen go through the key without some uncertainty, but the odds of success increase with patience and knowledge of a few special features.

Characteristics of the leaves are most important, and with practice nearly all the Minnesota hawthorns can be distinguished by their leaves alone. But only use leaves that grow from the short spurlike lateral shoots that come from the side of an older twig, not from a terminal shoot. And examine a representative sample of leaves from more than one branch.

The color of the anthers is also important to note. It will be either whitish (ranging from pure white to cream-white to pale yellow) or some shade of red (from bright magenta to slightly pink). The characteristic color will fade a day or two after the pollen is shed, and is not preserved on herbarium specimens, so the best way to see this character is to peel open a flower bud just before it would normally open on its own.

1. Thorns 1.5–3 cm long; hairs on lower surface of leaves restricted to axils of lateral veins; inflorescence glabrous; fruit ripening black .... *C. douglasii*
1. Thorns 3–10 cm long; hairs on lower surface of leaves (if present) not restricted to axils of lateral veins; inflorescence usually hairy, sometimes glabrous; fruit ripening red.
   2. Petioles with sessile red glands on margins; mature leaf blades usually < 6 cm long; compound thorns absent.
      3. Leaf bases acute to obtuse (forming a straight-sided angle with the petiole); petioles and lower leaf surface usually hairy (becoming glabrate by fall); sepals lined with 6–10 large glands or gland-tipped serrations per side; anthers usually white, occasionally pink .... *C. chrysocarpa*
      3. Leaf bases predominately rounded (with curving sides forming a broad smooth arc through the axis of the petiole); petioles and lower leaf surface usually glabrous, or with a few scattered hairs on upper surface of petioles; sepals entire or with 1–8 small glands per side; anthers pink, rarely whitish .... *C. macrosperma*
   2. Petioles without glands; mature leaf blades often > 6 cm long; compound thorns absent or present on main stem or lower branches.
      4. Second year portion of twigs gray; leaf bases with sides gradually tapered and often concave, resulting in a somewhat "winged" petiole; sepals lacking glands or with 1–3 small inconspicuous glands on each margin; mature leaf blades 2–4 cm wide .... *C. punctata*
      4. Second year portion of twigs brown (turning gray the 3rd year); leaf bases with sides abruptly tapered, rounded or truncate, not gradually tapered or concave, petioles clearly not winged; sepals with 3 or more glands or gland-tipped serrations on each margin; mature leaf blades 3.5–12 cm wide.
         5. Petioles hairy on upper surface only; leaf blades widest at or above the middle; bud scales bright coral red (best seen before the flowers are fully opened); the green twigs glabrous in the spring; inner face of individual nutlets with pits or cavities (excavated).
            6. Stamens 15–20; anthers 0.5–0.7 mm long .... *C. succulenta*
            6. Stamens 6–10; anthers 1–1.4 mm long .... *C. macracantha*
         5. Petioles hairy on all surfaces (often becoming glabrate by late season); leaf blades widest at or below the middle; bud scales brown or pinkish; green twigs hairy in the spring; nutlets not excavated.
            7. Petioles 8–17 mm long at maturity; the leaf blade 5–6.5 times longer than the petiole (blade length/petiole length = 5–6.5); blades elliptical or rhombic (widest at the middle); leaf base angled (straight sided); blade 3.3–6.5 cm wide at maturity; inflorescence with 15–45 flowers; corollas 12–18 mm across (spread flat); anthers pink to red; flowers appearing in June; fruits 6–9 mm long .... *C. calpodendron*
            7. Petioles 20–45 mm long at maturity; the blade 2–3.6 times longer than the petiole; blades ovate (widest below the middle); leaf base rounded, truncate, or angled; blade 6–12 cm wide at maturity; inflorescence with 6–17 flowers; corollas 16–30 mm across; anthers whitish; flowers appearing in May; fruits 9–20 mm long.
               8. Stamens 17–20; leaf margins incised 15–40% of the way to the midvein, producing lobes 8–25 mm long; compound thorns usually present on main stem (in 70% of specimens); twigs thick and coarse .... *C. mollis*
               8. Stamens 5–10; leaf margins incised 12–22% of the way to the midvein, producing lobes 5–9 mm long; compound thorns absent; twigs relatively slender .... *C. submollis*

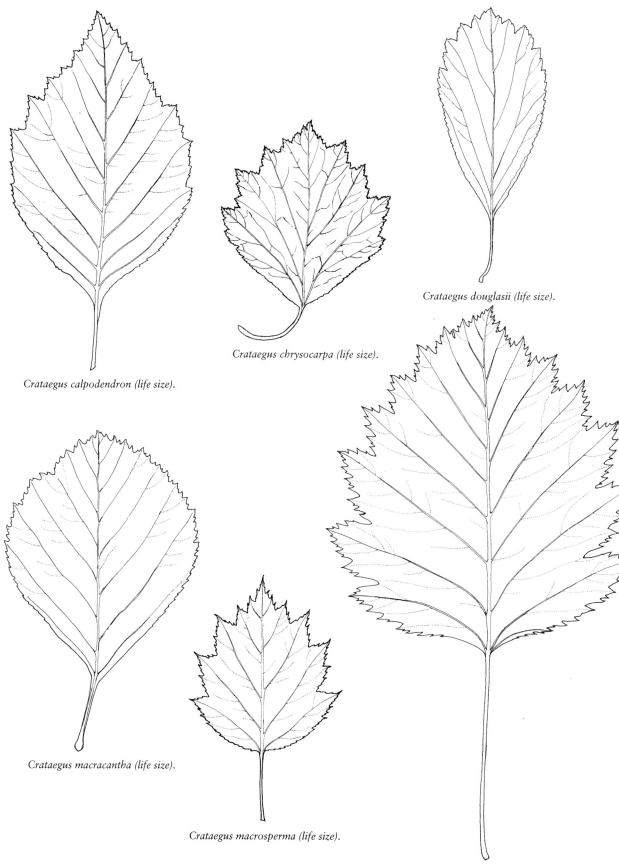

Crataegus calpodendron (life size).

Crataegus chrysocarpa (life size).

Crataegus douglasii (life size).

Crataegus macracantha (life size).

Crataegus macrosperma (life size).

Crataegus mollis (life size).

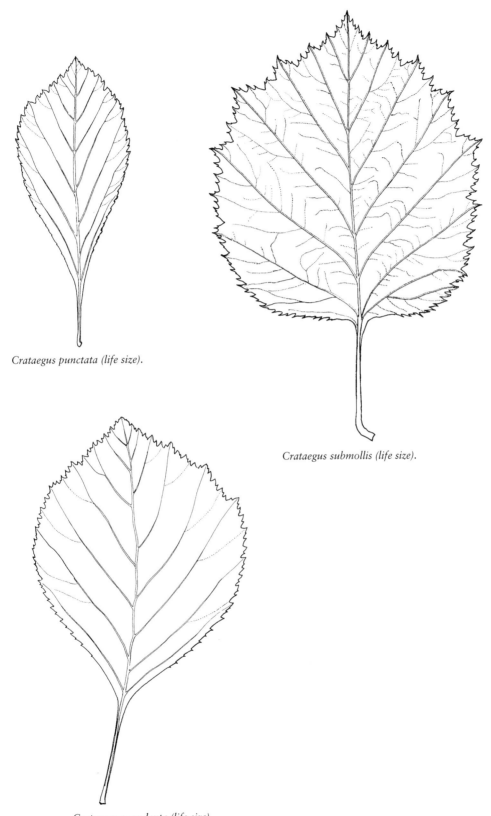

Crataegus punctata (life size).

Crataegus submollis (life size).

Crataegus succulenta (life size).

Crataegus calpodendron (Ehrh.) Medic.

Late hawthorn

[*C. tomentosa* DuRoi]

Tall **shrubs** or small **trees**, with 1–3 or more upright **stems** to 5.5 m tall and 9 cm dbh. Compound **thorns** present on lower portion of main stems; simple thorns abundant to sparse throughout or occasionally absent, 3.5–6 cm long. 2nd-year **branchlets** glabrous, brown to gray-brown; becoming gray the 3rd year. **Bark** thin, gray; broken into flat, narrow platelike scales. **Leaves** simple, alternate, deciduous. **Petioles** 8–17 mm long, densely to moderately hairy on all sides; glands lacking. Mature **leaf blades** elliptical to broadly elliptical or rhombic; 5–10 cm long, 3.3–6.5 cm wide; base acutely to obtusely angled or occasionally somewhat rounded, often slightly decurrent; apex acute to short-acuminate or occasionally subobtuse; margins with 2–7 pairs of small acute lobes 3–7 mm long, coarsely serrate, serrations with green callous tips; upper surface dark green, dull, with short, stiff appressed hairs; lower surface pale green, dull, with short, soft, erect or wavy hairs especially along the main veins. **Inflorescence** a terminal panicle with 15–45 flowers; peduncles, pedicels, and hypanthia densely hairy. **Flowers** bisexual, 5-merous, white; sepals glandular-serrate or glandular-laciniate, rarely entire; corolla 1.2–1.8 cm across; stamens 15–20; anthers pink to red; **anthesis** June 10–20; insect-pollinated. **Fruit** a broadly ellipsoidal pome; 6–9 mm long, 5.5–8 mm wide; orange-red; dull; maturing September 14–22; animal-dispersed. **Nutlets** 2–3. (*calpodendron*: urn-tree, for the shape of the fruit)

Identification

Late hawthorn is typically a large shrub or occasionally a small tree, with ascending branches, slender twigs, and numerous compound thorns on the lower portion of the trunk. It is the last Minnesota hawthorn to flower each year, usually during the second or third week in June, which is at least a week later than any other hawthorn. It also has the smallest fruit of any Minnesota hawthorn, only about 1/4 in (6–9 mm) in diameter. To be certain, look for the combination of 15–20 stamens, reddish anthers, relatively large pointed leaves, and petioles that are densely hairy on all sides.

Natural History

Late hawthorn is strongly associated with hardwood forests in the southeastern part of the state, where it is typically found in mesic, loamy soil with elms (*Ulmus* spp.), basswood (*Tilia americana*), ashes (*Fraxinus* spp.), or sugar maple (*Acer saccharum*). It does occur in alluvial soil in river valleys but usually not on active floodplains and not in fine silts or coarse sands. It also seems to be absent from historically fire-prone landscapes such as prairies, savannas, oak ecosystems, and pine forests.

Edge-grown plants often have multiple stems and may reach a height of about 18 ft (5.5 m). When suppressed in a forest understory, it usually has only a single stem 7–10 ft (2–3 m) tall. Suppressed specimens often persist for long periods and may flower frequently, if not every year, making this one of the most shade tolerant of the hawthorns. Seedlings, however, are rarely found in deep shade, indicating that openings or edges are required for reproduction.

Unfortunately nothing is known about the presettlement distribution or abundance of late hawthorn in Minnesota. Herbarium specimens and written records from the early years of settlement are sometimes insightful (Clements, Rosendahl, and Butters 1912) but in this case have proven erroneous. What we see on the landscape today is a few, scattered populations, each with just a handful of individuals.

Bark is thin, gray, and scaly—this stem is 3.5" (9 cm) dbh.

Leaves are relatively large and pointed.

Fruits are smallest of our hawthorns, only 1/4" (6–8 mm)—September 14.

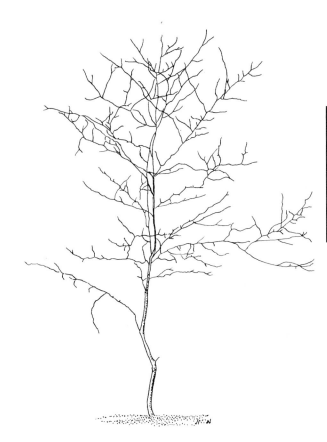

This is the last of the hawthorns to flower—June 12.

Compound thorn on main stem.

Crataegus chrysocarpa Ashe

Fireberry hawthorn

Midsize to large **shrubs** with 1–10 or more upright **stems** to 5.5 m tall and 16 cm dbh. Compound **thorns** absent; simple thorns usually abundant or occasionally sparse, 3.5–7 cm long. 2nd-year **branchlets** glabrous, brown; becoming gray the 3rd year. **Bark** thin, gray; broken into flat, narrow platelike scales. **Leaves** simple, alternate, deciduous. **Petioles** 1–2.5 cm long; hairy on all surfaces or occasionally just on upper surface, rarely glabrous, becoming glabrate by fall; a few to several marginal glands, or occasionally glands absent. Mature **leaf blades** ovate to somewhat elliptical or rhombic; 4–7 cm long, 3–5.5 cm wide (about 3/4 size at anthesis); base acutely to obtusely angled; apex obtusely to subacutely angled; margins with 2–5 pairs of small acute lobes 3–11 mm long, finely serrate, serrations tipped with small but often prominent dark glands; upper surface dark green, dull or somewhat shiny, with short, stiff appressed hairs or occasionally glabrous; lower surface pale green, dull, with hairs similar to upper surface but more concentrated along the main veins and somewhat longer and softer, occasionally glabrous or becoming glabrate by fall. **Inflorescence** a terminal panicle with 8–15 flowers; peduncles and pedicels hairy, hypanthia hairy or less often glabrous. **Flowers** bisexual, 5-merous, white; sepals glandular or glandular-serrate; corolla 1.4–2.2 cm across; stamens 6–10 or occasionally 15–20; anthers white or occasionally pink; **anthesis** May 15–28 in the south, May 25–June 10 in the north; insect-pollinated. **Fruit** a ± globose pome; 8.5–15 mm in diameter; red; dull or somewhat shiny; maturing August 20–September 5; animal-dispersed. **Nutlets** 2–5, mostly 3–4. (*chrysocarpa*: from the Greek *chrysos*, golden, and *carpos*, a fruit)

Identification

Fireberry hawthorn is always a shrub, never a tree; it is usually 6–10 ft (2–3 m) tall with multiple stems, ascending branches, and a rounded silhouette. It always has long, dark, simple thorns, never compound thorns. Leaf shape is variable, often leading to confusion with large-thorned hawthorn (*C. macracantha*) and eastern hawthorn (*C. macrosperma*).
Note: Most specimens have about 10 stamens, white anthers, hairy leaves, and hairy hypanthia. But some have about 20 stamens, and some have pink anthers. There is also a form from northern Minnesota that has both 20 stamens and pink anthers, as well as

glabrous leaves and hypanthia. Most of this variability can be accommodated by several of the 10 to 20 published varieties.

Natural History

Fireberry hawthorn occurs statewide and is by far the most common hawthorn in Minnesota, at least north of the Minnesota River valley. It is usually found along stable forest edges, in long-term forest openings, thin-canopy woodlands, and brushlands. In all habitats direct sunlight is essential; it will not survive long if overtopped by trees or taller shrubs. It is more forgiving of soil conditions, preferring mesic, loamy soils, but tolerating dry sites and poor soils better than other hawthorns. Under most conditions it grows slowly and can live 65+ years.

In presettlement times, prairie populations of fireberry hawthorn would have been limited to habitats in the fire shadow of lakes, the margins of wooded stream valleys, and other fire-protected habitats. It still occurs in those habitats, where those habitats can be found, but it has also expanded into a variety of seminatural grassy and "thickety" habitats that are a by-product of low-intensity agriculture such as intermittent cattle grazing. Actually, fireberry hawthorn does not typically form thickets on its own, but it does occur in thickets with other species, particularly slow-growing shrubs of similar size such as gray dogwood (*Cornus racemosa*), prickly ash (*Zanthoxylum americana*), beaked hazel (*Corylus cornuta*), or nannyberry (*Viburnum lentago*).

At peak anthesis on May 15—Washington County.

Fruits starting to turn from green to red—August 22.

Leaves typically have small, red glands on the petioles.

An edge-grown specimen 11' (3.4 m) tall—Washington County.

Stems may have simple thorns but never compound thorns.

Hawthorns   🦥   **153**

Crataegus douglasii Lindl.

Douglas hawthorn

Tall **shrubs** or small shrublike **trees**, with 1–5 or more upright or occasionally decumbent **stems**, to 7.7 m tall and 25 cm dbh. Compound **thorns** absent; simple thorns usually abundant, 1.5–3 cm long. 2nd-year **branchlets** glabrous, brown; becoming gray the 3rd year. **Bark** thin, gray; broken into flat, narrow platelike scales. **Leaves** simple, alternate, deciduous. **Petioles** 5–18 mm long, glabrous except for a few long hairs on the upper surface; often with a few red glands along the margins. Mature **leaf blades** obovate to elliptical, occasionally rhombic or obtrullate; 4–7 cm long, 2.5–5 cm wide; base acutely or occasionally obtusely angled; apex obtusely angled; margins with 1–5 pairs of small acute lobes 2–8 mm long, coarsely serrate, serrations tipped with small inconspicuous dark glands; upper surface dark green, dull or somewhat shiny, with short, stiff appressed hairs; lower surface pale green, dull, with tufts of relatively long straight or wavy hairs in the axils of the lower lateral veins, otherwise glabrous. **Inflorescence** a terminal panicle of 5–18 flowers; peduncles, pedicels, and hypanthia glabrous. **Flowers** bisexual, 5-merous, white; sepals glandular-serrate; corolla 1–1.5 cm across; stamens 5–10; anthers pale pink to nearly white; **anthesis** June 12–25; insect-pollinated. **Fruit** a broadly ellipsoidal pome; 11–15 mm long, 9–13 mm wide; black to purple-black; dull; maturing August 20–September 10; animal-dispersed. **Nutlets** 3–4, mostly 4. (*douglasii*: named for botanical explorer David Douglas, 1798–1834)

Identification

Douglas hawthorn is one of the largest hawthorns in Minnesota. It can easily become treelike in size, reaching 16–20 ft (5–6 m) in height, but it typically remains shrublike in form with multiple stems, ascending branches, and slender twigs. It lacks compound thorns, and the simple thorns are notably short, no more than 1 1/8 inch (3 cm) long. Its closest look-alike, and the only other hawthorn that regularly occurs with it, is fireberry hawthorn (*C. chrysocarpa*). Douglas hawthorn differs from it, and from all other Minnesota hawthorns, by the shortness of the thorns and the black color of the fruit.

Natural History

This species is unique among hawthorns in having the majority of its range in the mountains of western North America with only a small, isolated population around the upper Great Lakes. It seems likely that the climate-modifying effect of the Great Lakes in some way simulates the cordilleran conditions of the West, where Douglas hawthorn is reportedly common (Phipps, O'Kennon, and Lance 2003). It is certainly not common in Minnesota; in fact, it is usually considered rare here or at least habitat limited. The limiting factor appears to be the proximity of Lake Superior itself. All known populations are found within 5 or 10 miles of the lake in a narrow band from the Gooseberry River (Lake County) northeastward to the Canadian border at Grand Portage (Cook County), a distance of about 100 miles (162 km).

Within this narrow band it occurs primarily in streamside thickets with rocky, gravelly, or clayey substrates. These habitats may be briefly flooded in the spring and experience some scouring and sedimentation. Other habitats include bedrock outcrops, brushy meadows, and forest openings. All habitats have a relatively low risk of fire yet are exposed to periodic natural disturbances such as erosion, windthrows, and insect outbreaks. Direct sunlight seems to be a critical factor since reproduction apparently does not occur in a closed-canopy forest. In general, populations of Douglas hawthorn appear rather mobile and well adapted to habitat disturbances. At the same time, it is tenacious and relatively long-lived; there is credible evidence of larger individuals being at least 60 to 70 years old, possibly 80 to 90.

Not visible here are the small thorns, only about 1" (2–3 cm) long.

Leaf shape is most similar to fireberry hawthorn.

Multiple stems are common for this species.

These fruits will ripen black in September—August 28.

Crataegus macracantha Lodd. ex Loud.

Large-thorned hawthorn

[*C. succulenta* Schrad. ex Link var. *macracantha* (Lodd. ex Loud.) Egglest.]

Tall **shrubs** or small **trees**, with 1 or occasionally 2–6 upright **stems** to 6 m tall and 15 cm dbh. Compound **thorns** sometimes present on lower portion of main stems (in 38% of specimens); simple thorns always present and typically abundant throughout, 4–10 cm long. 2nd-year **branchlets** glabrous, brown to red-brown, shiny; becoming gray the 3rd or 4th year. **Bark** thin, gray; broken into flat, narrow platelike scales. **Leaves** simple, alternate, deciduous. **Petioles** 5–15 mm long, hairy on the upper surface only, becoming sparsely hairy or glabrate by late season; glands lacking. Mature **leaf blades** elliptical to broadly elliptical or rhombic, or obovate to broadly obovate; 4.5–9 cm long, 3.5–6.5 cm wide; base acutely to obtusely angled, occasionally somewhat decurrent; apex obtusely or occasionally acutely angled; margins without lobes or with 2–4 pairs of small lobes rarely exceeding 7 mm in length, serrate to finely serrate, glands at tips of serrations minute or not apparent; upper surface dark green, dull, with short, stiff appressed hairs; lower surface pale green, dull, with short, soft, wavy hairs concentrated along the larger veins. **Inflorescence** a terminal panicle of 10–30 flowers; peduncles, pedicels, and hypanthia hairy. **Flowers** bisexual, 5-merous, white; sepals glandular-serrate to glandular-laciniate; corolla 1.5–2 cm across; stamens 6–10; anthers white or pink with about equal frequency; **anthesis** May 24–June 15; insect-pollinated. **Fruit** a ± globular pome; 8–12 mm in diameter; red; dull or somewhat shiny; maturing August 20–September 20; animal-dispersed. **Nutlets** 2–3, rarely 4. (*macracantha*: large-thorned)

Identification

Large-thorned hawthorn is a large shrub or sometimes a small tree, with spreading or ascending branches, slender twigs, and extremely long, dark thorns. The thorns can be as long as 4 in (10 cm) and tend to be bent backwards (reflexed). Also, notice that when the leaves are just expanding in the spring, the bud scales are bright coral red. This is a character shared only with succulent hawthorn (*C. succulenta*). These two closely related species can be reliably separated only by features of the stamens (see key). Large-thorned hawthorn can also be confused with fireberry hawthorn (*C. chrysocarpa*), but it lacks the small red glands on the margins of the petiole, and the leaf

blades tend to be less deeply incised. Also, it sometimes has compound thorns on the main stem, which are never seen on fireberry hawthorn.

Natural History

The large-thorned hawthorn occurs statewide, but it is most common in the hardwood forest region of central Minnesota, where it favors heavy loam or alluvial soil, usually with oaks (*Quercus* spp.), aspens (*Populus* spp.), ashes (*Fraxinus* spp.), or basswood (*Tilia americana*). It also occurs in the coniferous forest region in thin, rocky or sandy soils, where it is associated with hardwoods or upland conifers. It even follows forested stream corridors westward into the prairie region. Its distribution and habitat preferences are very similar to those of fireberry hawthorn, but it is considerably less common.

Although large-thorned hawthorn is clearly a species of forested biomes, its seedlings cannot tolerate continuous shade and are rarely found under a closed forest canopy. Even under a canopy gap, they simply grow too slowly to compete successfully with saplings of most canopy species. As a result, reproduction is generally limited to the forest edge or to interior habitats where stochastic events give the odd seedling an unexpected opportunity. Those fortunate enough to get established can maintain themselves fairly well even if the canopy closes above them. They may not thrive under such conditions, but they may survive and flower regularly for many years.

Petals 5, stamens 6–10, anthers pink or white.

This stem is 4" (10 cm) in diameter; maximum is about 6" (15 cm).

Ripe fruit on September 2—Washington County.

Hawthorns 🍂 157

Crataegus macrosperma Ashe

Eastern hawthorn

Tall **shrubs** or occasionally small **trees**, with 1–5, or rarely more, upright **stems** to 5.5 m tall and 12 cm dbh. Compound **thorns** absent; simple thorns usually abundant, 3.5–5 cm long. 2nd-year **branchlets** glabrous, brown, becoming gray the 3rd year. **Bark** thin, gray; broken into flat, narrow platelike scales. **Leaves** simple, alternate, deciduous. **Petioles** 1–3 cm long, glabrous, or with a few scattered hairs on upper surface; marginal glands few to several, or rarely glands absent. Mature **leaf blades** ovate to broadly ovate or occasionally ovate-elliptical; 3–6.5 cm long, 2.5–5 cm wide; base rounded or less often obtusely angled, occasionally almost truncate; apex acutely angled or occasionally subobtuse; margins with 3–5 pairs of relatively large and conspicuous lobes 5–10 mm long, serrate, serrations tipped with small dark glands; upper surface dark green, dull, with short, stiff appressed hairs; lower surface pale green, dull, glabrous or occasionally glabrate. **Inflorescence** a terminal panicle of 6–12 flowers; peduncles and pedicels hairy or less often glabrous; hypanthia glabrous or rarely hairy. **Flowers** bisexual, 5-merous, white; sepals entire, or more often with a few shallow gland-tipped serrations; corolla 1.3–1.8 cm across; stamens 6–10 or less often 16–20; anthers pale pink to bright pink, rarely whitish; **anthesis** May 10–June 5; insect-pollinated. **Fruit** a ± globose pome; 8–14 mm in diameter; red; dull; maturing September 4–18; animal-dispersed. **Nutlets** 2–4, usually 4. (*macrosperma*: large-seeded)

Identification

Eastern hawthorn is a medium-size hawthorn that usually takes the form of a large shrub 8–10 ft (2.5–3 m) tall with strongly ascending branches. The leaves are relatively small and thin for a hawthorn and often have a reddish tinge when young. They are held at the ends of long, flexible petioles and tend to flutter in the wind almost like aspen leaves. Eastern hawthorn is most likely to be confused with the more common fireberry hawthorn (*C. chrysocarpa*) but differs consistently in a number of ways. The leaves are smaller, have rounded bases, are glabrous on the undersurface, and have more deeply incised margins (larger "lobes"). Also, the sepals typically have fewer and smaller marginal glands.

Note: Minnesota populations are quite variable and differ in a number of ways from populations farther

east. Minnesota plants tend to have hairy inflorescences and glandular sepals, which are characters not reported from elsewhere (Phipps and Muniyamma 1980), and specimens with 16–20 stamens (twice the normal number) are not uncommon here. Assigning such variable specimens to typical *C. macrosperma* represents a significantly expanded concept of the species, and perhaps they would be better treated as one or more separate varieties.

Natural History

Eastern hawthorn occurs over a fairly large portion of central and northern Minnesota, but it is relatively uncommon. It typically occurs as scattered individuals or in small family groups, rarely in large, structured populations. It appears to favor mesic, loamy or clayey soils and partial shade, but it is somewhat of an opportunist and a habitat generalist.

Although it is always associated with forest ecosystems, it seems to prefer partially open or brushy habitats, particularly long-term forest edges or forests that have been set back to an early successional stage by some major disturbance. It has also been found in the interior of thin-canopy oak/aspen (*Quercus/Populus*) woodlands and in savanna-like settings where there is little sign of disturbance but where a fair amount of sunlight still manages to reach the shrub layer.

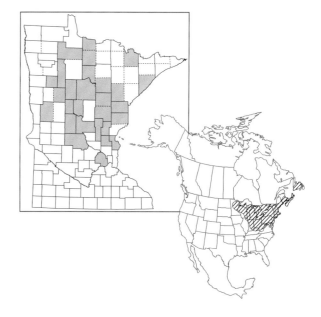

Immature leaves are often red-tinged, and notice the 20 bright pink anthers in each flower—May 21.

Fruits tend to taste mealy and have 4 stony nutlets—August 28.

Eastern hawthorn can have single or multiple stems.

Crataegus mollis (T. & G.) Scheele

Downy hawthorn

Small **trees**, with one or a few upright **stems** to 12 m tall and 47 cm dbh. Compound **thorns** usually present on lower portions of stem and larger branches (in 70% of specimens); simple thorns moderately abundant to sparse throughout or sometimes lacking (in 20% of specimens), 3–7 cm long. 2nd-year **branchlets** glabrous, brown or gray-brown; becoming gray the 3rd year; thick and coarse. **Bark** thin, gray; broken into flat, narrow platelike scales. **Leaves** simple, alternate, deciduous. **Petioles** 1–2 cm long at anthesis, becoming 2–4.5 cm at maturity; densely hairy on all surfaces, becoming sparsely hairy by late season; glands lacking. Mature **leaf blades** broadly to very broadly ovate; 7–12.5 cm long, 6–12 cm wide (about half-size at anthesis); base broadly rounded to nearly truncate, or occasionally somewhat cordate; apex obtusely to subacutely angled; margins with 1–6 pairs of relatively large acute to subacute lobes 8–25 mm long, coarsely serrate, glands at tips of serrations absent or inconspicuous; upper surface dark green, dull, with short, stiff usually appressed hairs; lower surface pale green, dull, with short, soft wavy hairs usually most dense along the larger veins. **Inflorescence** a terminal panicle of 8–17 flowers; peduncles, pedicels, and hypanthia hairy to densely hairy. **Flowers** bisexual, 5-merous, white; sepals glandular-laciniate; corolla 1.6–3 cm across; stamens 17–20; anthers white to pale yellow; **anthesis** May 5-25; insect-pollinated. **Fruit** a ± globose pome; 10–20 mm in diameter; scarlet to dull crimson; maturing September 12–October 5; animal-dispersed. **Nutlets** 5 or occasionally 4. (*mollis*: soft, in reference to the pubescent leaves)

Identification

Downy hawthorn is a small, stout tree usually armed with compound thorns. Forest-grown trees typically have a single stem and may reach 40 ft (12 m) in height and 10 inches (25 cm) in diameter. Open-grown specimens are usually shorter and tend to have multiple trunks that fork near the base and broad, rounded crowns. It can be difficult to tell one hawthorn species from another, but this one is fairly easy; look for the coarse, knotty twigs and the large, roundish leaves.

Natural History

This is the largest and most conspicuous of the state's hawthorns and the most common one in much of southern Minnesota. At the time of settlement, southern Minnesota was mostly fire-maintained prairie, which would seem to create a problem for downy hawthorn. Its thin bark cannot protect it from fire, and if top-killed, it resprouts weakly or not at all. There were, however, a few habitats that escaped fires such as wooded stream valleys, brushy ravines, and wooded fringes on the east side of large lakes. These fire-protected habitats were apparently reservoirs of downy hawthorn.

The prairies are now gone, and so are the wildfires, but small patches of the original fire-protected habitats remain, and they often have healthy populations of downy hawthorn. Still, examples such as this where downy hawthorn is found in a truly natural habitat are exceedingly rare. Where we find it today is mostly in habitats that originated from human activities and survive through benign neglect, such as intermittent pastures, fencerows, rural parks, and abandoned farmsteads. Although downy hawthorn does colonize these habitats when the opportunity arises, it does not do so with the speed or tenacity of shrubs like smooth sumac (*Rhus glabra*), wild plum (*Prunus americana*), or chokecherry (*Prunus virginiana*).

Flowers appear when the leaves are about half-grown—May 10.

Stems can reach 18.5" (47 cm) dbh; this one is 7" (18 cm) dbh.

A wild specimen captured in a rural Martin County park.

Fruits can measure 3/4" (2 cm) across—September 15.

Crataegus punctata Jacq.

White haw

Small **trees**, with a single upright **stem** to 9.4 m tall and 27 cm dbh, often forked near base. Compound **thorns** usually present on lower portion of main stem and larger branches (in 75% of specimens); simple thorns moderately abundant to sparse throughout, or absent (in 33% of specimens), 2.5–6 cm long. 2nd-year **branchlets** glabrous, ashy gray. **Bark** thin, gray or gray-brown; broken into flat, narrow platelike scales. **Leaves** simple, alternate, deciduous. **Petioles** 3–15 mm long or indistinct, densely to sparsely hairy on all surfaces, becoming glabrate by late season; glands lacking. Mature **leaf blades** obovate to obovate-elliptical; 4–7 cm long, 2–4 cm wide; base acute to attenuate (decurrent); apex obtuse to subacute, or less commonly acute; margins without lobes or with 2–4 pairs of small lobes rarely exceeding 5 mm in length, serrate, glands at tips of serrations small and inconspicuous; upper surface dark green, dull, with scattered soft appressed hairs; lower surface pale green, dull, hairs similar to upper surface but denser and concentrated more along larger veins (sometimes becoming glabrate in late season). **Inflorescence** a terminal panicle of 8–20 flowers; peduncles, pedicels, and hypanthia hairy, becoming glabrate by late season. **Flowers** bisexual, 5-merous, white; sepals with a few small sessile marginal glands, or glands lacking; corolla 1.6–2.3 cm across; stamens 16–20; anthers reddish or white with about equal frequency; **anthesis** May 25–June 15; insect-pollinated. **Fruit** a ± globular pome; 11–19 mm in diameter; dull crimson to maroon, rarely clear yellow in *f. aurea* Ait.; maturing September 15–October 5; animal-dispersed. **Nutlets** 2–4, mostly 3. (*punctata*: with dots)

Identification

White haw is the most consistently treelike of the hawthorns, usually reaching a height of 16–23 ft (5–7 m). It has a single slender trunk and horizontally layered branches that suggest an acacia tree on an African savanna. It exhibits this form whether open grown or forest grown. The 2nd-year twigs are ash gray rather than brown, and the leaves have a long, tapering base. The epithet "*punctata*" refers to the dots (punctae) that are abundant on the fruits of this species. These dots are actually lenticels and are present on the fruits of most, if not all, hawthorns.

Natural History

White haw occurs throughout the hardwood forest region of the state, but it is most common on the forested floodplains and river terraces of the southeast. Even though it seems to tolerate occasional spring flooding and moderate levels of sedimentation, it does not appear to be a floodplain specialist; its association with rivers may be incidental rather than adaptive. In fact, mesic upland habitats serve just as well, especially where the dominant trees are maples (*Acer* spp.), basswood (*Tilia americana*), elms (*Ulmus* spp.), or oaks (*Quercus* spp.). White haw is relatively slow growing and long-lived compared to other trees its size. Increment cores from trees in stable habitats sometimes show up to 70 annual rings.

White haw does not occur in areas that are historically prone to fires, such as the coniferous forest region, prairie region, or the Anoka Sand Plain. Its bark is too thin to protect it from fire, and older trees will not resprout if top-killed. It is also intolerant of continual shade, so it thrives only in brushy edge habitats or where cattle grazing has thinned the forest canopy. Individuals trapped under a closed canopy may survive for a number of years, even decades, but they gradually decline; they become spindly and fail to reproduce. Seedlings are practically never seen in a closed-canopy forest.

Flowers appear late, usually the first week of June.

Layered horizontal branches are characteristic of white haw.

Fruits tend to be maroon or dull crimson.

Compound thorns are on most (not all) stems.

Single stems are the rule for white haw, this one is 9" (23 cm) diameter.

Crataegus submollis Sarg.

Quebec hawthorn

Tall **shrubs** or small **trees**, with 1 or a few upright **stems** to 9 m tall and 15 cm dbh. Compound **thorns** absent; simple thorns moderately abundant, 3.5–7 cm long. 2nd-year **branchlets** glabrous, brown to gray-brown; becoming gray the 3rd year. **Bark** thin, gray; broken into flat, narrow platelike scales. **Leaves** simple, alternate, deciduous. **Petioles** 1.3–1.8 cm long at anthesis, becoming 2–3.7 cm at maturity; densely hairy on all surfaces, becoming sparsely hairy or glabrate by fall; marginal glands lacking or with 2–5 small reddish glands. Mature **leaf blades** ovate to broadly ovate or nearly orbicular; 6–9.5 cm long, 6–8.5 cm wide (about 3/4 size at anthesis); base truncate, rounded, or obtusely angled; apex obtusely to subacutely angled; margins with 3–5 pairs of small acute lobes 5–9 mm long, irregularly serrate, serrations tipped with small inconspicuous dark glands; upper surface dark green, dull, with short, stiff appressed hairs; lower surface pale green, dull, with soft wavy or appressed hairs, especially along main veins, often glabrate by fall. **Inflorescence** a terminal panicle of 6–15 flowers; peduncles, pedicels, and hypanthia hairy. **Flowers** bisexual, 5-merous, white; sepals glandular-serrate to glandular-laciniate; corolla 1.7–2.3 cm across; stamens 7–10; anthers creamy white; **anthesis** May 12–June 3; insect-pollinated. **Fruit** a globose to depressed-globose pome; 9–17 mm long, 10–20 mm wide; dull red; maturing September 3–25; animal-dispersed. **Nutlets** 3–5. (*submollis*: somewhat soft, presumably in comparison to the soft leaves of *C. mollis*)

Identification

Quebec hawthorn is a large shrub or small tree with spreading or ascending branches and slender twigs. The large, roundish leaves look something like those of downy hawthorn (*C. mollis*) but are generally smaller and have smaller lobes. The flowers are also similar to those of downy hawthorn but have roughly half the number of stamens (7–10 instead of 17–20). Other important differences are the relatively slender twigs and the lack of compound thorns.

Natural History

Relatively little is known about Quebec hawthorn in Minnesota except that it appears to be uncommon and somewhat cryptic. In fact, botanists overlooked it entirely until 1996. Even then it required years of careful study by specialists to reveal its true identity. What we now know, or think we know, is still too sketchy to support many conclusions.

We do know that a rather dispersed population extends for several miles on terraces along the Mississippi River in central Minnesota (Aitkin, Crow Wing, and Morrison counties), and there is a cluster of confirmed records from oak forests in northern Ramsey County. Elsewhere populations seem widely scattered and isolated, although more extensive field searches may show otherwise.

Habitats vary considerably, but all the sites are upland, and most are in brushy areas or along woodland margins. Other consistent features seem to be dry-mesic soil, usually sandy but sometimes loamy, partial shade, and association with early successional tree species such as oaks (*Quercus* spp.), trembling aspen (*Populus tremuloides*), green ash (*Fraxinus pennsylvanica*), or pines (*Pinus* spp.). Most sites are within the forested region of the state, but at least two are well within the historic prairie biome (Lac qui Parle and Rock counties). The significance of the prairie occurrences is unclear, but Quebec hawthorn does not appear to be part of the original prairie flora.

Leaf blade is nearly round, up to 3.75" (9.5 cm) long.

An open-grown specimen 26' (8 m) tall—Ramsey County.

Mature fruits are red, up to 3/4" (2 cm) across.

Each panicle has 6–15 flowers, each flower 10 stamens—May 12.

Multiple stems are not uncommon for Quebec hawthorn.

Crataegus succulenta Schrad. ex Link

Succulent hawthorn

Tall **shrubs** or small **trees**, with 1 or occasionally a few upright **stems** to 6.7 m tall and 15 cm dbh. Compound **thorns** often present on lower portion of main stems (in 50% of specimens); simple thorns typically abundant on branches and twigs, 3–9 cm long. 2nd-year **branchlets** glabrous, brown, glossy; becoming gray the 3rd or 4th year. **Bark** thin, gray; broken into flat, narrow platelike scales. **Leaves** simple, alternate, deciduous. **Petioles** 7–15 mm long, hairy on the upper surface only, becoming glabrate by late season; glands lacking. Mature **leaf blades** broadly elliptical to broadly obovate; 4.5–9 cm long, 3.5–7 cm wide; base acutely to obtusely angled, occasionally somewhat decurrent; apex obtusely or occasionally acutely angled; margins without lobes or with 2–4 pairs of small lobes rarely exceeding 6 mm in length, serrate to finely serrate, glands at tips of serrations minute or not apparent; upper surface dark green, dull, with scattered short, stiff appressed hairs; lower surface pale green, dull, with short, soft wavy hairs concentrated along the larger veins. **Inflorescence** a terminal panicle of 10–30 flowers; peduncles, pedicels, and hypanthia hairy. **Flowers** bisexual, 5-merous, white; sepals glandular-serrate to glandular-laciniate; corolla 1.4–2 cm across; stamens 15–20; anthers usually white but sometimes reddish or pinkish; **anthesis** May 25–June 12; insect-pollinated. **Fruit** a ± orbicular pome; 8–12 mm in diameter; red; dull or somewhat shiny; maturing August 25–September 15; animal-dispersed. **Nutlets** 2–3, rarely 4. (*succulenta*: succulent or fleshy, in reference to the fruit)

Identification

Succulent hawthorn (named for its fruit) is a large shrub or sometimes a small tree reaching heights of about 20 ft (6 m) and stem diameters of 6 inches (15 cm), with spreading or ascending branches, slender twigs, and extremely long, dark thorns. It is very similar to the more common large-thorned hawthorn (*C. macracantha*), but with smaller anthers (0.5–0.7 mm versus 1–1.4 mm) and about twice as many stamens (15–20, versus 6–10). Without flowers the two species are nearly impossible to tell apart. *Note:* It has been suggested that succulent hawthorn (a nonsexual species) may have arisen from large-thorned hawthorn (a sexual species) through hybridization (Muniyamma and Phipps 1984).

Natural History

This is a relatively uncommon hawthorn of southern and western Minnesota. It is associated with the loamy soils of maple-basswood (*Acer-Tilia*) forests and less often the sandy soils of oak (*Quercus*) forests. Although it is consistently associated with forest habitats, it does not typically occur in forest interiors. Instead it prefers forest edges, long-term forest openings, and areas of patch disturbance within a forest where the shrub layer receives a fair amount of sunlight. If overtopped by faster-growing saplings of canopy trees, it can usually survive and perhaps even produce flowers, but seedlings will not survive without more light.

The known occurrences of succulent hawthorn generally consist of only a few individuals scattered in loose colonies, rarely numbering more than a dozen plants at a single site. Invariably, fireberry hawthorn (*C. chrysocarpa*), large-thorned hawthorn (*C. macracantha*), or white haw (*C. punctata*) will be found in the vicinity and usually in greater numbers. Such "genus communities" are not unusual for hawthorns. Their origins are unclear but may be a result of the feeding patterns of birds, the primary dispersal agent of hawthorn seeds.

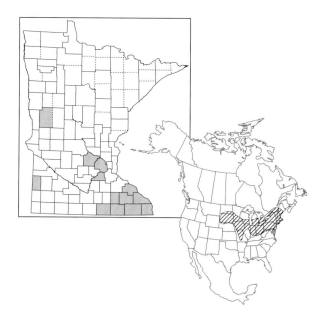

Distinguished by 15–20 stamens and unusually small anthers.

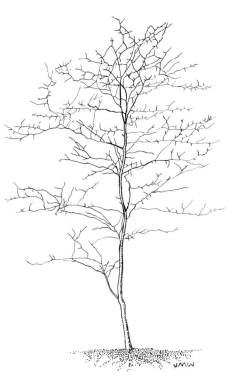

Fruits tend to be small, often only 3/8 " (1 cm) across.

Twig with leaves removed to show the 3.5 " (9 cm) thorns.

A single stem is the rule, multiple stems the exception.

Leaves tend to be roundish and finely serrate.

Dasiphora, shrubby cinquefoil

Rosaceae: Rose family

This is a genus of about 15 species of deciduous shrubs found in temperate regions of the Northern Hemisphere. There is a single species in North America, universally known as shrubby cinquefoil. For years it resided in the genus *Potentilla*, but there is growing agreement among taxonomists that it belongs elsewhere; *Dasiphora* and *Pentaphylloides* are the current contenders.

Dasiphora fruticosa (L.) Rydb.

Shrubby cinquefoil
[*Pentaphylloides fruticosa* (L.) Schwarz; *Potentilla fruticosa* L.]

Midsize **shrubs**, with upright **stems** to 1 m tall and 1 cm basal diameter, clonal by layering of lower branches. **Branchlets** of the current year reddish brown to purplish, hairy; 1-year-old branchlets gray to gray-brown, glabrous or glabrate. Outer **bark** gray-brown, often black-dotted, exfoliating in vertical strips to expose pale brown inner bark. **Leaves** palmately or short-pinnately compound, alternate, deciduous. **Petioles** 0.3–1.5 cm long, hairy; stipules long, papery, partially sheathing. **Leaflets** 3–7 (usually 5), sessile, the 3 terminal leaflets confluent at base; elliptical to narrowly elliptical or narrowly oblong-elliptical; 0.5–2 cm long, 1.5–6 mm wide; base tapered; apex acute to somewhat blunt; margins entire, revolute; upper surface dark green, moderately to densely covered with long silky hairs; lower surface pale green, otherwise similar to upper. **Flowers** bisexual, 5-merous, yellow; often borne singly or in clusters of 2–4, terminal; bractlets narrowly lanceolate to elliptical or oblong, alternating with and usually exceeding the sepals, 5–9 mm long; sepals lance-ovate, acuminate, 4–8 mm long; petals ovate to obovate or orbicular, 7–14 mm long; corolla 1.8–3 cm across (measured flat); stamens and carpels numerous; **anthesis** late May to late September; insect-pollinated. **Fruit** a compact head of densely hairy achenes surrounded by the persistent sepals and bractlets; maturing early July to late September; wind- and gravity-dispersed. (*fruticosa*: shrubby)

Identification

Shrubby cinquefoil is a small, bushy shrub, usually 2–3 ft (60–90 cm) tall, with bright yellow flowers and small compound leaves. It is distinctive enough, with or without flowers, that it probably will not be confused with anything else.
Note: This is a wide-ranging shrub occurring across much of North America, Europe, and Asia, and it exhibits considerable biological complexity. Although the species complex has been frequently studied, there is little agreement on the best taxonomic treatment (Davidson and Lenz 1989; Elkington 1969; Löve 1954). Cultivars are commonly used in urban and suburban landscaping and appear to have originated from wild populations in Europe and western North America. They do not seem to escape into the wild or hybridize with native populations.

Natural History

In the northeastern counties shrubby cinquefoil is found in crevices of bedrock outcrops along the shore of Lake Superior. In the northwest it is found in wet prairies, seepage swamps, and fens. The records from central and southern Minnesota are from calcareous fens and dry, dolomite cliffs. The similarities among these habitats are difficult to see, but basically shrubby cinquefoil is a plant of shallow calcareous wetlands and certain exposed bedrock formations, particularly those that are basic rather than acidic. In all habitats, shrubby cinquefoil needs direct sunlight from above and from the sides. It grows too slowly and is too short in stature to compete for sunlight with most wetland shrubs such as willows (*Salix* spp.) and dogwoods (*Cornus* spp.); it clearly prefers open areas among grasses or sedges.

Many populations, especially those in the northwestern counties, are in habitats subjected to periodic wildfire, often at intervals as short as 5–10 years. Although shrubby cinquefoil does resprout after fire, it is not directly benefited by fire; at least it is not stimulated to spread or reproduce as a result of fire. It is not a rapid colonizer and it is sensitive to disturbance within its habitat, especially disturbances to the soil and the hydrologic regime. For these reasons, its presence is a fairly good indicator of stable ecological conditions.

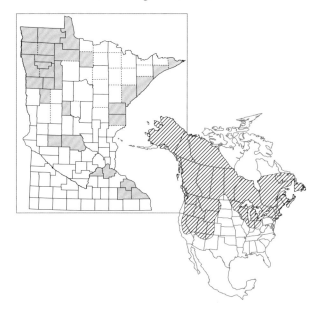

Flowers appear continually from late May through September.

Typical specimen from shore of Lake Superior, Cook County—July 6.

Fruit is a cluster of achenes enveloped by the sepals—September 21.

Shrubby cinquefoil   171

Diervilla, bush honeysuckle

Caprifoliaceae: Honeysuckle family

The bush honeysuckles are a North American genus of 3 species, all woody shrubs, with 1 species occurring in Minnesota. They have traditionally been placed in the family Caprifoliaceae along with the true honeysuckles, but it has recently been proposed that they be segregated in a new family, Diervillaceae (Backlund and Pyck 1998). (*Diervilla* is named for the French botanist N. Diéreville, who introduced the plant to Europe in 1699.)

Diervilla lonicera P. Mill.

Bush honeysuckle

Low to midsize **shrubs**, with upright or arching **stems** to 1 m tall; forming rhizomatous colonies. **Branchlets** green or reddish, glabrous or minutely hairy in decurrent lines. **Bark** grayish or brownish, becoming glabrous with age, older stems exfoliating. **Leaves** simple, opposite, deciduous. **Petioles** 3–12 mm long, ciliate. **Leaf blades** elliptical to ovate or lanceolate; 6–13 cm long, 2.5–7 cm wide; base rounded or tapered; apex long-acuminate; margins serrate, ciliate; upper surface dark green, glabrous or with short hairs on midvein; lower surface pale green, glabrous or hairy, hairs (if present) usually confined to midvein. **Flowers** bisexual, 5-merous, borne in short-stalked terminal and axillary cymes of 2–7; sepals bristlelike, 2–5.5 mm long, persistent in fruit; corolla tubular, the outer surface glabrous, the inner surface hairy, pale yellow turning orange, red, or scarlet with age, about 1–1.7 cm long; stamens 5, barely exserted, hairy; style 1, long-exserted, hairy; stigma capitate; **anthesis** mid-June to early September; insect-pollinated. **Fruit** a narrowly elliptical, ovate, or oblong capsule, with a long slender beak and persistent bristlelike sepals; brown or greenish; 1–1.5 cm long (excluding sepals); maturing early mid-July to early mid-September; gravity-dispersed. (*lonicera*: for its resemblance to the true honeysuckles in the genus *Lonicera*)

Identification

The stems and branches are typically rather sparse, and they tend to arch until the upper portions are parallel with the ground at about knee height, at least when growing singly. En masse they form a dense, luxurious coppice, although still only about waist high. The leaves are relatively large with serrate margins and a long, drawn-out tip. Except for the serrate leaves it superficially resembles the true honeysuckles (*Lonicera*). It is also easy to mistake bush honeysuckle for an herbaceous plant, but the stem is distinctly woody.

Note: Although typical specimens have nearly smooth leaves, specimens with leaves that are densely hairy on the undersurface are occasionally found in northern Minnesota. These have been named var. *hypomalaca* Fern. (Fassett 1942).

Natural History

Bush honeysuckle is ubiquitous in forests throughout much of Minnesota. It is especially common in the north, where it occurs in just about every upland forest type. It is less common in the south, where it occurs primarily in mesic hardwood forests on cool, north-facing slopes and deep ravines. It seems to prefer acidic substrates, especially rocky or well-drained mineral soil, but also cliffs, talus, and bedrock outcrops.

Bush honeysuckle does well in the interior of mature, undisturbed forests, where it successfully flowers and sets seed in deep shade. But it seems to be more abundant in forest openings or clearings, where it gets partial sunlight, and in forests that have been set back to an early successional stage by logging or fire (Wright and Bailey 1982). As long as the underground rhizomes are not damaged, it will usually survive and resprout vigorously. The rhizomes grow quickly and can become relatively long, almost qualifying as invasive. They are very competitive and can send up new stems even in stable habitats, often creating dense colonies 20 ft (6 m) or more across. The individual stems live only a few years, but established colonies seem to persist much longer. The long tubular flower is adapted for pollination by bumblebees and hawkmoths (Schoen 1977).

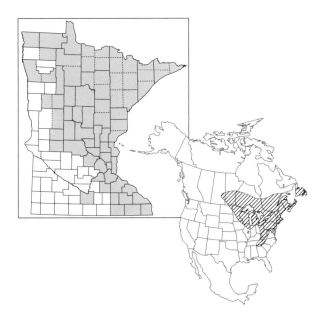

Note the persistent sepals at the tip of the fruit—September 12.

Flowers are yellow but may turn orange or scarlet—July 13.

A dense, rhizomatous colony from Lake County—July 13.

Dirca, leatherwood

Thymelaeaceae: Mezereum family

This is a small North American genus of 3 species. One is a rare shrub restricted to California (*D. occidentalis*); the second is even more rare and is found only in northeastern Mexico (*D. mexicana*), and the third is the common, widespread species that occurs in Minnesota (*D. palustris*). (*Dirca* is named for *Dirce*, a woman in Greek mythology who turned into a fountain after her murder.)

Dirca palustris L.

Leatherwood

Midsize to tall **shrubs**, with single upright **stems** to 3 m tall and 8 cm basal diameter. **Branchlets** coarse, greenish the 1st year becoming brown or gray-brown the 2nd, glabrous or occasionally sparsely hairy; nodes conspicuously swollen. **Bark** gray to brown, smooth, becoming rough near base of older stems. **Leaves** simple, alternate, deciduous. **Petioles** 1–3 mm long, glabrous. **Leaf blades** elliptical to obovate or nearly rhombic; 4–8 cm long, 2.5–5 cm wide; apex blunt to obtusely tapered; base tapered or rounded; margin entire; upper surface dark green, glabrous; lower surface pale green, glabrous or occasionally hairy. **Flowers** bisexual, 4-merous; borne on 2nd-year twigs in terminal or lateral drooping clusters of 2–4; emerging from large hairy bud scales that persist until the flowers fade; pedicels 1–2 mm long, lengthening somewhat in fruit, glabrous; hypanthium corolla-like, tubular, shallowly 4-lobed, pale yellow, 5–8.5 mm long; petals none; stamens 8, long-exserted; style 1, threadlike, long-exserted; **anthesis** mid-April to mid-May; insect-pollinated. **Fruit** a green drupe; ovate-elliptical; 9–12 mm long; maturing late May to mid-June; gravity-dispersed. **Seed** 1; black; shiny; about 6 mm long. (*palustris*: of swamps, a misnomer, at least in regard to its habitat in Minnesota)

Identification

Leatherwood shrub is unique in nearly all respects. Notice that the twigs have enlarged nodes giving them the look of a jointed insect leg. Also, the bark is extremely tough and leathery, yet the twigs themselves are very pliable, almost rubbery. There is so little lignin in the wood that the twigs can be easily tied in knots without breaking. The main stem branches repeatedly from near the base, and the branches are heavy and wide spreading, which gives leatherwood the appearance of a miniature tree, although it typically reaches a height of only 5–6 ft (1.5–2 m).

Natural History

Probably more than any other shrub, leatherwood is characteristically associated with old-growth, mesic, deciduous forests, particularly forests dominated by sugar maple (*Acer saccharum*), red oak (*Quercus rubra*), or basswood (*Tilia americana*) (Minnesota Department of Natural Resources 2003). Within such forests leatherwood is not particularly rare, although it seldom occurs in great abundance. Soils are typically deep, high-nutrient, mesic loams, or they may be sandy loams if there is a subsurface hardpan (such as a clay layer) to keep the surface mesic.

Leatherwood is perhaps the most shade tolerant shrub in Minnesota. In fact, it is one of the few species that can complete its entire reproductive cycle in the understory of a closed-canopy maple forest without the benefit of a canopy gap or other form of disturbance. It accomplishes this in part by flowering and leafing out early in the spring while the understory is still sunny. It does not colonize open habitats or early successional forests, and it is absent from fire-prone landscapes. Because of these attributes, a large, well-structured population of leatherwood is one of the best indicators of a stable, climax forest (Stearns 1951).

The yellow flowers emerge in early spring before the leaves unfold, and are pollinated by queen bumblebees. The resulting fruits, which are mature by early summer, each contain a single, shiny, black seed. Leatherwood is not known to have any specialized dispersal mechanism; the fruits apparently just fall to the ground, and the seed germinates the following spring. There is also some indication that mature leatherwood may reproduce by layering or by rhizomes (Graves 2004), but that possibility has not been fully investigated.

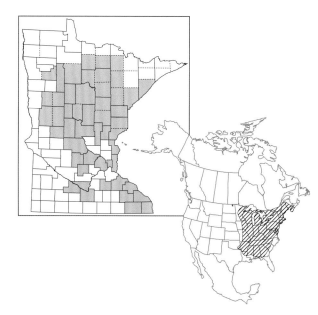

Note the blunt tip and smooth margins.

Leatherwood is among the first shrubs to flower—April 16.

Each fruit contains a single black, shiny seed—June 3.

Stems can reach about 3" (8 cm) diameter.

The enlarged nodes are characteristic of leatherwood.

A 3' (1 m) specimen in flower (leaves about half-grown)—May 7, Washington County.

Elaeagnus, Russian olive and silverberry

Elaeagnaceae: Oleaster family

This is a genus of about 45 species, primarily of Eurasia. One species is native to North America, and several others are naturalized. Minnesota has 1 native and 1 naturalized species. (*Elaeagnus* is from the Greek *elaea*, olive, and *agnos*, the chaste tree of southern Europe, *Vitex agnus-castus* L.)

Key to the Genus Elaeagnus *in Minnesota*

1. The youngest branchlets brown; the largest leaves usually greater than 2 cm wide, and 1.3–2.8 times as long as wide (l/w = 1.3–2.8), upper surface of leaves silvery green at maturity; thorns absent; sepals 2–3.5 mm long .... *E. commutata*
1. The youngest branchlets silvery white; leaves less than 2 cm wide, and 3–7 times as long as wide (l/w = 3–7), upper surface of leaves dull green at maturity; thorns often present; sepals 3.5–5 mm long .... *E. angustifolia*

Elaeagnus angustifolia L.

Russian olive

Small nonnative **trees**, with single upright **stems** to 10 m tall and 15 cm dbh; nonclonal. **Branchlets** of the current year densely covered with silvery scales and sometimes stellate hairs; 2nd-year branchlets shiny brown to reddish brown, glabrous; thorns 1–5.5 cm long, dark brown, glossy. **Leaves** simple, alternate, deciduous. **Petioles** 4–11 mm long, scaly or stellate-hairy. **Leaf blades** lanceolate to narrowly lanceolate or occasionally narrowly elliptical to narrowly lance-elliptical; 4–8 cm long, 1–2 cm wide, length/width 3–7; base tapered or less often rounded; apex acute to subacute; margins entire; upper surface dull green, with scattered to dense silvery scales or stellate hairs, occasionally glabrate; lower surface green-gray to silver-gray with dense silvery scales or stellate hairs. **Flowers** bisexual, 4-merous; 8–12 mm long; borne in clusters of 1–3 from leaf axils on growth of the current year; sepals triangular, 3.5–5 mm long, spreading, yellow on upper surface, silver-scaly on lower surface; petals absent; stamens 4; **anthesis** early June to early July; insect-pollinated. **Fruit** drupelike; dry and mealy; covered with silvery scales; 9–14 mm long; pit ellipsoidal, striated, 7–11 mm long; maturing mid-August to mid-September; animal-dispersed. (*angustifolia*: narrow-leaved)

Identification

Russian olive is a rather small, bushy tree commonly planted on roadsides and in parks in southern and western Minnesota. It reaches heights of about 33 ft (10 m) and has distinctive silvery leaves. The native silverberry (*E. commutata*) and buffaloberry (*Shepherdia argentea*) also have silvery leaves, but the leaves of silverberry are distinctly broader, and those of buffaloberry are opposite rather than alternate. *Note:* There are several cultivars being propagated commercially that vary in the shape of the leaves, the presence or absence of thorns, and the type of hairs that cover the twigs and leaves.

Natural History

Russian olive is native to southeastern Europe and western and central Asia. It was brought to America in the late nineteenth century for use as an ornamental and has since been widely planted, especially in the western states. It is easily transplanted and survives well under harsh conditions. It is drought resistant, cold tolerant, and it fixes atmospheric nitrogen. It is planted for windbreaks, erosion control, roadside ornament, the "improvement" of wildlife habitat (Borell 1962), and seemingly to just fill in treeless habitats. Highway engineers in particular consider it a panacea for roadsides because it tolerates salt pollution. Governmental land management agencies in general have made considerable use of it on public land. And yet, problems have emerged.

In the western states Russian olive has escaped cultivation and in some places it has taken over stream banks, lakeshores, and drainageways at the expense of native cottonwoods and willows (Randall and Marinelli 1996). Even though the fruits are attractive to birds, which spread the seeds in their droppings, the diversity of bird species in habitats infested with Russian olive is lower than in equivalent areas of native vegetation (Knopf and Olson 1984). In some cases, considerable efforts are now being expended to eradicate Russian olive from natural habitats.

Russian olive may pose similar problems in Minnesota. It has proven to be invasive in native prairies and has become naturalized in several of the western counties. It does not appear to have caused a great deal of ecological harm, at least not yet, but because of potential problems, it would seem wise to substitute native shrubs when plans might otherwise call for Russian olive.

Bark is rough and somewhat flaky—this stem is 6" (15 cm) diameter.

The fruits are dry and mealy—August 13.

A typical roadside specimen.

Flowers are yellow on the inside, silvery on the outside—June 9.

Russian olive

Elaeagnus commutata Bernh. ex Rydb.

Silverberry

Large **shrubs,** with upright **stems** to 3.5 m tall (reportedly to 5 m) and 6 cm basal diameter; clonal by root suckering and reportedly by stolons. **Branchlets** of the current year densely covered with shiny brown scales, which become dull ash gray the 2nd year; thorns absent. **Bark** gray to gray-brown, nearly smooth, becoming rough or scaly with age. **Leaves** simple, alternate, deciduous. **Petioles** 3–7 mm long, scaly. **Leaf blades** elliptical or occasionally ovate; 3.5–6.5 cm long, 1.5–3.5 cm wide, length/width 1.3–2.8; base rounded to tapered; apex acute to obtuse; margins entire; upper surface with reflective silvery scales; lower surface similar to upper but often with a few reddish scales. **Flowers** bisexual, 4-merous; 6–10 mm long; borne in clusters of 1–4 from leaf axils on growth of the current year; sepals triangular-ovate, 2–3.5 mm long, somewhat spreading, yellow on upper surface, silver-scaly on lower surface; petals absent; stamens 4; **anthesis** late May to early July; insect-pollinated. **Fruit** drupelike; broadly ellipsoidal to short-obovate, sides somewhat angled; dry and mealy; covered with silvery scales; 9–14 mm long; pit ellipsoidal, striated, 7–12 mm long; maturing early August to early September; animal-dispersed. (*commutata*: changeable)

Identification

Silverberry is a large, clonal shrub averaging 3–6 ft (1–2 m) tall with relatively short, stiff branches. The leaves are covered with highly reflective silvery scales that give both upper and lower surfaces a metallic appearance. The leaves of Russian olive (*E. angustifolia*) are also silvery but primarily on the lower surface, and the leaves are measurably narrower. Silverberry might also be mistaken for buffaloberry (*Shepherdia argentea*), but the leaves of silverberry are alternate, while those of buffaloberry are opposite. The fragrance of silverberry flowers is strong and potent and not easily forgotten. In fact, the scent from a large flowering clone can be detected from a considerable distance.

Natural History

Silverberry is occasional to frequent in the prairie region of northwestern Minnesota. It is usually found in dry or moist prairies, meadows, stream banks, brushy thickets, and even in thin-canopy stands of trembling aspen (*Populus tremuloides*) or balsam poplar (*Populus balsamifera*). Silverberry is also seen on stable roadsides, railroad rights-of-way and abandoned land, but it does not aggressively invade fallow fields or pastures.

The native habitats of silverberry are historically prone to frequent wildfire, typically occurring in the early spring every 3–10 years. Silverberry is exceptionally well adapted to this type of fire regime. Even though fire will often kill or damaged the existing stems, it will also stimulate sprouting of new stems from dormant buds on the roots. The new stems grow quickly, especially when sprouting from a well-established root system. Even without fire or other disturbance, silverberry will continue to produce new stems. Under ideal conditions this can lead to the development of substantial thickets, with hundreds of interconnected stems occupying an area 65 ft (20 m) or more across.

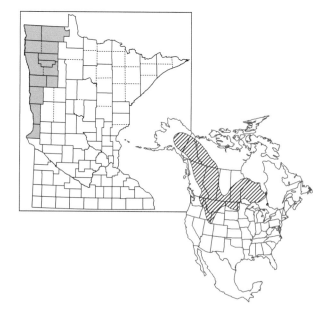

Leaves are comparatively broad, and silvery.

Flowers are strongly fragrant—June 6.

Note suckering tendencies—Mahnomen County.

Fruits are often abundant but unpalatable—August 1.

Empetrum, crowberry

Empetraceae [Ericaceae]: Crowberry family

The crowberries constitute a genus of 2 to 4 species of dwarf, evergreen shrubs occurring in southern South America and circumpolar in the Northern Hemisphere. Two species occur in North America, with 1 or possibly 2 species in Minnesota. (*Empetrum* is from the Greek *en*, upon, and *petros*, a rock, in reference to its habitat.)

Empetrum eamesii Fern. & Wieg. subsp. *atropurpureum* (Fern. & Wieg.) D. Löve

Purple crowberry
[*Empetrum atropurpureum* Fern. & Wieg.]

Dwarf **shrubs**, with prostrate **stems** to 80+ cm long; rooting at the nodes and forming mats. **Branchlets** brown; covered with dense white or brown curly hairs. **Bark** brown, flaky. **Leaves** simple; alternate; evergreen, persisting 1–2 years. **Petioles** short and broad, sometimes barely distinguishable from the blade; borne on a persistent peglike base. **Leaf blades** wide spreading to somewhat reflexed; tightly clustered, especially near tip of growing branchlets; oblong-linear to linear; 3.5–5 mm long, 0.8–1.3 mm wide; base somewhat tapered; apex blunt or rounded; margins entire, often with soft curly hairs; upper surface dark green, glabrous; lower surface similar to upper. **Flowers** bisexual or occasionally unisexual (female); inconspicuous; borne singly in axils of leaves on 1st-year branchlets; essentially sessile; sepals 3, about 1.5 mm long; petals absent; stamens 3, exceeding the sepals; **anthesis** June to July; insect-pollinated. **Fruits** spherical drupes; dark red to purplish; 4–7 mm across; with a persistent style; maturing late summer to early autumn; animal-dispersed. (*eamesii*: for botanist Edwin H. Eames, 1865–1948; *atropurpureum*: dark purple, in reference to the fruit)

Identification

Purple crowberry is a dwarf shrub with slender branches that creep over the ground forming a low ground cover. Because the leaves are evergreen and somewhat needlelike, it could be mistaken for a small, prostrate conifer. It is actually more closely related to the ericads (heaths), which include the cranberries (*Oxycoccus* spp.) and the bilberries (*Vaccinium* spp.). *Note:* Purple crowberries from Minnesota are mostly quite uniform in morphology and closely match other purple crowberries from the Lake Superior region. They typically have hairy, nonglandular branchlets and leaf margins, and red or purplish fruits. However, one specimen collected in 1948 has glabrous branchlets, leaves with numerous stipitate glands and dark, purple-black fruits. It closely matches specimens of black crowberry (*E. nigrum* L. subsp. *hermaphroditum* (Lange *ex* Hagerup) Böcher) from the Arctic. Efforts have been made to rediscover this species in the wild but without success, creating somewhat of a mystery. At this time it is uncertain if both black crowberry and purple crowberry occur in Minnesota. There is even disagreement over whether black crowberry and purple crowberry should be considered separate species (Löve 1960; Soper and Voss 1964; Moore, Harborne, and Williams 1970).

Natural History

The only known population of purple crowberry in Minnesota occurs on the Susie Island archipelago in Lake Superior (Cook County) (Butters and Abbe 1953). Although it grows on 3 of the 10 islands, the largest of these is no more than perhaps 200 acres in size, and the smallest only about 40 acres. The actual portion of the islands occupied by purple crowberry is smaller still, just the narrow zone along the shore where the forest meets the exposed bedrock. It is usually rooted in rock crevices with lichens, mosses, and low-stature vascular plants such as bird's-eye-primrose (*Primula mistassinica*), Hudson Bay eyebright (*Euphrasia hudsoniana*), or three-toothed cinquefoil (*Sibbaldiopsis tridentata*). It grows just out of reach of the waves but not so far back as to be shaded by the trees. Summer in this extreme habitat is cool and brief, and winter brings very cold temperatures, desiccating winds, and sometimes ice scouring. This is a harsh environment, often compared to arctic or alpine habitats.

The shoreline habitat of purple crowberry—Cook County.

The creeping branches form a matlike ground cover.

Epigaea, trailing arbutus

Ericaceae: Heath family

Epigaea is a small genus of dwarf shrubs with evergreen leaves and prostrate, vinelike stems. One species occurs in Japan, and 1 in North America. The closely related and possibly congeneric *Orphanidesia* has a single species that occurs in Eurasia. (*Epigaea* is from the Greek *epi*, upon, and *gaea*, the earth, in reference to its prostrate growth form.)

Epigaea repens L.

Trailing arbutus

Prostrate, vinelike **shrubs**, with slender cordlike **stems** to 80 cm long; creeping and rooting freely at the nodes. **Bark** brown, covered with brown bristly hairs, eventually becoming glabrous or glabrate, flaking in age. **Branches** few. **Leaves** simple; alternate; evergreen, persisting 1–2 years. **Petioles** 1–4 cm long, densely hairy. **Leaf blades** ovate to broadly elliptical or oblong, stiff and leathery; 2.5–7 cm long, 2–4.5 cm wide; base rounded to cordate; apex rounded; margins entire, ciliate; surfaces hairy, at least when young, reticulate veined, dark green above, somewhat paler beneath. **Flowers** structurally bisexual but functionally unisexual with some plants entirely male and others females, 5-merous; in compact terminal clusters of 1–8; pedicels 1–5 mm long; sepals lance-ovate, bristle-tipped, 5–8 mm long; corolla white to pale pink, tube slender, 6–12 mm long, lobes spreading, 4–9 mm long; stamens 10, barely exserted; style slightly shorter than the stamens; stigma 5-lobed; **anthesis** mid-April to late May; insect-pollinated. **Fruit** a 5-lobed capsule; densely hairy; spherical or depressed spherical; 5–8 mm in diameter; maturing early June to early mid-July, persisting after the seeds are dispersed. **Seeds** numerous; reddish brown; 0.4–0.6 mm long; ant-dispersed. (*repens*: creeping)

Identification

Trailing arbutus has slender, vinelike stems that trail along the surface of the ground and root at the nodes. The leaves are evergreen and can be seen all year, although they are often covered with moss or leaf litter and can be hard to spot. They will feel stiff and leathery and have conspicuous brown, bristly hairs on the margins. These coarse, brown hairs are also found on the stems and petioles. On close inspection, trailing arbutus will probably not be confused with another species. But if in doubt, note the white, tubular flowers, which are often described as smelling "spicy," even *tasting* spicy.

Natural History

Although trailing arbutus is fairly widespread in forested areas of northern Minnesota, its distribution is spotty, and it tends to occur in low numbers, even in what may seem like ideal habitat. Habitats are invariably in dry, sandy soil, usually where the dominant trees are jack pine (*Pinus banksiana*), red pine (*P. resinosa*), or northern pin oak (*Quercus ellipsoidalis*). Forests of this type historically experience ground fires as frequently as every 10 years, and crown fires every 80 years (Minnesota Department of Natural Resources 2003). In fact, both ground fires and canopy fires are considered necessary to perpetuate these types of forest. A ground fire will not harm the trees, but it will easily kill trailing arbutus (Wright and Bailey 1982). Exactly how the species manages to maintain a long-term presence under these conditions is not known, but perhaps the seeds survive buried beneath the surface and germinate after a fire.

Trailing arbutus flowers in late April or May and is pollinated by a variety of flying insects and ants (Clay and Ellstrand 1981). Then around the end of June the fruit matures and splits open, exposing hundreds of tiny, brown seeds embedded in a sweet, sticky, white placenta. The placental tissue and the seeds are quickly gathered by ants and taken to their nest (Clay 1983). The ants eat the placental tissue and discard the seeds, effectively spreading trailing arbutus. This is an apparent act of mutualism in which both the ants and trailing arbutus benefit. The process is called myrmecochory and is not uncommon among forest-dwelling herbaceous plants, but it is rare among woody plants. Another curious feature of trailing arbutus is the roots; they lack root hairs, so absorption of nutrients and water requires a mycorrhizal relationship. This is a mutualistic relationship with soil fungi (Wood 1961).

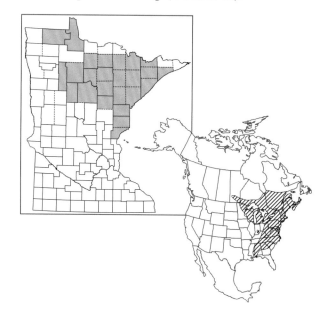

Flowers have a spicy fragrance, but can be hard to spot—May 3.

It is typical for only the leaves to show—Itasca County.

Fruits ripen in June, seeds are dispersed by ants—June 5.

Leaves are stiff and leathery, evergreen.

Euonymus, burning bush

Celastraceae: Staff-tree family

Euonymus is a large genus with 200+ species of shrubs and small trees found in North and Central America, Europe, Asia, and Australia. Five species are native to the United States, and 1 is native to Minnesota. (*Euonymus* is the classical name of the European spindle-tree, *Euonymus europaeus*.)

One Asian species, winged euonymus (*E. alatus*), is widely cultivated in southern Minnesota, especially in residential areas. It has become invasive in native forests farther east, actually as close as Iowa (Farrar 2001), and it could create ecological problems in Minnesota.

Euonymus atropurpureus Jacq.

Burning bush

Tall **shrubs** or small **trees**, with upright **stems** arising singly to 4 m tall and 3.5 cm dbh; forming rhizomatous colonies. **Branches** often few, spreading or ascending, with 4 longitudinal, corky lines or faint ridges, lines often persisting but becoming less pronounced in age. **Branchlets** greenish, glabrous. **Bark** gray, smooth or slightly rough. **Leaves** simple; opposite; deciduous. **Petioles** 0.7–1.6 cm long, glabrous or occasionally minutely hairy. **Leaf blades** elliptical to oblong-elliptical or slightly obovate; 6–15 cm long, 2.5–6.5 cm wide; base acute to subacute or occasionally rounded; apex acuminate; margins finely glandular-serrate; upper surface glabrous; lower surface with short hairs. **Flowers** bisexual, 4-merous; in glabrous, axillary cymes of 7–15; peduncle 2–5 cm long; pedicels 0.5–1 cm long; sepals reddish purple, broadly semicircular, 1–1.5 mm long; petals reddish purple, ovate, 2–4 mm long, wide spreading; style none; stigma 4-lobed; **anthesis** early June to early mid-July; insect-pollinated. **Fruit** a deeply 4-lobed, leathery capsule; 1.5–2 cm across; turning pink or red when ripe and splitting to expose 1–4 orange-red arils, each surrounding a single seed; maturing late September to late October; animal-dispersed. **Seeds** light brown, 6–8 mm long. (*atropurpureus*: dark purple, in reference to the flower)

Identification

Burning bush (named for its red autumn foliage) is a tall shrub, typically with a single stem 6–9 ft (2–3 m) high. The leaves are opposite, have finely serrate margins, and a narrow, pointed tip. They could be confused with leaves of choke-cherry (*Prunus virginiana*) or nannyberry (*Viburnum lentago*). The purple flower of burning bush is dramatic, although tiny and seldom noticed. The fruit, however, is bright pink and hard to miss. It is an intriguing structure with 4 lobes. Each lobe has a single red "seed" (actually an aril) that dangles below the leathery capsule after it opens in autumn. Also, the twigs and branches have 4 thin, corky, longitudinal ridges (sometimes visible only as faint lines) that make the twigs somewhat square in cross section.

Natural History

Burning bush is not a rare shrub, but it seldom occurs in much abundance, and it is usually inconspicuous until autumn when the leaves drop and the pink fruit become visible. Primary habitat is in forested river corridors, particularly on low terraces, floodplains, and the margins of sloughs. It can also be found on slopes and high ground, although less often. Shade will vary from moderate to none, with the most favorable conditions found under a thin canopy or in patchy shade along an edge. Spring flooding and moderate amounts of sedimentation are normal in most burning bush habitats and are easily tolerated, but do not look for it in permanently saturated soil. Adaptations to natural disturbances not withstanding, burning bush rarely appears in human-altered habitats such as roadsides, old fields, or pastures.

Seeds of burning bush are spread widely by birds that feed on the fruit. Established plants can also reproduce asexually by rhizomes, which spread horizontally 1–6 inches (2–15 cm) below ground (Musselman 1968). A healthy network of rhizomes can produce a number of interconnected aerial stems, resulting in the formation of a distinct colony (clone). The colonies are usually fairly open, rarely, if ever, thicketlike.

The rhizomes are not particularly aggressive or invasive, and the aerial stems are relatively slow growing. This is especially true in comparison to more aggressive and faster-growing rhizomatous shrubs such as the sumacs (*Rhus* spp.), gray dogwood (*Cornus racemosa*), and sand bar willow (*Salix interior*).

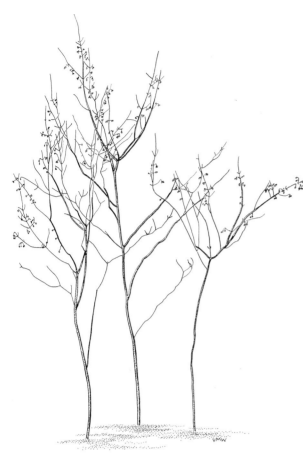

Note the finely serrate leaf margins and drawn-out tip.

Plump red arils dangle from the leathery capsule—November 20.

Four corky ridges run the length of each twig.

Flowers are striking but less than 3/8" (1 cm) across—June 19.

Stems arise singly but are connected underground.

Frangula, glossy buckthorn

Rhamnaceae: Buckthorn family

The genus *Frangula* includes 40 to 60 species of shrubs and small trees widespread in the New and Old Worlds, with 6 species native to the United States. None is native to Minnesota, but there is 1 European species, glossy buckthorn (*F. alnus*), that is naturalized here. The fern-leaved and fastigiated forms of that species are occasionally cultivated in Minnesota, but it is the wild-type form that has become naturalized. (*Frangula* is the classical Latin name for glossy buckthorn, *Frangula alnus*.)

    Frangula is often treated as a subgenus or section in the genus *Rhamnus*, but it consistently differs in a number of technical characters of the flowers and in the absence of bud scales (Kartesz and Gandhi 1994).

Frangula alnus P. Mill.

Glossy buckthorn
[*Rhamnus frangula* L.]

Nonnative, naturalized, small **trees** or tall **shrubs**, with single or multiple stems to 7 m tall and 10 cm dbh. **Bark** thin, gray to dark gray, made rough by pale, warty lenticels. **Branchlets** minutely hairy; brown the 1st year, brown with a gray flaky epidermis the 2nd year; thorns lacking. **Leaves** simple; alternate; deciduous. **Petioles** 0.5–2 cm long, hairy. **Leaf blades** obovate to elliptical; 4–7.5 cm long, 2.5–4 cm wide; base tapered; apex abruptly pointed or occasionally rounded; margins entire or minutely wavy; lateral veins 6–9 per side, curving near the margin; upper surface dark green, glossy, glabrous; lower surface somewhat paler than upper, dull, hairy on main veins or occasionally glabrous. **Inflorescence** a sessile umbel with 2–8 flowers; arising from leaf axils on 1st-year branchlets. **Flowers** bisexual; 5-merous; yellowish or greenish; 3–5 mm across; petals present; pedicels 3–9 mm long, glabrous or occasionally hairy; **anthesis** late May to mid-August; insect-pollinated. **Fruit** a blackish spherical drupe; 6–11 mm in diameter; maturing early August to late September; animal-dispersed. (*alnus*: the Latin name of the alders)

Identification

Glossy buckthorn is a large shrub or small tree with stems occasionally reaching 23 ft (7 m) in height and 4 inches (10 cm) in diameter. The small, yellowish flowers are rarely noticed, but the black berries are very conspicuous. They ripen in autumn and usually fall to the ground before winter unless they are eaten by birds first. Glossy buckthorn looks similar to common buckthorn (*Rhamnus cathartica*), except the leaves are alternate instead of opposite, and they have entire margins, not serrate. Also, the tips of the branchlets lack the thorns of common buckthorn.

Natural History

Like common buckthorn, glossy buckthorn is a native of Europe and was brought to North America in the early nineteenth century for gardens and hedges. It spread aggressively into native habitats and has now become a serious ecological problem in much of northeastern North America (Catling and Porebski 1994). In Minnesota, the problem is most urgent in wetlands, particularly tamarack (*Larix laricina*) swamps, shrub swamps, wet meadows, and fens. In time it displaces native shrubs such as willows (*Salix* spp.), dogwoods (*Cornus* spp.), and bog birch (*Betula pumila*) and inhibits the establishment and regeneration of native trees. It can even become so dense that it shades out grasses and sedges. Reproduction is only by seeds, which are produced in abundance and spread by birds.

The Minnesota invasion apparently began in the 1930s or perhaps earlier and seems to have originated from specimens cultivated in the Twin Cities area. Since then it has radiated outward, expanding its range slowly but inexorably every year. Glossy buckthorn has no known diseases or insect predators in North America, and there seem to be no ecological barriers to its continued spread. For these reasons it must be considered a serious threat to the ecological integrity of wetlands statewide.

Management options are few (Heidorn 1991; Post, McCloskey, and Klick 1989). It resprouts after cutting or burning, so control methods are generally limited to mechanical uprooting or treatment with chemical herbicides. Unfortunately, both of these techniques are practical only on a small scale. Large-scale options such as biocontrol are urgently needed. Like common buckthorn, glossy buckthorn is now listed as a restricted noxious weed under Minnesota statute, and its importation, sale, and transport are prohibited (Minnesota Rule 1505.0732).

Glossy leaves with smooth margins—August 16.

Note the pale, warty lenticels.

Flowers are bisexual; each is both male and female—June 9.

An unwelcome presence in any tamarack swamp—Anoka County.

Fraxinus, the ashes

Oleaceae: Olive family

The ashes comprise a genus of about 65 species of deciduous trees and rarely shrubs. They are distributed primarily in the temperate regions of the Northern Hemisphere, but they also extend southward into the tropics. There are about 18 species in the United States, and 3 in Minnesota. (*Fraxinus* is the classical Latin name for the ash tree.)

Key to the Genus Fraxinus *in Minnesota*

1. Lateral leaflets sessile (attached to the rachis at a tapered base), the point of attachment covered with a dense mat of tangled pale brown hairs; lower surface of leaflets with tangled pale brown hairs along the lower portion of midvein; the seed portion of the fruit (samara) flat, barely distinguishable from the wing portion; bark of young trees with soft corky ridges, older trees scaly; leaflets 9–11 .... *F. nigra*
1. Lateral leaflets on a discernable stalk, the point of attachment with ± straight white hairs or hairs lacking; lower surface of leaflets with ± straight whitish hairs along midvein, and sometimes over entire surface; the seed portion of the fruit ± circular in cross section, easily distinguishable from the flat wing portion; bark with distinct ridges and furrows that form a honeycomb pattern; leaflets 5–9.
    2. Stalk of lateral leaflets (petiolules) hairy, 1–4 mm long, winged; upper margin of leaf scar ± straight ....*F. pennsylvanica*
    2. Stalk of lateral leaflets glabrous, 5–10 mm long, not noticeably winged; upper margin of leaf scar concave .... *F. americana*

Fraxinus americana L.

White ash

Large **trees**, to 32 m tall and 83 cm dbh. **Branchlets** greenish or brownish to gray, glabrous, with whitish lenticels the 1st year. **Bark** moderately thick, light gray, developing narrow interlacing ridges and deep diamond-shaped or honeycombed furrows. **Leaves** pinnately compound; opposite; deciduous. **Petioles** 4–9 cm long, glabrous. **Petiolules** slender, 5–10 mm long, glabrous to sparsely hairy. **Leaflets** 5–9; elliptical to ovate or ovate-lanceolate; 9–14 cm long, 3–7 cm wide; base of lateral leaflets obtusely tapered to rounded; apex acuminate; margins serrate; upper surface dark green, glabrous; lower surface pale green, with ± straight white hairs along midvein and often the proximal portion of lateral veins. **Inflorescence** a panicle borne from leaf axils on branchlets of the previous year. **Flowers** unisexual with male flowers and female flowers on separate trees; corolla lacking; calyx 4-parted, minute; stamens 2, rarely 3; style 1; **anthesis** before the leaves appear, early to late May; wind-pollinated. **Fruit** a 1-seeded samara; spatulate; 2.5–4.5 cm long, 5–9 mm wide; the body (seedcase) ellipsoidal, ± circular in cross section; maturing late August to late September, often persisting on the tree through winter; wind-dispersed. (*americana*: of America)

Identification

White ash is a tall forest tree, with a straight, slender trunk and relatively small crown. It looks very much like the ubiquitous green ash (*F. pennsylvanica*). In fact, white ash is so cryptic in the presence of green ash that it went essentially unnoticed in Minnesota until 1966 (Johnson and Pauley 1967). Both trees have the same growth form and the same honeycomb pattern on the bark. But in green ash the stalk of each individual leaflet is short (less than 5 mm long) and usually winged with decurrent tissue from the blade. In white ash the stalk is usually longer and not noticeably winged. Also, the leaves of white ash usually turn wine red or bronze in the autumn; green ash turns yellow.

Natural History

White ash is comparatively uncommon in Minnesota, and is largely restricted to mesic deciduous forests in the southeast and east-central counties. It usually occurs as scattered individuals or in small groves, mixed with northern red oak (*Quercus rubra*), basswood (*Tilia americana*), sugar maple (*Acer saccharum*), green ash (*F. pennsylvanica*), or black ash (*F. nigra*). It prefers fertile, loamy soil on slopes along major streams. Unlike green ash, it rarely occurs on active floodplains or in wet depressions, and it does not seem to aggressively colonize open land. In Minnesota, at least, white ash occurs in the canopy of mid- or late-successional forests and often behaves as a climax species.

White ash are among the last trees to leaf out in the spring, usually after the flowers have appeared. The fruits are usually mature by the beginning of September and are released during autumn and winter; they germinate the following spring. Seedlings do well in the deep shade of a mature forest, at least for a few years, but they will eventually die unless a gap opens in the canopy allowing more light to penetrate. Given at least partial sunlight, white ash will grow quickly and live to a relatively old age (*fide* Burns and Honkala 1990).

*Sexes are separate, these flowers are female—
May 2.*

Flowers from a male tree—May 16.

*"Samara" is the term given to a
winged fruit—September 5.*

*Each leaf has 5–9 leaflets—they
turn wine-red in autumn.*

*A forest-grown white ash from
Olmsted County.*

Leaflets are on distinct stalks (petiolules).

*Note the honeycomb pattern on
this 23" (59 cm) dbh trunk.*

Ashes   **205**

Fraxinus nigra Marsh.

Black ash

Large **trees**, to 33 m tall and 84 cm dbh. **Branchlets** greenish brown, glabrous to gray, with dark lenticels the 1st year. **Bark** of young trees brown or gray, with soft corky ridges, becoming gray and scaly at maturity. **Leaves** pinnately compound; opposite; deciduous. **Petioles** 3–9 cm long, glabrous. **Petiolules** lacking. **Leaflets** 9–11; lanceolate to elliptical or occasionally oblong; 8–15 cm long, 2.5–6 cm wide; base of lateral leaflets obtusely tapered or sometimes rounded; apex acuminate; margins serrate; upper surface dark green, glabrous; lower surface somewhat paler than upper, with tangled, pale brown hairs along the lower portion of the midvein. **Inflorescence** a panicle borne from leaf axils on branchlets of the previous year. **Flowers** unisexual or bisexual with both on the same tree or each on separate trees; corolla lacking; calyx lacking; stamens 2; style 1; **anthesis** before the leaves appear, early to late May; wind-pollinated. **Fruit** a 1-seeded samara; spatulate to broadly linear; 2.5–4.5 cm long, 6–11 mm wide; the body (seedcase) flat in cross section, barely if at all distinguishable from the wing; maturing early July to early September; wind-dispersed. (*nigra*: black)

Identification

Black ash is a tall, slender tree with a relatively small crown, short branches, and stout twigs. The bark is silvery gray, fine textured, and somewhat scaly at maturity, not furrowed like the bark of other ashes. The compound leaves are large and rather droopy, looking more like those of walnut (*Juglans nigra*) or butternut (*J. cinerea*) than of the other ashes. But like all ashes, the leaves are opposite on the twig, not alternate. Also notice that the individual leaflets of black ash appear to be attached directly to the rachis; the leaflets of other ashes are attached by a short stalk.

Natural History

Black ash is a common tree throughout the forested region of Minnesota, especially northward. It occurs in all types of moist forests, but it is especially abundant on low river terraces, stream banks, seepage areas, moist depressions, and swamps. It also occurs on floodplains, but only where it is not subjected to silt deposition.

In upland habitats black ash usually occurs intermixed with basswood (*Tilia americana*), trembling aspen (*Populus tremuloides*), white spruce (*Picea glauca*), maples (*Acer* spp.), or a variety of other tree species. In this habitat type it can become a large tree, sometimes exceeding 100 ft (30 m) in height and 30 inches (76 cm) dbh.

In wet, swampy habitats it is a small, stunted or spindly tree, often no more than 30 ft (9 m) tall and 8 inches (20 cm) dbh, with only a few branches and a small, narrow crown. Under these conditions it may form pure stands, or it may be mixed with American elm (*Ulmus americana*), red maple (*Acer rubrum*), yellow birch (*Betula alleghaniensis*), or tamarack (*Larix laricina*). In swamps, it does best where the water is moving slowly rather than stagnant, or where the standing water is only seasonal.

Black ash saplings are moderately tolerant of shade, usually more so than green ash. And yet in most forest situations, saplings rarely reach the canopy without the benefit of a canopy gap to allow in more light. Black ash is notable in that it leafs out very late in spring, one of the last tree species to do so, and drops its leaves early in autumn. It is not the prolific seed producer that green ash is, nor is it as aggressive in colonizing open land.

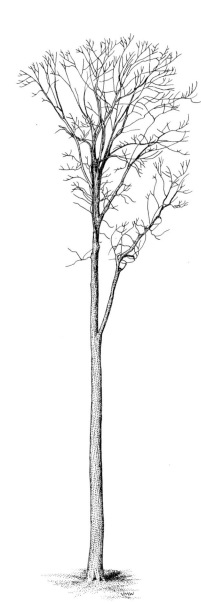

The female flowers just after pollination—May 2.

These male flowers have just released their pollen—May 2.

Fruits are flatter and broader than those of green ash.

Mature bark is silvery gray and fine textured.

Black ash is a tall, straight, canopy tree— Lake County.

Note that the leaflets are not stalked.

Ashes

Fraxinus pennsylvanica Marsh.

Green ash [red ash]

[*F. pennsylvanica* Marsh. var. *subintegerrima* (Vahl) Fern.]

Large **trees**, to 34 m tall and 119 cm dbh. **Branchlets** greenish brown to brown; glabrous or hairy; often with whitish lenticels the 1st year. **Bark** gray to brown, moderately thick, developing narrow interlacing ridges and irregular diamond-shaped or honeycombed furrows. **Leaves** pinnately compound; opposite; deciduous. **Petioles** 3–7 cm long; hairy on all surfaces or upper surface only, or glabrous. **Petiolules** stout, hairy, winged, 1–4 mm long or subsessile. **Leaflets** 5–9; lanceolate to elliptical, occasionally ovate or oblong; 7–13 cm long, 2–5 cm wide; base of lateral leaflets obtusely or acutely tapered or occasionally somewhat rounded; apex acuminate or occasionally acute; margins serrate; upper surface dark green, glabrous; lower surface pale green, with ± straight white hairs along the midvein and the proximal portion of the lateral veins, or the entire surface evenly hairy. **Inflorescence** a panicle borne from leaf axils on branchlets of the previous year. **Flowers** unisexual with male flowers and female flowers on separate trees; corolla lacking; calyx 4-parted, minute; stamens 2 or 3, rarely 4; style 1; **anthesis** as the leaves appear, mid-May to mid-June; wind-pollinated. **Fruit** a 1-seeded samara; spatulate or paddle-shaped; 2.5–4.5 cm long, 4–7 mm wide; the body (seedcase) narrowly cylindrical, ± circular in cross section; maturing early July to early September, sometimes persisting on the tree through winter; wind-dispersed. (*pennsylvanica*: of Pennsylvania)

Identification

Green ash is a large tree with a tall, thick trunk and a relatively small crown, and the bark has a honeycomb or diamond-shaped pattern. All three Minnesota ashes can be told apart by how the leaflets are attached to the rachis. Leaflets of white ash are attached by a relatively long, slender stalk, those of green ash by a short, winged stalk, and those of black ash have no stalk at all.

Note: There are two varieties of green ash in Minnesota; both occur statewide and in the same habitats. The more common (by a factor of perhaps 10 to 1) has nearly glabrous twigs and foliage, with hairs only along the midvein on the underside of the leaf. It has been segregated as var. *subintegerrima* (Vahl) Fern. and is called green ash. The typical variety (var. *pennsylvanica*) is uniformly hairy on the twigs and underside of the leaves and is called red

ash. Since there are no other apparent differences, most taxonomists no longer distinguish between the two and call the greater entity green ash.

Natural History

Green ash is one of the most common and ubiquitous trees in Minnesota, especially southward. It is most abundant on low river terraces, floodplains, and a variety of other moist habitats, often with American elm (*Ulmus americana*), box elder (*Acer negundo*), or plains cottonwood (*Populus deltoides* subsp. *monilifera*). It does not grow in swamps like black ash (*F. nigra*), but the two ashes may grow side by side in uplands. It prefers basic (calcareous) or weakly acidic soils and occurs in sand, silt, clay, or loam but not peat.

Green ash is tolerant of spring flooding and moderate levels of sedimentation, but it does not grow in permanently saturated soil. It does, however, tolerate drought and seems unaffected by the temperature extremes found in Minnesota. Young trees grow rapidly and resprout vigorously if cut or damaged, and they produce large numbers of seeds. Green ash is also one of the most effective colonizers of abandoned agricultural and urban lands, which only enhances its reputation as a tough, durable tree. In most situations seedlings do not survive under deep shade, which is consistent with its status as an early-successional species. But even in late-successional or climax forests, it manages to reproduce in low, moist areas or at the margins of open wetlands.

Flowers from a female tree—May 14.

Leaflets are attached by a short stalk (petiolule).

Leaves are compound, each with 5–9 leaflets.

Flowers from a male tree—May 13.

Contrast the shape of these fruits with those of black ash.

A 21" (53 cm) dbh trunk showing typical honeycomb bark.

Ashes

Gaultheria, snowberry and wintergreen

Ericaceae: Heath family

Gaultheria is a large genus of about 125 to 150 species of evergreen shrubs. They are found in eastern Asia, Australasia, and throughout the Americas. There are 6 species in the United States, and 2 in Minnesota. (*Gaultheria* is named for botanist and physician Jean-Francois Gaultier, 1708–56.)

Key to the Genus Gaultheria *in Minnesota*

1. Stems and branches creeping vinelike over the ground; leaves tiny, less than 1 cm long, the lower surface of the leaves with coarse bristlelike hairs (seen without magnification); flowers 4-merous; fruit white .... *G. hispidula*
1. Stems with upright branches to 15 cm tall; leaves at least 2 cm long, the lower surface of the leaves lacking hairs; flowers 5-merous; fruit red .... *G. procumbens*

Gaultheria hispidula (L.) Muhl.

Snowberry

Dwarf vinelike **shrubs**, with delicate creeping **stems** to 50 cm long, rooting at the nodes. **Stems** and **branches** brownish, with closely appressed bristlelike hairs. **Leaves** simple, alternate, evergreen. **Petioles** 0.5–1 mm long. **Leaf blades** broadly elliptical to nearly orbicular or occasionally ovate; 5–9 mm long, 3.5–6.5 mm wide; base acute to obtuse or rounded; apex obtuse to somewhat rounded, slightly apiculate; margins entire, revolute; upper surface dark green, glabrous; lower surface pale green, with a few to several closely appressed bristlelike hairs. **Flowers** bisexual, 4-merous, white; borne singly from the axils of ordinary leaves; peduncles nodding, 1.5–2.5 mm long, with 2 sepal-like bractlets at base of flower; calyx base with appressed bristlelike hairs, expanding to enclose the fruit; calyx lobes ovate to deltate, 0.5–1 mm long; corolla bell-shaped, the rounded lobes about 2 mm long; **anthesis** mid-May to early June; insect-pollinated. **Fruit** a white translucent berry 4–7 mm in diameter; hairy; maturing mid-July to mid-August; animal-dispersed. (*hispidula*: with small stiff hairs)

Identification

Snowberry is a dwarf shrub with tiny, roundish, evergreen leaves. The delicate stems and branches creep over the ground, often intermingling and forming small mats. The mats can be spotted easily, if looking at the ground, but the flowers are small and easily missed. Snowberry is most likely to be confused with one of the cranberries (*Oxycoccus macrocarpus* or *O. quadripetalus*) or perhaps twinflower (*Linnaea borealis* subsp. *americana*), but among these species only snowberry has stiff, brown, bristlelike hairs on the stems and the lower surface of the leaves (usually seen without magnification).

Natural History

Snowberry is relatively common in north-central and northeastern Minnesota in a region ecologists are now calling the Laurentian Mixed Forest Province (Minnesota Department of Natural Resources 2003). It seems to prefer *Sphagnum* swamps or bogs, often with black spruce (*Picea mariana*) or Labrador tea (*Rhododendron groenlandicum*). It is also common on mossy rocks and rotting logs in a variety of moist forest settings.

It thrives in very acidic, low-nutrient, and low-light conditions. But it is easily killed by fire, especially in drought years when fires are more frequent and more severe in swamps. Under these conditions fires often burn though the moss and organic layers down to mineral soil. Fires must be part of the regular disturbance cycle for snowberry since it lives almost exclusively in fire-prone landscapes.

Exactly how snowberry recolonizes habitats after a fire is not clear. The seeds are presumably spread by animals that eat the fruit, but the process has never been documented. However, once an individual becomes established in a suitable habitat, it spreads within that habitat by asexual reproduction, a process that is easily observed. The stems and branches creep along the ground, sending down roots every few inches (centimeters). When stems are broken or fragmented, the individual segments, if rooted, become autonomous and can found new colonies. The process is slow, but in the time interval between fires a single snowberry has the potential to spread over a sizable area.

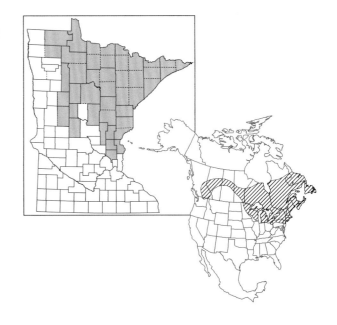

The fruit is a white, translucent berry—August 8.

The flower is no more than 1/8 " (3 mm) long—May 28.

The intermingling stems form a delicate mat.

Gaultheria procumbens L.

Wintergreen

Low or dwarf **shrubs**, with creeping woody rhizomes at or near the surface, producing at intervals upright leafy branches to 15 cm tall. **Branches** brown, with fine recurving hairs or glabrate. **Leaves** simple, alternate, evergreen; in clusters of 2–5 near the ends of the aerial branches. **Petioles** 2–5 mm long, hairy. **Leaf blades** elliptical to broadly elliptical or suborbicular, occasionally obovate; 2–4.5 cm long, 1.5–2.5 cm wide; base subacute to obtuse; apex obtuse to rounded, apiculate; margins with widely spaced bristle-tipped serrations, revolute; upper surface dark green, shiny, glabrous; lower surface pale green, dull, glabrous. **Flowers** bisexual, 5-merous, whitish; borne singly from the axils of ordinary leaves; peduncles nodding, 3–8 mm long, with 2 sepal-like bractlets at base of flower; calyx lobes ovate, minutely ciliate, 1–1.5 mm long; corolla urn shaped to short cylindrical, 6–8 mm long, the rounded lobes 1–2 mm long; **anthesis** late mid-July to late August; insect-pollinated. **Fruit** a bright red, berrylike capsule; 8–11 mm in diameter, with a strong flavor of wintergreen; maturing late August to late September, often held overwinter; animal-dispersed. (*procumbens*: lying on the ground)

Identification

Wintergreen is a dwarf, ankle-high shrub, with barely woody stems and shiny, evergreen leaves. The small white flowers are inconspicuous and hang down from the leaf axils. The fruits are red and relatively conspicuous and have a strong taste of wintergreen, but they are rarely produced in abundance. Wintergreen is most similar to pipsissewa (*Chimaphila umbellata* subsp. *cisatlantica*) or perhaps to the herbaceous bunchberry (*Cornus canadensis*). But the leaf margins of wintergreen have widely spaced bristle-tipped serrations, which is a character not seen in similar-looking plants.
Note: At one time the leaves of this plant were the commercial source of the compound known as wintergreen, which is now produced synthetically.

Natural History

Wintergreen is a fairly common plant in northern forests, particularly in dry, sandy soil, with jack pine (*Pinus banksiana*), red pine (*P. resinosa*), or sometimes northern pin oak (*Quercus ellipsoidalis*).

The soils are typically acidic, low in nutrients, and with a thin humus layer derived from decomposing pine needles. There is often significant moss or lichen cover and frequently blueberries (*Vaccinium* spp.), bracken fern (*Pteridium aquilinum*), or bearberry (*Arctostaphylos uva-ursi*). Although the soils are typically sandy and with little structure, they are characteristically stable and are not subject to significant erosion.

Wintergreen produces small, white flowers that are pollinated primarily by bumblebees (Reader 1977), but fruit production is reportedly low (Mirick and Quinn 1981). If this is the case, asexual reproduction may be more important than seed production in maintaining wintergreen populations. Asexual reproduction is accomplished by a tough, woody rhizome that grows horizontally just beneath the duff layer. As it grows, the rhizome sends shallow roots downward into the mineral layer, and leafy aerial shoots upwards. These aerial shoots grow to a height of about 6 inches (15 cm) and appear at intervals as great as 8–12 inches (20–30 cm). As the rhizome continues to grow and branch, a sizable colony can develop. In time, the colony may fragment and form additional colonies. This growth form would seem to make it vulnerable to ground fires, and pine forests are historically prone to ground fires. But wintergreen reportedly survives fire (Wright and Bailey 1982), although how it manages this is not known.

These fruits will turn bright red when ripe—August 28.

Nodding flowers hang singly from leaf axils—August 13.

A typical colony of wintergreen in a pine forest—Itasca County.

Gaylussacia, black huckleberry

Ericaceae: Heath family

This genus includes about 50 species of shrubs, mostly in South America, with 4 to 6 species in North America, and 1 in Minnesota. (*Gaylussacia* is named for the French chemist Louis Joseph Gay-Lussac, 1778–1850.)

Gaylussacia baccata (Wang.) K. Koch

Black huckleberry

Low to midsize **shrubs**, with erect or ascending **stems** to 1 m tall; forming rhizomatous colonies. **Branchlets** of the current year pale brown, hairy; 2nd-year branchlets reddish brown, hairy or glabrate. **Bark** smooth or the thin outer layer peeling, becoming dark purplish gray to blackish. **Leaves** simple, alternate, deciduous. **Petioles** 1–2.5 mm long, hairy. **Leaf blades** elliptical to obovate; 3–5.5 cm long, 1.3–2.5 cm wide; base acute; apex acute to subobtuse or blunt; margins entire, hairy; upper surface dark green, hairy on midrib, with small resinous dots; lower surface similar to upper, but pale green and with a greater number of resinous dots. **Flowers** bisexual, 5-merous, reddish, gland-dotted; borne in lateral racemes of 3–9 from leaf axils on twigs of the previous year; pedicels 3–7 mm long, glabrous or glabrate; sepals ovate to deltate, 0.5–1 mm long; corolla urn shaped to short-cylindrical, 4–6 mm long, the lobes 0.5–1 mm long and reflexed; style slightly exserted; **anthesis** mid-May to early June; insect-pollinated. **Fruit** a black, globose drupe; 6–8 mm across; maturing early August to mid-September; animal-dispersed. (*baccata*: with berries)

Identification

Black huckleberry is a tangled, bushy, understory shrub, usually knee high to waist high. It looks a lot like sweet lowbush blueberry (*Vaccinium angustifolium*), and the two species are likely to be found growing side by side. But black huckleberry is usually a larger shrub, and the leaves are marked with small, yellow, resinous dots, especially on the lower surface (seen with magnification). The fruits are also similar to those of blueberry, although they contain 10 hard nutlets that make them difficult to eat.

Natural History

Black huckleberry is common in the eastern states but quite rare in Minnesota, barely reaching the eastern counties. The few known occurrences in Minnesota are from well-drained, sandy soil or dry, sandstone outcrops in forests of northern pin oak (*Quercus ellipsoidalis*), jack pine (*Pinus banksiana*), or red pine (*P. resinosa*), usually in full or partial shade. Forests of this type are generally considered fire dependent (Minnesota Department of Natural Resources 2003). This means that the dominant tree species, in this case oak or pine, require periodic fires to reproduce. Not

surprisingly, black huckleberry is well adapted to fire, at least low-intensity ground fires (Matlack, Gibson, and Good 1993). Even though the aboveground stems will likely be consumed during a fire, dormant buds on the buried rhizomes survive and resprout vigorously. These rhizomes are key to the success of black huckleberry.

New populations are founded by seeds spread in the droppings of birds and other animals, but maintenance and expansion of existing populations is largely accomplished by the extensive system of long, horizontal rhizomes that grow just beneath the surface of the ground (Matlack, Gibson, and Good 1993). Rhizomes are branching underground stems that produce both aerial stems and roots. They allow a single pioneering plant of seedling origin to spread outward by what is essentially a process of asexual or clonal reproduction. If conditions are ideal, perhaps following a fire when competition for light or nutrients is reduced, rhizomatous growth can result in a large, dense clone of perhaps 1,000 square feet (100 square meters) or more, with hundreds of aerial stems sharing a common root system (Harper 1995). In time, the clone may fragment, producing independent, isolated patches. Yet no matter how isolated or independent they become, all the plants originated from 1 seed and are still considered members of the same clone. Any given site can encompass many clones or just a single very old, very fragmented clone.

Flowers are reddish and urn shaped—June 4.

A closer look would reveal yellow, resinous dots on the leaves.

Fruits can be eaten but the nutlets make it difficult—August 19.

*A red pine forest with groundcover of black huckleberry—
Pine County.*

Gleditsia, honey locust

Caesalpiniaceae [Fabaceae]: Bean family

Gleditsia is a genus of about 15 species of thorny, deciduous trees and in one case a shrub, distributed primarily in Asia and the Americas. There are 2 species in North America, and 1 in Minnesota. (*Gleditsia* is named for the German botanist Johann Gottlieb Gleditsch, 1714–86.)

Gleditsia triacanthos L.

Honey locust

Midsize **trees**, to 25 m tall and 45 cm dbh; armed with numerous large, simple and/or compound thorns to 20 cm long, thorns lacking in form *inermis* (Pursh) Schneid. **Branches** slender; spreading or ascending. **Branchlets** glabrous; initially greenish, becoming reddish brown or gray. **Bark** gray to nearly black, broken into scaly plates. **Leaves** compound, alternate, deciduous; 10–30 cm long; those on the elongate terminal shoots twice-pinnate, those on the short lateral shoots once-pinnate and clustered. **Petioles** 10–20 cm long, hairy to glabrate. **Leaflets** oblong-elliptical to oblong-lanceolate; 1.5–3.5 cm long, 0.5–1.2 cm wide; base obtuse to rounded; apex obtuse to blunt; margins with broad, shallow, gland-tipped serrations; surfaces sparsely hairy, often just on the midvein; lower surface somewhat paler than upper surface. **Flowers** generally unisexual, with each inflorescence either male or female, borne on the same or different plants; in elongate axillary racemes 3–8 cm long; perianth 3–5 mm long, yellowish green; stamens 5–7; **anthesis** late May to late June; insect-pollinated. **Fruit** a flat, oblong legume or pod; 15–40 cm long, 2.5–4 cm wide; 1–3 per peduncle; dark reddish brown at maturity, indehiscent; maturing late August to late September, held on the tree through winter; animal-dispersed. **Seeds** many, about 9 mm long and 5 mm wide. (*triacanthos*: three-thorned)

Identification

Honey locust is a medium-size forest tree with a straight, slender trunk and large compound leaves. The leaves look something like those of black locust (*Robinia pseudoacacia*) and Kentucky coffee tree (*Gymnocladus dioicus*), but the individual leaflets are much smaller. The very long pods are distinctive, as are the extremely large thorns (the largest of any native tree), but be aware that some individual trees lack thorns entirely.

Natural History

Native honey locust is known to have occurred at only one place in Minnesota: the Mississippi River bottoms in Houston County, about 3/4 of a mile (1 km) north of the Iowa border. The discovery was documented with a herbarium specimen collected by the botanist W. A. Wheeler (MINN #413) on July 25, 1899. An entry from his collection book for that date reads: "One tree; height 59 ft, circumference 3 ft from ground 6 ft. On island across slough from Reinhart's." The island is now submerged in the slack water pool behind lock and dam number 8, which was built by the U.S. Army Corps of Engineers in the 1930s. Since no other credible record exists, native honey locust may now be extinct in Minnesota.

Cultivars of honey locust have been planted in southern and central Minnesota since the latter half of the nineteenth century, usually as ornamentals around homes and in parks. Some of these specimens may now be 100+ years old, and if they were in a wooded area, could have produced a second generation of trees that are nearing maturity. So at this time, it could be difficult or even impossible to distinguish specimens of the native genotype from descendents of imported trees. However, to rediscover a native stand of this species in Minnesota would be of great scientific and historical interest, and a worthy mission.

Any large, forest-grown honey locust from the Mississippi or Missouri river drainages found in native bottomland habitats in the southern two or three tiers of counties could be native. Certainly an age, based on tree-ring counts, that predates settlement in the region (ca. 1850) would be persuasive if not conclusive. Also, though it hardly seems necessary to mention, trees found growing in rows or on city boulevards are not likely to be native.

A single leaf with approximately 150 leaflets.

A raceme of male flowers—June 9.

A raceme of female flowers—June 9.

The pods can reach 16" (40 cm) in length—September 5.

A well-armed honey locust near Ames, Iowa.

Gymnocladus, Kentucky coffee tree

Caesalpiniaceae [Fabaceae]: Bean family

Gymnocladus is a small genus with 4 species, all deciduous trees from temperate and tropical regions. Three species occur in Asia, and 1 in the eastern United States. Its closest relative is honey locust (genus *Gleditsia*). (*Gymnocladus* is from the Greek *gymnos*, naked, and *clados*, branch.)

Gymnocladus dioicus (L.) K. Koch

Kentucky coffee tree

Midsize **trees**, to 23 m tall and 74 cm dbh; clonal by root suckering. **Branches** spreading or weakly ascending, stout. **Branchlets** brown, coarse and knotty; glabrous. **Bark** of mature stems gray, with shallow fissures and flat plates that tend to curl at the edges. **Leaves** bipinnately compound, alternate, deciduous; 30–90 cm long. **Petiole** and rachis glabrous. **Leaflets** 40 or more, ovate to ovate-elliptical; 4–9 cm long, 2–4 cm wide; base rounded or occasionally obtuse; apex acute to short-acuminate; margins entire; upper surface dark green, sparsely hairy or glabrate; lower surface pale green, hairy, at least on larger veins. **Inflorescence** a loose terminal raceme 7–20 cm long, bearing 18–50 flowers. **Flowers** unisexual or bisexual, male and female usually on separate trees; 5-merous; hypanthium tubular, 8–15 mm long; sepals linear, 6–9 mm long, hairy; petals obovate, greenish white, 8–11 mm long, densely hairy; stamens 10; **anthesis** late May to late June; insect-pollinated. **Fruit** a thick, heavy pod; yellowish and leathery in summer, becoming reddish brown and woody by winter; irregularly oblong; 8–15 cm long, 3–5 cm wide, about 2 cm thick; maturing in autumn but persisting on tree until early spring; dispersal agent unknown. **Seeds** 4–7; hard-shelled; blackish brown; depressed spherical or slightly discoid; 1.5–2 cm long; embedded in a green, glutinous material. (*dioicus*: dioecious)

Identification

The key to identifying Kentucky coffee tree is understanding the large, compound leaf. It is the largest leaf of any tree in northern climates, nearly 3 ft (1 m) long and with as many as 100 separate leaflets. Do not mistake the individual leaflets for the entire leaf. The leaves of honey locust (*Gleditsia triacanthos*) and black locust (*Robinia pseudoacacia*) are similar, but the individual leaflets of Kentucky coffee tree are larger and have pointed tips. The large, strangely shaped pods are also unique, if not bizarre, and can usually be found on mature female trees all winter.

Natural History

Kentucky coffee tree is uncommon or rare wherever it occurs (Isely 1998), and it may be as close as Minnesota gets to having an enigmatic tree. It is found most often in hardwood forests on terraces of the Minnesota River, the Mississippi River below the Twin Cities, and a few major tributaries. These are raised terraces, well above the reach of normal flood events. Although it is clearly a forest tree, seedlings do not do well in the shade of a dense forest canopy; they generally need open ground and plenty of sun. But Kentucky coffee tree produces suckers directly from its roots, and the suckers seem to do fairly well in the shade. The genders are usually separate, meaning that each tree is either male or female. As a result, some sites are known to consist entirely of single-sex clones derived by root suckers from a single parent.

Kentucky coffee tree is notable as the last tree to leaf out in the spring and one of the first to drop its leaves in the fall. In fact, it is seen without leaves for so long (at least 7 months of the year) that healthy trees are often mistaken for dead. The pods are another mystery. No animal that currently shares its habitat is known to eat them or disperse the seeds within. The pods simply fall from the tree and eventually rot where they land. It has been theorized that the animal that evolved to disperse the seeds may have become extinct near the end of the Pleistocene Epoch about 13,000 years ago, when so many large North American mammal species became extinct (Barlow 2001). This could explain why Kentucky coffee trees have become so uncommon and the surviving populations so isolated and scattered.

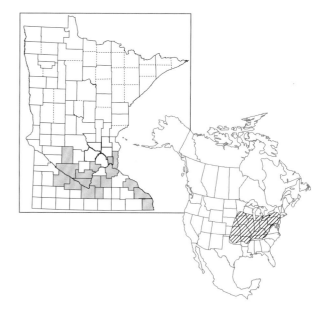

Pods are yellow in summer, brown by winter.

The undeveloped stamens indicate this flower is female—June 10.

Flowers can be unisexual or bisexual—June 10.

Note the smooth margins and narrow tip of each leaflet.

This is a single leaf with close to 100 leaflets.

Large, black seeds are imbedded in green, gelatinous material.

Trunks have distinctive "platy" bark—this one is 7" (18 cm) dbh.

Hamamelis, witch-hazel

Hamamelidaceae: Witch-hazel family

Hamamelis is a small genus with 4 to 6 species of deciduous shrubs from eastern Asia and eastern North America. Two species occur in the United States, and 1 in Minnesota. (*Hamamelis* is an ancient Greek name for a European shrub called medlar, *Mespilus germanica* L.)

Hamamelis virginiana L.

Witch-hazel

Small **trees** or tall **shrubs**, with multiple upright or ascending **stems** to 6 m tall and 8 cm dbh. **Branchlets** brown or gray; stellate hairy or glabrate by autumn. **Bark** of larger stems brown or gray-brown, rough. **Leaves** simple, alternate, deciduous. **Petioles** 6–18 mm long, with stellate hairs. **Leaf blades** broadly elliptical to nearly circular or obovate; 6–15 cm long, 4.5–10 cm wide; base rounded or slightly subcordate, asymmetrical; apex acute to short-acuminate or rounded; margins irregularly wavy; upper surface sparsely stellate hairy or glabrate, dark green; lower surface with scattered stellate hairs especially on veins, pale green. **Flowers** bisexual, 4-merous, sessile; 1–4 in axillary clusters; sepals brownish, ovate to elliptical, 2.5–3.5 mm long; petals yellow, ribbonlike, wavy or crinkly, 1–2 cm long; stamens 4, very short, alternating with 4 equally short staminodes; styles 2, short; **anthesis** peaking after the leaves have fallen in early October to early November; insect-pollinated. **Fruit** a woody capsule; 1–1.4 cm long; brown; short stellate hairy; maturing in autumn 1 year after pollination; opening explosively and dispersing seeds forcibly. **Seeds** 2 per capsule; black; shiny; ellipsoidal; 6–9 mm long. (*virginiana*: of Virginia)

Identification

Witch-hazel is a large shrub with multiple stems that may reach heights of 20 ft (6 m) and diameters of 3 inches (8 cm). The leaves and the growth form can be confused with American hazel (*Corylus americana*) and possibly round-leaved dogwood (*Cornus rugosa*). Two characters to remember are the "wavy" leaf margins and the star-shaped hairs on the twigs and leaves (seen with magnification). The flowers are certainly unique, but do not look for them until October.

Natural History

Witch-hazel is a common shrub farther east, but it is rare in Minnesota, just reaching the eastern counties. It occurs in the understory of dry to moist deciduous forests, typically with oaks (*Quercus* spp.), sugar maple (*Acer saccharum*), or basswood (*Tilia americana*). It easily survives and reproduces in a closed-canopy forest, but growth and flowering are reportedly increased under a canopy gap (Hicks and Hustin 1989).

Witch-hazel is peculiar in that the flowers open in the autumn, usually peaking about the time the leaves are falling. This may happen after the first frost, yet flying insects are still active and manage to pollinate the flowers. Although pollination occurs in the autumn, actual fertilization does not occur until the following spring (Flint 1957), so the fruits develop during the summer, like those of most spring-pollinated species. When the fruits are ripe in the autumn, they burst open, forcibly ejecting two smooth black seeds a distance of up to 33 feet (10 m) (Meyer 1997). Most seeds remain dormant in the soil for 18 months, germinating after two winters (Gaut and Roberts 1984).

Although the stems of witch-hazel will produce basal suckers, they all arise from a confined root crown and cannot generate new root crowns, so reproduction is entirely by seed. Individual stems are reported to reach 30 years of age (De Steven 1983), but since stems can be continually replaced by basal suckers, the root system could be much older than any of the stems.

Extracts of witch-hazel bark and leaves have a long history in traditional American medicine (Fulling 1953) and are still available commercially. However, the pharmaceutical value of witch-hazel has never been widely accepted.

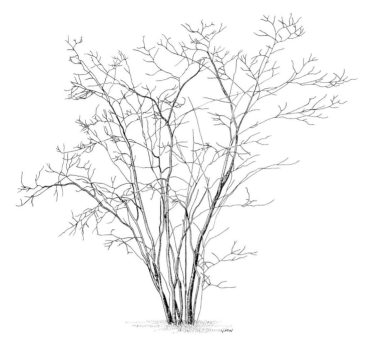

Stems reach about 3" (8 cm) in diameter and have rough bark.

Note the wavy leaf margins.

Capsules open explosively, launching seeds up to 33' (10 m).

Fruit is a woody capsule about 1/2" (1–1.4 cm) long—September 8.

Flowering reaches its peak in October.

Hudsonia, beach heath

Cistaceae: Rock-rose family

Beach heath is part of a small genus of 3 species, all low, mat-forming or mound-forming, evergreen shrubs of sand dunes in eastern North America. One species occurs in Minnesota. (*Hudsonia* is named for the English botanist William Hudson, 1730–93.)

Hudsonia tomentosa Nutt.

Beach heath

[*Hudsonia ericoides* L. subsp. *tomentosa* (Nutt.) Nickerson and Skog]

Low **shrubs**, with slender decumbent or prostrate **stems** to 30 cm long and 3 mm diameter; decumbent stems occasionally rooting at nodes. **Branches** numerous, diffuse, ascending; up to about 15 cm high. **Branchlets** initially greenish and densely hairy, becoming reddish brown and glabrous or glabrate. **Leaves** simple, alternate, evergreen; appressed and mostly overlapping, thereby appearing to clothe the branches; sessile; oblong to lance-oblong or lance-linear; 1–3 mm long, 0.3–0.6 mm wide; apex acute; margins entire; surfaces densely gray-hairy. **Flowers** bisexual, 5-merous, solitary at the ends of short lateral branches; peduncle 1.5–3 mm long, hairy; sepals fused into 3 unequal segments 3–4.5 mm long, hairy; petals bright yellow, oblong or narrowly obovate, 3–5 mm long; stamens 8–20, shorter than the petals; style 1.5–2 mm long, slender, glabrous; **anthesis** early June to early July; insect-pollinated. **Fruit** a smooth, brown, ovoid capsule; 3-valved; 2.5–3 mm long; enclosed in the densely hairy calyx; maturing early July to early August; gravity- and secondarily wind-dispersed. **Seeds** 1–3. (*tomentosa*: woolly, in reference to the leaves and branchlets)

Identification

Beach heath is a low, mat-forming, evergreen shrub, usually about ankle high. The actual leaves are reduced to tiny, green slivers that turn brown after the first summer and press tightly to the thin, wiry stem. Although beach heath is "evergreen" in the sense that the leaves last through winter, the overall color is more of a pale gray-green, even in summer. The entire plant would be inconspicuous were it not for its habit of growing in the open on bare sand. In fact, if it is not growing on bare sand, it is probably not beach heath.

Natural History

In Minnesota, beach heath is sometimes found on high, sandy beaches of large lakes, well beyond the reach of normal wave action, but most occurrences are on active sand dunes that are not directly associated with lakes. Such dunes are rare and local features in Minnesota, yet they can be found at several widely scattered locations across the state.

There are a few dunes in the northwestern counties, all of which formed from sand deposited on the shores of Lake Agassiz, a large, extinct glacial lake. There are also dunes on terraces of the Mississippi River that formed from sand deposited by streams of glacial meltwater originating from the Grantsburg sublobe. However, most dunes are found on the Anoka Sandplain (Cooper 1935), a large outwash plain in the east-central counties that also formed from sand carried by glacial meltwater, but in this case deposited over a broad, level plain (Wright 1972). In all cases, the sand arrived where it is now by water, yet the actual dunes were created by wind and began to form during a particularly warm, dry period about 8,000 years ago (*fide* Wovcha, Delaney, and Nordquist 1995).

Dunes are dynamic habitats with high crests and bowl-shaped depressions. The depressions are called blowouts and are generally devoid of vegetation except for beach heath. If these blowouts are not kept open by wind, they will become overgrown by grasses and other plants, and beach heath will disappear. On active dunes, beach heath can become nearly buried by blowing sand, but it produces new roots (adventitious roots) along the buried portions of the stem allowing it to continue to grow upwards. It seems that every intact, well-developed dune field in the state has a population of beach heath, but it should be noted that sand dunes are rare in Minnesota, and dunes with active blowouts are rarer still. Also, humans have a destructive tendency to plant pines on dunes or use them as a playground for off-highway vehicles.

Flowers are bright yellow, but tiny and rarely noticed—June 15.

Fruits remain enclosed in the shaggy calyx—July 23.

Beach heath on Minnesota Point in Lake Superior—St. Louis County.

Ilex, winterberry

Aquifoliaceae: Holly family

This genus includes 300 to 350 species of evergreen and deciduous trees and shrubs, occurring worldwide in temperate and tropical regions. About 25 species occur in North America, and 1 in Minnesota. (*Ilex* is the classical Latin name for the holly oak, *Quercus ilex*, which, to Linnaeus, resembled members of this genus.)

Ilex verticillata (L.) Gray

Winterberry

Tall **shrubs,** with multiple upright **stems** to 4 m tall and 5 cm basal diameter; clonal by root suckering. First-year **branchlets** greenish, glabrous or sparsely hairy; second-year branchlets shedding a thin, gray epidermal layer to reveal a smooth, brown surface. **Bark** of mature stems thin, gray to brownish, often mottled; roughened with pale, warty lenticels. **Leaves** simple, alternate, deciduous. **Petioles** 6–13 mm long, short-hairy. **Leaf blades** elliptical to ovate-elliptical; 5–10 cm long, 2–4.5 cm wide; base tapered; apex acute to acuminate; margins finely serrate; upper surface dark green, dull, sparsely hairy to glabrate, veins impressed or sunken; lower surface pale green, hairy, veins conspicuously protruding. **Flowers** bisexual or unisexual, plants may have only male or only female flowers, or flowers with both sexes; 5–8 merous; borne in small clusters from leaf axils on 1st-year branchlets; pedicels 1–2 mm long; sepals ciliate, less than 1 mm long; petals whitish, spreading or reflexed, 1.5–2 mm long; stamens as many as the petals and slightly shorter; style none, stigma capitate; **anthesis** mid-June to early July; insect-pollinated. **Fruit** a red, berrylike drupe; spherical; 5–8 mm in diameter; containing 3–6 bony nutlets; maturing early September to early October, remaining on the branchlet well into winter; animal-dispersed. (*verticillata*: whorled, for the arrangement of the flowers)

Identification

Winterberry is a tall, clonal shrub with slender twigs and dark green, serrate leaves. The veins are noticeably sunken above and protruding beneath, giving the leaves a "quilted" appearance. The tiny, pale flowers emerge after the leaves are fully developed and are rarely noticed. But the red berries are very conspicuous in fall and winter, especially after the leaves have fallen. They are held close to the stem, either singly or in small tight clusters.

Natural History

Winterberry is fairly common in much of the forested region of eastern Minnesota, especially in the east-central counties. It is usually found in brushy or forested wetlands that develop in shallow basins, often with tamarack (*Larix laricina*), speckled alder (*Alnus incana* subsp. *rugosa*), or various willows

(*Salix* spp.). Soil in these habitats is usually a thin layer of weakly acidic, sedge-derived peat over sand. Other wetland habitats include lakeshores, pond margins, and marsh edges.

All of these habitats may experience localized spring flooding from melting snow but this type of flooding doesn't cause much damage. It's a different story along major rivers, where fast-moving floodwater can leave some tree roots exposed by scouring and others buried under heavy sediments. These conditions are tolerated by floodplain specialists such as buttonbush (*Cephalanthus occidentalis*) and sandbar willow (*Salix interior*) but not winterberry.

A secondary habitat of winterberry is surface-dry uplands, specifically in areas of sandy, acidic soil and a high water table, often in the shade or partial shade of oaks (*Quercus* spp.), trembling aspen (*Populus tremuloides*), or pines (*Pinus* spp.).

The seeds of winterberry are spread widely in the droppings of birds, yet winterberry is slow to invade old fields or other early successional habitats. Once it is established, it can spread short distances by root suckers and it may form fairly dense clones, especially in upland habitats. But even under the best of circumstances, the stems will advance perhaps only a foot (30 cm) per year, and the clones are not usually large in extent. The individual stems are relatively slow growing and can live 25 to 30 years.

The fruits will remain on the branch through winter.

Female flowers form small clusters in axils of leaves—June 17.

Note the yellow anthers of the male flowers—June 19.

A typical 8' (2.5 m) tall specimen from Anoka County.

Multiple stems are the rule for winterberry.

Juglans, butternut and black walnut

Juglandaceae: Walnut family

Juglans is a genus of about 20 species of deciduous trees and shrubs found in temperate and subtropical regions of North America, South America, Europe, and Asia. Six species occur in the United States, and 2 in Minnesota. (*Juglans* is the classical Latin name for the European walnut; from *Jovis*, of Jove or Jupiter, and *glans*, nut.)

Key to the Genus Juglans of Minnesota

1. Terminal leaflet present and similar to lateral leaflets; pith of young twigs dark chocolate brown; leaf scars T-shaped (the upper margin ± straight); terminal buds 8–15 mm long (by August); upper surface of leaflets evenly hairy; fruit ± ellipsoidal in shape (distinctly longer than wide), covered with sticky glands .... *J. cinerea*
1. Terminal leaflet absent or poorly developed; pith of young twigs tan colored; leaf scars V-shaped (the upper margin notched); terminal buds 5–8 mm long; upper surface of leaflets with hairs (if any) confined to midvein; fruit ± spherical, not sticky .... *J. nigra*

Juglans cinerea L.

Butternut

Midsize to large **trees**, to 26 m tall and 63 cm dbh. 1st-year **branchlets** stout, green to greenish brown, with glandular and nonglandular hairs; 2nd-year branchlets brown, glabrate; pith dark chocolate brown, chambered; leaf scars T-shaped (the upper margin ± straight); terminal bud oblong, 8–15 mm long and 3–5 mm wide (by August). **Bark** moderately thick, gray to gray-brown, smooth when young, soon developing relatively narrow, flat-topped, interlacing ridges and broad shallow furrows. **Leaves** pinnately compound, alternate, deciduous. **Petioles** 3–9 cm long, with glandular and nonglandular hairs. **Leaflets** 11–17; ± sessile; terminal leaflet similar to lateral leaflets; ovate to lance-ovate or lance-oblong; 7–13 cm long, 3–5.5 cm wide; base rounded or nearly truncate, asymmetrical; apex acuminate; margins serrate; upper surface dark green, sparsely to moderately hairy; lower surface gray-green, hairy. **Inflorescence** unisexual, with male flowers and female flowers borne separately on the same branchlet. **Male flowers** numerous, borne on slender, pendulous catkins 6–12 cm long; catkins ± sessile, arising singly from leaf axils on branchlets of the previous year. **Female flowers** 3–7, borne on a short spike arising from the apex of branchlets of the current year; **anthesis** early May to early June; wind-pollinated. **Fruit** a nut enclosed in a thin indehiscent husk covered with sticky glandular hairs; ellipsoidal to obovoid, bluntly pointed; 5–8 cm long, 2.5–4 cm wide; seed sweet; maturing early August to early September; animal-dispersed. (*cinerea*: ashy gray, in reference to the bark)

Identification

Butternut is a medium to large tree with a slender trunk, relatively broad crown, and stout twigs. It is most similar to black walnut (*J. nigra*), but the two can be told apart by a number of characters, even in winter (see key). At a distance, butternut could also be mistaken for black ash (*Fraxinus nigra*), but butternut has alternate leaves (not just leaflets), and black ash has opposite.

Natural History

Until recently, butternut was a fairly common tree in mesic hardwood forests in southern Minnesota, but it never occurred as a dominant tree. It was usually seen as scattered individuals or in small groves, typically with oaks (*Quercus* spp.), black cherry (*Prunus serotina*), basswood (*Tilia americana*), sugar maple (*Acer saccharum*), or American elm (*Ulmus americana*). It seems to prefer loamy or alluvial soils or sandy soil if the water table is relatively near the surface. It was perhaps most common on elevated river terraces, although not on active floodplains where siltation and scouring occurred. Butternut is intolerant of shade, so it rarely reproduces in mature forests unless there is a substantial gap in the canopy to provide light for seedlings. The greatest recorded age of a butternut in Minnesota is 221 years (Hale 1996), which is probably near the maximum potential.

Butternut is very susceptible to butternut canker (*Sirococcus clavigignenti-juglandacearum* N.B. Nair, Kostichka & Kuntz), a lethal fungal disease of unknown origin. The disease was first reported in Wisconsin in 1967 (Renlund 1971) and reached southeastern Minnesota in the 1970s. It has since spread throughout the state and throughout the North American range of butternut. The fungus attacks the cambium, leaving a blackened elliptical area of dead cambium just beneath the bark (Ostry, Mielke, and Anderson 1996). When the number of cankers becomes too great, the branch or trunk becomes essentially girdled and dies. There is no known treatment or control, and few if any trees are immune. This tragic situation has progressed to the point where nearly all butternuts in Minnesota are now dead or dying.

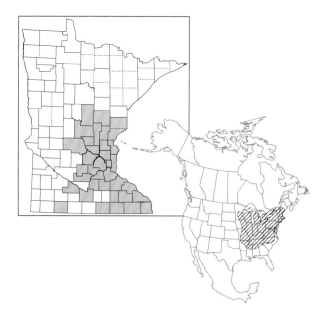

A single leaf with 13 sessile leaflets.

Female flowers are in a spike at tip of branch—May 24.

Male flowers are in a pendulous catkin—May 13.

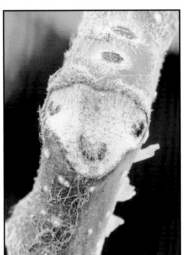

The top of the leaf scar is more or less straight (compare with black walnut).

Smooth-topped ridges are characteristic—this trunk is 11" (28 cm) dbh.

The fruits are 2–3" (5–8 cm) long, sticky to the touch—July 12.

Juglans nigra L.

Black walnut

Large **trees**, to 35 m tall and 100 cm dbh. First-year **branchlets** stout, greenish-brown, with glandular and nonglandular hairs; second-year branchlets brown or gray-brown, glabrate or sparsely glandular and hairy; pith tan colored, chambered; leaf scars V-shaped (the upper margin notched); terminal bud ovate, 5–8 mm long and nearly as wide (by August). **Bark** thick, gray to dark gray or gray-brown, developing coarse irregular ridges and deep furrows. **Leaves** pinnately compound, alternate, deciduous. **Petioles** 3–9 cm long, with glandular and often nonglandular hairs. **Leaflets** 12–18, ± sessile; terminal leaflet absent or poorly developed; ovate to lance-ovate or oblong-elliptical; 7–14 cm long, 3–6 cm wide; base rounded or nearly truncate, asymmetrical; apex acuminate; margins serrate; upper surface dark green, minutely glandular-hairy along the midvein; lower surface pale green, hairy along midvein and in axils of lateral veins. **Inflorescence** unisexual, with male flowers and female flowers borne separately on the same branchlet. **Male flowers** numerous, borne on slender pendulous catkins 4–10 cm long; catkins ± sessile, arising singly from leaf axils on branchlets of the previous year. **Female flowers** 1–4, borne on a short spike arising from the apex of branchlets of the current year; **anthesis** early May to early June; wind-pollinated. **Fruit** a nut enclosed in a thick, semifleshy, indehiscent husk; not glandular or sticky; ± spherical; 4.5–7 cm in diameter; seed sweet; maturing late August to late September; animal-dispersed. (*nigra*: black, in reference to the bark)

Identification

Black walnut is a large tree with a thick trunk and broad crown. It is most likely to be confused with butternut (*J. cinerea*); both have large compound leaves and a similar growth form, including characteristically stout twigs. They can be differentiated by the leaves or the fruit, and in winter by the bark or the leaf scars (see key).
Note: Since the earliest days of settlement, black walnut has been commonly planted somewhat north of its native range, both as a shade tree and for lumber. Although all of the mapped records represent wild populations, some of those north of the Minnesota River valley could be wild descendants of planted trees. Those south of the valley are undoubtedly native.

Natural History

Black walnut is widespread and locally common in southern Minnesota, especially in deep, well-drained, alluvial soils on slightly elevated floodplains. Common associates include American elm (*Ulmus americana*), rock elm (*U. thomasii*), hackberry (*Celtis occidentalis*), and green ash (*Fraxinus pennsylvanica*). It also occurs on forested slopes along streams and in a variety of other forest settings. In the best habitats it will grow rapidly and eventually reach a height of 100 ft (30 m) with a trunk diameter of 3 ft (91 cm). But because of their high timber value, tall, straight, forest-grown trees are seldom seen outside state parks or other protected areas.

In general, black walnut becomes established only where there are large openings in the forest canopy that allow direct sunlight to reach the forest floor. It rarely reproduces under a closed canopy because there is not enough sunlight for its seedlings to compete with seedlings of more shade-tolerant species. However, black walnut produces a water-soluble compound called juglone, which enters the soil through its roots, leaves, fruit, and bark and inhibits the growth of most other plant species, including the seedlings of other tree species (Lee and Campbell 1969). This phenomenon is called allelopathy; it is presumably a way to reduce competition.

The nut is enclosed in a thick, spherical husk—July 15.

Male catkins can reach 4" (10 cm) in length—May 23.

Note the pink stigmatic surface of the female flowers—May 24.

Dark gray and deeply furrowed bark—24" (61 cm) dbh.

The top of the leaf scar is notched.

Notice that the terminal leaflet does not develop.

Walnut

Juniperus, the junipers

Cupressaceae: Cypress family

The junipers comprise a genus of about 60 species of evergreen trees and shrubs, distributed widely in the Northern Hemisphere. Thirteen species occur in the United States, and 3 in Minnesota. (*Juniperus* is the classical Latin name for a species of juniper.)

Numerous cultivars of Old World junipers and of Rocky Mountain juniper (*J. scopulorum* Sarg.) are planted in Minnesota. Many are quite hardy here, even persisting long after cultivation, but none are known to be naturalized.

Key to the Genus Juniperus *in Minnesota*

1. Leaves in whorls of 3, sharp-pointed and needlelike, jointed at the base, not decurrent ....*J. communis* var. *depressa*
1. Leaves opposite (in 2s), usually scalelike (only juvenile leaves sharp-pointed and needlelike), not jointed at base, distinctly decurrent.
    2. Upright conical-shaped tree; peduncles straight; female cone ("berry") 3–6 mm across; seeds 1–2, occasionally 3 .... *J. virginiana*
    2. Low shrub with long prostrate branches rarely more than 25 cm tall; peduncles curved; female cone 5–8 mm across; seeds 3–5 .... *J. horizontalis*

Juniperus communis L. var. *depressa* Pursh

Common juniper

Midsize **shrubs**, lacking a main stem but with multiple decumbent, spreading, or ascending **branches** to 20 cm basal diameter, forming irregular circular patches up to 6 m across but rarely more than 1.5 m tall; branches occasionally layering, but clone formation rare. **Branchlets** yellowish green the 1st year, becoming orange-brown or reddish brown the 2nd year, glabrous. **Bark** thin, brown, flaking or peeling. **Leaves** in whorls of 3; evergreen, persisting about 4 years; linear-lanceolate to needlelike; divergent; 6–18 mm long, 1–1.8 mm wide; base jointed, not decurrent; apex sharply pointed; margins entire; upper surface uniformly green; lower surface green with a pale blue-glaucous longitudinal band. **Dioecious**, each shrub bearing either female cones (strobili) or male cones. Mature **male (pollen) cones** ellipsoidal to oblong; 2–3 mm long; composed of 6–12 cone scales, each bearing 3–5 pollen sacs; borne singly in leaf axils on 2nd-year branchlets; peduncles 0.5–1 mm long, with 4 scalelike leaves at base; releasing pollen early May to early June. Mature **female (seed) cones** irregularly spherical or broadly ellipsoidal; fleshy and berrylike; 6–10 mm in diameter; blue-green to blue-black, glaucous; borne singly on scaly peduncles about 1 mm long, from leaf axils on 2nd-year branchlets; maturing after 2 or 3 years but remaining closed; seeds 2–4 (usually 3); wind-pollinated, animal-dispersed. (*communis*: common; *depressa*: depressed, low-growing)

Identification

Common juniper, as it occurs in Minnesota, is a shrub with long branches that sweep along the ground and turn upwards at the tips. The branch tips can sometimes reach a height of 5 ft (1.5 m), but the shrub itself can be 20 ft (6 m) across; in all cases, it is wider than tall. The leaves are in whorls of 3 and have sharp points.
Note: Common juniper is the most widespread of the 60-or-so species of juniper, and is found across North America and Eurasia. It has 4 or 5 recognized varieties, but only the sprawling shrub variety (var. *depressa*) occurs in Minnesota. The typical variety (var. *communis*) is an erect tree found in Europe.

Natural History

Common juniper is not as common in Minnesota as its name might imply, nor is it rare. It can be found now and then in a variety of dry, open habitats such as sandy barrens, rocky slopes, bedrock outcrops, cliffs, and exposed ridgetops. It can also colonize abandoned fields, especially if the soil is sandy and well drained. It can even thrive in pastures, where cattle quickly learn to avoid it. But under normal conditions common juniper is not particularly invasive or aggressive.

Common juniper is somewhat tolerant of shade from deciduous trees, yet if overtopped, it will eventually lose vigor and decline. It is also sensitive to fire, and it will not resprout if top-killed. But the foliage does not ignite easily, and because the main branches are somewhat protected in the middle of the plant, large individuals often survive a typical grass fire.

Common juniper is very drought tolerant and also heat and cold tolerant, but not long-lived compared to eastern redcedar (*J. virginiana*). A maximum age of about 150 years has been reported (Marion and Houle 1996), but individuals more than 40 to 50 years old seem to be rare in Minnesota and are probably restricted to cliffs.

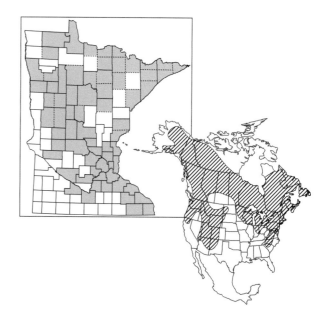

Characteristic growth form of common juniper in Minnesota—Anoka County.

These male strobili have just released their pollen—May 29.

Look in the leaf axils for the female strobili—May 29.

Bark is thin, brown, and flaky.

The berrylike seed cones ripen blackish after 2 or 3 years—September 4.

Juniperus horizontalis Moench

Creeping juniper

Low **shrubs**, with prostrate or decumbent stems and branches often several meters long, but rarely more than 25 cm tall and 2 cm diameter; forming clones by layering. **Branchlets** greenish the 1st year, becoming brown the 2nd year; glabrous; tightly clothed in overlapping scales for 2–5 years. **Bark** thin, brown to reddish brown; initially smooth but eventually flaking or peeling. **Leaves** opposite; evergreen, persisting 4–5 years; of two types: **juvenile leaves** as found on seedlings and vigorous shoots of mature plants subulate to needlelike; divergent; 3–6.5 mm long, 0.5–1 mm wide; base decurrent, not jointed; apex sharply pointed; margins entire; **adult leaves** ovate, scalelike; tightly appressed, crowded and overlapping; 1–3 mm long, 0.5–1.5 mm wide; base decurrent; apex acute; margins entire. **Dioecious**, each shrub bearing either female cones (strobili) or male cones. Mature **male (pollen) cones** ellipsoidal to oblong; 2.5–3.5 mm long; composed of 6–10 cone scales, each bearing 3–4 pollen sacs; borne singly at the tips of 2nd-year branchlets; sessile; releasing pollen late April to late May. Mature **female (seed) cones** irregularly spherical; fleshy and berrylike; 5–8 mm in diameter; bluish to blue-black, glaucous; containing 3–5 seeds; borne singly on curved, scaly peduncles 2–4 mm long, from 2nd-year branchlets; maturing the 2nd year but remaining closed; wind-pollinated, animal-dispersed. (*horizontalis*: lying flat, in reference to the growth form)

Identification

Creeping juniper is a low-growing groundcover with long, slender branches that hug the ground. New branchlets grow erect but are rarely more than 5–10 inches (15–25 cm) in height. In many ways it is a prostrate version of eastern redcedar (*J. virginiana*). In fact, the only reliable character that distinguishes the two species is growth form. Common juniper (*J. communis* var. *depressa*) is also a shrub, but it will usually be at least 3 ft (1 m) tall with upswept branch tips. The female cones of all junipers resemble small fleshy berries.

Natural History

In spite of being geographically widespread in Minnesota, creeping juniper is quite uncommon. Furthermore, it is invariably localized in small,

discontinuous habitats, typically sand dunes, sand barrens, and bedrock outcrops.

The long, prostrate branches lay directly on the ground, and if the conditions are right, they can send down new roots anywhere along their length. In this way they can enhance their water-collecting capacity and establish large clones that are better able to resist damage or injury. In fact, a single clone can form a dense carpet 60 ft (20 m) or more across. In favorable habitats the individual branches can grow relatively fast yet may live only 10–15 years. However, an entire interconnected clone can live much longer.

Creeping juniper requires direct sunlight at all stages of development and is easily shaded out by trees, other shrubs, and even tall grasses. It is also easily killed by ground fires and does not resprout. On the presettlement landscape it probably survived only in habitats where fuels were too light to carry a fire, or where there was some naturally occurring firebreak. Paradoxically, the suppression of wildfires that has accompanied settlement has not favored creeping juniper. Without fire, the previously open dunes and outcrops have become overgrown by trembling aspen (*Populus tremuloides*), eastern redcedar (*J. virginiana*), and various shrubs, or they have been deliberately planted with nonnative conifers. This has effectively crowded creeping juniper out of its native habitats, and unlike the other native junipers, it does not readily colonize human-created habitats.

Female strobili at time of pollination are tiny and rarely noticed—May 5.

Male strobili are at the tips of second-year branchlets—May 5.

Seed cones are the female strobili at maturity—August 24.

Creeping juniper forms a matlike groundcover—Polk County.

Juniperus virginiana L.

Eastern redcedar, red juniper

Midsize **trees**, with single upright stems to 19 m tall and 51 cm dbh. **Branchlets** greenish or yellow-green the 1st year, becoming brown the 2nd, glabrous; tightly clothed in overlapping scales for 2–4 years. **Bark** thin, brown, peeling lengthwise into long, narrow, fibrous strips. **Leaves** opposite; evergreen, persisting 4–6 years; of two different types: **juvenile leaves** subulate to needlelike; divergent; 4–9 mm long, 0.5–1 mm wide; base decurrent, not jointed; apex sharply pointed; margins entire; found on young trees and occasionally on vigorous shoots of older trees; **adult leaves** ovate, scalelike; tightly appressed, crowded and overlapping; 1–3 mm long, 0.5–1.5 mm wide; base decurrent; apex acute; margins entire. **Dioecious**, each tree bearing either female cones (strobili) or male cones. Mature **male (pollen) cones** oblong-cylindrical; 2–4 mm long; composed of 6–12 cone scales, each bearing 4–5 pollen sacs; borne singly at the tips of 2nd-year branchlets; peduncles 0.5–1 mm long, naked; releasing pollen late April to late May. Mature **female (seed) cones** irregularly spherical; fleshy and berrylike; 3–6 mm in diameter; blue-glaucous; containing 1–2 or occasionally 3 seeds; borne singly on straight scaly peduncles 1–5 mm long, from 2nd-year branchlets; maturing in autumn of the 1st year but often held on the tree a 2nd year; remaining closed; wind-pollinated, animal-dispersed. (*virginiana*: of Virginia)

Identification

Eastern redcedar is a small to midsize evergreen tree with a conical or pyramidal crown. The form and general aspect of this tree are distinctive and once learned, make recognition fairly simple. The foliage is green in summer but turns dark maroon or bronze in winter. Also, it is useful to know that the bluish "berries" that are so conspicuous in summer are actually cones (strobili) like those of other conifers, except they never open.

Natural History

Eastern redcedar is fairly common in southern Minnesota, especially in the southeast. It is a relatively small tree in this region, seldom more than about 50 ft (14 m) tall, but in the southern states it is reported to reach 120 ft (37 m) (Harlow et al. 1991). It is widely known for its aromatic, decay-resistant wood and for its extreme tolerance of drought. It is also known for its longevity, with reported ages of 475 years in Virginia (Larson 1997) and 369 years in Iowa (Anderson 1944). In Minnesota, it is found most commonly in dry, sterile, sandy or rocky soil, usually in the range of weakly acidic to moderately basic (calcareous).

In presettlement times it was probably restricted to sparsely vegetated marginal habitats like rock outcrops, cliffs, steep eroding banks, and the margins of bluff prairies. On more fertile sites it would have been outcompeted by hardwoods, and on prairies it would have been kept in check by wildfires. But settlement, and particularly agriculture, opened new habitats for eastern redcedar. It is able to invade old fields and abandoned or intermittent pastures, even where there is dense sod. Cattle avoid it at all costs, often allowing it to become unnaturally abundant in pastures, sometimes to the point of forming impenetrable thickets.

Eastern redcedar is considered fire sensitive; it has thin bark and does not resprout if the stem is killed. But a lack of fuel beneath the tree prevents most grass fires from reaching the trunk, so large trees often survive fire. Also, the foliage is notoriously slow to ignite, yet if ignited, the resins and volatile oils burn explosively.

Mature male strobili are only about 1/8" (2–4 mm) long—May 8.

Seed cones ripen blue their first autumn—August 16.

Female strobili at peak of receptivity—May 3.

Fibrous strips loosen from outer bark—14" (36 cm) dbh.

Junipers

Kalmia, bog laurel

Ericaceae: Heath family

Kalmia is a small North American genus of about 7 species of evergreen and deciduous shrubs and small trees. A single species occurs in Minnesota. (*Kalmia* is named for the botanical explorer Pehr Kalm, 1716–79.)

Kalmia polifolia Wang.

Bog laurel

Low or midsize **shrubs**, with single or multiple upright, ascending or somewhat decumbent **stems** to 70 cm tall. **Branchlets** flattened (2-angled); the nodes enlarged or at least prominent; minutely hairy, becoming glabrous by the 2nd year. **Bark** shedding a thin, gray epidermal layer to expose a smooth, reddish brown surface. **Leaves** simple, opposite or in whorls of 3; evergreen, persisting until the 2nd year. **Petioles** 2–3 mm long or more often indistinct. **Leaf blades** lanceolate to linear or narrowly oblong; 1.5–4 cm long, 4–12 mm wide, length/width 3–8; apex tapered; base tapered or rounded; margins entire, revolute; upper surface dark green, shiny, glabrous or minutely hairy along midvein; lower surface pale green or whitish, dull, densely and minutely hairy, often with glands on midvein. **Flowers** bisexual, 5-merous, pink to rose-purple or occasionally white; borne singly from the axils of the reduced upper leaves and forming a loose terminal cluster; pedicels 1.5–3.5 cm long, glabrous; sepals 2–3 mm long, ovate, with a conspicuous ring at base; corolla saucer-shaped, 9–16 mm across; stamens 10, 3–5 mm long; style 5–7 mm long; **anthesis** late mid-May to mid-June; insect-pollinated. **Fruit** a spherical, 5-valved capsule; 4–6 mm in diameter; maturing late mid-June to mid-July. **Seeds** numerous; whitish; about 2 mm long; linear; wind- and gravity-dispersed. (*polifolia*: with leaves like *Polium*, a genus in the family Lamiaceae)

Identification

Bog laurel is a knee-high bog shrub with thick, leathery, evergreen leaves and bright, purplish flowers. Wherever bog laurel is found there will likely be bog rosemary (*Andromeda glaucophylla*), Labrador tea (*Rhododendron groenlandicum*), and leatherleaf (*Chamaedaphne calyculata*). All are evergreen bog shrubs and will look somewhat alike. But in bog laurel the leaves are opposite rather than alternate, and each young twig is more or less flat, which makes it difficult or impossible to roll it between your fingers. Furthermore, at each internode the twig is flattened at an angle perpendicular to the section of twig in the previous internode, and the nodes themselves are somewhat enlarged and prominent.

Natural History

Bog laurel is common in a variety of acidic peatland habitats, principally poor fens, bogs, and muskeg.

These are boreal-type habitats that typically have carpets or hummocks of *Sphagnum* moss and often scattered tamarack (*Larix laricina*) or stunted black spruce (*Picea mariana*). As might be expected, bog laurel roots in the saturated peat below the living moss, yet in some cases the stem becomes nearly buried by the faster-growing moss, leaving only the tops exposed. Rather than being smothered, the buried portions respond by producing adventitious roots within the layer of living moss, turning a plight into an advantage.

Bog laurel is unusually sensitive to disturbances in its habitat, especially fire, drought, and nonseasonal flooding. It can also be crowded out by taller shrubs or encroaching trees, and it shows only a limited ability to colonize new habitats. Because of these sensitivities, the presence of bog laurel is usually a good indicator of a mature, stable habitat.

Pollination in the genus *Kalmia* is unusual, possibly unique, and worth a short description. In the flower bud the 10 anthers are pushed upwards by the growth of the filaments into corresponding pockets on the inside of the petals. As the petals open and expand, the anthers are held in the pockets, and the filaments are bent backward under tension. When a pollinator (usually a bee) lands on the corolla, one or more of the anthers are pulled from their pockets, and the filament suddenly snaps upwards, showering the insect with a cloud of pollen (Lovell and Lovell 1934).

Bog laurel in flower is hard to miss—June 6.

Each flower has 10 stamens and 1 style—June 6.

Leaves are dark green, and opposite each other on the stem.

Small, whitish seeds develop within each 5-valved capsule.

Bog laurel 🍃 257

Larix, tamarack

Pinaceae: Pine family

This genus contains about 10 species of deciduous trees, widely distributed in boreal and cold temperate regions of North America and Eurasia. Three species occur in the United States, and 1 in Minnesota. (*Larix* is the classical name for the European species.)

European larch (*L. decidua* P. Mill.) is sometimes planted in Minnesota as an ornamental. It is an upland species that differs from the native tamarack by having somewhat longer leaves and larger cones. It is said to occasionally escape cultivation, at least in the eastern part of the country.

Larix laricina (Du Roi) K. Koch

Tamarack

Midsize or rarely large **trees**, to 26 m tall and 84 cm dbh. **Branchlets** brown, glabrous. **Bark** relatively thin, orange-brown to brown or grayish; with rough, flaky scales. **Leaves** soft, needle-shaped; those on long shoots borne singly, those on short shoots (spurs) borne in tufts of 15–35; deciduous, turning yellow and falling each autumn; slender, straight, ± flat, with a prominent keel on the lower surface; 1.2–3 cm long, 0.3–0.6 mm wide; apex tapered or blunt; margins entire. **Monoecious**, with male cones (strobili) and female cones separate but on the same tree. Mature **male (pollen) cones** subglobose, 3–4 mm long; terminal on short shoots (spurs); pollen shed late April to late May. Mature **female (seed) cones** erect, subglobose to ovoid; 1–2 cm long; on a short, curved peduncle; borne from short shoots (spurs) on 1–4-year-old branchlets; maturing and shedding seeds late August to early October of the 1st year and persisting on the tree for another year or more; wind-pollinated. **Seeds** 2–3 mm long, with a broad, papery wing 4–6 mm long; wind- and gravity-dispersed. (*laricina*: larchlike; originally considered a pine)

Identification

Tamarack is a slender, midsize tree with relatively short, horizontal branches and a conical crown. The soft, needle-shaped leaves occur in tufts of 15 to 35. The needles of balsam fir (*Abies balsamea*) and the spruces (*Picea* spp.) are single, and those of pines (*Pinus* spp.) are in bundles of 2 or 5. The leaves of tamarack turn yellow and drop each autumn, making it the only deciduous conifer in Minnesota. In winter it is sometimes mistaken for a dead spruce.

Natural History

Tamarack is a common tree throughout most of its range in Minnesota, especially northward. It sometimes occurs in uplands but primarily in acidic, nutrient-poor wetlands, such as peat-filled basins, peaty lakeshores, and boggy stream margins. It often forms pure stands, or in the north it may be mixed with black spruce (*Picea mariana*), northern white cedar (*Thuja occidentalis*), or balsam fir (*Abies balsamea*). In the central and southern counties it is more likely to be found with hardwoods such as paper birch (*Betula papyrifera*), red maple (*Acer rubrum*), or black ash (*Fraxinus nigra*). Because it

cannot tolerate shade, it is never found in a forest understory, always in the overstory or scattered in the open.

Tamarack is reported to survive temperature extremes from −79°F to over 100°F (−63°C to 38°C) (Roe 1957) and live to an age of 335 years (Harlow et al. 1991). But it is vulnerable to prolonged flooding and is easily damaged by fire. Still, tamarack colonizes well after a fire, although it does not require large-scale disturbance to become established, even in stable habitats. In fact, it is usually the first tree to colonize sedge- or moss-dominated peatlands, generally preceding black spruce (Heinselman 1970).

Bearing tree data collected during the public land surveys in the latter half of the nineteenth century indicates that tamarack was the most abundant tree in Minnesota at the time of settlement, followed by trembling aspen (*Populus tremuloides*), bur oak (*Quercus macrocarpa*), and paper birch (*Betula papyrifera*); black spruce was fifth (U.S. Surveyor General 1847–1908). Since then, tamarack has declined dramatically, especially on upland sites. However, black spruce has increased, both in absolute and relative terms, and is now more abundant than tamarack. The cause of this reversal is not clear, but it is probably a combination of logging, fire suppression, and severe outbreaks of larch sawfly (*Pristiphora erichsonii* [Hartig]).

Female strobili showing red-tipped scales—June 9, Lake County.

Bark is covered with rough, flaky scales—7" (17 cm) dbh.

Seed cones are only about 1/2" (1–2 cm) long—August 18.

A pure stand of tamarack from Anoka County.

The male strobili sit atop short spurs—May 10, Anoka County.

Tamarack 🍂 **261**

Linnaea, twinflower

Caprifoliaceae: Honeysuckle family

This genus consists of a single polymorphic species, *Linnaea borealis*, which occurs in a nearly continuous band through the northern parts of Europe, Asia, and North America (circumboreal). Within this range, there is considerable variation in the leaves and flowers, much of which is geographically correlated. On this basis, the species has been split into three subspecies (Hultén 1968). The entity that occurs in Minnesota and across the northern part of North American is called subsp. *americana* (Forbes) Hult. ex Clausen (*Linnaea* is named for the Swedish naturalist Carolus Linnaeus, 1707–78.)

Linnaea borealis L. subsp. *americana* (Forbes) Hult. *ex* Clausen

Twinflower

[*L. americana* Forbes]

Dwarf vinelike **shrubs**, with slender creeping **stems** to 2+ m long and 0.5–2 mm diameter; rooting at the nodes. Stems and **branches** wiry, reddish brown, hairy. **Leaves** simple, opposite, evergreen, persisting about 2 years. **Petioles** 2–5 mm long, hairy. **Leaf blades** ovate to obovate or broadly elliptical to circular; 9–18 mm long, 7–15 mm wide; base contracted to the petiole and usually somewhat decurrent; apex blunt to rounded; margins with 1–4 broad, rounded teeth per side, or smaller leaves often entire; upper surface dark green, sparsely hairy especially near margins; lower surface pale green, glabrous or with a few scattered hairs. **Inflorescence** borne singly from the tips of short, erect, leafy branches; peduncle glandular-hairy, 3.5–8 cm long, forked near summit with each branch (pedicel) bearing a single nodding flower. **Flowers** bisexual, whitish to pink or purple; calyx 2–3 mm long, 5-lobed, glandular-hairy; corolla funnel-shaped, 8–12 mm long, shallowly 5-lobed, the outer surface glabrous, the inner surface hairy; stamens 4, included; style 1, exserted; **anthesis** early mid-June to early August; insect-pollinated. **Fruit** a small, dry, indehiscent capsule about 2 mm long, enclosed by two densely glandular bractlets; containing a single seed; ripening mid-July to late August; animal-dispersed. (*borealis*: northern; *americana*: of America)

Identification

Twinflower is a dwarf, evergreen shrub with slender, vinelike stems that creep along the ground. The upright branches are only a few inches high and produce a pair of nodding pink flowers that are held well above the leaves. The leaves are small, roundish, and opposite each other on the stem. The creeping stems and opposite leaves resemble those of partridgeberry (*Mitchella repens*), except each leaf has a shallow tooth near the summit. Snowberry (*Gaultheria hispidula*) and large cranberry (*Oxycoccus macrocarpus*) also have creeping stems, but their leaves are alternate.

Natural History

Twinflower is fairly common in the ground layer of a variety of northern forest types. This includes cool, mossy, conifer swamps as well as uplands and mixed hardwood-conifer forests. It typically roots in peat, humus, or decomposing woody material but also on mossy boulders, decaying stumps, and talus. The solitary occurrence in southern Minnesota is from an algific talus slope, which is a unique refuge for northern species that exists only on the Paleozoic Plateau.

The main stems, which can eventually reach lengths of 6 ft (2 m) or more, creep along the ground, rooting at the nodes. Every few inches the stems will produce a leafy upright branch that rises 4–5 inches (10–12 cm) and bears the flowers. If the main stems survive undisturbed for about 10 years, they will begin to decay and break apart, but the fragments are fully rooted by that time and can survive to grow new stems (Eriksson 1992). This is a form of asexual or clonal reproduction, and since seedling establishment is reportedly low (Eriksson 1992), this type of reproduction may be essential to maintain populations.

Twinflower is very sensitive to ground fire because it roots in the organic layer of the soil, which may be entirely consumed by a hot fire. If burned out of a habitat, it will slowly recolonize, presumably by seeds carried on the fur of small mammals. The process has never been documented but must be quite effective since twinflower is fairly common and widespread in fire-prone landscapes.

Pairs of nodding flowers are held well above the leaves—June 25.

The fruits are covered with sticky hairs.

Twinflower often forms dense patches; use bunchberries in background for scale—July 6.

Lonicera, the honeysuckles

Caprifoliaceae: Honeysuckle family

The honeysuckles comprise a genus of about 180 species of shrubs, climbing vines, and small trees. They are deciduous or rarely evergreen and are found in temperate and tropical regions throughout the Northern Hemisphere. In the United States there are about 17 native species and numerous naturalized species. Minnesota has 6 native and 3 naturalized species. (*Lonicera* is in honor of Johann Lonitzer, 1499–1569.)

The three naturalized honeysuckles were introduced from Asia, with good intentions, for use in landscaping. Ironically, they have also been used for "conservation" purposes such as wildlife cover and "living snow fences." Unfortunately, they have escaped into the wild, where they reproduce unimpeded by any natural biological controls and have proven disastrous for conservation. They are displacing native species and causing significant damage to the integrity of certain native ecosystems, especially oak ecosystems in central and southern Minnesota.

Amur honeysuckle [*L. maackii* (Rupr.) Herder] is another Asian shrub that was introduced into eastern North America for horticultural purposes. It has since spread aggressively throughout much of the East, having now reached parts of Wisconsin and Iowa (Luken and Thieret 1995). There seem to be few if any ecological barriers to prevent it from reaching Minnesota.

Key to the Genus Lonicera in Minnesota

1. A climbing or scrambling vine; twigs hollow with a white pith; the leaves just below the flowers fused at their base to form a single perfoliate disk-shaped leaf; flowers in whorls of 6, with 1–5 whorls on each of 1–3 terminal spikes arising from the center of the uppermost leaf.
    2. Margins of leaf blades with long cilia (0.5–1 mm long); 1st-year branchlets hairy .... *L. hirsuta*
    2. Margins of leaf blades sometimes hairy but not ciliate; branchlets glabrous.
        3. Anthers 3.8–4.8 mm long; leaf blades nearly circular in outline; upper surface of perfoliate leaves often blue-glaucous, at least near the center of the disk .... *L. reticulata*
        3. Anthers 2.5–3.5 mm long; leaf blades distinctly longer than wide; upper surface of perfoliate leaves not blue-glaucous .... *L. dioica*
1. An upright shrub; twigs hollow with a brown pith, or solid with a white pith; leaves not fused or perfoliate; flowers in pairs from the axils of ordinary leaves.
    4. Twigs solid, pith white; native shrubs.
        5. Leaf blades widest below the middle, glabrous on the upper surface; corolla tube 1–1.6 cm long, entire corolla (tube + lobes) 1.5–2.2 cm long. .... *L. canadensis*
        5. Leaf blades widest at or above the middle, hairy on the upper surface; corolla tube 0.2–0.6 cm long, entire corolla 0.6–1.4 cm long.
            6. Lower surface of leaf blade covered with a tangled mat of soft wavy hairs 0.1–0.4 mm long; leaf margin similarly hairy but not ciliate; peduncles erect or ascending, 1.5–2.5 cm long; corolla lobes strongly reflexed and longer than the tube; style hairy; floral bracts not apparent .... *L. oblongifolia*
            6. Lower surface of leaf blade with ± straight, stiff hairs 0.5–1 mm long; leaf margin with relatively long, stiff cilia; peduncles arching or drooping, 0.5–1.5 cm long; corolla lobes flared but not reflexed, shorter than the tube; style glabrous; floral bracts linear, 3–7 mm long .... *L. villosa*
    4. Twigs hollow, pith brown; nonnative shrubs frequently naturalized.
        7. Entire plant glabrous except for margins of leaf blades; bractlets at anthesis no more than half as long as the ovaries they subtend .... *L. tatarica*
        7. Entire plant ± hairy, particularly the lower leaf surface, petiole, peduncles, and 1st-year branchlets; bractlets at anthesis at least half as long as the ovaries they subtend.
            8. Leaves and peduncles moderately to densely hairy .... *L. morrowii*
            8. Leaves (at least the upper surface of the blade) and peduncles only sparsely hairy or glabrate .... *L. ×bella*

Lonicera ×*bella* Zabel

Bella honeysuckle

Nonnative, naturalized, tall **shrubs,** with single or multiple upright, ascending or arching **stems** to 4 m tall and 6 cm basal diameter. 1st-year **branchlets** green to brown, hairy or occasionally glabrate; 2nd-year branchlets brown to gray, glabrous or glabrate; pith brown, hollow. **Bark** thin, brown to gray, rough, often shredding or peeling. **Leaves** simple, opposite, deciduous. **Petioles** 2–6 mm long, hairy. **Leaf blades** ovate to lance-ovate or lance-oblong; the larger ones 3–5.5 cm long and 1.5–3 cm wide; apex acutely to obtusely tapered or occasionally rounded; base truncate to rounded or shallowly cordate; margins entire, hairy or sometimes ciliate; upper surface dark green, sparsely hairy to glabrate; lower surface pale green, hairy to sparsely hairy. **Flowers** bisexual, 5-merous, in close sessile pairs on peduncles that arise singly from leaf axils on 1st-year branchlets; peduncles 0.8–2 cm long, sparsely hairy to glabrate; floral bracts linear, 2–5 mm long at anthesis; bractlets oblong, 0.7–1.3 mm long, half to two-thirds as long at anthesis as the ovary they subtend; calyx 0.6–1 mm long; corolla funnel-shaped, white to pink, fading to yellow in age, 1.2–2.2 cm long, the lobes longer than the tube; **anthesis** early mid-May to early June; insect- and hummingbird-pollinated. **Fruit** a depressed-spherical berry; shiny or translucent; orange to red; 6–8 mm in diameter; maturing mid-June to mid-July; animal-dispersed. (×: denotes hybrid; *bella*: beautiful)

Identification

Bella honeysuckle is a large, dense shrub often over 6 ft (2 m) tall, with long, arching branches and stiff, slender twigs. It is the artificial hybrid of Tartarian honeysuckle (*L. tatarica*) and Morrow's honeysuckle (*L. morrowii*). Tartarian honeysuckle is hairless except for the leaf margins, and Morrow's honeysuckle is consistently and evenly hairy throughout. As might be expected, bella honeysuckle is more or less intermediate in hairiness. The actual pattern and abundance of hairs is variable, but at least the lower surface of the leaves and the flower stalks will have some hairs.

Natural History

Bella honeysuckle is the fertile hybrid between the Eurasian Tartarian honeysuckle (*L. tatarica*) and the Japanese Morrow's honeysuckle (*L. morrowii*) (Green 1966). It was created in cultivation for the horticultural trade, and like its parent species, has been widely planted in North America, including Minnesota. It has since escaped cultivation and spread aggressively to a variety of natural and seminatural habitats, including grasslands, woodlands, and thickets. It appears to be even more invasive than either of the parent species (Barnes and Cottam 1974).

Feral populations are now ubiquitous in southern and central Minnesota, with isolated colonies in the north. It is extremely invasive, and without natural predators it continues to expand and move into new habitats. In the process it easily displaces native species and disrupts ecological processes. Large infestations can create dense thickets several acres in size, which can seriously impede the reproduction of native forest trees, especially oaks, which need sunlight for their seedlings. The overall effect is to reduce biological diversity and alter the natural succession and regeneration of native forests and woodlands.

Control, much less eradication, is very difficult. However, the combined use of cutting and the careful application of an herbicide to the cut stumps has been used successfully on a limited scale; unfortunately it is impractical on a large scale. Also, the seeds are spread in the droppings of birds, so reinfestation is always a concern. Since it has proven to be a serious and persistent ecological pest, bella honeysuckle, like the other nonnative honeysuckles, should not be planted.

Flowers can be white or pink, and may fade to yellow—June 12.

Bark is thin, and brown or gray; wood is very hard.

Fruit is a red or orange berry 1/4" (6–8 mm) across—July 26.

A typical edge-grown specimen from Washington County—May 27.

Honeysuckles   **269**

Lonicera canadensis Marsh.

Fly honeysuckle

Midsize **shrubs,** with single or multiple upright or sprawling **stems** to 2 m tall and 2 cm basal diameter, clonal by layering. **Branchlets** glabrous, greenish to purplish the 1st year, becoming brown or gray the 2nd year; pith white, solid. **Bark** brown to gray, rough, often peeling or shredding in fibrous strips. **Leaves** simple, opposite, deciduous. **Petioles** 3–6 mm long, ciliate. **Leaf blades** ovate to lance-ovate or nearly elliptical; the larger ones 4.5–9 cm long and 2.5–5 cm wide; apex acute or blunt; base rounded to nearly truncate or shallowly cordate; margins entire, ciliate; upper surface dark green, glabrous; lower surface somewhat paler than upper, glabrous or sparsely hairy. **Flowers** bisexual, 5-merous; in sessile pairs on peduncles that arise singly from leaf axils on 1st-year branchlets; peduncles glabrous, 1–2 cm long; floral bracts lanceolate, 1.5–4.5 mm long; bractlets oblong, 0.1–1 mm long; calyx 0.2–0.6 mm long; corolla funnel-shaped, pale yellow to greenish yellow, 1.5–2.2 cm long, the tube longer than the lobes; **anthesis** early May to early mid-June; insect- and hummingbird-pollinated. **Fruit** a red, ovoid berry; 6–11 mm long; maturing early mid-June to early August; animal-dispersed. (*canadensis*: of Canada)

Identification

Fly honeysuckle is a medium-size forest shrub about waist or shoulder high. The leaves are opposite on the twig and have ciliate margins. The growth form is irregular: most often erect or semierect but sometimes sprawling or almost vinelike. It typically has only a few, thin branches, which gives the whole plant a rather sparse, open look. The pale yellow flowers appear in spring just as the leaves are expanding, and the bright red berries ripen by midsummer.

Natural History

Fly honeysuckle is nearly ubiquitous in forests throughout its range in Minnesota. It is most common in mesic or dry-mesic forests with either hardwoods or conifers. Soils are typically acidic, usually sandy or loamy, and often rocky. It also occurs, but somewhat less commonly, in lowland forests and swamp forests, where it may grow in moist or wet peat.

Fly honeysuckle is very tolerant of shade; it seems to have no difficulty flowering and setting seed in a closed-canopy forest. And yet under stable conditions most reproduction is vegetative (clonal), accomplished by a process called layering. This happens when a lower branch comes into contact with the soil and takes root. This new root crown may then send up vertical shoots. It is usually possible to find these rooted branches lying on the soil just beneath the leaf litter, often connecting two or more otherwise separate-looking shrubs. In this way, fly honeysuckle can form loose colonies sometimes several meters across that are, or were at one time, connected just beneath the surface.

Fly honeysuckle is considered fire adapted because it will resprout after a relatively cool fire, but the shallow roots and layered branches are killed by a hot ground fire (Ahlgren 1959). If it has been "burned out" of an area, it will eventually recolonize by seeds carried in the droppings of birds, just as the forest itself will regenerate. But it is not an aggressive colonizer, so it may take decades for large colonies to become reestablished.

Bark is gray or brown, often peeling or shredding.

Fruits are in pairs and never quite round—July 8.

A typical specimen will stand about 3' (1 m) tall.

Flowers are funnel-shaped and hang downward—May 9.

Lonicera dioica L.

Wild honeysuckle

Climbing **vines** or nearly self-supporting **shrubs**, with weakly twining, scrambling, or arching **stems** to 3.5 m tall and 2 cm diameter; clonal by layering. 1st-year **branchlets** glabrous, greenish; 2nd-year branchlets gray or brown; pith white, hollow. **Bark** gray or brown, peeling or shredding in long fibrous strips. **Leaves** simple, opposite, deciduous. **Petioles** lacking or to 1 cm long, often hairy. **Leaf blades** of two types: normal stem leaves oblong, elliptical, or obovate; the larger ones 5–9 cm long and 3–7 cm wide; apex rounded or blunt; base tapered or rounded; the uppermost 1–3 pairs of leaves on flowering branchlets fused at the base to form a single perfoliate leaf, usually rhombic or elliptical-oblong with tapered apices; margins of all leaves entire, lacking cilia; upper surface dark green, essentially glabrous; lower surface pale green or blue-glaucous, moderately to densely hairy, or occasionally glabrous. **Flowers** bisexual, 5-merous; in sessile whorls of 6, with 1–5 whorls aggregated on 1 (rarely 3) terminal spike; peduncles glabrous, 0.3–1.5 cm long, arising from the center of the uppermost perfoliate leaf; floral bracts 0.5–2 mm long; calyx less than 1 mm long; corolla tubular, purplish or rarely yellow, 1.5–2.5 cm long, the tube slightly longer than the lobes; **anthesis** early mid-May to early July; insect- and hummingbird-pollinated. **Fruit** an orange-red, spherical berry; 8–12 mm in diameter; maturing late June to early August; animal-dispersed. (*dioica*: dioecious)

Identification

Wild honeysuckle is a climbing or sprawling vine, or sometimes a rather formless, mounded shrub. It usually has dark purple flowers but sometimes yellow. The pair of leaves just below the flowers is fused at the base to form a single, disklike leaf with the stem in the center. In Minnesota, this particular feature is shared only with hairy honeysuckle (*L. hirsuta*) and grape honeysuckle (*L. reticulata*).
Note: The leaves are typically hairy on the underside, but occasionally glabrous specimens are found. These have been named *L. dioica* L. var. *glaucescens* (Rydb.) Butters.

Natural History

Wild honeysuckle is a fairly common vine, although it never seems to grow in great abundance. It can be considered a habitat generalist or an opportunist, taking advantage of any opening it can find. This includes forest edges, brushy thickets, rocky lakeshores, riverbanks, eroding slopes, and bluffs—anywhere it can get at least partial sunlight. Forest interiors seem to barely suffice; there is so little sunlight that stems may grow only 3 ft (1 m) long and produce just a few pairs of leaves and no flowers. Under more favorable conditions it can grow to perhaps 12 ft (3.5 m) in length and produce abundant flowers.

The stems and branches typically scramble over vegetation but not aggressively and not to the detriment of the supporting plants. Occasionally it will twine tightly on stems of shrubs or saplings that are 1–3 inches (2–8 cm) in diameter. Yet honeysuckle vines are short-lived; they generally die and fall away before the constricting vine can cause serious damage to its host.

The seeds of wild honeysuckle are carried in the droppings of birds, which is how it colonizes new habitats. But established plants generally maintain their presence, and spread short distances, by layering of stems and lower branches, which root upon contact with the soil. This will sometimes produce loose colonies but not dense thickets.

Flowers are usually purple, sometimes yellow—May 28.

Fruits ripen red—July 14.

Leaves on nonflowering stems are usually elliptical.

Wild honeysuckle climbing a black ash sapling—Pine County.

Lonicera hirsuta Eat.

Hairy honeysuckle

Climbing **vines**, with twining or scrambling **stems** to 5 m tall and 1 cm diameter; clonal by layering. 1st-year **branchlets** greenish, with gland-tipped and/or non–gland-tipped hairs; 2nd-year branchlets gray or brown, glabrate; pith white, hollow. **Bark** brown or gray-brown, eventually peeling in long fibrous strips. **Leaves** simple, opposite, deciduous. **Petioles** lacking, or to 1 cm long, hairy. **Leaf blades** of two types: normal stem leaves broadly elliptical to suborbicular, the larger ones 5.5–13 cm long and 3.5–7.5 cm wide; apex rounded or tapered; base rounded or tapered; the uppermost pair of leaves on flowering branchlets fused at base to form a single perfoliate leaf, usually rhombic or elliptical; margins of all leaves entire, long-ciliate; upper surface dark green, sparsely hairy to glabrate; lower surface pale green, moderately to densely hairy. **Flowers** bisexual, 5-merous; in sessile whorls of 6, with 1–5 whorls aggregated on each of 1–3 terminal spikes; peduncles glandular, 0.7–2 cm long, arising from the center of the uppermost perfoliate leaf; floral bracts 1–3 mm long; calyx less than 1 mm long; corolla tubular, yellow, 1.8–3 cm long, the tube longer than the lobes; **anthesis** mid-June to mid-July; insect- and hummingbird-pollinated. **Fruit** an orange-red, spherical berry; 8–13 mm in diameter; maturing late July to mid-September; animal-dispersed. (*hirsuta*: covered with coarse, stiff hairs)

Identification

Hairy honeysuckle is a climbing or scrambling vine with soft, velvety leaves and tubular, yellow flowers. The pair of leaves just below the flowers is fused at the base to form a single disklike leaf with the stem in the center. This is one of three native honeysuckle vines in Minnesota. All have the peculiar disklike leaves, but only hairy honeysuckle has cilia on the leaf margins.

Natural History

Hairy honeysuckle is fairly common within its geographic range, occurring with about equal frequency in upland forests and swamp forests, associated with either hardwoods or conifers. Although common, it is not usually abundant, and it rarely becomes prominent in any natural community. It is moderately tolerant of shade yet manages only minimal stem growth in deep shade. It grows larger and flowers more abundantly with increased sunlight, such as along a forest edge or under a canopy gap. In this way, it functions more as an opportunist, exploiting small patches of available habitat. It also seems to be somewhat transient; it grows rapidly but does not usually persist long in any one place.

Hairy honeysuckle can twine tightly on small diameter stems or branches, allowing it to climb to a height of at least 16 ft (5 m). Yet it is more often seen sprawling passively on shrubs or trailing along the ground. When trailing, it will root where the stem contacts the ground, especially in wetlands, and sends up new aerial shoots from the nodes. In this way, it will sometimes form loose colonies several meters across. It occurs mostly in fire-prone landscapes, and it will resprout after a "cool" fire, although its shallow roots and layered stems are killed by intense fires.

The long floral tube is designed for hummingbirds—July 18.

Mature fruit is a spherical berry about 3/8 " (8–13 mm) across—September 13.

A close look at the leaf margins would reveal long cilia.

Bark peels in long, fibrous strips.

Lonicera morrowii Gray

Morrow's honeysuckle

Nonnative, naturalized, tall **shrubs**, with single or multiple upright, ascending, or arching **stems** to 4 m tall and 8 cm basal diameter. 1st-year **branchlets** green to brown, hairy; 2nd-year branchlets brown to gray, glabrate, pith brown, hollow. **Bark** thin, brown to gray, rough, often peeling or shredding. **Leaves** simple, opposite, deciduous. **Petioles** 2–6 mm long, hairy. **Leaf blades** ovate to lance-ovate or lance-oblong; the larger ones 2.5–5 cm long and 1.5–2.7 cm wide; apex rounded or acutely to obtusely tapered; base truncate to rounded or shallowly cordate; margins entire, hairy or sometimes ciliate; upper surface dark green, evenly and moderately hairy; lower surface pale green, moderately to densely hairy. **Flowers** bisexual, 5-merous; in close sessile pairs on peduncles that arise singly from leaf axils on 1st-year branchlets; peduncles 1–2 cm long, hairy; floral bracts linear, 2–7 mm long at anthesis; bractlets oblong, 1.5–2 mm long, half to fully as long at anthesis as the ovary they subtend; calyx 0.8–1.5 mm long; corolla funnel-shaped, white to yellowish, 1.2–2 cm long, the lobes longer than the tube; **anthesis** mid-May to mid-June; insect- and hummingbird-pollinated. **Fruit** a depressed-spherical berry; translucent; yellowish to red; 6–8 mm diameter; maturing early July to early mid-August; animal-dispersed. (*morrowii*: for its discoverer James Morrow, 1820–65)

Identification

Morrow's honeysuckle is a large, bushy shrub with multiple stems, coarse, stiff branches, and fine twigs. The twigs and leaves are evenly covered with soft, downy hairs, and the flowers are usually white. The similar Tartarian honeysuckle (*L. tatarica*) is hairless (glabrous) except for the margins of the leaves. The hybrid between the two is called bella honeysuckle (*L. ×bella*), which falls somewhere between the two in terms of hairiness. The hybrid is actually more common in the wild than either parent, but it is usually mistaken for one or the other.

Natural History

Morrow's honeysuckle is a Japanese species imported into the United States by the horticulture trade in about 1875 (Rehder 1940). It is believed to have been brought to Minnesota sometime around 1900 or

shortly after. It was promoted as an ornamental shrub for rural landscaping, but it soon escaped into the wild and became established in grassy and brushy habitats and open woodlands. The vector is apparently birds that eat the fruit and spread the seeds in their droppings. It has since spread widely and is now found scattered throughout the southern half of the state. It apparently has no natural biological controls on this continent, and there seem to be no barriers to prevent it from spreading throughout the state.

Morrow's honeysuckle is ecologically invasive in the sense that it invades native habitats and displaces native species. In extreme cases it can dominant the shrub layer of woodlands, forming thickets so dense that very little light can penetrate, thereby shading out the plants beneath. This results in the degradation of wildlife habitat, the loss of biological diversity, and the disruption of ecological processes such as forest regeneration. The spread of Morrow's honeysuckle has been aided by Dutch elm disease, which has killed most of the canopy elms in hardwood forests throughout central and southern Minnesota. This opened up considerable habitat, much of which has been invaded by nonnative honeysuckle shrubs.

Control of Morrow's honeysuckle is difficult, especially in woodland habitats. It resprouts if cut or burned, but it can be killed by applying an appropriate herbicide to freshly cut stumps in mid or late summer.

Twigs have brown pith and a hollow core—May 21.

The twigs and leaves are covered with soft hairs—July 12.

A typical open-grown specimen from Freeborn County—May 30.

Stems branch repeatedly starting near the base.

Honeysuckles 277

Lonicera oblongifolia (Goldie) Hook.

Swamp fly honeysuckle

Midsize to tall **shrubs**, with single or multiple upright **stems** to 2 m tall and 2 cm basal diameter; clonal by layering. 1st-year **branchlets** greenish to brownish, minutely hairy; 2nd-year branchlets developing and shedding a thin gray epidermis, leaving a brown, glabrous surface beneath; pith white, solid. **Bark** gray or brown, rough, exfoliating in papery flakes or strips. **Leaves** simple, opposite, deciduous. **Petioles** 1–4 mm long, densely hairy, not ciliate. **Leaf blades** elliptical to obovate or oblong; the larger ones 3.5–8.5 cm long and 1.5–3 cm wide; apex tapered or occasionally rounded; base tapered; margins entire, finely hairy but not ciliate; upper surface green, moderately covered with fine woolly hairs 0.1–0.4 mm long; lower surface pale green, densely covered with a tangled mat of similar hairs. **Flowers** bisexual, 5-merous; in sessile pairs on erect or ascending peduncles that arise singly from leaf axils on 1st-year branchlets; peduncles minutely hairy, 1.5–2.5 cm long; floral bracts lacking; calyx lacking or rudimentary; corolla strongly bilabiate, tubular, pale yellow or whitish, 0.8–1.4 cm long, the lobes longer than the tube and reflexed; **anthesis** early June to early July; insect- and hummingbird-pollinated. **Fruit** a ± spherical, reddish berry; 7–11 mm in diameter; shiny and somewhat translucent; maturing early July to early August; animal-dispersed. (*oblongifolia*: with oblong leaves)

Identification

Swamp fly honeysuckle is generally a midsize shrub about knee high or waist high, with 1–3 stems and rather sparse branches. Exceptional specimens may reach 6 ft (2 m) in height and develop into a large, bushy shrub with many branches and fine branchlets. It is most likely to be confused with mountain fly honeysuckle (*L. villosa*); the two species commonly occur together, and they look very similar, especially the foliage and growth form. But swamp fly honeysuckle lacks cilia on the leaf margins, the peduncles are longer and more erect, and the two possess a different phenology and floral morphology (see key). Also, when comparing the two species side by side, notice that the leaves of swamp fly honeysuckle are a uniform pale green while those of mountain fly honeysuckle are usually darker, and may be suffused with red until midsummer.

Natural History

Swamp fly honeysuckle is fairly common in conifer swamps, shrub swamps, and sedge meadows and occasionally on lakeshores and stream banks. It is usually found in the open or under a thin canopy of tamarack (*Larix laricina*), northern white cedar (*Thuja occidentalis*), or sometimes black ash (*Fraxinus nigra*). The soils in these habitats typically consist of peat or sometimes loam, and the pH is moderately acidic. Soils will likely be wet, or at least moist, but not ponded or flooded except for short periods in the early spring. These conditions are indicative of what ecologists call swamps or fens; they are not the extremely acidic, nutrient-poor conditions found in true bogs, where members of the heath family (Ericaceae) typically dominate (Minnesota Department of Natural Resources 2003).

Individual stems typically reach an age of only 8 to 12 years, but new stems can arise if the older stems are damaged by fire or browsing. Lower branches will occasionally arch downward and root where they contact the ground, then send up new shoots from that point. This process is called layering, a form of clonal reproduction where apparently separate individuals are actually interconnected. This can result in small, loose colonies 3–10 ft (1–3 m) across consisting of perhaps a dozen or so "ramets," the term given to individual members of a clone.

Flowers stand erect, petals curve back—June 10.

Fruit is a red, translucent berry—July 21.

A typical specimen from a Beltrami County swamp.

Honeysuckles 🍂 **279**

Lonicera reticulata Raf.

Grape honeysuckle
[*Lonicera prolifera* (Kirchner) Rehder]

Climbing **vines**, with twining or scrambling **stems** to 8 m tall and 2 cm diameter; clonal by layering. 1st-year **branchlets** greenish, becoming brown, glabrous; 2nd-year branchlets gray or brown; pith white, hollow. **Bark** gray, the thin outer layer flaking or peeling. **Leaves** simple, opposite, deciduous. **Petioles** lacking or indistinct. **Leaf blades** of two types: normal stem leaves broadly elliptical to nearly circular, the larger ones 4.5–9 cm long and 3.5–8 cm wide; apex rounded; base rounded or clasping; the 2 or 3 uppermost pair of leaves on flowering branchlets fused at the base, each pair forming a single, ± circular perfoliate leaf; margins of all leaves entire and lacking cilia; upper surface dark green or the perfoliate leaves often blue-glaucous, glabrous or glabrate; lower surface pale green, sparsely to moderately hairy. **Flowers** bisexual, 5-merous; in sessile whorls of 6, with 1–5 whorls aggregated on each of 1–3 terminal spikes; peduncles glabrous, 1–3.5 cm long, arising from the center of the uppermost perfoliate leaf; floral bracts rudimentary or lacking; calyx vestigial, less than 0.5 mm long; corolla tubular, pale yellow, 1.8–2.5 cm long, the tube longer than the lobes; **anthesis** late May to late June; insect- and hummingbird-pollinated. **Fruit** a shiny, red, spherical berry; 8–12 mm in diameter; maturing mid-July to mid-September; animal-dispersed. (*reticulata*: reticulate)

Identification

Grape honeysuckle is a climbing or scrambling vine with pale yellow, tubular flowers. It has no tendrils or aerial roots; instead it climbs by twining its stem around a suitable support. The peculiar leaves are nearly circular in outline and have a rather stiff, leathery texture. The two or three upper pairs of leaves on each flowering twig are fused at the base, so that each pair forms a single disklike leaf with the stem passing through the center (perfoliate). There are three native honeysuckle vines in Minnesota, and they all have similar disklike leaves and all climb in the same fashion, but only grape honeysuckle has leaves so nearly circular in outline.

Natural History

Grape honeysuckle is rather uncommon in Minnesota, but it can be found occasionally in the hardwood forests in the southeastern counties. It seems to prefer upland sites with loamy or sometimes sandy loam soil, usually in the company of oaks (*Quercus* spp.), maples (*Acer* spp.), or basswood (*Tilia americana*).

It does poorly in perpetual shade; it seems to flourish only where it receives direct sunlight for at least a portion of the day such as in small openings and brushy thickets and along forest edges. Often these are transitional habitats recovering from some event, natural or otherwise, that opened the forest canopy and created an opportunity for a fast-growing but short-lived climber, a role that grape honeysuckle plays successfully.

Grape honeysuckle may twine on small branches or on stems of saplings. In this way it can climb to heights of at least 25 ft (8 m), but it apparently cannot reach the canopy of mature trees. It can also be seen scrambling over shrubs or trailing on the ground. Trailing stems are able to root where they come into contact with the soil and then sprout new aerial shoots. When this happens, a network of rooted stems, each with the potential to produce aerial shoots at their nodes, can create a small colony. Under the right conditions, these colonies can flourish and become thicketlike.

The bluish cast of the perfoliate leaves is diagnostic—September 18.

Note the strangely circular leaves on the nonflowering stem.

Leaves below the flowers are perfoliate (fused at base)—June 10.

Honeysuckles ❦ **281**

Lonicera tatarica L.

Tartarian honeysuckle

Nonnative, naturalized, tall **shrubs**, with single or multiple upright, ascending, or arching **stems** to 4.3 m tall and 7 cm basal diameter. 1st-year **branchlets** green to brown, glabrous; 2nd-year branchlets brown to gray, pith brown, hollow. **Bark** thin, brown to gray, rough, often peeling or flaking. **Leaves** simple, opposite, deciduous. **Petioles** 2–6 mm long, glabrous. **Leaf blades** ovate to lance-ovate or lance-oblong; the larger ones 3–7 cm long and 1.5–4 cm wide; apex acutely or obtusely tapered, or occasionally rounded; base truncate to rounded or shallowly cordate; margins entire, often with scattered cilia; upper surface dark green, glabrous; lower surface pale green, glabrous. **Flowers** bisexual, 5-merous; in close sessile pairs on peduncles that arise singly from leaf axils on 1st-year branchlets; peduncles 0.6–2.5 cm long, glabrous; floral bracts linear, 2–5 mm long at anthesis; bractlets roughly hemispherical, 0.6–1.1 mm long, one-third to half as long at anthesis as the ovary it subtends; calyx 0.5–1 mm long; corolla funnel-shaped, white to pink or purplish, 1–1.8 cm long, the lobes longer than the tube; **anthesis** mid-May to mid-June; insect- and hummingbird-pollinated. **Fruit** a depressed-spherical berry; shiny or translucent; orange to red; 6–10 mm in diameter; maturing early July to early mid-September; animal-dispersed. (*tatarica*: of Tatar; Tartarian)

Identification

Tartarian honeysuckle is a large, bushy shrub, often over 6 ft (2 m) tall. Open-grown specimens develop a hemispheric form with stiff, arching branches and numerous fine twigs. It is similar to the densely hairy Morrow's honeysuckle (*L. morrowii*) but has hairs only on the margins of the leaves. The two species have been hybridized to create bella honeysuckle (*L.* ×*bella*), which is actually more common than either of the parents.

Natural History

Tartarian honeysuckle, a native of Eurasia, was introduced into North America as a garden ornament as early as 1752 (Rehder 1940) and was apparently brought to Minnesota in the 1860s or 1870s. It quickly escaped cultivation, and by about 1900 it had become naturalized in the vicinity of the Twin Cities and Rochester. It is now firmly established in southern and central Minnesota and moving northward.

It readily invades marginal grassy and brushy habitats and native woodlands, especially oak woodlands. It seems to have few predators or diseases to keep populations in check, so once established it can quickly form dense thickets that exclude nearly all other species. In cases of severe infestations there is little, if any, reproduction of the native canopy trees or understory species, which effectively interrupts the natural cycles of forest succession and regeneration (Woods 1993). Many thousands of acres of native woodlands have now been severely damaged by nonnative honeysuckle shrubs (including Morrow's honeysuckle and bella honeysuckle). The severity of the problem is exceeded only by that of common buckthorn (*Rhamnus cathartica*).

Control methods have been less than effective; if cut, honeysuckles resprout tenaciously. Many land managers have resorted to herbicides, with only limited success. Because of the ease with which the nonnative honeysuckles spread and the severe ecological damage they cause, none of them should be planted, especially in rural areas. Any of the native dogwoods (*Cornus*) or viburnums (*Viburnum*) make much better landscaping choices.

Except for leaf margins, the entire plant is hairless—May 23.

The branching pattern can result in dense thickets.

Note that the bractlets are much shorter than the ovaries—May 23.

Fruits, like the flowers, are in sessile pairs—July 19.

An 8' (2.5 m) tall specimen from Anoka County—May 28.

Lonicera villosa (Michx.) J. A. Schultes

Mountain fly honeysuckle

[*L. caerulea* L. var. *villosa* (Michx.) T. & G.]

Low to midsize **shrubs**, with single or multiple upright **stems** to 1.5 m tall and 2 cm basal diameter; clonal by layering. 1st-year **branchlets** greenish to brown, finely and minutely hairy, often with long, coarse hairs interspersed; 2nd-year branchlets similar but epidermis darker, and soon exfoliating; pith white, solid. **Bark** brown, exfoliating in thin papery flakes or strips. **Leaves** simple, opposite, deciduous. **Petioles** 1–4 mm long, with fine minute hairs and long coarse hairs interspersed. **Leaf blades** elliptical to oblong or narrowly obovate; the larger ones 3–6.5 cm long and 1.2–3 cm wide; apex tapered, blunt, or somewhat rounded; base tapered or blunt; margins entire, with straight, stiff cilia 0.5–1 mm long; upper surface dark green, often suffused with red until midseason, sparsely to moderately covered with ± straight, stiff hairs 0.5–1 mm long; lower surface similar to upper but pale green and hairs usually denser. **Flowers** bisexual, 5-merous; in sessile pairs on arching or drooping peduncles that arise singly from leaf axils on 1st-year branchlets; peduncles hairy, 0.5–1.5 cm long; floral bracts 2, linear to narrowly lanceolate, 3–7 mm long; calyx vestigial, less than 0.5 mm long; corolla ± regular, funnel-shaped, pale yellow, 0.6–1 cm long, the lobes shorter than the tube; **anthesis** early May to early mid-June, the flowers emerging with the leaves or soon after; insect- and hummingbird-pollinated. **Fruit** an ovoid or broadly ellipsoidal berry derived from 2 fused ovaries; blue or blue-black, glaucous; 6–11 mm long; maturing early mid-June to late July; animal-dispersed. (*villosa*: covered with long, weak hairs)

Identification

Mountain fly honeysuckle is a smallish shrub with brown, shredding bark and dark green leaves. The entire plant stands only about knee high or waist high and has a rather sparse look (even large individuals rarely look bushy) causing it to be inconspicuous in most settings. The leaves and growth form look very much like swamp fly honeysuckle (*L. oblongifolia*), and the two species often grow side by side in the same habitat. But mountain fly honeysuckle has very distinctive cilia on the leaf margins. Also notice that the flowers appear at least two weeks earlier than those of swamp fly honeysuckle and have a different

morphology (see key). It may also be mistaken for a small willow, but all willows have alternate leaves, and all honeysuckles have opposite leaves.

Note: Minnesota's mountain fly honeysuckle is part of a circumpolar species complex with a very involved taxonomic history (Hultén 1970). There are as many as five varieties described under the North American name *Lonicera villosa,* and numerous varieties described under the Eurasian name *Lonicera caerulea.* If the complex is interpreted to be a single polymorphic species, then Minnesota's plants would be called *L. caerulea* var. *villosa.*

Natural History

Mountain fly honeysuckle is fairly common in mossy conifer swamps, usually with tamarack (*Larix laricina*), white cedar (*Thuja occidentalis*), or sometimes black spruce (*Picea mariana*). It is also found in fens, shrub swamps, and sedge meadows, perhaps with scattered willows (*Salix* spp.) or speckled alder (*Alnus incana* subsp. *rugosa*). It seems to be absent from highly acidic bogs and from seasonal wetlands that may dry out in late summer. It is usually found as scattered individuals or small clonal colonies that develop by layering of the lower branches.

Flowers hang downward, and petals don't curve back—May 23.

Fruit is blue or blackish, on a short, curved stalk—June 23.

Leaf margins have long, stiff cilia.

Bark exfoliates in thin, papery strips.

A typical specimen from a swamp in Cook County.

Honeysuckles 🍃 **285**

Malus, the apples

Rosaceae: Rose family

This genus contains about 55 species of deciduous trees and shrubs found in north temperate regions of Europe, Asia, and North America. About 10 species are native to the United States, and 1 species is native to Minnesota. (*Malus* is the classical Latin name for the apple tree.)

The domestic apple is derived mostly from *M. pumila* P. Mill. of Europe and western Asia and is occasionally feral on roadsides and in old fields throughout most of Minnesota. It apparently does not compete with the native *M. ioensis,* but they are probably interfertile and could possibly hybridize (Dickson, Kresovich, and Weeden 1991). Many other Old World *Malus* species and hybrids are cultivated in Minnesota for their ornamental flowers and fruits (Tietmeyer and Bristol 2002). None are known to be naturalized.

Malus ioensis (Wood) Britt.

Prairie crab-apple
[*Pyrus ioensis* (Wood) Bailey]

Tall **shrubs** or small **trees**, with single upright **stems** to 6 m tall and 11 cm dbh; clonal by root suckering. **Branches** numerous, spreading or ascending, stout, often with spur thorns. 1st-year **branchlets** woolly, becoming glabrous the 2nd or 3rd year, red-brown. **Bark** gray, somewhat scaly, the outer layer of older stems peeling and exposing a reddish inner layer. **Leaves** simple, alternate, deciduous. **Petioles** 0.8–2.5 cm long, woolly. **Leaf blades** ovate to elliptical or oblong; 3.5–7 cm long, 2–5 cm wide; base acute to obtuse or rounded; apex acute to obtuse or rounded; margins with coarse irregular serrations, and 0–3 pairs of shallow rounded or acute lobes, the basal lobes sometimes pronounced; upper surface dark green, woolly when young, becoming glabrate at maturity; lower surface pale green, persistently woolly. **Flowers** bisexual, 5-merous; 1–6 borne in a simple corymb; pedicels 0.8–3 cm long, woolly; sepals 3–6 mm long, lanceolate to triangular, densely woolly; petals 1.3–2 cm long, white to pink, glabrous; stamens 6–25; styles 5, woolly at base; **anthesis** mid-May to early June; insect-pollinated. **Fruit** a broadly ellipsoidal to subglobose pome; 2.5–4 cm in diameter; greenish; barely if at all edible; maturing early September to early October; animal-dispersed. (*ioensis*: of Iowa)

Identification

Prairie crab-apple is a large, thicket-forming shrub or sometimes a small tree, often with low, crooked branches and spur thorns. The large whitish or pinkish flowers are very conspicuous in late spring, but the tree is hardly noticed the rest of the year. The growth form, spur thorns, and peeling bark are similar to the native wild plum (*Prunus americana*), and the flowers could be mistaken for those of the domestic apple tree. The key difference is that the petioles and the underside of the leaves of prairie crab-apple are densely woolly. Also, the leaf margins may have shallow lobes near the base.

Natural History

An early observer in Fillmore County described prairie crab-apple as "common along the margin of prairies and in open valleys" (Winchell 1876). As brief as it is, this is perhaps the best, if not the only,

description of prairie crab-apple from the presettlement landscape of Minnesota. Today, the same landscape is dominated by agriculture, and although the prairies are gone, prairie crab-apple has managed to hang on. Current habitats include woodland borders, brushy thickets, and grassy openings, especially on river bottoms. The best habitats seem to be south of the Minnesota River valley, yet prairie crab-apple has been found as far north as the town of Elk River (Sherburne County).

It is usually found in sandy, loamy or relatively coarse, alluvial soil in the company of oaks (*Quercus* spp.), sumacs (*Rhus* spp.), prickly ash (*Zanthoxylum americanum*), or wild plum (*Prunus americana*). It can withstand drought and occasional spring flooding, and although mature plants can survive for a time under a moderately dense tree canopy, seedlings need direct sunlight.

Under ideal conditions, a mature prairie crab-apple can sprout multiple root suckers at distances up to 20 ft (6 m) from the main stem. Suckers are aerial stems that arise from adventitious buds on the roots of the parent plant. In this way it can form a dense thicket made impenetrable by the stiff, interlacing, horizontal branches and sharp spines. This growth form is probably what allows prairie crab-apple to resist browsing when its native habitat is used as a cattle pasture.

Flowers are similar to those of domestic apple—May 21.

Fruits can reach 1.5" (4 cm), but are barely edible—September 3.

The lobed leaf margin is diagnostic.

Stems can arise from seeds or by root suckering.

At peak anthesis on May 21—Wabasha County.

Prairie crab-apple   289

Menispermum, moonseed

Menispermaceae: Moonseed family

Moonseed belongs to a small genus of two closely related species: 1 in eastern North America, and 1 in eastern Asia. (*Menispermum* is from the Greek *mene* for moon, and *sperma* for seed; these are references to the crescent shape of the seed.)

Menispermum canadense L.

Moonseed

Climbing **vines**, with twining **stems** to 10 meters tall and 2 cm diameter; forming loose rhizomatous colonies. **Bark** sparsely hairy, green to greenish brown, developing short brown or gray ridges near base of older stems. Aerial **branches** few. **Leaves** simple, alternate, deciduous. **Petioles** 4–16 cm long; sparsely hairy, attaching slightly inside the margin of the blade (peltate). **Leaf blades** reniform, circular, or broadly ovate; 4–18 cm long, 6–22 cm wide; base cordate; apex acute to obtuse or rounded; margins with 1–3 pairs of shallow blunt lobes, otherwise entire; upper surface sparsely hairy to glabrate, dark green; lower surface sparsely hairy, pale green. **Flowers** unisexual, each inflorescence with either male flowers or female flowers; 4–8-merous; borne in axillary panicles of 15–50; whitish or greenish; pedicels 2–6 mm long; sepals elliptical, 2–3 mm long; petals obovate, 1.3–1.8 mm long; stamens 12–24 in male flowers, generally fewer and vestigial in female flowers; pistils 2–4, borne on a short stipe; stigmas sessile; **anthesis** early June to early July; insect-pollinated. **Fruit** a bluish black drupe; globose; 9–13 mm in diameter; glabrous; maturing mid-August to early October; animal-dispersed. **Seed** one, crescent shaped. (*canadense*: of Canada)

Identification

Moonseed is a climbing vine with large, soft, roundish leaves and a smooth, greenish stem. At first glance, the leaves may look like those of a native grape (*Vitis* spp.) or the herbaceous wild yam (*Dioscorea villosa*), but notice that the petiole of moonseed is attached slightly inside the margin of the leaf blade rather than at the very edge. The fruiting clusters appear grapelike, and they may remain on the plant over the winter. Even though they are eaten by wildlife, they are reportedly poisonous to humans (Young and Young 1992).

Natural History

Moonseed is a common vine of mesic hardwood forests throughout much of Minnesota, especially along rivers in the southern half of the state. As a forest vine it has the ability to survive in deep shade, yet it clearly prefers sunny edges or partial openings, where it may grow rapidly and luxuriantly. Soil types vary, but moist loam or alluvium seems to be preferred.

Moonseed can produce long horizontal rhizomes that grow just beneath the ground and send up aerial stems at intervals of 4–12 inches (10–30 cm). In this manner it can form small, loose colonies, often with multiple, intertwining stems. The stem, which is weak and cannot support itself, will typically grow along the ground or scramble over shrubs or herbaceous plants. It can also climb to heights of 33 ft (10 m), possibly more, by twining around a tree trunk. A suitable host tree will have a trunk no more than about 6 inches (15 cm) in diameter with either smooth or rough bark. Occasionally the vine becomes tight enough to cause some slight deformation in the trunk of the host tree, but the vine usually does not live long enough to kill or permanently disfigure a tree. The vines, in fact, are barely woody, but they overwinter well, although the terminal portion is sometimes killed in severe winters. The ecological role of moonseed seems to be that of a fast-growing, short-lived opportunist.

The long, yellow roots reportedly have a bitter taste and were used as ritual medicine by the Dakota Indians. They referred to the plant as "yellow medicine," which is the namesake of a county and a river in southwestern Minnesota (Upham 1969).

Fruits look like wild grapes but are reportedly poisonous—September 18.

Flowers are unisexual, these are female—June 20.

The vines can climb to a height of about 33' (10 m).

Moonseed

Morus, the mulberries

Moraceae: Mulberry family

The mulberries constitute a genus of about 10 species of deciduous trees and shrubs in temperate and tropical regions of North America, Europe, and Asia. Two species are native to the United States. Minnesota has 1 native species (now perhaps extirpated) and 1 naturalized species. (*Morus* is the classical Latin name for mulberry.)

Key to the Genus Morus *in Minnesota*

1. Lower surface of leaf with hairs only on main veins and in axils of main veins; upper surface often sparsely hairy on lower portion of basal veins, otherwise glabrous. Leaves mostly with deep and irregular lobes .... *M. alba*
1. Lower surface of leaf moderately to densely hairy over entire surface; upper surface with short, stiff appressed hairs scattered ± evenly and sparsely over the surface. Leaves all or mostly unlobed .... *M. rubra*

Morus alba L.

White mulberry

Nonnative, naturalized, small **trees**, to 15 m tall and 50 cm dbh. **Bark** initially thin, orange-brown, rough; becoming gray and developing angular ridges and furrows, the furrows often orange tinged. **Branchlets** green to green-brown; minutely hairy the 1st year, essentially glabrous the second. **Leaves** simple, alternate, deciduous. **Petioles** 1–5 cm long, hairy. **Leaf blades** ovate, often with deep and irregular lobes; 5–13 cm long, 3.5–9 cm wide; base cordate to truncate, often asymmetrical; apex acute to short acuminate; margins coarsely serrate; upper surface dark green, often sparsely hairy on proximal portions of basal veins, otherwise glabrous; lower surface somewhat paler than upper, hairy only on main veins and in axils of main veins. **Flowers** 4-merous; unisexual, each tree bearing either male flowers or female flowers; borne in catkins from buds on 1st-year branchlets. **Male catkins** relatively slender, drooping to pendulous, 1.5–4 cm long; peduncle hairy, 0.5–2 cm long; flowers numerous, sepals greenish, 1.5–2 mm long. **Female catkins** stout, stiff, 0.5–1 cm long at anthesis; peduncle hairy, 0.3–1 cm long; flowers several, ovary broadly ellipsoidal to ovoid, 1.5–2 mm long; style branches divergent; **anthesis** early May to early June; wind-pollinated. Individual **fruit** an achene enclosed by its enlarged, fleshy calyx; 1–3 mm long; the aggregate fruit a cylindrical syncarp 1.5–2.5 cm long; initially white then red then becoming blackish when mature or remaining pearly white; maturing mid-June to mid-July; animal-dispersed. (*alba*: white, in reference to a color form of the fruit)

Identification

White mulberry is a small, stout tree usually 30–40 ft (9–12 m) tall with spreading branches and a rounded or irregular-shaped crown. The leaves come in an odd assortment of shapes, usually with one or more asymmetrical, thumblike lobes at the base, or they are sometimes unlobed. The occasional unlobed leaf could be confused with a leaf of red mulberry (*M. rubra*); such leaves can be differentiated only by the pattern of hairs on the surface (see key). And do not be misled by the common names of mulberries. The fruits of white mulberry start out white, then turn red and finally black, but on some trees they stay white. The fruits of red mulberry follow the same progression but always end up black.

Natural History

White mulberry is native to China. It was introduced into the eastern United States in the nineteenth century or possibly earlier. The original intent may have been to support a silkworm industry, but the industry never took hold. The trees, however, quickly became naturalized and flourished.

It is said that white mulberry was carried westward by Russian Mennonites and was called "Russian mulberry" for many years (Green 1898). It was valued primarily as an ornamental tree but also for the edible fruit and as a windbreak or hedge tree. It was planted in southern Minnesota as early as 1880, and herbarium specimens indicate that it had become locally naturalized by 1920. It is now naturalized throughout the southern third of the state, and although it is rarely if ever planted anymore, the seeds continue to be spread in the droppings of birds.

White mulberry is particularly common in ruderal habitats such as abandoned agricultural fields, urban sites, parks, and industrial areas. It is also found scattered in seminatural habitats such as brushy thickets, forest margins, and floodplains. It does not seem to tolerate permanently wet soil or the deep shade of forest interiors. The inevitable concern about naturalized species is that they may invade natural habitats and displace the native species, but the threat posed by white mulberry at this time does not seem great.

Some fruits turn black when mature, others remain white—July 1.

Male flowers are in greenish catkins—May 24.

Nearly all leaves are deeply lobed.

Female flowers at peak on May 24.

Furrows between the ridges are orange-tinged—16" (40 cm) dbh.

Mulberries

Mulberries   **297**

Morus rubra L.

Red mulberry

Large **trees**, to 25 m tall and 80 cm dbh (as seen in Iowa). **Bark** initially thin, brown or orange-brown; becoming gray and developing flat, interlacing ridges and shallow, narrow furrows. **Branchlets** greenish to brown; minutely hairy through the second year, or glabrous. **Leaves** simple, alternate, deciduous. **Petioles** 1.5–3.5 cm long, hairy. **Leaf blades** broadly ovate, usually lacking lobes or occasionally with deep and irregular lobes; 12–22 cm long, 8–15 cm wide; base rounded to truncate or cordate; apex abruptly acuminate; margins coarsely serrate; upper surface dark green, with short, stiff, appressed hairs scattered ± evenly and sparsely over the surface; lower surface pale green, moderately to densely hairy over entire surface, palmately 3-veined from base. **Flowers** 4-merous; unisexual, each tree bearing either male flowers or female flowers; borne in catkins from buds on 1st-year branchlets. **Male catkins** slender, pendulous, 2–6 cm long; peduncle hairy, 1–2.5 cm long; flowers numerous, sepals greenish, tinged with red, 1.5–2.5 mm long. **Female catkins** stout, stiff, 1–2 cm long at anthesis; peduncle hairy, 0.8–1.6 cm long; flowers several, ovary broadly ellipsoidal to ovoid, 1.5–2 mm long; style branches divergent; **anthesis** early May to early June; wind-pollinated. Individual **fruit** an achene enclosed by its enlarged, fleshy calyx; 1.5–3.5 mm long; the aggregate fruit a cylindrical syncarp 1–3 cm long; initially white then red then blackish when mature; maturing late June to late July; animal-dispersed. (*rubra*: red, in reference to the fruit)

Identification

Red mulberry can become a moderately large tree, reaching heights of at least 80 ft (25 m) in central Iowa and perhaps as large in southern Minnesota. The leaves are large and soft, almost velvety, and shaped like those of the native basswood (*Tilia americana*) or the often-planted catalpa (*Catalpa speciosa*). The fruits are initially white, then turn red and ultimately black. It hybridizes easily with the naturalized white mulberry (*M. alba*).

Natural History

Red mulberry is basically a tree of forested floodplains, but it does not grow tall enough to compete with dominant floodplain trees such as plains cottonwood (*Populus deltoides* subsp. *monilifera*) and silver maple (*Acer saccharinum*). It seems to play the role of a fast-growing opportunist, exploiting canopy gaps, ecotones, woodland margins, stream banks, and other early successional habitats within a forested ecosystem. Its native habitat in Minnesota seems to be bottomlands and lower slopes along the Mississippi River.

There are only two documented occurrences of native red mulberry in Minnesota, both from Houston County. The first is a herbarium specimen collected by H. L. Lyon (MINN #368) on August 18, 1899, somewhere near the village of Jefferson along the Mississippi River. Lyon's notes read, "Specimen taken from sprouts growing from stump about 8 inches in diameter. Owner of land affirms that 'the tree was a mulberry before it was cut down.'" The second record is a herbarium specimen collected by C. O. Rosendahl and F. K. Butters (MINN #3890) on June 25, 1920, from "sandy soil, wooded hillside about 3 miles north of Jefferson."

Neither of these two sites has been relocated, and it is possible that native red mulberry no longer exists in Minnesota. There are a handful of undocumented reports (Rosendahl 1955; Ownbey and Morley 1991), but most of these can be traced to misidentified herbarium specimens or to unwarranted generalizations. Although red mulberry has occasionally been planted in Minnesota, probably from nursery stock originating from states south of Minnesota, it is not known to have spread from cultivation.

Each male catkin contains 20–50+ flowers—May 7.

Fruits start white then turn red then black—June 22.

Tight clusters of female flowers at anthesis—May 7.

Leaves lack the lobing of white mulberry.

Mature bark is gray with flat, scaly ridges. Ames, Iowa—15" (38 cm) dbh.

Mulberries

Myrica, sweet gale

Myricaceae: Wax-myrtle family

This genus includes 50 to 60 species of shrubs and small trees; they are widespread but occur mostly in the tropics. There are 7 species in the United States, and 1 in Minnesota. (*Myrica* is from the Greek *myrike,* the classical Latin name of some fragrant plant.)

Myrica gale L.

Sweet gale

Midsize **shrubs**, with multiple upright or ascending **stems** to 1.5 m tall and 3 cm basal diameter; clonal by root suckering. **Branches** numerous, ascending. **Branchlets** hairy, reddish brown. **Bark** brown, smooth or roughened with numerous small lenticels. **Leaves** simple, alternate, deciduous. **Petioles** 1–3 mm long, hairy or glabrous. **Leaf blades** aromatic; oblanceolate to obovate; 2–6.5 cm long, 0.8–2 cm wide; base tapered to attenuate; apex obtuse to rounded; margins with 1–5 pairs of teeth toward apex; upper surface dotted with minute yellow glands, hairy or glabrate; lower surface similar to upper. **Flowers** unisexual; male flowers and female flowers in separate catkins on the same or usually on different plants; borne laterally on leafless twigs of the previous season. **Male flowers** 12–25; in compact cylindrical catkins 0.8–1.8 cm long; each flower with 4–8 stamens, subtended by a single ciliate-margined, rhombic bract 2–3.5 mm long. **Female flowers** 15–35; in dense ovate or short-cylindrical catkins 0.5–1.5 cm long; each flower with 2 stigmas, subtended by a single ovate bract about 2 mm long, and by 2 bracteoles forming inflated winglike appendages; **anthesis** late April to late May; wind-pollinated. **Fruit** nutlike; ovate; flattened; 2.5–3 mm long; maturing early mid-July to mid-September; animal- and water-dispersed. (*gale*: an old generic name, bearing reference to an aromatic plant)

Identification

Sweet gale is a dense, bushy shrub, usually about waist high. The leaf has a short tip and a distinctive pale green color. It could be mistaken for a small willow, but the leaf of sweet gale is dotted with tiny, yellow glands (seen with a hand lens) and is strongly aromatic when crushed. The same features distinguish it from the bog heaths such as leatherleaf (*Chamaedaphne calyculata*) and Labrador tea (*Rhododendron groenlandicum*).

Natural History

Sweet gale is common on both boggy and rocky shores of many lakes and streams in the northeast. It typically roots right at the shoreline with the branches hanging over the water. It spreads vegetatively by layering of lower branches and reportedly by root suckers (Skene et al. 2000). This can lead to extensive colonies with numerous closely spaced stems that branch repeatedly beginning near the base. The result is often dense, luxurious thickets that line the shore. Such thickets are apparently undamaged by spring flooding, forest fires, herbivore browsing, and even severe winter ice conditions. As long as they are not overtopped by trees and water levels remain relatively constant, they may persist for decades, possibly longer.

Sweet gale also occurs in peatland habitats that are not directly associated with lakes or rivers, such as shrub swamps and sedge meadows, but such cases are the exception, not the rule. In all cases the most consistent habitat components are direct sunlight and a substrate that is wet, acidic, and relatively nutrient poor.

Sweet gale has a distinct advantage under these conditions because it is known to fix nitrogen (Rodriguez-Barrueco 1968), meaning it harbors colonies of symbiotic bacteria on its roots that can convert atmospheric nitrogen into nitrate, a form useful to plants. Alders (*Alnus* spp.) also have this ability, but the willows (*Salix* spp.), dogwoods (*Cornus* spp.), and most other shrubs in the region do not. This ability may give sweet gale a competitive edge in both boggy and sandy habitats where the availability of fixed nitrogen is believed to be a limiting factor.

These male flowers have just released their pollen—May 23.

Fruits are in short, stiff catkins on leafless twigs—July 18.

From the shore of McFarland Lake, Cook County.

Female flowers could be confused with those of a hazel.

Nemopanthus, mountain-holly

Aquifoliaceae: Holly family

Mountain-holly is the sole member of a monotypic genus endemic to eastern North America. It is very similar to the genus *Ilex* (the true hollies), and it is sometimes placed in that genus. (*Nemopanthus* is from the Greek *nema*, thread, *pous*, foot, and *anthos*, flower; these are apparently references to the slender peduncle.)

Nemopanthus mucronatus (L.) Trel.

Mountain-holly
[*Ilex mucronata* (L.) M. Powell, V. Savolainen & S. Andrews]

Tall **shrubs**, with single or multiple upright **stems** to 4.7 m tall and 5 cm dbh. **Bark** thin, gray or gray-green mottled, ± smooth or roughened with pale, warty lenticels. **Branchlets** slender, glabrous, brown to reddish brown, developing a gray, flaky epidermis the 2nd year. **Leaves** simple, alternate, deciduous. Petioles 4–12 mm long; glabrous, often purplish, somewhat winged. **Leaf blades** obovate, elliptical, or oblong; 3-5.5 cm long, 1.5–2.5 cm wide; base acutely or obtusely tapered or irregularly rounded; apex obtusely tapered to rounded or occasionally acute, mucronate; margins entire or remotely serrate, especially near apex; upper surface dark green, glabrous; lower surface pale green, glabrous. **Flowers** 4-merous, minute; unisexual, each tree bearing either male flowers or female flowers, or occasionally bisexual (reportedly); borne singly from leaf axils on 1st-year branchlets; peduncles slender, glabrous, 1–3 cm long; calyx absent; petals yellowish or greenish, straplike, 1.5–2 mm long; stamens about as long as the petals; style none, stigma capitate; **anthesis** when leaves are about half grown, from mid-May to early June; insect-pollinated. **Fruit** a dull, reddish to maroon or purplish, berrylike drupe; ± spherical; 6–9 mm in diameter; containing 4–5 bony nutlets; maturing late July to early September; animal-dispersed. (*mucronatus*: with a mucro; a short, abrupt point at the tip of the leaf)

Identification
Mountain-holly is a tall shrub, usually in the range of 6–12 ft (2–3.5 m), with multiple erect stems. The leaves are comparatively small, with smooth surfaces and entire or nearly entire margins. Also, the petioles are characteristically reddish or purplish. The bark and general growth form are most like speckled alder (*Alnus incana* subsp. *rugosa*), but the leaves of speckled alder are much larger and have serrate margins.

Natural History
Mountain-holly is generally uncommon in Minnesota and is restricted to scattered wetland habitats in the east-central counties. It occurs most often in thinly forested or shrub-dominated swamps with tamarack (*Larix laricina*), black ash (*Fraxinus nigra*), or

speckled alder (*Alnus incana* subsp. *rugosa*). Soils vary from weakly to moderately acidic and usually consist of thin peat or sometimes wet sand or loam. Swamps of this type may develop in isolated basins or as part of larger wetland complexes. They often experience flooding for brief periods in the spring but are not prone to significant erosion or sedimentation.

Mountain-holly reproduces primarily by seeds that are transported in the droppings of birds, but it can also spread short distances by the process of layering. Layering begins when a normal, upright stem lies flat on moist ground (this seems to happen periodically but exactly how is not really clear). The stem then produces roots along its length and sends up a second generation of stems. A network of layered stems can produce a relatively large colony with dozens of upright stems. The colony is collectively called a clone, and although individual stems may live for perhaps 35 years, the clone itself is self-perpetuating and can be much older.

Well-established clones of mountain-holly appear to compete successfully with shrubs of similar size, such as bog birch (*Betula pumila*), dogwoods (*Cornus* spp.), and some of the willows (*Salix* spp.). But speckled alder is taller, faster growing, and more aggressive. If present, it will usually dominate the habitat, relegating mountain-holly to edges or small, unoccupied gaps.

Each female flower sits atop a curiously long peduncle—June 8.

Leaves are smooth and usually less than 2" (5 cm) long.

Male flowers are distinguished by their yellow anthers—June 3.

Fruits are reddish, about 1/4" (6–9 mm) across—August 8.

Bark resembles speckled alder—this stem is 1.5" (4 cm) diameter.

Mountain-holly   🍂   **307**

Ostrya, ironwood

Betulaceae: Birch family

This genus contains 5 to 10 species of deciduous trees, mostly in temperate regions of North America, Europe, and Asia. Three species are found in the United States, and 1 in Minnesota. (*Ostrya* is the classical Greek name for the European hop-hornbeam, *Ostrya carpinifolia* Scop.)

Ostrya virginiana (P. Mill.) K. Koch

Ironwood

Small or midsize **trees**, to 22 m tall and 37 cm dbh. **Bark** thin, brown or gray; with fine rectangular scales or flat, narrow, scaly ridges. First-year **branchlets** brown; hairy and often stipitate-glandular, becoming glabrous or glabrate the 2nd year. **Leaves** simple, alternate, deciduous or marcescent. **Petioles** 2–9 mm long; hairy and often stipitate-glandular. **Leaf blades** narrowly ovate or elliptical; 7–12 cm long, 3–6 cm wide; base rounded, blunt or somewhat cordate; apex acuminate; margins sharply serrate or double serrate; upper surface dark green, sparsely to moderately hairy; lower surface pale green, moderately hairy, especially on larger veins and in axils of lateral veins. **Inflorescence** unisexual, with separate male catkins and female catkins on the same branch. **Male catkins** slender, pendulous, 2–7 cm long; borne in terminal clusters of 1–4; formed in late summer and expanding with the leaves the following spring. **Female catkins** 3–5 mm long at anthesis; borne singly at the tips of 1st-year branchlets; **anthesis** late April to late mid-May; wind-pollinated. **Fruit** a small, ovoid nutlet enclosed in an inflated, papery, pouchlike bract 1–2.5 cm long; loosely arranged in a hoplike strobilus 3–5 cm long, and containing 8–22 bracts; maturing early August to early September and shed individually and intermittently through autumn and winter; wind- and gravity-dispersed. (*virginiana*: of Virginia)

Identification

Ironwood is a small or midsize tree, usually with a single, slender trunk that remains distinct to near the top of the tree. The branches are also slender and held horizontally, and the bark is thin and relatively fine textured. The leaves could be mistaken for those of an elm (*Ulmus* sp.), but the margins are more finely serrate than elm, and the leaf base is symmetrical. Perhaps the most unique feature is the hoplike fruit. They are often seen on the tree in autumn and winter, long after the leaves have fallen. It is also worth noting that at least some of the branches may hold the dried and shriveled leaves all winter; the oaks (*Quercus* spp.) are the only other Minnesota trees that normally do this.

Natural History

Ironwood is a common subcanopy tree in upland hardwood forests over most of Minnesota, especially in late-successional or climax forests. In presettlement times it was abundant only in the "Big Woods" region in the south-central part of the state (Daubenmire 1936; U.S. Surveyor General 1847–1908). It now appears to be more widespread, or at least more abundant in areas where it was uncommon before. The reasons for this trend are not clear.

Ironwood seems to prefer loamy or sandy soil, typically beneath a canopy of red oak (*Quercus rubra*), basswood (*Tilia americana*), American elm (*Ulmus americana*), or sugar maple (*Acer saccharum*). It does not occur in swamps or on floodplains, indicating sensitivity to flooding or sedimentation, and it does not invade old fields, pastures, or other nonforested areas.

Ironwood is extremely tolerant of shade. In fact it is one of the few tree species that is adapted to complete its entire life cycle in the shade of larger trees. Not only does it flower and set seed in deep shade, the seeds will germinate, and the saplings will grow to maturity without any large-scale disturbance; this clearly qualifies ironwood as a climax species.

It is relatively slow growing in its natural habitat, but when cultivated in the open as a specimen tree, it grows rapidly. It is considered to be relatively short-lived, although it can reach 100 years (Young 1934), possibly more.

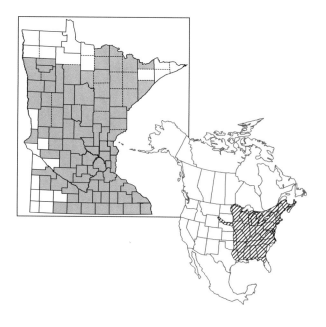

Red, threadlike stigmas reveal the female flowers—May 13.

There is a small nutlet in each pouchlike bract—July 22.

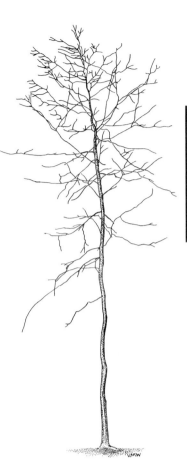

Male catkins resemble those of birch, a close relative—May 15.

The bark has flat, narrow, scaly ridges—this trunk is 9" (23 cm) dbh.

Leaves are elmlike but the bases are more symmetrical.

Oxycoccus, the cranberries

Ericaceae: Heath family

The cranberries constitute a circumboreal genus of 2 to 4 species. All are dwarf, vinelike, evergreen shrubs. Two of the species occur in Minnesota. American botanists have often included the cranberries in the genus *Vaccinium* along with the blueberries and bilberries, but they are kept separate here primarily on the basis of flower morphology and growth form. (*Oxycoccus* refers to a sour berry.)

Key to the Genus Oxycoccus *in Minnesota*

1. Leaves tapered to an acutely-angled tip; the largest leaf blades mostly less than 1 cm long; pedicels naked except for two tiny, reddish, scalelike bracts about 0.5 mm wide, usually borne at or below the middle of the pedicel .... *O. quadripetalus*
1. Leaves with a blunt or rounded tip; the largest leaf blades more than 1 cm long; pedicels with two small, usually green, leaflike bracts 1–2 mm wide, usually borne above the middle of the pedicel .... *O. macrocarpus*

Oxycoccus macrocarpus (Ait.) Pers.

Large cranberry
[*Vaccinium macrocarpon* Ait.]

Low or dwarf vinelike **shrubs**, with slender creeping **stems** to 1.5 m long, eventually rooting at the nodes. **Branches** erect or ascending, to 15 cm tall; initially brown, hairy or glabrous, eventually the thin outer layer splits to reveal a smooth, red-brown inner layer. **Leaves** simple, alternate, evergreen, persisting at least 2 years. **Petioles** glabrous, 1–2 mm long. **Leaf blades** elliptical to oblong; 9–16 mm long, 3–7 mm wide; base blunt to rounded; apex blunt to rounded or occasionally obtusely tapered; margins entire, somewhat revolute; upper surface dark green (becoming reddish brown in winter), shiny, glabrous; lower surface pale green, moderately to barely glaucous, glabrous. **Flowers** 4-merous, bisexual, white to pink; borne singly from axils of closely spaced bracts at the base of shoots of the current year, the shoots growing beyond the flowers; pedicels 1.5–3.5 cm long, hairy, bearing 2 ovate, green, leaflike bracts 3–5 mm long and 1–2 mm wide, usually borne above the middle of the pedicel; corolla lobes lanceolate, 6–9 mm long, strongly reflexed at maturity; **anthesis** late mid-June to late mid-July; insect-pollinated. **Fruit** a globose berry; 10–16 mm in diameter; turning red between early August and early September but held on the branches over winter; after-ripening being completed by the following spring; dispersed by water or animals. (*macrocarpus*: large-fruited)

Identification

Large cranberry is one of two species of true cranberry (genus *Oxycoccus*) that grow wild in Minnesota. The other is conveniently known as small cranberry (*O. quadripetalus*). Both are low-growing, dwarf shrubs with vinelike stems that trail over the ground. Their flowers and growth form are essentially identical. The main difference lies in the size and shape of the leaves, those of large cranberry being slightly larger and having rounded tips.

Natural History

Large cranberry is fairly common in the forested regions of Minnesota, especially in the central counties. The best habitats are tamarack (*Larix laricina*) swamps with well-developed hummocks or carpets of *Sphagnum* moss; it is occasionally found on floating sedge mats as well. These habitats are only moderately acidic, with pH values of 4.8–6.1 (Vander Kloet 1988) and with relatively high levels of mineral nutrients.

The more common small cranberry favors the highly acidic black spruce (*Picea mariana*) bogs, where the pH may be as low as 2.5, and mineral nutrients are practically nonexistent (Vander Kloet 1988). The degree of acidity in any given habitat has a profound influence on plant distribution and is how ecologists distinguish between swamps and bogs (Minnesota Department of Natural Resources 2003). Because of the different habitat requirements, the two species rarely occur together.

Both species of cranberry produce leafy upright branches about 4 inches (10 cm) tall that bear the flowers. They also produce long, horizontal branches 2.5 ft (75 cm) or more in length that trail over the surface. The trailing branches can root at the nodes and form new branches, thereby expanding the colony.

Large cranberry is the cranberry of commerce. It is cultivated in large artificial wetlands, mostly in Wisconsin, Massachusetts, New Jersey, and Oregon (Eck 1990). Wild populations are not harvested on a large scale because they do not usually produce fruit in enough abundance.

Flowers alone cannot distinguish this from small cranberry—July 5.

The wild version of grocery-store cranberries—October 4.

Leaves have a blunt or rounded tip.

Branches are usually about 4" (10 cm) tall, and stand erect.

Cranberries 🍃 **315**

Oxycoccus quadripetalus Gilib.

Small cranberry
[*Vaccinium oxycoccos* L.]

Low or dwarf vinelike **shrubs**, with slender creeping **stems** to 75+ cm long, eventually rooting at the nodes. **Branches** erect or ascending, to 15 cm tall; initially brown, minutely hairy or occasionally glabrous, eventually the epidermal layer splits to reveal a smooth, red-brown inner layer. **Leaves** simple, alternate, evergreen, persisting at least 2 years. **Petioles** ± glabrous, 0.5–1.5 mm long. **Leaf blades** ovate to elliptical or oblong-ovate to oblong-elliptical; 7–10 mm long, 2.5–5 mm wide; base rounded; apex acutely tapered; margins entire, revolute; upper surface dark green, shiny, glabrous; lower surface pale green to whitish green, strongly glaucous, glabrous. **Flowers** 4-merous, bisexual, white to pink; borne singly from axils of closely spaced bracts at the base of shoots of the current year, the shoots often not developing beyond the flowers, giving the impression of a terminal raceme; pedicels 1.5–5 cm long, hairy, bearing 2 linear, reddish, scalelike bracts 1–2.5 mm long and about 0.5 mm wide, usually borne at or below the middle of the pedicel; corolla lobes lanceolate, 5–7 mm long, strongly reflexed at maturity; **anthesis** early June to mid-July; insect-pollinated. **Fruit** a globose berry; ripening red; 7–12 mm in diameter; maturing late July to early September but held on the branches over winter; dispersed in early spring by water or animals. (*quadripetalus*: with 4 petals)

Identification

Small cranberry is a tiny, vinelike shrub with thin, wiry stems. They creep over the tops of bog mosses and can be surprisingly hard to spot. The leaves are no more than 3/8 inch (10 mm) long and remain green all year. They look much like the leaves of large cranberry (*O. macrocarpus*) but are measurably smaller and have pointed tips. The runners, not the flowers, could be confused also with those of snowberry (*Gaultheria hispidula*). Both can form delicate mats with interlacing stems, but the leaves of snowberry are more round in outline and have dark, bristlelike hairs on the lower surface.

Natural History

Small cranberry is a wide-ranging circumboreal bog species. It is quite common in Minnesota, even more common than large cranberry (*O. macrocarpus*), at

least in the north. It is found primarily in *Sphagnum*-dominated bogs with stunted black spruce (*Picea mariana*) or tamarack (*Larix laricina*) and in nonforested bogs of the type commonly called muskeg. It is also found on floating bog mats and in rare cases on wet sandy beaches of oligotrophic lakes or on mossy boulders. These are very acidic habitats with pH values in the range of 2.5–3.8 and with very low nutrient levels (Vander Kloet 1983). It rarely occurs with large cranberry, which favors similar but less acidic habitats. Although the berries of small cranberry are similar in eating quality to those of large cranberry, they are slightly smaller and are rarely gathered by people.

Small cranberry produces two types of branches. One type grows upright to a height of about 2–4 inches (5–10 cm) and produces the flowers. The other type functions as a runner or stolon and grows horizontally over the top of the moss for a distance of 2.5 ft (75 cm) or more. These runners can root at the nodes although the roots barely penetrate more than a few inches (centimeters) into the living moss layer. The roots may not reach the saturated peat below, but they can reach the water that is conducted upward between the stems of the living moss. When the moss dries in times of drought, small cranberry may suffer badly, although for a bog plant it is surprisingly well adapted to desiccation. In fact, some features such as the thick epicuticular waxes that cover the stomata are adaptive features shared with desert plants (Vander Kloet 1988).

The 2 red bracts on each flower stalk are diagnostic—June 18.

The fruits are 1/4–1/2" (7–12 mm) across, and note the small, pointed leaves—September 22.

Cranberries   🌿   **317**

Parthenocissus, Virginia creeper and woodbine

Vitaceae: Grape family

This genus includes 10 to 15 species of climbing vines from temperate regions of North America and Asia. Three species are native to the United States, and 2 are found in Minnesota. (*Parthenocissus* is from the Greek *parthenos*, virgin, and *cissos*, ivy; this is a translation of the common name, Virginia creeper.)

Boston ivy [*Parthenocissus tricuspidata* (Sieb. & Zucc.) Planch.], a native of Japan and China, is sometimes planted around houses for ornament, but it is barely hardy in Minnesota and does not appear to survive in the wild.

Key to the Genus Parthenocissus *in Minnesota*

1. Inflorescence branching dichotomously, lacking a central axis; branchlets and petioles glabrous; tendrils 4–15 cm long, with 1–3 branches, the tips pointed or blunt; aerial roots absent .... *P. vitacea*
1. Inflorescence with a distinct central axis; branchlets and petioles hairy; tendrils 1–4 cm long, with 2–10 branches, the tips developing adhesive disks; aerial roots present on main stem .... *P. quinquefolia*

Parthenocissus quinquefolia (L.) Planch.

Virginia creeper

High-climbing **vines**, with tendril-bearing **stems** to 27 m tall and 7 cm diameter. **Branchlets** of the current year brown to yellow-brown, hairy; 2nd-year branchlets brown, hairy. **Aerial roots** abundant on stem and main branches. **Tendrils** at nodes opposite a leaf; 1–4 cm long, with 2–10 branches, the tips developing adhesive disks. **Bark** gray, rough. **Leaves** palmately compound, alternate, deciduous. **Petioles** 4–16 cm long, hairy. **Leaflets** 4 or 5 (usually 5); ± elliptical; 6–12 cm long, 3–6 cm wide; base tapered; apex acuminate; margins sharply serrate; upper surface dark green, moderately to sparsely covered with short, stiff hairs; lower surface similar to upper but paler. **Inflorescence** a large compound cyme with a distinct central axis, 8–15 cm tall with 25–200+ flowers. **Flowers** bisexual, 5-merous, greenish; pedicels glabrous or hairy, 2–5 mm long, turning red in fruit; calyx reduced to a collarlike disk; petals elliptical to oblong, 2.5–3.5 mm long, reflexed, the tips cucullate; **anthesis** late June to late July; insect-pollinated. **Fruit** a ± globose, blue or blue-black berry; 4–8 mm in diameter; maturing early to late September; animal-dispersed. (*quinquefolia*: with 5 leaves, or leaflets in this case)

Identification

Confusion between Virginia creeper and woodbine (*P. vitacea*) is common. They are both climbing vines with nearly identical leaves and flowers, and they both produce small tendrils that attach to their host tree. But in the case of Virginia creeper the tendrils are only 3/4–1 1/2 inches (1–4 cm) long and have 2 to 10 branches. The tip of each tendril branch will develop an adhesive disk when it contacts a host. In contrast, the tendrils of woodbine are 1 1/2–6 inches (4–15 cm) long but branch only once or maybe twice, and the tips do not normally produce adhesive disks. Instead, they usually attach by twining around a small twig or by forcing the tip into a crevice in the bark of its host and then expanding to fill the crevice. Relying on the presence or absence of adhesive disks often leads to misidentification because the expanded tip may look like a disk, and under certain circumstances woodbine may actually produce disks. Rely instead on the length of the tendrils and the number of tendril branches. Also, Virginia creeper has stems that produce aerial roots that adhere tightly to the host tree. The only other Minnesota vine that has

aerial roots is common poison ivy (*Toxicodendron radicans* subsp. *negundo*), which differs by having 3 leaflets instead of 5.

Natural History

Virginia creeper is relatively uncommon in Minnesota, being found primarily in mature hardwood forests in the southeast portion of the state. It is certainly much less common than woodbine (*P. vitacea*) and exploits a slightly different ecological niche. Woodbine will climb tall trees, but more commonly it sprawls over the ground, low shrubs, rock piles, and fences and is quick to invade disturbed habitats. It flowers and fruits abundantly in just about any situation.

Virginia creeper, on the other hand, is largely restricted to the interior of mature forests, at least in Minnesota. It specializes in climbing the dominant canopy trees and produces flowers only when it has reached well into the crown of its host. With the combination of tendrils and aerial roots it will sometimes cling so tightly to its host that the two may appear to have almost grown together. The relationship does not appear to harm the tree, but the adhesive that bonds the tendrils to the tree is so strong that if the tendril is pulled hard, the bark will break before the tendril or the bond.

Inflorescence has a distinct central axis (compare to woodbine)—July 30.

Fruits are smaller than those of woodbine—September 25.

Each leaf has 5 leaflets attached to the same point (palmate).

Using aerial roots to climb an oak.

Parthenocissus vitacea (Knerr) Hitchc.

Woodbine

[*P. inserta* (Kerner) K. Fritsch]

High-climbing or sprawling **vines**, with tendril-bearing **stems** to 22 m tall and 12 cm diameter. **Branchlets** of the current year brown to yellow-brown, glabrous; 2nd-year branchlets brown, glabrous. **Aerial roots** lacking. **Tendrils** at nodes opposite a leaf; 4–15 cm long, with 1–3 branches, the tips pointed or blunt, occasionally somewhat dilated or rarely with adhesive disks. **Bark** gray, rough, becoming coarse and deeply fissured on older stems. **Leaves** palmately compound, alternate, deciduous. **Petioles** 4–15 cm long, essentially glabrous. **Leaflets** 4 or 5 (usually 5); roughly elliptical; 6–12 cm long, 3–6 cm wide; base tapered; apex acuminate; margins sharply serrate or double-serrate; upper surface dark green, glabrous or with a few hairs on main veins; lower surface pale green, glabrous. **Inflorescence** a compound cyme lacking a distinct central axis, 3–7 cm tall with 25–75 flowers. **Flowers** bisexual, 5-merous, greenish; pedicels glabrous, 2–5 mm long, turning red in fruit; calyx reduced to a collarlike disk; petals elliptical to oblong, 3–4 mm long, reflexed, the tips cucullate; **anthesis** late mid-June to late July; insect-pollinated. **Fruit** a ± globose, blue-black berry; 6–10 mm in diameter; maturing late August to late September; animal-dispersed. (*vitacea*: like *vitis*, the grape, in reference to the similarity of the berries)

Identification

There seems to be chronic confusion about the differences between woodbine and Virginia creeper (*P. quinquefolia*). Woodbine has long, sinuous tendrils that branch only once or twice and generally lack adhesive disks at their tips. The tendrils can twine around small branches 1/2–3/4 inch (1–2 cm) in diameter, or when the tip of the tendril enters a crevice in rough bark, it can expand and wedge itself in. The tendrils are very durable and may outlast the stem. The tendrils of Virginia creeper are shorter, weaker, and more highly branched, and they develop adhesive disks at the tips whenever they encounter a substrate to adhere to. Also, Virginia creeper has aerial roots on the stems that adhere to its host, and it has hairs on the twigs and petioles. Lastly, the inflorescence of Virginia creeper has a continuous central axis rather than the dichotomously branched

inflorescence of woodbine; this is a subtle but reliable difference.

Natural History

Woodbine is basically a vine of hardwood forests, where it is often seen hanging ropelike from tall, mature canopy trees. Its skills, however, are hardly limited to climbing trees. When growing in the open, which it often does, it will sprawl over fences, rock piles, shrubs, and herbaceous vegetation and flower profusely. The seeds are widely distributed in the droppings of birds, and seedlings seem to pop up everywhere, especially under bird roosts.

In the absence of physical support the stems of woodbine will creep along the ground, producing roots and leaves at each node. The leaves grow upright and with the stem out of sight, give the appearance of being individual herbaceous plants rather than interconnected components of a woody vine. When one of these creeping stems encounters a tree or other suitable host, it will climb upwards using its deceptively strong tendrils.

Woodbine is fast growing in direct sunlight but grows slower in deep shade. Among woody vines, which are typically short-lived, woodbine appears to be moderately long-lived, although it is very difficult to determine the age of a vine.

The inflorescence branches dichotomously—July 7.

Bark becomes thick and coarse—this stem is 4.25" (11 cm) diameter.

Petals are "boat" shaped—July 7.

Leaves turn maroon in autumn—September 7.

Fruits can be very abundant—September 5.

Physocarpus, ninebark

Rosaceae: Rose family

This genus includes 5 to 10 species of deciduous shrubs found in North America and Asia. There are 5 species in the United States, and 1 in Minnesota. (*Physocarpus* is from the Greek *physa,* bladder, and *karpos,* fruit, in reference to the inflated pod.)

Physocarpus opulifolius (L.) Maxim.

Ninebark

Tall **shrubs**, with 1–4 upright or arching **stems** to 3.3 m tall and 3 cm basal diameter. **Branches** numerous, upright to ascending. **Branchlets** initially greenish, becoming brown then gray; glabrous or nearly so. **Bark** of older stems with multiple loose, outer layers peeling in thin, papery sheets, the outermost layer ashy gray, and the inner reddish brown. **Leaves** simple, alternate, deciduous. **Petioles** 0.8–3 cm long, glabrous or stellate-hairy. **Leaf blades** ovate; 4–7.5 cm long, 2.5–6 cm wide; base obtuse to truncate or rounded, occasionally somewhat cordate; apex acute to obtuse or blunt; margins 3–lobed, irregularly dentate; upper surface stellate-hairy or glabrate, dark green; lower surface glabrous or somewhat stellate-hairy, pale green. **Flowers** bisexual, 5-merous; 15–50, borne in hemispheric, terminal corymbs 2–6 cm across; pedicels 1–2 cm long, stellate-hairy; sepals stellate-hairy, triangular, 2–3 mm long; petals white, glabrous or glabrate, ± circular, 2.5–3.5 mm long; stamens 20–40; pistils 3–5; **anthesis** late May (south) to early August (northeast); insect-pollinated. **Fruit** an inflated follicle; borne in clusters of 3–5 within a hemispheric corymb 5–8 cm across; each follicle about 1 cm long; ovate to elliptical; glabrous or stellate-hairy; maturing mid-July to early September. **Seeds** 3–4, shiny; pale green; apparently gravity-dispersed. (*opulifolius*: with leaves like *Opulus*, in reference to the European *Viburnum opulus*)

Identification

Ninebark is a large, bushy shrub, commonly 6 ft tall (2 m) or taller. Open-grown specimens typically develop long, arching branches and a rounded silhouette, while forest-grown plants are generally sparser and tend to grow more erect. Identification is pretty simple; it is usually enough to note the peeling bark, three-lobed leaves, or papery pods. But also notice that the leaves, flowers, and sometimes the pods are covered with small stellate hairs. At a magnification of 10×, each hair is seen to branch in a radiating star pattern. This feature is not unique, but it is unusual.

Note: There is considerable variation in the degree of hairiness of the pods and lower surface of the leaves. Specimens from the north shore of Lake Superior have nearly hairless pods (Butters and Abbe 1953) and would be considered var. *opulifolius*. Those with

permanently hairy pods are found in the central and southeastern counties and have been segregated as var. *intermedius* (Rydb.) Robins. Not all botanists believe the formal distinction is warranted (Voss 1985).

Natural History

Ninebark is found in upland woods, rocky shores, bluffs, riverbanks, rock outcrops, and sometimes brushy wetlands. It usually occurs in places that receive direct sunlight for at least a portion of the day, but it is occasionally found in shady forest interiors. It seems to fill the role of a fast-growing, relatively short-lived opportunist that takes advantage of thinly vegetated, transitional habitats and ecotones. These could be considered early successional or disturbance-dependent habitats. Disturbance, in this case, is the result of natural forces such as soil erosion, wind exposure, or fire.

Although ninebark is broadly adapted and populations seem quite mobile, it is not an aggressive shrub, nor is it particularly common. In fact, the only place in Minnesota where it could be considered common is the bedrock outcrops along the north shore of Lake Superior; elsewhere it is somewhat sporadic. It reproduces only by seed; however, the function of the inflated pod and the mode of seed dispersal are unclear.

A typical specimen from the shore of Lake Superior—Lake County.

Each fruit is a papery pod (follicle) borne in small clusters—July 19.

Outer layer of bark peels in thin, papery sheets.

Flowers are arranged in dense, hemispheric corymbs—July 18.

Picea, the spruces

Pinaceae: Pine family

The spruces constitute a genus of about 35 species of evergreen trees, occurring primarily in north temperate regions of North America and Eurasia. Seven species are native to the United States, and 2 are native to Minnesota. (*Picea* is the classical Latin name for a spruce or fir tree, from *picis*, pitch.)

In addition to Minnesota's two native species, cultivars of Colorado spruce (*P. pungens* Engelm.) and Norway spruce (*P. abies* (L.) Karst.) are widely grown in the state and often persist at old homesites.

Key to the Genus Picea in Minnesota

1. Twigs hairy; needles (leaves) often <10 mm long, tips obtuse or blunt; mature seed cones 1.5–3 cm long .... *P. mariana*
1. Twigs hairless; needles >10 mm long, tips acute or sharp-pointed; mature seed cones 2.5–6 cm long .... *P. glauca*

Picea glauca (Moench) Voss

White spruce

Large **trees**, to 37 m tall and 84 cm dbh. **Bark** thin; gray; with rough, flaky scales. **Branchlets** pale yellowish brown the first year, becoming brown the 2nd; glabrous. **Leaves** needlelike; borne singly in a tight spiral pattern; evergreen, persisting 7–10 years; straight or slightly curved; roughly 4-sided in cross section; 10–22 mm long, 0.6–1.1 mm wide; borne on a persistent peglike base; apex sharp-pointed or merely acute; margins entire. Trees monoecious, with male **cones** (strobili) and female cones borne separately on the same tree. Mature **male (pollen) cones** oblong-cylindrical; 0.8–1.5 cm long; borne terminally, or laterally on 2nd-year branchlets, predominately in the lower portion of the crown; pollen shed early May to early June. Mature **female (seed) cones** pendulous; oblong-ellipsoidal to oblong-cylindrical; 2.5–6 cm long; short stalked; borne terminally or in leaf axils on 2nd-year branchlets, predominately in the upper portion of the crown; maturing and shedding seeds in autumn of the first year and falling from the tree soon after; wind-pollinated. **Seeds** 2–3.5 mm long, with a broad papery wing 6–10 mm long; wind- and gravity-dispersed. (*glauca*: blue-green, in reference to the young leaves)

Identification

White spruce is a tall, slender evergreen with a narrow, conical crown. The branches are relatively short and tend to be horizontal; the lower branches often droop. It differs from black spruce (*P. mariana*) by having hairless twigs and longer cones. Both spruces differ from balsam fir (*Abies balsamea*) by having needles (leaves) that are attached to a raised peglike base rather than flush with the twig, and by having scaly bark.

Natural History

White spruce is a common forest tree in most of northern and central Minnesota. While black spruce typically grows in wetlands, white spruce grows primarily in uplands, particularly in loamy, rocky or alluvial soils. It prefers moist conditions but also grows in dry sites, especially if the soil is relatively deep and fertile. Under typical forest conditions white spruce is somewhat slow growing, but it lives longer than balsam fir and at least as long as the pines. The oldest white spruce in Minnesota are thought to be in the Boundary Waters Canoe Area Wilderness. They are estimated to be at least 300 years old (Heinselman 1973). White spruce nearly 1,000 years old have been reported from above the Arctic Circle (Giddings 1962).

White spruce is very tolerant of shade and can easily grow under a canopy of early-successional species such as trembling aspen (*Populus tremuloides*) and paper birch (*Betula papyrifera*). Being taller and longer-lived, white spruce will eventually overtop them and form a new canopy. White spruce can also reproduce under a canopy of its own species, which surprisingly few trees can do. This gives it the ability to continually replace itself in the canopy, which qualifies it as a true climax species. It typically shares the canopy with a small number of other climax species, particularly balsam fir (*Abies balsamea*) and northern white cedar (*Thuja occidentalis*).

Mature forests of white spruce are very susceptible to fire in dry years. Not surprisingly, the seeds of white spruce germinate and grow well on the bare mineral soil left after a fire. But unlike the pines, white spruce does not require fire or any major disturbance to reproduce. Its seeds germinate well on a variety of surfaces in undisturbed forests, such as humus, rotting logs, and moss (Buell and Niering 1957). Mature white spruce trees usually survive infestations of spruce budworm that typically kill balsam fir trees (Heinselman 1973), and white spruce is rarely infected with dwarf mistletoe (*Arceuthobium pusillum*), which can be so deadly to black spruce (Hawksworth and Weins 1972).

Male strobili are shed soon after releasing their pollen—May 12.

Seed cones are longer than those of black spruce.

Female strobili are usually found in upper part of crown—May 5.

Each leaf (needle) is attached to a raised, peglike base.

Bark is gray with rough, flaky scales— trunk is 19" (49 cm) dbh.

A typical white spruce from Cook County.

Spruces ❧ 331

Picea mariana (P. Mill.) B.S.P.

Black spruce

Small or midsize **trees**, to 25 m tall and 48 cm dbh. **Bark** thin; gray or brownish; with rough, flaky scales. **Branchlets** pale brown the 1st year, becoming brown the 2nd; hairy. **Leaves** linear or needlelike; borne singly in a dense spiral pattern; evergreen, persisting 7–10 years; straight or slightly curved; roughly 4-sided in cross section; 5–14 mm long, 0.8–1.5 mm wide; borne on a persistent peglike base; apex obtuse or blunt, occasionally acute; margins entire. Trees monoecious, with male **cones** (strobili) and female cones borne separately on the same tree. Mature **male** (**pollen**) **cones** subglobose to oblong; 1–1.5 cm long; borne terminally, or laterally on 2nd-year branchlets, predominately in the lower portion of the crown; pollen shed early May to mid-June. Mature **female** (**seed**) **cones** pendulous; subglobose to ellipsoidal; 1.5–3 cm long; short stalked or ± sessile; borne terminally or in leaf axils of 2nd-year branchlets, predominately in the upper portion of the crown; maturing in autumn of the first year and persisting on the tree for many years while shedding seeds intermittently; wind-pollinated. **Seeds** 2–3 mm long, with a broad papery wing 5–8 mm long; wind- and gravity-dispersed. (*mariana*: a Latin derivative of *Maria*, in reference to Maryland, although this species does not occur there)

Identification

Black spruce is a rather small, slender evergreen with short, horizontal, or drooping branches. The surest and quickest way to tell it from white spruce (*P. glauca*) is by the short, stout hairs on the twigs (may require a hand lens). A rare hybrid between black spruce and white spruce was found near Cromwell (Carlton County) in 1955 (Little and Pauley 1958).

Natural History

In Minnesota, black spruce is now the most abundant tree species growing on peat soil, having surpassed tamarack (*Larix laricina*) within historical times (U.S. Surveyor General 1847–1908). These peatland habitats include both bogs and swamps.

True bogs receive all their water directly from rainfall and as a result, are extremely acidic and nutrient poor. They are generally devoid of trees except for scattered or stunted black spruce. Under these harsh but stable conditions black spruce may

live 250 years but grow no more than 20 ft (6 m) tall and 2 inches (5 cm) in diameter. Swamps, in contrast to bogs, receive at least some water that has flowed through mineral soil, so swamps are not as acidic or as nutrient poor as bogs. Black spruce will grow faster and larger in swamps than in bogs, but in swamps it will have to compete with tamarack, balsam fir (*Abies balsamea*), or northern white cedar (*Thuja occidentalis*). In the northeastern counties black spruce sometimes occurs in dry uplands, mostly in thin soil over bedrock or boulders (Ohman and Ream 1971).

In peatlands, the gradual upward accumulation of peat can cause the shallow roots of black spruce to become buried deeper (some say this happens when the weight of the tree causes it to gradually sink into the peat), then the roots will likely die from poor aeration. But black spruce has the unusual ability to develop a new layer of roots above the dead layer. Over time, older trees may end up with several layers of dead roots beneath the living roots (Vincent 1965).

Large stands of black spruce are very susceptible to fire in drought years. But seed cones occur at the top of tall trees and often survive fire, even if the tree itself is killed. In fact, they may continue to release viable seeds for 3 or 4 years and eventually regenerate the stand (Ahlgren 1959). Dwarf mistletoe (*Arceuthobium pusillum*) is a parasitic plant that uses black spruce as its primary host and may kill trees, even whole stands (Hawksworth and Weins 1972).

A female strobilus (cone) at the time of pollination—June 21.

Black spruce typically holds dead branches.

Seed cones persist on the tree for several years.

Male strobili (pollen cones) about 1/2" (10–15 mm) long—June 21.

Compare the hairy twig with the smooth twig of white spruce.

A typical stand of black spruce from Cook County.

Pinus, the pines

Pinaceae: Pine family

The pines comprise a genus of about 100 species, all needle-leaved trees or shrubs. They are found throughout the northern hemisphere with about 38 species native to the United States, and 3 native to Minnesota. (*Pinus* is the classical Latin name for a pine tree.)

In addition to the 3 native pines, several species of nonnative pines are sometimes planted for landscaping purposes and occasionally for timber production. Of these, European Scots pine (*P. sylvestris* L.) is probably the most common. It has needles in bundles of 2 like the native red pine, but the needles are shorter, less than 4 inches (10 cm) long, and the bark of the upper trunk and branches is conspicuously orange or reddish and distinctly flaky.

Key to the Genus Pinus *in Minnesota*

1. Needles (leaves) in bundles of 5; cones slender, 8–20 cm long; bark usually ridged and furrowed .... *P. strobus*
1. Needles in bundles of 2; cones stout, 3–6 cm long; bark scaly.
    2. Needles 2–6 cm long; bark uniformly gray to gray-black .... *P. banksiana*
    2. Needles 10–15 cm long; bark with conspicuous patches of reddish brown or orange-brown .... *P. resinosa*

Pinus banksiana Lamb.

Jack pine

Midsize to occasionally large **trees**, to 31 m tall and 50 cm dbh; **branches** spreading or ascending, the crown conical to oblong or irregularly rounded. **Bark** relatively thin; gray or gray-black or sometimes brownish; with irregular scaly ridges or plates, somewhat flaky. **Branchlets** brown, glabrous. **Leaves** needlelike; spirally arranged in bundles of 2; evergreen, persisting for 2–3 years; relatively stout and stiff, somewhat curved and often slightly twisted, channeled (U-shaped in cross section); 2–6 cm long, 1–1.7 mm wide; apex acute; margins minutely serrate; all surfaces with faint longitudinal lines of stomata; bundle sheaths 2–5 mm long, persistent. Trees monoecious, with separate male **cones (strobili)** and female cones on the same tree. Mature **male (pollen) cones** cylindrical, 1–1.5 cm long; borne in dense clusters at the base of 1st-year branchlets; pollen shed in May or June. Mature **female (seed) cones** conical, usually pointed forward and incurved before opening, becoming ovoid, divergent, and ± symmetrical after opening; 3–6 cm long; sessile; maturing the 2nd year but typically remaining closed for several years or indefinitely, or until released by fire; persisting on the tree after seeds are released; wind-pollinated. **Seeds** 3–4 mm long, with a thin, papery wing 1–1.2 cm long; wind- and gravity-dispersed. (*banksiana*: named for English botanist Sir Joseph Banks, 1743–1820)

Identification

Jack pine is the only Minnesota pine with short needles. They rarely measure more than 2 1/2 inches (6 cm) long and are packed in bundles of 2. They are also rather thick and stiff and usually curved. The unopened cones tend to grow parallel to the branch, often with the tip curving inward. The bark is usually dark gray and scaly, sometimes almost flaky.

Natural History

Jack pine is on average the smallest of Minnesota's three native pines, and the most abundant. It is particularly common on outwash plains and sandy glacial lake plains in central Minnesota. If the soils are very sandy, with low nutrient levels and little organic matter, then jack pine may grow in pure stands. On better soils it might be mixed with any of the other native pines or with bur oak (*Quercus macrocarpa*) or northern pin oak (*Q. ellipsoidalis*).

It is often portrayed as a small, scraggly, short-lived tree. Yet under favorable conditions, in places like Scenic State Park (Itasca County), it can grow to a stately 100 ft (31 m) tall. And a specimen in the Boundary Waters Canoe Area Wilderness (Superior National Forest) has been aged at 243 years (Heinselman 1973). Where it is not protected, jack pine is usually cut for pulp before reaching 65 years.

Jack pine seedlings need direct sunlight; they cannot survive in the shade of a forest canopy, not even a canopy of other jack pine. Species that are more tolerant of shade, such as white spruce (*Picea glauca*), will eventually come up through the understory and replace the jack pine, limiting its dominance to a single generation. This course of events is normally reversed by periodic crown fires, which strongly favor the return of jack pine (Ahlgren 1976). The reason is that most mature jack pine have at least some cones that are tightly sealed with resin (called "serotinous") that melts only during the heat of a fire (Gauthier, Bergeron, and Simon 1993). Although the fire may kill the trees, the seeds survive and are released soon after the fire passes. They find an ideal seedbed in the ashes of the previous forest and grow quickly. In other words, large, pure stands of even-aged jack pine invariably originate from a crown fire that destroyed the previous stand of jack pine, an event called a "stand-replacing fire."

A cluster of male strobili—June 3.

Bark is typically gray with scaly or flaky ridges.

Seed cones often curve back toward the branch.

These female strobili have recently been pollinated—June 3.

A stand of jack pine in Koochiching County.

Pinus resinosa Ait.

Red pine

Large **trees**, to 37 m tall and 100 cm dbh; with nearly horizontal **branches** and a narrow, oblong or ellipsoid-shaped crown. **Bark** relatively thick; gray with patches of reddish brown to orange-brown; with loose, flaky or scaly plates. **Branchlets** brown, glabrous. **Leaves** needlelike; spirally arranged in bundles of 2; evergreen, persisting for 4–5 years; slender, straight, barely if at all twisted, channeled (U-shaped in cross section); 10–20 cm long, about 1 mm wide; apex acute; margins minutely serrate; all surfaces with faint longitudinal lines of stomata; bundle sheaths 8–20 mm long, persistent. Trees monoecious, with separate male **cones (strobili)** and female cones borne on the same tree. Mature **male (pollen) cones** cylindrical to ellipsoidal, 1.3–1.8 cm long; borne in dense clusters at the base of 1st-year branchlets; pollen shed late May to mid-June. Mature **female (seed) cones** stiffly divergent from the stem; ± symmetrical, conical-ovoid before opening, broadly ovoid to nearly globose after opening; 3.5–6 cm long; essentially sessile; maturing in the autumn of the 2nd year, and releasing seeds through autumn, winter, and the following spring, usually falling from the tree later the same year or the following year; wind-pollinated. **Seeds** 3–5 mm long, with a thin, papery wing 1–1.5 cm long; wind- and gravity-dispersed. (*resinosa*: resinous)

Identification

The bark of red pine is always distinctive. It has gray, scaly plates and, true to its name, conspicuous patches of orange-brown or reddish brown color. The dark green needles are larger and coarser than those of white pine (*P. strobus*) and are in bundles of 2, not 5. The needles are also brittle, causing them to break cleanly when bent.
Note: The misnomer "Norway pine" is sometimes applied to this species. It has been traced to early settlers who confused the native red pine with Scots pine (*P. sylvestris*), which is native to Norway and most of northern and central Europe. The native red pine occurs only in North America and was officially designated the Minnesota state tree in 1953.

Natural History

Red pine is a tall, slender tree reaching a maximum height of about 120 ft (37 m) in Minnesota.

Maximum age can only be guessed, but a living specimen near Sea Gull Lake in the Boundary Waters Canoe Area Wilderness (Cook County) is known to be 407 years old (Heinselman 1973). Red pine is most common on dry or dry-mesic, sandy, acidic soils. It seems to prefer flat or gently rolling terrain and is often found on low, sandy ridges along lakeshores. It occurs in pure stands or mixed with white pine (*P. strobus*), jack pine (*P. banksiana*) or northern pin oak (*Quercus ellipsoidalis*). Red pine is considered an early successional species because it is intolerant of shade and is dependent on fire for large-scale reproduction (Ahlgren 1976).

Red pine was once very abundant in Minnesota, but the best trees and the largest stands had been cut by the early twentieth century. The combination of logging and the slash fires that followed tended to increase trembling aspen (*Populus tremuloides*), and in some cases jack pine, at the expense of red pine (Ohman et al. 1978). Current forest conditions, as well as forest management practices, continue to favor aspen. As a result, there is relatively little natural red pine reproduction occurring in Minnesota. But because red pine is so often planted (more than any other tree in Minnesota), it is commonly seen in parts of the state where it would not naturally occur, usually in straight-rowed, single-species plantations.

Seed cones are short, and they point away from the branch.

Each male strobilus is a simple pollen-making organ—June 12.

The female strobili (cones) catch wind-borne pollen—June 12.

A stand of red pine in Itasca County.

Bark typically has patches of orange-brown color.

Pinus strobus L.

Eastern white pine

Large **trees**, to 41 m tall and 140 cm dbh; with nearly horizontal upswept **branches**, and a somewhat flat-topped crown. **Bark** thick, gray with a purplish cast; with either scaly plates or blocky ridges. **Branchlets** brown; hairy, becoming glabrous or glabrate the 3rd year. **Leaves** needlelike; spirally arranged in bundles of 5; evergreen, persisting for 2 years; slender, straight, 3-angled (roughly triangular in cross section); 5–10 cm long, 0.5–0.8 mm wide; apex acute; margins minutely serrate; faint longitudinal lines of stomata visible only on upper surface; bundle sheaths 10–15 mm long, shed early the 1st year. Trees monoecious, with separate male **cones (strobili)** and female cones borne on the same tree. Mature **male (pollen) cones** ellipsoidal, 8–12 mm long; borne in dense clusters at the base of 1st-year branchlets; pollen shed in May or June. Mature **female (seed) cones** pendent; cylindrical to narrowly cylindrical or narrowly lance-cylindrical, often slightly curved; 8–20 cm long; on stalks 1.5–3 cm long; maturing and shedding seeds in the autumn of the 2nd year and falling from the tree soon after; wind-pollinated. **Seeds** 3–5 mm long, with a thin, papery wing 1.8–2.5 cm long; wind- and gravity-dispersed. (*strobus*: ancient Latin name for some unrelated tree)

Identification

Compared to red pine (*P. resinosa*), the needles of eastern white pine are smaller and softer and have a finer texture, and they are in bundles of 5, not 2. Also, the crown of white pine tends to be somewhat flat topped instead of round topped. The bark is uniformly grayish with a purplish cast and often with distinct ridges, while the bark of red pine is scaly or platy and has patches of orangish or reddish brown color.

Natural History

Eastern white pine is a tall, massive tree reaching a maximum height of about 133 ft (41 m) in Minnesota but reportedly reaching 220 ft (68 m) in New England (Harlow et al. 1991). And it may reach an age of 450 years (*fide* Burns and Honkala 1990). It prefers mesic soils and grows well in sand, clay, or loam. On sandy soils, it commonly occurs mixed with red pine (*P. resinosa*) or jack pine (*P. banksiana*), or often both. On better soils, it usually occurs with hardwoods, typically oaks (*Quercus* spp.) or paper birch (*Betula papyrifera*).

Crown fires occurring at intervals of 100 to 200 years, along with more frequent ground fires, are generally needed to perpetuate large stands of eastern white pine (Heinselman 1973). Without this fire regime, stands are eventually replaced by species that are more tolerant of shade but less tolerant of fire, such as white spruce (*Picea glauca*), balsam fir (*Abies balsamea*), and certain hardwoods. In this sense, eastern white pine is considered a fire-dependent species, but that holds true only for large stands. Scattered individuals or small groves of eastern white pine that occur in a matrix of other tree species may have originated in small openings caused by windfalls, lightning strikes, or other localized disturbance rather than fire.

White pine blister rust is a disease caused by the parasitic fungus *Cronartium ribicola* J. C. Fisch. It entered the United States from Europe in about 1906 and reached Minnesota in 1916 (Miller, Kimmey, and Fowler 1959). It is usually fatal to eastern white pine and cannot be effectively controlled or treated. For this reason eastern white pine is rarely used in reforestation or plantations anymore. And for a variety of reasons, mostly related to human management of forests, natural reproduction is very poor. All this has led to a tragic situation; disease coupled with fire suppression, deer predation, and years of unsustainable logging practices have pushed native populations of eastern white pine into a steep decline.

Long, slender seed cones hang downward—August 13.

These female strobili will develop into the seed cones—June 18.

A mature white pine from Carlton County.

The male strobili are seen only briefly in late spring—June 18.

A 22" (55 cm) dbh trunk showing characteristic bark pattern.

Populus, poplars, aspens and cottonwoods

Salicaceae: Willow family

This genus includes about 40 species of deciduous trees, widespread throughout the Northern Hemisphere. There are about 8 species in North America, and 4 in Minnesota. (*Populus* is the classical Latin name.)

In addition to the native species, a number of European poplars are sometimes planted in Minnesota for ornamental purposes. The European white poplar (*P. alba* L.) is a large, coarse tree with a broad crown. The leaves look something like those of the native bigtooth aspen (*P. grandidentata*) except the underside is densely covered with white hairs, even at maturity. European white poplar is occasionally planted around urban lakes and in parks, but it spreads by root suckers and can become a nuisance. There is also some concern that it may become invasive.

Lombardy poplar (*P. nigra* L. var. *italica*) is a large tree with close-set, erect branches that form a narrow, spirelike or columnar crown. It was a popular ornamental tree in the past, but it is very susceptible to disease and is rarely planted today. It is often replaced by upright clones of gray poplar (*P. ×canescens*), an artificial hybrid between white poplar and the Eurasian aspen (*P. tremula*).

Recently, fast-growing artificial hybrids involving a number of different aspens and poplars have been developed by the forestry industry for large-scale biomass and fiber production. "Siouxland" poplar is a heavily promoted hybrid between the North American cottonwood (*P. deltoides*) and the European black poplar (*P. nigra*). There are also several commercially available aspen hybrids created by crossing the Eurasian aspen and the North American trembling aspen (*P. tremuloides*).

Key to the Genus *Populus* in Minnesota

1. Petioles distinctly flattened in cross section, especially near the attachment with the blade, glabrous or hairy at base only; leaf blades no more than 1/3 longer than wide (l/w = 0.8–1.3), lower surface of blades a uniform pale green color.
   2. Leaf blades broadly triangular in outline, with long narrow tips; leaf bases distinctly truncate; teeth on leaf margins gland tipped; axis of catkins glabrous; mature capsules 7–11 mm long, with 3–4 valves .... *P. deltoides* subsp. *monilifera*
   2. Leaf blades broadly ovate to nearly round, with short narrow tips; leaf bases rounded or occasionally somewhat truncate; teeth not gland tipped; axis of catkins hairy; mature capsules 3–6 mm long, with 2 valves.
      3. Leaf margins with 4–12 teeth per side, each tooth 3–4 mm long; leaves densely white-woolly (tomentose) when just expanding, glabrous when full size .... *P. grandidentata*
      3. Leaf margins with 20–50 teeth per side, each tooth 0.5–1.5 mm long; leaves glabrous at all stages of development .... *P. tremuloides*
1. Petioles roundish or channeled in cross section, minutely and evenly hairy; leaf blades at least 1/3 longer than wide (l/w = 1.3–2.3), lower surface often with blotchy copper-colored stains .... *P. balsamifera*

Populus balsamifera L.

Balsam poplar

Large or midsize **trees**, to 25 m tall and 64 cm dbh; clonal by root suckering. 1st-year **branchlets** greenish, usually hairy; 2nd-year branchlets brown, hairy or glabrate. **Bark** greenish brown and somewhat smooth when young, becoming gray or gray-brown and developing flat-topped ridges and narrow furrows in age. **Leaves** simple, alternate, deciduous. **Petioles** roundish in cross section, with a shallow channel on upper surface, 2–5 cm long, minutely hairy. **Leaf blades** ovate to ovate-lanceolate; 6–10 cm long, 3–7 cm wide, length/width 1.3–2.3; base rounded or occasionally cordate; apex acute or acuminate; margins with 30–55 small rounded teeth per side, each tooth with a small imbedded gland; upper surface dark green, essentially glabrous; lower surface pale green, usually with blotchy copper-colored stains, essentially glabrous. **Flowers** borne in unisexual **catkins**, each tree bearing either male catkins or female catkins; from lateral buds on 2nd-year branchlets; appearing before the leaves. **Male catkins** pendulous, 4–9 cm long, ± sessile. **Female catkins** pendulous, 6–16 cm long, nearly sessile, rachis hairy; **anthesis** early May to early June; wind-pollinated. **Fruit** a 2-valved ovoid capsule; 5.5–9 mm long; stipes 0.5–1 mm long; releasing seeds late May to late June; wind-dispersed. (*balsamifera*: balsam-bearing)

Identification

Balsam poplar is a fairly tall, slender tree with relatively short, ascending branches and stout twigs. It is similar to the aspens (*P. tremuloides* and *P. grandidentata*) but can be recognized quickly by the shape of the leaf and by the blotchy, copper-colored resin stains on the underside of the leaf. The copper color can actually be seen from some distance when the wind blows. Also note the large buds; they are coated with a sticky, yellow, aromatic resin called "balm of Gilead" in the pharmaceutical trade.

Natural History

Balsam poplar occurs throughout the forested region of central and northern Minnesota. It is especially prominent in the aspen parkland and transitional hardwood forests in the northwestern counties, where it is one of the principal tree species along the prairie-forest border. It prefers moist sites, often along lakeshores or on river terraces or at the margins of swamps or marshes. Soil types range from loamy to silty or clayey, even sandy if the water table is near the surface. Balsam poplar is fast growing and relatively short-lived. Individual trees remain vigorous for 50 to 75 years and usually die by 100; a maximum age of 200 years has been reported (Viereck 1970).

Like the aspens, balsam poplar is an early successional species that occurs primarily in fire-prone landscapes. Fire kills or damages the standing trees but stimulates suckering (sprouting) from the long, shallow roots and also provides a good seedbed for seedling establishment. The new suckers, or seedlings, grow rapidly and soon replace the previous stand. In the absence of fire or other major disturbance, balsam poplar will sucker very little, and seedlings will not survive. If that happens, late-successional tree species, which are characteristically longer-lived and more shade tolerant, will become established in the understory and eventually replace the balsam poplar by overtopping it or simply outliving it. Fire is the natural mechanism for reversing this process of forest succession, but since human settlement that role has largely been taken over by clear-cutting.

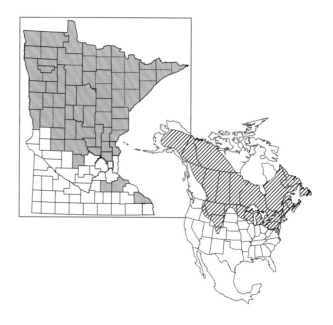

Postpollination female flowers with developing ovaries.

A mature 13" (33 cm) dbh tree showing furrowed bark.

Lower surface of leaf shows copper-colored stain.

Bottom half of these male catkins have shed their pollen—May 23.

Female flowers showing red stigmas—May 12.

Populus deltoides Marsh. subsp. *monilifera* (Ait.) Eckenw.

Plains cottonwood

[*P. deltoides* Marsh. var. *occidentalis* Rydb.; *P. sargentii* Dode]

Large **trees**, to 40 m tall and 2 m dbh; not clonal. **Branchlets** glabrous; greenish the 1st year, green-brown the 2nd. **Bark** thick, coarse, gray or brown, with long angular ridges and deep furrows. **Leaves** simple, alternate, deciduous. **Petioles** flat in cross section, at least near the summit, 4–8 cm long, glabrous. **Leaf blades** deltate; 5–10 cm long, 5.5–11 cm wide, length/width 0.8–1.1; base truncate; apex long-acuminate; margins with 12–30 rounded teeth per side, each tooth with a small gland; upper surface bright green, glabrous; lower surface similar to upper but often slightly paler. **Flowers** borne in unisexual **catkins**, each tree bearing either male catkins or female catkins; arising from lateral buds on 2nd-year branchlets; appearing before the leaves. **Male catkins** stout, pendulous, 5–12 cm long, ± sessile. **Female catkins** slender, pendulous, 6–12 cm long in flower, becoming 9–17 cm long in fruit, ± sessile, rachis glabrous; **anthesis** early April to early May; wind-pollinated. **Fruit** a 3- or 4-valved ovoid capsule; 7–11 mm long; stipes 3–5 mm long; releasing seeds late mid-May to early mid-June; wind- and water-dispersed. (*deltoides*: triangular, in reference to the leaf; *monilifera*: resembling a string of beads)

Identification

Plains cottonwood can become a huge tree with massive limbs and thick, coarse bark. It can be distinguished from balsam poplar (*P. balsamifera*) and the aspens (*P. tremuloides* and *P. grandidentata*) by the shape of the leaf alone, especially by the broad, squared-off base and the long, drawn-out tip. *Note:* Eastern cottonwood (*P. deltoides* subsp. *deltoides*) is a closely related subspecies, occurring to the east and south of Minnesota, reportedly coming no closer than central Illinois (Eckenwalder 1977). Because the morphological differences are clinal and the two subspecies intergrade, both subspecies are represented on the accompanying North American map.

Natural History

Plains cottonwood is probably the most massive tree species in Minnesota (white pine runs a close second), commonly measuring as much as 120 ft (37 m) in height and 5 ft (1.5 m) in diameter. It is also said to be the fastest-growing tree in North America (Cooper and Van Haverbeke 1990). But the branches are

brittle and easily broken by wind or ice, and by 100 years most trees show considerable damage and decay. A maximum age of 200 years has been estimated (Harlow et al. 1991), but the true age of older trees is difficult to determine.

Plains cottonwood is an early successional species commonly found on floodplains and along streams and lakeshores in southern and western Minnesota. Seasonal flooding presents no problem for cottonwood; even the sedimentation and scouring that often accompanies flooding is easily tolerated. Shade, however, is not tolerated at any stage of growth.

On large floodplains cottonwood often grows in pure stands or mixed with silver maple (*Acer saccharinum*), boxelder (*Acer negundo*), or peach-leaved willow (*Salix amygdaloides*). It also colonizes surface-dry upland sites, such as fencerows, field margins, and gravel pits, but it is susceptible to drought and under these circumstances it probably survives only where the groundwater is near the surface.

Plains cottonwood reproduces only by seed; it does not produce root suckers as the aspens and poplars do. But a single tree can produce up to 48 million seeds (Cooper and Van Haverbeke 1990), which are released in late May just as spring floodwaters are receding. The newly exposed sand and silt make an ideal seedbed, allowing the seeds to germinate almost immediately and grow as much as 2 1/2 ft (80 cm) by autumn of the 1st year.

Female flowers at peak anthesis—April 22.

These capsules are about ready to release their seeds.

A broad, squared-off base and drawn-out tip.

Note the red anthers on these male catkins—April 11.

Thick, angular ridges and deep furrows—40" (102 cm) dbh, Ramsey County.

Populus grandidentata Michx.

Bigtooth aspen

Large **trees**, to 29 m tall and 60 cm dbh; clonal by root suckering. **Branchlets** brown, initially hairy, becoming glabrous by the end of the 1st year. **Bark** of younger trunks thin, smooth, greenish yellow to olive-green, eventually becoming thick and gray with prominent ridges and furrows. **Leaves** simple, alternate, deciduous. **Petioles** flat in cross section, at least near summit, 4–8 cm long, glabrous, or hairy near base. **Leaf blades** broadly ovate to nearly orbicular; 5–10 cm long, 4.5–9 cm wide, length/width 1–1.3; base rounded to somewhat truncate; apex obtuse to acute; margins with 4–12 large blunt teeth per side, teeth lacking glands; upper surface dark green, densely white-woolly when immature, becoming glabrous before reaching full size; lower surface similar but pale green and retaining woolly hairs somewhat longer. **Flowers** in unisexual **catkins**, each tree bearing either male catkins or female catkins; arising from lateral buds on 2nd-year branchlets; appearing before the leaves. **Male catkins** pendulous, 2.5–9 cm long, sessile. **Female catkins** slender, pendulous, 3–8 cm long in flower, becoming 9–15 cm long in fruit, sessile, rachis hairy; **anthesis** late mid-April to mid-May; wind-pollinated. **Fruit** a two-valved ovoid capsule; 3–5 mm long; stipes 0.8–1.7 mm long; releasing seeds late May to mid-June; wind-dispersed. (*grandidentata*: large-toothed)

Identification

Bigtooth aspen is a tall, slender tree with a narrow crown and short, stout branches. It is similar to trembling aspen (*P. tremuloides*), except the leaves are somewhat larger on average (but still tremble in the wind) and have fewer but larger teeth. Also, the leaves appear later in the spring and are densely white-woolly when just unfolding, giving the whole tree a ghostly appearance. European white poplar (*P. alba*) is sometimes planted in the region and also has white-woolly leaves, but it retains the wooliness, at least on the underside of the leaves; bigtooth aspen loses it when the leaves are about half grown. Natural hybrids between bigtooth and trembling aspen (= *P.* ×*smthii* Boivin) are known but not common (Barnes and Pregitzer 1985).

Natural History

Bigtooth aspen is fairly common throughout most of the forested region of Minnesota, especially in the central and east-central counties. Yet nowhere is it as common as the closely related trembling aspen. The ecology and life history of the two aspens are similar, but bigtooth aspen is more narrowly adapted, preferring moist, loamy or sandy-loam soil. It is typically found as small, scattered clones of one or two dozen trees in a matrix of other hardwood species such as oaks (*Quercus* spp.), paper birch (*Betula papyrifera*), basswood (*Tilia americana*), red maple (*Acer rubrum*), or trembling aspen.

Bigtooth aspen is a pioneer species that initially becomes established by seed on bare, moist soil and then spreads by root suckering. In fact, the vast majority of bigtooth aspen trees seen in a forest are actually clones that originated as root suckers rather than seedlings. As it turns out, seedlings are quite rare (Barnes 1966). Suckers are generally produced at the margins of the stand, so the stand expands outward until it encounters competition from other trees, then suckering generally stops. If the standing trunks are removed, usually by fire or clear-cutting, the roots will again sprout suckers and begin a new generation, but this is the only way bigtooth aspen can produce a second generation on the site of the first. If the trees are left undisturbed, other tree species that are more shade tolerant will usually become established in the understory and eventually overtop or outlive the bigtooth aspen.

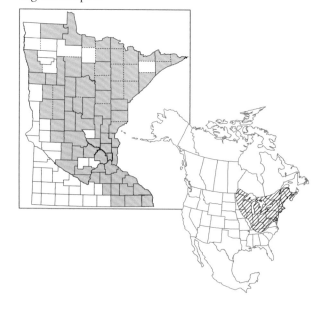

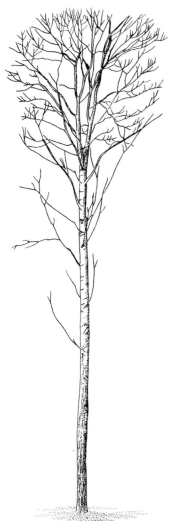

The name "bigtooth" comes from the jagged leaf margin.

These male flowers have shed nearly all their pollen—May 5.

Note the broad, red stigmas on these female catkins—April 29.

A 21" (54 cm) dbh specimen showing mature bark.

Young trees have smooth, greenish bark.

Populus tremuloides Michx.

Trembling aspen

Large **trees**, to 32 m tall and 67 cm dbh; clonal by root suckering. **Branchlets** brown or greenish brown, glabrous. **Bark** of young trees thin, pale grayish green to whitish green or nearly white, smooth, eventually becoming thick, gray or brown, and developing broad flat ridges and shallow furrows, at least near the base of older trees. **Leaves** simple, alternate, deciduous. **Petioles** flat in cross section, at least near summit, 3–7 cm long, glabrous. **Leaf blades** broadly ovate to depressed orbicular; 3.5–7.5 cm long, 3–7.5 cm wide, length/width 0.9–1.2; base broadly rounded to somewhat truncate; apex abruptly short-acuminate; margins with 20–50 blunt teeth per side, teeth lacking glands; upper surface dark green, glabrous; lower surface pale green, glabrous. **Flowers** in unisexual **catkins**, each tree bearing either male catkins or female catkins; arising from lateral buds on 2nd-year branchlets; appearing before the leaves. **Male catkins** pendulous, 3–8 cm long, sessile. **Female catkins** pendulous, 3–6 cm long in flower, becoming 4–15 cm long in fruit, sessile, rachis hairy; **anthesis** early April to early mid-May; wind-pollinated. **Fruit** a 2-valved ovoid capsule; 3.5–6 mm long; stipes 0.7–1.5 mm long; releasing seeds early mid-May to early June; wind-dispersed. (*tremuloides*: resembling *P. tremula* for the trembling of the leaves)

Identification

Trembling aspen is a tall, slender tree with short, stout branches and a narrow crown. The petiole is unusually long, and it is flattened in a direction perpendicular to the plane of the leaf, so the leaf tends to flutter, or "tremble," in the wind. The bark is usually greenish or sometimes white like paper birch (*Betula papyrifera*), but it never peels like birch.

Natural History

Trembling aspen is said to be the most widespread tree in North America (Harlow et al. 1991). True or not, it certainly is the most abundant tree in Minnesota, although when the first settlers arrived, it apparently ranked second behind tamarack (*Larix laricina*) (U.S. Surveyor General 1847–1908). It grows in a wide range of habitat types but mostly in dry to moist uplands in sandy to sandy-loam soil. It is an early successional species that grows quickly and rarely lives beyond 100 years, although a maximum

age of 200 years has been reported (Heinselman 1973). It is intolerant of shade and in the absence of disturbance is eventually replaced by more shade-tolerant species such as white spruce (*Picea glauca*), balsam fir (*Abies balsamea*), sugar maple (*Acer saccharum*), or red maple (*A. rubrum*).

The key to aspen ecology is its phenomenal ability to spread vegetatively by sprouting stems from its shallow root system, a process called root suckering (Barnes 1966). In this way, a single tree established by seed can produce hundreds of trees spread over an acre or more. Since all the stems originate from a common root system, they are genetically identical and collectively called a clone. Suckering and subsequent clone formation are greatly stimulated by fire and by clear-cutting. The history of logging and slash fire in the early part of the twentieth century favored a tremendous increase in trembling aspen at the expense of the pines (Ahlgren 1976). So, in effect the vast expanses of trembling aspen seen in northern Minnesota today are the legacy of pine logging a century ago.

The forest tent caterpillar (*Malacosoma disstria* Hbn.), a native insect, has widespread outbreaks every 10 to 15 years, which last from two to five years (Duncan and Hodson 1958). During outbreaks they can defoliate entire stands of trembling aspen over huge areas, sometimes for three consecutive years. Each time the trees will releaf and are rarely killed.

Female flowers at peak receptivity, note the red stigmas—April 8.

These male flowers have recently shed their pollen—April 11.

These mature capsules are releasing their seeds—May 29.

Bark starts smooth, becomes furrowed near base.

The flattened petiole causes the leaves to "tremble" in the wind.

A mature stand along the Tomahawk Road, Lake County.

Prunus, plums and cherries

Rosaceae: Rose family

The plums and cherries make up a genus of about 200 species of deciduous trees and shrubs. They occur mainly in north temperate regions, with about 50 species native to the United States, and 7 native to Minnesota. (*Prunus* is the classical Latin name for the plum tree.)

In addition to the native species, many nonnative *Prunus* cultivars are grown in Minnesota for their ornamental value or edible fruits. Some of the most common include European bird cherry (*P. padus*), purple-leaf sand cherry (*P.* ×*cistena*), nanking cherry (*P. tomentosa*), Amur chokecherry (*P. maackii*), and sour cherry (*P. cerasus*). None of these are known to be naturalized in the state.

The cherries, particularly choke-cherry (*P. virginiana*), host the "black knot" fungus *Apiosporina morbosa* (Schwein.: Fr.) Arx., which produces conspicuous elongated black galls that may kill an infected twig but usually do little harm to the plant.

Key to the Genus *Prunus* *in Minnesota*

1. Sepals 2–4 mm long; petals 6–14 mm long; branches bearing stout spines (not usually seen in herbarium specimens); fruit 2–3 cm in diameter, with a shallow longitudinal groove; the pit somewhat flattened and ± 2-edged (plums).
    2. Leaf margin with rounded serrations, each serration with a dark, sessile gland embedded in the summit; leaf blades broad, no more than twice as long as wide (l/w ≤ 2); margin of sepals lined with glands or glandular serrations, at least on the distal half; sepals usually glabrous, or hairy on the upper (inner) surface only .... *P. nigra*
    2. Leaf margin with sharply pointed serrations, glands absent; leaf blades proportionately narrower, more than twice as long as wide (l/w > 2); margin of sepals lacking glands, or occasionally with a few glands at the apex; sepals usually hairy, or sometimes glabrous on the lower (outer) surface .... *P. americana*
1. Sepals 0.5–2 mm long; petals 2.5–6.5 mm long; branches lacking spines; fruit 0.5–1.2 cm in diameter, not grooved; the pit ± spherical with no edges (cherries).
    3. Inflorescence an umbel or shortened corymb with 1–6 flowers.
        4. A shrub rarely more than 1.5 m (5 ft) tall; leaf tips acute or obtuse; margin of leaf blades with serrations on upper (distal) 3/4 only; serrations not gland tipped; flowers in umbel-like clusters of 1–3; pedicels less than 1.5 cm long.
            5. Youngest portion of the twigs minutely hairy; leaf tips usually obtuse .... *P. susquehanae*
            5. Twigs glabrous; leaf tips usually acute.
                6. Leaves mostly oblanceolate, 1–1.5 cm wide, base long-tapered ..... *P. pumila* var. *pumila*
                6. Leaves mostly elliptical to obovate, 1.5–2.3 cm wide, base tapered but not long-tapered .... *P. pumila* var. *besseyi*
        4. A small tree often to 6 m (20 ft) tall; leaf tips acuminate; margin of leaf blades with serrations extending to the base; serrations each tipped with a distinct reddish or yellowish gland; flowers in shortened corymbs of 3–6; pedicels at least 1.5 cm long .... *P. pensylvanica*
    3. Inflorescence an elongated raceme with 20–60 flowers.
        7. Sepals glandless, or with at most 2–4 marginal glands; sepals persistent on fruit; lower surface of leaf blades glabrous, or with rust-colored hairs along the lower portion of the midvein, hairs not noticeably concentrated in axils of lateral veins; leaf blades relatively slender (length/width = 2–3); serrations on leaf margins incurved or appressed and generally blunt with a dark, callous, glandlike tip .... *P. serotina*
        7. Sepals lined with 10 or more glands; sepals not persistent on fruit; lower surface of leaf blades with scattered whitish or yellowish hairs, typically concentrated in the axils of the lateral veins; leaf blades proportionately broader (length/width = 1.5–2); serrations on leaf margins straight with a sharp slender tip .... *P. virginiana*

Prunus americana Marsh.

American wild plum

Tall **shrubs** or small **trees**, with single or multiple upright **stems** to 6 m tall and 11 cm dbh; clonal by root suckering. **Branches** wide-spreading, usually bearing stout spines up to 6 cm long. **Branchlets** brown to gray, glabrous or with short dense hairs that may persist for several years. **Bark** dark gray to gray-brown, ± smooth on younger stems, becoming rough and often curling or peeling in thick strips. **Leaves** simple, alternate, deciduous. **Petioles** 0.8–1.7 cm long, hairy to densely hairy, sometimes with 1 or 2 dark sessile glands near summit. **Leaf blades** elliptical to somewhat obovate; 5.5–10 cm long, 3–4.5 cm wide, length/width 2–2.5; base tapered or narrowly rounded; apex acuminate; margins with a single or double row of sharply pointed, nonglandular serrations; upper surface dark green, glabrous or glabrate; lower surface somewhat paler than upper, sparsely to moderately hairy, especially on main veins. **Flowers** bisexual, 5-merous; borne in sessile umbels of 1–4; pedicels 0.7–1.8 cm long, glabrous or hairy; sepals 2–3.5 mm long, margins lacking glands or with a few glands at apex, upper surface hairy, lower surface glabrous or hairy; petals white, 6–11 mm long; **anthesis** early May to early June; insect-pollinated. **Fruit** a 1-seeded drupe; red to purple; roughly spherical; 2–3 cm in diameter; maturing early mid-August to mid-September; animal-dispersed. (*Americana*: American)

Identification

This is the familiar wild plum that is so conspicuous on roadsides, especially in May when it is covered with large white flowers. It is a large, thicket-forming shrub or sometimes a small tree, usually 10–15 ft (3–5 m) tall, with coarse, spiny branches and an open crown. It closely resembles Canada plum (*P. nigra*), except the leaves are proportionately narrower, and the leaf serrations are sharply pointed rather than blunt. It is also very similar to big-tree plum (*P. mexicana* S. Wats.), which occurs just to the south of Minnesota.

Natural History

American wild plum is relatively common in what was historically the prairie region of Minnesota. Agriculture has now supplanted the actual prairie, but before that happened, wild plum was probably found in brushy coulees and ravines, in the fire shadow of lakes, and in river valleys where the frequency of wildfire was relatively low. It would probably not have been found on the open prairie, where fires typically occurred every 3 to 5 years. Today, wildfires have been effectively suppressed, even on the few remaining patches of real prairie. This allows wild plum to find habitat in just about any piece of open land that manages to remain idle for even a few years. This includes roadsides, utility rights-of-way, abandoned field and pastures. It is occasionally found in forested regions where human activities have created brushy openings or a permanent forest edge.

Soils are generally sandy or loamy and range from dry to moist and from calcareous (basic) to slightly acidic. The more strongly acidic soils are favored by the closely related Canada plum (*P. nigra*). American wild plum is also adapted to floodplains, where it tolerates moderate levels of spring flooding and associated sedimentation.

American wild plum is fast growing and relatively long-lived, sometimes reaching an age of 50 to 60 years. If not constrained by competition, it will produce long, invasive roots that can send up shoots (suckers) as much as 15 ft (5 m) from the parent stem. In time it can form dense thickets 30 ft (9 m) or more across that are made impenetrable by wide-spreading, intermingling branches that are armed with sharp spines. These thickets resist fire, browsing by cattle, and invasion by other woody species and can persist for decades.

The flowers appear with the leaves—May 7.

Fruits fall from the tree when ripe—September 3.

Wild American plum on a floodplain in Houston County—May 7.

Thick strips of bark loosen, then curl.

Leaves are narrower than those of Canada plum.

Prunus nigra Ait.

Canada plum

Tall **shrubs** or small **trees**, with single or multiple upright **stems** to 5 m tall and 7 cm dbh; clonal by root suckering. **Branches** spreading to ascending, usually bearing stout spines up to 5 cm long; compound spines sometimes developing on main stems. **Branchlets** reddish brown or gray, glabrous or rarely hairy. **Bark** gray, initially smooth, becoming rough and peeling on older stems. **Leaves** simple, alternate, deciduous. **Petioles** 0.8–1.5 cm long, sparsely to densely hairy, with 1 or a few dark sessile glands near summit. **Leaf blades** broadly elliptical to obovate; 6–11 cm long, 4–7 cm wide, length/width 1.3–2; base tapered or broadly rounded; apex abruptly acuminate; margins with a double row of blunt serrations each with a dark sessile gland embedded in the summit; upper surface dark green, sparsely hairy, at least on larger veins; lower surface pale green, hairy, often densely so, especially on veins. **Flowers** bisexual, 5-merous; borne in sessile umbels of 1–3(4); pedicels 0.6–1.8 cm long, glabrous or occasionally hairy; sepals 2.5–4 mm long, margins with glands or glandular serrations, at least on distal half, upper surface glabrous or occasionally hairy, lower surface glabrous; petals white, occasionally streaked with pink, 9–14 mm long; **anthesis** early May to early June; insect-pollinated. **Fruit** a single-seeded drupe; reddish to crimson or purplish; roughly spherical; 2–3 cm in diameter; maturing mid-August to late mid-September; animal-dispersed. (*nigra*: black, in reference to the bark)

Identification

Canada plum is a large shrub or sometimes a small, coarse tree, usually 9–13 ft (3–4 m) tall, with a short, forking trunk, spreading branches, and dark gray, peeling bark. It produces conspicuous clusters of large white flowers in May and large reddish or purplish fruit in late August. It is very similar to the more common American wild plum (*P. americana*), but the leaves are more rounded in outline, and the margins have blunt serrations with a small gland embedded in the summit of each tooth.

Natural History

Canada plum occurs throughout most of the forested region of Minnesota, but its distribution is somewhat spotty, especially in the south. It is generally not as common as American wild plum (*P. americana*), which in many ways could be considered its prairie analog. The ranges of the two species overlap in a wide swath that runs diagonally through the state, and although the populations do intermingle, they remain distinct; there does not seem to be any hybridization.

Canada plum occurs exclusively in forest ecosystems, yet it does not thrive under a closed forest canopy. Instead it prefers long-term forest openings, forest margins, clearings, open-canopy woodlands, and brushy habitats where there may be only scattered trees. It is primarily associated with hardwoods, usually oaks (*Quercus* spp.), trembling aspen (*Populus tremuloides*), or paper birch (*Betula papyrifera*), and secondarily with upland conifers.

The best habitats seem to have moderately acidic, well-drained, sandy soil. Canada plum is not found in wetlands, although it does occur on river terraces and elevated floodplains if it can remain beyond the reach of flooding and sedimentation. Habitats seem to be chosen opportunistically and colonized fairly quickly; yet even with its suckering capabilities, Canada plum spreads too slowly to be considered aggressive.

Leaves are noticeably broad compared to American wild plum.

Small glands line the margins of the sepals.

Fruits are sweet but have a large pit—August 11.

Flowers can be an inch (2.5 cm) across—May 31.

A roadside colony of Canada plum—May 8.

Prunus pensylvanica L. f.

Pin cherry

Small **trees**, with single upright **stems** to 10 m tall and 16 cm dbh; clonal by root suckering. **Branchlets** red or reddish brown, glabrous or rarely hairy, developing a thin, gray, flaky epidermis. **Bark** thin, gray or reddish brown, smooth except for conspicuous horizontal lenticels. **Leaves** simple, alternate, deciduous. **Petioles** 1–2 cm long, glabrous or occasionally hairy, with 1–3 sessile red glands near summit. **Leaf blades** ovate to elliptical or oblong-lanceolate; 5–9 cm long, 2–4 cm wide, length/width 2–3; base tapered or somewhat rounded; apex acuminate; margins with a single row of fine and often irregularly shaped serrations, each tipped with a red or yellow gland; upper surface dark green, glabrous; lower surface pale green, hairy along main veins or glabrate. **Flowers** bisexual, 5-merous, borne in umbel-like clusters or shortened corymbs of 3–6, subtended by several glandular-serrate bracts to 5 mm long; pedicels 1.5–2 cm long, glabrous; sepals 1.3–2 mm long, glabrous, marginal glands absent; petals white, 3.5–6 mm long; **anthesis** early May to mid-June; insect-pollinated. **Fruit** a 1-seeded drupe; shiny red; spherical; 5–8 mm in diameter; maturing early July to late mid-August; gravity- and animal-dispersed. (*pensylvanica*: of Pennsylvania)

Identification

Pin cherry is a small tree, usually 15–25 ft (5–8 m) tall, with long, slender branches and a narrow crown. The bark of young trees often has a distinctive metallic sheen and is smooth except for conspicuous orange lenticels (thin, corky, horizontal ridges). When pin cherry is in flower, it can be mistaken for a plum (*P. americana* or *P. nigra*) or a serviceberry (*Amelanchier* spp.).

Natural History

Pin cherry is a common understory tree that occurs throughout the forested region of Minnesota, especially northward. It prefers mesic to dry-mesic loamy soil and occurs in association with both hardwoods and conifers. Yet, for an understory tree it is remarkably intolerant of shade. In fact, it is abundant only in forests that are recovering from some catastrophic disturbance that has removed the overstory trees and allowed more light to reach the understory. The cause may be fire, a windstorm, or clear-cutting.

Under such conditions pin cherry will grow rapidly, yet it will rarely reach a height of more than about 33 ft (10 m) or live more than 25 to 35 years. By the time the pin cherries are starting to die out, saplings of the next generation of canopy trees are beginning to overtop them. This speeds their decline and suppresses any reproduction. When the forest matures and the canopy closes, there will be few, if any, pin cherry left. But the pin cherry will have left behind an astonishing amount of dormant seed buried in the soil (called a seed bank). As many as 450,000 viable seeds per acre have been reported, and they can remain dormant for as long as 50 years (Marks 1974). If the inevitable disturbance happens during that time, and the canopy is removed again to allow more light to reach the forest floor, the buried seeds of pin cherry will germinate, and the cycle will be renewed. Pin cherry is one of a very few tree species to employ this strategy.

This strategy was especially effective during the past century, when human settlement created a landscape with large areas of semipermanent open or brushy habitats, such as cut-over forests, abandoned farmland, utility rights-of-way, and transportation corridors—all ideal habitats for pin cherry.

Flowers are smaller than those of plums—May 20.

Fruits are about 1/4" (5–8 mm) across and bright red—July 28.

A small colony of pin cherry in Pine County—May 20.

Bark is smooth except for corky lenticels—this stem is 4" (10 cm) diameter.

Cherries   🍃   **359**

Prunus pumila L. (including var. *pumila* and var. *besseyi* (L. H. Bailey) Waugh)

Sand cherry

Low or midsize **shrubs** with 1 to several upright or decumbent **stems** to 1.7 m tall and 2 cm basal diameter; clonal by layering. **Branchlets** brown to reddish brown, glabrous, developing a thin, gray, flaky epidermis. **Bark** brown to gray, smooth or somewhat roughened with horizontal lenticels. **Leaves** simple, alternate, deciduous. **Petioles** 0.5–1.2 cm long, glabrous, often with 1 or 2 dark sessile glands near summit. **Leaf blades** narrowly elliptical to narrowly elliptical-obovate in var. *besseyi*, or oblanceolate in var. *pumila*; 3.5–5.5 cm long, 1.1–2.1 cm wide; base acutely to long-acutely tapered; apex acutely tapered; margins with a single row of sharply pointed nonglandular serrations on the distal 3/4 of the blade; upper surface dark green, glabrous; lower surface pale green, glabrous. **Flowers** bisexual, 5-merous, borne in sessile umbels of 1–3; pedicels 0.5–1.1 cm long, glabrous; sepals 1.4–1.8 mm long, glabrous, with a few marginal glands on distal half; petals white, 3–6 mm long; **anthesis** early May to mid-June; insect-pollinated. **Fruit** a 1-seeded drupe; black or purplish black; ± spherical to broadly ellipsoidal; 8–12 mm across; maturing early July to mid-August; animal-dispersed. (*pumila*: dwarf)

Identification

Sand cherry typically grows in small clumps and produces multiple stems, each stem no more than about waist high. It is very similar to Appalachian dwarf cherry (*P. susquehanae*), but the twigs are smooth, not hairy. Also, the leaves tend to be proportionately narrower and more sharply pointed. The leaves of both species differ from those of the other native cherries and plums by having a relatively broad tip and margins that are serrate only on the upper half or three-quarters.

Note: Two varieties of sand cherry occur in Minnesota (see key at beginning of chapter). Variety *pumila* is quite rare and is known to occur only on sand dunes in Wabasha, Washington, Winona, and St. Louis (Park Point in Duluth) counties. Variety *besseyi* is much more common and occurs in a variety of habitats (including sand dunes) and in all the counties indicated on the map except St. Louis County, where only variety *pumila* is known. Also see the note under *P. susquehanae*.

Natural History

Sand cherry occurs scattered throughout much of Minnesota, but it is apparently absent from the northeastern counties, where the closely related Appalachian dwarf cherry occurs. Both species need direct sunlight and occur in dry, sandy or rocky soils. But sand cherry seems to prefer calcareous or circumneutral limestones, sandstones, and soils derived from those rock types. Appalachian dwarf cherry is associated with the more acidic granites, basalts, and gabbros. Because of Minnesota's geological history, the more acidic rock exposures are found predominately in the northeast, and the less acidic and calcareous materials are found in the west and south, which may explain why the distributions of the two species barely overlap.

Habitats of sand cherry include dunes, sand barrens, savannas, gravel hill prairies, bedrock outcrops, and openings in pine forests. It is usually associated with clump-forming prairie grasses and herbaceous plants rather than other woody species. It easily withstands drought and temperature extremes, and it resprouts after fire or browsing. But sprouts may take 2 to 4 years to regain their vigor and produce flowers.

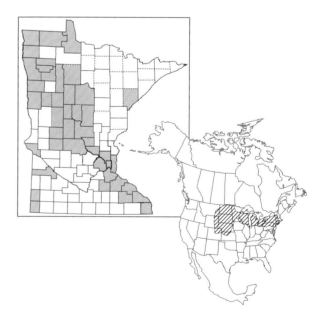

Flowers at peak on May 22 in Pine County.

Fruit is a black "drupe" about 3/8" (8–12 mm) across—August 4.

Bark is dark, with conspicuous lenticels.

Leaves tend to have a slender, tapering base, especially var. pumila.

A large specimen from Minnesota Point in St. Louis County.

Cherries ❧ **361**

Prunus serotina Ehrh.

Black cherry

Large **trees**, to 30 m tall and 65 cm dbh; nonclonal. **Branchlets** brown to reddish brown, glabrous or occasionally hairy at base. **Bark** brown to gray, initially smooth, but soon splitting into thick, flat scales with out-turned edges. **Leaves** simple, alternate, deciduous. **Petioles** 1–2.2 cm long, glabrous or rarely hairy, with 1 or a few sessile glands near summit. **Leaf blades** elliptical to oblong-elliptical or occasionally somewhat ovate or obovate; 6–12 cm long, 2.5–5 cm wide, length/width 2–3; base tapered or somewhat rounded; apex acuminate; margins with a single row of incurving or appressed serrations, each serration blunt except for a dark, callous, glandlike tip; upper surface dark green, glabrous; lower surface pale green, glabrous or with rust-colored hairs along the proximal half or third of the midvein. **Flowers** bisexual, 5-merous; 20–60 borne in an elongate raceme 5–11 cm long; pedicels 3–8 mm long, glabrous; sepals 0.5–1 mm long, margins with 2–4 glands or glandless, glabrous, persistent in fruit; petals white, 2.5–3.5 mm long; **anthesis** mid-May to mid-June; insect-pollinated. **Fruit** a 1-seeded drupe; black; spherical or oblate; 7–11 mm in diameter; maturing early August to early September; gravity- and animal-dispersed. (*serotina*: late-coming, an apparent reference to the fruit)

Identification

Black cherry is a relatively large canopy tree with a slender, sinuous trunk and a smallish crown. It produces long racemes of fragrant white flowers in late spring just as the leaves are reaching full size. By late summer it will have small, black fruits about 3/8 inch (1 cm) across. Saplings are easily confused with choke-cherry (*P. virginiana*), a common shrub that also produces long racemes of white flowers. But the leaves of black cherry are generally narrower and more elliptical than those of choke-cherry. Also, on the undersurface of the leaf there is often a distinctive fringe of rust-colored hairs running along both sides of the midvein near the base.

Natural History

Black cherry is a common forest tree in central and southern Minnesota, especially in dry-mesic, sandy or loamy soils. Without exception, these are well-drained upland sites, not swamps or active floodplains. It rarely forms pure stands; instead, it occurs scattered in the canopy or understory of midsuccessional forests with oaks (*Quercus* spp.), red maple (*Acer rubrum*), aspens (*Populus* spp.), or paper birch (*Betula papyrifera*).

Black cherry survives drought fairly well, but the bark is thin, which leaves the underlying cambium very susceptible to fire. After a fire or logging (a more realistic fate for black cherry), sprouts will usually arise from stumps, especially stumps of younger trees.

Black cherry is moderately tolerant of shade, especially when young. In fact, seedlings compete well under a thin canopy of oaks and aspen, especially in low-nutrient soils. However, it does not survive more than a few years in the deep shade of sugar maple (*Acer saccharum*) or basswood (*Tilia americana*). The greatest number of seedlings is generally found in moist, partially shaded conditions near a parent tree. But the seeds are spread widely in the droppings of birds, and seedlings seem to pop up everywhere, not just in forests but in old fields, brushy thickets, abandoned pastures, and gardens.

Black cherry grows rapidly when young and can live for 200 or more years. In Minnesota, a black cherry 80 ft (25 m) tall with a trunk 20 inches (50 cm) in diameter is considered a large tree, but in New York and Pennsylvania black cherries reportedly reach 129 ft (40 m) in height and 7 ft (2.2 m) in diameter (Harlow et al. 1991).

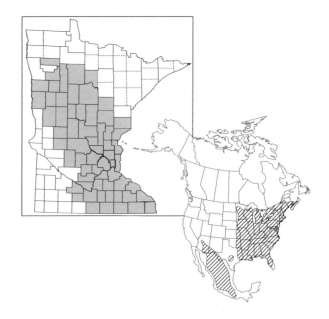

Fruits mature in August but don't last long—
August 22.

Flowers are abundant and fragrant—June 3.

Leaves are similar to choke-cherry but more
slender.

Bark has flat scales with out-turned edges—
17" (43 cm) dbh.

Prunus susquehanae Willd.

Appalachian dwarf cherry

[*P. cuneata* Raf.; *P. pumila* var. *cuneata* (Raf.) L.]

Low or midsize **shrubs**, with single or multiple upright or ascending **stems** to 1 m tall; clonal by layering. **Branchlets** brown to reddish brown, minutely hairy for 3 or more years. **Bark** brown to gray, smooth or somewhat rough. **Leaves** simple, alternate, deciduous. **Petioles** 0.3–1 cm long, glabrous or sometimes hairy, often with 1 or 2 dark sessile glands near summit. **Leaf blades** elliptical to elliptical-obovate; 4–5.5 cm long, 1.4–2.3 cm wide; base acutely tapered; apex obtusely or subacutely tapered, or somewhat rounded; margins with a single row of sharply pointed, nonglandular serrations on the distal 3/4; upper surface dark green, glabrous; lower surface pale green, glabrous. **Flowers** bisexual, 5-merous, borne in sessile umbels of 1–3; pedicels 0.7–1.7 cm long, glabrous; sepals 1.5–2 mm long, glabrous, with a few marginal glands on distal half; petals white, 3.5–6.5 mm long; **anthesis** mid-May to late mid-June; insect-pollinated. **Fruit** a 1-seeded drupe; black; ± spherical; 8–12 mm in diameter; maturing mid-July to late August; animal-dispersed. (*susquehanae*: of the Susquehanna River)

Identification

Appalachian dwarf cherry is a smallish shrub usually no more than waist high, often much smaller. The individual flowers are also rather small, but they are often abundant and conspicuous. They appear in the spring just as the leaves are beginning to expand. It can be told from the closely related sand cherry (*P. pumila*) by the covering of minute hairs on the twigs (requires magnification), and by the slightly broader and more blunt-tipped leaves.
Note: The taxonomy of the dwarf cherries (represented in Minnesota by *P. pumila* and *P. susquehanae*) has been hotly debated for at least a hundred years. Minnesota plants have at times been divided into as many as three separate species (*P. besseyi*, *P. pumila*, and *P. susquehanae*), or treated as a single polymorphous species (*P. pumila s.l.*). The treatment here basically follows that of Catling, McKay-Kuja, and Mitrow (1999). For an alternative treatment, see Rohrer (2000).

Natural History

Appalachian dwarf cherry occurs scattered throughout most of the northern forest region of Minnesota, extending southward to the Anoka Sandplain, just north of the Twin Cities. It is not an abundant species, but it does occur with some regularity in suitable habitats. Requirements seem to include direct sunlight and a substrate of acidic sand or acidic bedrock such as granite, slate, or gabbro. It is not known to occur on calcareous limestones or sandstones, or on the soil derived from those rock types.

Appalachian dwarf cherry does not compete well in the shade of trees or larger shrubs, but it may be found with other low-stature shrubs such as bush honeysuckle (*Diervilla lonicera*) or blueberry (*Vaccinium angustifolium*). These conditions are typically associated with sand savannas, openings in jack pine (*Pinus banksiana*) woodlands, rocky lakeshores, and bedrock "balds."

Appalachian dwarf cherry is very tolerant of heat and drought. Under conditions of severe moisture stress, it will remain green and successfully produce flowers and fruit even though the leaves of other plants become dried and brown. It spreads by layering and will resprout if stems are damaged by fire or browsing.

Flowers appear before the leaves are half-grown—May 30.

These fruits will turn black when ripe—August 10.

The leaves tend to be broader than those of sand cherry.

Prunus virginiana L.

Choke-cherry

Tall **shrubs** or small **trees**, with multiple or occasionally single upright **stems** to 8 m tall and 15 cm dbh; clonal by root suckering. **Branchlets** brown to gray-brown or reddish brown, glabrous or hairy. **Bark** thin, gray or brownish, smooth or rough; with pale lenticels. **Leaves** simple, alternate, deciduous. **Petioles** 1–2 cm long, glabrous or sometimes hairy, with 1 or a few dark glands near summit. **Leaf blades** broadly elliptical to obovate; 5.5–10 cm long, 3–6 cm wide, length/width 1.4–2; base rounded or blunt; apex short-acuminate; margins with a single row of fine, straight serrations, each serration with slender, sharp, usually noncallous tip; upper surface dark green, glabrous or glabrate; lower surface pale green, with whitish or yellowish hairs typically concentrated in the axils of the lateral veins. **Flowers** bisexual, 5-merous; 20–50 borne on an elongate raceme 5–10 cm long; pedicels 4–8 mm long, glabrous; sepals 0.5–1.5 mm long, margins lined with 10 or more red glands or glandular serrations, not persistent in fruit; petals white, 2.5–4.5 mm long; **anthesis** early May to mid-June; insect-pollinated. **Fruit** a 1-seeded drupe; red-purple to blackish; spherical; 8–11 mm in diameter; maturing mid-July to late August; animal-dispersed. (*virginiana*: of Virginia)

Identification

Choke-cherry is typically a large, bushy shrub with multiple stems 7–16 ft (2–5 m) tall. At times it will take the form of a small tree with a single twisted or leaning stem reaching a maximum height of about 25 ft (8 m). The leaves are conspicuously reddish tinged in the spring but turn dark green by summer. Confusion with black cherry (*P. serotina*) is common because the flowers and leaves are similar. A number of characters can be use to separate the two species (see key at beginning of chapter), but also be aware that black cherry develops into a large tree and begins flowering about a week later than choke-cherry.

Natural History

Choke-cherry is one of the most common and ubiquitous shrubs in Minnesota. The maps show it to be the only woody species (so far) that has been vouchered in every Minnesota county and subcounty. Choke-cherry is typically a forest edge species, but it also does well in forest interiors, particularly under

oaks (*Quercus* spp.), paper birch (*Betula papyrifera*), and aspens (*Populus* spp.), which by their nature have rather thin canopies. It does not do as well under the thicker canopies of maples (*Acer* spp.) and basswood (*Tilia americana*), and it is not common on active floodplains. And in the jargon of foresters, it does not respond aggressively if "released" from a suppressing overstory.

Choke-cherry is also found in nonforested regions; in fact it can usually be found wherever there are patches of brush along a stream or ravine, or a narrow strip of trees along a lakeshore. It is even found in degraded habitats such as roadsides, fence-rows, old fields, and intermittent pastures. But it would be a mistake to think of choke-cherry as a ruderal species. Actually, it is a highly adaptable, highly integrated inhabitant of Minnesota's natural landscape.

Choke-cherry is relatively slow growing but quick to colonize if the opportunity arises, and it is tenacious once established. If the stems are browsed, cut, or burned, new stems will sprout vigorously from the roots. Even without disturbance it will usually sucker and form relatively small, dense clones. Choke-cherry spreads slowly compared to more aggressive clonal shrubs such as sumacs (*Rhus* spp.), prickly ash (*Zanthoxylum americanum*), American wild plum (*Prunus americana*), and red raspberry (*Rubus idaeus* var. *strigosus*).

Flowers are in long racemes like black cherry—May 11.

Too bitter for humans, birds love the fruits, most don't last this long—Sept. 11.

This stem is 4" (10 cm) in diameter— about average.

A typical edge-grown specimen 6.5' (2 m) tall—Anoka County.

Leaves are finely serrate, broader than those of black cherry.

Quercus, the oaks

Fagaceae: Beech family

The oaks include about 400 species of deciduous and evergreen trees and shrubs. They occur worldwide with 90 species in the United States, and 7 in Minnesota. (*Quercus* is the classical Latin name for an oak tree, meaning "beautiful tree.")

This is the largest genus of trees in North America, and except for the aspens (*Populus* spp.), the oaks may be the most abundant trees in Minnesota. The state's oaks fall into two major groups: the red oak group (section *Lobatae*) and the white oak group (section *Quercus*). The red oak group has leaves with pointed lobes and bristle tips. They produce acorns that stay on the tree for two growing seasons (16 months). The acorns fall to the ground in the autumn of the 2nd year and germinate the following spring. This group includes northern pin oak (*Q. ellipsoidalis*), northern red oak (*Q. rubra*), and black oak (*Q. velutina*).

The white oak group has leaves with rounded lobes and no bristles. They produce acorns that mature at the end of the first growing season (4 months). The acorns fall to the ground the first autumn and germinate immediately. This group includes bur oak (*Q. macrocarpa*), white oak (*Q. alba*), swamp white oak (*Q. bicolor*), and chinkapin oak (*Q. muhlenbergii*).

Oaks hybridize easily within their own group but not with members of another group. The cross between northern red oak and northern pin oak is fairly common in Minnesota; other crosses are relatively rare.

Acorn production varies greatly from year to year. A particularly large acorn crop is usually followed by 2 to 4 years with little or no production. This pattern is typically synchronized within each species over large geographic areas, with each species being on a different cycle (Sork and Bramble 1993). Bur oak seems to be on a 2-year cycle and had good acorn crops statewide in 1994, 1996, 1998, 2000, and 2002, with poor crops in the intervening years. White oak and northern red oak appear to be on a 3-year cycle, and had good crops statewide in 1994, 1997, and 2000. The cycles of all oak species seemed to converge in 2000 with an extraordinary combined crop of acorns throughout Minnesota and much of the Midwest. Predictably, 2001 was a poor year for acorn production; no species produced an abundant crop.

This phenomenon is called mast-fruiting, and an acorn crop taken as a whole is called mast. It has been suggested that weather conditions control the synchronicity of mast-fruiting, but the cyclical aspect is likely inherent within each species and is apparently an evolved survival strategy. The survival benefits of mast-fruiting are not known, but it is often speculated that in years of little or no acorn production, populations of seed predators (squirrels, deer, etc.), may decline; then in years of large mast production there are fewer seed predators, and they are easily satiated, allowing large numbers of acorns to survive and germinate.

Oak wilt is a serious disease caused by a nonnative fungus (*Ceratocystis fagacearum* [T. W. Bretz] J. Hunt) that results in the blockage of the water-conducting system of the tree (Hepting 1971). Unable to bring water from the roots to the leaves, the tree wilts and dies. Although all oak species are susceptible, northern red oak, northern pin oak, and black oak are especially vulnerable and usually die within a few weeks. White oak, bur oak, and swamp white oak may survive for several years, dying one branch at a time. The disease and the disease organism are very similar to Dutch elm disease, which has all but wiped out the native elms (*Ulmus* spp.).

The fungus causing oak wilt is transported by sap-feeding beetles ("picnic beetles") that are attracted to fresh wounds on oak trees. Once an infection starts, it can spread from tree to tree through naturally grafted roots. The disease cannot be cured, but it can be controlled to some extent by preventing wounding of oak trees and by severing the root connections between infected and healthy trees (Holman 1987). Oak wilt occurs statewide, but the greatest concentration of infected trees is in an area surrounding the Twin Cities Metropolitan Area, with Anoka and Sherburne counties often cited as the hardest hit (Pokorny 1999).

Another threat to oaks is the gypsy moth (*Lymantia dispar*). It did not occur in North America until 1869, when it was accidentally introduced into Massachusetts. Since then it has gradually spread south and west, recently reaching Minnesota. The larvae of the moth feed on the leaves of oaks, basswood (*Tilia americana*), alders (*Alnus* spp.), aspens (*Populus* spp.), hawthorns (*Crataegus* spp.), and other native trees, but oaks suffer the most (Katovich and Haack 1991). Although entire stands can be defoliated very quickly, they will usually leaf out again the same year. Healthy trees can usually withstand repeated defoliation for 2 or 3 consecutive years, but they eventually weaken and become susceptible to diseases.

1. Leaf blades with blunt or rounded lobes, the lobes not bristle-tipped; the scales covering the acorn cup with a prominent keel or bump on the back; lower surface of leaf blades glabrous (*Q. alba*), or with a uniform covering of minute stellate-appressed hairs; acorns maturing in 1 year.
   2. Margins of leaf blades with deep sinuses extending at least half the distance to the midvein.
      3. The underside of mature leaves glabrous, smooth to the touch .... *Q. alba*
      3. The underside of mature leaves uniformly covered with minute stellate-appressed hairs, usually velvety to the touch.
         4. Acorns borne at the ends of short peduncles no more than 0.5 cm long; acorn cups with a prominent fringe of curly awns 1–12 mm long; leaf margins with large and irregular primary lobes that often bear smaller secondary lobes; the deeper sinuses often with broad, flat bottoms; lower surface of leaf blades covered with minute stellate-appressed hairs only; twigs developing corky ridges after 3–5 years .... *Q. macrocarpa*
         4. Acorns borne at the ends of long peduncles 3–7 cm long; acorn cups lacking a fringe, or with a sparse fringe of ± stiff awns no more than 1 mm long; leaf margins with small and usually regular lobes that lack secondary lobes; the sinuses usually with narrow, rounded bottoms; lower surface of leaf blades covered with two types of hairs: minute stellate-appressed hairs (as in *Q. macrocarpa*) interspersed with longer, erect, 1–4-rayed, fascicled hairs; twigs not corky .... *Q. bicolor*
   2. Margins of leaf blades with shallow sinuses extending less than half the distance to the midvein.
      5. Acorns borne at the ends of long peduncles 3–7 cm long; acorn cup comprising 50–65% of the total length of the acorn; lower surface of leaf blades with two types of hairs: minute stellate-appressed hairs interspersed with longer, erect, 1–4-rayed, fascicled hairs .... *Q. bicolor*
      5. Acorns borne at the ends of short peduncles less than 1 cm long; acorn cup comprising 35–50% of the total length of the acorn; lower surface of leaf blades with only minute stellate-appressed hairs .... *Q. muhlenbergii*
1. Leaf blades with acutely pointed lobes, each lobe bristle-tipped; the scales covering the acorn cup flat; lower surface of leaf blades with hairs only in tufts in the axils of the lateral veins; acorns maturing in 2 years.
   6. The deepest sinuses on the margin of leaf blade extending 65–90% of the distance to the midvein; upper surface of the leaf shiny; acorn cup ± dome-shaped in side view, at least 2/3 as tall as wide, the cup making up at least half the total length of the acorn; terminal bud somewhat angled when seen in a cross section through the lower half; the petioles and green branchlets densely hairy when the leaves are just expanding in the spring.
      7. Inner surface of acorn cup ± glabrous, or with a ring of hairs around the scar; tips of scales on acorn cup flat and appressed; terminal buds (after August 1) 2–4 mm long, glabrous or hairy on upper half .... *Q. ellipsoidalis*
      7. Inner surface of acorn cup uniformly hairy; tips of scales on acorn cup loose, those near the rim with tips curled back; terminal buds (after August 1) 4–7 mm long, uniformly hairy
      .... *Q. velutina*
   6. The deepest sinuses extending 45–70% of the distance to the midvein; upper surface of the leaf dull; acorn cup ± flat-topped in side view, only 1/4 to 1/2 as tall as wide, the cup making up less than half the total length of the acorn; terminal bud ± circular in cross section; the petioles and green branchlets sparsely hairy or glabrous when the leaves are just expanding .... *Q. rubra*

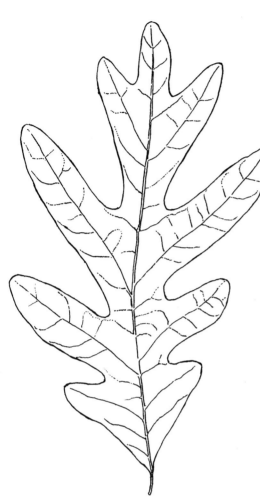

Quercus alba *(life size)*.

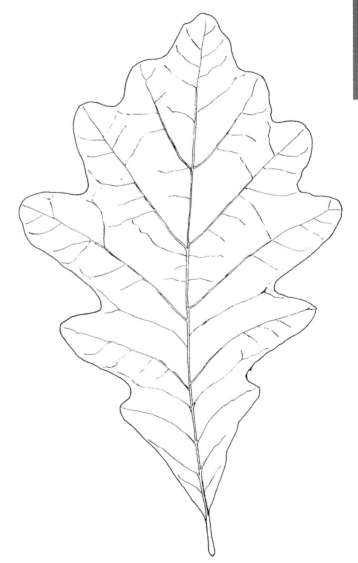

Quercus bicolor *(life size)*.

Quercus ellipsoidalis *(life size)*.

Quercus muhlenbergii *(life size)*.

Quercus macrocarpa *(life size)*.

Quercus rubra *(life size)*.

Quercus velutina *(life size)*.

Quercus alba L.

White oak

Large **trees**, to 29 m tall and 100 cm dbh. **Bark** of mature trees light gray, relatively thin; trunks with narrow, flat-topped or scaly ridges separated by narrow, shallow furrows; branches with large, scalelike plates. **Leaves** simple, alternate, deciduous or marcescent. **Petioles** 1–2.5 cm long, glabrous or glabrate. **Leaf blades** 9–17 cm long, 6–12 cm wide; base acutely to obtusely tapered; each margin with 3–5 large primary lobes and 0–5 smaller secondary lobes, the ultimate lobes with rounded apices; the deepest sinuses extending 50–95% of the distance to the midvein; upper surface dark green, dull or glossy, glabrous; lower surface pale green, dull, glabrous at maturity, or occasionally with a few simple appressed hairs along the main veins. **Flowers** unisexual, with male flowers and female flowers borne separately on the same branch. **Male flowers** in slender, pendulous catkins 3–8 cm long, from buds on branchlets of the previous year. **Female flowers** 1–3 on a short peduncle from leaf axils on branchlets of the current year; **anthesis** early to late May; wind-pollinated. **Fruit** (acorn) an ovoid-ellipsoidal to oblong nut 1.7–2.5 cm long, 1.1–1.7 cm wide; with a scaly, dome-shaped or bowl-shaped cup at the base, cup 25–50% of the total length of the nut plus cup, fringe lacking, the inner surface of cup uniformly hairy, the scales on the cup with a prominent dorsal bump; peduncle to 1.5 cm long; maturing late mid-August to late September of the 1st year; animal-dispersed. (*alba*: white, in reference to the light-colored bark)

Identification

The leaves of white oak have deep sinuses and rounded lobes like those of bur oak (*Q. macrocarpa*), but in white oak the lobing is more uniform and continues to the tip of the leaf. Curiously, the trunk has fine-textured, scaly bark, while the branches have large, coarse plates that are loose at the edges. The mature bark of the other oaks is more or less uniform throughout the tree. Hybrids between bur oak and white oak are known in Minnesota but are not common.

Natural History

White oak is a large forest tree reaching heights of nearly 100 ft (30 m) in Minnesota and reportedly 150 ft (46 m) farther east (*fide* Burns and Honkala 1990). It is relatively common in the east-central and southeastern counties, where it prefers deep, well-drained, acidic soils, usually sand or sandy loam. It typically occurs mixed with bur oak and northern pin oaks (*Q. ellipsoidalis*) and often trembling aspen (*Populus tremuloides*). It has a deep root system and is very drought resistant, but it is sensitive to flooding and sedimentation. White oak is slow growing, even in comparison to other oaks, and is among the longest-lived (500 to 600 years).

Although mature white oaks can be killed outright by fire, saplings will resprout vigorously. But like most oaks they cannot survive prolonged shade. This creates a situation in nature where white oak forests regenerate only after a catastrophic fire kills the canopy trees thereby "releasing" the saplings from the shade of the previous generation. These are called "stand-replacing" fires, and without them the dominant oaks would eventually be replaced by more shade-tolerant trees that do not need to be released, such as sugar maple (*Acer saccharum*), basswood (*Tilia americana*), elms (*Ulmus* spp.), and possibly northern red oak (*Q. rubra*).

This is a textbook explanation of forest succession that probably describes white oak in Minnesota until the time of settlement. Since then, forest fires have been suppressed to the point where regeneration of oak forests is at the mercy of artificial mechanisms. So instead of stand-replacing fires we now have stand-replacing clear-cuts, with less than satisfactory results.

There are 1–3 female flowers atop each peduncle—May 29.

Acorn has a long nut set in a scaly cup—August 28.

Rounded lobes and deep sinuses.

Male flowers are in long, tangled catkins—May 29.

Bark is light gray with narrow furrows—18 " (45 cm) dbh.

Oaks   **377**

Quercus bicolor Willd.

Swamp white oak

Large **trees**, to 24 m tall and 70 cm dbh. **Bark** of mature trees gray or brownish gray, thick, with flat-topped or scaly ridges separated by deep furrows. **Leaves** simple, alternate, deciduous. **Petioles** 0.5–2.5 cm long, hairy. **Leaf blades** 10–19 cm long, 7–11 cm wide; base acutely tapered; each margin with 3–9 small to midsize rounded or blunt lobes, generally lacking secondary lobes, the deepest sinuses usually extending 15–50% of the distance to the midvein; upper surface dark green, glossy, glabrous or glabrate; lower surface pale green or grayish, dull, densely hairy with minute, appressed-stellate hairs interspersed with longer, erect, 1–4-rayed fascicled hairs. **Flowers** unisexual, with male flowers and female flowers borne separately on the same branch. **Male flowers** in slender, pendulous catkins 2–8 cm long, from buds on branchlets of the previous year. **Female flowers** 1–3 on a long peduncle from leaf axils on branchlets of the current year; **anthesis** early to late May; wind-pollinated. **Fruit** (acorn) a broadly ovoid or ellipsoidal nut 1.7–2.4 cm long, 1.3–1.7 cm wide; with a scaly, dome-shaped cup at the base, cup 50–65% of the total length of the nut plus cup, occasionally with a sparse fringe of ± stiff awns up to 1 mm long, the inner surface of the cup uniformly hairy; the scales of the cup with a prominent dorsal bump; borne on a peduncle 3–7 cm long; maturing mid-August to late mid-September of the 1st year; animal-dispersed. (*bicolor*: two-colored, in reference to the leaves)

Identification

Swamp white oak is most likely to be confused with bur oak (*Q. macrocarpa*), but the leaves have smaller lobes, and the lobes are more uniform in size and shape. Also, the two species have a different pattern of hairs on the underside of the leaves (see key); and notice that the acorns of swamp white oak are on a long, slender stalk (peduncle). The two species sometimes grow side by side and hybridize freely (Bray 1960).
Note: There are recurring reports of native swamp white oak in the Minnesota River valley as far upstream as Granite Falls (Yellow Medicine County) and from scattered locations elsewhere in central Minnesota (Little 1971; Ownbey and Morley 1991). Most of these reports have been traced to misidentified herbarium specimens of bur oak.

Although plausible, there is no convincing evidence that swamp white oak has ever occurred naturally in the Minnesota River valley.

Natural History

Swamp white oak is a slow growing, relatively long-lived (300+ years) canopy tree. It is now rare in Minnesota and is apparently restricted to lowland forests on the floodplain of the Mississippi River. Historically it occurred as far upstream as the Twin Cities area, but it has not been found above Wabasha (Wabasha County) for many years.

Most of its habitat was lost early in the twentieth century when a series of eight locks and dams were completed on the river. They turned the Mississippi from a free-flowing river into a series of interconnected navigation pools. The only original forests that survived intact were immediately downstream from the dams, where the water levels remained more-or-less natural. This is predominately where swamp white oak occurs today. Its shallow root system is particularly well adapted to survive regular spring flooding and accompanying sedimentation. It typically occurs mixed with plains cottonwood (*Populus deltoides* subsp. *monilifera*), silver maple (*Acer saccharinum*), river birch (*Betula nigra*), or sometimes bur oak (*Q. macrocarpa*).

Female flowers ready to receive pollen—May 24.

Only swamp white oak has acorns on long stalks—September 9.

Leaves are like white oak but sinuses are shallower.

These male flowers have just released their pollen—May 24.

Bark is deeply furrowed—this trunk is 27" (68 cm) dbh.

Oaks

Oaks 379

Quercus ellipsoidalis E. J. Hill

Northern pin oak; Hill's oak

Large **trees**, to 31 m tall and 110 cm dbh. **Bark** of mature trees gray or gray-brown, thick, broken into relatively short, blocky ridges separated by deep or shallow furrows. **Leaves** simple, alternate, deciduous or marcescent. **Petioles** 2–4.5 cm long, glabrous or glabrate. **Leaf blades** 7–14 cm long, 6.5–13 cm wide; base obtusely tapered or truncate; each margin with 2–4 primary lobes and 9–22 secondary lobes, each lobe acutely pointed and bristle-tipped; the deepest sinuses extending 65–90% of the distance to the midvein; upper surface glossy, dark green, glabrous or glabrate; lower surface dull, pale green, with tufts of hairs in the axils of the lateral veins, otherwise glabrous. **Flowers** unisexual, with male flowers and female flowers borne separately on the same branch. **Male flowers** in slender, pendulous catkins 4–10 cm long, from buds on branchlets of the previous year. **Female flowers** 1–3 on a short peduncle from leaf axils on branchlets of the current year; **anthesis** early May to early June; wind-pollinated. **Fruit** (acorn) an ellipsoidal or ovoid nut 1.2–1.7 cm long, 0.8–1.3 cm wide; with a scaly, dome-shaped cup at the base; the cup 2/3 to fully as high as wide, comprising 50–65% of the total length of the nut plus cup; the scales on the cup flat, with appressed tips, the inner surface of the cup glabrous or rarely with a ring of hairs around the scar; maturing mid-August to mid-September of the 2nd year; animal-dispersed. (*ellipsoidalis*: ellipsoidal, in reference to the shape of the nut)

Identification

Confusion with northern red oak (*Q. rubra*) is chronic, and indeed the two species look very similar and will even hybridize. But the leaves of northern pin oak usually have deeper sinuses and are shinier on the upper surface. Also, the acorns are usually smaller and proportionately narrower, and the acorn cup covers a greater portion of the nut.
Note: Northern pin oak seems to be the source of recurrent claims that the more southeasterly scarlet oak (*Q. coccinea* Munch.) occurs naturally in Minnesota, which it does not. It comes no closer than the southeast corner of Wisconsin (Nixon 1997).

Natural History

Northern pin oak is a common species in Minnesota, probably more common than northern red oak,

especially in remnants of the original savannas and woodlands that occur on sandy outwash plains and gravelly moraines in central Minnesota. In contrast, northern red oak will typically be more common on the heavier, loamy soils in fire-protected landscapes. And yet the two species are sometimes found together in mixed stands on the same soil with the same fire history. Northern pin oak is generally less tolerant of shade than is red oak but it is more tolerant of drought; neither species tolerates flooding or sedimentation. Compared to other oaks, northern pin oak is moderately fast growing and relatively short-lived.

Although northern pin oak was not recognized by science until 1899, there are earlier historical accounts from Minnesota that seem to refer to this species and describe its ecological role in the presettlement landscape: "There is a species of oak that appears like red oak (*Q. rubra*) that frequents the outskirts of the Big Woods. It is sometimes associated with the bur oak in the 'openings,' and sometimes is found in company with the trembling aspen. It makes a smaller tree generally than the bur oak" (Winchell 1875). And from Fillmore County: "This is the oak that is abundant as underbrush and small trees. It often forms thickets skirting the outlines of a prairie. Large trees are found in the heavy timber in the NW portion of the County" (Winchell 1876).

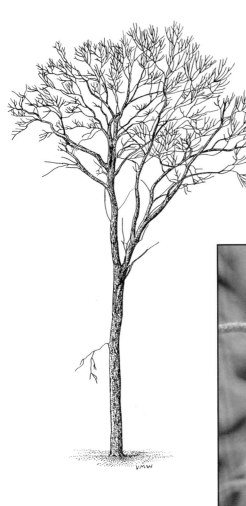

Look for female flowers among the new leaves—May 14.

Deep sinuses and bristle-tipped lobes.

A typical forest-grown tree from Washington County.

Bark is broken into short, blocky ridges—30" (76 cm) dbh.

The male flowers are in catkins just below the leaves—May 8.

The nut is small and sits deep in the cup—August 27.

Quercus macrocarpa Michx.

Bur oak

Large **trees**, to 34 m tall and 110 cm dbh. **Bark** of mature trees gray, thick to very thick, with coarse, scaly ridges separated by deep furrows. **Leaves** simple, alternate, deciduous. **Petioles** 1–3 cm long, hairy. **Leaf blades** 11–20 cm long, 7–15 cm wide, often grotesquely large on basal sprouts; base acutely to obtusely tapered; each margin with 2–6 large, irregular, primary lobes and often 2–10 smaller, secondary lobes, the ultimate lobes with rounded apices, the deepest sinuses usually in the lower half of the blade and extending 50–95% of the distance to the midvein; upper surface dark green, sparsely hairy or glabrate; lower surface pale green or gray, densely and uniformly hairy with minute appressed-stellate hairs. **Flowers** unisexual, with male flowers and female flowers borne separately on the same branch. **Male flowers** in slender, pendulous catkins 2–6 cm long, from buds on branchlets of the previous year. **Female flowers** 1–3 on a short peduncle from leaf axils on branchlets of the current year; **anthesis** early May to early June; wind-pollinated. **Fruit** (acorn) an ovoid or ellipsoidal to broadly ellipsoidal nut 1.4–2.2 cm long, 1–1.6 cm wide; with a scaly, dome-shaped cup at the base comprising 60–80% of the total length of the nut plus cup, cup with a fringe of soft, curly awns up to 12 mm long, the inner surface of cup uniformly hairy; the scales on the cup with a prominent dorsal keel or bump; peduncle 1–5 mm long; maturing early August to early mid-September of the 1st year; animal-dispersed. (*macrocarpa*: large-fruited, more applicable to the southern form)

Identification

Bur oak can usually be told by the deep sinuses in the lower half of the leaf. They may reach nearly to the midvein and have a broad, flat bottom. The upper half of the leaf usually has shallower sinuses but not always. The leaves of white oak (*Q. alba*) are similar, but the sinuses are usually more uniform in shape and depth. Also, the underside of a bur oak leaf is densely hairy and velvety to the touch, while a white oak leaf is smooth.
Note: The thick outer bark is sometimes shed in large patches (also seen in white oak) leaving conspicuous patches of relatively smooth inner bark. This condition is caused by a saprophytic fungus (*Corticium maculare*) and apparently does not harm the tree.

Natural History

Bur oak is the most common and ubiquitous oak in Minnesota. It occurs statewide but more commonly in the southern and western counties. It is extremely drought tolerant, slow to moderate growing and long-lived (400+ years). The largest specimens grow in deep soil on river terraces and slightly elevated floodplains. This type of riverine habitat may experience occasional spring flooding of short duration, but not sedimentation. Bur oak even follows the major river valleys westward into the prairie region, and it is the only oak that does. However, it does not occur just in river valleys; it does well in just about all upland landforms.

Since bur oak is intolerant of shade, closed stands rarely regenerate without some major disturbance that allows more light to reach the seedling layer, and that disturbance is usually fire. If young trees are top-killed by fire, they will resprout vigorously and repeatedly from massive root systems, resulting in shrublike "grubs" with root systems centuries old. As few as 12 to 15 years without fire is enough for a grub to grow into a tree with thick fire-resistant bark (Weaver and Kramer 1932). Because of its adaptation to fire, bur oak is usually the dominant tree wherever prairie grades into forest, particularly in the fire-maintained savannas of southern and western Minnesota.

A grove of savanna-grown bur oak in Anoka County.

There are usually 1 or 2 deep sinuses in lower half of leaf.

There isn't much to the female flowers, mostly stigmas—May 30.

A harmless fungus causes outer bark to slough—18" (45 cm) dbh.

The male catkins produce wind-borne pollen—May 19.

The fringe of curly awns gives bur oak its name—August 22.

Quercus muhlenbergii Engelm.

Chinkapin oak

Large **trees**, to 30 m tall and 60 cm dbh (estimated potential for Minnesota). **Bark** of mature trees gray, relatively thin, with scaly, flat-topped ridges separated by narrow, shallow furrows. **Leaves** simple, alternate, deciduous. **Petioles** 1–3 cm long, sparsely hairy to glabrous. **Leaf blades** 7–15 cm long, 4–8 cm wide; base obtusely tapered to blunt or nearly truncate; each margin with 8–14 acute to blunt gland-tipped teeth or small lobes, the deepest sinuses usually extending 10–25% of the distance to the midvein; upper surface dark green, glabrous; lower surface pale green, minutely and uniformly hairy with abundant or sparse appressed-stellate hairs. **Flowers** unisexual, with male flowers and female flowers borne separately on the same branch. **Male flowers** in slender, pendulous catkins 3–8 cm long, from buds on branchlets of the previous year. **Female flowers** 1–3 on a short peduncle from leaf axils on branchlets of the current year; **anthesis** in May (dates imperfectly known for Minnesota); wind-pollinated. **Fruit** (acorn) an ovoid to oblong nut 1.5–2 cm long, 1–1.4 cm wide; with a scaly, dome-shaped cup at the base comprising 35–50% of the total length of the nut plus cup, cup with little if any fringe, the inner surface of the cup uniformly hairy; the scales of the cup with a prominent dorsal keel or bump; sessile or borne on a peduncle to 8 mm long; maturing August-September of the 1st year (dates imperfectly known for Minnesota); animal-dispersed. (*muhlenbergii*: named for American botanist G. H. E. Muhlenberg, 1753–1815)

Identification

The leaves of chinkapin oak are relatively long and narrow with a continuous row of small, gland-tipped lobes along the margin. It keys closest to swamp white oak (*Q. bicolor*), but the two probably will not be confused, especially if acorns are present. If still in doubt, compare the bark and even the habitats. Chinkapin oak will be on high, dry uplands, while swamp white oak will be on floodplains.

Natural History

Native chinkapin oak has been found only once in Minnesota. The discovery was made by the early botanist W. A. Wheeler on July 15, 1899, in Section 19, Crooked Creek Township, Houston County.

Wheeler described two small trees in some detail: one was 9 ft (2.8 m) tall, the other 10 ft (3.1 m) tall. He documented the discovery with authenticated herbarium specimens.

The site is on a dry southwest-facing hillside at an elevation of about 850 ft (283 m). The soil is calcareous and coarse textured, derived from Prairie du Chien dolomite (a limestone). At the time of the discovery the habitat was apparently open and prairielike, or possibly savanna-like, with a few scattered trees or oak grubs. This is a natural community type maintained by a combination of wildfire, thin soil, and a steep southwest exposure (it follows that chinkapin oak is both fire tolerant and drought resistant but generally intolerant of shade).

The site has since grown into a substantial forest, a common fate for savannas deprived of wildfire. It is now dominated by several species of oak (only chinkapin oak is missing), hickories (*Carya* spp.), black cherry (*Prunus serotina*), and American elm (*Ulmus americana*). No one knows for sure what happened to the chinkapin oaks, but they have not been seen since the original discovery. Some say they were cut for fence posts or trampled by cattle, but more likely they were overgrown or crowded out when the habitat succeeded from savanna to forest.

Female flowers are nearly hidden at base of new leaves—May 5.

The male catkins can reach about 3" (8 cm) in length—May 2.

Bark is gray with scaly, flat-topped ridges— 19" (48 cm) dbh, southwest Wisconsin.

Acorn is an ovoid nut in a scaly, dome-shaped cup— September 5.

Narrow leaf with shallow, evenly-spaced sinuses.

Oaks 🍂 **385**

Quercus rubra L.

Northern red oak
[*Q. borealis* Michx.; *Q. maxima* Ashe]

Large **trees**, to 33 m tall and 106 cm dbh. **Bark** of mature trees gray or gray-brown, thick, broken into long, smooth, flat-topped ridges separated by deep or shallow furrows. **Leaves** simple, alternate, deciduous or marcescent. **Petioles** 2–5 cm long, glabrous. **Leaf blades** 10–18 cm long, 8–14 cm wide; base obtusely tapered or nearly truncate; each margin with 2–4 primary lobes and 5–18 secondary lobes, each lobe acutely pointed and bristle tipped; the deepest sinuses extending 45–70% of the distance to the midvein; upper surface dull, dark green, glabrous; lower surface dull, pale green, with tufts of hairs in the axils of the lateral veins, otherwise glabrous. **Flowers** unisexual, with male flowers and female flowers borne separately on the same branch. **Male flowers** in slender, pendulous catkins 4–9 cm long, from buds on branchlets of the previous year. **Female flowers** borne singly or in pairs on a short peduncle from leaf axils on branchlets of the current year; **anthesis** early May to late May; wind-pollinated. **Fruit** (acorn) a broadly ovoid nut 1.6–2.5 cm long and 1.3–2.3 cm wide; with a scaly, flat or depressed dome-shaped cup at the base; the cup 1/4 to 1/2 as high as wide, comprising 25–50% of the total length of the nut plus cup; the scales on the cup flat, with appressed tips, the inner surface of cup glabrous or with a few scattered hairs; maturing mid-August to mid-September of the 2nd year; animal-dispersed. (*rubra*: red, in reference to the autumn foliage)

Identification

The leaves are very similar to those of northern pin oak (*Q. ellipsoidalis*) and to a lesser extent black oak (*Q. velutina*), but the sinuses are usually shallower and the upper surface is dull. Leaves alone cannot always distinguish northern red oak, but mature acorns are usually conclusive. The nuts themselves are relatively large and proportionately broad but with a small, flat cup that is shaped more like a plate than a cup and seems to barely cover the base of the nut. The bark is also different, usually with broader and flatter ridges that are not broken into short segments like the bark of northern pin oak or black oak. Hybrids between northern red oak and northern pin oak are relatively common in central Minnesota.

Natural History

Northern red oak is a common forest tree, especially in the southern half of the state. It occasionally reaches heights of 110 ft (33 m) in Minnesota, but it reportedly reaches 160 ft (49 m) farther to the east and south (Harlow et al. 1991). Among the oaks it is relatively fast growing and moderately long-lived (300+ years). It prefers deep, well-drained, loamy or clayey soils, yet it can also be found in drier, sandy soils. It is known to be susceptible to fire and drought (*fide* Burns and Honkala 1990), which has apparently kept it out of the prairie region, and it is susceptible to flooding and sedimentation, which keeps it off floodplains.

It is abundant only in mesic hardwood forests, particularly the type known as the "Big Woods," where it occurs in the canopy with sugar maple (*Acer saccharum*), basswood (*Tilia americana*), American elm (*Ulmus americana*), and green ash (*Fraxinus pensylvanica*). A dense climax forest of this type is an unusual place to find any oak since they generally need more light to reproduce. The seedlings and especially the saplings have a difficult time surviving the perpetual shade (Bray 1956). And yet somehow northern red oak has managed to maintain a continuing presence within this large, forested matrix without the need for major landscape-level disturbance such as fire. This ability is indicative of a true climax species, and perhaps this is the only oak in Minnesota deserving of the title.

The male catkins are conspicuous en masse—May 12.

Like northern pin oak except the sinuses are shallower.

Large, broad nut in a small, flat cup is diagnostic—August 24.

The tiny flecks of red give away the female flowers—May 12.

Note the long, flat-topped ridges—trunk is 19" (48 cm) dbh.

Quercus velutina Lam.

Black oak

Large **trees**, to 27 m tall and 70 cm dbh. **Bark** of mature trees gray to gray-brown or nearly black, thick, broken into short ridges or irregular blocks separated by deep furrows. **Leaves** simple, alternate, deciduous or marcescent. **Petioles** 2.5–6 cm long, glabrous or glabrate. **Leaf blades** 9–17 cm long, 8–16 cm wide; base obtusely tapered or truncate; each margin with 3–4 primary lobes and 8–20 secondary lobes, each lobe acutely pointed and bristle-tipped; the major sinuses extending 65–85% of the distance to the midvein; upper surface glossy, dark green, glabrous or glabrate; lower surface dull, pale green, with tufts of hairs in the axils of the lateral veins, otherwise glabrous. **Flowers** unisexual, with male flowers and female flowers borne separately on the same branch. **Male flowers** in slender, pendulous catkins 6–11 cm long, from buds on branchlets of the previous season. **Female flowers** 1–5 on a short peduncle from leaf axils on branchlets of the current year; **anthesis** early May to late May; wind-pollinated. **Fruit** (acorn) an ovoid to subglobose nut 1.2–2 cm long, 1–1.5 cm wide; with a scaly, dome-shaped cup at the base, the cup 3/4 to fully as high as wide, comprising 50–75% of the total length of the nut plus cup; the scales on the cup flat, with loose tips, those near the rim of the cup with tips curled back; the inner surface of the cup uniformly hairy; maturing mid-August to mid-September of the 2nd year; animal-dispersed. (*velutina*: velvety, the reference is obscure)

Identification

Black oak is easily confused with northern pin oak (*Q. ellipsoidalis*) and to a lesser extent northern red oak (*Q. rubra*). But the inner surface of the acorn cup has a dense, uniform covering of small hairs (magnification needed) that the other species do not have. Also, the tips of the scales near the rim of the cup are loose and tend to curl back. It is known to hybridize with both northern pin oak and northern red oak, but it is unclear how common such hybrids are in Minnesota.

Natural History

Black oak is locally common in the southeastern counties, especially on terraces and slopes along the Mississippi River and major tributaries. It competes most successfully in the driest, sandiest habitats; in

fact, with the possible exception of eastern redcedar (*Juniperus virginiana*), it may be the most drought-tolerant tree in Minnesota.

Black oak is most often found in open woodlands and savannas in highly erodable and droughty soils, particularly on south-facing slopes, ridgetops, and sand barrens. Under the most severe conditions it may grow no taller than about 40 ft (12 m), with a stout, crooked trunk and short, gnarled branches. Few other species can compete under these conditions, enabling black oak to continually replace itself and act as an edaphic climax species.

With better soil and moisture conditions it can become a relatively tall, straight tree with a broad crown and a maximum height in Minnesota of about 90 ft (27 m). Under these more favorable conditions it can create a closed canopy forest, typically in association with other oak species and shagbark hickory (*Carya ovata*). But black oak is generally intolerant of shade and usually cannot reproduce under a closed canopy. After one generation it will likely be succeeded by more shade-tolerant species that become established in the understory and gradually replace the black oaks as they die. In presettlement times this process of forest succession would likely have been set back by periodic wildfires, which favored the regeneration of oak forests. Since settlement, fires have been almost totally suppressed, resulting in very little oak regeneration.

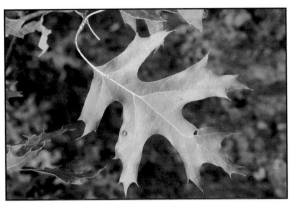

The leaf is very hard to tell from northern pin oak.

The cup is at least half the length of the acorn—August 25.

The male flowers are little more than anthers on a string—May 8.

Female flowers emerging from leaf axils—May 8.

Note short, blocky ridges and blackish color— 22" (56 cm) dbh.

Rhamnus, the buckthorns

Rhamnaceae: Buckthorn family

The buckthorns are a genus of 90 to 110 species of deciduous and evergreen trees and shrubs, distributed mostly in temperate regions of the Northern Hemisphere with a few in the tropics. Six species are native to the United States, and 1 to Minnesota. There is also one naturalized species in Minnesota. (*Rhamnus* is from the Greek *rhamnos*, the name for some species in this genus.)

The taxonomic classification of *Rhamnus* often encompasses a distinct group of plants segregated into subgenus *Frangula*. This includes the shrub commonly known as glossy buckthorn, which would be known as *Rhamnus frangula* L. under this broad classification. In the classification used here, *Frangula* is treated as a distinct genus, so glossy buckthorn becomes *Frangula alnus* P. Mill. It is believed that this classification better reflects evolutionary relationships.

Key to the Genus Rhamnus *in Minnesota*

1. Leaves usually opposite or subopposite (occasionally alternate), lateral veins 3–4 per side; branchlets often ending in a sharp thorn; leaf blade 2.5–6 cm long; petioles 1–3.5 cm long; flowers 4-merous; a large nonnative shrub commonly over 3 m tall .... *R. cathartica*
1. Leaves distinctly alternate, lateral veins 5–8 per side; thorns lacking; leaf blade 5–12 cm long; petioles 0.5–1.5 cm long; flowers 5-merous; a small native shrub usually less than 1 m tall .... *R. alnifolia*

Rhamnus alnifolia L'Her.

Alder-leaved buckthorn

Midsize **shrubs**, with multiple decumbent or upright **stems** to 2.3 m long (usually < 1 m vertical height) and 2.5 cm basal diameter; clonal by layering. **Bark** thin, reddish brown to gray or gray-black, somewhat rough. **Branchlets** minutely hairy; greenish to brown the 1st year, brown with a gray, flaky epidermis the 2nd year; thorns lacking. **Leaves** simple, alternate, deciduous. **Leaf blades** elliptical to ovate or lance-ovate; 5–12 cm long, 2–6 cm wide; base tapered or somewhat rounded; apex acute to short-acuminate; margins with glandular or eglandular serrations; lateral veins 5–8 per side; upper surface dark green, sparsely hairy to essentially glabrous; lower surface somewhat paler than upper, hairy to sparsely hairy. **Inflorescence** a sessile umbel with 1–3 flowers; arising from leaf axils on 1st-year branchlets. **Flowers** functionally unisexual, with male flowers and female flowers on separate plants; 5-merous; greenish yellow; minute, 1.5–3 mm across; petals lacking; pedicels 2–5 mm long, glabrous or occasionally minutely hairy; **anthesis** mid-May to mid-June; insect-pollinated. **Fruit** a blackish, spherical or ovoid drupe; 6–9 mm across; maturing mid-July to late mid-August; animal-dispersed. (*alnifolia*: with leaves like *Alnus*, the alder)

Identification

Alder-leaved buckthorn is a native shrub, usually about knee high or waist high with stems no more than an inch (2.5 cm) in diameter. The leaves are dark green with serrate margins and 5–8 conspicuous lateral veins. The flowers are small and green and rarely noticed. Although alder-leaved buckthorn is related to the infamous European buckthorns (*Rhamnus cathartica* and *Frangula alnus*), there is no reason for confusion. Except for technical similarities between the flowers, they look quite different.

Natural History

Alder-leaved buckthorn is found nearly throughout the forested region of Minnesota, although it is rare south of about Anoka County. Northward it becomes fairly common in appropriate habitats. This includes a variety of wet or moist sites, such as conifer swamps, wet woods, moist uplands, brushy meadows, and marshes. In most habitats the sunlight is filtered by a thin canopy of trees or by tall, widely spaced shrubs; other habitats may be open and receive full sunlight. Substrates are either peat or mineral soil and usually range from weakly to moderately acidic. These habitats are typically in fire-prone landscapes, but how alder-leaved buckthorn responds to fire is not known.

Alder-leaved buckthorn is most often seen in multistemmed clones 1–2 m (3–6 ft) across that are formed by layering of stems and lower branches. This is a process in which the lower portion of the stems spread outward along the ground and send down roots where they contact moist soil. At the same time, the branches continue to grow upright, at least from the tips. New root crowns formed in this manner can then become the center of continued growth, allowing the clone to expand outward. The process of clone formation is not particularly rapid, but in time, and if not constrained by competition, it can result in loose but continuous clones up to 15 m (50 ft) across. The largest stems in the center of well-established clones are sometimes as much as 20 years old, which may be near the maximum age normally reached by individual stems. But by then many of the outer stems are no longer connected to the original root system and are living independently.

A typical colony; the tiny flowers are barely visible—June 8.

Stems are rarely as much as an inch (2.5 cm) in diameter.

Fruits are black drupes about 1/4" (6–9 cm) across—August 14.

Flowers are functionally unisexual; these are male—May 24.

Rhamnus cathartica L.

Common buckthorn

Nonnative, naturalized, small **trees** or tall **shrubs**, with 1 or a few upright **stems** to 11 m tall and 16 cm dbh. **Branchlets** minutely hairy or sometimes glabrous; green to brownish green the 1st year, brown with a gray, flaky epidermis the 2nd; thorns often developing at the ends of short, lateral branchlets. **Bark** thin, dark gray to blackish; smooth when young, becoming rough and scaly or peeling in age. **Leaves** simple, opposite to subopposite or sometimes alternate, deciduous. **Petioles** 1–3.5 cm long, hairy. **Leaf blades** elliptical to broadly elliptical, oblong or obovate; 2.5–6 cm long, 1.8–4 cm wide; base tapered or rounded; apex abruptly pointed or rounded; margins with gland-tipped serrations; lateral veins 3–4 per side, curving toward the apex; upper surface dark green, sparsely hairy; lower surface pale green, hairy to sparsely hairy. **Inflorescence** a sessile umbel with 1–5 flowers; arising from near the base of 1st-year branchlets. **Flowers** functionally unisexual, with male flowers and female flowers on separate trees; 4-merous; greenish or yellowish green, 4–6 mm across; petals present; pedicels 3–8 mm long, glabrous or rarely minutely hairy; **anthesis** mid-May to mid-June; insect-pollinated. **Fruit** a blackish, spherical drupe; 5–8 mm across; maturing late August to late September, often held into winter; animal-dispersed. (*cathartica*: purging, the effect of the berries if eaten)

Identification

Common buckthorn is usually a large, bushy shrub, but it can also grow to be a small tree 35 ft (11 m) tall. The bark is initially smooth, then becomes rough and scaly like that of black cherry (*Prunus serotina*). Also notice that most branchlets end in a short, hard thorn. Oddly, the leaves do not change color in the autumn; they stay bright green even after a hard frost, and the blackish berries are held on the tree most of the winter unless eaten by birds.

Natural History

Common buckthorn was brought to North America from its native Europe sometime prior to 1850. It was intended for use as a hedge plant, but it proved to be extremely invasive and quickly escaped into the wild. It has been naturalized in Minnesota since at least the 1930s, possibly earlier, and has now spread over most of the state.

It is adapted to nearly all upland soil types and moisture regimes; it is drought resistant and flood tolerant and has no natural biological controls on this continent. It grows quickly in the open and in brushy habitats. It even thrives under a canopy of forest trees, especially oaks. In fact, it can form nearly impenetrable thickets in oak forests, where it easily outcompetes native shrubs for light and moisture.

Control is very difficult. Young trees (less than 1 inch diameter) have shallow root systems and can be pulled up by hand. But larger plants must be mechanically uprooted or treated with herbicides (Dziuk 1998). If they are only cut or burned, they will resprout vigorously and control will become even more difficult.

Common buckthorn spreads only by seed, which it does with great proficiency. Forests can become carpeted with seedlings, as many as 500,000 per acre (*fide* Moriarty 1998), leaving room for little else. This effectively eliminates reproduction of the native trees and shrubs and greatly reduces the abundance and diversity of herbaceous plants. The function of local ecosystems becomes seriously impaired with long-term consequences for the succession and regeneration of forests. For these reasons, common buckthorn is now listed as a restricted noxious weed under Minnesota law and cannot be imported, sold, or transported in the state (Minnesota Rule 1505.0732).

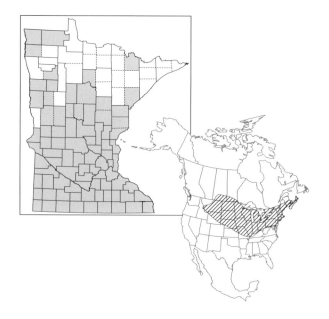

Flowers are yellowish green, these are from a female tree—June 9.

Male flowers, each less than 1/4" (4–6 mm) across—June 9.

Bark is smooth when young, starts to peel in age.

Fruits will stay on the tree all winter if not eaten first—September 20.

Notice that common buckthorn is still green on November 11.

Rhododendron, Labrador tea

Ericaceae: Heath family

The rhododendrons are a large genus of about 800 species, mostly in temperate regions of the Northern Hemisphere, especially Asia. About 30 species occur in North America, and 1 in Minnesota. (*Rhododendron* is from the Greek for rose tree.)

Minnesota's single native species, Labrador tea (*Rhododendron groenlandicum* [Oeder] Kron & Judd), has long resided in the segregate genus *Ledum*, a small group of 3 to 5 boreal species. The current trend toward monophyletic taxonomy would seem to justify combining *Ledum* with *Rhododendron* (Kron and Judd 1990).

Most of the other species of *Rhododendron* are poorly adapted to Minnesota's harsh winters. However, in 1957, the Minnesota Landscape Arboretum established a *Rhododendron* breeding program, focusing primarily on the development of cold-hardy deciduous azaleas. Cultivars released by this program during the past 40-plus years are now becoming quite popular (Pellett and De Vos 1978; Moe and Pellett 1986).

Rhododendron groenlandicum (Oeder) Kron & Judd

Labrador tea
[*Ledum groenlandicum* Oeder]

Midsize **shrubs**, with upright stems to 1 m tall; clonal. 1st-year **branchlets** with a dense covering of long, copper-colored hairs, the hairs turning gray the 2nd year and persisting for 3–5 years. **Bark** gray. **Leaves** simple, alternate, evergreen. **Petioles** 2–4 mm long, densely hairy. **Leaf blades** narrowly elliptical to broadly linear or oblong-linear; 2.5–5.5 cm long, 0.6–1.7 cm wide; base tapered or blunt, sometimes rounded; apex tapered or blunt; margins entire, strongly inrolled; upper surface dark green, glabrous or sparsely hairy along the sunken midvein; lower surface densely white-woolly the 1st year, the hairs becoming copper-colored the 2nd year. **Flowers** bisexual, 5-merous, white; borne in terminal umbel-like clusters of up to 40; pedicels slender, 1–2.5 cm long, minutely hairy and glandular; calyx much reduced, with minute rounded lobes about 0.2 mm long; corolla spreading, 7–10 mm across (measured flat), petals obovate; **anthesis** late May to late mid-June; insect-pollinated. **Fruit** a 5-celled capsule; narrowly ellipsoidal with a persistent style; 5–7 mm long; splitting from the base upwards; maturing mid-August to mid-September and shedding seeds in autumn and winter; gravity-dispersed. (*groenlandicum*: of Greenland)

Identification

Labrador tea is a waist-high bog shrub with fragrant, evergreen leaves and round-topped clusters of white flowers. Notice that the leaves are smooth and dark green above, but the undersides have a dense covering of copper-colored hairs and inrolled margins. Once these characters are learned, a quick look at the leaf is usually all that is needed for positive identification.

Natural History

Labrador tea is a common and characteristic shrub of peatlands, particularly bogs, conifer swamps, and certain types of fens. These habitats may be forested with tamarack (*Larix laricina*) or black spruce (*Picea mariana*) or with nothing larger than waist-high shrubs. Typically, *Sphagnum* moss will be present and will often carpet the ground. In densely forested habitats or where tall shrubs such as speckled alder (*Alnus incana* subsp. *rugosa*) dominate, Labrador tea tends to favor small openings or edges, usually staying out of deep shade.

Although peatlands are its primary habitat, Labrador tea will sometimes be found on a shoreline in wet sand or among rocks. In this type of habitat it may be exposed to ice scouring or seasonal flooding, which seem to cause it few problems. It is, however, susceptible to floods that deposit sediments or erode the soil from around its roots. It is also vulnerable to ponding that occurs behind beaver dams and poorly designed roads.

Labrador tea apparently spreads underground, probably by layering of lower branches or by the growth of rhizomes. Because of this, it will form discernable colonies that can expand slowly outwards, eventually finding and exploiting unoccupied patches of habitat. Yet it is not invasive or aggressive, and it does not rapidly colonize new habitats. Once it does become established, it seems to persist, at least if the habitat remains stable. In general, it seems little bothered by normal weather extremes, animal browsing, and "cool" fires that burn quickly and leave the soil undamaged; an intense fire may burn down into the peat layer and kill the roots.

Notice the long, copper-colored hairs on the stem—June 8.

A common sight in bogs throughout Minnesota.

The capsules split open from the base—September 2.

Labrador tea   🍂   **399**

Rhus, the sumacs

Anacardiaceae: Cashew family

The sumacs are a wide ranging genus of deciduous trees and shrubs with as many as 100 species. There are about 12 species in the United States, and 2 in Minnesota. It is closely related to the genus *Toxicodendron* (poison sumac and the poison ivies), but it is nontoxic. (*Rhus* is the classical Greek and Latin name of the sumac.)

In addition to Minnesota's native species, the fragrant sumac (*R. aromatica* Ait.), native to the south and east of Minnesota, is widely planted here, especially its low-growing cultivars such as "Gro-low."

Key to the Genus Rhus *in Minnesota*

1. Twigs and petioles densely hairy; hairs on the fruit long and slender (0.5–3 mm long) .... *R. hirta*
1. Twigs and petioles glabrous; hairs on the fruit short and club shaped (0.1–0.3 mm long) .... *R. glabra*

Rhus glabra L.

Smooth sumac

Large shrubs or small trees, with upright stems to 6 m tall and 10 cm dbh; clonal by root suckering. Bark thin, gray or brownish, smooth or made rough by large lenticels. Branches relatively few, stout, weak. Branchlets green the 1st year, brown the 2nd; glabrous. Leaves pinnately compound, alternate, deciduous. Petioles 4–9 cm long, glabrous. Leaf blades 17–35 cm long, 11–25 cm wide. Leaflets 9–23; sessile; lanceolate to lance-oblong; 6–12 cm long, 2–3.5 cm wide; base rounded; apex acuminate; margins sharply serrate; upper surface dark green or blue-green, hairy on midvein only; lower surface pale green, glabrous. Inflorescence an erect, terminal panicle (thyrse) 7–19 cm long, the female panicle about half the size of the male; hairy. Flowers 5-merous; unisexual, each plant bearing either male flowers or female flowers; pedicels 1–2 mm long, hairy; sepals 1.3–2.2 mm long, hairy or glabrate; petals 2–3.5 mm long, longer on male flowers than on female, yellowish green, hairy; stamens 5; styles 3; anthesis late June to late July; insect-pollinated. Fruit a slightly flattened, 1-seeded drupe 3.5–5 mm broad; with a dense covering of short, stout, metallic red hairs, 0.1–0.3 mm long; maturing late July to early September, often retained over winter and through the following summer; animal-dispersed. (*glabra*: smooth, without hairs)

Identification

Smooth sumac is a large, spreading shrub with almost tropical-looking compound leaves and smooth, stout twigs. It is very similar to the common staghorn sumac (*R. hirta*), except the twigs and petioles are smooth, not hairy. Naturally occurring hybrids between the two sumacs (named *R.* ×*borealis*) are fairly common and have twigs that are somewhat hairy the 1st year but smooth the 2nd (Hardin and Phillips 1985).

Natural History

Smooth sumac is common throughout most of the forested region of Minnesota as well as the prairie region. It is particularly common in clearings and openings in woodlands and along woodland edges, rock outcrops, dry prairies, riverbanks, and lakeshores. It also occurs on elevated portions of floodplains, but it does not tolerate frequent or prolonged flooding. It prefers sandy, rocky, or loamy soil, usually where conditions are basic (calcareous) or weakly acidic.

Smooth sumac is a fast-growing, early successional species that opportunistically invades large open areas. To succeed it needs direct sunlight and plenty of room. In forested regions it will eventually be shaded out by taller trees, and in the case of functioning prairies it will be kept in check by periodic wildfire. So under presettlement conditions it probably had an ephemeral and widely scattered presence within a large landscape area. But in the human-altered landscape of today it is a common and more-or-less permanent feature of roadsides and abandoned fields.

Once established, smooth sumac spreads rapidly by suckers that sprout from long, shallow roots that grow horizontally just beneath the soil surface (Gilbert 1966). In a short time it can form large clones 150 ft (46 m) or more across, with hundreds of interconnected stems and a dense canopy that shades out everything beneath. The individual stems reach their full height of 12–16 ft (4–5 m) in 10 years or less and rarely live more than 25 years. As the older stems at the center of the clone eventually die, new ones sprout at the periphery, so a clone may be much older than any of the stems. It resprouts vigorously after an initial fire or cutting, but it eventually weakens with frequent burning or cutting.

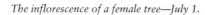
Each leaf has 9–13 serrate-margined leaflets.

The fruits mature 6–7 weeks after pollination—August 22.

The inflorescence of a female tree—July 1.

Quite different from the velvety branchlet of staghorn sumac.

Compare these with the shaggy fruit of staghorn sumac—August 22.

Stems can get about 4" (10 cm) in diameter.

Rhus hirta (L.) Sudworth

Staghorn sumac
[*R. typhina* L.]

Large **shrubs** or small **trees**, with upright stems to 11 m tall and 19 cm dbh; clonal by root suckering. **Bark** thin, gray or gray-brown, smooth or made rough by large lenticels. **Branches** relatively few, stout, weak. **Branchlets** green the 1st year, brown the 2nd; with a dense covering of long, velvety hairs, becoming glabrate only after several years. **Leaves** pinnately compound, alternate, deciduous. **Petioles** 4–9 cm long, densely hairy. **Leaf blades** 18–40 cm long, 11–24 cm wide. **Leaflets** 13–27; sessile; lance-oblong to lanceolate or lance-linear; 6–13 cm long, 1.5–4 cm wide; base rounded; apex acute to acuminate; margins sharply serrate; upper surface dark green or blue-green, sparsely hairy to glabrate; lower surface pale green, hairy, especially on midvein. **Inflorescence** an erect, terminal panicle (thyrse) 6–18 cm long, the female panicle about half the size of the male; densely hairy. **Flowers** 5-merous; unisexual, each plant bearing either male flowers or female flowers; pedicels 1–2 mm long, glandular-hairy; sepals 0.7–1.7 mm long, glandular-hairy; petals 2–3.3 mm long, longer on male flowers than on female, greenish white, hairy or glabrate; stamens 5; styles 3; **anthesis** mid-June to mid-July; insect-pollinated. **Fruit** a slightly flattened, 1-seeded drupe; 3.5–5 mm broad; with a dense covering of long, slender, metallic red hairs 0.5–3 mm long; maturing early August to late September, often retained over winter and through the following summer; animal-dispersed. (*hirta*: hairy)

Identification

Staghorn sumac is a large shrub or sometimes a small tree, with sharply serrate compound leaves. The stout, velvety branches are mostly pith and easily broken. The individual fruits are small and shaggy with metallic red hairs and are packed into dense, glistening, cone-shaped clusters. Staghorn sumac is so distinctive it can only be confused with smooth sumac (*R. glabra*), but the twigs are velvety with long, soft hairs, not smooth. Hybrids between the two sumacs (named *R.* ×*borealis*) are fairly common; they have twigs that are somewhat hairy the 1st year but smooth the 2nd (Hardin and Phillips 1985).

Natural History

Staghorn sumac is common in Minnesota, although somewhat less common than smooth sumac

(*R. glabra*). The two species are ecologically very similar and often grow side by side at forest edges, in openings, clearings, abandoned fields, and bluff prairies, and on riverbanks, lakeshores, and roadsides. Both are early successional species that grow rapidly but do not live very long. Comparing the two, staghorn sumac has a more restricted range in Minnesota and is more characteristic of the forested region of the state. This may indicate a greater sensitivity to fire or drought, which were more prevalent on the prairies.

Although staghorn sumac is a species of forested ecosystems, it cannot compete for light in a stable forest or with established saplings of forest trees; it thrives only in the open. With enough space it can establish a dense colony formed by suckers that sprout from long, horizontal roots. A colony formed in this way is called a clone. Clones may eventually consist of hundreds of stems and form a dense canopy 15 to 30 ft (5–9 m) tall that excludes all competitors. In the absence of disturbance, clones may persist for decades, but they eventually break up and are replaced by longer-lived and usually more shade-tolerant species.

The sumacs are among the last woody species to leaf out in spring and among the first to shed their leaves in autumn. In most areas, the leaves are already turning bright crimson in late August and begin to fall by mid-September.

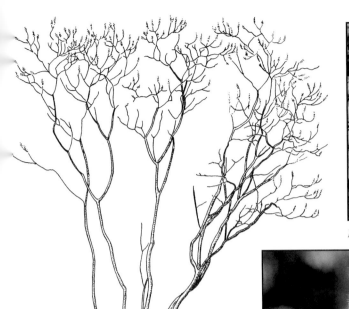

It's hard to tell staghorn from smooth sumac at this distance.

Perhaps suggestive of a stag's "horn" in velvet.

This female inflorescence is about half the size of the male—July 1.

This specimen is 14' (4.3 m) tall; they can reach 35' (11 m) in Minnesota—Anoka County.

This stem is 5.5" (14 cm) in diameter— about average.

Fruits have a dense covering of metallic-red hairs—August 24.

Ribes, gooseberries and currants

Grossulariaceae: Gooseberry family

The genus *Ribes* includes about 150 species of shrubs, distributed mostly in temperate regions of the northern hemisphere and South America. About 48 species are native in the United States, and 9 are native in Minnesota. (*Ribes* is from the Arabic *ribas*, which originally applied to a species of rhubarb.)

Golden currant (*R. aureum* Pursh var. *villosum* DC.) is a western plant that is sometimes reported as native to Minnesota, but there is no documented evidence to support the claim.

Although members of the genus are sometimes planted for ornament, and the fruits are sometimes eaten, they would be obscure were it not for their role as the alternate host of *Cronartium ribicola* J. C. Fisch., a parasitic fungus responsible for white pine blister rust. The disease is usually fatal to eastern white pine (*Pinus strobus*) but cannot be transmitted directly from pine to pine without a species of *Ribes* as an intermediary (Miller, Kimmey, and Fowler 1959).

The disease, which originated in Europe, was first detected in North America in 1906 and in Minnesota in 1916 (Ritter 1941). It was first thought that the only way to protect the pines was to eradicate all native and cultivated *Ribes* growing within 900 feet (277 m) of white pine. That was the maximum distance the spores can travel from *Ribes* to pine, or so it was thought for many years. There were, at that time, about 1 million acres of white pine in Minnesota, and in 1917 the Department of Conservation (now the Department of Natural Resources) began *Ribes* eradication efforts that continued yearly into the 1950s.

By 1951, the last year summary statistics were published, an incredible 235,499 person days had been expended digging and pulling 73,444,723 individual *Ribes* on 404,877 acres of forest land (Minnesota Department of Conservation 1932–52). An unknown number were also killed by spraying of 2,4–D (2,4–Dichlorophenoxyacetic acid) and other chemical herbicides. The effort was justified by having "protected" 173,027 acres of white pine. Eradication efforts were eventually phased out when it was realized that the spores can travel up to a mile, not the 900 feet previously thought. The benefits of nearly 40 years of *Ribes* eradication were deemed negligible, but the damage to the native populations of *Ribes* was never assessed.

Key to the Genus Ribes in Minnesota

1. Flowers 1–3 per inflorescence; pedicels not jointed at base of flower; styles hairy, at least near the base; stems usually with bristles or spines or both [the gooseberries (subgenus *Grossularia*)].
   2. Ovary with stiff gland-tipped hairs, becoming nonglandular prickles in fruit; sepals shorter than the calyx tube; 2nd-year branchlets hairy .... *R. cynosbati*
   2. Ovary and fruit without gland-tipped hairs or prickles; sepals longer than the calyx tube; 2nd-year branchlets glabrous or hairy.
      3. Style more than 10 mm long; filaments 8.5–11 mm long; sepals 5–7.5 mm long; nodal spines well developed and prominent .... *R. missouriense*
      3. Style less than 10 mm long; filaments 1.5–4.5 mm long; sepals 2.5–5 mm long; nodal spines absent or poorly developed.
         4. Filaments 3–4.5 mm long; anthers exerted beyond the petals (stamens 1.5–2 times as long as the petals); leaf blades with only nonglandular hairs; floral bracts with hairs along margin but usually lacking glands; branchlets glabrous .... *R. hirtellum*
         4. Filaments 1.5–2.5 mm long; anthers about equaling the petals; leaf blades occasionally with small stalked glands in addition to nonglandular hairs; floral bracts with glands along the margin; 1st- and 2nd-year branchlets usually hairy .... *R. oxyacanthoides*
1. Flowers 2–18 per inflorescence; pedicels jointed at base of flower; styles glabrous; stems lacking bristles or spines (except *R. lacustre*) [the currants (subgenus *Ribes*)].
   5. Stems densely bristly .... *R. lacustre*
   5. Stems without bristles, prickles, or spines.
      6. Leaf blades with small, bright yellow, resinous dots, at least on the lower surface; 2nd- and 3rd-year branchlets hairy, and with yellow, resinous dots; sepals greater than 2.7 mm long.
         7. Style 5–7.5 mm long; filaments greater than 1 mm long; petals 2.7–4 mm long, more than half as long as the sepals; pedicels 1.5–4.5 mm long, shorter than the subtending bract; yellow glandular dots present on both upper and lower surface of leaves .... *R. americanum*
         7. Style 1.1–2 mm long; filaments less than 1 mm long; petals 1–1.5 mm long, less than half as long as the sepals; pedicels 4.3–6 mm long, longer than the subtending bract; yellow glandular dots present only on lower surface of leaves .... *R. hudsonianum*
      6. Leaf blades without bright yellow, resinous dots; 2nd- and 3rd-year branchlets not hairy, and without yellow, resinous dots; sepals less than 2.7 mm long.
         8. Ovary and fruit covered with gland-tipped hairs; style 1–1.8 mm long; leaf blades 3.5–7 cm wide; racemes ascending .... *R. glandulosum*
         8. Ovary and fruit glabrous; style less than 1 mm long; leaf blades 5–10 cm wide when mature; racemes drooping .... *R. triste*

Ribes americanum P. Mill.

Wild black currant

Midsize **shrubs**, with multiple ascending, arching, decumbent or trailing **stems** to 2.5 m long, rooting at the tips and along the length; spines or bristles absent. 1st- and 2nd-year **branchlets** hairy, with yellow glandular dots; becoming smooth as the thin outer layer flakes off in age. **Leaves** simple, alternate, deciduous. **Leaf blades** 2.5–5 cm long, 2.5–5.5 cm wide; with 3–5 palmate lobes; base rounded, truncate, or shallowly cordate; margins with pointed serrations; upper surface dark green, sparsely hairy to glabrous, with yellow glandular dots; lower surface pale green, hairy, with numerous yellow glandular dots. **Flowers** bisexual, 5-merous; 4–16 in drooping racemes; floral bracts 4.7–8.5 mm long, exceeding the pedicels; pedicels woolly, jointed at summit, 1.5–4.5 mm long; calyx tube 2.8–5 mm long; sepals greenish-yellow, 4–5.5 mm long; petals greenish-white, 2.7–4 mm long, about equaling the stamens; filaments 2–2.5 mm long; ovary glabrous; style 5–7.5 mm long, not divided, glabrous; **anthesis** early May to mid-June; insect-pollinated. **Fruit** a smooth, black berry; 6–10 mm in diameter; maturing early July to late August; animal-dispersed. (*americanum*: of America)

Identification

Wild black currant is a bushy, multistemmed shrub, usually about waist high or sometimes shoulder high. The stems initially grow erect but arch toward the ground when they get long. It has no spines or bristles, and the crushed leaves have no distinctive odor. It does have distinctive yellow, resinous dots on the twigs and both surfaces of the leaves (seen with a hand lens). Northern black currant (*R. hudsonianum*) is similar, but it has yellow dots only on the lower surface of the leaves.

Natural History

Wild black currant is the most common and widespread currant in Minnesota, especially in the southern half of the state. It occurs in a wide range of wet or moist habitats, including lakeshores, riverbanks, shallow marshes, brushy woodland edges, and occasionally woodland interiors. It seems to favor full sunlight or partial shade and soils that range from moderately acidic to basic. This includes sandy, silty, and loamy soils and sometimes shallow

peat. It also seems well adapted to floodplains, where it shows a high tolerance for spring flooding and sedimentation. It will even colonize nonnative habitats such as abandoned hay meadows, intermittent pastures, and ditch banks.

In fact, wild black currant can become rather aggressive in certain ruderal habitats, especially in species-depleted sites where competition is low but light and nutrients are high. Under these conditions, the stems may grow 6 ft (2 m) or longer and arch downward. Where they touch the ground, they will root and send up new stems, a process called tip-rooting. If this process is repeated often enough, a single plant can eventually spread to form a tangled thicket 8–10 ft (2.5–3 m) across.

It is much less aggressive in diverse native communities, especially in the shade. Under these conditions it will appear as relatively small, scattered individuals or in sparse, open colonies. The individual stems rarely live more than about 4 to 6 years, but the root crown can continue to sprout stems for much longer.

Gooseberries have 1–3 flowers, the currants up to 18—May 29.

Fruits ripen smooth and black—August 26.

Branches lack spines and bristles—June 2.

Ribes cynosbati L.

Prickly gooseberry

Midsize **shrubs**, with multiple ascending, arching or trailing **stems** to 2 m long, rooting at the tips and along the length; nodal spines and internodal bristles usually present. 1st- and 2nd-year **branchlets** hairy, becoming smooth as the thin outer layer is shed in age. **Leaves** simple, alternate, deciduous. **Leaf blades** 1.8–5.5 cm long, 2–5.5 cm wide; with 3–5 palmate lobes; base usually cordate; margins with rounded serrations; upper surface dark green, hairy, with occasional intermixed gland-tipped hairs; lower surface pale green, otherwise similar to upper surface. **Flowers** bisexual, 5-merous; borne in clusters of 1–3; floral bracts 1–2.5 mm long, shorter than the pedicels; pedicels with both gland-tipped and non–gland-tipped hairs, not jointed at summit, 3–15 mm long; calyx tube 3–5 mm long; sepals greenish, sometimes tinged with purple, 2.5–4 mm long; petals white, 1–2 mm long, slightly exceeded by the stamens; filaments 1–2 mm long; ovary with stiff, gland-tipped hairs; style 4.5–7 mm long, the upper third divided, hairy on the lower half; **anthesis** late April to early June; insect-pollinated. **Fruit** a dull, red or purplish berry; 8–14 mm in diameter; usually with stiff, broad-based prickles, or rarely smooth; maturing early July to mid-August; animal-dispersed. (*cynosbati*: from the Greek meaning dog brier)

Identification

Prickly gooseberry is a small to midsize shrub, usually with multiple stems about 3 ft (1 m) high. The stems often have sharp spines at the nodes and stiff, slender bristles between the nodes. The ovary at the base of the flower is usually covered with stiff hairs that harden into long, firm prickles by the time the fruit ripens in midsummer. It is most likely to be confused with Missouri gooseberry (*R. missouriense*) and swamp gooseberry (*R. hirtellum*).

Natural History

Prickly gooseberry is a common understory shrub in hardwood forests throughout most of Minnesota. It typically occurs in moist, loamy soils under oaks (*Quercus* spp.), maples (*Acer* spp.), basswood (*Tilia americana*), or ashes (*Fraxinus* spp.), but it is occasionally found on floodplains and in swamps. As a point of distinction, this is one of the few shrubs that can thrive beneath a closed canopy of sugar

maples, which cast the densest shade of any Minnesota tree. To accomplish this, prickly gooseberry greens up and flowers in early May before the canopy trees leaf out. This early start gives it a chance to complete much of its annual growth cycle before the forest interiors are subjected to deep shade.

The seeds of prickly gooseberry are spread by a variety of birds, enabling it to move quickly into new habitats. These new arrivals are not normally aggressive, at least not in deep shade, but once established they can be very persistent; they can even spread slowly by vegetative means. This happens when the stems become long and arch downward or trail along the ground. The stems respond by rooting where they contact moist soil, creating new root crowns that can sprout additional aerial shoots.

Reproducing in this fashion is a slow and uncertain process; under stable forest conditions it allows the population to replace individuals that are lost to normal attrition, but not much more. The situation is different in grazed woodlands. Cattle avoid prickly gooseberry, perhaps because of the bristly stems, giving it a competitive advantage over more palatable species. Under these conditions prickly gooseberry can become unnaturally abundant, even to the point of forming small thickets.

Note the short sepals and the hairy ovary—April 30.

Smallish leaves with round-tipped lobes, bristly stems.

The hairs on the ovary become prickles on the fruit—August 1, Wright County.

Gooseberries and Currants 🍃 **411**

Ribes glandulosum Grauer

Skunk currant

Low to midsize **shrubs**, with 1 or a few ascending, arching, or trailing **stems** to 2 m long, trailing stems rooting along their length; spines and bristles absent. 1st- and 2nd-year **branchlets** glabrous, the thin outer layer exfoliating with age. **Leaves** simple, alternate, deciduous. **Leaf blades** 2.5–5 cm long, 3.5–7 cm wide, with 3–5 palmate lobes; base cordate to deeply cordate; margins with pointed serrations; upper surface dark green, glabrous, without glands; lower surface pale green, glabrous or with scattered hairs, short stalked glands usually present along main veins. **Flowers** bisexual, 5-merous; 6–15 in ascending racemes; floral bracts 1.3–2.5 mm long, shorter than the pedicels; pedicels with red, gland-tipped hairs, jointed at summit, 3–6.5 mm long; sepals pale green or yellowish, 1.6–2.5 mm long; calyx tube 0.5–1 mm long; petals pinkish or purplish, 0.8–1.2 mm long, about equaling the stamens or a little shorter; filaments 0.5–1 mm long; ovary with red, gland-tipped hairs; style 1–1.8 mm long, divided to the base, glabrous; **anthesis** early May to mid-June; insect-pollinated. **Fruit** a translucent red berry; 6–10 mm in diameter; with stiff, gland-tipped hairs; maturing mid-June to mid-July; animal-dispersed. (*glandulosum*: glandular, in reference to the fruit)

Identification

Although a considerable portion of the plant may be trailing over the ground, there will be at least one upright branch that produces the flowers and fruits, which makes identification pretty simple: If the flowers and fruits are covered with stiff, gland-tipped hairs, it is either skunk currant or bristly black currant (*R. lacustre*), and if the stem has no bristles, then it can only be skunk currant. True to its name, the leaves and the inner bark have a distinctive skunklike odor when crushed or scraped, and even the fruits are tainted with the odor.

Natural History

Skunk currant is relatively common in the ecological region of Minnesota known as the Laurentian Mixed Forest Province (Minnesota Department of Natural Resources 2003). The province is characterized by broad areas of coniferous forest, hardwood forest, conifer bogs, and swamps. Within this habitat matrix, skunk currant needs only to find some degree of

shade and a wet or moist substrate such as peat, woody humus, heavy loam, or even mossy rocks. Suitable sites are usually moderately or weakly acidic.

These conditions can be met in a variety of upland and lowland habitats, and they need not be in stable, climax forests. Skunk currant is an adaptable colonizer, capable of a certain amount of mobility. However, it does not readily colonize habitats where the soil has been recently and severely disturbed, or where erosion or sedimentation are actively occurring.

The stems of skunk currant are weak; by the time they reach a height of about 2 ft (60 cm) they can no longer support themselves and end up lying on the ground. These newly horizontal stems may become covered with leaf litter or overgrown by mosses, which stimulates them to produce roots along their length. The rooted stems then send up vertical branches from the nodes, which grow erect for a few years until they too can no longer support themselves and become horizontal on the ground. This process of vegetative spreading is called layering; it is an effective way to exploit habitats that may be inhospitable to establishment by seed. Skunk currant even employs this strategy on rocks, where stems will root in crevices and then trail across the rocks, rooting again when they come to another crevice.

Note the red, gland-tipped hairs on the ovary—May 17.

Fruits taste much like a skunk smells—June 26.

From a white cedar swamp in Cook County—July 6.

The inflorescence stands upright, does not droop—May 17.

Gooseberries and Currants ❧ **413**

Ribes hirtellum Michx.

Swamp gooseberry

Midsize **shrubs**, with multiple upright, arching or sprawling **stems** to 1.5 m long, rooting at the tips and along the length; nodal spines usually absent or poorly developed; internodal bristles usually present but typically sparse, eventually shed with the outer layer of bark. 1st- and 2nd-year **branchlets** glabrous, the thin outer layer exfoliating with age. **Leaves** simple, alternate, deciduous. **Leaf blades** 1–3 cm long, 1.5–3.5 cm wide; with 3–5 palmate lobes; base tapered, rounded or nearly truncate; margins with pointed serrations; upper surface dark green, sparsely hairy or glabrate, without glands; lower surface pale green, sparsely to moderately hairy, without glands. **Flowers** bisexual, 5-merous; borne in clusters of 1–3; floral bracts 1–2 mm long, shorter than the pedicels; pedicels glabrous, not jointed at summit, 2–5 mm long; calyx tube 1.8–3 mm long; sepals greenish or yellowish, often tinged with purple, 2.5–4 mm long; petals white, sometimes tinged with purple, 1.7–2.5 mm long, exceeded by the stamens; filaments 3–4.5 mm long; ovary glabrous; style 5.5–7.5 mm long, the upper half divided, hairy on the lower half; **anthesis** early mid-May to early June; insect-pollinated. **Fruit** a greenish to purplish berry; 7–11 mm in diameter; smooth; maturing early July to mid-August; animal-dispersed. (*hirtellum*: with small, stiff hairs)

Identification

At first glance there is not much to distinguish swamp gooseberry from the other gooseberries; it is another sparse-looking, bristly shrub with multiple erect or arching stems about waist high. It can be particularly difficult to tell this species from the less common northern gooseberry (*R. oxyacanthoides*), especially after the flowers have withered. So have a good hand lens ready, and be prepared to study the key carefully. Also be aware that swamp gooseberry can hybridize with both northern gooseberry and prickly gooseberry (*R. cynosbati*). Such hybrids, although apparently rare, are reported to occur wherever the geographic ranges of the parent species overlap (Sinnott 1985).

Natural History

Swamp gooseberry is fairly common in shallow wetlands, particularly tamarack (*Larix laricina*) swamps. It also occurs in shrub swamps with willows (*Salix* spp.), dogwoods (*Cornus* spp.), or speckled alder (*Alnus incana* subsp. *rugosa*), and in sedge meadows, marshes, wet woods, and lakeshores. It can even be found on ditch banks, utility rights-of-way, and other disturbed habitats, although it should not be considered an aggressive colonizer.

The preferred soil seems to be wet peat or sometimes wet mineral soil or coarse humus. Conditions are usually weakly to moderately acidic and not prone to alluvial flooding, or at least not prone to flooding that deposits sediments or causes scouring. Shade, in moderation, is tolerated, as long as there is direct sunlight for at least a portion of the day.

Under certain conditions the stems will arch to the ground and root at the tips, or become horizontal on the ground and root along the whole length of the stem. This results in the establishment of adventitious root crowns that can sprout new stems and live independently from the parent plant. This is a form of vegetative or clonal reproduction that allows a single plant to spread without the necessity of flowering and fruiting. Most if not all species of gooseberries are able to reproduce in this way, but sizable colonies of swamp gooseberry produced in this manner are not common.

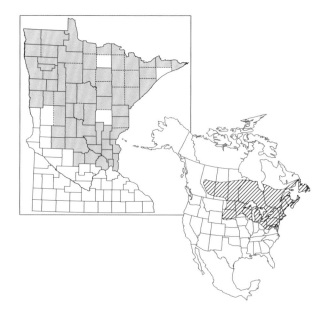

Stamens protrude farther than those of northern gooseberry—May 22.

Fruit is a smooth, purplish berry about 3/8" (7–11 mm) across.

Stems are typically about waist high.

Ribes hudsonianum Richards.

Northern black currant

Midsize **shrubs**, with multiple upright or ascending **stems** to 1 m tall; spines and bristles absent. 1st- and 2nd-year **branchlets** hairy, with scattered yellow, glandular dots; becoming smooth as the thin outer layer splits and exfoliates with age. **Leaves** simple, alternate, deciduous. **Leaf blades** 2.5–6 cm long, 3–7 cm wide; with 3–5 palmate lobes; base cordate; margins with pointed serrations; upper surface dark green, sparsely hairy or glabrate, without glands; lower surface pale green, moderately to densely hairy, with many yellow glandular dots. **Flowers** bisexual, 5-merous; 8–18 in ascending racemes; floral bracts 0.8–2.2 mm long, shorter than the pedicels; pedicels sparsely hairy to nearly glabrous, jointed at summit, 4.3–6 mm long; sepals white, 2.8–4 mm long; calyx tube lacking, or up to 0.5 mm long; petals white, 1–1.5 mm long, about equaling the stamens; filaments 0.5–0.9 mm long; ovary glabrous, smooth except for yellow, glandular dots; style 1.1–2 mm long, the upper third divided, glabrous; **anthesis** mid-May to mid-June; insect-pollinated. **Fruit** a smooth, blue-black berry; 7–11 mm in diameter; maturing early July to early September; animal-dispersed. (*hudsonianum*: of the Hudson Bay region)

Identification

Northern black currant is one of only two *Ribes* in Minnesota that have bright yellow, resinous dots on the leaf surface (seen with a hand lens); the other is wild black currant (*R. americanum*). But in northern black currant the dots occur only on the lower surface of the leaf. Also note the foul-smelling foliage, sometimes detectable from a distance.

Natural History

Northern black currant is a species of cold climates, ranging as far north as the Arctic Circle. With one important exception, it gets no farther south in Minnesota than about the latitude of Duluth. It is a rather scarce plant, which makes habitat preferences difficult to categorize, but it seems to favor peat soil in conifer swamps, usually with tamarack (*Larix laricina*) or northern white cedar (*Thuja occidentalis*). It has also been found in moist, mineral soil in upland forests, usually where shade is intermittent rather than continuous.

The disjunct populations in the southeast (Fillmore County) occur in a unique habitat type called algific (cold-producing) talus slopes. These rare habitats are small, usually a fraction of an acre, and occur only on certain north-facing, forested slopes in the stream-dissected Paleozoic Plateau. They owe their unique character to a continuous supply of cold air that originates in persistent underground ice reservoirs insulated in the karst formation. The cold air arrives at the surface through a network of fissures in the underlying limestone bedrock. Once at the surface, the cold air flows downslope over the surface of the ground, creating boreal-like growing conditions.

These habitats are believed to have been created during the last glacial advance. When the glaciers retreated northward about 14,000 years ago, plants began to migrate northward too and eventually recolonized the deglaciated area, including the algific talus slopes. As the regional climate warmed, conditions on the algific talus slopes remained relatively unchanged providing a boreal-like refugia for cold-loving species. After all this time they still harbor relict populations of not only northern black currant but other northern plant species such as twinflower (*Linnaea borealis*) and balsam fir (*Abies balsamea*).

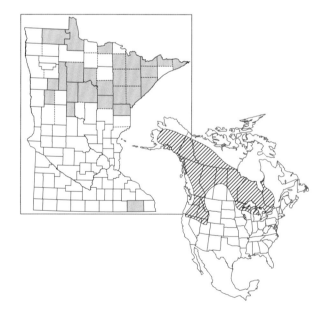

Fruits are smooth, become black when ripe—July 20.

The undersides of the leaves have tiny, yellow dots.

A large specimen will stand about 3' (1 m) tall.

Flowers are white, bell shaped—May 25, Fillmore County.

Ribes lacustre (Pers.) Poir.

Bristly black currant

Midsize **shrubs**, with multiple upright, ascending or arching **stems** to 1 m tall; with nodal spines and dense internodal bristles. 1st- and 2nd-year **branchlets** glabrous or occasionally minutely hairy, becoming smooth when the thin outer layer exfoliates with age. **Leaves** simple, alternate, deciduous. **Leaf blades** 2–5 cm long, 2.5–5 cm wide; with 3–5 deep palmate lobes; base cordate; margins with rounded teeth; upper surface dark green, with scattered gland-tipped hairs often interspersed with nonglandular hairs; lower surface pale green but otherwise similar. **Flowers** bisexual, 5-merous; 2–6 in arching or drooping racemes; floral bracts 2.2–4 mm long, shorter than the pedicels; pedicels with nonglandular hairs intermixed with red, gland-tipped hairs, jointed at summit, 3–6 mm long; calyx tube 0.5–1.2 mm long; sepals 2–2.8 mm long; petals pinkish, 1–2 mm long, about equaling the stamens; filaments 1.1–1.5 mm long; ovary with red, gland-tipped hairs; style 1.5–1.7 mm long, the upper third or half divided, glabrous; **anthesis** late May to early mid-June; insect-pollinated. **Fruit** a purple-black berry; ± spherical; 5–10 mm in diameter; covered with reddish, gland-tipped hairs; maturing early mid-July to late August; animal-dispersed. (*lacustre*: of lakes)

Identification

The most striking feature of bristly black currant is the extremely bristly stem. It is far more bristly than any other Minnesota currant or gooseberry. Another important feature is the red, gland-tipped hairs that cover the flowers and fruit. This is a character shared only with skunk currant (*R. glandulosum*). The two also share a distinctive and disagreeable skunk-like odor, which unfortunately taints even the fruit.

Natural History

This is basically a boreal and subarctic species that seems only marginally adapted to the temperate conditions found in Minnesota. It occurs sporadically in the coniferous forest region in the northern half of the state. And although evidence is scanty, populations appear to be small and ephemeral, usually consisting of only a few scattered individuals at any given site. Known records, of which there are few, are split about evenly between two seemingly different habitat types: rocky habitats such as cliffs,

talus, and rock ledges, and wetland habitats in conifer swamps.

Swamp habitats typically have a thin or interrupted canopy of northern white cedar (*Thuja occidentalis*), black spruce (*Picea mariana*), or tamarack (*Larix laricina*) and a ground cover of mosses and sedges. The soil is normally wet peat, and sunlight is typically subdued or patchy. Habitats with these conditions tend to be relatively stable over time, and by their nature have a low risk of fire, flooding, or drought.

Conditions in exposed rocky habitats seem quite different; the substrate itself may be unstable, often crumbling and eroding away. There is very little actual soil, and the plants appear to be rooted in small crevices or cracks. Any plant growing there is likely to be exposed to extremes in moisture and temperature conditions.

Note the tiny, glandular flowers and the bristly stem—June 8.

The flowers are no more than 3/16" (5 mm) across—June 8.

Fruits are covered with reddish, gland-tipped hairs—July 27.

Stems are upright, about waist high.

Gooseberries and Currants 🍃 **419**

Ribes missouriense Nutt.

Missouri gooseberry

Midsize **shrubs**, with numerous upright, arching, or trailing **stems** to 2.5 m tall, rooting at the tips and along the length; nodal spines prominent, to 2 cm long, stout; internodal bristles strong, abundant on lower half or third of stem, usually absent from upper portion. 1st-year **branchlets** hairy, 2nd-year branchlets glabrous, the thin outer layer exfoliating with age. **Leaves** simple, alternate, deciduous. **Leaf blades** 1.5–4 cm long, 2–4.5 cm wide; with 3–5 palmate lobes; base obtusely tapered to truncate; margins with pointed or rounded serrations; upper surface sparsely hairy, without glands; lower surface moderately to densely hairy, without glands. **Flowers** bisexual, 5-merous; in loose clusters of 1–3; floral bracts 2–3 mm long, shorter than the pedicels; pedicels glabrous, not jointed at summit, 3–13 mm long; calyx tube 1.5–3 mm long; sepals greenish yellow, 5–7.5 mm long; petals white, 2–3 mm long, greatly exceeded by the stamens; filaments 8.5–11 mm long; ovary glabrous; style 11–15 mm long, the upper quarter to half divided, hairy, at least near base; **anthesis** late April to early June; insect-pollinated. **Fruit** a dark purple or blackish berry; dull; spherical or short-ellipsoidal; 8–15 mm in diameter; smooth; maturing early mid-July to mid-August; animal-dispersed. (*missouriense*: of Missouri)

Identification

Full-grown specimens of Missouri gooseberry range from 3 to 8 ft (1–2.5 m) tall, with multiple stems and a jumble of long, tangled branches that arch toward the ground. The armature is formidable with large, stout spines at the nodes; the lower portions also have slender bristles between the nodes. The closest look-alike is probably prickly gooseberry (*R. cynosbati*), which also has nodal spines and internodal bristles. The fruits and flowers of the two species differ in a number of ways (see key) and are probably the easiest way to tell them apart.

Natural History

Missouri gooseberry is a common shrub in hardwood forests, where it thrives in deep shade. It does especially well on forested floodplains, seemingly unaffected by spring flooding and accompanying sedimentation. Surprisingly, it is at least as common in the prairie region, where it occurs in a variety of habitats including brushy thickets, shelterbelts, and woodlots. It even occurs in unburned grasslands, where it competes in the open with exotic and native grasses. This is probably a recent turn of events; the presettlement prairies would have burned every few years, relegating Missouri gooseberry to gallery forests along rivers and other fire-protected habitats.

Although Missouri gooseberry will colonize abandoned agricultural land, it will do so with no great haste and not until a stable cover is established. In general, acidic soils seem to be avoided; otherwise soil type does not appear to be a limiting factor. Alluvial deposits such as sand and silt are exploited just as readily as loams. Moisture conditions are also diverse and range from dry to moist or seasonally flooded.

Perhaps because of its sharp spines, Missouri gooseberry is generally able to resist cattle grazing. In fact, established colonies may increase with grazing pressure as the cattle reduce the more palatable competition. Under these circumstances it may spread aggressively by the process of layering and tip-rooting and ultimately form dense thickets. It is not uncommon to see overgrazed woodlots with a solid ground cover of Missouri gooseberry. This does not happen in ungrazed native habitats where high species diversity keeps competition intense.

Long, projecting stamens distinguish Missouri gooseberry—May 8.

Fruits turn blackish when ripe—July 20.

The nodal spines are formidable.

Multiple stems with strong, sharp bristles.

A 7' (2.2 m) specimen at peak anthesis—April 22, Houston County.

Gooseberries and Currants 🌿 **421**

Gooseberries and Currants

Ribes oxyacanthoides L.

Northern gooseberry

Midsize **shrubs**, with multiple upright, arching or trailing **stems** to 1.5 m tall, rooting at the tips and along the length; nodal spines usually present but variable; internodal bristles present, or absent on upper portions. 1st- and 2nd-year **branchlets** minutely hairy or glabrate, becoming smooth as the thin outer surface exfoliates with age. **Leaves** simple, alternate, deciduous. **Leaf blades** 1.5–4 cm long, 2–4 cm wide; with 3–5 palmate lobes; base tapered, truncate or somewhat cordate; margins with rounded or pointed serrations; upper surface dark green, sparsely to moderately hairy with small, stalked glands occasionally intermixed; lower surface pale green, usually more densely hairy than upper surface. **Flowers** bisexual, 5-merous; in clusters of 1–3; floral bracts 1–2 mm long, shorter than the pedicels; pedicels glabrous or occasionally hairy or glandular, not jointed at summit, 1–5 mm long; calyx tube 2–4 mm long; sepals greenish or yellowish, 2.5–5 mm long; petals white, 2–3 mm long; about equaling the stamens; filaments 1.5–2.5 mm long; ovary glabrous; style 5.5–8 mm long, the upper one-third divided, hairy on lower half; **anthesis** early mid-May to mid-June; insect-pollinated. **Fruit** a berry; 6–11 mm in diameter; greenish purple; smooth; maturing late mid-July to mid-September; animal-dispersed. (*oxyacanthoides*: like *Crataegus oxyacantha*, a European hawthorn, in reference to the leaf shape or possibly the spines)

Identification

Northern gooseberry is a relatively small, prickly shrub, usually no more than about 4 ft (1.2 m) tall, with stems that ultimately arch toward the ground. It is very similar to swamp gooseberry (*R. hirtellum*), and a close examination of the flowers will be needed to distinguish between the two (see key). Fresh flowers are best, but the dried flowers that often persist on top of the fruit until the middle or end of summer are usually adequate. Hybrids between the two species have been reported (Sinnott 1985) and possess morphological characteristics intermediate between the two parents.

Note: A contemporary revision of the gooseberries (Sinnott 1985) has divided *R. oxyacanthoides* into five subspecies. All the subspecies are endemic to North America, but only subsp. *oxyacanthoides* occurs in Minnesota.

Natural History

Northern gooseberry is widespread in North America, but it appears to be somewhat spotty in Minnesota. It may be most common in the northeast, especially along the north shore of Lake Superior, but there appears to be a chance of finding it almost anywhere in the northern two-thirds of the state. Because it is often difficult to tell from the common swamp gooseberry, it is rarely identified in the field, which means that most of what we know about its distribution and abundance must be inferred from incidental herbarium specimens.

Northern gooseberry has been found most often on rocks, or in rocky, gravelly, or sandy soil, sometimes on lakeshores. It might also occur in forested or brushy swamps but probably not in deeply shaded forests. It is more likely to be localized in an opening or along an exposed edge where it receives at least partial sunlight.

Under favorable conditions the tips of the branches can arch to the ground and tip-root, or trail along the surface and root at the nodes. Rooted branches tend to sprout additional stems, creating a colony or even a small thicket of several seemingly independent shrubs.

Flower structure is key to learning the gooseberries.

Fruits are edible but don't count on finding many—August 26.

Stems grow upright or arch, reach lengths of nearly 5' (1.5 m).

Gooseberries and Currants 🐌 **423**

Ribes triste Pall.

Swamp red currant

Midsize **shrubs**, with 1 or a few ascending, spreading or trailing **stems** to 1 m tall, rooting at the tips and along the length; spines and bristles absent. 1st-year **branchlets** sparsely hairy, 2nd-year branchlets glabrous, the thin outer surface flaking off with age. **Leaves** simple, alternate, deciduous. **Leaf blades** 4–9 cm long, 5–10 cm wide; with 3–5 palmate lobes; base cordate to truncate; margins with rounded or pointed serrations; upper surface sparsely hairy to glabrate, glands absent; lower surface moderately to densely hairy, glands absent. **Flowers** bisexual, 5-merous; 6–15, in arching or drooping racemes; floral bracts 0.7–1.5 mm long, shorter than the pedicels; pedicels hairy and often bearing scattered stalked glands, jointed at summit, 2–5 mm long; calyx tube lacking or up to 0.5 mm long; sepals greenish or yellowish and flecked with purple, 1.2–2.2 mm long; petals rose purple, 0.3–1 mm long, about equaling the stamens; filaments 0.4–0.6 mm long; ovary glabrous; style 0.5–1 mm long, the upper one-third divided, glabrous; **anthesis** early May to early June; insect-pollinated. **Fruit** a bright red berry; 5–9 mm in diameter; smooth; maturing late June to early August; animal-dispersed. (*triste*: sad or dull-colored; the reference unclear)

Identification

Many of the currants have long, arching stems, but those of swamp red currant are generally short and upright, often only knee high. Also, most currants have black fruit, or in the case of skunk currant (*R. glandulosum*) the fruit is red but covered with gland-tipped hairs. Only swamp red currant has fruit that is both bright red and smooth. Also notice that the inflorescence of swamp red currant droops and that of skunk currant is nearly erect. Shade-grown leaves can be relatively large and may be suggestive of mountain maple (*Acer spicatum*) or thimbleberry (*Rubus parviflorus*).

Natural History

Swamp red currant is relatively common in conifer swamps, especially with tamarack (*Larix laricina*). It also occurs in hardwood swamps and occasionally in moist, upland forests. Soils tend to be moderately acidic and composed of peat, woody humus, or sometimes moist loam; in cool, moist situations it can even be found on rocks. It seems to be absent from strongly acidic habitats such as heath bogs and muskegs, and from floodplains that are subjected to sedimentation.

Filtered sunlight is perhaps favored, but swamp red currant can survive and reproduce in perpetual shade. Under ideal conditions it can become relatively abundant, although it never seems to be aggressive.

The stems of swamp red currant always begin erect, but arch or lean as they get longer and eventually lie horizontal on the ground. When the newly horizontal stems become overgrown by moss or covered by leaf litter, they take root along their length. It is from the nodes of these horizontal stems that will come the next generation of erect stems. Eventually the new erect stems become horizontal and begin the process over again. This is a process of vegetative reproduction called layering, which can result in extensive colonies several square yards (meters) in extent.

Racemes hang downward—June 6.

Like skunk currant but without gland-tipped hairs—June 6.

Ripe fruits are bright, translucent red—July 19.

This is as big as swamp red currant usually gets.

Gooseberries and Currants   🌿   **425**

Robinia, black locust

Fabaceae: Bean family

This genus includes 4 species of deciduous trees and shrubs native to parts of the United States and northern Mexico. None are native to Minnesota, but a single species has been introduced here and has become naturalized. (*Robinia* is named for French herbalist Jean Robin [1550–1629] and his son Vespasian Robin [1579–1662].)

Robinia pseudoacacia L.

Black locust

Nonnative, naturalized, large **trees**, to 27 m tall and 65 cm dbh; clonal by root suckering. **Branchlets** initially greenish and hairy, becoming brown and glabrous by the 2nd year; **spines** in pairs at nodes, to 2 cm long, broad-based, sharp. **Bark** thick; brown or gray; with long, interlacing ridges and deep, irregular furrows. **Leaves** pinnately compound, alternate, deciduous. **Petioles** 1–3.5 cm long, sparsely to moderately hairy. **Leaf blades** 8–20 cm long. **Leaflets** 11–19, opposite or subopposite, elliptical to oblong, 2–6 cm long, 1–3 cm wide; base tapered to rounded; apex blunt to rounded; margins entire; upper surface dark green, hairy or glabrate; lower surface pale green, with short, stiff, appressed hairs. **Inflorescence** a drooping raceme 5–13 cm long, with 8–30 flowers; borne from leaf axils on 1st-year branchlets. **Flowers** bisexual, 5-merous; pedicels 5–10 mm long, hairy; calyx 4–8 mm long, hairy, the triangular lobes shorter than the tube; petals 1.5–2.2 cm long, white; stamens 10; style 1; **anthesis** late mid-May to mid-July; insect-pollinated. **Fruit** a brown legume or pod; narrowly oblong to linear, flat; glabrous; 3–11 cm long, 1–1.5 cm wide; maturing early August to early September; pods opening and shedding seeds while still on the tree, the empty pods often persisting through winter. **Seeds** 2–10, about 5 mm long; animal- and gravity-dispersed. (*pseudoacacia*: false acacia)

Identification

Black locust is a tall, slender tree with a narrow crown, coarse bark, and sharp spines on the branches. The large compound leaves look something like those of honey locust (*Gleditsia triacanthos*) and Kentucky coffee tree (*Gymnocladus dioica*), and saplings could be mistaken for false indigo (*Amorpha fruticosa*) or prickly ash (*Zanthoxylum americanum*). Although they all share some characteristics, only black locust has the combination of leaflets with rounded tips and entire (not toothed) margins, and branches with sharp spines.

Natural History

Black locust is native only in the Ozark and Appalachian regions of the eastern United States, but it has been widely planted and naturalized beyond its original range (Isely and Peabody 1984). It was brought to Minnesota in about 1860, possibly earlier, and was originally promoted for use in erosion control, as a windbreak, and for fuel, lumber, and fence posts. Although it is seldom planted anymore, it has persisted and spread.

It spreads to new habitats by seed, usually becoming established in abandoned fields and roadsides. It also does well along forest borders and in forest interiors where there are gaps in the canopy. Once established it spreads aggressively by root suckers, and without intervention it can quickly form large stands. It seems to prefer loamy, nonacidic soil, either moist or dry, but with little encouragement it will grow in just about any soil that is not saturated for extended periods.

Because of its invasive nature, black locust has now become a serious ecological problem, especially in mesic hardwood forests in the lower Mississippi River valley. In places like Beaver Creek Valley State Park (Houston County) and Afton State Park (Washington County), groves of large, mature black locust occupy significant portions of the forest canopy that would otherwise be occupied by native species such as oaks (*Quercus* spp.), maples (*Acer* spp.), basswood (*Tilia americana*), and ashes (*Fraxinus* spp.).

Most control efforts consist of repeated cutting, girdling, or burning, but black locust resprouts vigorously (Anderson and Brown 1980). It is often necessary to resort to chemical treatment. Because of very real ecological concerns, black locust should not be planted in rural areas; even in urban areas there are many native species better suited.

Paired spines at base of leaf.

The thick, coarse bark of a 21" (53 cm) dbh black locust.

Each inflorescence has up to 30 pea-like flowers—June 22.

The fruit is a legume or pod 2–4" (3–11 cm) long—August 30.

Each leaf is pinnately compound, with 11–19 round-tipped leaflets.

Rosa, the roses

Rosaceae: Rose family

The roses comprise a large genus with an estimated 120 or more species throughout the Northern Hemisphere. There are 18 to 20 species native to the United States, and 4 native to Minnesota. (*Rosa* is the classical Latin name for rose.)

There are two additional species that may occur in Minnesota: Pasture rose (*R. carolina*) and swamp rose (*R. palustris*). Both are eastern species that appear to range no farther west than Wisconsin, yet it is possible that undiscovered native populations of one or both species may exist in our eastern counties.

There are a number of cultivated rose species that persist after cultivation and may have the potential to spread somewhat beyond where they were planted. With one possible exception, none are known to have become fully naturalized in Minnesota. The one to watch is multiflora rose (*R. multiflora*). It was introduced into southern Minnesota relatively recently, and there are some indications it may be spreading. The states to our east and south are having serious ecological problems with multiflora rose (Evans 1983; Farrar 2001); it is very invasive and difficult to control. Every effort should be made to ensure this species does not become established in Minnesota.

Key to the Genus Rosa in Minnesota

1. Stems and branches with a pair of strong broad-based prickles just below most or at least some nodes, these prickles are distinctly larger than other prickles that may (or may not) be scattered throughout; sepals often less than 2.5 mm wide at base (range: 2–3 mm) .... *R. woodsii*
1. Stems and branches lacking distinct pairs of larger prickles just below nodes, prickles either all ± alike and not restricted to nodes, or prickles absent; sepals 2.5 mm wide or wider (range: 2.5–5 mm).
   2. Stipules with a continuous row of numerous tiny glands along the entire margin; petioles and rachis of leaf blade also with stalked glands; the lower (outer) surface of sepals usually nonglandular; flowers usually solitary (occasionally in clusters of 2 or 3) .... *R. acicularis*
   2. Stipules lacking marginal glands or with a few glands scattered on the distal portion; petioles and rachis usually lacking glands; the lower (outer) surface of sepals usually with conspicuous stalked glands; flowers in clusters of 1–8.
      3. Bristles occurring throughout the plant, including growth of the current year; leaflets usually 9 (range: 7–11); flowers in clusters of 3–8; pedicels often hairy; stems mostly herbaceous, often dying back to the ground each winter and resprouting each spring, reaching about 50 cm tall, flowers borne at the tips of these herbaceous sprouts .... *R. arkansana*
      3. Bristles usually on lower portion of stem only, absent from growth of the current year; leaflets usually 7 (range: 5–9); flowers in clusters of 1–4; pedicels glabrous; stems long-lived and often reaching 2 m tall, flowers borne on lateral branches from the woody stem .... *R. blanda*

Rosa acicularis Lindl. subsp. *sayi* (Schw.) Lewis

Prickly wild rose

Midsize **shrubs**, with 1 or a few upright **stems** to 2.5 m tall and 1.75 cm diameter; stems and woody branches reddish brown; with stiff slender bristles throughout, including growth of the current year; forming loose rhizomatous colonies. **Leaves** pinnately compound, alternate, deciduous. **Petioles** 2–4 cm long, glandular and hairy. **Stipules** adnate, margins with a continuous row of tiny, stalked glands, otherwise entire. **Leaf blades** 5–10 cm long, 5–9 cm wide. **Leaflets** 5–7, elliptical to oblong; 2.7–4.7 cm long, 1.5–2.8 cm wide; base obtuse to rounded; apex acute to obtuse or rounded; margins single- or minutely double-serrate, gland-tipped, primary teeth 12–18 per side; upper surface dark green, glabrate; lower surface pale green, hairy, sometimes slightly glandular. **Flowers** bisexual, 5-merous; borne singly or occasionally in 2s or 3s at the ends of lateral branches of woody stems; pedicels 1–3.5 cm long, glabrous; sepals 1.7–2.2 cm long, 3–5 mm wide at base, the lower (outer) surface usually nonglandular; petals pink or red, 2–3 cm long and about as wide; stamens and styles numerous; **anthesis** early June to early July; insect-pollinated. **Fruit** a red, globose, berrylike structure (hip) 1–2 cm in diameter; maturing late July to mid-September; animal-dispersed. (*acicularis*: needlelike)

Identification

There are two common roses in the northeastern counties: prickly wild rose, which has bristles on the stems and branches, and smooth wild rose (*R. blanda*), which has bristles only on the lower portion of the stem. Less common is prairie wild rose (*R. arkansana*), which resembles bristly wild rose by being bristly throughout, but it is a much smaller plant that lacks glands on the petiole.
Note: Prickly wild rose is by far the widest ranging rose, and it is the only rose native to both North America and Eurasia. Because the North American population differs from the Eurasian in a number of minor morphological characters, it has been segregated as subsp. *sayi* (Lewis 1959).

Natural History

Prickly wild rose is fairly common in the northeastern counties, certainly more common than the other native roses, but it is rare or absent elsewhere. It occurs in a variety of upland habitats, usually with pines (*Pinus* spp.) or hardwoods such as trembling aspen (*Populus tremuloides*) and paper birch (*Betula papyrifera*). Because it does not tolerate deep shade, it is usually found in partial openings, under a canopy gap, or along an exposed forest margin. It is also common in brushy thickets and on lakeshores, beaches, rock outcrops, and cliffs. Soil conditions are normally acidic and range from moist to dry; textures range from sandy or rocky to clayey.

Prickly wild rose is not particularly aggressive in natural habitats, but it does invade roadsides, old log landings, utility rights-of-way, and other disturbed sites. Competition is typically reduced in these settings, allowing it to spread quickly by underground rhizomes. Once established in this way it can be very persistent. In fact, the rhizomes sometimes survive clear-cutting and other land-clearing attempts and resprout vigorously. It also resprouts after a "cool" fire, but the rhizomes are often killed by an intense fire. Perhaps because of the prickly stems, it is not heavily browsed by deer or other herbivores.

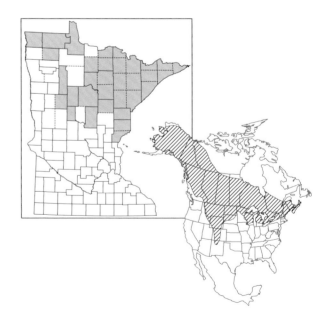

The fruit (hip) begins turning red in late July.

Flowers are up to 2 .75 " (7 cm) across—July 2.

Each leaf has 5–7 leaflets.

The whole stem is bristly, even the new growth.

Rosa arkansana Porter

Prairie wild rose
[*R. suffulta* Greene]

Low **shrubs**, with 1 or a few upright **stems** to 50 cm tall (occasionally to 1 m) and 5 mm diameter; stems greenish the 1st year, becoming reddish brown to dark purple the 2nd year; with stiff slender bristles throughout, including growth of the current year; forming loose rhizomatous colonies. **Leaves** pinnately compound, alternate, deciduous. **Petioles** 1.5–3 cm long, hairy, not glandular. **Stipules** adnate, margins with a few scattered glands on the distal portion, or occasionally glandular-serrate. **Leaf blades** 6.5–9.5 cm long, 4–5.5 cm wide. **Leaflets** 7–11 (usually 9), obovate or occasionally elliptical; 2–3.5 cm long, 1.2–2 cm wide; base acute to obtuse or rounded; apex rounded or occasionally obtuse; margins single-serrate with 7–15 teeth per side; upper surface dark green, glabrous to hairy; lower surface pale green, hairy. **Flowers** bisexual, 5-merous; 3–8 borne at the ends of herbaceous 1st-year stems, or on lateral branches of woody stems; pedicels 1–2 cm long, often hairy; sepals 1.4–2.2 cm long, 2.5–3.5 mm wide at base, the lower (outer) surface usually glandular; petals pink, 1.5–2.5 cm long and about as wide; stamens and styles numerous; **anthesis** early June to early August; insect-pollinated. **Fruit** a red, globose, berrylike structure (hip) 1–1.5 cm in diameter; maturing late July to mid-September; animal-dispersed. (*arkansana*: of Arkansas, the species described from the valley of the Arkansas River in Colorado)

Identification

Prairie wild rose is most likely to be mistaken for prickly wild rose (*R. acicularis*) or wild rose (*R. woodsii*). But prairie wild rose usually (not always) occurs on open prairies, and it is smaller than the other roses, often no more than about knee high. It also tends to produce flowers at the tips of herbaceous shoots that rise directly from the roots, rather than from branches of a woody stem.
Note: A few specimens from southeastern Minnesota have glandular pedicels; this is a character not typical of prairie wild rose. They are suspected to be part of a fertile hybrid population between prairie wild rose and pasture rose (*R. carolina*), which is an eastern species that does not quite reach Minnesota.

Natural History

Prairie wild rose is found commonly in native prairies throughout the prairie region of Minnesota and occasionally in open, prairielike habitats within forested regions. Although it is a versatile plant, it seems to prefer dry, sandy or gravelly soil, usually in direct sunlight and in the company of grasses and herbaceous plants. When overgrown by brush or trees, it tends to lose vigor. It is unusually tolerant of high temperatures and desiccation and will often remain green and produce flowers even under drought conditions. And true to its prairie origins, it will resprout vigorously after a fire and invariably produce flowers the same year. But even without fire the stems often die back in the fall, and new stems sprout from rhizomes the following year. Occasionally stems will live two or three years and become woody.

Prairie wild rose becomes established by seeds, which are spread primarily in the droppings of birds. It does this quite successfully in native habitats but not very well in roadsides, abandoned fields, or other nonnative habitats. Once a colony is established, it expands by the growth of underground rhizomes. These rhizomes are tough and generally very persistent even though the aboveground shoots are short-lived and seem somewhat transient.

Prairie wild rose is often no more than knee high—July 3.

Each leaf has 7–9 (usually 9) leaflets.

The berrylike fruit of a rose is commonly called a "hip"—September 9.

Rosa blanda Ait.

Smooth wild rose

Mid to tall **shrubs**, with 1 or a few upright **stems**, to 2.2 m tall and 2 cm diameter; stems and woody branches initially reddish brown to dark purple-brown, smooth, becoming gray and rough with age; with stiff, slender bristles on lower portions of the stem, the upper portion, especially the growth of the current year, usually without bristles; forming loose rhizomatous colonies. **Leaves** pinnately compound, alternate, deciduous. **Petioles** 1.5–3 cm long, hairy, nonglandular or sometimes with a few scattered glands. **Stipules** adnate, margins with a few scattered glands on the distal portion or glands absent. **Leaf blades** 6–9 cm long, 5–7 cm wide. **Leaflets** 5–9 (usually 7), elliptical to obovate; 2.5–4 cm long, 1.5–2.2 cm wide; base acute to obtuse or rounded; apex obtuse to rounded; margins single-serrate with 10–17 teeth per side; upper surface dark green, sparsely hairy; lower surface pale green, sparsely hairy to hairy. **Flowers** bisexual, 5-merous; 1–4 borne at the ends of lateral branches of woody stems; pedicels 1–2 cm long, glabrous; sepals 1.5–2.5 cm long, 2.5–4 mm wide at base, the lower (outer) surface or margins usually glandular; petals pink or reddish, 2–3 cm long and about as wide; stamens and styles numerous; **anthesis** early June to late June; insect-pollinated. **Fruit** a red, globose, berrylike structure (hip) 1–2 cm in diameter; maturing early August to mid-September; animal-dispersed. (*blanda*: mild or bland, in reference to the lack of bristles on the upper portion of the stem)

Identification

Smooth wild rose generally lacks bristles on the new twigs, although the lowest portion of the stem is almost always bristly. The other native roses are similar except they have bristles throughout, even on the new growth. Be aware that smooth wild rose hybridizes freely with wild rose (*R. woodsii*), creating fertile crosses (named *R. ×dulcissima* Lunnell) that possess characters intermediate between the parents; these can be very difficult to identify.

Natural History

Smooth wild rose is by far the most common native rose in Minnesota. It is ubiquitous throughout the state in a variety of upland habitat types, including prairies, open woodlands, forest margins, and brushy thickets. It will also invade roadsides, fencerows, rock piles, and old fields. It can tolerate direct sunlight and moderate amounts of shade, but it does poorly in deep shade. Soil requirements seem minimal; sandy soil may be preferred, although it grows well in loamy or clayey soil too, even in crevices in rock outcrops. Conditions range from dry to moist, and from basic (calcareous) to weakly acidic.

The stems are rather weak and have difficulty staying upright if they get too long. But when the stems are supported by surrounding vegetation, they can easily reach 6.5 feet (2 m) in height. They typically appear singly or in tight clumps of 2 to 4. Each stem, or clump of stems, arises from a distinct root crown, yet all the root crowns in an area may be interconnected by a common rhizome system. These rhizome systems can become quite extensive although not particularly invasive. Even where competition is minimal, the stems are rarely numerous enough to form a discernable colony and never a dense thicket.

The individual stems sometimes live 10 years but probably not much longer. However, rhizome systems can be very tenacious and live significantly longer than the individual stems. They usually survive fire, cutting, and a surprising amount of aboveground disturbances, ultimately sending up several generations of stems.

Flowers are often produced in abundance—May 19.

Fruits remain on the branch all winter or until eaten— September 11.

Each of the 5–9 leaflets has a serrate margin and rounded tip.

In spite of the common name, only new growth is smooth.

Rosa woodsii Lindl.

Wild rose

[*R. fendleri* Crép.; *R. macounii* Greene]

Mid to tall **shrubs**, with 1 or a few upright **stems** to 2.5 m tall and 2 cm diameter; upper portion of stems and woody branches reddish brown to dark purple, smooth, becoming gray and rough with age; usually with a pair of strong, broad-based prickles just below the nodes (infrastipular), and often with smaller more slender prickles scattered throughout; rhizomatous. **Leaves** pinnately compound, alternate, deciduous. **Petioles** 1.5–3.5 cm long, hairy, often with a few scattered glands. **Stipules** adnate, margins usually glandular-serrate at least on distal portion. **Leaf blades** 4.5–7.5 cm long, 4–5.5 cm wide. **Leaflets** 7–9 (usually 7), obovate to elliptical; 2.2–3.5 cm long, 1.3–1.8 cm wide; base acute to obtuse; apex rounded; margins single-serrate with 12–20 teeth per side; upper surface dark green, sparsely hairy; lower surface pale green, hairy. **Flowers** bisexual, 5-merous; 2–4 borne at the ends of lateral branches of woody stems; pedicels 1–2 cm long, glabrous or sparsely hairy; sepals 1–2 cm long, 2–3 mm wide at base, the lower (outer) surface usually glandular; petals pink to reddish, 1.5–2.5 cm long and nearly as wide; stamens and styles numerous; **anthesis** early June to early July; insect-pollinated. **Fruit** a reddish, ± globose, berrylike structure (hip) 0.8–1.8 cm in diameter; maturing early mid-August to mid-September; animal-dispersed. (*woodsii*: named for English botanist Joseph Woods, 1776–1864)

Identification

In Minnesota, wild rose is the only species with infrastipular prickles. These may be inconspicuous among the other prickles (if other prickles are present), but look for a pair of somewhat larger and stiffer prickles just below the nodes. Swamp rose (*R. palustris*) and pasture rose (*R. caroliniana*) also have infrastipular prickles, but they are eastern species that are thought to range no farther west than Wisconsin. *Note:* The complex evolutionary relationship between *R. woodsii* and *R. blanda* has been a matter of much confusion. In an effort to explain this complexity, Lewis (1962), in a classic study, concluded that the western *R. woodsii* and the eastern *R. blanda* meet in Minnesota and the Dakotas, where they hybridize freely. After examining Minnesota specimens, Lewis concluded that no "pure" *R. woodsii* occurs in Minnesota. Yet some specimens (those fitting the description presented here) were in the opinion of Lewis close enough to pure *R. woodsii* to be called by that name. Those specimens closer to *R. blanda* were to be called *R. blanda*, and the remaining specimens were called by their hybrid name, *R.* ×*dulcissima*.

A recent reappraisal (Joly and Bruneau 2007) came to a different conclusion: Based on morphological and molecular data, *R. woodsii* and *R. blanda* are indistinguishable and should be considered a single species, called *R. blanda*. This alternative treatment, whatever its value, came too late for full consideration in this book, but it will likely be welcomed by Minnesota botanists who have tired of struggling with the identification of these plants.

Natural History

Wild rose is not particularly rare in Minnesota, but it is somewhat cryptic, making its true status difficult to determine. It appears to be more common in the western counties, although it may have the potential to be found throughout most of the state. Habitats are usually found along forest margins and openings, usually with pines (*Pinus* spp.), oaks (*Quercus* spp.), or trembling aspen (*Populus tremuloides*), but it is also found in brushy or grassy habitats. Soil pH tends to be basic (calcareous) or moderately acidic, and textures range from sandy to loamy or clayey. Moisture conditions vary from dry to moist.

Flower color ranges from pale pink to deep red—July 6.

A pair of prickles just below each node indicates wild rose.

Each leaf is pinnately compound with 7–9 (usually 9) leaflets.

Each fruit (hip) contains numerous tiny seeds—September 11.

Rubus, blackberries and raspberries

Rosaceae: Rose family

Rubus is a very large and complex genus of woody and semiwoody shrubs. Species number perhaps 750 worldwide. There are about 200 to 250 species in the United States, mostly in the eastern half, with 33 native species and 2 named hybrids currently known in Minnesota. (*Rubus* is from the Latin *ruber,* for red, in reference to the fruit.)

    Rubus is by far the largest genus of woody plants in Minnesota. Although a few Minnesota species have been domesticated and are cultivated for their fruit, all those species found growing wild in Minnesota are evidently native. Furthermore, they all seem to be restricted to their original geographic ranges and, to varying degrees, to remnants of their original habitats. Some species of *Rubus,* notably the highbush blackberries and raspberries, do colonize habitats that have been altered by human activities if the alterations were not too great.

    The genus *Rubus* as it occurs in Minnesota can be broken down into 5 easily recognized subgenera:

- *Cyclactis* (2 species and 1 hybrid: the dwarf raspberries)
- *Chamaemorus* (1 species: cloudberry, *Rubus chamaemorus*)
- *Anaplobatus* (1 species: thimbleberry, *Rubus parviflorus*)
- *Idaeobatus* (2 species and 1 hybrid: the raspberries)
- *Rubus* (27 species: the highbush blackberries, dewberries, and bristle-berries)

    By far, the largest subgenus is *Rubus,* known collectively as the blackberries. The blackberries that occur in Minnesota can be divided further into three broad groups that roughly correspond to taxonomic sections. These groups can be identified by growth form and other gross morphological features easily seen in the field. In fact, it is highly recommended that any attempt to identify an unknown specimen begin with critical observations of the mature plant growing in its native habitat. These groups are as follows:

1. The highbush blackberries (9 species, including sections *Alleghenienses, Canadenses*, and *Arguti*). The canes (stems) of these plants are thick and heavy, often 6+ ft (2 m) in length. They generally grow upright but tend to lean or arch as they grow longer. Prickles, when present, have a broad base and a sharp tip (shaped like a cat's claw but not so curved) that can easily tear skin. Their characteristic habitat is dry, sandy soil in woodlands and woodland margins. Populations of most highbush blackberries are quick to exploit habitat opportunities and tend to be mobile as local populations but stable as metapopulations. They typically flower in June, with the fruit ripening in August.
2. The dewberries (6 species, section *Flagellares*). The canes of dewberries can be very long, in some cases nearly 10 ft (3 m), but they are slender and relatively weak; they cannot support their entire length. Instead of growing upright, they trail along the ground for at least a portion of their length and root at the tips. Tip-rooting is what defines the dewberries. Prickles tend to be sharp and hard but smaller than those of the highbush blackberries and sometimes lacking the broad base (then they are shaped more like a needle than a cat's claw). Dewberries tend to occur in dry, sandy soil, usually in partially wooded or savannalike settings. They also typically flower in June, with fruit ripening in August.
3. The bristle-berries (12 species, sections *Setosi* and *Hispidi*). The canes of the bristle-berries are relatively short, usually about 3 ft (1 m) in length, and they are often rather weak. They generally stand more or less upright, although they may arch over and sometimes lie passively on supporting vegetation. They do not normally trail along the ground like the dewberries, and they do not ordinarily tip-root. (*R. fulleri*, the lone Minnesota member of section *Hispidi*, sometimes called the groundberries, is the exception; were it not for its habit of tip-rooting, it would be placed in section *Setosi*.) Some bristle-berries have hard, strong prickles like the dewberries, but most have only stiff bristles. The bristles are sharp but usually not strong enough to penetrate skin. Bristle-berries typically occur in open habitats, often in shallow wetlands, and in sandy or peaty soil. Most flower in July, with fruits ripening in August or September.

When attempting to identify blackberries, it is essential to remember that the canes (stems) are biennial; they live for only two years. During the first year, the cane will produce only leaves and is called a primocane. The 2nd year, the same cane will produce flowers and is then called a floricane. Since most blackberry plants produce canes every year, there will be both floricanes and primocanes present on the same plant at the same time. It is very important to have a sample of both a primocane and a floricane from the same plant when attempting to use the key; a fragment will not do.

Note: For purposes of citation, Mark P. Widrlechner is first author of the *Rubus* treatment, and Welby R. Smith second author. Widrlechner is responsible for the taxonomic and nomenclatural content of the treatment, and Smith is responsible for the natural history sections. The descriptions and keys were prepared jointly and derived largely from a set of approximately 300 herbarium specimens collected in Minnesota by Smith between 1993 and 2004 (on deposit in MIN, ISC, MO, and WIS), and secondarily by specimens from Iowa and Wisconsin. The North American range maps were prepared by Smith under the direction of Widrlechner.

1. Flowering stems herbaceous, usually < 50 cm tall; stems lacking bristles or prickles; flowers 1–4 per inflorescence.
    2. Leaves simple, with shallow rounded lobes; fruits yellowish when ripe (subg. *Chamaemorus*, cloudberry) .... *R. chamaemorus*
    2. Leaves compound with three distinct leaflets; fruits red (subg. *Cyclactis*, the dwarf raspberries).
        3. Plants producing long sterile runners, often 1 m or more in length by midsummer; flowering stem usually > 15 cm tall; flowers 2–4; petals white or rarely pale pink, 4–8 mm long; apex of leaflets acute .... *R. pubescens*
        3. Plants not producing runners; flowering stem usually < 15 cm tall; flowers single; petals pink to rose-colored, > 10 mm long; apex of leaflets obtuse .... *R. arcticus* subsp. *acaulis*
1. Flowering stems woody (canes), usually > 50 cm tall (or long, if prostrate); stems often with bristles or prickles, sometimes without; flowers usually more than 4.
    4. Primocane leaves simple, each leaf with 3 or 5 lobes; canes lacking bristles or prickles; flowers 3–5 cm across (spread flat) (subg. *Anaplobatus*, thimbleberry) .... *R. parviflorus*
    4. Primocane leaves compound, each leaf with 3 or 5 separate leaflets, individual leaflets not lobed, or occasionally with 2 or 3 lobes; canes often with bristles or prickles, sometimes without; flowers usually smaller.
        5. Primocane leaves with 3 or 5 leaflets, either palmately or pinnately compound; lower surface of leaflets whitish or silvery colored; petals generally < 7 mm long; ripe fruits separating from the core (receptacle of the flower) (subg. *Idaeobatus*, the raspberries).
            6. Petioles and inflorescence usually with gland-tipped hairs; canes erect to high-arching, not tip-rooting; primocane leaves usually pinnately compound with 5 leaflets, sometimes 3; fruit red when ripe; canes with stiff slender bristles, lacking broad-based prickles
            .... *R. idaeus* var. *strigosus*
            6. Petioles and inflorescence lacking gland-tipped hairs; canes ultimately arching to the ground, where the tips take root; primocane leaves usually with 3 leaflets, if 5 leaflets, then palmately compound; fruit purple-black when ripe; canes lacking slender bristles, but broad-based prickles present .... *R. occidentalis*
        5. Primocane leaves with 3 or 5 leaflets, always palmately compound; lower surface of leaflets green or pale green; petals generally > 7 mm long; ripe fruits not separating from the core (subg. *Rubus*, the blackberries).
            7. Canes (at least the terminal third of the mature floricane) prostrate or trailing along the ground and rooting at the tips.
                8. Canes with stiff bristles rather than hard prickles, those numbering 8–20+ per cm of cane; gland-tipped hairs interspersed with bristles on the cane and also present in inflorescence (§ *Hispidi*, a bristle-berry) .... *R. fulleri*
                8. Canes with hard prickles only, either broad-based or aciculate, numbering 0–5 per cm of cane; gland-tipped hairs usually absent (present only in the rare *R. ithacanus*) (§ *Flagellares*, the dewberries).
                    9. Lower surface of fully expanded primocane leaves velvety to the touch (moderately to densely hairy).
                        10. Pedicels with both gland-tipped hairs and non–gland-tipped hairs; primocanes often with at least a few gland-tipped hairs .... *R. ithacanus*
                        10. Pedicels with only non–gland-tipped hairs, and those sometimes sparse; canes glabrous.

11. Primocane leaflets usually 5, central leaflet 8–15 cm long, 6–11 cm wide, the base often cordate or at least subcordate; floricanes robust, forming a large mounding tangle, diameter frequently > 4 mm .... **R. satis**
11. Primocane leaflets usually 3, central leaflet 7–9 cm long, 4–6 cm wide, the base rounded or blunt; floricanes whiplike, prostrate or trailing, diameter 2.5–4 mm .... **R. ferrofluvius**
9. Lower surface of fully expanded primocane leaves smooth to the touch (sparsely hairy or nearly glabrous).
    12. Primocane leaves with 3 leaflets.
        13. Inflorescence ascendate; central leaflet on primocane leaves 5–8 cm long, 3–5.5 cm wide .... **R. steelei**
        13. Inflorescence a condensed corymb or cymule; central leaflet on primocane leaves 7–9 cm long, 4–6 cm wide .... **R. ferrofluvius**
    12. Primocane leaves usually with 5 leaflets (early-season leaves may have 3 leaflets).
        14. Inflorescence ascendate; pedicels often > 4 cm long; apex of primocane central leaflet abruptly short-acuminate; primocane leaves flat, lateral veins not prominent .... **R. multifer**
        14. Inflorescence a condensed corymb or raceme; pedicels < 4 cm long; apex of central leaflet gradually acuminate; primocane leaves plicate along the prominent lateral veins .... **R. plicatifolius**
7. Canes erect, arching or sometimes reclining on other vegetation, but not trailing along the ground and not usually tip-rooting.
    15. Canes with aciculate (needle-shaped) prickles only, lacking broad-based (shaped like a cat's claw although not always curved) prickles, or sometimes broad-based prickles present on *R. wisconsinensis*; prickles varying in strength, but most not strong enough to tear skin, usually > 3.5 prickles per cm of cane; canes usually ≤ 1.3 m long (§ *Setosi*, the bristle-berries).
        16. Primocanes, and often petioles, with gland-tipped hairs, obvious at 10×; prickles 10–45+ per cm of cane.
            17. Inflorescence a condensed raceme (rarely a corymb); primocane leaves with 5 leaflets, base of central leaflet rounded .... **R. regionalis**
            17. Inflorescence a raceme, corymb or sometimes a compound corymb; primocane leaves with 5 or 3 leaflets, base of central leaflet rounded or tapered.
                18. Bristles 10–19 per cm of cane, too weak to penetrate skin; primocane leaves with 3 or 5 leaflets; inflorescence a compound corymb, lacking prickles; tips of primocane leaflets abruptly acuminate .... **R. dissensus**
                18. Bristles 20–75+ per cm of cane, strong enough to penetrate skin; primocane leaves with 5 leaflets; inflorescence usually a raceme or simple corymb, occasionally a compound raceme, with obvious prickles; tips of primocane leaflets gradually acuminate .... **R. groutianus**
        16. Canes and petioles lacking gland-tipped hairs; prickles often < 10 per cm of cane (sometimes more in *R. uniformis*).
            19. Lower surface of leaves velvety to the touch (moderately to densely hairy).
                20. Pedicels with gland-tipped hairs; central leaflet of primocane leaves elliptical with a rounded base; inflorescence a raceme; prickles weak .... **R. semisetosus**

20. Pedicels lacking gland-tipped hairs; central leaflet of primocane leaves often obovate with a tapered base; inflorescence a raceme or corymb (often a compound corymb); prickles strong .... *R. missouricus*

19. Lower surface of leaves smooth to the touch (sparsely hairy to nearly glabrous).

21. Stipules on primocane leaves large and prominent, 2–3.5 cm long, and often notched on the margin; pedicels with gland-tipped hairs .... *R. stipulatus*

21. Stipules < 2 cm long, not notched; pedicels with or without gland-tipped hairs.

22. Inflorescence a corymb or cyme; pedicels lacking gland-tipped hairs or occasionally a few at the distal end.

23. Primocane leaves predominately with 3 leaflets; prickles 8–30 per cm of cane; pedicels < 1.5 cm long .... *R. uniformis*

23. Primocane leaves predominately with 5 leaflets (early leaves may have 3); prickles often < 8 per cm of cane; pedicels often > 1.5 cm long.

24. Prickles 2.5–5 per cm of cane, too weak to tear skin; central leaflet of primocane leaves typically elliptical or obovate, the tip abruptly short-acuminate, creating a "shouldered" effect .... *R. wheeleri*

24. Prickles 4–9 per cm of cane, strong enough to tear skin; central leaflet of primocane leaves ovate or elliptical, the tip gradually acuminate, the body of leaflet therefore rounded rather than "shouldered" .... *R. wisconsinensis*

22. Inflorescence typically a raceme; pedicels with gland-tipped hairs or without.

25. Pedicels with gland-tipped hairs; primocane central leaflets elliptical or ovate (widest at or below the middle) and proportionately broad (l/w < 1.8); sepals 8–10 mm long; prickles strong, 3–6 per cm of cane .... *R. superioris*

25. Pedicels only occasionally with gland-tipped hairs; primocane central leaflets tending to be elliptical or obovate (widest at or above the middle) and proportionately narrow (l/w > 1.8); sepals 5–6 mm long; prickles weak, 5–20 per cm of cane .... *R. vermontanus*

15. Canes with broad-based prickles, or rarely canes smooth; prickles strong enough to tear skin, < 3.5 per cm of cane; canes often > 1.3 m long.

26. Pedicels with coarse gland-tipped hairs and slender non–gland-tipped hairs, gland-tipped hairs also sometimes present on petioles and growing portions of primocanes; lower surface of primocane leaves velvety to the touch (§ *Alleghenienses*, the highbush blackberries).

27. Inflorescence a relatively narrow raceme 8–22 cm long and 3–7 cm wide, at least twice as long as wide; sepals ≤ 8 mm long .... *R. allegheniensis*

27. Inflorescence a relatively broad raceme 6–18 cm long, 6–10 cm wide, less than twice as long as wide; sepals > 7 mm long.

      28. Central leaflet of primocane leaves widest below the middle (broadly ovate), usually at least 3/4 as wide as long (w/l ≥ 0.75) .... *R. rosa*

      28. Central leaflet of primocane leaves usually widest at the middle (elliptical), about 2/3 as wide as long (w/l = 0.66) .... ***R. alumnus***

26. Pedicels lacking gland-tipped hairs although non–gland-tipped hairs may be present, even abundant, gland-tipped hairs also lacking on petioles and canes; lower surface of primocane leaves velvety or smooth.

    29. Lower surface of primocane leaflets essentially glabrous, or at most with sparse hairs on mid and lateral veins, and smooth to the touch; prickles few or none (§ *Canadenses*, the highbush blackberries).

      30. Inflorescence typically a leafy corymb with 2–8 flowers; canes with 1–3 prickles per 2 cm of cane, prickles also often on petioles and pedicels .... ***R. acridens***

      30. Inflorescence a raceme with 4–16 flowers; canes with 0–2 prickles per 2 cm of cane, petioles sometimes with prickles (*R. quaesitus*) but pedicels lacking prickles.

        31. Canes lacking prickles entirely, or with up to 1 prickle per 2 cm of cane, prickles absent from petioles .... ***R. canadensis***

        31. Canes with up to 2 prickles per 2 cm of cane, prickles also present on petioles .... ***R. quaesitus***

    29. Lower surface of primocane leaflets densely hairy, velvety to the touch; prickles abundant or few (§ *Arguti*, the highbush blackberries)

      32. Central leaflet of primocane leaves ± elliptical (widest at the middle, excluding the narrow tip), about twice as long as wide, including the narrow tip (l/w = 1.8–2.1); inflorescence an elongate raceme 6–15 cm long with 8–20 flowers; prickles on the canes up to 7 mm long .... ***R. ablatus***

      32. Central leaflet of primocane leaves ovate (widest below the middle), about 1 1/2 times as long as wide (l/w = 1.4–1.6); inflorescence a short raceme or corymb 3–7 cm long with 2–10 flowers; prickles on canes up to 5 mm long.

        33. Inflorescence an irregular cluster or a condensed leafy corymb; margins of primocane leaves irregularly serrate or jagged-incised .... ***R. recurvans***

        33. Inflorescence usually a short, leafy raceme; margins of primocane leaves regularly serrate .... ***R. frondosus***

Rubus ablatus Bailey

A species of highbush blackberry

Midsize **shrubs**, with biennial **canes** to 2 m long, semierect or ascending the 1st year, arching the 2nd; clonal by root suckering, not known to tip-root. Canes glabrous; **prickles** broad-based, moderately abundant, 0.3–1.5 per cm of cane, mostly straight, 4–7 mm long. Primocane **leaves** palmately compound with 5 leaflets; central **leaflet** elliptical or occasionally elliptical-ovate or elliptical-oblong, 7–13 cm long, 4.5–8.5 cm wide, base rounded or shallowly cordate, apex long-acuminate or caudate, margins sharply serrate, upper surface thinly hairy, lower surface velvety-hairy. **Petioles** glabrous or with sparse nonglandular hairs, armed with small declined or decurved prickles to 3 mm long; stipules linear to linear-lanceolate or filiform, 10–15 mm long. **Inflorescence** a moderately broad, elongate raceme 6–15 cm long, 4–7 cm wide, with 8–20 flowers; pedicels and peduncle with dense nonglandular hairs and occasionally a few aciculate prickles. **Flowers** bisexual, 5-merous, 2.2–4(5) cm across; sepals 6–9 mm long, triangular to triangular-oblong, apex acuminate or apiculate; petals white, elliptical to ovate; **anthesis** early to late June; insect-pollinated. **Fruit** an aggregate of black drupelets; short-cylindrical or ± globose; 8–15 mm across; maturing late July to late August; animal-dispersed. (*ablatus*: distinguished by its broad petals)

Identification

The canes generally range from 3–6 ft (1–2 m) in length and are well armed with broad-based prickles. They tend to stand semierect unless weighed down by ripe fruit, which develop in elongate racemes. The central leaflet of each primocane leaf is relatively narrow and elliptical in shape, and it has a long drawn-out tip. It is also velvety to the touch. In many ways, *R. ablatus* resembles a nonglandular version of *R. alleghemiensis*, and in fact the two will often occur side by side. A specimen that outwardly resembles *R. ablatus* that was collected in Pine County is suspected to actually be a hybrid between *R. alleghemiensis* and *R. canadensis*.

Note: Davis, Fuller, and Davis (1969b) treated *R. ablatus* as a synonym of *R. laudatus* A. Berger. However, Widrlechner (1998) maintained the distinction between the two species because the primocane leaflets of *R. ablatus* are acuminate to long-acuminate rather than acute to short-acuminate

as is typical for *R. laudatus*, and there is some degree of geographic separation, with *R. laudatus* being more southern.

Natural History

Rubus ablatus is found at scattered locations in eastern Minnesota, most commonly in the east-central counties. Typical soil type is well-drained sand or sandy loam, which tends to be acidic and relatively nutrient poor. Occasionally it is found on loamy glacial tills, which tend to be more calcareous and fertile. Habitats are usually associated with woodlands or savannas, most often with oaks (*Quercus ellipsoidalis* or *Q. macrocarpa*), trembling aspen (*Populus tremuloides*), or depending on the location, jack pine (*Pinus banksiana*), eastern white pine (*P. strobus*), or paper birch (*Betula papyrifera*).

R. *ablatus* thrives best in partial shade, typically along a forested border or in a grassy opening. It also does well in a woodland interior if it gets direct sunlight for at least a portion of the day. It typically occurs with other highbush blackberries, such as *R. alleghemiensis* or *R. recurvans*, but it is usually the least abundant. Like all the highbush blackberries it spreads by rhizomes and will sometimes form large and relatively dense colonies (clones).

Inflorescence is a nonglandular raceme—June 5.

Canes can reach 6' (2 m) in length—June 9.

Primocane leaves have 5 leaflets, and the central one is elliptical.

Fruits are about 1/2" (8–15 mm) long—August 18.

Rubus acridens Bailey

A species of highbush blackberry

Midsize **shrubs**, with biennial **canes** to 2 m long, ascending or arching the 1st year, arching to low arching the 2nd; clonal by root suckering, not known to tip-root. Canes glabrous; **prickles** aciculate, weak, scattered, 0.5–1.5 per cm of cane, straight or declined, 2–3 mm long. Primocane **leaves** palmately compound with 5 leaflets; central **leaflet** elliptical to ovate, 10–13 cm long, 6–9 cm wide, base subcordate to cordate, apex acuminate, margins sharply serrate or sometimes double-serrate, upper surface glabrous except for scattered hairs near margin, lower surface with scattered hairs on mid and lateral veins, often with rusty brown midveins. **Petioles** glabrous, often with a few small, weak, prickles; stipules linear, 11–15 mm long. **Inflorescence** a leafy corymb or rarely a raceme, with 2–8 flowers; pedicels and peduncles with sparse nonglandular hairs and aciculate prickles. **Flowers** bisexual, 5-merous, 2.5–4 cm across; sepals 10–12 mm long, narrowly ovate to oblong, apex caudate; petals white, ovate or elliptical; **anthesis** mid-June to early July; insect-pollinated. **Fruit** an aggregate of black drupelets, ± globular, 8–15 mm across; maturing mid-August to early September; animal-dispersed. (*acridens*: sharply dentate, in reference to the leaf margins)

Identification

R. acridens has ascending or arching canes that reach a length of about 6 ft (2 m). It is similar to *R. canadensis* but with 2–8 flowers in a condensed corymb rather than 4–16 in a raceme. And while *R. canadensis* is notable for having leaves with essentially no hairs, and canes with no prickles, *R. acridens* tends to have slightly hairy leaves and canes with at least a few prickles.
Note: Davis, Fuller, and Davis (1969a) included *R. acridens* in *R. kennedyanus* Fern., concluding that the differences separating the two were minor.

Natural History

R. acridens is currently to known to occur only in Minnesota. It was first discovered in Itasca State Park (Clearwater County) in 1944 and eventually found in a handful of other locations in northern Minnesota. Nothing that closely matches this species has been found in any other state, making it one of a very few plant species endemic to Minnesota. Furthermore, it appears to be relatively uncommon, possibly rare.

Its entire range is depicted on the Minnesota map provided here, which reveals it to be distinctly northern in distribution, occurring entirely within the Laurentian Mixed Forest Province. It appears to be the only Minnesota blackberry that is absent from the sand plains of east-central Minnesota. Additional field work might reveal a different pattern, but for now it remains an anomaly.

Relatively little is known about this species, although its habitat preferences and natural history appear to follow the pattern seen in related species of highbush blackberries. That means it tends to be associated with upland hardwood forests of the type typically dominated by trembling aspen (*Populus tremuloides*) or paper birch (*Betula papyrifera*), or it may occur with one or more of the native pines (*Pinus* spp.). Habitats are usually in partial shade and well-drained sandy or sandy loam soil, and on level terrain rather than steep slopes or ravines.

A typical inflorescence has only 2–8 flowers—June 28.

Prickles are needle-shaped and rather sparse.

Central leaflet has a heart-shaped base and a drawn-out tip.

Fruits, still red on August 19, will turn black by September.

Blackberries and Raspberries **449**

Rubus allegheniensis Porter

A species of highbush blackberry

Midsize or tall **shrubs**, with biennial **canes** to 3.7 m long, semierect or arching the 1st year, arching the 2nd; clonal by root suckering, not known to tip-root. Canes occasionally with gland-tipped hairs scattered on distal portion of primocane but typically lacking nonglandular hairs; **prickles** broad-based, moderately abundant to abundant, 0.1–3 per cm of cane, straight or somewhat decurved, 4–6 (8) mm long. Primocane **leaves** palmately compound with 5 or rarely 3 leaflets; central **leaflet** elliptical to elliptical-ovate or ovate; 8.5–13.5 cm long, 4–9 cm wide, base subcordate to cordate, apex acuminate to long-acuminate or caudate, margins serrate, upper surface thinly hairy, lower surface velvety-hairy. **Petioles** with sparse to dense nonglandular hairs and sometimes gland-tipped hairs, armed with broad-based decurved prickles to 3 mm long; stipules linear to linear lanceolate, 6–12 (16) mm long. **Inflorescence** an elongate, cylindrical raceme 8–22 cm long, 3–7 cm wide, with 7–25 flowers; pedicels and peduncle with short, dense, nonglandular hairs, longer gland-tipped hairs, and sometimes aciculate or broad-based prickles. **Flowers** bisexual, 5-merous, 2.5–4.8 cm across; sepals 5–8 mm long, triangular-elliptical, apex acuminate to caudate, often glandular; petals white, elliptical to ovate; **anthesis** late May to early July; insect-pollinated. **Fruit** an aggregate of black drupelets, globular to short-cylindrical, 8–15 mm wide, 8–18 mm long; maturing late July to early September; animal-dispersed. (*allegheniensis*: of the Allegheny Mountains)

Identification

The canes of *R. allegheniensis* are particularly long, often in the range of 6–10 ft (2–3 m), and have large, sharp prickles. The central primocane leaflet is elliptical or slightly ovate in outline, and the underside is velvety to the touch. Both *R. ablatus* and *R. alumnus* are similar, but *R. ablatus* lacks gland-tipped hairs in the inflorescence, and *R. alumnus* has a measurably broader inflorescence. Specimens have been collected in Pine County that may be hybrids between *R. allegheniensis* and *R. canadensis* although they key to *R. ablatus*.

Note: Widrlechner (1998) compiled a list of 23 relevant synonyms for this species, too many to include here.

Natural History

R. allegheniensis is a broadly adapted species that occurs throughout much of the forested region of the state. It is certainly the most widespread and in many places the most common blackberry. It is usually associated with early or midsuccessional forests of oaks (*Quercus* spp.), trembling aspen (*Populus tremuloides*), paper birch (*Betula papyrifera*), or pines (*Pinus* spp.). And although it clearly prefers well-drained, sandy, acidic soil, it is sometimes found in loamy or even clayey soils that may be somewhat basic (calcareous).

It can be found in the relatively deep shade of forest interiors, a habitat too shady for most other blackberries. However, it is more common in the intermittent shade along a forest edge. It is also found in brushy ecotones, recently cutover forest land and even in abandoned fields or pastures that are reverting back to forest. It also does well under power lines and along rights-of-way that have been cut through forests, especially if those corridors are kept open by mechanical brush cutting rather than by herbicides. *Rubus allegheniensis* is also one of the species benefiting from the openings in forests caused by oak wilt disease, a fungal infection fatal to oaks.

Each inflorescence is a narrow, glandular raceme—June 2.

Fruits ripen from late July to early September.

Canes can reach 12' (3.7 m) in length; this one is a primocane.

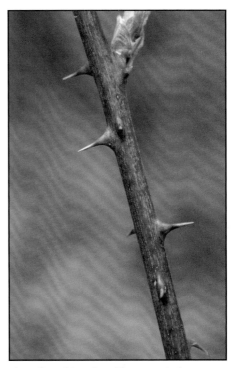

Sharp, broad-based prickles are typical.

Blackberries and Raspberries 🌿 451

Rubus alumnus Bailey

A species of highbush blackberry

[*R. facetus* Bailey; *R. impos* Bailey; *R. apianus* Bailey; *R. licitus* Bailey; *R. bellobatus* Bailey; *R. fernaldianus* Bailey; *R. miriflorus* Bailey; *R. ostryifolius* Bailey; *R. parcifrondifer* Bailey; *R. pubifolius* Bailey; *R. corei* Bailey]

Midsize or occasionally tall **shrubs**, with biennial **canes** to 2.7 m long, semierect or arching the 1st year, arching the 2nd; clonal by root suckering, not known to tip-root. Canes occasionally with gland-tipped hairs scattered on distal portion of the primocane but lacking nonglandular hairs; **prickles** broad-based, moderately abundant, 0.7–1.5 per cm of cane, straight or somewhat decurved, 4–8 mm long. Primocane **leaves** palmately compound with 5 leaflets; central **leaflet** elliptical to elliptical-oblong, 8.5–15.5 cm long, 5–10 cm wide, base cordate to subcordate, apex acuminate, margins sharply serrate, upper surface thinly hairy, lower surface velvety-hairy. **Petioles** with sparse to dense nonglandular hairs and sometimes gland-tipped hairs, armed with broad-based decurved prickles to 4 mm long; stipules linear to linear-lanceolate, 7–15 mm long. **Inflorescence** a wide-flaring leafy raceme 6–18 cm long, 6–10 cm wide, with 5–19 flowers; pedicels and peduncle with dense nonglandular hairs, gland-tipped hairs, and scattered aciculate prickles. **Flowers** bisexual, 5-merous, 2.5–5 cm across; sepals 6–10 mm long, triangular to narrowly triangular, apex acuminate to caudate, often glandular; petals white, ovate to broadly ovate or elliptical; **anthesis** early June to early July; insect-pollinated. **Fruit** an aggregate of black drupelets, short-cylindrical, 9–18 mm wide, 12–21 mm long; maturing late July to late August; animal-dispersed. (*alumnus*: student or pupil)

Identification

The canes are semierect or arching, sometimes over 6 ft (2 m) in length, with large, velvety leaves and very long, very sharp prickles. Note that the flowers/fruits are on particularly long pedicels, often more than 1.5 inches (4 cm) long, which creates a broad, flaring raceme. It most closely resembles *R. rosa* but differs primarily by the shape and proportions of the central leaflet of the primocane leaves. It could also be mistaken for *R. alleghensis*, but *R. alleghensis* has a narrower raceme (shorter pedicels) and smaller sepals. *Note:* There are specimens from northwestern Minnesota that may key to this species but show characteristics that indicate possible hybridization

with an unknown species in section *Canadenses*, possibly *R. acridens*, such as thinner pubescence on the lower surface of leaflets, reduced prickle density, and a rusty-colored midvein.

Like *R. rosa*, many cultivars have been derived from this species (*fide* Widrlechner 1998), and also like *R. rosa*, this species is probably a polyploid derivative of *R. alleghensis* (Hodgdon and Steele 1966).

Natural History

Rubus alumnus is a forest species, found primarily with upland hardwoods such as oaks (*Quercus* spp.) or trembling aspen (*Populus tremuloides*), and sometimes conifers, particularly the native pines (*Pinus* spp.) or occasionally white spruce (*Picea glauca*). It is typically found in intermittent shade in partial clearings, under thin canopies, and along forest edges. Soils are invariably sandy and acidic, and range from dry to mesic.

Rubus alumnus typically occurs in genus communities with other highbush blackberries such as *R. alleghensis*, *R. ablatus*, and *R. recurvans* and sometimes with dewberries or bristle-berries such as *R. satis* and *R. wisconsinensis*. In stable habitats these communities can become highly structured, although *R. alumnus* is usually only a minor component.

Canes can reach 9' (2.7 m) in length and arch over—June 10.

Canes bear only leaves the first year, flowers the second.

Straight, broad-based prickles— very sharp.

Inflorescence is a broad, glandular raceme—June 10.

Fruits turn black in August.

Rubus arcticus L. subsp. *acaulis* (Michx.) Focke

Arctic dwarf raspberry
[*R. acaulis* Michx.]

Low **shrubs**, with annual **stems** to 15 cm tall, ± erect, sparsely hairy to glabrate, lacking bristles, prickles, or glands; forming small rhizomatous colonies. **Leaves** alternate, deciduous, ternately compound. Central **leaflet** rhombic to elliptical or obovate, 2–4.5 cm long, 1.5–3.5 cm wide, base cuneate, apex subacute to obtuse or blunt, margins irregularly serrate or infrequently double-serrate, the basal third often entire, upper surface green, sparsely hairy to glabrate, lower surface pale green, glabrous or glabrate. **Petioles** 2–6 cm long, sparsely hairy to glabrate; stipules narrowly ovate or elliptical, 4–8 mm long. **Flowers** bisexual (unisexual in subsp. *arcticus*), 5-merous; borne singly at apex of stem; peduncle 1–4 cm long, sparsely hairy to glabrate; sepals narrowly triangular with attenuated tip, 5–10 mm long, erect at anthesis but ultimately reflexed; petals pink to rose-colored or purplish, obovate to narrowly obovate, 15–25 mm long, erect, clawed; **anthesis** late May to late June; insect-pollinated. **Fruit** an aggregate of red drupelets, globular, 6–10 mm across; maturing early July to mid-August; animal-dispersed. (*arcticus*: of the arctic; *acaulis*: without a stem)

Identification

Arctic dwarf raspberry is essentially a herbaceous species; it reaches a height of just 4–6 inches (10–15 cm) and is woody only at the base. Each stem produces a single pink or rose-colored flower and 2 or 3 leaves, and each leaf is divided into 3 leaflets. Except for the pink flower, it can easily be mistaken for one of the native strawberries (*Fragaria* spp.), and sterile specimens often are. Sterile specimens are also confused with the closely related dwarf raspberry (*R. pubescens*), but the tips of its leaflets are blunter, and its stems do not develop the long, slender runners of dwarf raspberry. Hybrids between the two species (named *R.* ×*paracaulis* Bailey) have been found in Minnesota, but they are quite rare. The hybrid flower color is variable but usually some shade of pink, and the shape of the central leaflet is somewhere between the rather blunt tip of arctic dwarf raspberry and the narrower, acute tip of dwarf raspberry.
Note: This is a wide-ranging, circumpolar species with several intergrading populations (Hultén 1971). The Eurasian plants, and some populations in Alaska, are considered subsp. *arcticus*. The widespread North American plants, including those in Minnesota, are designated subsp. *acaulis*. A third population in Alaska and adjacent portions of Canada is named subsp. *stellatus*.

Natural History

Arctic dwarf raspberry is found in many of the peatland areas of northern Minnesota, primarily in the north-central and northwestern counties. Populations are often small and somewhat transient, and the species as a whole is rather uncommon or at best occasional. It typically grows in wet *Sphagnum*-dominated habitats of the type commonly called bogs, but which ecologists prefer to call swamps or poor fens. It is sometimes found in the open or more often with widely spaced black spruce (*Picea mariana*), tamarack (*Larix laricina*), or maybe northern white cedar (*Thuja occidentalis*). These are wet, acidic, low-nutrient habitats with full or partial sunlight. The habitats are characteristically stable; they are not strongly affected by drought or prone to flooding, frequent fire, or most other stochastic, landscape-level events. In this context they would be considered late-successional or climax communities.

A single pink flower 4–6" (10–16 cm) above the ground—June 9.

Only one fruit per stem—July 28.

Leaflet has a blunt or obtuse tip—compare with dwarf raspberry.

Except for the pink flower, it resembles wild strawberry.

Rubus canadensis L.

A species of highbush blackberry
[*R. besseyi* Bailey]

Midsize **shrubs**, with biennial **canes** to 2 m long, erect or arching the 1st year, arching the 2nd; clonal by root suckering, not known to tip-root. Canes glabrous; **prickles** absent or sparse, 0–0.5 per cm of cane, declined, 1–3 mm long, broad-based. Primocane **leaves** palmately compound with 5 leaflets; central **leaflet** elliptical, 9.5–14.5 cm long, 5.5–8 cm wide, base rounded, subcordate or cordate, apex long-acuminate or caudate, margins serrate to sharply serrate, upper surface glabrous except for scattered hairs near margin, lower surface glabrous or with a few hairs along mid and lateral veins, midvein often rusty-colored. **Petioles** glabrous, unarmed or with very small, weak prickles; stipules linear to filiform, to 12 mm long. **Inflorescence** a raceme 6–15 cm long with 4–16 flowers; pedicels and peduncle with sparse, nonglandular hairs. **Flowers** bisexual, 5-merous, 2.5–4 cm across; sepals 6–9 mm long, triangular to narrowly triangular, apex acuminate or caudate; petals white, ovate to broadly ovate; **anthesis** mid-June to mid-July; insect-pollinated. **Fruit** an aggregate of black drupelets, globular to short-cylindrical, 9–16 mm wide, up to 2 cm long, maturing mid-August to early September; animal-dispersed. (*canadensis*: of Canada)

Identification

The canes of *R. canadensis* tend to be rather slender and are sometimes dark purple in color. They start out more or less erect but ultimately arch or lean, but not so far as to touch the ground. The inflorescence is a raceme, similar in form to *R. allegheniensis* although somewhat smaller and without the gland-tipped hairs. In fact, this species is usually characterized as entirely lacking hairs and prickles, which is not quite true; some legitimate specimens will have perhaps 3 or 4 weak, scattered prickles on the canes and barely noticeable hairs on the leaves and inflorescence. *Rubus acridens* and *R. quaesitus* are closest to *R. canadensis* in the key, but they are distinctly prickly.

Note: A suspected hybrid between *R. canadensis* and *R. allegheniensis* has been found in Pine County; it most closely resembles *R. ablatus*.

Natural History

R. canadensis has a generally northern range, which includes the region north of Lake Superior. It is not particularly common in Minnesota, although there is a cluster of records from Pine County, where it could be described as locally common in appropriate habitats. Even in the best habitats it never seems to occur in great numbers; instead, it is usually found as scattered individuals or small colonies, often with other species of highbush blackberry such as *R. ablatus*, *R. allegheniensis*, and *R. recurvans*.

R. canadensis is most often associated with early or midsuccessional forests of trembling aspen (*Populus tremuloides*), paper birch (*Betula papyrifera*), pines (*Pinus* spp.), or sometimes white spruce (*Picea glauca*). It does well in a forest interior, at least if the canopy is thin enough to allow some sunlight to reach the shrub layer. Marginal habitats are perhaps better, particularly a forest edge, brushy clearing, or opening. Habitats are usually on level or gently rolling terrain in mesic, sandy or rocky soil.

Inflorescence is a nonglandular raceme—June 10.

Fruits change from green to red to black—August 19.

Leaves feel smooth, and canes lack prickles.

Rubus chamaemorus L.

Cloudberry

Low **shrubs**, with annual herbaceous **stems** to 30 cm tall, erect and unbranched; somewhat hairy, often minutely so; lacking glands, bristles, and prickles; forming extensive rhizomatous clones. **Leaves** simple, alternate, deciduous; somewhat leathery, 1–3 per stem. **Petioles** sparsely hairy, 3–7 cm long; stipules broad or nearly circular, gland-margined, 1–5 mm long, somewhat foliaceous. **Leaf blades** roughly circular to reniform, with 3–7 (usually 5) rounded lobes, palmately veined; 4–11 cm long, 6–12 cm wide; base cordate to broadly cordate; margins finely dentate; upper surface dark green, glabrous or glabrate, with impressed veins; lower surface pale green or gray-green, hairy on veins. **Flowers** unisexual, with separate male flowers and female flowers borne on different plants (dioecious); 5- or 4-merous; solitary on terminal peduncle 2–5 cm long, peduncles with soft nonglandular hairs and scattered gland-tipped hairs; sepals ovate with acuminate tips, 5–12 mm long, hairy and usually sparsely glandular; petals white, 6–14 mm long, obovate to elliptical; **anthesis** early June to early July; insect-pollinated. **Fruit** an aggregate of a few large drupelets, at first reddish becoming translucent yellow or amber-colored when ripe, 1–2 cm across, maturing late July to late August; animal-dispersed. (*chamaemorus*: from the Greek *chamae*, on the ground, and the Latin *morus*, the mulberry tree)

Identification

The aerial stems of cloudberry are essentially herbaceous and rise to a height of only 4–12 inches (10–30 cm). There are just 1–3 leaves per stem and at most 1 flower. The leaves are simple, not compound, with shallow, rounded lobes and finely toothed margins. The leaves can be confused with those of swamp red currant (*Ribes triste*) and possibly skunk currant (*R. glandulosum*), but the lobes are more rounded.

Natural History

Cloudberry is common in true boreal and arctic habitats across the northern portions of North America, Europe, and Asia, exhibiting a nearly continuous circumpolar distribution (Hultén 1971). It becomes rare at latitudes as far south as Minnesota, and in fact it was not discovered here until 1954 (Lakela 1954). Since then it has been found at only a few additional locations and is considered very rare in the state.

The Minnesota habitats are all peat bogs, usually with a thin to moderate canopy of black spruce (*Picea mariana*) and a carpet of *Sphagnum* moss. Associated species include common ericaceous shrubs, such as Labrador tea (*Rhododendron groenlandicum*) and bog laurel (*Kalmia polifolia*). These habitats are moderately to strongly acidic, with low levels of nutrients and only patchy sunlight. Farther north, it is known to thrive in open (nonforested) habitats.

Reproduction by seed does occur and is essential for dispersal, but it is apparently uncommon (Korpelainen 1994). The main mode of reproduction is vegetative. This is accomplished by an extensive system of branched rhizomes that grow just beneath the surface of the moss and send up herbaceous aerial stems from the nodes. Each aerial stem produces 1 to 3 leaves and occasionally 1 flower. Studies have shown rhizomes can be up to 33 ft (10 m) long, and comprise from 92–97% of the biomass of the clone (*fide* Korpelainen 1994). It has also been shown that the actual number of clones in any population is typically low (Korpelainen 1994), and there is evidence that male clones predominate (Ågren 1988). It is even possible that a small "population" may consist of a single, diffuse clone, which would be all male or all female even if the clone consisted of hundreds of stems. This could be especially significant in Minnesota, where populations are particularly small and isolated, and where conservation is a concern.

Leaves are simple, and have rounded lobes.

Fruits have only a few drupelets, and ripen yellowish—
August 15.

These female flowers look little different than the males—June 17.

A black spruce bog inhabited by cloudberry—Cook County.

Rubus dissensus Bailey

A species of bristle-berry

Midsize **shrubs**, with biennial **canes** to 1.3 m long, arching to low-arching the 1st year, low-arching to prostrate the 2nd; clonal by root suckering, not normally tip-rooting. Canes usually with a few gland-tipped hairs on upper portion of primocane; **prickles** aciculate, abundant, 10–19 per cm of cane, weak, mostly declined, 2.5–4 mm long. Primocane **leaves** with 3 or 5 leaflets, central **leaflet** elliptical or somewhat ovate to obovate, 7.5–10 cm long, 4.5–5.5 cm wide, base rounded or tapered, apex abruptly acuminate to short-acuminate, margins coarsely serrate, upper surface glabrous or with a few hairs near margin, lower surface glabrous or with hairs along mid and lateral veins. **Petioles** with declined aciculate prickles, fine nonglandular hairs, and sometimes coarse gland-tipped hairs; stipules linear, 15–25 mm long. **Inflorescence** a compound corymb with up to 26 flowers; pedicels with both gland-tipped and non–gland-tipped hairs, and at least a few small aciculate prickles. **Flowers** bisexual, 5-merous, 2–3 cm across; sepals 6–9 mm long, with a few gland-tipped hairs, narrowly triangular to narrowly elliptical, apex apiculate or caudate; petals white, elliptical to obovate; **anthesis** late June to mid-July; insect-pollinated. **Fruit** an aggregate of black drupelets, ± globose, 7–12 mm across; maturing late July to late August; animal-dispersed. (*dissensus*: from *dis*, the opposite of, and *sensus*, in the sense of)

Identification

The upper portions of the 1st-year canes (primocanes) and sometimes the petioles have at least a few gland-tipped hairs mixed in with the bristles. In this way it is most like *R. regionalis*, *R. groutianus*, and *R. fulleri* but differs by consistently having a compound, corymb-type inflorescence. Close attention must be paid to the habit of the canes; they will arch or lie prostrate on surrounding vegetation, but they will not characteristically trail along the ground or tip-root. Any hint of tip-rooting could indicate *R. fulleri*, but the primocane leaves of *R. fulleri* tend to have 3 leaflets rather than 5, and the central leaflet tends to be wider than that of *R. dissensus*.
Note: R. dissensus may represent a more lightly armed form of *R. groutianus*.

Natural History

Rubus dissensus, as described here, appears to be very rare throughout its range, including Minnesota. It is currently known only from specimens collected in Kalamazoo County, Michigan, Iron County, Wisconsin, and 5 counties in east-central Minnesota. Still, it seems likely that it occurs at undiscovered points in between, especially when considering the spotty history of *Rubus* field surveys and the cryptic nature of the bristle-berries.

The species was first discovered in Minnesota during statewide surveys in 1996 and 1997; it was previously unknown in the state. Most populations were found in moist meadows that are dominated by fine-leaved sedges, particularly woolly sedge (*Carex pellita*) and wiregrass (*Carex lasiocarpa*), but populations sometimes extend into portions of adjacent upland prairie dominated by big bluestem (*Andropogon gerardii*) or porcupine-grass (*Hesperostipa spartea*) along with various forbs. Soils are more-or-less acidic and range from peaty to sandy. These habitats were historically kept clear of trees by periodic wildfires started by lightning strikes. This appears to suit *R. dissensus*, which thrives in full sunlight. To date, *R. dissensus* has not been found in human-degraded habitats, at least not in habitats that have a recent history of livestock grazing or soil disturbances.

Flowers are about an inch (2–3 cm) across—June 27.

Canes arch over the ground or lie gently on the surface.

This pattern of branching is called a compound corymb—August 5.

Prickles are sharp but weak.

Blackberries and Raspberries   **461**

Rubus ferrofluvius Davis, Fuller & Davis

A species of dewberry

Low **shrubs**, with biennial **canes** to 2.4 m long, trailing; clonal by root suckering and by tip-rooting. Canes glabrous; **prickles** aciculate or barely broad-based, 0.7–3.5 per cm of cane, recurved, 1–3 mm long. Primocane **leaves** palmately compound with 3 leaflets, the lateral ones often lobed; central **leaflet** ovate to elliptical or broadly elliptical, 7–9 cm long, 4–6 cm wide, base rounded or blunt, apex acuminate to long-acuminate, margins serrate or double-serrate, upper surface thinly hairy to nearly glabrous, lower surface usually moderately hairy but can vary from thinly hairy to velvety-hairy. **Petioles** with scattered, nonglandular hairs and usually several small, recurved prickles; stipules lanceolate, 10–20 mm long. **Inflorescence** a condensed corymb or cymule with 2–8 flowers; pedicels with sparse to moderately dense nonglandular hairs and rarely a small prickle or two, but lacking gland-tipped hairs. **Flowers** bisexual, 5-merous, 2.5–3.5 cm across; sepals 6–7 mm long, triangular or triangular-elliptical, the apex acute to apiculate; petals white, elliptical to oblong; **anthesis** mid-May to mid-June; insect-pollinated. **Fruit** an aggregate of black drupelets; globose to short-conical or short-cylindrical; 8–14 mm wide, 10–15 mm long; maturing mid-July to late August; animal-dispersed. (*ferrofluvius*: iron river; named for the type locality, near Iron River, Bayfield County, Wisconsin)

Identification

As in all the dewberries, the canes of *R. ferrofluvius* trail along the ground and root at the tips, and from the rooted tips new canes can arise the following year. But unlike most dewberries, the primocane leaves have only 3 leaflets rather than 5, and the lateral leaflets usually have pronounced lobes. Among Minnesota dewberries only *R. steelei* has similarly shaped leaves, but the leaves of *R. steelei* tend to feel smooth rather than velvety. Also, the inflorescence of *R. ferrofluvius* is typically a condensed corymb with 2–8 flowers, most closely resembling that of *R. plicatifolius*.

Note: Voss (1983) incorrectly noted that the publication of *R. ferrofluvius* was invalid because the authors designated two collection numbers for the type specimen (Davis, Fuller, and Davis 1982). In fact, both numbers refer to the same specimen; this was a method of notation consistently practiced by these collectors for joint collections.

Natural History

Although there are several records of *Rubus ferrofluvius* scattered across east-central and northeastern Minnesota, populations appear to be concentrated in the Anoka Sandplain just north of the Twin Cities. Most are from savannas, open woodlands, and forest margins, usually in association with trembling aspen (*Populus tremuloides*), northern pin oak (*Quercus ellipsoidalis*), or, farther north, jack pine (*Pinus banksiana*). The immediate habitat is usually grassy or brushy and receives full or partial sunlight; soils are most often dry and sandy. A few of these populations extend onto soils that appear to have been plowed or heavily pastured in the past. The far northern records (St. Louis County) are from outcrops of igneous bedrock.

Like all the dewberries, *Rubus ferrofluvius* is clonal, spreading above ground by stolons (through the process of tip-rooting) and evidently underground by root suckering. The resulting colonies are usually small and diffuse, but they sometimes become tangled thickets as much as 60 ft (20 m) across.

Rubus ferrofluvius seems to tolerate drought and temperature extremes, even fire. Although the canes are easily consumed in a typical ground fire, they resprout from the root crowns. In fact, the maintenance of populations may be enhanced by periodic dormant-season burns.

Floricanes hug the ground, flower from mid-May to mid-June.

Each primocane leaf has 3 leaflets, with the lateral ones lobed at base.

Canes trail along the gound as much as 8' (2.4 m) then tip-root— August 4.

Rubus frondosus Bigel.

A species of highbush blackberry

[*R. sativus* (Bailey) Brainerd; *R. fandus* Bailey; *R. folioflorus* Bailey; *R. pratensis* Bailey]

Midsize **shrubs**, with biennial **canes** to 1.5 m long, high-arching the 1st year, low-arching the 2nd; clonal by root suckering, not known to tip-root. Canes glabrous; **prickles** broad-based, rather sparse, 0.5–1.2 per cm of cane, straight or decurved, 2–5 mm long. Primocane **leaves** palmately compound with 5 or occasionally 3 leaflets; central **leaflet** elliptical-ovate, ovate, or suborbicular, 8–14 cm long, 6–11 cm wide, base cordate to subcordate, apex acuminate to long-acuminate, margins serrate, upper surface thinly hairy, lower surface velvety-hairy. **Petioles** glabrous, armed with declined aciculate prickles to 3 mm long; stipules linear to linear-lanceolate, 10–18 mm long. **Inflorescence** a leafy raceme or sometimes a corymb, with 2–10 flowers; pedicels and peduncle with moderately dense nonglandular hairs and rarely aciculate prickles. **Flowers** bisexual, 5-merous, 2–3.5 cm across; sepals 6–10 mm long, triangular-elliptical, apex acuminate or apiculate; petals white, obovate; **anthesis** early to late June; insect-pollinated. **Fruit** an aggregate of black drupelets, globose, 10–16 mm across; maturing mid-July to mid-August; animal-dispersed. (*frondosus*: leafy)

Identification

The canes of *Rubus frondosus* are normally 3–4.5 ft (1–1.5 m) long. They initially grow erect but eventually arch at least somewhat. The longer floricanes may arch nearly to the ground, but they do not trail along the ground or tip-root. The inflorescence is a compact raceme of 2 to 10 flowers usually overtopped by the leaves. The central leaflet of each primocane leaf is broadly ovate with a heart-shaped (cordate) base, and the lower surface is velvety to the touch. *R. frondosus* is very similar to the more common *R. recurvans*, and some specimens can be difficult to distinguish (see key). It bears a lesser resemblance to *R. rosa* and *R. satis*.

Natural History

Rubus frondosus is fairly common in parts of central Minnesota, particularly in what was historically the fire-maintained oak-aspen (*Quercus-Populus*) ecosystem that skirted the prairies. Today, the best habitats are usually found along woodland margins, in long-term forest openings, ecotones between grasslands and woodlands, and other marginal habitats where there is full sunlight or partial shade. Soils are primarily dry or dryish with a sandy texture.

Maintenance of these habitats was one function of natural ecosystems that has been lost with fire suppression. But to some extent, makeshift habitats are now provided as a by-product of logging, road building, "brushing" of utility corridors and rights-of-way, low-intensity farming, and a variety of other human activities. This is especially true for activities that tend to create brushy borders in otherwise wooded terrain but do not greatly alter the woodland character of the soil.

These habitat types are magnets for several species of highbush blackberries, including *R. allegheniensis*, *R. ablatus*, *R. recurvans*, *R. alumnus*, and *R. rosa*. In fact, it is not unusual to find 4 or 5 species forming a stable genus community wherever habitat conditions are ideal. Indeed, these communities are surprisingly stable, with anecdotal evidence of some persisting relatively unchanged for at least 50 years. This may be attributable, in part, to the root-suckering growth form of blackberries. Suckering allows the establishment of dense clones, which can be effective in resisting encroachment from competing tree saplings and shrubs, at least if aided by periodic disturbances, such as fire, that set back forest succession.

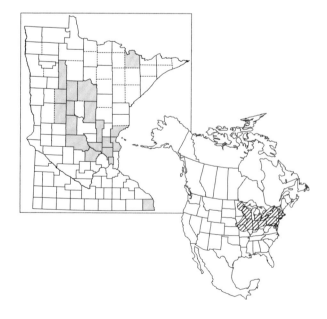

The inflorescence is a small, nonglandular raceme—June 27.

Healthy canes get about 4.5' (1.5 m) long, then arch over.

Fruits ripen about 6 weeks after pollination—August 4.

Blackberries and Raspberries   🌿   **465**

Rubus fulleri Bailey

A species of bristle-berry
[*R. setosus* Bigl. var. *rotundior* Bailey; *R. exter* Bailey]

Low **shrubs**, with biennial **canes** to 1.5 m long, ascending or arching the 1st year, low-arching, prostrate, or trailing the 2nd; clonal by root suckering and often tip-rooting. Canes frequently with dense, gland-tipped hairs, at least on primocane; armed with weak, aciculate **prickles** or stiff bristles, 8–20+ per cm of cane, 2–5 mm long. Primocane **leaves** palmately compound with 3 or 5 leaflets (usually 3); central **leaflet** broadly elliptical, elliptical-ovate, or obovate, 6–9.5 cm long, 4–8 cm wide, base rounded or subcordate, apex acute to short-acuminate, margins serrate or sharply serrate, upper surface glabrous and somewhat glossy, lower surface nearly glabrous or sparsely hairy on main veins, dull. **Petioles** with gland-tipped hairs, weak aciculate prickles, and sometimes fine, soft, nonglandular hairs; stipules lanceolate to linear-lanceolate, 10–25 mm long. **Inflorescence** an open corymb or sometimes a raceme, with 5–20 flowers; pedicels and peduncle with short, dense, nonglandular hairs, longer gland-tipped hairs, and stiff bristles. **Flowers** bisexual, 5-merous, 1.8–3.5 cm across; sepals 4–6 mm long, ovate-elliptical with an apiculate tip, often with gland-tipped hairs; petals white, ovate to obovate or oblong; **anthesis** mid-June to mid-July; insect-pollinated. **Fruit** an aggregate of black drupelets, ± globose, 10–15 mm across; maturing early to late August; animal-dispersed. (*fulleri*: named for its discoverer, American botanist Albert Fuller)

Identification

The 1st-year canes (primocanes) start erect, but by mid-August they will have reached about 3 ft (1 m) in length and begun to arch toward the ground. When the tip reaches the ground, it will take root if soil and moisture conditions permit. This may be the only character that separates closely related species, so it is essential to examine several healthy, undamaged canes to establish if the plant is truly a "tip-rooter." If a specimen of *Rubus fulleri* is not recognized as a tip-rooter, it will probably key to *R. dissensus*. Also note that the canes have soft, gland-tipped hairs intermixed with stiff bristles (most conspicuous on the upper portions of 1st-year canes). The only similar Minnesota species that have glandular canes are *R. regionalis*, *R. groutianus*, and *R. dissensus*. *Note:* The proposal by Davis, Fuller, and Davis (1982) to combine *R. fulleri* with *R. wheeleri* in

section *Setosi* is not followed here because *R. fulleri* is fundamentally a tip-rooting plant, and the shape of its leaf does not closely resemble that of *R. wheeleri* (Widrlechner 1998).

Natural History

Rubus fulleri is found almost exclusively on sand plains in the central and east-central counties, typically in habitats called swales or wet meadows. These are shallow wetlands sustained by a high water table, and have a ground layer of sedges, broad-leaved herbaceous plants, and often scattered shrubs. Adjacent uplands may also be suitable if there is direct sunlight and little competition. *Rubus fulleri* is known to be very sensitive to livestock grazing and changes in groundwater levels and does not readily colonize grossly disturbed habitats.

The best habitats are essentially remnants of the original oak savanna ecosystem that existed in the region before settlement. There is a whole suite of similar "bristle-stemmed" *Rubus* species that typically occur with *R. fulleri* in habitats of this type. They include *R. stipulatus*, *R. uniformis*, *R. semisetosus*, *R. vermontanus*, *R. dissensus*, and perhaps one or two others that are still poorly known. They often dominate the low-shrub layer with large clones integrated into complex and highly structured communities, or segregated into zones along moisture and light gradients.

Inflorescence is a simple corymb with gland-tipped hairs—July 2.

Primocanes arch to the ground, then tip-root.

Canes are covered with dense prickles and gland-tipped hairs.

Fruits turn black in August.

Rubus groutianus Blanchard

A species of bristle-berry
[*R. discretus* Bailey]

Midsize **shrubs**, with biennial **canes** to 1.3 m long, erect or arching the 1st year, arching the 2nd; clonal by root suckering, not known to tip-root. Canes with varying numbers of stiff, gland-tipped hairs, especially the primocane; **prickles** aciculate, abundant to very abundant, 20–75+ per cm of cane, declined, decurved, or occasionally straight, varying in strength but some strong enough to tear skin, 2–5 mm long. Primocane **leaves** palmately compound with 5 leaflets; central **leaflet** elliptical or occasionally elliptical-ovate or elliptical-obovate, (6)7–11.5 cm long, 3.5–6.5(8) cm wide, base tapered or rounded, apex acuminate, rarely "shouldered," margins serrate to irregularly double-serrate, upper surface nearly glabrous, lower surface thinly hairy, primarily on main veins, smooth to the touch. **Petioles** with hairs sometimes present, these may be gland-tipped and/or non–gland-tipped; armed with numerous aciculate prickles; stipules lanceolate to lance-linear, 10–18 mm long. **Inflorescence** a small condensed raceme or corymb at the end of a leafy branch or occasionally a compound corymb, with 5–28 flowers; pedicels and peduncle with a few soft, nonglandular hairs, stiff, gland-tipped hairs, and numerous straight, aciculate prickles (spicules) 2–4 mm long. **Flowers** bisexual, 5-merous, 2–3 cm across; sepals 5–7 mm long, elliptical to ovate-elliptical, apiculate, often with gland-tipped hairs; petals white, elliptical to obovate; **anthesis** mid-June to mid-July; insect-pollinated. **Fruit** an aggregate of black drupelets, ± globose, 8–14 mm across; maturing mid-August to early September; animal-dispersed. (*groutianus*: in honor of American bryologist A. J. Grout)

Identification

The canes of *R. groutianus*, if not winter-damaged, are usually about 3 ft (1 m) long and arch over at about knee height. The prickles are exceptionally dense and are intermixed with gland-tipped hairs, giving the canes a "shaggy" look. Also, the prickles are rather strong and stiff for a bristle-berry, sometimes strong enough to tear skin. These characters are also seen to varying degrees in *R. regionalis*, *R. dissensus*, and *R. fulleri*.

Natural History

Rubus groutianus is currently known from only two locations in Minnesota. The record from Pine County is based on a herbarium specimen collected somewhere north of Hinckley in 1959 by the noted batologist Albert Fuller and described on the herbarium label only as a "dense patch in field." That population has not been relocated and may now be gone. The population in Wadena County was found during a survey in 1999 and revisited as recently as 2003. It occurs at the edge of a jack pine forest in dry, sandy soil and nearly full sunlight. The 1999 survey found bristle-berries as a group to be fairly common in Wadena County, but found *R. groutianus* at only one location.

Few conclusions can be drawn from this rather sparse history, but assuming *R. groutianus* has a greater presence than we currently know, and that it behaves similar to closely related species, then some things can be surmised. It probably has a range in east-central Minnesota that encompasses several counties but would be localized in nonagricultural habitats on sand plains or possibly sandy moraines. The predominant trees would likely be northern pin oak (*Quercus ellipsoidalis*), pines (*Pinus* spp.), or trembling aspen (*Populus tremuloides*), and there would be dewberries and other bristle-berries present, such as *R. ferrofluvius*, *R. plicatifolius*, and *R. uniformis*. Local conditions would likely include level or gently rolling terrain, full sunlight or partial shade, and well-drained sandy soil or perhaps moister soil at the edge of a groundwater-maintained wetland.

Inflorescence can be simple or compound—July 13.

*Fruits are about 1/2" (8–14 mm) long and ripen black—
August 28.*

Primocane leaves have 5 leaflets, and are smooth to the touch.

Blackberries and Raspberries 🌿 **469**

Rubus idaeus L. var. *strigosus* (Michx.) Maxim.

Wild red raspberry

[*R. strigosus* Michx.; *R. idaeus* subsp. *strigosus* (Michx.) Focke]

Midsize **shrubs**, with erect to high-arching biennial **canes** to 1.7 m long; not tip-rooting but forming rhizomatous colonies. Canes with gland-tipped hairs (at least on upper portion of primocane) and stiff bristles; **bristles** 15–50+ per cm of cane, straight or declined, 1–3.5 mm long; **prickles** absent. Primocane **leaves** palmately compound with 3 leaflets, or pinnately compound with 5 leaflets; central **leaflet** elliptical to ovate, occasionally 3-lobed, the larger ones 6–11 cm long, 4–7 cm wide, base rounded or cordate, apex acuminate, margins single- or double-serrate, upper surface dark green, sparsely hairy to glabrate, lower surface gray-green or silvery gray, densely hairy. **Petioles** with gland-tipped hairs and stiff bristles; stipules lanceolate, linear, or filiform, 5–10 mm long. **Inflorescence** a simple or compound leafy corymb with 3–8 flowers, and sometimes with solitary flowers in lower leaf axils; pedicels 5–35 mm long, with stiff bristles and gland-tipped hairs. **Flowers** bisexual, 5-merous; 8–12 mm across; sepals 5–9 mm long, ovate-triangular with a caudate tip, often glandular, ultimately reflexed; petals white, narrowly oblong to obovate, 4–7 mm long, erect; **anthesis** late May to early July; insect-pollinated. **Fruit** an aggregate of red drupelets; often separating when ripe, hemispheric, 13–17 mm across; maturing mid-July to late August; animal-dispersed. (*idaeus*: of Mt. Ida; *strigosus*: with straight, stiff, appressed hairs)

Identification

The canes of wild red raspberry are usually about 3 ft (1 m) tall and erect, or the upper portion may arch somewhat. They are covered with stiff, bristly hairs interspersed with softer, gland-tipped hairs. The canes of black raspberry (*R. occidentalis*) are much longer and arch all the way to the ground, and they have no gland-tipped hairs. And instead of stiff bristles, they have sharp, broad-based prickles that can easily pierce skin. Wherever substantial numbers of the two species occur together, there will likely be hybrids (*R.* ×*neglectus* Peck). Physical characteristics of hybrids tend to be intermediate between the two parents, but they always have at least a few gland-tipped hairs on the upper portion of the primocane. *Note:* *R. idaeus* var. *idaeus* is native to Europe and western Asia (Hultén 1971) and differs from North American varieties by lacking gland-tipped hairs. The variety native to eastern North American, including Minnesota, is recognized here as var. *strigosus* and is replaced by one or more similar varieties west of the Great Plains.

Natural History

Wild red raspberry is one of the most common and ubiquitous shrubs in Minnesota, especially in the northern two-thirds of the state. It prefers full sunlight or partial shade in a variety of dry to moist habitats, including young hardwood forests, grassy or brushy ecotones, meadows, swamps, lakeshores, woodland edges, and openings. Soils can be sandy, loamy, rocky, or peaty and range from circumneutral to acidic.

Wild red raspberry establishes quickly by seed and then spreads rapidly by long, underground rhizomes. It often develops dense thickets that can outcompete herbaceous vegetation and even impede the establishment of forest trees. The tough rhizomes easily survive fire (Ahlgren 1959) and resprout vigorously. In fact, colonies can expand substantially in response to fire. It even survives the severe soil disturbance that often accompanies logging, allowing it to become abundant in cutover land. This phenomenon is perhaps augmented by a long-lived seed bank that reportedly can remain viable in the soil for 100 years (Whitney 1982).

Gland-tipped hairs are visible on the pedicels—June 15.

Fruits ripen red from mid-July to late August.

Primocanes are erect, and leaves pinnately compound.

Blackberries and Raspberries   **471**

Rubus ithacanus Bailey

A species of dewberry

[*R. schoolcraftianus* Bailey; *R. pauper* Bailey; *R. florenceae* Bailey; *R. pityophyllus* S. J. Smith; *R. pohlii* Bailey]

Low to midsize **shrubs**, with biennial **canes** to 3 m long, arching and mounding; clonal by root suckering and tip-rooting. Canes with a few gland-tipped hairs, at least on the distal end of the primocanes; **prickles** broad-based, sparse to moderately abundant, 0–2 per cm of cane, straight or slightly decurved, 2–5 mm long. Primocane **leaves** palmately compound with 5 or rarely 3 leaflets; central **leaflet** elliptical-rhombic, elliptical-ovate, or ovate, 8–14 cm long, 6–9 cm wide, base rounded, subcordate or rarely cordate, apex acuminate to long-acuminate, margins sharply double-serrate, upper surface thinly hairy, lower surface moderately hairy to velvety-hairy. **Petioles** armed with decurved, broad-based prickles, 2–4 mm long. **Inflorescence** ascendate or racemose, rarely corymbose, with 5–15(20) flowers; pedicels and peduncle with gland-tipped hairs, nonglandular hairs, and sometimes aciculate prickles. **Flowers** bisexual, 5-merous, 2.5–4 cm across; sepals narrowly triangular, apex often caudate; petals white, ovate; **anthesis** early June to early July; insect-pollinated. **Fruit** an aggregate of black drupelets, globose to short-cylindrical, 10–15 mm long; maturing late July to late August; animal-dispersed. (*ithacanus*: of Ithaca, New York, the type locality)

Identification

Rubus ithacanus is a mounding dewberry with long canes that arch over and trail along the ground, ultimately rooting at the tips. The canes are strong and prickly and can easily reach 6 ft (2 m) in length; one exceptional cane measured 9.5 ft (3 m). The primocane leaves have prickly petioles and 5 large, velvety leaflets. The inflorescence takes a variety of forms, but it is usually rather compact, with 5–12 large flowers. Overall, *R. ithacanus* most closely resembles *R. satis*, but with gland-tipped hairs in the inflorescence and with larger and often more abundant prickles. If it is not recognized as a tip-rooter, it will probably key to one of the highbush blackberries such as *R. alleghaniensis*, *R. ablatus*, or *R. rosa*.

Natural History

Very little is known about *Rubus ithacanus* in Minnesota other than it appears to be quite rare. To date, only two historical and one modern record have been verified, and direct field observations are limited to a single site in Isanti County. Any conclusions about the distribution and habitat preference of *R. ithacanus* would be conjectural, but it does appear to follow the pattern of other dewberries.

It seems to be a forest species widely distributed in eastern Minnesota, probably occurring on broad sandplains and sandy moraines in association with bur oak (*Quercus macrocarpa*), white oak (*Q. alba*), northern pin oak (*Q. ellipsoidalis*), or trembling aspen (*Populus tremuloides*). It seems to show a preference for sandy soil, dry or moist, and intermittent rather than continual shade.

If *Rubus ithacanus* is found again in Minnesota, and experience tells us it could be found again if field searches are intensified, it will probably be integrated into a community with other blackberries and dewberries such as *R. satis*, *R. alleghaniensis*, *R. ablatus*, and *R. recurvans*. A situation like that would require each plant in the community to be examined carefully with patience and a critical eye. In that way, and only in that way, will rarities like *R. ithacanus* be discovered.

The flowers are in a glandular raceme—June 14.

Primocane leaves typically have 5 large, velvety leaflets.

A cool summer resulted in poor fruit production—August 23.

Strong, sharp prickles make canes tricky to handle.

Rubus missouricus Bailey

A species of bristle-berry

[*R. mediocris* Bailey]

Midsize **shrubs**, with biennial **canes** to 1.5 m long, erect to arching the 1st year, low-arching the 2nd; clonal by root suckering, not known to tip-root. Canes glabrous; **prickles** aciculate, 1–5(8) per cm of cane, straight or declined, 2–5 mm long, often strong enough to tear skin. Primocane **leaves** palmately compound with 5 leaflets (early leaves may have 3 leaflets); central **leaflet** elliptical to obovate-elliptical, 7–10(11) cm long, 4–5.5 cm wide, base tapered to rounded, apex acuminate, margins sharply and somewhat irregularly serrate, upper surface thinly hairy to nearly glabrous, lower surface densely hairy, velvety to the touch. **Petioles** with hooked prickles and sparse, nonglandular hairs; stipules lanceolate, 15–20 mm long. **Inflorescence** varying from a large, compound corymb to a reduced, simple corymb or raceme, with 7–20 flowers; pedicels with moderate to dense nonglandular hairs but lacking gland-tipped hairs, rarely with a few stiff bristles. **Flowers** bisexual, 5-merous, 2.5–4 cm across; sepals 5–7 mm long, ovate-elliptical, apiculate to caudate; petals white, broadly elliptical to obovate; **anthesis** mid-June to early July; insect-pollinated. **Fruit** an aggregate of black drupelets, ± spherical to short-conical, 12–17(19) mm across, to 20 mm long; maturing early to late August; animal-dispersed. (*missouricus*: of Missouri; the type locality being near Lake City, Jackson County, Missouri).

Identification

Compared to the other bristle-berries, *R. missouricus* is particularly large and robust, with large, sharp prickles that are often strong enough to tear skin. The leaflets are usually elliptical in outline, although the central leaflet of the primocane leaves is often narrowly obovate, an unusual shape for a bristle-berry. Also, the undersides of the leaflets are velvety to the touch. The only other bristle-berry with velvety leaves is *R. semisetosus*, which differs by having glandular inflorescences.

Note: Previous reports of *R. missouricus* from Minnesota (Widrlechner 1998; Davis, Fuller, and Davis 1968a) were based upon fragmentary herbarium specimens that although very close, do not conclusively match this species. The only unequivocal

population known at the time of this writing was discovered near Blaine in Anoka County in 2003.

Natural History

The true status of *R. missouricus* in Minnesota is somewhat of a mystery. The only known population is isolated in a small, remnant habitat on the Anoka Sandplain just north of the Twin Cities. The site is a groundwater-sustained sedge meadow on moist sand in nearly full sunlight. It is growing intermingled with other bristle-berries, such as *R. stipulatus*, *R. vermontanus*, and *R. fulleri*, scattered willow shrubs (*Salix* spp.), hardhack (*Spiraea tomentosa*), and bog birch (*Betula pumila*).

Elsewhere in its range, at least in Iowa and Missouri, *R. missouricus* is considered an indicator of upland prairie and savanna habitats, not wetlands. In Iowa, it has even been found in dry hillside prairies in well-drained sandy or gravelly soil (Widrlechner 1998).

With continued searching, *R. missouricus* may turn up at other locations in Minnesota, perhaps even in prairie habitats, but years of searching have so far turned up only this one.

Each inflorescence can have 7–20 flowers—June 20.

Central leaflet of each primocane leaf is elliptical or obovate.

The weight of ripe fruit may cause the inflorescence to droop—August 16.

A species of dewberry

Low **shrubs**, with biennial **canes** to 2.5 m long, initially erect but becoming prostrate or trailing by the end of the 1st year; clonal by root suckering and frequently tip-rooting. Canes glabrous; **prickles** aciculate or barely broad-based, often rather sparse, 1–3.5 per cm of cane, curved or declined, 2–3 mm long. Primocane **leaves** palmately compound with 5 or rarely 3 leaflets; central **leaflet** ovate to suborbicular, 6–9 cm long, 5–7 cm wide, base rounded to subcordate, apex acuminate or short-acuminate, sometimes abruptly so, margins coarsely serrate, upper surface sparsely hairy, lower surface sparsely to moderately hairy. **Petioles** with curved prickles and sparse to moderately abundant nonglandular hairs; stipules linear to linear-lanceolate, 10–19 mm long. **Inflorescence** ascendate with 1–6 flowers; pedicels relatively long, with soft, nonglandular hairs. **Flowers** bisexual, 5-merous, 2.5–3.5 cm across; sepals about 6 mm long, oblong, apex acuminate or apiculate; petals white, elliptical to oblong or occasionally obovate; **anthesis** late May to mid-June; insect-pollinated. **Fruit** an aggregate of black drupelets, globose to short-conical, 12–16 mm across; maturing mid-July to mid-August; animal-dispersed. (*multifer*: fruitful)

Identification

The canes of *Rubus multifer* are commonly over 5 ft (1.5 m) long and sometimes over 7 ft (2.2 m), but they are weak and usually trail along the ground their entire length, and since the inflorescence and leaves are relatively small, the entire plant is easily hidden in tall grass. The canes will frequently root at the tip, in the typical fashion of dewberries, but not until sometime in August when they have reached their full length. The prickles tend to be short and rather weak, and many do not last into the second year. The primocane leaves almost always have 5 leaflets, and they are relatively small and roundish with an abruptly short-pointed tip. *Rubus multifer* is most likely to be mistaken for *R. steelei*, a somewhat less robust dewberry that characteristically has only 3 leaflets and stouter prickles. It is also common to see herbarium specimens misidentified as *R. flagellaris*, a species not found in Minnesota but coming as close as southwestern Wisconsin (Widrlechner 1998).

Natural History

Rubus multifer is locally common on the Anoka Sand Plain but unusual elsewhere. The most vigorous populations seem to be found in isolated remnants of indigenous oak savanna or oak-aspen woodlands. These habitats typically have scattered groves of bur oak (*Quercus macrocarpa*), northern pin oak (*Q. ellipsoidalis*), or trembling aspen (*Populus tremuloides*) with intervening prairielike habitats and shallow wetlands. In this situation, *R. multifer* is usually rooted in dry or slightly moist sand, or occasionally in crevices of granite outcrops (Stearns and Benton counties), or in thin soil over sandstone bedrock (Washington County). It typically avoids direct tree cover, preferring full sunlight among grasses or partial shade among shrubs.

Spring wildfires ignited by lightning strikes were common in these habitats until about the turn of the twentieth century. By then, the continuous savanna ecosystem had been fragmented by farm fields and roads and more recently by residential developments. Fire, which is now understood to be essential to the health of the savannas, is sometimes used as a management tool to restore and enhance native savanna vegetation, at least in those isolated patches that have been saved for conservation purposes. *Rubus multifer*, as well as the other dewberries and blackberries that are native to savannas, respond very well to periodic fire, especially dormant-season fire at intervals of 4 to 8 years. Under these conditions, *R. multifer* can become very competitive with grasses and broad-leaved herbaceous plants, even developing large, luxuriant clones 10–20 ft (3–6 m) across.

A portion of a floricane with ascendate inflorescences—June 9.

Fruit production is often poor—August 3.

Central leaflet of primocane leaf is roundish with a short, abrupt tip.

Authentic oak savanna in Anoka County—excellent dewberry habitat.

Rubus occidentalis L.

Black raspberry

Midsize or tall **shrubs**, with arching biennial **canes** to 4 m long, clonal by tip-rooting. Canes with prickles but lacking hairs, glands, and bristles; **prickles** broad-based, 0.2–1 per cm of cane, straight or decurved, 3–5 mm long. Primocane **leaves** palmately compound with 3 or rarely 5 leaflets, lateral leaflets occasionally with a basal lobe; central **leaflet** ovate to ovate-elliptical, the larger ones 6–12 cm long, 4–9 cm wide, base rounded to cordate, apex acute to acuminate, margins coarsely double-serrate, upper surface dark green, glabrous or glabrate, lower surface whitish or silvery gray, densely hairy. **Petioles** lacking hairs, glands, and bristles but usually bearing a few broad-based prickles 1–2 mm long; stipules filiform, 4–8 mm long. **Inflorescence** a simple or compound leafy corymb with 5–15 flowers; pedicels 8–20 mm long, with aciculate or broad-based prickles and fine hairs, gland-tipped hairs lacking. **Flowers** bisexual, 5-merous; sepals 5–9 mm long, triangular-ovate to triangular-elliptical, with a caudate tip, hairy but lacking glands; petals white, narrowly obovate, 2–5 mm long; **anthesis** mid-May to late June; insect-pollinated. **Fruit** an aggregate of black or purple-black drupelets; not easily separating, hemispheric, 12–15 mm across; maturing early July to late August; animal-dispersed. (*occidentalis*: western, i.e., of the New World)

Identification

Black raspberry is similar to wild red raspberry (*R. idaeus* var. *strigosus*), but it is a larger and coarser shrub, and the undersides of the leaves are more silvery-colored. Also, the canes have sharp, hooked prickles that can easily tear skin and often exceed 10 ft (3 m) in length. They ultimately arch over until the tips reach the ground and then take root. In contrast, the canes of wild red raspberry are much shorter and remain more or less erect, and they never tip-root. Also be aware that the fruits of black raspberry are red until they ripen in July. When the two native raspberries grow together, they will invariably hybridize (= *R.* ×*neglectus* Peck). In a mixed population, hybrids can be just as abundant as the parents.

Natural History

Black raspberry is common in the southern portion of the state, becoming rare and widely scattered going northward. Most habitats are loosely associated with upland hardwood forests, particularly forest edges and forest clearings where direct sunlight is available for at least a portion of the day. Increased shade may slow growth and ultimately inhibit flowering and fruiting.

Birds effectively spread the seeds to a variety of other habitats as well, including brushy thickets, abandoned fields or pastures, utility corridors, rights-of-way, and fencerows. The largest plants seem to be on loamy soils that range from weakly acidic to basic (calcareous). Soils must also be well drained or at least not saturated for extended periods of time.

Before settlement, black raspberry was probably a savanna species, living in the ecotones created by the mosaic of native woodlands and prairies. Most savanna species did not fair well when the landscape was converted to agricultural uses, but black raspberry seems preadapted to the current species-depleted landscape. For instance, it flowers and produces seeds nearly every year, and the seedlings grow quickly, even in a dense sod, and not only do the prickly canes resist browsers, they resprout vigorously if cut or burned. When freed from normal ecosystem constraints, the canes can become quite aggressive, almost combative. They do this by forming large, prickly loops or arches that are rooted at both ends; these loops can eventually overlap and intermingle to create impenetrable thickets 20–30 ft (6–9 m) across.

Inflorescence is well armed with sharp prickles.

Canes can grow 13' (4 m) in first year, but live only 2 years.

Fruits are similar to those of wild red raspberry but ripen black.

Only second-year canes produce flowers—May 31.

Blackberries and Raspberries   🍂   **479**

Rubus parviflorus Nutt.

Thimbleberry

Midsize **shrubs**, with erect biennial **canes** to 2 m high; forming rhizomatous colonies, not tip-rooting. Canes glandular-hairy the 1st year becoming glabrate and exfoliating the 2nd, lacking prickles and bristles. **Leaves** simple, alternate, deciduous. **Petioles** 6–18 cm long, with gland-tipped hairs; stipules lanceolate, 6–20 mm long. **Leaf blades** 5- or sometimes 3-lobed; 10–30 cm long and about as wide; base cordate or deeply cleft; apices acute to short-acuminate or suboptuse; margins irregularly serrate or double-serrate; palmately veined; upper surface green, sparsely hairy; lower surface somewhat paler than upper, hairy to sparsely hairy, glandular on main veins. **Inflorescence** a leafy corymb of 2–9 flowers. **Flowers** bisexual, 5-merous, 3.5–5+ cm across; pedicels 1–4 cm long, with dense gland-tipped hairs; sepals ovate to triangular, 1–1.8 cm long including a long, caudate tip, glandular on the backs, white-tomentose within; petals white, broadly obovate to nearly circular, 1.5–2.5 cm long; **anthesis** late June to late July; insect-pollinated. **Fruit** an aggregate of red or pinkish drupelets, broadly hemispheric, 1.5–2 cm across; maturing early August to mid-September; animal-dispersed. (*parviflorus*: small-flowered, an unfortunate misnomer)

Identification

Thimbleberry is a conspicuous leafy shrub, usually 4–6 ft (1–2 m) tall, with large white flowers and salmon-colored fruits. The fact that the leaves are simple, not compound, and that the stems have no bristles or prickles should eliminate any confusion with the blackberries or raspberries. There could still be some confusion with the leaves of mountain maple (*Acer spicatum*) and red maple (*A. rubrum*), and possibly with American high-bush cranberry (*Viburnum trilobum*), except that the leaves of thimbleberry are alternate while the others are opposite.
Note: Fassett (1941) recognized 19 forms based on variation in leaf pubescence and texture, and trichome morphology. At least 7 of these forms have been found in Minnesota, with f. *bifarius* (Fern.) Fassett, a soft-pubescent form, and f. *glabrifolius* Fassett, a glabrous form, the most common.

Natural History

Thimbleberry occurs scattered throughout much of northeastern Minnesota, but it is common only near the shore of Lake Superior. It is associated with a variety of upland forest types, most often with early successional trees, such as trembling aspen (*Populus tremuloides*) or paper birch (*Betula papyrifera*).

Although thimbleberry is essentially a forest species, it is most abundant following a large-scale disturbance, such as fire, that removes the forest canopy. This temporarily reduces competition for light and possibly nutrients, to which thimbleberry responds by aggressively resprouting from below-ground rhizomes. In this way it sometimes forms dense colonies 100 ft (30 m) or more across. Fire is just one stimulus; thimbleberry can also become abundant in cutover forest land, in artificial or natural clearings, under utility lines, and on roadsides, talus slopes, boulder fields, and a variety of other early-successional habitats.

The presence of thimbleberry in the Great Lakes region as a whole is somewhat of a puzzle. It is basically a western species with only small isolated populations in this region. How this came about is a matter of speculation, but at one time the range was probably continuous and then became fragmented by glacial activity and subsequent climate changes.

Flowers can be 2" (5 cm) across, and reach their peak in July.

Leaves are up to a foot (30 cm) across and shaped like a maple leaf.

Fruits ripen red—August 28.

Rubus plicatifolius Blanch.

A species of dewberry

[*R. semierectus* Blanch.; *R. rhodinsulanus* Bailey; *R. coloniatus* Bailey; *R. victorinii* Bailey; *R. botruosus* Bailey; *R. problematicus* Bailey; *R. prior* Bailey; *R. rosendahlii* Bailey; *R. exutus* Bailey]

Low **shrubs**, with biennial canes to 2.2 m long; low-arching to mounding, ultimately trailing; clonal by root suckering and tip-rooting. Canes glabrous; **prickles** aciculate or nearly broad-based, 1–5 per cm of cane, declined or sometimes decurved, 3–4 mm long. Primocane **leaves** palmately compound with usually 5 leaflets, sometimes 3 or rarely 7; central **leaflet** elliptical, elliptical-ovate or ovate, 7–10 cm long, 4–7 cm wide, base rounded, subcordate or cordate, apex acuminate, margins coarsely serrate, upper surface nearly glabrous, lower surface thinly hairy yet smooth to the touch. **Petioles** with small declined or decurved prickles, nonglandular; stipules linear-lanceolate to linear, 9–18 mm long. **Inflorescence** a corymb or raceme, with 3–8 flowers; pedicels short, less than 4 cm long, pedicels and peduncle with sparse nonglandular hairs and aciculate prickles. **Flowers** bisexual, 5-merous, 2.5–4.2 cm across; sepals 5–6 mm long, ovate-triangular or elliptical, apex apiculate or acuminate; petals white, elliptical to broadly elliptical or oblong; **anthesis** early to late June; insect-pollinated. **Fruit** an aggregate of black drupelets, ± globose or short-cylindrical, 10–17 mm wide, 10–19 mm long; maturing late July to late August; animal-dispersed. (*plicatifolius*: plicate-leaved)

Identification

Rubus plicatifolius is a trailing tip-rooter with slender canes reaching 7 ft (2.2 m) in length. The canes will always have some prickles, but they may be scattered and rather weak. The "plicate" aspect of the leaves can be difficult to see, but it means that the leaflets are slightly folded or angled at each lateral vein, something like a Japanese fan, giving the margins a slightly "ruffled" look. This same leaf plication is sometimes seen in late-season leaves of *R. frondosus* and in some of the bristle-berries (section *Setosi*). Occasionally *R. wisconsinensis* will tip-root, in which case it will likely key to *R. plicatifolius*.
Note: Hodgdon and Steele (1966) and Gleason and Cronquist (1991) treat *R. plicatifolius* as a synonym of *R. recurvicaulis* Blanch., a similar but larger, mounding species restricted to the northeastern

United States and adjacent Canada. Widrlechner (1998) believes the relationships between the two taxa deserve further study before combining the two can be justified.

Natural History

Rubus plicatifolius is one of the more common and widespread dewberries in the northeastern United States (Widrlechner 1998). It appears to be common even as far west as Wisconsin, but it becomes rather scarce in Minnesota. Most of the Minnesota records are from grassy, prairielike habitats associated with oak savannas in the east-central counties. These are usually sunny or partially shaded spots where competition is minimal. Soils are usually dry or sometimes moist, though always sandy and always acidic.

The oak savanna ecosystem was the predominant landscape feature on sandy outwash plains in this area before settlement. It is possible that *R. plicatifolius* was common then, but it seems to have not fared well since. Today it is found only in remnant habitats that have survived more or less unaltered; it apparently does not succeed in habitats that have a history of agriculture or livestock grazing.

Without flowers it can easily hide in tall grass—June 15.

As in all Rubus, *the fruit is not a berry but an aggregate of drupelets.*

There are 3–8 flowers in a corymb or raceme—June 15.

Primocanes can trail over the ground for 7' (2.2 m) before tip-rooting.

Blackberries and Raspberries   483

Rubus pubescens Raf.

Dwarf raspberry
[*R. triflorus* Richards.]

Low **shrubs**, with annual or partially biennial **stems**, hairy, but lacking glands, bristles, and prickles. **Sterile stems** slender and whiplike, trailing and rooting at the tips and nodes, to 2.8 m long; herbaceous, or more often the basal portion becoming lignified and persisting a 2nd year. **Flowering stems** ± erect, to 30 cm tall; herbaceous; arising from the root crown or from the lower nodes of a 2nd-year sterile stem. **Leaves** alternate, deciduous, ternately compound. Central **leaflet** borne on a short petiolule, rhombic, 3–8 cm long, 2–5 cm wide, base cuneate, apex acute, margins double-serrate or irregularly single-serrate, the basal third often entire, upper surface dark green, glabrous to sparsely hairy, lower surface somewhat paler than the upper, sparsely to moderately hairy; the lateral leaflets ± sessile, asymmetrically ovate or lobed. **Petioles** hairy, 2–8 cm long or lacking in the inflorescence; stipules oblanceolate to obovate or elliptical, 5–15 mm long. **Flowers** bisexual, 5-merous; borne singly or in a loose terminal cluster of 2–4; sepals ovate to narrowly triangular, 3–6 mm long, apex acute to acuminate, ultimately reflexed; petals whitish or pale pink, narrowly obovate, 4–8 mm long; **anthesis** mid-May to late June; insect-pollinated. **Fruit** an aggregate of red to dark red drupelets, globose, 5–12 mm across; maturing late June to early August; animal-dispersed. (*pubescens*: hairy)

Identification

Dwarf raspberry is a low-growing shrub, barely woody, with white or occasionally pinkish flowers. It produces two types of stems: a long, slender, sterile stem that creeps over the forest floor for 6–8 ft (2–2.5 m), rooting at the tips and nodes, and a flowering stem that rises more or less vertically to a height of about 12 inches (30 cm). Since nothing about dwarf raspberry looks at all bushy or shrubby, it is sometimes mistaken for a herbaceous species, usually one of the native strawberries (*Fragaria* spp.) or cinquefoils (*Potentilla* spp.). A much closer match is the somewhat rare arctic dwarf raspberry (*R. arcticus* subsp. *acaulis*); these two will even hybridize (the hybrid is named *R. ×paracaulis*). Yet arctic dwarf raspberry lacks long, whiplike runners, has larger flowers that are pink or rose-colored, not white, and a slightly different leaflet shape.

Natural History

Dwarf raspberry is common in a variety of habitats throughout the forested region of the state, including upland forests, swamp forests, shrub swamps, and open habitats like fens and meadows. Soil conditions are usually moist or wet but occasionally dry, and range from sandy to loamy or peaty. Conditions tend to be moderately to weakly acidic or sometimes slightly basic (calcareous).

The annual runner hugs the forest floor, creeping along for perhaps 8 ft (2.5 m), rooting at the nodes, yet only the basal portion of the runner will survive winter. The next year the flowering stem is produced from the nodes of the surviving portion of the runner and directly from the root crown. The flowering stems grow erect but remain herbaceous and die back in autumn.

The flowering stem clearly serves to produce seeds for sexual reproduction, but the purpose of the runner might not be obvious; after all, it remains sterile and dies at the end of each season. But as it creeps over the ground, it can send down roots from each node. Even though the runner dies, the series of roots it leaves behind survive the winter and send up shoots the following year. This is a very effective method of asexual reproduction, which can lead to an intricate network of runners crisscrossing the forest floor.

This is about as large as the flowering stem gets, no more than 1' (30 cm) tall.

Flowers are small and in clusters of 2–4—May 19.

Leaves are trifoliate, fruits small and red—July 22.

Blackberries and Raspberries   **485**

Rubus quaesitus Bailey

A species of highbush blackberry

Midsize **shrubs**, with biennial **canes** to 1.8 m long, ascending or arching the 1st year, arching or low-arching the 2nd; clonal by root suckering, not known to tip-root. Canes generally glabrous, or rarely with a few gland-tipped hairs; **prickles** broad-based but slender, 1.5–6 per cm of cane, straight or slightly declined, 3–6 mm long. Primocane **leaves** palmately compound with 5 leaflets; central **leaflet** elliptical or occasionally elliptical-ovate or elliptical-obovate, 10–12 cm long, 5.5–7.5 cm wide, base rounded to subcordate, apex acuminate to long acuminate or caudate, margins sharply serrate, upper surface glabrous except for scattered hairs near margin, lower surface glabrous or with a few hairs along mid and lateral veins, midvein often rusty-colored. **Petioles** glabrous or with a few fine hairs, armed with slender, recurved, broad-based prickles; stipules linear to linear-lanceolate, 12–18 mm long. **Inflorescence** a raceme with 7–15 flowers; pedicels and peduncle with a moderate number of soft, nonglandular hairs and occasionally a few gland-tipped hairs, prickles absent or rarely with a few fine, aciculate prickles. **Flowers** bisexual, 5-merous, 2.3–3.5 cm across; sepals 6–8 mm long, ovate-triangular, apex long-apiculate to caudate; petals white, obovate to elliptical; **anthesis** mid-June to mid-July; insect-pollinated. **Fruit** an aggregate of black drupelets, globular to short-cylindrical, 10–20 mm long; maturing early August to early September; animal-dispersed. (*quaesitus*: sought out, special)

Identification

Normal canes of *Rubus quaesitus* range from 2–5 ft (0.6–1.5 m) long and tend to arch or lean, but they do not trail along the ground or tip-root. They have strong, sharp, broad-based prickles of the type that distinguish the highbush blackberries from the bristle-berries. In general appearance, *R. quaesitus* looks something like the common *R. allegheniensis*, but its leaves are smooth to the touch, not velvety, and the inflorescence lacks gland-tipped hairs. It differs from *R. canadensis* by having canes with more than just 3 or 4 prickles.

Note: Most morphological characters place *R. quaesitus* intermediate between *R. canadensis* in section *Canadenses* and possibly *R. jennisonii* (a species not known to occur in Minnesota) in section *Arguti*, but its taxonomic relationships are unclear.

Natural History

Little is known about *R. quaesitus* other than it is apparently rare throughout its range. There are authenticated specimens from only a few locations in New Brunswick, Wisconsin, and Minnesota. It was first discovered in Minnesota by Albert Fuller in 1958 at a *Rubus*-rich site in Kanabec County. The site was revisited in 2003, but *R. quaesitus* could not be found.

The only other known site was discovered in 1998 in Carlton County. As a measure of its rarity, this was the only discovery of *R. quaesitus* among 500 or more *Rubus* populations investigated during a statewide field survey. The population is small but apparently well established in a mature forest of trembling aspen (*Populus tremuloides*) and paper birch (*Betula papyrifera*). The soil is mesic sandy-loam, and sunlight is filtered or patchy for most of the day.

Little more can be said about *R. quaesitus*; there is no published information about its ecology, natural history, or habitat preferences other than a meager note crediting it with producing unusually large fruit, even in poor blackberry years (Davis, Fuller, and Davis 1969a), an observation that cannot be confirmed.

Each inflorescence is a nonglandular raceme—June 28.

Primocane leaves are smooth to the touch.

Fruits ripen black in August, 7–15 per raceme.

Rubus recurvans Blanch.

A species of highbush blackberry

[*R. recurvans* var. *subrecurvans* Blanch.; *R. difformis* Bailey; *R. heterogeneus* Bailey; *R. weigandii* Bailey]

Midsize **shrubs**, with biennial **canes** to 1.7 m long, nearly erect or arching the 1st year, arching or nearly prostrate the 2nd; clonal by root suckering and rarely by tip-rooting. Canes glabrous; **prickles** broad-based, rather small and often sparse, 0.5–3.5 per cm of cane, straight or declined, 2–3.5 mm long. Primocane **leaves** palmately compound with 5 or occasionally 3 leaflets; central **leaflet** ovate or elliptical, 7–14 cm long, 6–9 cm wide, base cordate to subcordate, apex acuminate to long-acuminate, margins sharply and jaggedly serrate, upper surface sparsely hairy, lower surface velvety-hairy. **Petioles** glabrous, armed with small curved prickles to 3 mm long; stipules linear to linear-lanceolate, 10–15 mm long. **Inflorescence** a compact, leafy, corymb, or less often a short raceme, with 3–10 flowers; pedicels and peduncle with moderate to dense nonglandular hairs and often with fine, aciculate prickles. **Flowers** bisexual, 5-merous; 2–3.5 cm across; sepals 6–11 mm long, ovate to oblong-triangular with an abruptly long-pointed tip, or sometimes foliaceous and 20 mm long; petals, white, obovate; **anthesis** mid-June to early July; insect-pollinated. **Fruit** an aggregate of black drupelets, short-cylindrical to globose, 8–12 mm wide, 8–15 mm long; maturing late July to mid-August; animal-dispersed. (*recurvans*: recurving, in reference to the arching canes)

Identification

The canes of *Rubus recurvans* typically grow upright until they reach a height of about 3 ft (1 m), then they begin to arch. They sometimes arch low, but they do not normally trail along the ground or root at the tips. Broad-based prickles are usually small and sparse, though nearly always present. The inflorescence is typically a short, leafy cluster with only 3 to 10 flowers, but it can vary greatly. The leaves found among the flowers are irregularly shaped, often with extremely jagged serrations. In nearly all other aspects it is very similar to *R. frondosus*, and at times it can be difficult to tell the two apart (see key).

Natural History

Rubus recurvans is one of the more common highbush blackberries, especially in the band of hardwood forests that runs diagonally through the state from the southeast to the northwest. It is most often found in sandy soil and partial shade along woodland fringes and in forest openings and remnant savannas, usually in the company of northern pin oak (*Quercus ellipsoidalis*), trembling aspen (*Populus tremuloides*), or sometimes jack pine (*Pinus banksiana*).

Historically, these were fire-maintained habitats that existed because of periodic ground fires and in some cases crown fires. *Rubus recurvans*, like most Minnesota blackberries, is well suited to these conditions. If the canes are killed by fire, the root crown resprouts vigorously. It can then exploit the increased light and nutrient availability that follow a fire by increasing seed production and clonal growth.

Wildfires have been greatly suppressed in recent decades and now play only a minor role in *Rubus* ecology. However, the adaptations to fire have to some extent preadapted many of the highbush blackberries, including *R. recurvans*, to current conditions. For example, they are sometimes able to respond to logging operations as they would to a fire, and they occasionally find suitable habitat under power lines and along rights-of-way that have been cut through forest land and maintained as perpetual brushland.

Canes can reach 5.5' (1.7 m) long and arch over—June 17.

Margins of primocane leaflets are sharply and jaggedly serrate.

The inflorescence is a compact corymb with 3–10 flowers—June 17.

Fruits ripen black between late July and mid-August.

Blackberries and Raspberries 🌿 **489**

Rubus regionalis (Bailey) Bailey

A species of bristle-berry

Midsize **shrubs**, with biennial **canes** to 1.2 m long, initially erect, then arching or becoming nearly prostrate; clonal by root suckering, not known to tip-root. Canes with gland-tipped hairs and stiff gland-tipped bristles, at least on upper portion of primocane; **prickles** aciculate, often very dense, 10–45 per cm of cane, straight or declined, 1–4 mm long, varying greatly in size and strength. Primocane **leaves** palmately compound with 5 leaflets; central **leaflet** elliptical, 7–8.5 cm long, 4–5.5 cm wide, base rounded, apex short-acuminate to acuminate, margins serrate, upper surface glabrous, lower surface nearly glabrous, veins impressed. **Petioles** with both gland-tipped and non–gland-tipped hairs, and densely armed with aciculate prickles; stipules linear to lance-linear, 10–18 mm long. **Inflorescence** usually a condensed raceme or rarely a corymb, with 7–22 flowers; peduncle and pedicels with gland-tipped hairs and non–gland-tipped hairs; bracts stipulelike, to 1 cm long. **Flowers** bisexual, 5-merous, 2.3–3.5 cm across; sepals 5–8 mm long, with gland-tipped hairs, elliptical to narrowly triangular, apex acuminate to apiculate; petals white, elliptical to ovate; **anthesis** late June to mid-July; insect-pollinated. **Fruit** an aggregate of black drupelets, ± globose, 8–12 mm across; maturing mid-August to early September; animal-dispersed. (*regionalis*: regional)

Identification

The bristly stem of *R. regionalis* immediately identifies it as a bristle-berry. Of the 12 or so bristle-berries in Minnesota, only 4 (*R. regionalis*, *R. dissensus*, *R. groutianus*, and *R. fulleri*) have gland-tipped hairs on the petioles and the primocanes. Identification is usually pretty easy to this point, then it gets difficult. In most cases, the inflorescence of *R. regionalis* is a condensed raceme; the other species are corymbose. It may take a careful examination of several mature floricanes to determine this. For whatever reason, all 4 species are more-or-less rare in Minnesota.

Natural History

Rubus regionalis appears to be quite rare in Minnesota. There are, in fact, only a small handful of verified records, too few to get a clear picture of its habitat preferences or distribution patterns. This may change when a more thorough survey of potential habitats is completed, but for now we can make only broad assumptions. Unlike most bristle-berries, *R. regionalis* does not seem to be primarily a savanna species, although there are one or possibly two records from savannalike habitats. Rather, it appears to be more closely associated with conifer forests, particularly with pines (*Pinus* spp.). There is even one record from a subboreal habitat near the Canadian border.

Local conditions are probably more important habitat factors than the larger ecosystem type. At this finer scale, *R. regionalis* seems to prefer open or partially shaded habitats, particularly where forests transition to meadow or brushland. Within these transition zones, or ecotones, it forms small colonies, usually with numerous tangled, bristly canes sprawled on adjacent vegetation. Soils are usually sandy and nutrient poor, either moist or dry.

Primocane leaves have 5 leaflets, the central one elliptical in shape.

Fruits are often small, less than 1/2" (8–12 mm) long—August 29.

Canes are covered with stiff bristles and gland-tipped hairs.

Flowers are in a short, glandular raceme—June 29.

Rubus rosa Bailey

A species of highbush blackberry
[*R. eriensis* Bailey]

Midsize or occasionally tall **shrubs**, with biennial **canes** to 2.5 m long, erect or arching the 1st year, arching the 2nd; clonal by root suckering, not known to tip-root. Canes with gland-tipped hairs, at least on distal portion of primocane; **prickles** broad-based, large, and strong, 0.3–3 per cm of cane, straight or decurved, 6–8 mm long. Primocane **leaves** soft and clothlike, palmately compound with 5 leaflets; central **leaflet** broadly ovate or suborbicular, 9.5–17 cm long, 8.5–13 cm wide, base rounded to cordate, apex acuminate, margins serrate, upper surface thinly hairy, lower surface velvety-hairy. **Petioles** often with gland-tipped hairs, armed with decurved, broad-based prickles to 4 mm long; stipules linear to lanceolate, 12–20 mm long. **Inflorescence** a leafy raceme or compound corymb with 5–24 flowers; pedicels and peduncle with nonglandular hairs, gland-tipped hairs, and variously shaped prickles. **Flowers** bisexual, 5-merous, 3.5–5 cm across; sepals 7–10 mm long, triangular, tips acuminate to caudate, often bearing gland-tipped hairs; petals white, ovate to broadly ovate or elliptical; **anthesis** late May to late June; insect-pollinated. **Fruit** an aggregate of black drupelets, short-cylindrical to short-conical, 8–16 mm wide, 12–20 mm long; maturing mid-July to late August; animal-dispersed. (*rosa*: resembling a rose)

Identification

Rubus rosa is a very large, very robust blackberry with thick, heavily armed canes up to 8 ft (2.5 m) in length. The canes often arch parallel to the ground at about waist or chest height and may have large branches—a feature worth noting. The inflorescence is densely covered with gland-tipped hairs, and the leaves are very large and velvety, almost clothlike. It has the largest flowers and perhaps the largest fruit of any Minnesota blackberry. It is most similar to *R. alumnus*, except the central leaflet of its primocane leaves is broadly ovate rather than elliptical.

Note: Rubus rosa is reported to be the wild source of many horticultural varieties selected and cultivated for their fruit (Bailey 1944). But none of the wild populations studied in Minnesota appear to be holdovers or obvious descendents of cultivated plants.

The form of *R. rosa* in which the flowers form a compound corymb instead of a wide raceme is restricted to north-central Minnesota and represents an expanded concept of the species.

Natural History

Rubus rosa is found most commonly in the mixed hardwood-conifer forests in the north-central counties, usually in dry, sandy soil with oaks (*Quercus* spp.), trembling aspen (*Populus tremuloides*), paper birch (*Betula papyrifera*), or any of the native pines (*Pinus* spp.). It is well adapted to early successional habitats, perhaps even more than the other highbush blackberries. Populations establish quickly on forestland after the canopy has been removed or thinned by a fire or windstorm and then spread aggressively underground, even forming dense thickets if left unimpeded. These colonies resist grazing by native and domesticated animals and resprout if cut or burned. And yet, these colonies are typically short-lived, eventually being overtopped and shaded out by the next generation of canopy trees.

Today the predominant force disturbing forest canopies is the practice of clear-cutting, to which *R. rosa* seems preadapted. It also does well on grassy or brushy roadsides adjacent to forests, and along utility corridors that have been cut through forests, and potentially other places where human activities keep forest succession set back to an early stage.

Flowers are exceptionally large, can be 2" (5 cm) across—June 10.

Fruits are large; stalks have gland-tipped hairs—August 15.

Primocane leaflets are large, broad, and velvety.

Rubus satis Bailey

A species of dewberry
[*R. densipubens* Bailey; *R. onustus* Bailey]

Low to midsize **shrubs**, with biennial **canes** to 2.6 m long, initially erect, becoming low-arching or mounding and ultimately trailing; clonal by root suckering and by tip-rooting. Canes glabrous; **prickles** broad-based, relatively small, scattered, 0.5–1.5 per cm of cane, decurved, 1.5–3.5 mm long. Primocane **leaves** palmately compound with 5 or occasionally 3 leaflets; central **leaflet** ovate to wide-ovate or elliptical-ovate, 8–15 cm long, 6–11 cm wide, base subcordate to cordate, apex acuminate to long-acuminate, margins sharply serrate, upper surface sparsely hairy, lower surface moderately hairy to velvety-hairy. **Petioles** with a few small, decurved prickles and sometimes scattered nonglandular hairs; stipules linear to linear-lanceolate, 10–14 mm long. **Inflorescence** a relatively small and compact cyme, corymb, or occasionally a raceme, with 3–10 flowers; pedicels and peduncle with long, soft, nonglandular hairs, and rarely 1 or 2 small prickles. **Flowers** bisexual, 5-merous; about 3.2–4.5 cm across; sepals 6–7 mm long, ovate-triangular, apex acuminate; petals white, elliptical to broadly elliptical or oblong; **anthesis** early to late June; insect-pollinated. **Fruit** an aggregate of black drupelets, globose to short-cylindrical, 9–17 mm wide, 10–18 mm long; maturing mid-July to mid-August; animal-dispersed. (*satis*: enough or sufficient; the reference is obscure)

Identification

The flowers of *R. satis* are notably large, on average the largest among the dewberries. But the flower clusters are relatively small and compact and are usually surpassed by the large and abundant leaves. The primocane leaves are especially large, and the lower surfaces are distinctly velvety to the touch. The prickles are not unusually long or abundant, but they are sharp enough and strong enough to tear skin. If *R. satis* were not recognized as a tip-rooter, it would probably key to *R. frondosus*.
Note: Davis, Fuller, and Davis (1968b) treated *R. satis* as a synonym of *R. ithacanus* Bailey, but *R. ithacanus* has gland-tipped hairs, whereas the type specimen of *R. satis* lacks them, which seems to be sufficient reason for maintaining the distinction (Widrlechner 1998).

Natural History

As a group, dewberries are not particularly common in Minnesota, but among them *R. satis* is perhaps the most common. It is typically found in sandy soil that is dry or at least well drained at the surface, and usually in the company of oaks (*Quercus* spp.), trembling aspen (*Populus tremuloides*), or occasionally jack pine (*Pinus banksiana*). Forest edges, where there is often often less competition for sunlight, are preferred to forest interiors. *Rubus satis* resprouts after fire and often persists after clear-cutting, but it is not aggressive and cannot compete directly with taller perennial shrubs, especially clonal species such as American hazel (*Corylus americana*) and gray dogwood (*Cornus racemosa*).

The dewberries, which in Minnesota number 6 species, all have long canes that characteristically root at their tips, usually in August of the 1st year. *Rubus satis* accomplishes this by "mounding" first. That is, the canes first grow upright then arch to the ground, creating a loop or mound about waist high. When the tips reach the ground, they take root, or they trail along the ground for some distance and then root. This produces looping arches or mounds, and if there are enough canes involved, then the result can be a prickly thicket resembling rolls of barbed wire.

3–10 flowers in a small, compact cluster—June 18.

Canes will form a large, tangled mound.

Tight clusters of fruit ripen between mid-July and mid-August.

Rubus semisetosus Blanch.

A species of bristle-berry

Low or midsize **shrubs**, with biennial **canes** to 1.3 m long (usually < 1 m), initially erect, becoming arching to low-arching or prostrate; clonal by root suckering, not known to tip-root. Canes glabrous; **prickles** aciculate, abundant to sparse, 1.5–5 per cm of cane, straight or declined, 2.5–4 mm long. Primocane **leaves** palmately compound with 5 or sometimes 3 leaflets; central **leaflet** elliptical or occasionally elliptical-ovate, 6–11 cm long, 3.5–6 cm wide, base rounded to blunt or rarely subcordate, apex acute to acuminate, margins sharply serrate, upper surface glabrous or nearly so, lower surface densely hairy, velvety to the touch. **Petioles** with slender, aciculate prickles and scattered, nonglandular hairs; stipules lanceolate, 10–15 mm long. **Inflorescence** a leafy raceme with 7–20 flowers; pedicels with short, dense, nonglandular hairs and at least a few gland-tipped hairs, and occasionally stiff bristles. **Flowers** bisexual, 5-merous, 2–3.4 cm across; sepals 4–8 mm long, triangular to triangular-ovate, apiculate, with nonglandular hairs and usually glandular hairs; petals white, ± elliptical; **anthesis** mid-June to mid-July; insect-pollinated. **Fruit** an aggregate of black drupelets, ± globose, 8–13 mm across; maturing early August to early September; animal-dispersed. (*semisetosus*: half bristly)

Identification

The canes of *Rubus semisetosus* are typically 2–3 ft (60–100 cm) in length and usually arch at about knee height, but they do not trail along the ground, and they do not tip-root. They have a moderate number of slender, needle-shaped prickles, which tend to be rather weak and usually break on contact rather than puncture the skin. The leaves are dull and somewhat thick, and the lower surfaces are velvety to the touch rather than smooth. Among the 12 bristle-stemmed *Rubus* (the "bristle-berries") that constitute sections *Setosi* and *Hispidi* in Minnesota, only 2 have velvety leaves: *R. semisetosus* and *R. missouricus*.

Natural History

Scattered outlying populations of *Rubus semisetosus* have been found as far north as Aitkin County, some of them in tamarack swamps. While there is no reason to discount the more northerly occurrences, most populations occur in savanna remnants farther south, particularly on sand plains in Anoka, Isanti, and Sherburne counties. Savanna populations usually grow in moist sand along the margins of groundwater-fed swales or marshes but also in surface-dry uplands that are just above the water table. These are usually grass- or sedge-dominated habitats, often with scattered brush, such as American hazel (*Corylus americana*) and prairie willow (*Salix humilis*), or groves of trembling aspen (*Populus tremuloides*) or oaks (*Quercus* spp.). Because of the low nutrient content of the sandy soils, the vegetation is often rather sparse, which seems to suit *R. semisetosus*. It clearly does best in direct sunlight or partial shade where competition is minimal.

Rubus semisetosus is apparently sensitive to livestock grazing and does not compete well with the weeds that typically follow human disturbance. It is usually found in stable native habitats with diverse, well-structured plant communities. Because of conversion to agricultural uses, and more recently to residential and commercial uses, such habitats have become exceedingly rare. Perhaps more importantly, these habitats have been reduced to small fragments that are isolated from the ecosystem processes, such as fire, that are needed to maintain them. Without fire, they quickly succeed to a closed-canopy forest and lose their characteristic savanna flora. For these reasons, *R. semisetosus* and many other savanna species are now quite rare.

Inflorescence is a leafy raceme with 7–20 flowers—June 30.

Fruits tend to be small; they ripen black in August.

Primocanes are about 3' (1 m) long; they arch but don't tip-root.

Blackberries and Raspberries   497

Rubus steelei Bailey

A species of dewberry

[*R. connixus* Bailey; *R. cordialis* Bailey; *R. currulis* Bailey; *R. austrinus* Bailey; *R. dives* Bailey]

Low or midsized **shrubs**, with biennial **canes** to 1.8 m long, initially erect or low-arching, eventually trailing; clonal by root suckering and tip-rooting. Canes glabrous; **prickles** broad-based, sparse to moderately abundant, 0.5–2 per cm of cane, decurved, weak, 1–2 (3) mm long. Primocane **leaves** palmately compound with 3 or occasionally 5 leaflets; central **leaflet** ovate to broadly elliptical or nearly orbicular, 5–8 cm long, 3–5.5 cm wide, base rounded or subcordate, apex acuminate or short-acuminate, margins coarsely serrate or double-serrate, upper surface nearly glabrous, lower surface sparsely to moderately hairy but not velvety to the touch. **Petioles** with sparse, nonglandular hairs and small, declined or decurved, aciculate prickles; stipules linear to linear-lanceolate, 5–12 mm long. **Inflorescence** ascendate with 1–5 flowers; pedicels and peduncle with nonglandular hairs and occasionally 1 or a few small prickles. **Flowers** bisexual, 5-merous, 2.3–3.8 cm across; sepals 6–10 mm long, triangular to elliptical, apex caudate or acuminate; petals white, elliptical to narrowly obovate; **anthesis** late May to late June; insect-pollinated. **Fruit** an aggregate of black drupelets, globose or short-cylindrical, 10–15 mm across; maturing late July to late August; animal-dispersed. (*steelei*: named for American botanist Edward S. Steele, 1850–1942)

Identification

Rubus steelei is a small dewberry, almost delicate in comparison to other Minnesota dewberries. But like the others, the canes lie prostrate or trail along the ground, sometimes reaching a length of almost 6 ft (1.8 m), and in August their tips take root. The inflorescence is relatively sparse, usually with only 2 to 4 flowers. The leaves are somewhat unusual in that they typically have only 3 leaflets, and on average the leaflets are smaller than those of related species, usually just 2–3 inches (5–8 cm) in length. The leaves and growth form are most similar to *R. multifer*, which differs most obviously by having 5 leaflets instead of 3.

Note: Specimens collected from southern and central Minnesota are a very close match for specimens from other parts of the country, but those collected in northern Minnesota are subtly different and may represent a distinct genetic race.

Natural History

Rubus steelei is rather unusual among the dewberries in that it occupies a geographic area extending from northern Minnesota south to Texas; an impressive range of latitudes. Not surprisingly, habitats vary somewhat with latitude, but in Minnesota they seem to have some things in common, such as well-drained sandy or rocky soil, partial shade, and a forest setting with oaks (*Quercus* spp.), pines (*Pinus* spp.), or trembling aspen (*Populus tremuloides*). Actually, forest interiors may be too shady for *R. steelei* unless gaps in the canopy allow at least intermittent sunlight to reach the forest floor. Other than canopy gaps, favorable conditions are sometimes found in savannas and in brushy transition zones along woodland margins, lakeshores, and outcrops of igneous bedrock.

Although the habitat types are varied and seemingly common, *R. steelei* itself appears to be uncommon, and populations often consist of only a few individuals. This could also be an artifact of cursory surveys and a lack of resolve by botanists to seek out hard-to-identify plants. Remember, this is a small, inconspicuous shrub, easily hidden among herbaceous vegetation and perhaps overlooked more often than not.

Each inflorescence has just 1–5 flowers—June 2.

Primocane leaves have only 3 leaflets, each just 2–3" (5–8 cm) long.

Fruits are about 1/2" (10–15 mm) across—July 29.

Rubus stipulatus Bailey

A species of bristle-berry

Low to midsize **shrubs**, with biennial **canes** to 1.5 m long, arching to nearly prostrate; clonal by root suckering, rarely, if ever, tip-rooting. Canes glabrous; **prickles** aciculate, usually sparse, 1.5–7 per cm of cane, straight or declined, very fine and often weak, 1–3 mm long. Primocane **leaves** palmately compound with 5 or occasionally 3 leaflets; central **leaflet** elliptical, 6–11 cm long, 4–7 cm wide, base rounded or tapered and ultimately blunt, apex short-acuminate, margins irregularly serrate or double-serrate, upper surface glabrous except for scattered hairs along margin, lower surface usually with at least some hairs on main veins. **Petioles** glabrous or nearly so, prickles few, weak; stipules lanceolate, conspicuously large, 2–3.5 cm long, often notched on margin. **Inflorescence** a raceme or an open corymb, with 5–19 (35) flowers; bracts often prominent and resembling the stipules; pedicels and peduncle with short, dense, nonglandular hairs and longer, sparser, gland-tipped hairs, also small scattered prickles. **Flowers** bisexual, 5-merous, 2–3 cm across; sepals triangular to triangular-ovate, about 6 mm long, apex apiculate or acuminate, densely hairy and sparsely glandular; petals white, elliptical to obovate; **anthesis** mid-June to early July; insect-pollinated. **Fruit** an aggregate of black drupelets, globose, 8–14 mm across; maturing early to late August; animal-dispersed. (*stipulatus*: with prominent stipules)

Identification

Normal canes of *R. stipulatus* tend to be about 3 ft (1 m) long and generally arch so that the upper portion is parallel to the ground at about knee height. The canes may also appear to lie passively on surrounding vegetation, but they do not trail along the ground or root at the tips. The primocane leaves normally have 5 leaflets and are smooth to the touch, and the inflorescence has glandular hairs. However, the real defining feature of *R. stipulatus* is the very large stipules that are often notched on the margin. *Note:* Davis, Fuller, and Davis (1982) treat *R. stipulatus* as a synonym of *R. dissensus*, but a number of characters, including the large notched stipules, seem to distinguish this species.

Natural History

Rubus stipulatus appears to be one of the rarer species of bristle-berry in Minnesota. It is rare not only in Minnesota but throughout its range, which encompasses only small parts of Minnesota, Wisconsin, and formerly Iowa (Widrlechner 1998). Prior to settlement, the portion of Minnesota where *R. stipulatus* now occurs was occupied by an oak savanna ecosystem. It was essentially a level sandplain with scattered oaks (*Quercus macrocarpa* and *Q. ellipsoidalis*) and perhaps groves of trembling aspen (*Populus tremuloides*) within a matrix of prairie and shallow groundwater sustained wetlands.

These wetlands, the habitat usually associated with *R. stipulatus*, are open, sunny places dominated by fine-leaved sedges and rushes. The rooting zone is usually moist to wet sand or a thin layer of sedge-derived peat over sand. Conditions are typically weakly acidic and nutrient poor. Aside from being bristle-berry havens, these habitats support a highly diverse community of specialized plants, including a disproportionate number of regionally rare species.

Since settlement, the original savanna ecosystem has been largely supplanted by agricultural fields and more recently by suburban developments. Wetlands have survived only to the extent that they could not be drained or filled and were able to resist the invasion of nonnative species, particularly reed canary grass (*Phalaris arundinacea*).

Note the prominent bracts in the inflorescence—June 24.

Primocanes reach nearly 5' (1.5 m) in length and arch low.

Fruits ripen black in August.

Large, notched stipules give this bristle-berry its name.

Rubus superioris Bailey

A species of bristle-berry

Midsize **shrubs**, with biennial **canes** to 1.3 m long, semierect or arching; clonal by root suckering, not known to tip-root. Canes glabrous; **prickles** aciculate, 3–6 per cm of cane, straight or declined, fairly strong, 2.5–4 mm long. Primocane **leaves** palmately compound with 5 or sometimes 3 leaflets; central **leaflet** elliptical to ovate, 7.5–11 cm long, 4.4–7.5 cm wide, l/w 1.46–1.58, base rounded or subcordate, apex acuminate to long-acuminate, margins serrate or double-serrate, upper surface nearly glabrous, lower surface sparsely hairy. **Petioles** with aciculate prickles, glandless; stipules linear-lanceolate, 11–15 mm long. **Inflorescence** a short and somewhat condensed raceme with 3–12 flowers; pedicels and peduncle with a few stiff bristles and with both nonglandular hairs and gland-tipped hairs, but neither abundant. **Flowers** bisexual, 5-merous, 2–3.5 cm across; sepals 6–10 mm long, glandular, narrowly triangular, apex acuminate or caudate; petals white, elliptical to short-oblong or obovate; **anthesis** late June to mid-July; insect-pollinated. **Fruit** an aggregate of black drupelets, ± globose, 9–15 mm across; maturing early August to early September; animal-dispersed. (*superioris*: in reference to Lake Superior, near where it was first found)

Identification

The canes of *Rubus superioris* can reach 4 ft (1.3 m) in length, although it seems the upper half is often winter-killed. Like the other bristle-berries, they generally grow at an ascending angle, or they may arch at about knee height, but they do not normally lie prostrate or trail along the ground, and they do not tip-root. No single character separates *R. superioris* from the 11 other species of bristle-berries found in Minnesota, but look for the following combination of characters: gland-tipped hairs on the inflorescence but not on the canes, the lower leaf surface smooth rather than velvety, and the largest stipules well under 2 cm in length.

Natural History

Surveys have discovered scattered populations of *R. superioris* across much of northern Minnesota, generally in landscapes dominated by early or midsuccessional forests of trembling aspen (*Populus tremuloides*), paper birch (*Betula papyrifera*), or any

of the native pines (*Pinus* spp.). Most populations seem to be rather small and localized, usually in grassy meadows or forest openings, typically in full sunlight or partial shade. Soils are most often sandy or rocky and usually dry but occasionally moist. In a few cases it has been found growing in thin, coarse-textured soil over granite bedrock. Habitats like these do not seem in short supply, especially in the northern half of the state, and yet *R. superioris* appears to be rather uncommon.

Among the bristle-berries, *R. superioris* is the most northerly in distribution, perhaps indicating some special adaptation to harsh environmental conditions. In general, it is the canes, not the roots, that are most vulnerable to severe winters. Any portion of the cane exposed to the cold, dry air above the snow will likely be damaged. Buds on the portion of the cane that is below the snow line will usually survive and in spring may grow with increased vigor as if to compensate for the damage. Although nearly all of the blackberries risk a certain amount of dieback in severe winters, the bristle-berries as a group seem to suffer the most.

Glandular racemes at peak on June 31—Lake County.

Primocane leaves typically have 5 smooth leaflets.

On August 21 these fruits were ripe or nearly so.

Rubus uniformis Bailey

A species of bristle-berry

Low or midsize **shrubs**, with biennial **canes** to 1.5 m long, initially erect but soon arching or becoming nearly prostrate; clonal by root suckering, not normally tip-rooting. Canes glabrous; **prickles** aciculate, 8–30 per cm of cane, straight or declined, weak, 1.5–3 mm long. Primocane **leaves** palmately compound with 3 leaflets, the lateral leaflets often lobed; central **leaflet** elliptical to elliptical-obovate, 6.5–9.5 cm long, 3.5–6 cm wide, base tapered or rounded, apex acuminate to short-acuminate, margins serrate, upper surface glabrous or with a few scattered hairs near margin, lower surface moderately to sparsely hairy. **Petioles** with aciculate prickles and moderately abundant nonglandular hairs, lacking gland-tipped hairs; stipules linear to lanceolate, 10–18 mm long. **Inflorescence** a condensed corymb with 3–11 flowers, occasionally branching; pedicels short, often less than 1 cm long, gland-tipped hairs lacking, non–gland-tipped hairs dense, prickles occasional. **Flowers** bisexual, 5-merous, 2–3 cm across; sepals 5–7 mm long, triangular, apex caudate or apiculate, densely hairy; petals white, elliptical to obovate; **anthesis** mid-June to mid-July; insect-pollinated. **Fruit** an aggregate of black drupelets, ± globose, 8–15 mm across; maturing early August to early September; animal-dispersed. (*uniformis*: not varying)

Identification

The canes of *Rubus uniformis* are often rather short and weak, usually only 20–40 inches (50–100 cm) long, and they are always bristly, sometimes very bristly. These characters immediately identify it as one of the bristle-berries (1 among 12). Dealing with the bristle-berries can be frustrating, but this one has two important and conspicuous features. The primocane leaves, even the late-season leaves, consistently have only 3 leaflets, and the inflorescence is unusually small and compact (and nonglandular).

Natural History

Rubus uniformis is fairly common in east-central Minnesota, especially on the Anoka Sandplain, at least where remnant native habitats still persist. It seems to be a consistent component of shallow, sedge-dominated wetlands or wetland margins, typically in moist sand or thin peat over sand. These habitats are usually dominated by fine-leaved sedges and grasses, such as wiregrass (*Carex lasiocarpa*) and Canada bluejoint (*Calamagrostis canadensis*), and have a diverse assemblage of forbs. It may also be found in upland prairielike settings and in grassy forest openings, especially where the water table is near the surface.

Rubus uniformis is small enough to be partially shaded by tall grasses and broad-leaved herbaceous plants, which does not seem to hinder it. The denser shade of overhanging shrubs or trees is a different matter and is usually avoided. Yet, even under ideal conditions *R. uniformis* is not an aggressive or a dominant plant; rhizomatous colonies can sometimes measure 30–40 ft (9–12 m) across and still be hard to detect.

The habitats of *R. uniformis* often abound with highbush blackberries, dewberries, and bristle-berries. Species such as *R. allegheniensis*, *R. recurvans*, *R. fulleri*, *R. multifer*, *R. semisetosus*, and several others typically occur together and form complex and intricate communities. This is especially true where habitats show even a slight range of topographic relief resulting in subtle moisture gradients.

Small, compact clusters of flowers is characteristic—June 24.

Fruits can be hidden by tall grass—August 7.

Most bristle-berries have 5 leaflets, but Rubus uniformis *has only 3.*

Rubus vermontanus Blanchard

A species of bristle-berry
[*R. unanimus* Bailey; *R. malus* Bailey; *R. deaneanus* Bailey; *R. singulus* Bailey]

Midsize **shrubs**, with biennial **canes** to 1.1 m long, arching or low-arching; clonal by root suckering, not known to tip-root. Canes glabrous; **prickles** aciculate, often moderately abundant, 5–20 per cm of cane, declined, 2–4 mm long, not strong enough to tear skin. Primocane **leaves** palmately compound with 5 or 3 leaflets, if 3 the lateral pair often shallowly lobed; central **leaflet** elliptical or sometimes obovate or elliptical-obovate, 7.5–8 cm long, 3–4.5 cm wide, l/w 1.8–2.4, base rounded or tapered, apex acuminate, margins sharply serrate, upper surface ± glabrous, lower surface nearly glabrous, strongly veined. **Petioles** lacking hairs and glands, armed with fine aciculate prickles; stipules linear, 9–14 mm long. **Inflorescence** a relatively compact raceme, with 5–10 flowers; pedicels and peduncle with scattered, nonglandular hairs and occasionally gland-tipped hairs, weakly armed with aciculate prickles. **Flowers** bisexual, 5-merous, 2–3 cm across; sepals 5–6 mm long, narrowly triangular to narrowly ovate, hairy and with a few prickles, apiculate to acuminate; petals white, elliptical or somewhat obovate; **anthesis** late June to late July; insect-pollinated. **Fruit** an aggregate of black drupelets, spherical to somewhat conical, 8–13 mm across; maturing early August to early September; animal-dispersed. (*vermontanus*: of Vermont; the type locality in Windham County, Vermont)

Identification

The canes of *R. vermontanus* are bristly and usually get about 3 ft (1 m) long. They invariably arch, sometimes low to the ground, but they do not tip-root. These are essential characters seen in most of the bristle-berries. But the primocane leaflets of *R. vermontanus* are noticeably narrow in comparison to the other bristle-berries; even the largest are usually less than 1 3/4 in (4.5 cm) wide and are smooth to the touch. Also, the shape is elliptical or even obovate in outline. These leaf characters are easily seen in comparison with other bristle-berries and will quickly pare down the field of candidates.

Natural History

Although not common in Minnesota, *R. vermontanus* can be found occasionally in appropriate habitat, which seems to be remnants or facsimiles of savannas.

In this part of the world, a savanna is an ecosystem with scattered groves of oak (*Quercus macrocarpa* or *Q. ellipsoidalis*), trembling aspen (*Populus tremuloides*), or jack pine (*Pinus banksiana*) set in a matrix of prairie and shallow wetlands. The prairie portions usually have dry, sandy soil and are dominated by native grasses, such as big bluestem (*Andropogon gerardii*) and porcupine grass (*Hesperostipa spartea*). The wetlands may have a thin layer of peat over sand and are typically dominated by fine-leaved sedges, such as woolly sedge (*Carex pellita*), or grasses, such as Canada bluejoint (*Calamagrostis canadensis*), and maybe with scattered willow (*Salix* spp.) shrubs. This is a dynamic system kept functioning by periodic wildfires. In this setting, *R. vermontanus* occurs in both the shallow wetlands and in the upland prairies but always in sunlight.

True savannas are very rare these days; most were unceremoniously cleared for agriculture as soon as the settlers ran out of more desirable land. Those that escaped the plow were often deprived of fire and grew into dense woodlands, losing the prairie component and sometimes the wetlands as well. When these woodlands are intensively grazed by cattle, the trees start to die from soil compaction and are replaced by domestic pasture grasses. For a time this may create a visual approximation of a savanna (i.e., a grassland with scattered trees). But it would be a mistake to assume that this in any way re-creates a true savanna environment.

The inflorescence is a compact raceme with 5–10 flowers—July 2.

Fruits will ripen over a 2–3 week period in August.

Primocane leaflets are characteristically narrow and smooth; canes are bristly.

Rubus wheeleri Bailey

A species of bristle-berry
[*R. semisetosus* Blanch. var. *wheeleri* Bailey]

Midsize **shrubs**, with biennial **canes** to 1+ m long, erect to arching; clonal by root suckering, rarely if ever tip-rooting. Canes glabrous; **prickles** aciculate, often sparse and weak, 2.5–5 per cm of cane, straight or declined, 3–5 mm long. Primocane **leaves** palmately compound with 5 or rarely 3 leaflets; central **leaflet** elliptical to obovate, 7–10 cm long, 4.5–7 cm wide, base tapered to rounded or subcordate, apex short-acuminate, often abruptly so, margins serrate, upper surface nearly glabrous, lower surface thinly hairy on veins, smooth to the touch. **Petioles** with sparse, nonglandular hairs and usually a few weak prickles. **Inflorescence** a corymb or cyme, or sometimes approaching a broad, open raceme; with 4–12 flowers; pedicels and peduncle usually with stiff bristles or weak, aciculate prickles, thinly hairy and glandless or with a few gland-tipped hairs just below the calyx. **Flowers** bisexual, 5-merous, 2.3–3.8 cm across; sepals usually with gland-tipped hairs; petals white, elliptical to ovate or obovate; **anthesis** mid- to late June; insect-pollinated. **Fruit** an aggregate of black drupelets, ± globose 8–15 mm in diameter; maturing mid-August to early September; animal-dispersed. (*wheeleri*: named for Bailey's mentor, Charles F. Wheeler)

Identification

Two important characters separate *Rubus wheeleri* from the 11 other bristle-berries that occur in Minnesota. First, the pedicels normally lack gland-tipped hairs (determined with a hand lens). There may be a few at the very top of the pedicels, but that does not rule out *R. wheeleri*. This character alone puts it in a small group of bristle-berries that includes *R. uniformis*, *R. missouricus*, and *R. wisconsinensis*. Next, look closely at the shape of the central leaflet of a primocane leaf; the body is often elliptical in outline or sometimes even obovate, meaning that it is widest above the middle, and it has a short, abrupt tip.

Natural History

The geographic range of *Rubus wheeleri* appears to fall within the forested region of the state where the dominant trees are usually oaks (*Quercus* spp.), trembling aspen (*Populus tremuloides*), or occasionally jack pine (*Pinus banksiana*). Although its

habitat requirements are poorly known, *R. wheeleri* seems to prefer open, grassy or sedgy habitats, such as forest clearings and edges, meadows, and ecotones between wetlands and uplands. Soil conditions seem to be sandy or peaty and range from dry to moist.

Currently, *Rubus wheeleri* is known in Minnesota only from single sites in Anoka, Benton, Todd, and Wadena counties. There are also herbarium specimens collected in the 1950s from a site in St. Louis County that resemble *R. wheeleri* and may in fact be this species, but there is some doubt that cannot be settled without relocating the population.

The easiest conclusion to be drawn is that *R. wheeleri* is quite rare in Minnesota. While this may be true, there is still a lot of field work to be done. Large areas of apparently suitable habitat remain to be searched, and areas searched once often need to be searched a second time. Although this can be said for many of the bristle-berries and dewberries, the rarer ones like *R. wheeleri* need special attention. They usually occur intermixed with populations of more common species and will be overlooked unless special efforts are made to find them.

This type of inflorescence is called a corymb—June 20.

Canes are usually less than 3' (1 m) long.

Primocane leaves have 5 broad leaflets, each with an abrupt tip.

Fruits are beginning to ripen on August 20—Benton County.

Rubus wisconsinensis Bailey

A species of bristle-berry

[*R. minnesotanus* Bailey; *R. latifolius* Bailey; *R. setospinosus* Bailey]

Midsize **shrubs**, with biennial **canes** to 1.9 m long, initially erect, but eventually arching, mounding, or becoming prostrate; clonal by root suckering and occasionally by tip-rooting. Canes glabrous; **prickles** aciculate or nearly broad-based, varying in strength but often strong enough to tear skin, 4–9 per cm of cane, declined or decurved, 2.5–4 mm long. Primocane **leaves** palmately compound with 5 or occasionally 3 leaflets; central **leaflet** ovate to broadly elliptical or suborbicular, 7–11 cm long, 5–9 cm wide, base rounded to cordate, apex acuminate, margins sharply and somewhat irregularly serrate, upper surface nearly glabrous, lower surface nearly glabrous to moderately hairy. **Petioles** glabrous or with sparse, nonglandular hairs only, and with strongly curved prickles; stipules lanceolate to linear-lanceolate, 13–20 mm long. **Inflorescence** usually a condensed corymb with 2–12 flowers; pedicels and peduncle with aciculate prickles and moderately abundant nonglandular hairs. **Flowers** bisexual, 5-merous, 2.5–4.5 cm across; sepals 6–8(12) mm long, ovate-elliptical, apex apiculate, acuminate or caudate; petals white, elliptical or somewhat ovate or obovate; **anthesis** early June to early July; insect-pollinated. **Fruit** an aggregate of black drupelets, globose or short-cylindrical, 10–17 mm wide, 10–20 mm long; maturing late July to late August; animal-dispersed. (*wisconsinensis*: of Wisconsin, the type locality in Waushara County, Wisconsin)

Identification

The canes of *R. wisconsinensis* are typically 3 to 4 ft (1 to 1.2 m) long, but occasionally reach 6 ft (1.9 m). They usually arch over, forming a loop or "mound" at about knee or waist height, with the far portion lying passively on surrounding vegetation or the soil surface. The canes do not usually tip-root, although that phenomenon has been seen in 3 of 14 populations studied in Minnesota. Often the canes are densely armed with long, sharp prickles that fall somewhere between aciculate (needle shaped) and broad-based. They vary in strength but are usually strong enough to tear skin, making the canes very difficult to handle. Leaflets of the primocane leaves tend to be proportionately broad, almost circular in outline, and coarsely serrate.

Note: The most vigorous canes of *R. wisconsinensis* can have prickles similar in strength to those of the highbush blackberries in section *Arguti*, which may have led Gleason and Cronquist (1991) to place *R. wisconsinensis* in synonymy with *R. pensilvanicus* Poiret. But members of section *Arguti* have leaves that are velvety beneath, and they generally flower earlier than does *R. wisconsinensis* (Widrlechner 1998).

Natural History

Rubus wisconsinensis occurs at scattered locations in eastern and central Minnesota but most commonly on the level or gently rolling terrain of the Anoka Sandplain just north of the Twin Cities. It is typically associated with remnants of the presettlement oak-aspen (*Quercus* spp.-*Populus tremuloides*) ecosystem. When intact and full-functioning, this was a fire-maintained system encompassing a mixture of savannas, woodlands, brushlands, and shallow wetlands.

Within this habitat mosaic, *Rubus wisconsinensis* seems rather mobile and eclectic in choice of habitats. It is usually found in brushy meadows or at the margins of woodlands or wetlands where it receives full sunlight. But it is also found in woodland openings and under a thin forest canopy where the sunlight is only intermittent. Soils are generally acidic and range from sandy to loamy or sometimes peaty, and from moist to dryish.

Flowers appear between early June and early July.

These fruits were still red on August 5, and will turn black by September—Ramsey County.

Canes commonly arch over to form a "mound."

Prickles are thin, but often strong enough to tear skin.

Salix, the willows

Salicaceae: Willow family

The willows comprise a large genus with about 450 species of deciduous trees and shrubs. They occur worldwide but primarily in north temperate, boreal, and arctic regions of the Northern Hemisphere. There are 103 species in North America (Argus 1997), and 18 species currently known to be native to Minnesota. There are also at least 3 European tree willows that are now naturalized in the state. (*Salix* is the classical Latin name for the willows.)

There is at least one additional native species that may have been overlooked in Minnesota. It is *Salix pseudomyrsinites* Anderss., a tall shrub common in upland habitats north of Minnesota. It has not yet been found here, but based on its geographical distribution in North America, it could be here (Argus, personal communication).

One species deliberately left out of this treatment is white willow (*Salix alba*). White willow is a European tree that was introduced into North America during the colonial era. It is reported to be naturalized across much of the continent (Argus 1986), including Minnesota (Ownbey and Morley 1991). But after a careful examination of the relevant herbarium specimens and a statewide field survey, no evidence could be found that it is naturalized in Minnesota. It is not certain it was ever even planted here. Clearly, the "white willow" that was brought west with the early homesteaders and was commonly used for windbreaks on Minnesota prairies by the late nineteenth century (Records 1913) was mostly, if not entirely, a hybrid between true white willow and crack willow (*S. fragilis*) (Upham 1884). The hybrid, named whitecrack willow (*S. ×rubens*), originated in Europe and has been propagated for centuries by cuttings (Meikle 1984).

Even outside of cultivation, polyploidy is common in willows, which suggests that naturally occurring hybridization is important in willow evolution. And there is evidence that first-generation (F1) hybrid willows may be relatively common in nature but not always morphologically discernable (Hardig et al. 2000). Individual specimens that do not seem to fit any species just right or seem intermediate between two species may be hybrids, or simply extreme expressions of the natural variability of an otherwise stable species, or possibly an individual influenced by unusual environmental conditions.

The treatment of the willows presented here follows closely the taxonomic concept of George Argus (1997). Dr. Argus guided this study of willows and generously examined all of the willow specimens collected during the course of this study (numbering more than 700), which form the basis of this treatment.

Key to Female (Pistillate) Specimens of Salix in Minnesota

1. Capsules hairy.
    2. Catkins appearing before the leaves appear (precocious), leaves < half-grown when seeds are released; catkins sessile or borne at the tips of short branchlets up to 1 cm long.
        3. Stipes of mature capsules > 1 mm long; styles 0.1–1 mm long (usually 0.6 mm or less).
            4. Mature capsules 2.5–4 mm long, essentially beakless .... *S. sericea**
            4. Mature capsules 4–10 mm long, tapered to a long distinct beak.
                5. Catkins 3–8 cm long; floral bracts 1.5–2.5 mm long; 2nd-year branchlets usually glabrous or at least glabrous in patches; stipes 2–3 mm long .... *S. discolor*
                5. Catkins 1–3.5 cm long; floral bracts 0.8–2 mm long; 2nd-year branchlets evenly woolly; stipes 1–2.5 mm long.
                    6. Catkins usually > 2 cm long; leaves with stipules (the leaf scars on the stem will have scars of stipules at each end) .... *S. humilis* var. *humilis*
                    6. Catkins usually < 2 cm long; leaves lacking stipules .... *S. humilis* var. *tristis*
        3. Stipes of mature capsules ≤ 1 mm long; styles 0.6–1.8 mm long.
            7. The underside of leaves (if present) densely and evenly covered with long, white, silky hairs, the hairs persistent on mature leaves; stipes 0.6–1 mm long; twigs ± brittle at base .... *S. pellita*
            7. The underside of leaves (if present) glabrous or sparsely covered with straight or wavy, white or reddish hairs, the hairs (if any) falling off before the leaves are half-grown; stipes 0.2–1 mm long (usually < 0.6 mm); twigs flexible at base .... *S. planifolia*
    2. Catkins appearing at the same time as the leaves (coetaneous), leaves fully developed when seeds are released; catkins sessile or borne at the tips of flowering branchlets up to 15 cm long.
        8. Catkins borne at the ends of flowering branchlets 2–15 cm long (usually > 4 cm); floral bracts usually shed before the capsules reach maturity or soon after; leaf blades narrowly linear, 8–25 times longer than wide, with regularly spaced conspicuous serrations on margins .... *S. interior*
        8. Catkins sessile or borne on flowering branchlets up to 2.8 cm long; floral bracts persistent; leaf blades 2–12 times longer than wide, margins serrate, serrulate, crenate or entire.
            9. Catkins borne at the ends of flowering branchlets 1–2.8 cm long; leaf margins serrulate .... *S. maccalliana*
            9. Catkins sessile or borne on flowering branchlets < 1.5 cm long; leaf margins sometimes serrate but more often entire or with inrolled margins.
                10. Styles 0–0.5 mm long; stipes 1.5–5 mm long.
                    11. Leaf blades 1.8–3.3 times as long as wide (l/w = 1.8–3.3); mature catkins 2.5–6 cm long (usually > 3); floral bracts yellowish or tan .... *S. bebbiana*
                    11. Leaf blades at least 4 times as long as wide (l/w ≥ 4); mature catkins 1–3 cm long; floral bracts brown .... *S. petiolaris*
                10. Styles 0.6–1.8 mm long; stipes ≤ 1.5 mm long.

12. Floral bracts brown to pale yellowish brown; lower surface of leaves with a dense woolly covering of long, tangled, white hairs (occasionally glabrous); branchlets not glaucous; a small shrub of swamps and fens (peat soil), < 1.5 m tall .... *S. candida*

12. Floral bracts dark brown to blackish; lower surface of leaves covered with relatively long, straight, silky hairs 0.5–1 mm long that lie ± flat and in one direction; branchlets often glaucous (with a bluish white, waxy coating) in small patches; a tall shrub of sand or gravel shores and banks (mineral soil), > 1.5 m tall .... *S. pellita*

1. Capsules glabrous.

13. Leaf blades narrowly linear (sides parallel), 8–25 times longer than wide (l/w = 8–25), 16–36 times longer than the petiole (leaves often appearing sessile); catkins borne at the ends of leafy branchlets that are usually > 4.5 cm long (range: 2–15 cm) .... *S. interior*

13. Leaf blades not narrowly linear (sides curving or tapering), 1.2–11 times longer than wide (l/w = 1.2–11), < 16 times longer than the petiole; catkins sessile or borne at the ends of branchlets that are ≤ 5 cm long.

14. Stipes mostly > 2 mm long; leaf tips acute to somewhat rounded; leaf blades 1.2–4.3 times as long as wide.

15. Catkins 1.3–3 cm long; petioles of fully developed leaves 2–8 mm long; leaf margins entire; leaves glabrous or occasionally young unfolding leaves hairy .... *S. pedicellaris*

15. Catkins 3–9 cm long; petioles of fully developed leaves 6–20 mm long; leaf margins serrulate; leaves hairy at least on the petiole or lower portion of midrib.

16. Catkins sessile or borne at the ends of flowering branchlets ≤ 0.5 cm long, catkins appearing before the leaves (precocious); styles 0.6–1.8 mm long; floral bracts dark brown to blackish .... *S. pseudomonticola*

16. Catkins borne at the ends of flowering branchlets 0.5–3 cm long, catkins appearing with the leaves (coetaneous); styles 0.1–0.5 mm long; floral bracts tan .... *S. pyrifolia*

14. Stipes mostly < 2 mm long; leaf tips acute to acuminate; leaf blades 2–11 times as long as wide.

17. Mature capsules 7–11 mm long (measured along the curve if the capsule has split open and the valves are reflexed); seeds released in July or later .... *S. serissima*

17. Mature capsules 3–7 mm long; seeds usually released before July.

18. Catkins sessile or borne at the ends of flowering branchlets that are ≤ 1 cm long.

19. Styles 0.6–1.8 mm long; the larger leaf blades 1.4–2.8 times as long as wide (l/w = 1.4–2.8) .... *S. pseudomonticola*

19. Styles 0.2–0.6 mm long; the larger leaf blades 2.5–6 times as long as wide (l/w = 2.5–6) .... *S. eriocephala*

18. Catkins borne at the ends of flowering branchlets that are usually > 1 cm long.

20. Leaves glabrous at all stages of development; leaf blades usually < 3 times as long as wide (l/w < 3); cultivated trees, rarely escaped .... *S. pentandra*

20. Leaves hairy to some extent (carefully examine leaves that are just unfolding and the petioles of older leaves); leaf blades often > 3 times as long as wide (l/w > 3); common native or nonnative trees or shrubs.

21. Mature capsules 5–7 mm long; leaf blades 2.3–4.8 times as long as wide (l/w = 2.3–4.8); bud scales orange, usually persistent at base of branchlet; shrubs or small trees no more than 6 m tall .... *S. lucida*

21. Mature capsules 3–6 mm long; leaf blades 3–11 times as long as wide (l/w = 3–11); bud scales yellowish or brownish, not persistent; large or midsize trees often 10+ m tall.

22. Styles 0.3–0.8 mm long; leaves densely covered with long, straight, silky hairs when just unfolding (*S.* ×*rubens*), or occasionally glabrous (*S. fragilis*); bud scales fused.
  23. Stipes 0.5–1.5 mm long, 2–3 times as long as the subtending nectary; immature leaf blades usually glabrous, or sparsely hairy as they are just unfolding .... *S. fragilis*
  23. Stipes 0.5–0.8 mm long, 1.5–2 times as long as the subtending nectary; immature leaf blades hairy even after they unfold, but generally becoming glabrous by the time they reach full size .... *S.* ×*rubens*
22. Styles 0.1–0.4 mm long; unfolding leaves glabrous, or with patches of relatively short, kinky hairs; bud scales free with overlapping margins.
  24. Stipes 1.5–2.5 mm long; the larger leaves 3–6 times as long as wide; leaves glaucous beneath (made lighter in color by a cloudy, bluish white, waxy coating) .... *S. amygdaloides*
  24. Stipes 0.5–1.5 mm long; the larger leaves 5–11 times as long as wide; leaves not glaucous beneath (appearing the same color on both the upper and lower surfaces) .... *S. nigra*

Key to Male (Staminate) Specimens of Salix *in Minnesota*

1. Stamens 3 or more per flower.
  2. Catkins slender, 4.5–7.5 times as long as wide (l/w = 4.5–7.5), and loosely flowered with 12–30 flowers per cm; flowers tufted and more or less whorled along the rachis; medium-size trees.
    3. Leaf blades at anthesis 5–7 times as long as wide (l/w = 5–7), not glaucous beneath (appearing to be the same color on both upper and lower surfaces) .... *S. nigra*
    3. Leaf blades at anthesis 3–5 times as long as wide (l/w = 3–5), glaucous beneath (made lighter in color by a cloudy, bluish white, waxy coating) .... *S. amygdaloides*
  2. Catkins thickish, 2–4.5 times as long as wide (l/w = 2–4.5), and densely flowered with 35–50+ flowers per cm; flowers not appearing whorled or tufted on the rachis; shrubs or trees.
    4. Immature leaves often with scattered hairs when just unfolding, but hairs soon falling off; stipules usually ≥ 1 mm long, even on young leaves; bud scales orange, conspicuous .... *S. lucida*
    4. Immature leaves glabrous; stipules minute or absent; bud scales brownish or yellowish, inconspicuous.
      5. Blades of leaves on flowering branchlets usually > 2.5 times as long as wide (l/w > 2.5), a native shrub with slender stems rarely > 2 m tall .... *S. serissima*
      5. Blades of leaves of flowering branchlets usually < 2.5 times as long as wide (l/w < 2.5), a cultivated tree often 10 meters tall .... *S. pentandra*
1. Stamens 2 per flower.
  6. Catkins appearing before the leaves (precocious).
    7. Catkins 0.5–2 cm long.
      8. Catkins 1–2 cm long; leaves with stipules (the leaf scars on the stem will bear scars of stipules at each end) .... *S. humilis* var. *humilis*
      8. Catkins 0.5–1.1 cm long; leaves lacking stipules .... *S. humilis* var. *tristis*
    7. Catkins 1.5–4 cm long.
      9. Floral bracts 0.8–1.5 mm long; filaments hairy at base; twigs very brittle at base .... *S. sericea**
      9. Floral bracts 1–2.5 mm long; filaments hairy or not; twigs ± flexible at base.

10. Emerging leaves (if present) densely covered with long, straight, silver-colored hairs that persist on mature leaves .... *S. pellita*

10. Emerging leaves (if present) with sparse, often short and kinky hairs that soon fall off.
    11. Catkins subtended by 1 or a few green bracts .... *S. planifolia*
    11. Catkins subtended by 1 or a few yellowish or colorless bracts.
        12. Filaments 2–4 mm long, glabrous .... *S. pseudomonticola*
        12. Filaments 5–9 mm long, often with a few hairs at base .... *S. discolor*

6. Catkins appearing at the same time as the leaves (coetaneous) or after the leaves (serotinous).
    13. Blades of the largest emerging leaves proportionately narrow, ≥ 4 times as long as wide (l/w ≥ 4).
        14. Leaf blades linear, 8–25 times as long as wide, not glaucous on the lower surface (upper and lower surfaces the same color); catkins borne on flowering branchlets 1.5–18 cm long, often branched and bearing secondary catkins .... *S. interior*
        14. Leaf blades 4–11 times as long as wide, glaucous on the lower surface (made lighter in color by a cloudy, bluish white, waxy coating); catkins sessile or borne on branchlets 0.1–1.3 cm long, not branched.
            15. Catkins 3.3–6.5 cm long, borne on flowering branchlets 5–12 mm long; each flower subtended by 2 nectaries; large trees.
                16. Pubescence (if any) restricted to the 1 or 2 leaves at the tip of the vegetative branchlets that are just unfolding, older leaves essentially glabrous .... *S. fragilis*
                16. Pubescence occurring on the 1 or 2 unfolding leaves, but also persisting on the 2 or 3 leaves directly below that are larger but have not yet reached full size .... *S. ×rubens*
            15. Catkins 1–3 (4.5) cm long, sessile or borne on flowering branchlets ≤ 5 mm long; each flower subtended by 1 nectary; small or large shrubs.
                17. The lower surface of the emerging leaves covered with a dense, tangled mat of white, woolly hairs; a small shrub usually ≤ 1.5 m tall .... *S. candida*
                17. The lower surface of emerging leaves glabrous or with relatively long, straight silky hairs that lie ± flat and in one direction; a large shrub often > 1.5 m tall .... *S. petiolaris*
    13. Leaves broader, usually < 4 times as long as wide (l/w < 4).
        18. Margins of leaf blades entire.
            19. Leaves and branchlets ± glabrous; filaments glabrous; a small shrub usually < 1.5 m tall .... *S. pedicellaris*
            19. Leaves and branchlets hairy; filaments hairy near base; a large shrub or small tree > 1.5 m tall .... *S. bebbiana*
        18. Margins of leaf blades distinctly toothed or serrulate (often minutely so).
            20. Leaf blades 1.5–3.2 times as long as wide (l/w = 1.5–3.2), leaf bases rounded or subcordate .... *S. pyrifolia*
            20. Leaf blades 2.5–6 times as long as wide (l/w = 2.5–6), leaf bases tapered.
                21. Catkins slender, 4.5–8 times as long as wide (l/w = 4.5–8); trees with trunks at least 10 cm dbh.
                    22. Pubescence (if any) restricted to the 1 or 2 leaves at the tip of the vegetative branchlets that are just unfolding, older leaves essentially glabrous .... *S. fragilis*
                    22. Pubescence occurring on the 1 or 2 unfolding leaves, but also persisting on the 2 or 3 leaves directly below that are larger but have not yet reached full size .... *S. ×rubens*

21. Catkins stout, 2–4.5 times as long as wide (l/w = 2–4.5); shrubs with stems < 10 cm dbh.
  23. Filaments hairy below the middle; catkins borne on flowering branchlets 3–13 mm long; twigs reddish .... *S. maccalliana*
  23. Filaments glabrous; catkins borne on flowering branchlets 0–5 mm long; twigs usually yellowish or pale brownish, occasionally reddish .... *S. eriocephala*

Key to Nonflowering Specimens of Salix in Minnesota

1. Leaves proportionately slender, the blades usually ≥ 5 times as long as wide (l/w ≥ 5).
  2. Lower surface of mature leaves so densely hairy as to obscure the leaf surface.
    3. Lower surface of leaves covered with a tangled mat of white or gray, woolly hairs; a small shrub usually < 1.5 m tall.
      4. The larger leaf blades 5–10 cm long; petioles 3–10 mm long; stipules present although sometimes as small as 2 mm long; occurring in wet peat soils (swamps, fens, etc.) .... *S. candida*
      4. The larger leaf blades 2.5–5 cm long; petioles 0.5–3 mm long; stipules absent; occurring in dry mineral soils (prairies, pine forests, etc.) .... *S. humilis* var. *tristis*
    3. Lower surface of leaves covered with relatively long, straight, silky hairs that lie ± flat and in one direction; a medium to large shrub usually > 1.5 m tall.
      5. Margins of leaf blades crenulate, or entire and revolute; secondary veins of larger leaves impressed above; branchlets often glaucous (with patches of a bluish white, waxy covering) .... *S. pellita*
      5. Margins of leaf blades serrate or serrulate, not revolute; secondary veins of larger leaves protruding above; branchlets not glaucous .... *S. sericea**
  2. Lower surface of mature leaves glabrous or hairy but not so densely hairy as to obscure the surface of the leaf.
    6. Leaves linear (sides parallel), the blades 8–25 times longer than wide (l/w = 8–25); leaves not glaucous on lower surface (the lower surface the same color as the upper surface) .... *S. interior*
    6. Leaves narrowly ovate, elliptical or lanceolate (sides curving or tapering), the blades 5–11 times longer than wide (l/w = 5–11); leaves glaucous or not (paler on the lower surface, or the same color on both surfaces).
      7. Leaves not glaucous (the upper and lower surfaces the same color); bud scale margins free and overlapping .... *S. nigra*
      7. Leaves glaucous on lower surface (the lower surface a paler color than the upper); bud scale margins fused.
        8. Glands not present at the junction of leaf blade and petiole; common native shrubs.
          9. Stipules prominent and persistent; 2nd-year twigs usually yellowish or pale brown, occasionally reddish .... *S. eriocephala*
          9. Stipules absent, or minute and deciduous early; twigs dark red-brown or red-purple .... *S. petiolaris*
        8. Glands present at the junction of the leaf blade and petiole; nonnative trees.
          10. Hairs (if any) restricted to the 1 or 2 leaves that are just unfolding at the tips of the branchlets, older leaves essentially glabrous; mature leaves glossy on the upper surface, coarsely serrate .... *S. fragilis*

10. Hairs occurring on the 1 or 2 unfolding leaves, but also persisting on the 2 or 3 leaves directly below that have nearly reached full size; mature leaves glossy or dull, finely serrate .... *S. ×rubens*

1. Leaves proportionately broader, usually < 5 times as long as wide (l/w < 5).
12. Mature leaves ± hairy, at least on the upper surface of the petioles.
13. Pubescence consisting of moderate length white or reddish hairs scattered ± uniformly across the lower surface of the leaf blade, although sometimes more dense along the midvein and larger lateral veins, the upper surface occasionally hairy as well; leaf tips obtuse to acute.
14. Leaf blades 2.2–3.3 times longer than wide, 4–8 times longer than the petioles .... *S. bebbiana*
14. Leaf blades 2.5–5+ times longer than wide, 8–13 times longer than the petioles.
15. Margins of leaf blades entire and revolute, or with 1–3 rounded teeth per cm of leaf margin; lower surface of blade covered with short, tangled hairs; twigs flexible and tenacious at base .... *S. humilis*
15. Margins of leaf blades serrate or serrulate, with 4–8 sharp teeth per cm of leaf margin; lower surface of blade covered with long, straight, silky hairs; twigs very brittle at base .... *S. sericea**
13. Pubescence consisting of short white or gray hairs on the upper surface of the petiole, and often extending at least part way up the midvein of the blades, but not occurring uniformly across the leaf blade; leaf tips acute to acuminate.
16. Leaves with prominent glandular dots or lobes where the petiole joins the blade (on upper surface); tips of later leaves (those closest to the ends of the branchlets) long-acuminate to caudate .... *S. lucida*
16. Leaves lacking prominent glands where the petiole joins the blade; tips of leaves acute to acuminate.
17. Stipules small (< 1 mm long) or not apparent; upper surface of leaf blades dark green and glossy; 2nd-year twigs bright red and glossy.
18. Leaf blades 2–4 cm wide at maturity, 1.5–3.2 times as long as wide (l/w = 1.5–3.2), base rounded to cordate, lower surface blue-gray ..... *S. pyrifolia*
18. Leaf blade 0.8–2.5 cm wide at maturity, 2.5–5 times as long as wide (l/w = 2.5–5), base tapered, lower surface green .... *S. maccalliana*
17. Stipules often large and conspicuous (> 1 mm long); upper surface of leaf blades usually dull; 2nd-year twigs yellow to brown or red, dull or occasionally glossy.
19. Leaf margins crenate, with 2–4 teeth per cm (measured near the middle of a well-developed blade) .... *S. discolor*
19. Leaf margins serrate to serrulate, with 5–10 teeth per cm.
20. Leaf blades 3–6 times as long as wide (l/w = 3–6), tips long-acuminate; petiole and midvein of leaves pale yellow or greenish .... *S. eriocephala*
20. Leaf blades 1.5–3 times as long as wide (l/w = 1.5–3), tips acute to abruptly short-acuminate; petiole and midvein of leaves often red .... *S. pseudomonticola*
12. Mature leaves glabrous, or occasionally with a few hairs on the upper surface near the base of the blade or on the midrib.
21. Leaf margins entire.
22. The larger leaf blades 2–6 cm long, 0.6–2 cm wide; tips sometimes acute but more often blunt or slightly rounded; a small shrub usually < 1.5 m tall .... *S. pedicellaris*
22. The larger leaf blades 3.5–8 cm long, 1–2.8 cm wide; tips acute; a large shrub ≤ 3.5 m tall .... *S. planifolia*

21. Leaf margins serrate, serrulate, or crenate.
    23. Leaf tips acuminate (drawn to a narrow point, with concave sides).
        24. Leaves glossy above; glands present at the junction of leaf blade and petiole, these glands at least as prominent as those along the margins of the blade; bud scale margins fused.
            25. Leaf tips long-acuminate (at least those on later leaves); stipules usually present until August, 1–6 mm long, green and leaflike .... *S. lucida*
            25. Leaf tips short-acuminate; stipules often absent or minute, usually ≤ 1 mm long.
                26. Leaf blades < 3 times as long as wide (l/w < 3); a cultivated tree often 10 m tall .... *S. pentandra*
                26. Leaf blades > 3 times as long as wide (l/w > 3); a native shrub not > 3 m tall .... *S. serissima*
        24. Leaves ± dull above; glands not present at the junction of leaf blade and petiole, or if 1 or 2 glands present, they are no more prominent than those along the margin of the blade; bud scale margins free and overlapping .... *S. amygdaloides*
    23. Leaf tips acute (forming a straight-sided angle < 90 degrees).
        27. Leaf margins finely serrulate with 5–10 teeth per cm .... *S. pyrifolia*
        27. Leaf margins essentially entire, crenulate or coarsely serrate with 0–5 teeth per cm.
            28. Leaves tending to be obovate (widest above the middle), upper surface usually dull; 2nd-year twigs often hairy, at least in patches .... *S. discolor*
            28. Leaves elliptical (widest at the middle), upper surface glossy; 2nd-year twigs glabrous .... *S. planifolia*

*A single herbarium specimen of *Salix sericea* (silky willow) was collected in a wetland along the Root River in Forestville State Park (Fillmore County) in 1982 by Michael Tenney (#330B). The specimen (on deposit at MIN) contains only a twig with leaves and was not correctly identified until 1996 when it was examined by George Argus. This is the only verified record of this species in Minnesota at the time of this writing. The author has made repeated attempts to relocate the species at the original collection site and in suitable habitats nearby, but without success. The species is known to be native to adjacent portions of Wisconsin and Iowa, and the author accepts it as a member of Minnesota's native flora. However, there is simply too little information available at this time to present a useful treatment beyond its inclusion in the key.

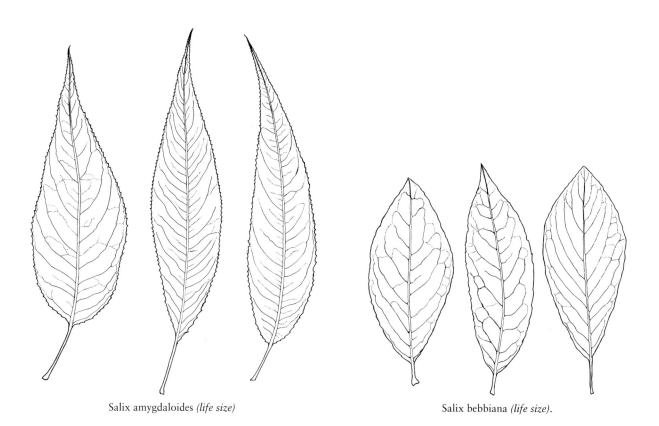

Salix amygdaloides *(life size)*

Salix bebbiana *(life size)*.

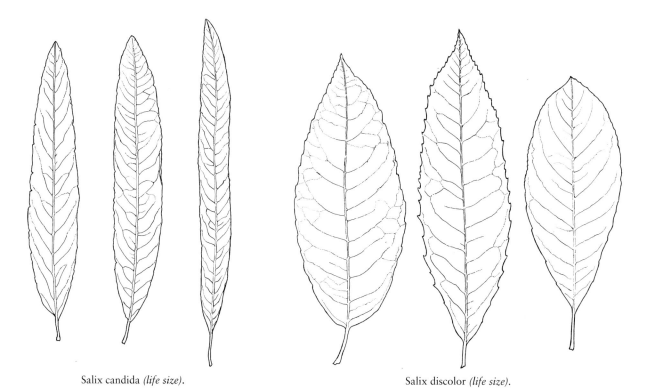

Salix candida *(life size)*.

Salix discolor *(life size)*.

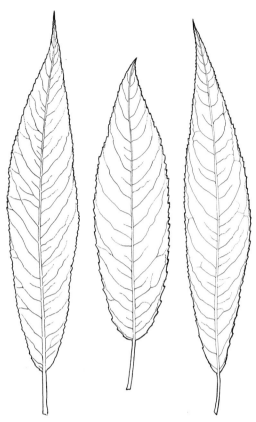

Salix eriocephala *(life size)*.

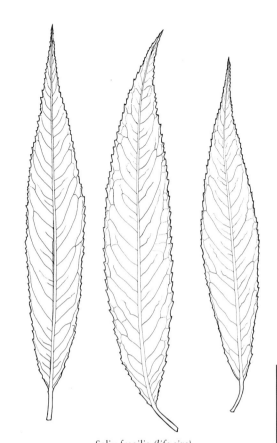

Salix fragilis *(life size)*.

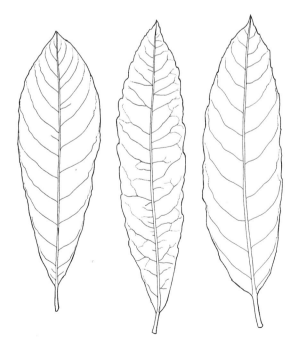

Salix humilis *var.* humilis *(life size)*.

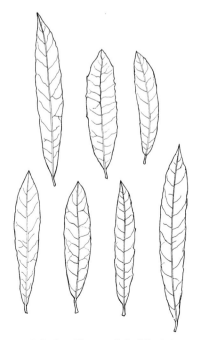

Salix humilis *var.* tristis *(life size)*.

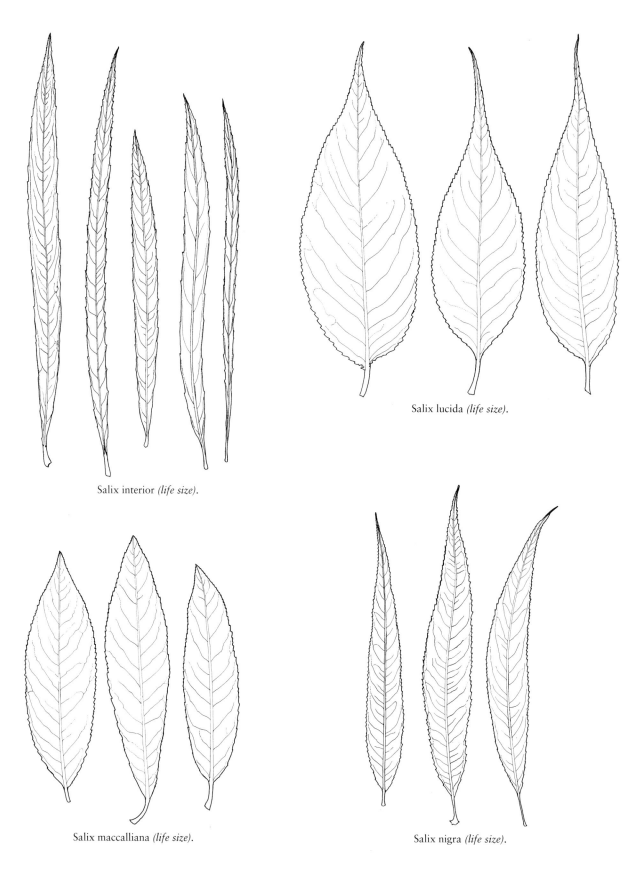

Salix lucida *(life size)*.

Salix interior *(life size)*.

Salix maccalliana *(life size)*.

Salix nigra *(life size)*.

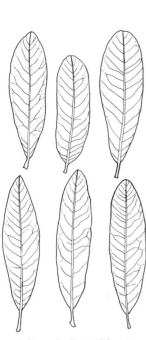

Salix pedicellaris *(life size)*.

Salix pellita *(life size)*.

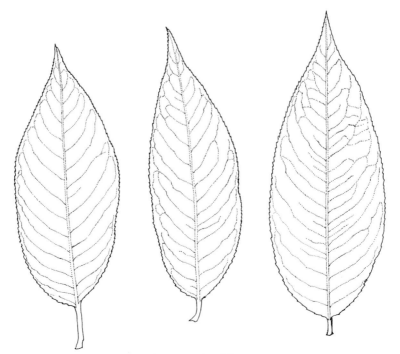

Salix pentandra *(life size)*.

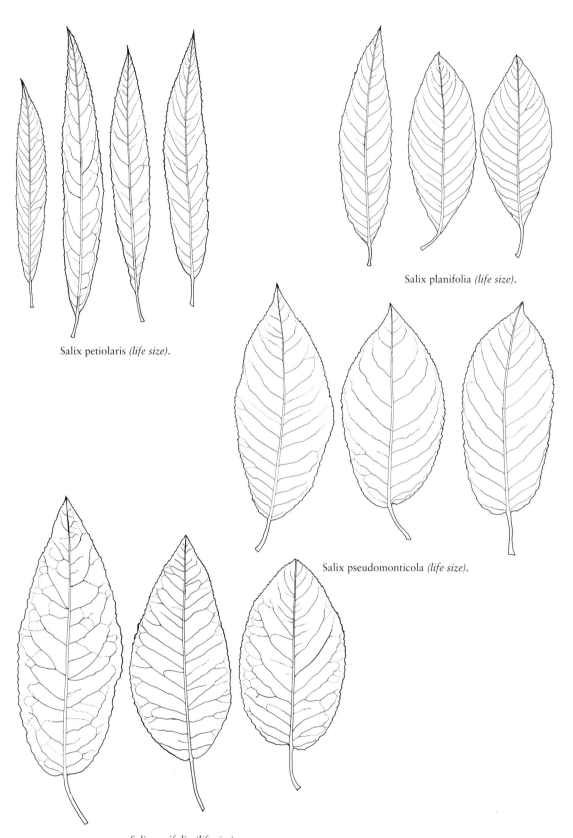

Salix petiolaris *(life size)*.

Salix planifolia *(life size)*.

Salix pseudomonticola *(life size)*.

Salix pyrifolia *(life size)*.

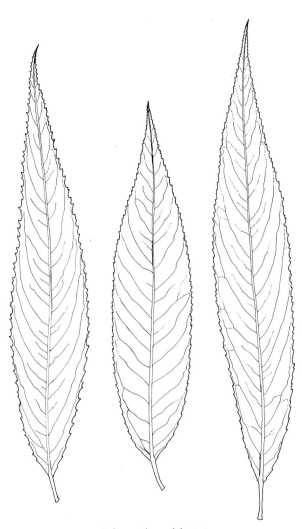

Salix ×rubens *(life size)*.

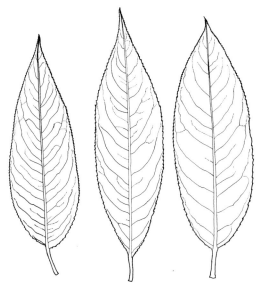

Salix serissima *(life size)*.

Salix amygdaloides Anderss.

Peach-leaved willow

Midsize **trees,** with 1 or a few upright, leaning, or decumbent **trunks,** to 22 m tall and 75 cm dbh. 1st-year **branchlets** greenish or yellowish, glabrous; 2nd-year branchlets brownish, glabrous. **Bark** gray, with deep, broad furrows and narrow, interlacing ridges. **Leaves** simple, alternate, deciduous. **Petioles** 5–15 mm long, glabrous, lacking enlarged glands at summit; stipules none or minute, rarely up to 1 cm long on vigorous shoots. Mature **leaf blades** lanceolate to ovate-lanceolate or narrowly elliptical; the larger ones 6–12 cm long and 1.2–3.3 cm wide, length/width 3–6; apex long-acuminate to caudate; base tapered or somewhat rounded; margins serrulate; upper surface dark green, glabrous; lower surface pale green or pale blue-green (glaucous), glabrous; immature leaf blades reddish or yellowish green, with patches of relatively short, kinky hairs when just unfolding, or occasionally glabrous. **Flowers** borne in unisexual **catkins,** each tree bearing either male catkins or female catkins (dioecious); appearing with the leaves or slightly after. **Male catkins** 3–6 cm long; borne on flowering branchlets 0.8–2 cm long; stamens 3–7, filaments hairy on lower half; bracts as in female catkins but persistent; nectaries 2 or more. **Female catkins** 2.5–9 cm long; borne on flowering branchlets 1–3.5 cm long; mature **capsules** glabrous, 3–5.5 mm long; styles 0.1–0.3 mm long; stipes 1.5–2.5 mm long; bracts pale yellow, 1.5–2.8 mm long, deciduous soon after flowering; nectary 1; **anthesis** early May to mid-June; wind- and insect-pollinated; **seeds** released early June to early July, wind-dispersed. (*amygdaloides*: like *Amygdalus*, the old generic name for the peach tree, which the leaves resemble)

Identification

The native peach-leaved willow is one of five tree willows that grow wild in Minnesota. This does not count any of the "weeping" cultivars that are commonly planted but do not seem to escape. Confusion about the wild trees results from the cryptic presence of whitecrack willow (*S.* ×*rubens*). This is a European hybrid that has been naturalized in Minnesota for perhaps 125 years but gone largely unrecognized. It is almost always misidentified as peach-leaved willow, but a close examination will reveal that when the new leaves of peach-leaved willow are just unfolding, they have thin patches of relatively short, kinky hairs or no hairs at all. The new leaves of whitecrack willow are densely covered with long, white, silky hairs. This difference can be seen from early spring well into summer. With practice, the two species can be told apart from a distance; the leaves of peach-leaved willow are not as shiny or as rigid as those of whitecrack willow; they even tend to droop a bit.

Natural History

Peach-leaved willow is the predominant native tree willow in Minnesota. It is likely to be found wherever there is seasonal flooding, especially along major rivers where floodwaters carry heavy sediment loads. These floodplains are typically forested with plains cottonwood (*Populus deltoides* subsp. *monilifera*) and silver maple (*Acer saccharinum*), with lesser amounts of peach-leaved willow and sometimes black willow (*S. nigra*). Peach-leaved willow is also one of the more important pioneers of lakeshores, riverbanks, marshes and swales, and even abandoned agricultural land in low-lying or flood-prone areas.

Forest-grown specimens typically have a single tall, straight trunk, but open-grown trees will often have multiple trunks that lean diagonally or even horizontally. The branches of exposed trees often suffer considerable damage from ice and wind. They are weak and brittle and often litter the ground after a storm. The seeds are released in June and germinate quickly on bare moist ground, particularly on exposed sandy or silty deposits left by receding floodwaters. The seedlings grow rapidly but need full sunlight to reach maturity; they will not survive under a closed canopy. In ideal habitat, peach-leaved willow will grow rapidly and can become quite large but will probably live no more than about 100 years (*fide* Burns and Honkala 1990).

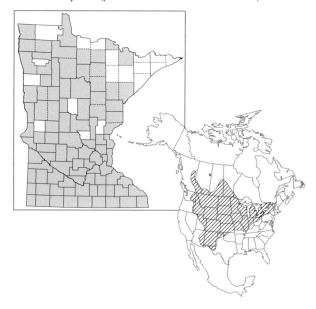

Deep furrows and interlacing ridges on a 21" (53 cm) dbh trunk.

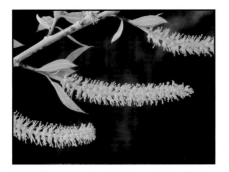

Male flowers are in whorls on a long, slender catkin—May 14.

Long, slender leaves are dark green above, pale green beneath.

These female catkins have begun releasing their seeds—June 22.

A typical open-grown specimen from Ramsey County.

Salix bebbiana Sarg.

Bebb's willow
[*S. rostrata* Richards]

Tall **shrubs** or small **trees**, with single or multiple upright **stems** to 7 m tall and 18 cm dbh. 1st-year **branchlets** greenish, hairy; 2nd-year branchlets red-brown, hairy or glabrate. **Bark** gray, rough, becoming coarsely furrowed in age. **Leaves** simple, alternate, deciduous. **Petioles** 0.5–1.2 cm long, hairy, lacking glands at summit; stipules usually less than 2 mm long, deciduous early. Mature **leaf blades** elliptical to elliptical-ovate or obovate; the larger ones 3–8 cm long and 1.5–3.2 cm wide, length/width 2.2–3.3; apex acute or occasionally obtuse; base acute to obtuse; margins entire to crenate or irregularly serrate, slightly revolute; upper surface dark green, hairy or sometimes glabrate; lower surface pale green or gray-green, hairy or glabrate; immature leaves reddish or yellowish green, densely hairy. **Flowers** borne in unisexual **catkins**, each shrub bearing either male catkins or female catkins (dioecious); appearing with the leaves or slightly before. **Male catkins** 1–3 cm long; essentially sessile or on short flowering branchlets 1–6 mm long; stamens 2, filaments hairy near base; bracts as in female catkins; nectary 1. **Female catkins** 2.5–6 cm long; borne on flowering branchlets 3–15 mm long; **capsules** hairy, 4–9 mm long; styles 0.1–0.3 mm long; stipes 2–4 mm long; bracts yellowish to tan, 1.2–2.5 mm long, persistent after flowering; nectary 1; **anthesis** early May to early mid-June; wind- and insect-pollinated; **seeds** released late mid-May to early July, wind-dispersed. (*bebbiana*: named for willow specialist M. S. Bebb, 1833–95)

Identification

Bebb's willow is typically a large, bushy shrub with multiple stems, or it can be a small, contorted tree with a single stem. It sometimes reaches heights of 22 ft (7 m) and stem diameters of 7 inches (18 cm). The mature female catkins have very slender capsules and an open, airy appearance, and when they are abundant, they give the entire shrub a characteristic gray-green cast. It is most often confused with pussy willow (*S. discolor*), and indeed the two often occur side by side and are similar in size and form. But the leaves of Bebb's willow are hairy (at least on the undersides), and those of pussy willow are smooth.

Natural History

Bebb's willow is a consistent and often abundant component of wetlands statewide. It is particularly common in swamps, meadows, lakeshores, stream banks, fens, prairie swales, and marshes. Indeed, a complete list of habitats would include nearly every wetland type in Minnesota except the most acidic bogs. It does especially well in permanently saturated peat soils with low levels of dissolved oxygen, but it does not do well if its roots become covered with sediment as might be the case on a floodplain.

Bebb's willow is an effective colonizer of newly formed wetlands such as ditches, breached beaver ponds, and low-lying farmland, but it is not as aggressive as pussy willow (*S. discolor*), slender willow (*S. petiolaris*), or sandbar willow (*S. interior*). It occasionally appears in uplands, mostly at the edges of forests or in forest openings, where it may persist if not shaded out by taller trees.

The wood is occasionally attacked by a fungus (*Valsa sordida* Nitschke), which leaves diamond-shaped depressions in the stems. This is the source of "diamond willow" used in furniture, canes, and other handicrafts (Lutz 1958). The fungus, however, is not specific to Bebb's willow; it also infects pussy willow, heart-leaved willow (*S. eriocephala*), and possibly other willows as well.

A female Bebb's heavily laden with catkins—May 8, Anoka County.

A female catkin with slender, "beaked" capsules—June 6.

Leaves have heavily textured surfaces; lower surface is hairy.

A large, old specimen with a basal diameter of 13" (33 cm).

Male catkins fall soon after releasing their pollen—May 18.

Salix candida Flüggé

Sage-leaved willow

Low or midsize **shrubs**, with 1 or a few upright **stems** to 2 m tall and 1.5 cm basal diameter; forming loose colonies by layering of stems and lower branches. 1st-year **branchlets** greenish or yellowish, hairy to woolly; 2nd-year branchlets brown, glabrous or glabrate. **Bark** gray or brown, smooth to rough. **Leaves** simple, alternate, deciduous. **Petioles** 3–10 mm long, hairy, lacking glands at summit; stipules foliaceous, 2–3 (-11) mm long. Mature **leaf blades** linear to narrowly oblong, sometimes narrowly lanceolate or oblanceolate; the larger ones 5–10 cm long and 0.6–1.8 cm wide, length/width 4.5–11; apex acute; base acute to attenuate; margins entire and revolute; upper surface dark green, glabrate or bearing tufts of white, woolly hair; lower surface densely and persistently white-woolly, or occasionally glabrous or glabrate and appearing pale green; immature leaf blades yellowish, woolly. **Flowers** borne in unisexual **catkins**, each shrub with either male catkins or female catkins (dioecious); appearing with the leaves or slightly before. **Male catkins** 1–1.5 cm long; subsessile or on short flowering branchlets to 5 mm long; stamens 2, filaments glabrous; bracts as in female catkins; nectary 1. **Female catkins** 2–5.5 cm long; borne on flowering branchlets 2–15 mm long; **capsules** covered with short, dense, woolly hairs, 3.5–6 mm long; styles 0.6–1.5 mm long; stipes 0.1–1.2 mm long; bracts pale to dark brown, 1–1.5 mm long, persistent after flowering; nectary 1; **anthesis** late April to early June; wind- and insect-pollinated; **seeds** released mid-May to mid-June, wind-dispersed. (*candida*: white, for the underside of the leaves)

Identification

Sage-leaved willow is one of the smallest willows in Minnesota, usually only about 3 ft (1 m) in height and often with only a few leaf-bearing twigs. The dense woolly covering on the underside of the leaf is very distinctive, but occasionally the leaf is smooth. In that case, the long, slender shape of the leaf, the tapering base, and entire margins become diagnostic.

Natural History

Sage-leaved willow is fairly common but only in rather specific habitat types. These are usually calcareous or circumneutral peatlands, such as sedge meadows, floating sedge mats, calcareous fens, and minerotrophic conifer swamps. It seems to be absent from acidic habitats, even weakly acidic habitats. It typically grows in the company of fine-leaved sedges and short-stature herbaceous plants, giving the impression that it does not compete well with larger shrubs. Although suitable habitats are often small and localized, they are characteristically stable. They may occasionally burn in wildfires, but they are not strongly influenced by cyclic disturbances such as floods or droughts, so ecological succession proceeds very slowly.

In such a stable habitat there may be few opportunities for seedlings to become established, creating a situation that may require specialized strategies for populations of small, short-lived species such as sage-leaved willow. In this case, the strategy is asexual reproduction accomplished by a process called layering. Layering begins when a lower branch or stem is forced to the ground by some external factor, and takes root where it contacts moist soil. It then sends up new shoots of its own, eventually breaking the connection with the parent plant. In time, and if repeated, this process can produce a fairly large but typically diffuse colony of autonomous individuals, each individual a clonal copy of the founder. Although the individual aerial stems rarely live more than 8 to 10 years, the collective clone itself may persist much longer. It is possible to recognize loose colonies 20–25 ft (6–8 m) across that apparently developed in this way.

Woolly capsules cause female catkins to look white—May 5.

Most of these male flowers have already released their pollen—May 5.

Leaves are long and narrow—green above, white-woolly beneath.

Salix discolor Muhl.

Pussy willow

Tall **shrubs** or small **trees**, with single or multiple upright **stems** to 10 m tall and 20 cm dbh. 1st-year **branchlets** yellowish to greenish or brownish, hairy or less often glabrous; 2nd-year branchlets brown, usually glabrous. **Bark** gray, rough, furrowed in age. **Leaves** simple, alternate, deciduous. **Petioles** 6–20 mm long, minutely hairy or occasionally glabrous, lacking glands at summit; stipules often minute but up to 8 mm or more on vigorous shoots. Mature **leaf blades** oblanceolate, elliptical or obovate; the larger ones 4–10.5 cm long and 1.5–3.5 cm wide, length/width 2.5–4; apex acute; base acute to obtuse; margins crenate to serrate; upper surface dark green, glabrous or glabrate; lower surface similar to upper but pale green (glaucous); immature leaf blades reddish or greenish, usually with white and/or rust-colored hairs. **Flowers** borne in unisexual **catkins**, each tree bearing either male catkins or female catkins (dioecious); appearing before the leaves. **Male catkins** 2–3.5 cm long; sessile; stamens 2, filaments glabrous or hairy at base; bracts as in female catkins; nectary 1. **Female catkins** 3–8 cm long; sessile or on flowering branchlets to 1 cm long; **capsules** hairy, 5–9 mm long; styles 0.3–1 mm long; stipes 2–3 mm long; bracts black to brown, 1.5–2.5 mm long, persistent after flowering; nectary 1; **anthesis** mid-April to mid-May; wind- and insect-pollinated; **seeds** released early May to late mid-June, wind-dispersed. (*discolor*: of another color, in reference to the upper and lower surfaces of the leaves)

Identification

Pussy willow is usually a large, coarse shrub with multiple bushy stems. But it can also take the dimensions of a small tree with a single irregular trunk 5–7 inches (12–17 cm) in diameter and 20–25 ft (6–8 m) tall. It becomes very conspicuous in early spring when it produces large, robust catkins, well before any leaves emerge. The leaf shape is most similar to Bebb's willow (*S. bebbiana*) and planeleaf willow (*S. planifolia*).

Natural History

Pussy willow is common and abundant in wetlands throughout most of Minnesota; it is rare only in the Prairie Coteau region in the southwest corner of the state. Typical habitats include marshes, riverbanks, lakeshores, swales, fens, conifer swamps, hardwood swamps, and occasionally marginal upland habitats. It is also a major and often dominant component of shrub swamps, typically with Bebb's willow (*S. bebbiana*), slender-leaved willow (*S. petiolaris*), red-osier dogwood (*Cornus sericea*), speckled alder (*Alnus incana* subsp. *rugosa*), and a variety of other wetlands shrubs.

It occurs in both mineral soil and peat soil, within a pH range from basic (calcareous) to moderately acidic; it seems to be absent only from strongly acidic habitats. It is relatively tolerant of drought and short-duration spring flooding but not of prolonged flooding or sedimentation. It generally needs direct sunlight for at least a portion of the day and is rarely found in deep shade.

Most willows are opportunists in the sense they can rapidly and effectively colonize newly created habitats, and pussy willow is particularly good in this role. It gains a foothold quickly and competes successfully with all latecomers, even speckled alder, which grows just as quickly and can spread underground. It resists damage by wind and ice and resprouts after fire and after browsing by deer, moose, or beaver. It does not spread vegetatively, but it does produce abundant seeds, which, like all willow seeds, can be carried on the wind for great distances.

Young leaves are suffused with red, but soon become dark green.

Male shrub at peak anthesis—April 15, Anoka County.

These male flowers were releasing pollen on April 16—Ramsey County.

Female catkins appear long before the leaves—April 22.

Stems branch repeatedly beginning near the base.

Pussy willow is a large, dense shrub or small tree.

Salix eriocephala Michx.

Heart-leaved willow
[*S. cordata* Muhl.; *S. rigida* Muhl.]

Tall **shrubs,** with numerous upright **stems** to 7 m tall and 20 cm basal diameter. 1st-year **branchlets** greenish to yellowish, hairy; 2nd-year branchlets yellow to yellow-brown or reddish, often blotchy, glabrous or glabrate. **Bark** gray, smooth or somewhat rough. **Leaves** simple, alternate, deciduous. **Petioles** 6–19 mm long; short-hairy, especially on upper (adaxial) surface; lacking glands at summit; stipules foliaceous, prominent and persistent, 5–10 mm long or longer on vigorous shoots. Mature **leaf blades** narrowly oblong to narrowly elliptical or narrowly lance-elliptical; the larger ones 6–12 cm long and 1–3 cm wide, length/width 3–6; apex acuminate; base acute to blunt or rarely subcordate; margins serrulate; upper surface dark green, glabrous or sparsely hairy along lower portion of midvein; lower surface similar to upper but pale green (thinly glaucous); immature leaf blades hairy, reddish or occasionally yellowish green. **Flowers** borne in unisexual **catkins,** each plant bearing either male catkins or female catkins (dioecious); appearing with or slightly before the leaves. **Male catkins** 1.5–4.5 cm long, sessile or on short flowering branchlets to 5 mm long; stamens 2, filaments glabrous; bracts as in female catkins; nectary 1. **Female catkins** 2–6 cm long, sessile or on short flowering branchlets to 1 cm long; **capsules** glabrous, 3–7 mm long; styles 0.2–0.6 mm long; stipes 1–2 mm long; bracts brown, 0.6–2 mm long, persistent after flowering; nectary 1; **anthesis** mid-April to late May; wind- and insect-pollinated; **seeds** released mid-May to late mid-June, wind-dispersed. (*eriocephala*: woolly-headed)

Identification

Heart-leaved willow is a large shrub with multiple stems arising from a single, compact base. Typical specimens are in the range of 10–15 ft (3–4.5 m) tall, while exceptional specimens can reach 22 ft (7 m). If not crowded, the stems will fan out, creating a hemispheric form and eliminating all doubt that this is a shrub and not a tree. The leaf shape is extremely variable and can resemble those of black willow (*S. nigra*) and slender-leaved willow (*S. petiolaris*), except it has prominent stipules. In spite of its common name, the leaves of heart-leaved willow are rarely, if ever, heart-shaped.

Note: One-year-old twigs (twigs in their second growing season) of var. *eriocephala* are uniformly reddish. Specimens with yellow or brownish twigs or patches of yellow or brown color have been named var. *famelica* (C.R. Ball) Dorn. Both varieties occur throughout the same range in Minnesota and in the same habitats, although var. *famelica* is more frequent.

Natural History

Heart-leaved willow is a common shrub in Minnesota wetlands, at least in wetlands that occur within the prairie and hardwood forest regions. It appears to be rare or absent in the coniferous forest region, where the wetlands tend to be more acidic. This is especially true in the northeast corner of the state, where pussy willow (*S. discolor*) and slender-leaved willow (*S. petiolaris*) are the common willows.

Wet loamy soils seem to be preferred, yet heart-leaved willow can also be found in sand, silt, clay, or thin peat. Typical habitats include prairie swales, wet meadows, shallow marshes, ditches, stream banks, lakeshores, and floodplains. It seems to tolerate flooding and sedimentation better than most willow shrubs, but like all willows it is intolerant of shade and grows best in the open. Scattered individuals can occasionally be found in marginal upland habitats, especially in areas with a near-surface water table.

Each male catkin has more than 100 individual flowers—April 22.

Note the persistent stipules at the base of each leaf.

Heart-leaved willow needs direct sunlight and plenty of room.

Female flowers are similar to pussy willow but are hairless—May 22.

Multiple stems arise from a compact base.

Salix fragilis L.

Crack willow

Nonnative, naturalized, midsize **trees,** with 1–3 upright or ascending **trunks,** to 20 m tall and 100 cm dbh. 1st-year **branchlets** yellowish, sparsely hairy or glabrous; second-year branchlets yellow to yellow-brown, glabrous. **Bark** gray or gray-brown, with coarse ridges and deep furrows. **Leaves** simple, alternate, deciduous. **Petioles** 5–20 mm long, glabrous or sparsely hairy, with prominent stalked glands or glandular lobes at summit; stipules small, ± ovate with acuminate apex, deciduous very early. Mature **leaf blades** narrowly elliptical to lanceolate or oblong-lanceolate; the larger ones 7–18 cm long and 1.3–3 cm wide, length/width 4–7.5; apex long-acuminate to caudate; base tapered or somewhat rounded; margins serrate to coarsely serrate; upper surface dark green, glossy, glabrous; lower surface pale green to pale blue-green, dull, glabrous; immature leaf blades yellowish green or reddish, usually glabrous or with a few long, silky hairs. **Flowers** borne in unisexual **catkins,** each tree bearing either male catkins or female catkins (dioecious); appearing with the leaves. **Male catkins** 3.3–6 cm long; borne on flowering branchlets 0.5–1.1 cm long; stamens 2, filaments hairy on lower half; bracts as in female catkins; nectaries 2. **Female catkins** 3.5–8 cm long; borne on flowering branchlets 0.8–2 cm long; **capsules** glabrous, 4–5 mm long; styles 0.5–0.8 mm long; stipes 0.5–1.5 mm long; bracts greenish or pale yellow, 1–3 mm long, deciduous after flowering; nectaries 2; **anthesis** early May to early June; wind- and insect-pollinated; **seeds** released late May to late June, wind-dispersed. (*fragilis*: fragile)

Identification

Crack willow is a midsize tree with a stout trunk, deeply furrowed bark, and large, shiny, coarsely serrate leaves. It is one of three tree willows introduced from Europe and naturalized in Minnesota. The others are bay willow (*S. pentandra*) and whitecrack willow (*S. ×rubens*). Telling crack willow from bay willow by the shape of the leaves is not very difficult, but whitecrack willow is a different matter. It originated as a hybrid between crack willow and white willow (*S. alba*) and exists in a bewildering number of forms. Perhaps the easiest way to tell them apart is by examining the young leaves that are just unfolding. Those of whitecrack willow have a dense covering of long, silky hairs, while those of crack willow will have few, if any, hairs.

Natural History

Crack willow is native to northern and northwestern Asia Minor and is extensively naturalized in Europe, from where it was introduced into North America. It was evidently brought to Minnesota in the latter half of the nineteenth century for use in windbreaks and as a fuel source for prairie homesteads (Records 1913). At the time, all the imported tree willows were apparently called "white willow," although it is clear now that most were actually whitecrack willow (*S. ×rubens*) (Upham 1884), with lesser amounts of crack willow and very little true white willow (*S. alba*). As a group, these willows were easily transplanted, fast-growing, and readily coppiced: a seemingly perfect tree for the style of agriculture practiced by the early prairie settlers.

The first documented occurrence of naturalized crack willow (based on herbarium specimens) was from the south shore of Minnesota Lake in Faribault County in 1891. The tree was described as about 12 feet (3.7 m) tall and was probably no more than 10 years old. In the intervening 100 plus years, naturalized crack willow has turned up at a few scattered locations, mostly lakeshores and riverbanks in southern and western Minnesota. Unlike whitecrack willow, it seems that true crack willow, as described above, is not particularly invasive in Minnesota.

Female catkins can reach 3" (8 cm) in length—May 3.

Male catkins are long and slender—May 3.

Leaves are long, rigid, coarsely serrate, and shiny.

A 21" (54 cm) dbh crack willow showing coarse, furrowed bark.

Salix humilis Marsh.

Prairie willow

Midsize or tall **shrubs**, with multiple upright, ascending, or decumbent **stems** to 3 m tall and 5 cm basal diameter; clonal by layering. 1st-year **branchlets** yellow-green to brownish, hairy to densely woolly; second-year branchlets brown, hairy to glabrate, occasionally remaining hairy into the 3rd year. **Bark** gray, smooth or somewhat rough. **Leaves** simple, alternate, deciduous. **Petioles** 0.5–7 mm long, hairy, lacking glands at summit; stipules to 11 mm long, or absent in var. *tristis*. Mature **leaf blades** narrowly to broadly oblanceolate, obovate, or sometimes oblong; the larger ones 2.5–9 cm long and 0.5–3 cm wide, length/width 2.5–6; apex acute to obtuse or somewhat rounded; base acute; margins entire, subentire, undulate or crenate; upper surface dark green, hairy to glabrate; lower surface pale green to gray-green, densely hairy to woolly or glabrate; immature leaf blades yellowish green, woolly. **Flowers** borne in unisexual **catkins**, each plant bearing either male catkins or female catkins (dioecious); appearing before the leaves. **Male catkins** 0.5–2 cm long; sessile; stamens 2, filaments glabrous or hairy; bracts as in female catkins; nectary 1. **Female catkins** 1–3.5 cm long; subsessile or on short flowering branchlets to 10 mm long; **capsules** hairy, 5–10 mm long; styles 0.1–0.4 mm long; stipes 1–2.5 mm long; bracts 0.8–1.6 mm long, brown to dark purple or nearly black, persistent after flowering; nectary 1; **anthesis** mid-April to mid-May; wind- and insect-pollinated; **seeds** released early mid-May to mid-June, wind-dispersed. (*humilis*: low growing)

Identification

Prairie willow is a midsize or tall shrub, with slender, erect stems, usually about 6 ft (2 m) tall. The leaves are relatively narrow, and the undersides are usually covered with dense, woolly hairs. The leaves of pussy willow (*S. discolor*) are similar, except they are generally hairless at maturity.

Note: There are two varieties of prairie willow in Minnesota. Variety *humilis* usually gets to be 6 ft (2 m) tall and has relatively large leaves. The diminutive variety *tristis* (Ait.) Griggs is rarely more than 3 ft (1 m) tall and has smaller and proportionately narrower leaves (see key). They are found in roughly the same habitat types, although variety *humilis* is more common by a factor of at least 20 to 1. It also appears that only variety *humilis*

occurs in the north central and northeastern counties. All photos on the facing page are variety *humilis*.

Natural History

Prairie willow is fairly common in portions of the state, especially in pine forests of the central and northern counties, and in brushy or savannalike habitats along the prairie-forest border in the western and southern regions. It is, in fact, the only willow in Minnesota that specializes in dry, upland habitats. It does particularly well in gravelly or sandy soil, even sand dunes and rock outcrops, and has the ability, rare among upland species, to spread vegetatively by the process of layering. Although it is among the most shade tolerant of willows, it still does not do well in continual deep shade.

Prairie willow occurs almost exclusively in fire-prone landscapes. It responds to fire by resprouting vigorously and flowering abundantly the following spring. A natural history survey of Fillmore County in 1875 gives a rare early account of the role of prairie willow in vegetation succession following the suppression of wildfire on the prairie: "The area covered by native timber is steadily increasing. A large proportion of the county is covered with bushes which are composed of hazel, aspen, oak (2 sorts) and, where these are wanting, a species of low willow seems to come up first after the prairie fires are stopped" (Winchell 1876).

Typical specimen from a pine forest in Hubbard County.

Male catkins get their yellow color from the anthers—May 3.

Female catkins beginning to release seeds on May 22.

This leaf shape is oblanceolate—characteristic of prairie willow.

Salix interior Rowlee

Sandbar willow

[*S. exigua* Nutt. subsp. *interior* (Rowlee) Cronq.]

Tall **shrubs** or rarely small **trees**, with numerous upright **stems** to 6.5 m tall and 9 cm dbh; forming dense colonies (clones) by root suckers. 1st-year **branchlets** yellowish or greenish, glabrous or sparsely hairy; 2nd-year branchlets red-brown or gray-brown, glabrous. **Bark** gray, smooth or somewhat rough. **Leaves** simple, alternate, deciduous. **Petioles** 1–7 mm long, glabrous or hairy, lacking glands at summit; stipules minute or absent. Mature **leaf blades** linear to narrowly oblong; the larger ones 6–15 cm long and 3–11 mm wide, length/width 8–25; apex acute to acuminate; base acute to acuminate; margins remotely serrulate to subentire; upper surface dark green, glabrous or hairy; lower surface similar to upper; immature leaf blades yellowish green or often reddish, with long, silky hairs. **Flowers** borne in unisexual **catkins**, each plant bearing either male catkins or female catkins (dioecious); appearing with the leaves or after, later catkins are on longer branchlets and often bear lateral secondary catkins. **Male catkins** 2–5 cm long; borne on flowering branchlets 1.5–18 cm long; stamens 2, filaments hairy on lower half; bracts as in female catkins but persistent; nectaries 2. **Female catkins** 3–7 cm long; borne on flowering branchlets 2–15 cm long; **capsules** hairy or glabrous, 5–9 mm long; styles 0–0.1 mm long; stipes 0.5–1 mm long; bracts yellowish to tan, 1.5–3.5 mm long, deciduous after flowering; nectary 1; **anthesis** early May to early July; insect- and wind-pollinated; **seeds** released early June to late August, wind-dispersed. (*interior*: inland)

Identification

Sandbar willow is a large shrub with slender, erect stems and short, flexible branches. Occasionally the tallest stems will approach 20 ft (6 m) in height and take on the proportions of a small tree. The extreme narrowness of the leaves distinguishes sandbar willow from all others. The leaves of slender-leaved willow (*S. petiolaris*) are nearly as narrow but are distinctly two-toned; the upper surface is dark green, and the lower is pale green or gray. Those of sandbar willow are the same color on both surfaces.

Natural History

Sandbar willow is very common in Minnesota, even in the prairie region. It is found in a variety of habitats, including riverbanks, sandbars, floodplains, lakeshores, prairie swales, and shallow marshes. It usually occurs on sand, silt, or loam, rarely on clay or shallow peat. It is quite adept at colonizing abandoned fields, especially in flood-prone areas or where the water table is near the surface. But it is most aggressive on exposed sandbars and mudflats that are created by receding floodwaters. In fact, seasonal flooding and heavy sedimentation strongly favor both the establishment and maintenance of sandbar willow colonies. However, it does not tolerate stagnant water, and it is easily shaded out by overhanging trees. Ideal habitats are especially common on the broad floodplains along the Mississippi and Minnesota rivers, where it is possible to find monotypic stands an acre or more in size.

The origin of these stands can be explained by the process of root suckering. In other words, the stems originate from adventitious buds that develop anywhere along the long horizontal roots, rather than from a single root crown like other willows. This can result in a thicket of erect stems so dense that it is often compared to the hairs on a dog. In these cases it is likely that all the stems arose from a single founder and remain connected underground through a common root system. The individual stems grow quickly and may flower in just 2 or 3 years, but they rarely live more than 12 years. They flower first in early May, just as the leaves are appearing, then again in mid-June to early July after a flush of vegetative growth.

Early-season male catkins are on short stalks—May 21.

Late-season female catkins may have a secondary catkin—July 6.

No other Minnesota willow has leaves so slender.

A typical colony on a sandbar along the Mississippi River.

Salix lucida Muhl.

Shining willow

Tall **shrubs** or small **trees,** with multiple upright **stems** to 6 m tall and 15 cm basal diameter. 1st-year **branchlets** yellow to yellow-green, glabrous or sometimes sparsely hairy, glossy; second-year branchlets similar. **Bark** gray; smooth, becoming rough in age. **Leaves** simple, alternate, deciduous. **Petioles** 5–13 mm long, glabrous or hairy, glandular dots or lobes prominent at base of blade and occasionally at summit of petiole; stipules foliaceous, 1–6 mm long. Mature **leaf blades** lanceolate, lance-ovate or sometimes elliptical-ovate; the larger ones 4–14 cm long and 1.4–3.5 cm wide, length/width 2.3–4.8; apex of later leaves long-acuminate or caudate, earlier leaves acute to acuminate; base tapered to rounded; margins serrulate; upper surface dark green, glabrous or occasionally glabrate, glossy; lower surface similar to upper, but slightly paler; immature leaves yellowish green or reddish, glabrous or with deciduous white or rust-colored hairs. **Flowers** borne in unisexual **catkins,** each plant bearing either male catkins or female catkins; appearing with the leaves. **Male catkins** 1.7–5 cm long; borne on flowering branchlets 1–2.5 cm long; stamens 3–6, filaments hairy near the base; bracts as in female catkins; nectaries 2. **Female catkins** 1.3–5 cm long; borne on flowering branchlets 1.3–3 cm long; **capsules** glabrous, 5–7 mm long; styles 0.5–0.8 mm long; stipes 0.5–2 mm long; bracts pale yellow or tan, 1.5–3 mm long, deciduous soon after flowering; nectary 1 or more; **anthesis** early May to early mid-June; insect- and possibly wind-pollinated; **seeds** released late May to late June, wind-dispersed. (*lucida*: shining, in reference to the leaves)

Identification

Shining willow is a large shrub or occasionally a small, bushy tree reaching a maximum height of about 20 ft (6 m). It is very conspicuous in May because of the large, bright yellow male (pollen-bearing) catkins. The orange bud scales are also large and conspicuous and persist for a few weeks after they open in the spring. Another useful feature is the long, drawn-out tip of the mid- and late-season leaves, and the glossy leaf surface. Also notice that where the petiole joins the leaf blade, there is a cluster of enlarged glands and often a small tuft of tangled hairs. Leaves of autumn willow (*S. serissima*) are similar, but they lack the tangle of hairs, and the leaf tips are shorter.

Natural History

Shining willow is occasional to frequent in a variety of wetland habitats throughout most of the forested region of the state, especially north of the Twin Cities. Typical habitats include sandy or marshy lakeshores, riverbanks, wet meadows, swales, and shrub swamps. It seems to prefer loamy soils, but it also occurs in shallow peat. Soil conditions range from slightly basic (calcareous) to moderately acidic; it is absent from strongly acidic habitats such as bogs. Seasonal flooding is not a deterrent as long as the floodwaters are relatively free of sediments.

Shining willow is usually seen as scattered individuals mixed with other shrubs rather than in pure stands. In fact, shining willow is not a significant component of any homogeneous or stable plant community type; it is more of an opportunist that exploits transitional or edge habitats. It competes well with shrubs its own height, but it is generally intolerant of shade from above. This makes it a fairly good colonizer of newly created habitats such as roadside ditches, and of newly created gaps in established habitats. It is fast growing and resprouts vigorously if stems are damaged or killed.

These female flowers were pollinated during previous week—May 20.

Leaves are smooth, shiny, and have long, drawn-out tips.

The large, male catkins are conspicuous for a brief period in May.

Salix maccalliana Rowlee

McCalla's willow

Tall **shrubs**, with multiple upright **stems** to 4.5 m tall and 4 cm dbh; occasionally clonal by layering of lower branches. 1st-year **branchlets** reddish, glabrous or glabrate; second-year branchlets red to red-brown, glabrous, shiny. **Bark** brownish to gray-brown, smooth or somewhat rough in age. **Leaves** simple, alternate, deciduous. **Petioles** 4–15 mm long; sparsely hairy on adaxial (upper) surface, often somewhat ciliate; lacking glands at summit; stipules reduced to small, glandular lobes, 0.2–0.6 mm long. Mature **leaf blades** elliptical to narrowly elliptical or sometimes oblong or obovate; the larger ones 4–8 cm long and 0.8–2.5 cm wide, length/width 2.5–5; apex acute to somewhat acuminate; base acute to obtuse; margins serrulate; upper surface dark green, shiny, glabrous to glabrate; lower surface pale green, dull, glabrous to glabrate or sparsely hairy near base; emerging leaves green, shiny, sparsely hairy. **Flowers** borne in unisexual **catkins**, each plant bearing either male catkins or female catkins (dioecious); appearing with the leaves. **Male catkins** 1.5–3 cm long; borne on flowering branchlets 0.3–1.3 (–2.5) cm long; stamens 2, filaments hairy near base; bracts as in female catkins; nectaries usually 2–4. **Female catkins** 2–6 cm long; borne on flowering branchlets 1–2.8 cm long; **capsules** densely hairy, 6–11 mm long; styles 0.8–1.2 mm long; stipes 0.8–3 mm long; bracts 2–4 mm long, tan or yellow-green, becoming brownish, persistent after flowering; nectary 1; **anthesis** early to late May; wind- and insect-pollinated; **seeds** released late May to late June, wind-dispersed. (*maccalliana*: named for William C. McCalla)

Identification

McCalla's willow is a visually striking shrub; it has multiple upright stems in the range of 6–14 ft (2–4.5 m) tall, short ascending branches, and shiny red twigs. The leaves are dark green and shiny, with finely serrate margins. The willow closest in appearance is probably autumn willow (*S. serissima*), but the petioles of autumn willow are completely hairless, while those of McCalla's willow are sparsely hairy. The leaves of planeleaf willow (*S. planifolia*) are, like McCalla's willow, smooth and shiny but have entire margins, and a glaucous (blue-gray) lower surface.

Natural History

McCalla's willow is rather uncommon in Minnesota and is apparently restricted to shallow wetlands in the northwestern counties, particularly shrub swamps, shrubby fens, and sedge meadows. Soils are usually calcareous or circumneutral sedge-derived peat or sometimes wet loam. It seems that the strongly acidic and nutrient-poor conditions in bogs are beyond its tolerance. Even in the best habitats McCalla's willow is never abundant; instead, it is usually scattered among the more common and aggressive slender-leaved willow (*S. petiolaris*) or pussy willow (*S. discolor*). Although these habitats may be influenced by cyclical droughts and by localized spring flooding, they are basically stable environments with little or no history of human influence. In Minnesota, McCalla's willow rarely, if ever, occurs in abandoned agricultural land, roadsides, or other grossly disturbed habitats.

Under ideal conditions a vigorous, well-established individual can produce dozens of stems that can grow to a height of at least 14 ft (4.5 m) and live 20 to 25 years. But individual stems rarely achieve such an age or size in Minnesota. They are often browsed heavily by deer or moose and are frequently top-killed by wildfire or more often by prescribed burns intended to improve wildlife habitat. McCalla's willow responds to this sort of damage by resprouting vigorously and repeatedly, if necessary, from a diffuse root crown and from layered branches.

Female flowers about 3 weeks after fertilization—June 10.

These male flowers are just starting to release pollen—May 23.

Female flowers at time of fertilization—May 23.

Characteristic red twigs and dark green, shiny leaves.

Salix nigra Marsh.

Black willow

Small or midsize **trees**, with 1 or a few upright, leaning, or decumbent **trunks**, to 25 m tall and 45 cm dbh. 1st-year **branchlets** greenish, glabrous or sometimes hairy; second-year branchlets brownish, glabrous. **Bark** gray, with narrow furrows and broad, flat-topped ridges. **Leaves** simple, alternate, deciduous. **Petioles** 3–12 mm long, hairy or glabrate, glands sometimes present at summit but not conspicuously enlarged; stipules foliaceous, 2–10 mm long, or absent. Mature **leaf blades** linear to narrowly lanceolate; the larger ones 6–15 cm long and 0.8–2 cm wide, length/width 5–11; apex acuminate to long-acuminate or caudate; base tapered or somewhat blunt; margins serrulate; upper surface dark green, essentially glabrous; lower surface similar to upper; immature leaf blades glabrous or with patches of relatively short, kinky, white or rust-colored hairs when just unfolding. **Flowers** borne in unisexual **catkins**, each tree bearing either male catkins or female catkins (dioecious); appearing with the leaves or slightly after. **Male catkins** 1.7–7.5 cm long; borne on flowering branchlets 0.4–1.5 cm long; stamens 3 or more, filaments hairy on lower half; bracts as in female flowers but persistent after flowering; nectaries usually 2 or more. **Female catkins** 3–7 cm long; borne on flowering branchlets 1–3.5 cm long; **capsules** glabrous, 3–5 mm long; styles 0.1–0.4 mm long; stipes 0.5–1.5 mm long; bracts pale yellow, 1–3 mm long, deciduous after flowering; nectary 1; **anthesis** late mid-May to early mid-June; wind- and insect-pollinated; **seeds** released early June to early July, wind- and water-dispersed. (*nigra*: black)

Identification

Black willow is a small or midsize tree with slender branches and an irregular crown. The leaves tend to hang downward on the branch, but the branches themselves do not droop, certainly not like the cultivated weeping willows. It is often confused with peach-leaved willow (*S. amygdaloides*) or sometimes with one of the naturalized European tree willows (*S. ×rubens* or *S. fragilis*). But the leaves of black willow are usually smaller and proportionately narrower, and notice that the upper and lower surfaces are the same dark green color. The leaves of the other tree willows are distinctly paler on the lower surface than on the upper.

Natural History

Black willow is locally common in southern and central Minnesota, where it inhabits a variety of low, wet, sunny habitats such as lakeshores, pond margins, shallow marshes, and especially floodplains. It is able to withstand the prolonged inundation and sedimentation associated with floods better than any other tree species in Minnesota (Gill 1970).

It sometimes grows as a tall canopy tree in mixed-species floodplain forests, but it is more common in the open on riverbanks, oxbows, or strands. In these exposed, unstable habitats it is often undercut by streams or partially uprooted by the scouring action of floods, and it may have broken limbs or ice-scarred trunks. This sometimes results in the larger trunks lying on the ground, where they may trap flood-borne sediments. They can then form new roots from adventitious buds and begin to send up vertical branches that may become tree-size in time.

Black willow is a supremely adapted pioneer. The seeds germinate very quickly in full sunlight and on moist soil, especially sandy or silty alluvium (McLeod and McPherson 1973), but seeds are not the only way it reproduces. The twigs are very brittle at the base; they will break off in a strong wind and take root wherever the wind or water takes them. In this way it readily colonizes flood-prone fields, abandoned hay meadows, and ditches. The greatest age reported for a black willow is only 85 years (*fide* Burns and Honkala 1990).

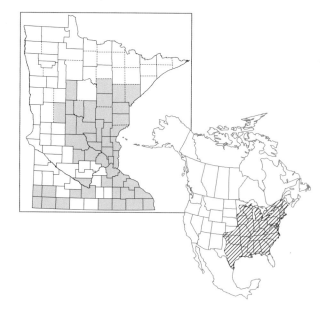

Leaves are slender, and tend to hang downward.

Male catkins are long and slender—May 24.

These female catkins were beginning to release seeds on June 21.

*Bark has broad, flat-topped ridges—this trunk is 18"
(46 cm) dbh.*

Salix pedicellaris Pursh

Bog willow

[*S. pedicellaris* Pursh var. *hypoglauca* Fern.]

Low or midsize **shrubs**, with 1 or a few upright **stems** to 1.7 m tall and 1 cm basal diameter; branches few or none; forming loose colonies by layering of stems and lower branches. 1st-year **branchlets** yellow-brown to brown, glabrous or minutely hairy; second-year branchlets brown to red-brown, glabrous. **Bark** gray, smooth or slightly rough. **Leaves** simple, alternate, deciduous. **Petioles** 2–8 mm long, glabrous or minutely hairy, lacking glands at summit; stipules minute or not apparent. Mature **leaf blades** oblong, elliptical-oblong, or obovate; the largest ones 2–6 cm long and 0.6–2 cm wide, length/width 2.2–4.3; apex acute to obtuse or rounded; base acute to obtuse or blunt; margins entire, sometimes revolute; upper surface dark green, glabrous, reticulate-veined; lower surface pale green or gray-green, glabrous; immature leaf blades yellowish green or reddish, glabrous or sparsely hairy. **Flowers** borne in unisexual **catkins**, each plant bearing either male catkins or female catkins (dioecious); appearing with the leaves. **Male catkins** 0.5–2 cm long; borne on flowering branchlets 0.3–1.5 cm long; stamens 2, filaments glabrous; bracts as in female catkins; nectary 1. **Female catkins** 1.3–3 cm long; borne on flowering branchlets 1–4 (–5) cm long; **capsules** glabrous, 3–7 mm long; styles 0.1–0.2 mm long; stipes 2–3 mm long; bracts tan to yellowish, sometimes with a reddish tinge, 0.8–1.6 mm long, persistent after flowering; nectary 1; **anthesis** early May to early June; wind- and insect-pollinated; **seeds** released late mid-May to early July, wind-dispersed. (*pedicellaris*: having pedicels)

Identification

Bog willow is a small, inconspicuous shrub, usually with a single stem about 3 ft (1 m) tall and a few short branches. It is sometimes small enough to be hidden among coarse-leaved sedges and is often overlooked. But its appearance is usually distinctive, especially the small size and peculiar shape of the leaves—look for smooth, blunt-tipped leaves with entire margins. It probably will not be mistaken for another willow, but at first glance it could be taken for swamp fly honeysuckle (*Lonicera oblongifolia*) or mountain fly honeysuckle (*L. villosa*), except the leaves are alternate, not opposite.

Natural History

Bog willow occurs frequently, but never abundantly, in a variety of moderately to weakly acidic peatlands, such as sedge meadows, floating sedge mats, shrub swamps, and open-canopy conifer swamps. It does not seem to tolerate shading or crowding and does not compete directly with larger shrubs or trees. Instead, it is usually found in more open spots among sedges and mosses. In many respects, bog willow is the ecological counterpart of sage-leaved willow (*S. candida*), which has a similar natural history but tends to occur in nonacidic peatlands. The two species rarely occur together in the same habitat.

Habitats of the type preferred by bog willow are generally stable, in an ecological sense, meaning that the species composition and community structure change very little over time. This provides few opportunities for colonization by seed and favors species that reproduce asexually (clonally). Few species of willow are so equipped, but bog willow accomplishes this by layering. Layering, in this case, occurs when mosses (typically *Sphagnum*) overgrow the lower branches, which then sprout adventitious roots within the living moss and continue to grow. In this way, bog willow can maintain itself and even spread short distances without the need for periodic disturbances to open gaps for seedbeds.

Female catkins are only about one inch (1.3–3 cm) long—May 5.

An unusually robust specimen 4' (1.2 m) tall—Itasca County.

Male catkins appear with the leaves in May.

Salix pellita (Anderss.) Anderss. ex Schneid.

Satiny willow

Tall **shrubs** or small **trees**, with single or multiple upright **stems** to 4(5) m tall and 10 cm basal diameter. 1st-year **branchlets** yellow-brown, glabrous or glabrate; second-year branchlets dark red-brown, glabrous, often glaucous in patches. **Bark** gray, smooth or somewhat rough. **Leaves** simple, alternate, deciduous. **Petioles** 3–12 mm long, glabrous or hairy, lacking glands at distal end; stipules minute and deciduous early. Mature **leaf blades** narrowly elliptical to lance-elliptical or lance-linear; the larger ones 5–12 cm long and 0.7–2 cm wide, length/width 4.5–11; apex narrowly acute to somewhat acuminate; base acute; margins entire or crenulate, revolute; upper surface dark green, sparsely hairy to glabrate; lower surface with dense silky, white hairs or rarely glabrate; immature leaf blades yellowish green or reddish-tinged, with dense silky hairs or rarely glabrous. **Flowers** borne in unisexual **catkins**, each plant bearing either male catkins or female catkins (dioecious); appearing before the leaves or with the leaves. **Male catkins** 2–3 cm long; sessile or subsessile; stamens 2, filaments glabrous or hairy at base; bracts as in female catkins; nectaries 1 or 2. **Female catkins** 2.2–8 cm long; sessile or borne on flowering branchlets to 5 mm long; **capsules** covered with long, straight, silvery hairs, 4–6 mm long; styles 0.8–1.5 mm long; stipes 0.6–1 mm long; bracts 1–2.5 mm long, dark brownish to blackish, persistent after flowering; nectary 1; **anthesis** early to late May; wind- and insect-pollinated; **seeds** released late May to late June. (*pellita*: from *pellis* for skin, the reference vague)

Identification

Satiny willow is a large, coarse shrub or potentially a small tree. The leaves are relatively long and narrow with a dense covering of straight, silky hairs on the lower surface. The leaves are somewhat like those of sage-leaved willow (*Salix candida*), but the hairs are straight and lie flat rather than curled and tangled. Rare variants of satiny willow that lack the dense hairs could be confused with slender-leaved willow (*S. petiolaris*). Notice that the youngest twigs of satiny willow often have patches of a bluish white, waxy coating (glaucous), which can be a useful character when leaves are not present.

Natural History

Satiny willow is a boreal or subboreal species, barely reaching Minnesota from the north. Little is known about this species in the state, except that it is clearly very rare. There are just a handful of verified records dating back to its discovery at Lake Vermilion in northern St. Louis County by the Arthur, Bailey, Holway expedition in 1886. Willows, however, generally go unrecognized except by specialists, of whom there are few, so it could be that satiny willow has been overlooked during routine floristic surveys.

All of the records to date are from the northeastern corner of the state on sandy or rocky shores of large lakes or on banks and gravel bars of streams. It does not appear to be an obligate wetland plant and would probably not be found in swamps, marshes, or bogs. Habitats that might be suitable for satiny willow may have some protection from wildfire but would likely be exposed to fluctuating water levels and forces such as erosion and ice scouring.

There would seem to be no shortage of this habitat type in the northeastern counties. It is a region of rugged relief and relatively young, glacially scoured landscapes ranging from 12,000 to 25,000 years old (Ojakangas and Matsch 1982). The streams are generally short with steep gradients, and the numerous lakes occur in bedrock basins with often rocky or bouldery shores. Perhaps a more thorough botanical survey of the region will reveal a previously hidden niche for satiny willow.

The female flowers, and later the capsules, are densely hairy—May 26.

Long, narrow leaves with silky hairs on lower surface.

Each male catkin has hundreds of flowers—May 24.

Bark is gray and smooth, or somewhat rough.

Salix pentandra L.

Bay willow

Introduced and possibly naturalized midsize **trees**, with 1 or a few upright **trunks**, to 18 m tall and 40 cm dbh. 1st-year **branchlets** yellowish or greenish, glabrous; second-year branchlets yellow or brownish, glabrous, shiny. **Bark** gray, with narrow ridges and moderately deep furrows. **Leaves** simple, alternate, deciduous. **Petioles** 5–12 mm long, glabrous, with enlarged glandular dots or lobes at summit; stipules minute or rarely to 3 mm long on vigorous shoots. Mature **leaf blades** elliptical to lanceolate; the larger ones 5–13.5 cm long and 2–5 cm wide, length/width 2–4; apex acuminate; base rounded; margins serrulate; upper surface dark green, glabrous, very shiny; lower surface pale green, glabrous, dull; immature leaves reddish, glabrous. **Flowers** borne in unisexual **catkins**, each tree bearing either male catkins or female catkins (dioecious); appearing with the leaves or slightly after. **Male catkins** 2.5–8.5 cm long; borne on flowering branchlets 1.2–3 cm long; stamens 3 or more, filaments hairy on lower half; bracts as in female catkins; nectaries 2. **Female catkins** 3.5–7 cm long; borne on flowering branchlets 2–9 cm long; **capsules** glabrous, 3–7 mm long; styles 0.4–0.6 mm long; stipes 0.5–1.6 mm long; bracts tan, 2–4 mm long, deciduous after flowering; nectaries 1 or 2; **anthesis** early May to late May; wind- and insect-pollinated; **seeds** released early June to late July, wind-dispersed. (*pentandra*: with 5 stamens)

Identification

Bay willow is a midsize European tree usually seen only in cultivation. The branches are typically ascending or spreading, not drooping, and they produce an irregular bushy crown. The leaves are broader than those of the other tree willows, and the margins are more finely serrate. Also, the leaves are stiff and very shiny, as are the twigs. There are two native shrub willows that have similar leaves that could cause some confusion: Shining willow (*S. lucida*), which has a longer leaf tip, and autumn willow (*S. serissima*), which has a somewhat narrower leaf.

Natural History

Bay willow is native to northern Europe and was brought to North America sometime in the eighteenth century for use in ornamental plantings and windbreaks. It is not planted in Minnesota very often, but it is sometimes used in rural landscaping, especially on lakeshore property. It is valued for the appearance of the dark green, glossy leaves, and it seems to be hardy throughout most of Minnesota. The twigs are flexible and do not seem to litter the ground after a windstorm like those of other tree willows, but older specimens do tend to develop broken or deformed limbs and a weather-beaten form.

There are only a few documented cases in Minnesota of bay willow escaping into native habitats, mostly along lakeshores and stream banks and in shallow marshes. It does not appear to be as invasive as whitecrack willow (*S. ×rubens*), which has a similar history of introduction but has proven to be extremely invasive. Although bay willow does not seem to pose a significant ecological threat, that could change over time. Given the potential risk to important lakeshore habitats, it would be wise to plant only native willows in rural areas.

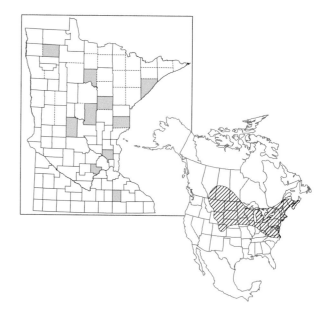

Female catkins release seeds in midsummer—July 26.

Note the stiff, shiny leaves.

Male catkins can be over 3" (2.5–8.5 cm) long—May 17.

Mature trees have coarse, furrowed bark—this trunk is 14" (36 cm) dbh.

Salix petiolaris J. E. Smith

Slender-leaved willow
[*Salix gracilis* Anderss.]

Tall **shrubs**, with numerous upright **stems** to 4 m tall and 4 cm basal diameter. 1st-year **branchlets** greenish or brownish, hairy; second-year branchlets dark red-brown or red-purple, glabrous or glabrate. **Bark** gray, smooth or slightly rough. **Leaves** simple, alternate, deciduous. **Petioles** 3–11 mm long, hairy or rarely glabrous; lacking glands at summit; stipules absent, or rudimentary and deciduous early. Mature **leaf blades** linear to lanceolate or narrowly oblong to narrowly elliptical; the larger ones 3.8–11 cm long and 0.6–1.9 cm wide, length/width 4–9; apex acute to acuminate; base acute; margins serrate to subentire; upper surface dark green, sparsely hairy to glabrous; lower surface pale green to grayish (glaucous), hairy to glabrate; immature leaf blades with long, silky hairs. **Flowers** borne in unisexual **catkins**, each plant bearing either male catkins or female catkins (dioecious); appearing with the leaves or slightly before. **Male catkins** 1–3 cm long, sessile or borne on flowering branchlets to 4 mm long; stamens 2, filaments glabrous or hairy at base only; bracts as in female catkins; nectary 1. **Female catkins** 1–3.5 cm long, borne on flowering branchlets 2–7 mm long; **capsules** hairy, 4–8 mm long; styles lacking or up to 0.3 mm long; stipes 1.5–4 mm long; bracts 1–2 mm long, brown or yellowish brown, persistent after flowering; nectary 1; **anthesis** late April to late May; wind- and insect-pollinated; **seeds** released late May to late mid-June, wind-dispersed. (*petiolaris*: pertaining to the petiole)

Identification

Slender-leaved willow is a tall shrub, sometimes reaching 13 ft (4 m) in height, with numerous slender, erect stems that arise from a rather diffuse base. The long, narrow leaves are dark green on the upper surface and a distinctive pale gray-green on the lower. The leaves of black willow (*S. nigra*) are similar but are dark green on both surfaces. The leaves of heart-leaved willow (*S. eriocephala*) are also similar but are usually broader and have noticeable stipules.

Natural History

Slender-leaved willow is probably the most common and abundant willow in Minnesota, often dominating or codominating large wetland tracts. In fact, most "willow swamps" owe their character and structure to this species. Other habitats include sedge meadows, shallow marshes, prairie swales, lakeshores, riverbanks, and roadside ditches. It will also colonize poorly drained soils in abandoned agricultural land. On occasion it can even be found in upland habitats, mostly in open or brushy woodlands, but it needs a fair amount of light and usually does not last long in direct competition with upland trees or shrubs.

Slender-leaved willow is typically found in deep to shallow peat or in wet loamy soils. Conditions range from somewhat basic (calcareous) to moderately acidic. The strongly acidic conditions that exist in bogs and muskegs seem beyond its tolerance. It is also intolerant of flood-borne sediments, which can smother its roots. This is an important factor on the floodplains of rivers that carry a heavy silt load such as the Minnesota River and the Mississippi River downstream of the Twin Cities.

Slender-leaved willow spreads only by seed, which it does very effectively, even in stable, competitive habitats where it is difficult for most willows to get a foothold. Stems that are killed by fire, cutting, or heavy browsing are quickly replaced by new stems sprouting from dormant buds on the root crown but, regardless of circumstances, individual stems do not seem to live much longer than about 15 years.

Note the dark twig and stout female catkins—May 29.

Leaves are dark green above, but pale, gray-green beneath.

Slender-leaved willow from a meadow in Washington County.

Male catkins appear briefly between late April and late May.

Salix planifolia Pursh

Planeleaf willow

Tall **shrubs,** with multiple upright **stems** to 4 m tall and 8 cm basal diameter. 1st-year **branchlets** greenish in spring, becoming red by autumn, sparsely hairy or glabrous; second-year branchlets red to red-brown, glossy (often drying dull brown), glabrous. **Bark** greenish to gray, smooth or slightly rough. **Leaves** simple, alternate, deciduous. **Petioles** 3–13 mm long, glabrous or glabrate, lacking glands at summit; stipules usually less than 3 mm long or absent. Mature **leaf blades** elliptical to narrowly elliptical; the larger ones 3.5–8 cm long and 1–2.8 cm wide, length/width 2.5–4.5; apex acute; base acute; margins crenulate to entire, somewhat revolute especially near base; upper surface dark green, glossy, glabrous or glabrate; lower surface blue-gray (glaucous), dull, glabrous or glabrate; immature leaf blades yellowish green, glossy, moderately hairy to glabrous. **Flowers** borne in unisexual **catkins,** each plant bearing either male catkins or female catkins (dioecious); appearing before the leaves. **Male catkins** 1–4 cm long; sessile or subsessile; stamens 2, filaments glabrous or hairy at base; bracts as in female catkins; nectary 1. **Female catkins** 2–6 cm long; sessile; **capsules** hairy, 2.5–6 mm long; styles 0.6–1.8 mm long; stipes 0.2–1 mm long; bracts, 1–2.5 mm long, dark brown to black, persistent after flowering; nectary 1; **anthesis** late April to early June; wind- and insect-pollinated; **seeds** released mid-May to late June, wind-dispersed. (*planifolia*: flat-leaved)

Identification

Planeleaf willow is a moderately tall, bushy shrub, averaging about 6 ft (2 m) in height, with multiple upright or leaning stems and shiny, reddish twigs. Compared to pussy willow (*S. discolor*), the leaves are smaller, stiffer, and shinier, especially in the spring. They are also more likely to be elliptical in shape and have entire margins. Also, pussy willow easily reaches the dimensions of a small tree with thick stems and coarse bark; planeleaf willow is a shrub about half the size of a large pussy willow, and it has slender stems and relatively smooth bark.

Natural History

Planeleaf willow is relatively common in the northeast and occasional elsewhere, but it never seems to be abundant. In fact, it is rarely if ever a dominant or even a codominant species; that role is usually filled by the larger and more aggressive pussy willow (*S. discolor*) or slender-leaved willow (*S. petiolaris*). Typical habitats include nonforested wetlands such as shrub swamps, sedge meadows, brushy fens, lakeshores, and stream banks. The soil is always wet and usually peaty but not the extremely acidic peat found in true bogs.

The larger populations seem to be found in fire-prone landscapes or at least in landscapes where the major vegetation patterns developed in response to fire. That may or may not be significant, but planeleaf willow does resprout vigorously when top-killed by fire or by browsing. It also seems to tolerate a certain amount of spring flooding although not sedimentation.

Compared to most of its associates, planeleaf willow is not a large shrub; the stems average only about 6 ft (2 m) tall and 1 in (2.5 cm) in diameter. But if the stems manage to grow beyond the reach of deer and moose, they can reach 11–13 ft (3.5–4 m) in height and 3 in (8 cm) in diameter, and live to an age of about 20 years. The outer stems of a clump often appear to lean and may eventually become horizontal on the ground and root along their length (a process called layering). These rooted stems may send up new aerial stems and ultimately produce a loosely interconnected colony as much as 15 ft (5 m) across.

Female catkins may not always "fill out"—May 9.

Male catkins are sessile; each flower has 2 stamens—May 2.

Two important characteristics: reddish twigs and shiny leaves.

Stems are typically multiple—bark is gray, and rough or smooth.

Salix pseudomonticola Ball

False mountain willow

Tall **shrubs**, with multiple upright **stems** to 3.5 m tall and 3 cm basal diameter. 1st-year **branchlets** yellow-green to reddish, hairy; second-year branchlets brownish to reddish, glabrous or glabrate. **Bark** gray, somewhat rough. **Leaves** simple, alternate, deciduous. **Petioles** 7–30 mm long; often reddish; hairy, especially on upper (adaxial) surface; lacking glands at summit; stipules foliaceous, persistent, 8–20 mm long. Mature **leaf blades** ovate to elliptical or oblong; the larger ones 4–11 cm long and 2.5–6 cm wide, length/width 1.4–2.5; apex acute to abruptly acuminate; base cordate to rounded; margins serrulate; upper surface dark green, glabrous or hairy on lower portion of midvein; lower surface pale green or gray-green, glabrous; immature leaf blades strongly reddish, hairy to sparsely hairy. **Flowers** borne in unisexual **catkins**, each plant bearing either male catkins or female catkins (dioecious); appearing before the leaves. **Male catkins** 1.5–4 cm long; sessile; stamens 2, filaments glabrous; bracts as in female catkins; nectary 1. **Female catkins** 3–9 cm long; sessile or borne on flowering branchlets to 0.5 cm long; **capsules** glabrous, 4–7 mm long; styles 0.6–1.8 mm long; stipes 1–2.5 mm long; bracts 1–2.4 mm long, dark brown to blackish, sometimes bicolored, persistent after flowering; nectary 1; **anthesis** early May to mid-May; wind- and insect-pollinated; **seeds** released late May to early June, wind-dispersed. (*pseudomonticola*: from *pseudo*, false, and *monticola*, mountain-dwelling; for its resemblance to *Salix monticola* Bebb)

Identification

False mountain willow is a large shrub with multiple bushy stems reaching a height of about 11 ft (3.5 m) in Minnesota but reportedly reaching 20 ft (6 m) farther west (Dorn 1975). When in the field, look for the broad, finely serrate leaves, large stipules, and strongly red-colored juvenile leaves. Even the mature leaves will usually have a reddish petiole and midvein. The leaves of balsam willow (*S. pyrifolia*) are similar but lack the prominent stipules, and those of heart-leaved willow (*S. eriocephala*) are not as broad or as reddish.

Natural History

False mountain willow was not known to occur in Minnesota until 1993, when a series of previously misidentified herbarium specimens collected between 1939 and 1952 along the St. Louis River near Fond du Lac (St. Louis County) were correctly identified by Robert Dorn. Since 1993 it has been found at another location along the St. Louis River in Carlton County and at several locations in the northwestern counties. The populations in the northwest appear to be continuous with populations in Canada, but the populations along the St. Louis River seem to be anomalous disjuncts.

In the northwest, it occurs in wet mineral soil and shallow peat in wet brush prairies and shrub swamps, usually in the company of pussy willow (*S. discolor*), Bebb's willow (*S. bebbiana*), and heart-leaved willow (*S. eriocephala*). This habitat type is common in that region, and yet false mountain willow appears to be rare or at least uncommon. Habitats along the St. Louis River are more difficult to characterize but appear to be wet seeps on clay banks or hillsides, in sunny or partially shaded forest openings.

Little is known about the ecology of false mountain willow in Minnesota, although populations in the northwest have been observed to resprout vigorously after fire and after heavy browsing by moose and deer.

A typical false mountain willow in moose habitat—Marshall County.

Note the large, leaflike stipules.

Look for broad leaves, serrate margins, and red petioles.

Female catkins are precocious, sessile; capsules are hairless—May 9.

Willows 🌿 **559**

Salix pyrifolia Anderss.

Balsam willow

Tall **shrubs**, with multiple upright **stems** to 3 m tall and 4 cm basal diameter; occasionally forming loose colonies by layering of lower branches. 1st-year **branchlets** greenish to reddish, minutely hairy or glabrate; second-year branchlets red to red-brown, glabrous, glossy. **Bark** gray, smooth or somewhat rough. **Leaves** simple, alternate, deciduous. **Petioles** 7–23 mm long, often reddish, hairy or glabrate, lacking glands at summit; stipules less than 1 mm long or absent. Mature **leaf blades** ovate to lance-ovate or elliptical; the larger ones 4–10 cm long and 2–4 cm wide, length/width 1.5–3.2; apex acute to short-acuminate; base rounded to cordate; margins serrulate or undulate; upper surface dark green, glabrous and glossy; lower surface blue-gray (glaucous), glabrous or occasionally sparsely hairy, dull; immature leaf blades reddish (drying yellowish green), glabrous or sparsely hairy. **Flowers** borne in unisexual **catkins**, each plant bearing either male catkins or female catkins (dioecious); appearing with the leaves. **Male catkins** 2–5 cm long; borne on flowering branchlets 2–7 mm long; stamens 2, filaments glabrous or hairy at base only; bracts as in female catkins; nectary 1. **Female catkins** 3–9 cm long; borne on flowering branchlets 0.5–3 cm long; the reduced leaves on catkin-bearing branchlets broad, apex obtuse to rounded; **capsules** glabrous, 5–8 mm long; styles 0.1–0.5 mm long; stipes 2–4 mm long; bracts 1–3 mm long, tan, persistent after flowering; nectary 1; **anthesis** mid-May to mid-June; wind- and insect-pollinated; **seeds** released early mid-June to early mid-July, wind-dispersed. (*pyrifolia*: with pear-shaped leaves)

Identification

The stems of balsam willow are often less than 6 ft (2 m) tall and pencil thin. They arise from a rather diffuse base and typically have only a few branches, which gives the entire plant a rather delicate, open appearance. Unlike some willows, this one is easily learned without resorting to technical details. The first thing people notice is the shiny red petioles and twigs. This contrasts with the leaf blades, which are dark green above and blue-gray beneath and have reticulate venation. Also, the leaves are proportionately broad for a willow and often have a slightly heart-shaped base. They are initially thin and translucent and

strongly red-tinged, but they become thick and almost leathery when they mature.

Natural History

Balsam willow is perhaps most common in conifer swamps with tamarack (*Larix laricina*) or black spruce (*Picea mariana*). It is also a consistent although minor component of most shrub swamps, but being smaller than the dominant willows, it is easily crowded out. Other habitats include lakeshores, riverbanks, floating peat mats, and marshes. It is not an aggressive colonizer, especially of ruderal habitats, so it is rarely seen on ditch banks or in flooded fields. And since it shows a clear preference for wet, acidic peat soil, the occasional appearance in upland habitats may be accidental or opportunistic and probably ephemeral.

Balsam willow may be delicate in appearance, but it persists tenaciously in stable, late-successional habitats where competition excludes most newcomers. Its ability to reproduce and spread by layering of the lower branches may be key. Also, with a well-established root system it can survive fire or heavy browsing and resprout the following year. And yet, balsam willow seems to be sensitive to sedimentation and abnormal changes in water levels, particularly nonseasonal flooding and drought.

Capsules are smooth, and will mature in early summer—May 3.

Note shape of small leaves at base of male catkins—May 18.

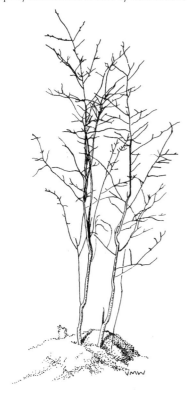

Relatively broad leaves, red petioles, and no visible stipules.

Stems are usually less than 10' (3 m) tall and 1.5" (4 cm) diameter.

Salix ×*rubens* Schrank

Whitecrack willow

Nonnative, naturalized, large **trees**, with 1–5 upright, leaning or decumbent **trunks**, to 30 m tall and 116 cm dbh. 1st-year **branchlets** yellow or yellow-brown, hairy; second-year branchlets yellow to yellow-green or brownish, glabrous or glabrate, shiny or dull. **Bark** gray or gray-brown, with deep furrows and coarse ridges. **Leaves** simple, alternate, deciduous. **Petioles** 6–18 mm long, hairy, usually with enlarged glandular dots or lobes at summit; stipules small, deciduous early. Mature **leaf blades** narrowly elliptical to oblong-elliptical or lanceolate; the larger ones 7–15 cm long and 1.3–3 cm wide, length/width 4–7; apex acuminate to long-acuminate or caudate; base acute; margins serrate to serrulate; upper surface dark green, shiny or dull, glabrous or glabrate; lower surface pale green or pale blue-green, dull, glabrous or glabrate; immature leaf blades reddish or yellowish green, covered with long, silky hairs at first, becoming glabrous. **Flowers** borne in unisexual **catkins**, each tree bearing either male catkins or female catkins (dioecious); appearing with the leaves or slightly after. **Male catkins** 3.5–6.5 cm long; borne on flowering branchlets 0.6–1.2 cm long; stamens 2, filaments hairy on lower half; bracts as in female catkins; nectaries 2. **Female catkins** 5–9 cm long; borne on flowering branchlets 0.5–2.5 cm long; **capsules** glabrous, 4–6 mm long; styles 0.3–0.8 mm long; stipes 0.5–0.8 mm long; bracts pale yellow or tan, 1–2.8 mm long, deciduous after flowering; nectary 1; **anthesis** early May to early June; wind- and insect-pollinated; **seeds** released late May to late June, wind- and water-dispersed. (*rubens*: reddish)

Identification

Whitecrack willow can become a massive tree with a broad, rounded crown. For years it was mistaken for the native peach-leaved willow (*S. amygdaloides*), but it is actually a hybrid of two European trees: white willow (*S. alba*) and crack willow (*S. fragilis*) (Meikle 1984). It exists like a chameleon alongside peach-leaved willow, yet the two can be told apart with practice. The mature leaves of whitecrack willow are smooth, but when just unfolding, they are covered with long, straight, silvery hairs. The unfolding leaves of peach-leaved willow have patches of relatively short, crinkly, white or reddish hairs, or occasionally no hairs at all. The differences are easiest to see in early or midsummer when each twig will have both fully expanded leaves

and newly emerging leaves. The common willow tree seen in the winter with bright yellow twigs is apparently a variety of this species (*S.* ×*rubens* nothovar. *basfordiana* (Scaling ex Salter) Meikle).

Natural History

Whitecrack willow was brought to North America from Europe in the eighteenth century, possibly earlier, and came to Minnesota with the early settlers. It was called "white willow" (Upham 1884) and was widely planted with box elder (*Acer negundo*) and plains cottonwood (*Populus deltoides* subsp. *monilifera*) as a windbreak and as fuel for prairie homesteads (Records 1913). There were financial incentives offered by both the federal and state governments to plant trees on the otherwise treeless prairie, and "white willow" was considered one of best. Unfortunately, it escaped into native habitats and has since spread to nearly every part of Minnesota. It is now common in a variety of wetland habitats, but it is most invasive on riverbanks and active floodplains, where it competes directly with the native willow trees.

Although whitecrack willow does produce flowers, the seeds are apparently sterile. But its twigs, which are very brittle at the base and break in a strong wind, are carried on water and wind and they will root tenaciously when they contact moist soil (Shafroth et al. 1994). This method of vegetative propagation is common among willows that specialize in riparian habitats, but whitecrack willow evidently does it better than any of Minnesota's native willows.

Male catkins are large and conspicuous, but fade quickly—May 11.

The gray-green color gives away whitecrack willow in late season—Freeborn County.

Female flowers are in very long, slender catkins—May 24.

Bark has deep furrows and coarse ridges—this trunk is 22" (56 cm) dbh.

Leaves are slender, stiff, and usually dull.

Willows 🪶 **563**

Salix serissima (Bailey) Fern.

Autumn willow

Tall **shrubs,** with single or multiple upright **stems** to 3 m tall and 4 cm basal diameter. 1st-year **branchlets** yellowish, glabrous; 2nd-year branchlets yellow to yellowish brown or sometimes reddish, shiny, glabrous. **Bark** brown to gray, smooth. **Leaves** simple, alternate, deciduous. **Petioles** 3–13 mm long, glabrous, glandular dots conspicuous at summit; stipules minute, often reduced to a single gland or absent. Mature **leaf blades** elliptical to lanceolate or oblong-lanceolate; the larger ones 4.5–9.5 cm long and 1–3.5 cm wide, length/width 2.5–6; apex of later leaves acuminate to long-acuminate, earlier leaves acute to short-acuminate; base tapered or narrowly rounded; margins finely and regularly serrulate; upper surface dark green, shiny, glabrous; lower surface, pale green, dull, glabrous; immature leaf blades reddish or yellowish green, glabrous. **Flowers** borne in unisexual **catkins,** each plant bearing either male catkins or female catkins; appearing with the leaves or after. **Male catkins** 1.5–4.7 cm long; borne on flowering branchlets 0.5–3.5 cm long; stamens 3 or more (usually 5), filaments hairy on lower half; bracts as in female catkins but persistent; nectaries 2 or more. **Female catkins** 2–5 cm long; borne on flowering branchlets 1–5 cm long; **capsules** glabrous, 7–11 mm long; styles 0.3–1 mm long; stipes 1–2 mm long; bracts pale yellow, 1.2–4 mm long, deciduous after flowering; nectary 1; **anthesis** mid-May to mid-June; wind- and insect-pollinated; **seeds** released early July to late October, wind-dispersed. (*serissima*: late-coming, in reference to the maturation of the capsules)

Identification

Autumn willow is a comparatively small willow, usually no more than about 6 ft (2 m) tall. The leaves are glossy, completely hairless, and have finely serrate margins. There are two species with similar leaves: McCall's willow (*S. maccalliana*) and shining willow (*S. lucida*). Be aware that the early-season leaves of autumn willow and shining willow will have shorter tips than leaves produced later in the year, so do not compare early-season leaves of one specimen with late-season leaves of a different specimen. True to its name, autumn willow is the only willow in Minnesota still holding catkins in autumn.

Natural History

Although autumn willow is not uncommon in Minnesota, it is not a major element in any plant community. Instead, it seems to occur as widely scattered individuals or in small, sparse populations. Most habitats are in shallow peat or occasionally wet mineral soil, and include calcareous fens, sedge meadows, conifer swamps, and shrub swamps. Conditions are usually weakly acidic or pH-neutral, but it does surprisingly well in strongly basic (calcareous) habitats, even to the point of rooting in marl deposits where the pH may be above 8.0.

It is intolerant of shade and most often grows in the open, usually in competition with sedges or herbaceous plants. It does not seem to compete well in dense shrub-dominated communities; it is easily crowded out by taller and more aggressive shrubs. Under all conditions it seems to be relatively short-lived. In fact, it is difficult to find individuals with stems more than 8 to 12 years old. It also seems that populations are rather mobile or even transient, perhaps more so than other willows. It reproduces only by seed and seems to rely on periodic small-scale disturbances to open microhabitats for seed germination.

Autumn willow produces flowers in the spring like the other willows, but it does not release the majority of its seeds until late summer or autumn. Often the capsules are still plump and full of seeds after the leaves are shed in the autumn, and sometimes even after the snow falls.

A well-developed autumn willow from a Marshall County fen.

Females are pollinated in spring, but release seeds in autumn—May 31.

Leaves are shiny and serrulate—compare with McCalla's willow.

Multiple slender stems are characteristic.

Male catkins are as large as the female catkins—May 29.

Sambucus, the elderberries

Caprifoliaceae: Honeysuckle family

The elderberries, or elders, form a genus of about 20 species of deciduous shrubs, small trees, and rarely perennial herbs found in temperate and subtropical regions of both hemispheres. There are 5 species in the United States, and 2 in Minnesota. (*Sambucus* is the classical Latin name for the European elder, *S. nigra*; it is believed to have originated from the Greek *sambuke*, a stringed musical instrument thought to be made of the wood of elder.)

Key to the Genus Sambucus *in Minnesota*

1. First-year branchlets (< 1 year old) glabrous; 2nd-year branchlets (1–2 years old) with white pith; leaflets usually 7, occasionally 5; petioles hairy in the channel on the upper surface, otherwise glabrous; inflorescence flat-topped, 9–18 cm across, wider than tall; flowering July to August; fruit black, ripening August to September .... *S. nigra* subsp. *canadensis*

1. First-year branchlets with short stiff hairs; 2nd-year branchlets with brown pith; leaflets usually 5, occasionally 7; petioles evenly hairy on all surfaces; inflorescence pyramidal, 3–8 cm across, taller than wide; flowering in May; fruit red, ripening June to July .... *S. racemosa*

Sambucus nigra L. subsp. *canadensis* (L.) R. Bolli

American elderberry

[*S. canadensis* L.]

Tall **shrubs**, with multiple erect or arching **stems** to 4 m tall and 9 cm dbh; clonal by stolons and reportedly by root suckers or rhizomes. **Branchlets** of the current year greenish, glabrous, with white pith; 1-year-old branchlets grayish to brownish, glabrous, pith also white. **Bark** grayish brown, ± smooth or rough in age, marked with warty lenticels. **Leaves** pinnately compound, opposite, deciduous. **Petioles** 3–7 cm long, hairy in the channel on the upper surface, otherwise glabrous. **Petiolules** 0–6 mm long. **Leaflets** 7 or occasionally 5; ovate or lance-ovate to elliptical or occasionally somewhat oblong; 5–12 cm long, 2.5–5.5 cm wide, the terminal leaflet somewhat larger than the lateral; base rounded to acute, usually symmetrical; apex acuminate; margins sharply serrate; upper surface dark green, sparsely short-hairy at least on midvein; lower surface pale green, short-hairy on veins, or occasionally nearly glabrous. **Inflorescence** a ± flat-topped terminal cyme 9–18 cm across, with 200–400 flowers; peduncle 6–14 cm long. **Flowers** bisexual, 5-merous, white; sepals triangular to oblong, about 0.5 mm long; corolla 3.5–7 mm across; filaments 1–2 mm long; **anthesis** early July to mid-August; insect-pollinated. **Fruit** a drupelike berry with 3–5 stonelike seeds, globose, 5–6 mm in diameter, ripening purplish black; maturing early August to mid-September; animal-dispersed. (*nigra*: black; *canadensis*: of Canada)

Identification

American elderberry is a tall, spreading shrub with weak, arching stems. The most conspicuous features are the large compound leaves and the clusters of foul-smelling white flowers. It looks much like red-berried elder (*S. racemosa*), but the flowers are in flat-topped clusters and appear in midsummer rather than early spring, and the berries are black rather than red. An infallible test any time of the year is the color of the pith in 2nd-year twigs. It is pure white in American elderberry, but yellowish brown in red-berried elder.

Natural History

American elderberry is widespread and relatively common in southern Minnesota, especially the southeast. There are also scattered records from the north, but they appear to be transient outposts that originate from seeds spread in the droppings of far-ranging birds. It commonly grows in wet or moist spots on floodplains, along streams, at the edge of marshes, and in grassy meadows. It has shallow roots that do well in saturated, oxygen-poor soils, especially in basic (calcareous) or circumneutral silt, loam, or peat.

The need for direct sunlight and freedom from competition seems critical for American elderberry. It does not compete successfully in the shade of trees, and under most circumstances it does not compete well in established shrub communities either. Slower-growing, but longer-lived shrubs such as willows (*Salix* spp.), speckled alder (*Alnus incana* subsp. *rugosa*), or red-osier dogwood (*Cornus sericea*) tend to dominate such habitats, providing few opportunities for a fast-growing but short-lived pioneer like American elderberry.

It usually does better in early successional, species-poor habitats dominated by grasses or sedges, particularly abandoned farmland in low-lying areas, swales in utility corridors that are kept open by periodic brush-cutting, and the banks of roadside ditches. Under favorable conditions it can form sizable colonies 30 ft (9 m) or more across, but it is more often seen as single shrubs or small colonies.

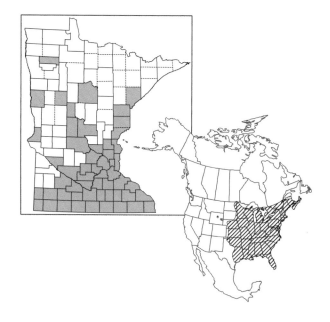

Branches will droop under the weight of ripe fruit—
September 13.

The flat-topped inflorescence can be 7" (18 cm) across—July 15.

Stems are weak and covered with warty lenticels.

A sizeable colony growing with reed canary grass—Ramsey County.

569

Sambucus racemosa L.

Red-berried elder

[*S. pubens* Michx.; *S. racemosa* L. subsp. *pubens* (Michx.) House]

Tall **shrubs**, with multiple erect or arching **stems** to 4.3 m tall and 12 cm dbh; clonal by root suckers or rhizomes, and reportedly stolons. **Branchlets** of the current year greenish brown, short-hairy, with white pith; 1-year-old branchlets grayish to brownish, glabrous, pith brown. **Bark** gray; young stems smooth except for enlarged warty lenticels, older stems becoming rough with thin, narrow, platelike scales. **Leaves** pinnately compound, opposite, deciduous. **Petioles** 2.5–6 cm long, evenly short-hairy on all surfaces. **Petiolules** 3–15 mm long. **Leaflets** 5 or occasionally 7; ovate to lance-ovate or elliptical to oblong; 5–12 cm long, 2–5 cm wide, the lateral leaflets somewhat larger than the terminal; base rounded to acute, asymmetrical; apex acuminate; margins sharply serrate; upper surface dark green, sparsely short-hairy at least on midvein; lower surface pale green, short-hairy especially on main veins. **Inflorescence** a pyramidal or ovate, terminal cyme 3–8 cm across, with 100–200 flowers; peduncle 2–9 cm long. **Flowers** bisexual, 5-merous, whitish; sepals triangular to oblong, about 0.5 mm long; corolla 3.5–6 mm across; filaments 0.5–1.5 mm long; **anthesis** late April to early June; insect-pollinated. **Fruit** a drupelike berry with 3–5 stonelike seeds, globose, 4–7 mm in diameter, ripening bright red; maturing mid-June to late July; animal-dispersed. (*racemosa*: with racemes)

Identification

Red-berried elder is a rather large, coarse shrub with tangled, arching stems, brittle branches and stout, pithy twigs. It is similar in size and form to American elderberry (*S. nigra* subsp. *canadensis*) but differs by a number of reliable characters (see key). One character that can be seen at any time of the year is the color of the pith in 2nd-year branchlets; it is distinctly yellowish brown in red-berried alder compared to pure white in American elderberry.

Natural History

Red-berried elder is a common understory shrub in mesic or moist forests throughout most of the state, especially the eastern half. Although usually associated with hardwoods, it also occurs with conifers. It is very tolerant of shade and easily survives under a closed canopy, but it generally does better along an edge or under a canopy gap. It also occurs along stream banks, lakeshores, and at the edge of marshes and swamps. Soils are usually loamy but sometimes sandy or rocky, and range from acidic to basic (calcareous).

In a stable forest interior it is slow growing and is usually seen as single scattered individuals. But if released from competition, it can quickly spread underground and form extensive colonies of a dozen or more plants. Under all circumstances, individuals seem short-lived, rarely surviving much beyond 10 or 15 years.

The leaves start expanding early in the spring, often before the end of April. This happens before most other shrubs show any sign of life and well before leaves of the canopy trees appear. The leaves also stay late into the autumn, usually remaining bright green until the first hard frost. This extended growing season may help explain the success of red-berried elder in shady understories.

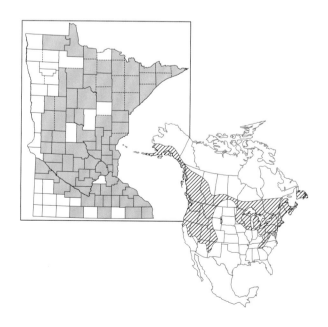

Fruits turn bright red in midsummer.

An edge-grown specimen from Cook County.

Inflorescence 1–3 " (3–8 cm) across, and pyramid shaped—May 8.

Stems can reach 14' (4.3 m) in height and nearly 5 " (12 cm) dbh.

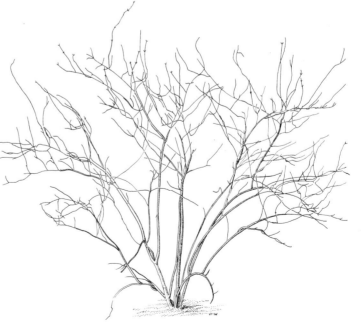

Shepherdia, the buffaloberries

Elaeagnaceae: Oleaster family

The buffaloberries comprise a strictly North American genus of 3 species, of which 2 occur in Minnesota. (*Shepherdia* is named for English botanist John Shepherd, 1764–1836.)

Key to the Genus Shepherdia *in Minnesota*

1. The largest leaf blades 1.8–3.3 cm wide and 1.7–2.6 times as long as wide (l/w = 1.7–2.6); branchlets of the current year reddish brown; thorns absent; upper surface of leaves with scattered stellate hairs or hairless (requires magnification); flowers opening when the leaves are 1/4 to 1/2 grown .... *S. canadensis*
1. The largest leaf blades 0.8–1.7 cm wide and 2.6–4.5 times as long as wide (l/w = 2.6–4.5); branchlets of the current year silvery; thorns usually present at the tips of short branchlets; upper surface of leaves covered with ± circular scales (requires magnification); flowers opening before the leaves appear .... *S. argentea*

Shepherdia argentea (Pursh) Nutt.

Silver buffaloberry

Large **shrubs** or small **trees**, with upright **stems** to 5 m tall and 10 cm basal diameter; forming rhizomatous colonies. **Branchlets** formed during the current year covered with silvery translucent scales, which flake off the 2nd year; thorns occasional to frequent, occurring at the tips of short branchlets 2–7 cm long. **Bark** gray-brown, rough, exfoliating in age. **Leaves** simple, opposite, deciduous. **Petioles** 3–10 mm long, scaly. **Leaf blades** oblong to narrowly elliptical or lanceolate; 3–5 cm long, 0.8–1.7 cm wide, length/width 2.6–4.5; base tapered; apex blunt; margins entire; upper surface green, moderately covered with colorless, sessile scales; lower surface pale gray-green, densely covered with colorless and brownish, sessile scales. **Inflorescence** a short, crowded cluster of 2–7 flowers borne from nodes on 2nd-year wood. **Flowers** 4-merous, unisexual (dioecious) with each plant having either male flowers or female flowers; perianth 2–6 mm across, greenish on the upper (inner) surface, white-scaly on the lower surface; stamens 8; **anthesis** mid-April to mid-May, flowers opening before the leaves appear; insect-pollinated. **Fruit** an achene enclosed in the enlarged fleshy calyx, appearing berrylike or drupelike, elliptical to ± globose, red, 5–9 mm across; maturing mid-July to mid-August, persisting through winter if not eaten; animal-dispersed. (*argentea*: silvery)

Identification

Silver buffaloberry is a relatively large shrub, reaching a height of 12–15 ft (4–5 m). The stiff, coarse branches often end with a sharp thorn, and notice that the narrow, blunt-tipped leaves are opposite on the stem rather than alternate. The flowers appear in early spring before the leaves emerge, but they are small and inconspicuous. The fruits, however, are bright red and often very conspicuous. They mature in mid to late summer, and if not eaten, they may persist on the branches through winter.

Natural History

Silver buffaloberry is a characteristic shrub of the plains and semiarid regions of western North America, barely reaching the western edge of Minnesota. It occurs here in remnant prairie habitats, especially in ravines and coulees and along streams and creeks. Yet occurrences in Minnesota are rare or at least uncommon; the reasons for this are not entirely understood. Soils are usually sandy or loamy or sometimes clayey and range from circumneutral to somewhat calcareous or even slightly saline or alkaline. Nodules on the roots are known to fix atmospheric nitrogen (Rodriguez-Barrueco 1968), and if the stems are killed by fire or grazing, they resprout vigorously from buried rhizomes and root crowns.

It is sometimes found as a solitary shrub but more often in rhizomatous colonies with dozens or even hundreds of interconnected stems. It may also be found as a component of semipermanent shrub communities with species such as chokecherry (*Prunus virginiana*), American plum (*P. americana*), wolfberry (*Symphoricarpos occidentalis*), or fireberry hawthorn (*Crataegus chrysocarpa*).

The fruit and foliage of silver buffaloberry are eaten by ungulates, formerly bison and elk, which is probably how the seeds were dispersed on the presettlement landscape. However, seedlings on the modern landscape have been reported as rare or even nonexistent (Looman 1984), and it is unclear how, or if, seed dispersal occurs now. This means that existing plants are primarily clones that may actually trace their seedling origin to the presettlement past. Such stubborn persistence is possible because rhizome systems can live much longer than the individual stems, which may survive only 20 or 25 years (Looman 1984).

Note the stamens on these male flowers, and the thorn tip—April 25.

Genders are separate; these flowers are from a female tree—April 25.

The fruits often persist through the winter—July 21.

Bark is rough; it eventually peels and exfoliates.

Buffaloberries 🌿 **575**

Shepherdia canadensis (L.) Nutt.

Canada buffaloberry

Large **shrubs,** with multiple upright or arching **stems** to 3.2 m tall and 4.5 cm basal diameter. **Branchlets** formed during the current year covered with reflective brown to reddish brown scales, which become dull gray the 2nd year and eventually flake off; thorns lacking. **Bark** dark gray, rough. **Leaves** simple, opposite, deciduous. **Petioles** 4–8 mm long, scaly. **Leaf blades** ovate to lanceolate or lance-elliptical; 4–7 cm long, 1.8–3.3 cm wide, length/width 1.7–2.6; base rounded or occasionally tapered; apex blunt; margins entire; upper surface dark green, sparsely covered with sessile white stellate hairs, or sometimes glabrate; lower surface pale gray-green, densely covered with stalked, silver-white, stellate hairs interspersed with stalked brown scales. **Inflorescence** a short spike of 5–12 flowers borne from nodes on 2nd-year wood. **Flowers** 4-merous, unisexual (dioecious), with each plant having either male flowers or female flowers; perianth 3–5 mm across, greenish on the upper surface, brown scaly on the lower surface; stamens 8; **anthesis** early mid-May to early June, flowers opening as the leaves are expanding; insect-pollinated. **Fruit** an achene enclosed in the enlarged fleshy calyx, appearing drupelike or berrylike, elliptical to ± globose, shiny red, 5–9 mm across; maturing late June to early August; animal-dispersed. (*canadensis*: of Canada)

Identification

Canada buffaloberry is a striking shrub and not likely to be confused with anything else that occurs in northern forests. The leaves are rather stiff and rigid with a distinctive blunt tip and entire margins. The upper surface is dark green, but the lower surface is covered with dense silvery hairs and scattered brown scales. The young twigs and buds are covered with reflective reddish scales, and even the bright red fruits (considered unpalatable) have a few scales.

Natural History

Canada buffaloberry is primarily a shrub of boreal and mountain regions, reaching Minnesota sporadically from the north. It is essentially a forest species, but it does not do well in deep shade; it seems to thrive only under a thin canopy or along an exposed edge. It is known to prefer calcareous substrates, which limits its distribution even further,

especially in the northeast where substrates tend to be acidic. It also has the unusual ability to produce nodules on its roots that can convert atmospheric nitrogen into nitrate, a form useful to plants (Rodriguez-Barrueco 1968).

There are a few records from forests near Lake Superior in the Duluth area, but most are from the northern border region. They range from Cook County in the northeast to Kittson County in the northwest. Those in the northeast occur in a coniferous forest landscape, usually in forests of pines (*Pinus* spp.) but also with hardwoods, especially on steep, rocky bluffs, rocky ledges, and outcrops. This is a fire-maintained landscape, but the interval between wildfires is relatively long, perhaps 100–150 years.

Habitats in the northwestern counties are in an aspen parkland landscape, specifically in dry to mesic soil in open groves of trembling aspen (*Populus tremuloides*) that develop within a prairie matrix. In this region the normal interval between wildfires is relatively short, possibly just 5–10 years. This is significant because if Canada buffaloberry is top-killed by fire it will resprout from the root crown, but not vigorously, and it may take several years to fully recover and flower again (Hamer 1996).

Female flowers on brown, scaly twigs—May 23

Fruits look appealing but are considered unpalatable—July 11.

Each plant has either male or female flowers; these are male—May 23.

Note rounded base and blunt tip.

Buffaloberries 🌿 **577**

Buffaloberries

Sibbaldiopsis, three-toothed cinquefoil

Rosaceae: Rose family

This North American genus contains a single species, a small shrub segregated from the otherwise herbaceous genus *Potentilla* by Rydberg in 1898. It is still maintained as *Potentilla* in most regional plant manuals. (*Sibbaldiopsis* is for its resemblance to the genus *Sibbaldia*: named for Sir Robert Sibbald, 1641–1722.)

Sibbaldiopsis tridentata (Ait.) Rydb.

Three-toothed cinquefoil
[*Potentilla tridentata* Ait.]

Low **shrubs,** with perennial woody caudex and upright herbaceous **stems** to 27 cm tall, stems greenish to reddish green, hairy. **Caudex** creeping or trailing and often branching, clothed in the persistent stipules and petioles of previous years, brown, hairy. **Leaves** palmately trifoliate, alternate, evergreen. **Petioles** of basal leaves to 6 cm long, disarticulating at the blade and persisting; petioles of midcauline leaves shorter; upper cauline leaves sessile and involucre-like; stipules sheathing, with 2 lanceolate or subulate lobes, persistent. **Leaflets** 3, sessile, oblanceolate to narrowly obovate; 1.2–3.5 cm long, 0.5–1.3 cm wide; base acute; apex with 2–5 lobes (usually 3), otherwise margins entire; upper surface dark green, sparsely hairy to glabrate; lower surface pale green, moderately to sparsely hairy. **Flowers** bisexual, 5-merous, white; borne in open cymes of 3–25; bractlets narrowly elliptical to lanceolate, 2–5 mm long; sepals triangular-ovate, acuminate to apiculate, 2.5–4 mm long; petals obovate to orbicular, 4–7 mm long; corolla 0.9–1.4 cm across (measured flat); stamens and carpels numerous; **anthesis** mid-June to late July; insect-pollinated. **Fruit** a compact head of achenes surrounded by the persistent sepals and bractlets, maturing early mid-July to late August; gravity-dispersed. (*tridentata*: 3-toothed, in reference to the tips of the leaves)

Identification

Three-toothed cinquefoil is a low shrub, usually about 6–8 inches (15–20 cm) tall with small, white flowers and rather unusual leaves. Each leaf is divided into 3 separate leaflets, and the tip of each leaflet has 3 teeth. They have a somewhat thick and leathery texture and are generally considered evergreen. The base of the plant is woody, qualifying it as a shrub, or in some terminology a "subshrub," but the rest of the plant is herbaceous and dies back each winter. This makes it more likely to be confused with a true herbaceous species, possibly one of the wild strawberries (*Fragaria vesca* subsp. *americana* or *F. virginiana*) or herbaceous cinquefoils (*Potentilla* spp).

Natural History

Although three-toothed cinquefoil appears to be dispersed throughout the forested region of the state, it is actually restricted to rather unusual habitats. These are typically dry, "barren" habitats on bedrock outcrops, cliffs, sandplains, beaches, or dunes. Habitats may have scattered oaks (*Quercus* spp.), jack pine (*Pinus banksiana*), or eastern redcedar (*Juniperus virginiana*), but more often there is only a sparse cover of grasses, sedges, or lichens.

The nature of the substrate varies from nearly pure sand to bedrock of granite, sandstone, dolomite, or basalt. They all tend to be low in fertility and range from slightly basic (calcareous) to moderately acidic; there is usually little if any true soil. Although the habitats are not prone to fire or flooding, they are regularly exposed to extreme temperatures and desiccating conditions. A good example is the bedrock outcrops on the shore of Lake Superior, where three-toothed cinquefoil is fairly common.

Ideal habitat on the rocky shoreline of Lake Superior—July 1.

Achenes (seeds) are enclosed within the dried sepals—August 22.

Each leaf has 3 leaflets, and each leaflet has 3 teeth.

Three-toothed cinquefoil 581

Smilax, bristly greenbrier

Smilacaceae: Greenbrier family

Bristly greenbrier belongs to a genus of 250 to 350 species of predominately climbing vines; most are woody, but some are herbaceous. They are distributed widely in tropical and temperate regions of the world, with 22 species in the United States and 4 in Minnesota, but only 1 Minnesota species is woody. (*Smilax* is an ancient Greek name of a woody vine.)

Smilax tamnoides L.

Bristly greenbrier

[*Smilax tamnoides* L. var. *hispida* Fern.; *S. hispida* Muhl. ex Torr.]

Climbing **vines**, with single or multiple **stems** to 10 m tall and 2 cm diameter; surface of stems green, becoming brown in age; the lower portion densely covered with blackish, needlelike prickles of varying forms 1–8 mm long; forming colonies by short or moderately long rhizomes, sending up stems at intervals of 10–20 cm. **Branches** few or many; usually prickly, sometimes smooth. **Leaves** simple, alternate, deciduous. **Petioles** 6–18 mm long, glabrous, somewhat winged, with a persistent dilated base bearing a pair of slender tendrils to 10 cm long. **Leaf blades** ovate to broadly lance-ovate; 6–16 cm long, 4–13 cm wide; base rounded or cordate; apex acute to short-acuminate; margins fringed with minute jagged teeth; surfaces glabrous, with 5–7 conspicuous longitudinal veins. **Inflorescence** a hemispheric umbel of up to 25 flowers, borne on a long glabrous peduncle; peduncles arising singly from leaf axils on 1st-year branchlets. **Flowers** 3-merous; unisexual, with each plant bearing either male flowers or female flowers (dioecious); greenish yellow; petals and sepals strap shaped, 4–7 mm long in male flowers, averaging somewhat shorter in female flowers; stigmas 3; **anthesis** late May to late June; insect-pollinated. **Fruit** a black globose berry, 5–8 mm in diameter; maturing early August to early October; animal-dispersed. (*Tamnoides*: like *Tamnus*, bryony)

Identification

Bristly greenbrier is a climbing vine with broad leaves, and stems with sharp, slender bristles. The stems never develop real bark, so they remain more or less green. This could cause confusion with the nonwoody species of greenbrier that occur in Minnesota (Mangaly 1968). They all have leaves with a similar shape and parallel venation, and all have at least a vinelike form, but only bristly greenbrier has bristles and climbs to a height of more than about 6 ft (2 m). In fact, this is the only bristly climbing vine in Minnesota.

Natural History

Bristly greenbrier is fairly common in southern Minnesota, especially on forested floodplains. It often forms dense, tangled, multistemmed colonies that hang curtainlike from the lower branches of forest

trees, sometimes from a height as great as 35 ft (10 m). Spring flooding and moderate levels of sedimentation are often features of its habitat and do not seem to deter it. It also seems to tolerate shade fairly well, although in deep shade it takes the form of a limp, passive sprawler.

The prickles vary greatly in form, even on a single stem. They range from thin, weak, and bristlelike, to somewhat broad-based and strong, but they're always sharp. They easily penetrate clothing and have the habit of breaking off in the skin and causing a persistent irritation and sometimes infection.

The tendrils are unique in that they come from the base of the petioles, and although the leaf blade itself is shed each fall, the lower portion of the petiole and the tendrils remain. They become hard and very strong, and they last for several years. Being a monocot, bristly greenbrier does not produce secondary tissue, therefore the stems never reach a great diameter or produce bark, and in fact they are relatively short-lived. How long they live is not known, but probably only 5–10 years.

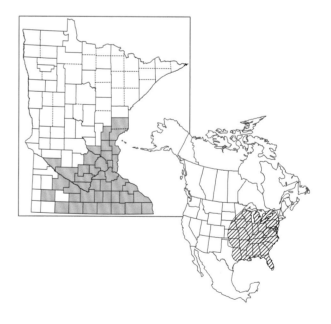

Flowers are in hemispheric umbels, these are female—June 9.

*Flowers from a male vine display yellow anthers—
June 14.*

*Fruits attach to a common point, a configuration called
an "umbel."*

Prickles vary in size and shape but all are sharp.

Note the parallel veins on the leaf blades.

Bristly greenbrier   **585**

Solanum, European bittersweet

Solanaceae: Nightshade family

Solanum is a large genus with well over 1,000 species, including many familiar garden plants such as the potato (*S. tuberosum*). They are predominately herbaceous and distributed widely, although mostly in tropical America. About 80 species occur in the United States, but almost a third are nonnative weeds from Europe and South America. Minnesota has perhaps 2 native species (both herbaceous) and an additional 4 nonnative weeds (1 woody). (*Solanum* is the classical Latin name of nightshade.)

Solanum dulcamara L.

European bittersweet

Naturalized nonnative climbing **vines**, with sprawling or twining **stems** to 4 m long and 1 cm basal diameter; woody only near the base. **Branches** few or many. **Branchlets** pale green to yellowish or brownish, glabrous or hairy. **Bark** of mature stems thin, brown to gray. **Leaves** simple, alternate, deciduous. **Petioles** glabrous or hairy, 1.5–4 cm long. **Leaf blades** ovate, 4–10 cm long, 2.5–6 cm wide; base rounded to truncate, cordate or hastate; apex acute to acuminate; margins with 1–4 (usually 2) prominent lobes or auricles near the base, or unlobed, entire; surfaces bright green, glabrous or hairy. **Inflorescence** a long-peduncled cyme with 10–25 flowers; lateral or terminal. **Flowers** bisexual, 5-merous; sepals greenish or bluish, 2–3 mm long, the lobes less than 1 mm long; petals blue or violet, rarely white, reflexed, 6–10 mm long; anthers 5–7 mm long, yellow, converging in a central column surrounding the protruding style; **anthesis** throughout the season, May to September; insect-pollinated. **Fruit** a shiny red berry with thin, translucent skin, ovoid or ellipsoidal, 8–11 mm long, 2-celled; maturing early July to late October; animal-dispersed. **Seeds** numerous. (*dulcamara*: from the Latin *dulcis*, sweet; and *amarus*, bitter, in reference to the roots, which are said to taste sweet at first, then bitter)

Identification

European bittersweet is a short, scrambling vine, usually 6–9 ft (2–3 m) long. The flowers are similar in structure to those of a potato or tomato, with the blue petals reflexed backwards and a bright yellow column of anthers projecting forward. At least some of the leaves toward the end of the stem will be deeply lobed, often in unique shapes. Despite the common name, European bittersweet is unrelated to American bittersweet (*Celastrus scandens*).
Note: Among all the cases of poisonous plants being ingested by children and reported to Hennepin Regional Poison Center, this species ranks among the highest. Although the actual degree of toxicity of the ripe berries is reportedly low (Hornfeldt and Collins 1990), it is wise to avoid eating any part of the plant.

Natural History

This species is native to most of Europe, where it inhabits damp woods and riverbanks. Europeans have used it to treat a variety of ailments; at one time it was even thought to protect against witches (Grigson 1955). It was brought to North America from Europe during colonial times (*fide* Mills et al. 1994), presumably for medicinal purposes. But there is no indication that it was extensively used for any purpose. It has, however, spread rapidly on its own and become naturalized over the northern half of the country. It is now fairly common in Minnesota, especially as an urban weed around buildings and in industrial areas. But it also invades native habitats, especially marshes, swamps, pond margins, and wet woods, where it shows a fairly high degree of shade tolerance. Although it is invasive, it is not abundant enough in natural habitats to be considered a serious ecological problem, at least not yet.

The stem is pliant and tough but too weak to grow upright unless supported from the sides by grasses or herbaceous plants. Yet, it may eventually clamber over other vegetation or climb as high as 13 ft (4 m) by twining on shrubs or saplings. The seeds are spread widely by birds and can germinate under a variety of moist conditions. It is short-lived but fast growing, often flowering the first year from seed. Individual stems can flower continuously from May to September, and it is not unusual to find both ripe fruit and new flowers on the same stem.

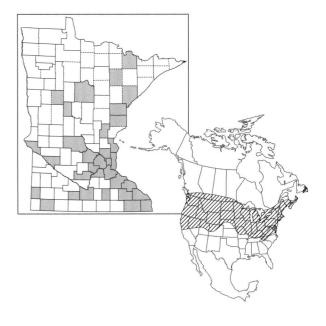

Flowers bear a family resemblance to those of tomato—July 15.

Note the prominent lobes at the base of each leaf.

Fruits are known to cause poisoning in children—September 10.

Sorbus, the mountain-ashes

Rosaceae: Rose family

This genus includes about 260 species of trees and shrubs. They occur predominately in temperate and subtropical regions of Asia but also in Europe and North America. The United States has 9 native and perhaps 3 naturalized species; Minnesota has 2 native and 1 naturalized species. (*Sorbus* is the classical Latin name for the European service-tree, *S. domestica.*)

Key to the Genus Sorbus *in Minnesota*

1. Leaflets 4–8 cm long, the lower surface glabrous, or sparsely hairy on main veins; apex of leaflets with an elongated terminal tooth creating a long, slender point; petioles 3–6 cm long; petioles, ovaries, and sepals glabrous or sparsely hairy; winter buds (seen all summer, fall, and winter) glabrous or with short, crinkly, brown or yellow hairs concentrated near tip or along margins of the scales.
    2. Lateral leaflets 3.3–4 times as long as wide (length/width = 3.3–4); lower surface of leaflets usually glabrous; inflorescence sparsely hairy to glabrate; flowers 5–8 mm across (measured flat with petals spread to maximum width); fruits 5–7 mm in diameter .... *S. americana*
    2. Lateral leaflets 2.5–3.2 times as long as wide (length/width = 2.5–3.2); lower surface of leaflets sparsely hairy, at least on main veins; inflorescence moderately hairy; flowers 7–12 mm across; fruits 8–12 mm in diameter .... *S. decora*
1. Leaflets 2.5–4 cm long, the lower surface uniformly hairy; terminal tooth not elongated; petioles 1.5–3 cm long; petioles, ovaries, and sepals moderately to densely hairy; winter buds uniformly covered with long, silky white hairs
    .... *S. aucuparia*

Sorbus americana Marsh.

American mountain-ash

Tall **shrubs** or small **trees**, with single or multiple upright **stems** to 12 m tall and 25 cm dbh. **Branchlets** of the current year greenish to brownish, glabrous; 2nd-year branchlets red-brown, glabrous. **Bark** thin, silver-gray to brown-gray; smooth, developing platelike scales on older stems, eventually peeling. **Buds** glabrous or with short, crinkly, brown or yellow hairs concentrated near the tip or along margins of the scales. **Leaves** pinnately compound, alternate, deciduous. **Petioles** 3.5–6 cm long; glabrous to glabrate or occasionally sparsely hairy. **Leaflets** 11–19; sessile; oblong to lance-oblong or narrowly elliptical; 4–8 cm long, 1–2 cm wide, length/width 3.3–4; base acute to obtuse; apex acuminate to short-acuminate; margins sharply serrate, with 18–30 serrations per side; upper surface dark green, glabrous or occasionally glabrate; lower surface pale green, glabrous or rarely sparsely hairy. **Inflorescence** a compound terminal cyme 5–13 cm across. **Flowers** bisexual, 5-merous, white; peduncles and pedicels sparsely hairy to glabrate; sepals triangular, 0.5–1 mm long, essentially glabrous; petals obovate to nearly orbicular, 2–3.5 mm long; corolla 5–8 mm across (measured flat); ovary glabrous; **anthesis** late mid-June to late July, insect-pollinated. **Fruit** a subglobose pome, 5–7 mm in diameter, red; maturing mid-August to mid-September, persistent through winter; animal-dispersed. (*americana*: of America)

Identification

American mountain-ash is typically a small tree, 15–20 ft (4–6 m) tall with spreading branches and large compound leaves. It is easily confused with showy mountain-ash (*S. decora*), differing only by degree in a number of small and variable characters (see key). Try to use all the available characters, but if only leaves are present, take careful measurements of several typical leaflets and note the length-to-width ratio, which is the length of the leaflet divided by the width. The leaflets of American mountain-ash are proportionately narrower with a l/w ratio of 3.3–4 compared to showy mountain-ash at 2.5–3.2.

Natural History

American mountain-ash occurs in a variety of habitats, mostly forests and swamps but also rocky lakeshores, cliffs, and talus. Typical soils are weakly to moderately acidic and range from shallow peat to sand or gravel. Although its size would categorize American mountain-ash as an understory tree, it does not exhibit the degree of shade tolerance one might expect of an understory tree. It seems to prefer forest edges or partial openings where it gets at least some direct sunlight. It is also found in successional shrub-dominated habitats that often develop after logging or fire, typically with alders (*Alnus* spp.), mountain maple (*Acer spicatum*), beaked hazel (*Corylus cornuta*), or saplings of canopy trees. These are roughly the same growing conditions favored by showy mountain-ash, and in fact the two species will sometimes grow side by side.

Habitats occur primarily in fire-prone landscapes where normal fire frequency may vary from 20 to 100 years. After a fire, stump sprouts and seedlings will both appear the 1st year, but reproduction is not dependent on fire (Ahlgren 1959). Regardless of the habitat or fire history, American mountain-ash is rarely abundant and not very aggressive, meaning it does not do well in direct competition with other trees. In fact, it is usually crowded out or shaded out before it reaches its maximum size of 35–40 ft (10–12 m). The fruits are often abundant and stay on the tree all winter or until eaten; they are a critical food source for many migrating and resident bird species (Martin, Zim, and Nelson 1951).

Flowers are in large clusters called compound cymes—July 12.

Mountain-ash provides important food for migrating birds—September 13.

Each fruit is a "pome," same as an apple—September 13.

Bark starts smooth, and becomes scaly or peely with age.

Sorbus aucuparia L.

European mountain-ash

Introduced and naturalized small **trees**, with single upright **stems** to 15 m tall and 25 cm dbh. **Branchlets** of the current year greenish to brownish, hairy; 2nd-year branchlets red-brown, glabrous. **Bark** thin, light gray, smooth, becoming rough with age. **Buds** uniformly covered with long, silky, white hairs. **Leaves** pinnately compound, alternate, deciduous. **Petioles** 1.5–3 cm long, hairy. **Leaflets** 11–15; sessile; narrowly elliptical to oblong-elliptical; 2.5–4 cm long, 0.7–1.8 cm wide, length/width 2.2–3.5; base obtuse to rounded or occasionally nearly truncate; apex acute; margins sharply serrate or double serrate with 13–21 serrations per side; upper surface dark green, hairy to sparsely hairy; lower surface pale green, hairy to densely hairy. **Inflorescence** a compound terminal cyme 4–11 cm across. **Flowers** bisexual, 5-merous, white; peduncles and pedicels moderately to densely hairy; sepals roughly triangular to ovate, 1–1.5 mm long, hairy or occasionally glabrous; petals ovate to nearly orbicular, 3.5–5.5 mm long; corolla 7.5–12 mm across (measured flat); ovary hairy; **anthesis** late May to early June; insect-pollinated. **Fruit** a subglobose pome, 7–11 mm in diameter, red to scarlet; maturing late mid-August to early October, persistent through winter; animal-dispersed. (*aucuparia*: bird-catching, in reference to the appeal of the fruit)

Identification

European mountain-ash is similar in appearance to the native mountain-ashes (*S. americana* and *S. decora*). All are small, stout trees with pinnately compound leaves and clusters of white flowers. But the leaves and leaflets of the European species are somewhat smaller than those of the American species, and the underside is densely hairy. Also, the tip of the leaflet lacks the elongate terminal tooth of the native species. Although there are many horticultural forms in commerce, the plants that are turning up in native habitats seem to most closely resemble the typical form that grows wild in Europe.

Natural History

This small tree is native to forests throughout most of Europe, especially in mountainous areas. It has long been planted in European cities because of the attractive foliage and white flowers. It was introduced to North America during colonial times and was probably brought to Minnesota in the mid to late nineteenth century. Although it is sometimes recommended for wildlife plantings, it is mostly used as a specimen tree in urban and suburban residential lots and on commercial property. Not surprisingly, the fruits are eaten by birds and carried into habitats far beyond where it was planted.

It first began appearing in native habitats around 1900 and has spread slowly ever since. It seems well adapted to the forests of central and southern Minnesota and behaves much the way the native mountain-ashes do in northern Minnesota. It is not yet abundant enough to displace native species or to disrupt forest succession or ecological processes, but it seems to posses the necessary characteristics to do so. In fact, there seem to be few ecological barriers to prevent its further spread. For example, it produces abundant seeds, has an efficient dispersal agent (birds), is preadapted to the climate and soils, and has few if any predators or parasites here.

Spontaneous hybridization with the native species of mountain-ash could also become a problem. Experience with other species has taught us that hybrids sometimes possess invasive abilities greater than either parent and can possess the ability to swamp local gene pools.

Single stems are the rule; they may reach 50´ (15 m) in height.

Flowers appear in late spring or early summer.

These fruits were orange on August 25, then turned red in October.

Sorbus decora (Sarg.) Schneid.

Showy mountain-ash

Tall **shrubs** or small **trees**, with single or multiple upright **stems** to 13 m tall and 30 (40) cm dbh. **Branchlets** of the current year greenish to brownish, glabrous or hairy; 2nd-year branchlets brownish, glabrous. **Bark** thin, silver-gray to gray-brown; smooth, developing platelike scales on older stems, eventually peeling. **Buds** glabrous or with short, crinkly, brown or yellow hairs usually concentrated near the tip or along margins of the scales. **Leaves** pinnately compound, alternate, deciduous. **Petioles** 3–6 cm long, sparsely hairy or occasionally glabrate. **Leaflets** 11–17; sessile; oblong to lance-oblong or elliptical; 4.5–8 cm long, 1.5–2.5 cm wide, length/width 2.5–3.2; base obtuse to rounded or occasionally nearly truncate; apex acute to short-acuminate; margins sharply serrate, with 15–25 serrations per side; upper surface dark green glabrous or glabrate; lower surface pale green, sparsely hairy at least on main veins. **Inflorescence** a compound terminal cyme 5–14 cm across. **Flowers** bisexual, 5-merous, white; peduncles and pedicels moderately hairy or occasionally sparsely hairy; sepals triangular, 1–1.5 mm long, essentially glabrous; petals ovate, 3–4.5 mm long; corolla 7–12 mm across (measured flat); ovary glabrous to sparsely hairy; **anthesis** early June to early mid-July; insect-pollinated. **Fruit** a subglobose pome, 8–12 mm in diameter, red to red-orange; maturing mid-August to late mid-September, persistent through winter; animal dispersed. (*decora*: handsome)

Identification

Showy mountain-ash is a small, stout tree with spreading branches and often a dense crown. It can be very conspicuous in early summer when it is covered in large, flat-topped clusters of white flowers and again in the autumn when the fruits ripen. It is easily mistaken for American mountain-ash (*S. americana*); they look very much alike and may occur in the same habitat. But the two can be told apart by a number of characters, even without flowers or fruit (see key).

Natural History

Showy mountain-ash occurs in a variety of mostly open-canopy, upland forests as well as swamp forests, brushy openings, lakeshores, rock outcrops, cliffs, and talus. It is commonly seen along the shore of Lake Superior, but elsewhere it is only occasional or infrequent. It is not a consistent or characteristic component of any homogeneous community type. Yet it still manages to maintain a presence at the landscape level by exploiting edges, ecotones, and early successional habitats that are all features of the fire-maintained forests of northern and central Minnesota. Although young mountain-ash do resprout if top-killed by fire, they are not particularly favored by fire except to the extent that fire may reduce competition for light or release nutrients into the soil.

The fruits are often abundant and persist all winter or until eaten by birds. Since birds spread the seeds over great distances, seedlings are commonly found in a variety of unsuitable habitats and locations (usually under bird roosts), where they may survive a few years but rarely reach maturity. Under favorable conditions showy mountain-ash can reach the stature of a small tree 35–42 ft (10–13 m) in height, but even then they will eventually be overtopped by larger trees, particularly mid- or late-successional species such as white spruce (*Picea glauca*), balsam fir (*Abies balsamea*), or pines (*Pinus* spp.). Once trapped in the understory, showy mountain-ash will eventually decline from lack of light.

Few trees are more deserving of the name "showy"—July 1.

Fruits are larger than those of American mountain-ash—August 26.

Multiple stems are common; some reach 42´ (13 m) in height.

A weather-beaten specimen from the shore of Lake Superior.

Spiraea, meadowsweet and hardhack

Rosaceae: Rose family

This genus includes 70 to 80 species of deciduous shrubs found in temperate regions of the Northern Hemisphere, particularly Asia. About 6 species are native to the United States, and 2 are native to Minnesota. There are also several nonnative *Spiraea* grown as ornamentals in Minnesota, but none is currently known to escape cultivation here. (*Spiraea* is from the Greek *speira,* meaning wreath.)

Key to the Genus Spiraea *in Minnesota*

1. Flowers some shade of pink or purple; leaves proportionately broad (length/width = 2–3.2), the lower surface with a dense covering of yellow-brown, woolly hairs (tomentum) .... *S. tomentosa*
1. Flowers white; leaves proportionately narrower (length/width = 3.5–6), the lower surface glabrous or with a few scattered white hairs .... *S. alba*

Spiraea alba DuRoi

Meadowsweet

Midsize **shrubs**, with multiple upright **stems** to 2.2 m tall and 1.5 cm basal diameter. **Branches** few to numerous, slender, strongly ascending. 1st-year **branchlets** brown, minutely hairy or glabrate; 2nd-year branchlets brown or gray, glabrous. **Bark** gray or brown, smooth. **Leaves** simple, alternate, deciduous. **Petioles** 1–5 mm long or barely distinguishable, minutely hairy. **Leaf blades** narrowly elliptical to narrowly obovate or oblanceolate, occasionally somewhat oblong; 3–7.5 cm long, 0.8–1.8 cm wide, length/width 3.5–6; base acutely tapered or somewhat decurrent; apex acutely tapered or occasionally somewhat blunt; margins coarsely serrate; upper surface dark green, sparsely short-hairy to glabrate; lower surface similar to upper but slightly paler. **Inflorescence** an elongate or pyramidal terminal panicle, with numerous flowers. **Flowers** bisexual, 5-merous, white; peduncles and pedicels densely to moderately short-hairy; sepals triangular, 0.7–1.6 mm long, spreading; petals ovate to orbicular, 2–3 mm long, spreading; **anthesis** early July to late August; insect-pollinated. **Fruit** a cluster of 4–6 small follicles, each 2.5–3.5 mm long, glabrous; maturing early September to mid-October, splitting open in October or November and shedding seeds during the winter; gravity-dispersed. (*alba*: white)

Identification

Meadowsweet is a medium-size shrub rarely more than 6 ft (2 m) tall, with slender stems and stiffly ascending branches. The leaf margins are coarsely serrate, and both upper and lower surfaces are essentially the same dark green color. It is rather inconspicuous until the clusters of small white flowers appear in mid to late summer; then it should be easy to tell from other species, especially the pink-flowered hardhack (*S. tomentosa*).

Note: There is a similar eastern species, *S. latifolia* (Ait.) Borkh. [*S. alba* var. *latifolia* (Ait.) Dippel] that differs from *S. alba* by having a glabrous inflorescence and by having leaves that are proportionately broader (l/w = 2–3), more coarsely serrate, and with a more blunt apex. Convincing specimens of *S. latifolia* have not yet been found in Minnesota, but it is not difficult to find specimens that appear intermediate between the two species in one or more of these characters. These intermediates seem to occur throughout the range of *S. alba* in Minnesota.

Natural History

Meadowsweet is fairly common in Minnesota, but it is rarely abundant and never dominant. It is somewhat of an opportunist and typically occurs in open or brushy wetlands that are weakly acidic or somewhat basic (calcareous), such as meadows, shallow marshes, rocky or swampy shores, wet prairies, and swales. These are typically grass- or sedge-dominated habitats in shallow peat or wet mineral soil. Occasionally it is found in dry upland habitats such as sand dunes and rock outcrops.

Meadowsweet does not tolerate shade, and it does not compete well with larger shrubs. In the company of willows (*Salix* spp.) or dogwoods (*Cornus* spp.) it tends to occupy gaps or openings where it is not crowded. Even though it is not aggressive, it will eventually colonize abandoned pastures and low-lying agricultural land if there already exists a stable cover of grasses or sedges.

It seems that individual stems rarely live more than about 10 years, even less where there are browsers such as deer, rabbits, or hares or where the land is managed with fire. If stems are killed by fire or browsing, new stems will sprout but only from dormant buds on existing root crowns. Stems do not sprout adventitiously from the roots or from rhizomes.

Leaves are slender, and coarsely serrate.

Each fruit is a cluster of 4–6 small follicles—September 13.

A large, bushy specimen from Carlton County—August 2.

Tall spires of white flowers appear from mid to late summer.

Meadowsweet   🌿   **601**

Spiraea tomentosa L.

Hardhack

Midsize **shrubs**, with single or multiple upright **stems** to 1.3 m tall and 1 cm basal diameter. **Branches** few, short. 1st-year **branchlets** with a dense, yellow-brown tomentum; 2nd-year branchlets glabrous or with remnant patches of tomentum, brown to reddish brown. **Bark** gray-brown, smooth. **Leaves** simple, alternate, deciduous. **Petioles** 1–4 mm long, tomentose. **Leaf blades** elliptical to narrowly elliptical; 3–5.5 cm long, 1–2.2 cm wide, length/width 2–3.2; base tapered; apex tapered or blunt; margins coarsely serrate; upper surface dark green, with scattered short, straight hairs; lower surface with a dense, yellow-brown tomentum. **Inflorescence** a tall spirelike terminal panicle with numerous flowers. **Flowers** bisexual, 5-merous, pink to purple or magenta; peduncles and pedicels densely tomentose; sepals triangular, 0.5–1 mm long, reflexed; petals ovate to orbicular, 1–1.5 mm long, spreading; **anthesis** early mid-July to late mid-August; insect-pollinated. **Fruit** a cluster of 5 tiny follicles, each 2–3 mm long, with remnant patches of tomentum; maturing early September to mid-October, splitting open in October or November and shedding seeds during winter; gravity-dispersed. (*tomentosa*: with a tomentum, or a dense covering of woolly hairs, in reference to the twigs and underside of the leaves)

Identification

Hardhack is a small or medium-size shrub, usually about waist high. It typically has only a few stems or branches and may appear almost herbaceous. The tall spire of pinkish or magenta flowers is usually conspicuous, actually striking, and very distinctive. Also note the strong color contrast between the upper and lower surfaces of the leaf. The upper surface is dark green, but the lower surface has a dense, yellow-brown tomentum (soft, matted hairs). This tomentum also occurs on the new twigs and the inflorescence.

Natural History

Hardhack is fairly common on the Anoka Sandplain, but elsewhere it is local and infrequent. It occurs almost exclusively in acidic wetlands, such as tamarack swamps, shrub swamps, sedge meadows, marshes, sandy shores, and swales, usually in peat or wet sandy soil. It is intolerant of shade and is usually found in direct sunlight with grasses and sedges, or in openings between widely scattered shrubs. Hardhack does not readily invade roadsides, ditch banks, old fields, or other ruderal habitats.

Hardhack occurs almost exclusively in fire-prone landscapes, or at least in remnants of landscapes that were fire prone before settlement. This hardly seems a coincidence since hardhack is not only adapted to survive fire but needs frequent fire to keep its habitat open and free of encroaching trees and shrubs; dense growth of willows (*Salix* spp.), dogwoods (*Cornus* spp.), or speckled alder (*Alnus incana* subsp. *rugosa*) will easily crowd it out. After a fire it will resprout vigorously and even flower the first summer. The suppression of wildfire and the reluctance of some land managers to use prescribed fire as a management tool have cost many species, hardhack among them, precious habitat.

Where fires are frequent, hardhack may become quite abundant, eventually forming sizable colonies. But with frequent fire hardhack will not accumulate much woody growth, forcing it to function more like a herbaceous plant. Even in the absence of fire individual stems are short-lived, rarely lasting more than 5 to 7 years. Actually, entire plants seem somewhat transient even while established populations appear stable, at least where sizable habitats remain intact and functional.

The pinkish or magenta flowers are striking and distinctive—August 2, Anoka County.

Each fruit is a cluster of 5 tiny follicles—September 14.

Contrast the leaf shape with that of meadowsweet.

Upper surface of leaf is dark green; the lower surface is much lighter.

Staphylea, bladdernut

Staphyleaceae: Bladdernut family

The bladdernut genus includes 10 species of trees and shrubs widely distributed in temperate regions of Eurasia and North America; 2 species occur in the United States and 1 in Minnesota. (*Staphylea* is from the Greek *staphyle*, a cluster of grapes, in reference to the flowers.)

Staphylea trifolia L.

Bladdernut

Tall **shrubs** or rarely small **trees**, with single or multiple upright **stems** to 5 m tall and 5 cm dbh; forming colonies by root suckering, and by layering and tip-rooting of lower branches. **Branchlets** glabrous; green the 1st year, brown the 2nd; developing whitish lenticels after 2–4 years. **Bark** of mature stems brown or gray with prominent white stripes; smooth or somewhat rough on older stems. **Leaves** ternately compound, opposite, deciduous. **Petioles** 4–12 cm long at maturity, sparsely hairy or glabrate. **Leaflets** 3, ovate to elliptical or broadly elliptical; 5–10 cm long, 3–6 cm wide; the lateral leaflets nearly sessile, the terminal leaflet on a long stalk; base tapered to rounded; apex abruptly acuminate; margins finely serrate; upper surface dark green, glabrous or sparsely hairy; lower surface pale green, hairy. **Flowers** bisexual; 5-merous; borne in drooping terminal clusters of 5–12; pedicels 6–14 mm long, jointed midway, glabrous or sparsely hairy; sepals whitish, oblong, 5–8 mm long; petals whitish, narrowly obovate, 7–9 mm long; stamens 5, barely exceeding the petals; styles 3; **anthesis** early May to late May; insect-pollinated. **Fruit** an inflated 3-lobed capsule, papery and bladderlike at maturity, 3–6 cm long, 2–4 cm in diameter; each lobe with 1–4 pale brown, shiny **seeds** that eventually become loose and rattle within the bladder; maturing mid-August to late September, persisting on the branch into winter; dispersal mechanism unknown. (*trifolia*: with 3 leaves, or in this case with 3 leaflets)

Identification

Bladdernut is a fairly tall, coarse shrub with multiple stems and stout branches. The flowers and fruits are quite distinctive, especially the inflated pod, which is often compared to a Japanese lantern. Also look for white streaks or flecks on the bark. The leaves might appear ordinary except they are ternately compound, meaning that each leaf is made up of 3 essentially identical leaflets. If this fact is recognized, then identification becomes even easier; if not, the leaves might be confused with those of burning bush (*Euonymus atropurpureus*) or choke-cherry (*Prunus virginiana*).

Natural History

Bladdernut is a characteristic understory shrub of forests on floodplains and river terraces in southeastern Minnesota. It is also found in upland forests, including slopes, forested ravines, and level terrain. It occurs under just about every species of late-successional hardwood tree, including maples (*Acer* spp.), ashes (*Fraxinus* spp.), oaks (*Quercus* spp.), elms (*Ulmus* spp.), and basswood (*Tilia americana*). While it might be a mistake to call bladdernut common, it is not rare. It is conspicuous only the spring when it is flowering, and again in early winter when the pods are exposed.

Bladdernut easily survives short-duration spring flooding along rivers and even moderate amounts of sedimentation, but it does not survive in stagnant water or in permanently saturated soils, and it is apparently sensitive to fire. It does well in deep shade, often managing to flower and fruit without the advantage of direct sunlight. It does even better along a forest edge or under a canopy gap where it receives more sunlight. If unconstrained by competition, it will spread vegetatively by root suckering and layering of lower branches. With enough room (and time), a colony can expand to perhaps 33 ft (10 m) in diameter.

Bladdernut also reproduces by seed, which raises questions about the peculiar shape of the pod. It is an inflated, papery structure with 3 downward-pointing lobes. Each lobe contains 1 to 4 seeds, which eventually become loose and rattle around inside the pod. The actual function of the pod is a mystery, but presumably it plays some role in the dispersal of the seeds.

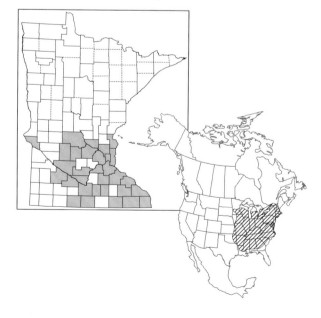

Flowers hang downward in clusters of 5–12—May 29.

The leaf is trifoliate, meaning it has 3 separate leaflets.

The curious bladderlike pods rattle when dry—August 22.

Bark has prominent whitish markings.

Bladdernut   🍂   **607**

Symphoricarpos, snowberry and wolfberry

Caprifoliaceae: Honeysuckle family

Symphoricarpos is a small genus, with 1 species in Central China and about 12 species in North America. Two species are known to be native in Minnesota. (*Symphoricarpos* is from the Greek *symphorein*, to bear together; and *carpos*, fruit, in reference to the clustered drupes.)

    Symphoricarpos orbiculatus Moench (coral-berry) is a southeastern species with red fruits. It is native in parts of Iowa (Eilers and Roosa 1994) and reported to be escaped from cultivation in Wisconsin (Wetter et al. 2001). It is sometimes cultivated in Minnesota, and there are occasional reports of it occurring wild in southern Minnesota (Ownbey and Morley 1991; Rosendahl 1955), yet there is no strong evidence that it is either native or naturalized in Minnesota.

Key to the Genus Symphoricarpos *in Minnesota*

1. Flowers on pedicels 0.5–2 mm long; style 1.5–3 mm long, not extending beyond the mouth of the corolla; flowers in terminal clusters of 2–10 (and sometimes single in the axils of upper leaves); leaf blades 1.5–4.5 cm long, the margins entire; petioles 1–3 mm long .... *S. albus*
1. Flowers sessile; style 6–10 mm long, extending well beyond the mouth of the corolla; flowers in both terminal and axillary clusters of 6–20; leaf blades 4–7.5 cm long, the margins often undulate; petioles 4–7 mm long .... *S. occidentalis*

Symphoricarpos albus (L.) Blake

Snowberry

Midsize **shrubs**, with upright **stems** to 1 m tall and 1.5 cm basal diameter; forming loose rhizomatous colonies. 1st-year **branchlets** red-brown, hairy; 2nd-year branchlets gray-brown, black-dotted, hairy. **Bark** thin, the gray epidermal layer splitting to reveal a smooth purplish layer beneath. **Leaves** simple, opposite, deciduous. **Petioles** 1–3 mm long, hairy. **Leaf blades** ovate to broadly elliptical; 1.5–4 cm long, 1–3 cm wide; base rounded to obtuse; apex rounded to blunt or occasionally obtuse; margins entire; upper surface dark green, sparsely hairy to glabrate; lower surface pale green, hairy. **Flowers** bisexual, 4- or 5-merous, whitish to pink; borne in terminal clusters of 2–10 or singly in the axils of the upper leaves; pedicels 0.5–2 mm long; calyx about 1 mm long, lobes ciliate; corolla campanulate, 5–7 mm long, the lobes shorter than the tube; stamens not quite reaching the mouth of the corolla (included); style 1.5–3 mm long, glabrous, about half as long as the corolla, stigma capitate; **anthesis** mid-June to mid-July; insect-pollinated. **Fruit** a berrylike drupe, ± globose, 6–10 mm in diameter, white; nutlets 2; maturing late July to early September; animal-dispersed. (*albus*: white)

Identification

Snowberry, as it occurs in Minnesota, is a smallish shrub, usually about knee high. It has small, roundish leaves and white, berrylike fruit. Wolfberry (*S. occidentalis*) is similar, and where the ranges of the two species overlap, they will sometimes occur together. When compared side by side, snowberry is generally a smaller, less robust shrub, with smaller leaves, shorter petioles, and more slender branches. Although they are clearly different, it sometimes requires a close examination to tell the two apart (see key).

Note: Native Minnesota snowberry belongs to variety *albus*, which occupies the range depicted on the accompanying North America map. There is also a western variety (var. *laevigatus* (Fern.) Blake) that ranges from Alaska to California. It is a much taller plant with glabrous leaves and twigs, and it seems to be the horticulturally preferred variety. It is occasionally planted in Minnesota, and under certain conditions it may escape cultivation but it is not known to be naturalized.

Natural History

Snowberry occurs primarily in the forested region of Minnesota, where it favors dry, sunny, or partially shaded habitats. It is particularly common in open-canopy forests with red pine (*Pinus resinosa*) or jack pine (*P. banksiana*). It is also associated with hardwoods, especially early-successional types such as trembling aspen (*Populus tremuloides*), paper birch (*Betula papyrifera*), and northern pin oak (*Quercus ellipsoidalis*). Other habitats include savannas, barrens, rock outcrops, and prairie-forest ecotones. It does not seem to compete well in dense shrub-dominated communities or in the deep shade of a closed-canopy forest. Soils always seem to be acidic, usually with a sandy or rocky texture.

All of these habitats are fire maintained or at least fire prone. Not surprisingly, snowberry has the ability to resprout from rhizomes and root crowns if the stems have been consumed in a typical ground fire. However, a particularly intense fire fueled by years of accumulated organic material can kill the shallow rhizomes. The rhizomes grow horizontally just beneath the surface and send up aerial shoots along their length, sometimes producing discernable colonies. Yet, by their nature, these rhizomatous colonies spread slowly and are usually rather sparse. They are not aggressive or invasive.

Stamens and style stay neatly hidden within the corolla—July 13.

The name "snowberry" aptly describes the fruit—August 13.

Leaves are no more than 1.5" (4 cm) long and have smooth margins.

The entire plant may be only knee high.

Snowberry   🌿   **611**

Symphoricarpos occidentalis Hook.

Wolfberry

Midsize **shrubs**, with single or multiple **stems** to 1.7 m tall and 2 cm basal diameter; forming rhizomatous colonies. 1st-year **branchlets** red-brown, hairy; 2nd-year branchlets gray-brown, black-dotted, glabrous or minutely hairy. **Bark** thin, the gray outer layer splitting to reveal a reddish brown layer beneath. **Leaves** simple, opposite, deciduous. **Petioles** 4–7 mm long, hairy. **Leaf blades** ovate to elliptical; 4–7.5 cm long, 2.5–4.5 cm wide, often larger on fast-growing shoots; base rounded to obtuse; apex acute to obtuse or blunt; margins entire to undulate-crenate or occasionally with large irregular lobes on fast-growing shoots; upper surface dark green, sparsely hairy to glabrate; lower surface pale green, hairy to sparsely hairy. **Flowers** bisexual, 4- or 5-merous, whitish to pinkish; borne in compact terminal and axillary clusters of 6–20; pedicels lacking; calyx 1–1.5 mm long, lobes ciliate; corolla campanulate, 5.5–8 mm long, the lobes usually longer than the tube; stamens reaching just beyond the mouth of the corolla (exserted); style 6–10 mm long, usually long-hairy near the middle, reaching well beyond the mouth of the corolla (exserted), stigma capitate; **anthesis** mid-June to early mid-August; insect-pollinated. **Fruit** a berrylike drupe, ± globose; 6–9 mm in diameter; whitish green, becoming dry, blackish and gall-like; nutlets 2; maturing early August to mid-September, often persisting through the winter and even the following summer; animal-dispersed. (*occidentalis*: western)

Identification

Wolfberry is a midsize shrub, usually about waist high. It differs from the similar snowberry (*S. albus*) by having larger leaves that are more likely to have wavy margins and by having larger clusters of flowers. The flowers themselves differ by a number of technical characters, but even without a hand lens it is easy to see that the stamens and especially the style protrude out from the corolla. In snowberry they are hidden within the corolla. The fruits ripen by the middle of September, but if not eaten by an animal they will remain clustered along the stem all winter and into the following summer. They will eventually turn black and become dry, at which point they may resemble insect galls.

Natural History

Wolfberry is one of the few woody plants that occurs primarily on open prairies. Secondary habitats include savannas and open woods, especially the early-successional oak-aspen (*Quercus-Populus*) woodlands that occur in the prairie-forest transition zone. Other habitats that might be described as local niche habitats include exposed ridges, bluffs, eroding slopes, ravines, and rock outcrops. It competes well in dry or moist soil, usually loam or sandy loam that has a pH ranging from basic (calcareous) to slightly acidic.

Wolfberry is a tenacious shrub; once established it can resist drought, wildfire, even heavy browsing. If the stems are killed, as in a fire, the dense network of underground rhizomes will send up an even greater number of tall, vigorous replacement shoots. These new shoots will typically flower and set seed the 1st year after the fire (Anderson and Bailey 1979). In this way, periodic fire at a frequency of perhaps once every 3 to 5 years can favor the spread of wolfberry, although annual burning will usually reduce it. Wolfberry may also increase when cattle are overgrazed on prairies because cattle avoid it, even when hungry, but will eat or trample the competition.

Where overgrazing or fire suppression has been a problem, wolfberry can form large, dense rhizomatous colonies (clones) over 650 ft (200 m) in diameter (Pelton 1953). In such situations, individual stems may live 13 years, and rhizomes 40 years (Pelton 1953), but the collective clone could live for centuries.

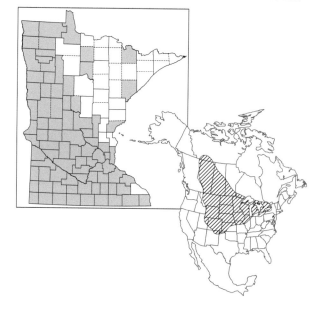

The stamens and style project out from the corolla—August 6.

Leaves can become 3" (7.5 cm) long.

Fruits eventually become black and gall-like if not eaten—September 5.

Flowers are in terminal and axillary clusters of 6–20—August 10.

Wolfberry 🌿 **613**

Taxus, yew

Taxaceae: Yew family

The yews comprise a genus of about 10 species; all are evergreen trees or shrubs distributed primarily in north temperate regions of Europe, Asia, and North America. Three species are native to North America, and 1 is native to Minnesota. (*Taxus* is from the Greek *taxos*, the classical name of the European yew tree, *T. baccata*.)

In addition to the native yew, there are at least 2 nonnative yews occasionally planted in Minnesota as ornament shrubs: Japanese yew (*T. cuspidata* Sieb. & Zucc.) and *T.* ×*media* Rehd., the hybrid between Japanese yew and European yew (*T. baccata* L.). Neither is known to escape cultivation in Minnesota.

Taxus canadensis Marsh.

Canada yew

Midsize **shrubs**, lacking a main stem, but with multiple ascending, spreading or prostrate **branches** originating from a single base; to 2 m tall and 7 cm basal diameter; forming colonies by layering of lower branches. **Branchlets** green and glabrous the 1st year, becoming brownish the 2nd year. **Bark** of mature stems thin, brown to reddish, somewhat scaly or flaky. **Leaves** simple, alternate, evergreen. **Petioles** 1–2 mm long, glabrous. **Leaf blades** nonresinous, linear, ± flat, 1–2.5 cm long, 1–3 mm wide; base tapered or rounded; apex contracted to a sharp tip; margins entire, often inrolled; surfaces glabrous with the midvein protruding on both upper and lower surfaces. **Strobili** unisexual, male and female separate, usually on the same plant, sometimes on different plants. **Male strobilus** borne singly from leaf axils; about 4 mm long; consisting of several pollen sacs projecting from a cuplike cluster of tiny scales; pollen released mid-April to mid-May, wind-pollinated. **Female strobilus** inconspicuous; borne singly from leaf axils; about 3 mm long; consisting of a single minute ovule subtended by 3 pairs of scales borne on a short stalk. **Mature ovule** consisting of a single brown seed about 4 mm long, surrounded by a fleshy, scarlet, cuplike aril 5–10 mm long, with an opening at the apex; maturing June to September; animal-dispersed. (*canadensis*: of Canada)

Identification

Canada yew is an evergreen shrub that reaches a height of about 6 ft (2 m). It looks much like a shrub version of balsam fir (*Abies balsamea*), but the leaves of yew are sharply pointed, while those of balsam fir are blunt. The fleshy, red aril looks like the berry of an angiosperm but has a hole at the top. It looks quite different from the reproductive structure of any other conifer and is unique to yew. Although the fleshy portion of the aril is edible, the seed itself and the rest of the plant are reportedly poisonous (Hils 1993).

Natural History

Canada yew is a widespread but somewhat uncommon shrub. In the southern part of the state it is found almost exclusively on cool, moist, north-facing forested slopes, especially on talus slopes in limestone karst areas. In the central and northern counties, it occurs most often in forested swamps. These swamps are not the same as bogs; they are usually located in peat-filled basins with an inflow of mineral-rich water. There is usually a ground cover of mosses and sedges and a canopy of tamarack (*Larix laricina*) or northern white cedar (*Thuja occidentalis*) with perhaps scattered black ash (*Fraxinus nigra*) or birches (*Betula* spp.).

Canada yew is notable for thriving in continual deep shade, easily completing its entire life cycle without benefit of direct sunlight. It is not an aggressive colonizer, and well-structured populations seem to be restricted to fairly stable habitats where deep shade keeps competition minimal.

The lower branches spread widely from the base of the shrub and will root on contact with the ground. When this happens, a new root crown is created that may in time produce more aerial shoots and establish itself independent of the parental shrub. This is a process of clonal reproduction called layering. In this way, a single shrub can gradually spread to form a dense colony of clones as much as 100 ft (30 m) across. But yew is slow growing, and clonal growth rarely keeps up with deer predation, which is severe and has a very strong influence on the current distribution and abundance of yew in Minnesota.

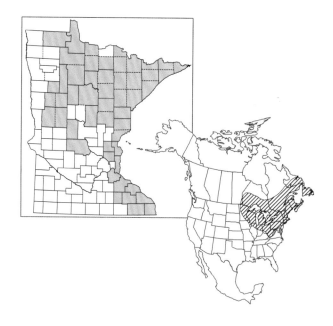

Each female strobilus contains a single ovule—April 30.

Pollen is released from male strobili in April or May.

The "berry" is really an aril with an opening at the top—June 25.

Canada yew looks like a shrub version of balsam fir.

Bark is thin, rough, and sometimes scaly.

Thuja, northern white cedar

Cupressaceae: Cypress family

This genus includes 5 species; all are evergreen trees from North America and eastern Asia. Two species occur in the United States, and 1 in Minnesota. (*Thuja* is the classical Greek name of a juniper.)

Thuja occidentalis L.

Northern white cedar

Midsize **trees**, to 25 m tall and 123 cm dbh. **Branchlets** initially clothed in overlapping green leaf bases, becoming bare after 2–3 years; developing flat, fanlike sprays. **Bark** thin, silvery gray, developing long, thin, interlacing ridges that may loosen and exfoliate. **Leaves** scalelike with decurrent bases; opposite, with 2 pairs arranged in 4 ranks, the lateral pair sharply folded and clasping the flat facial pair, the dorsal surface of the flat scales producing a resin-filled blister; remaining green for 1 year, then becoming brown, but persisting for another 1–2 years; tightly appressed, crowded and overlapping; 2–6 mm long; glabrous, bright green. Monoecious with separate male **cones** and female cones on the same branch. **Male (pollen) cones** borne singly at the tips of lateral branchlets; roughly spherical, about 1.5 mm long; releasing pollen late April to mid-May, and persisting for about 1 year. **Female (seed) cones** borne singly at the tips of lateral branchlets; ovate to oblong, 8–15 mm long at maturity; wind-pollinated; maturing and releasing seeds in autumn of the 1st year, but remaining on the branch through winter. **Seeds** oblong, 3–5 mm long, with a pair of thin, papery wings, wind-dispersed. (*occidentalis*: western, i.e., of the Western Hemisphere)

Identification

Northern white cedar is a stout, midsize tree, rarely more than 75 ft (23 m) tall in Minnesota. It has short branches, a conical crown, and silvery gray bark. The actual trunk tapers noticeably and often seems to twist or spiral. The individual leaves are small and scalelike, similar to those of eastern redcedar (*Juniperus virginiana*), yet the ultimate branch is a flat, soft spray.
Note: Wild northern white cedar is the source of the commercial arborvitae, which has more than 120 named cultivars available in every imaginable size and shape (Chambers 1993).

Natural History

Northern white cedar is locally common in parts of northern and east-central Minnesota, where its primary habitat is peat swamps. In fact, it is often the dominant tree in swamps where conditions are only slightly acidic; if conditions are strongly acidic, the dominant trees are more likely to be black spruce (*Picea mariana*) or tamarack (*Larix laricina*) (Petraborg 1969). It also grows in moist, upland forests, on rocky lakeshores, rock outcrops, and cliffs. On cliffs it grows very slowly and often has severely stunted and deformed trunks.

Two important characteristics qualify northern white cedar as a climax species. First, saplings are very tolerant of deep shade. This gives them the ability to survive for many years in a forest understory waiting for a gap to open in the canopy and then grow quickly to fill the gap. Second, its seeds germinate well on rotting logs and moss in undisturbed forests. These capabilities allow northern white cedar to continually replace itself in the canopy without the need for fire or other major disturbance to "restart" the successional process (Grigal and Ohmann 1975).

The oldest living tree in Minnesota is believed to be a northern white cedar growing on the shore of Basswood Lake (Lake County). The center of the trunk has become pulpy with decay, but the outer portion is solid and contains 400 rings. Based on this, its age has been estimated to be over 1,100 years (Ahlgren and Ahlgren 2001), but there is no way to know for sure. Still older is a dead northern white cedar on a cliff on the Niagara Escarpment in Ontario aged at 1,653 years, making it the oldest known tree in eastern North America (Kelly, Cook, and Larson 1994).

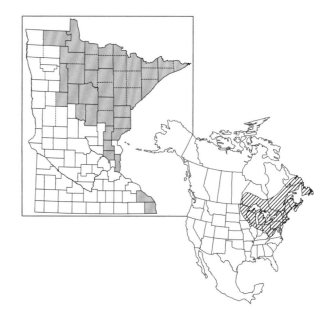

Northern white cedar from an old-growth forest in Lake County.

Mature cones release seeds in autumn of their first year—August 26.

Male and female cones are on same branch; these are female—May 9.

Male cones are tiny, about 1/16" (1.5 mm) long—May 9.

Twigs form flat, soft "sprays."

Tilia, basswood

Tiliaceae: Linden family

This genus contains 40 to 50 species of deciduous trees found mainly in temperate regions of the Northern Hemisphere. The United States has a single polymorphic species. (*Tilia* is the classical Latin name of the European linden, probably derived from the Greek *ptilon*, for wing, in reference to the winglike bract of the fruit.)

European lindens, most often cultivars of littleleaf linden (*T. cordata* Mill.), are commonly grown as boulevard trees in Minnesota, but are not known to be naturalized in the state.

Tilia americana L.

Basswood

Large **trees**, with single upright **stems**, or multiple stems from basal sprouts, to 35 m tall, and 121 cm dbh. **Branches** ascending, ultimately arching. 1st-year **branchlets** glabrous, green to brown, becoming gray the 2nd or 3rd year. **Bark** of young trees thin, smooth and gray, becoming moderately thick and developing ridges and furrows in age. **Leaves** simple, alternate, deciduous. **Petioles** 3–7 cm long, glabrous. **Leaf blades** of flowering branches broadly ovate to nearly orbicular; 7–15 cm long, 5–13 cm wide, often much larger on basal sprouts; base cordate or truncate, often asymmetrical; apex abruptly acuminate; margins sharply serrate, each tooth with an elongate tip; upper surface dark green, glabrous; lower surface pale green, glabrous except for small tufts of brownish hairs in the axils of the main veins. **Flowers** bisexual, 5-merous; borne in axillary cymes of 5–17, each inflorescence subtended by a membranous spatulate bract 5–10 cm long to which the peduncle is fused for about half its length; pedicels glabrous or glabrate, 5–10 mm long; sepals ovate, 3.5–6 mm long, minutely hairy; petals yellowish, narrowly elliptical to oblong, 6–9 mm long, glabrous; stamens about 60; style 1; **anthesis** early July to early August; insect-pollinated. **Fruit** a spherical, woody, nutlike drupe 6–9 mm in diameter, minutely hairy; maturing mid-August to mid-September; wind- and gravity-dispersed. (*americana*: of America)

Identification

Basswood is a tall canopy tree with high-arching branches and a relatively small crown. It produces fragrant clusters of cream-colored or yellowish flowers in midsummer, which become woody, pea-size fruits in late summer. The shape and large size of the leaf is distinctive, and notice that the trunk often has persistent suckers growing from the base. Basswood is sometimes confused with littleleaf linden (*Tilia cordata* Mill.), a European tree that is often planted on city boulevards but not found in the wild.

Natural History

Basswood is a common canopy tree in mesic deciduous forests throughout most of the state, especially in deep, fertile, loamy soil in the southern and central counties (Daubenmire 1936). It is often codominant in late-successional forests with sugar maple (*Acer saccharum*), red oak (*Quercus rubra*), and formerly American elm (*Ulmus americana*) and in early-successional forests with bur oak (*Quercus macrocarpa*) and green ash (*Fraxinus pennsylvanica*).

Basswood thrives on alluvial soil in river corridors, especially on slightly elevated portions of floodplains that are just beyond the reach of repeated or long-duration spring flooding and sedimentation. It is relatively fast growing and long-lived and can become very large. Good habitats typically produce trees 100–115 ft (30–35 m) tall with diameters of 3 ft (1 m) or more.

Basswood is unusual among Minnesota canopy trees because it flowers in midsummer instead of spring, and it is insect-pollinated rather than wind-pollinated (Anderson 1976). As a result, seeds are produced in great numbers, and they germinate under a wide variety of forest conditions. Still, most basswood trees in a stable forest originate from basal sprouts, not from seed (Bray 1956). These basal sprouts, also called suckers, are the large persistent stems produced from the base of mature basswood trees once they have reached the canopy. These "replacement stems" surround the main trunk, and when the trunk dies or is blown over, one or more will grow rapidly and take its place in the canopy.

Leaf is large and asymmetrical with narrow tip and serrate margin.

Fragrant flowers appear in July, and are bee-pollinated.

Bark develops long ridges and narrow furrows—23" (59 cm) dbh.

Pea-size "drupes" float to the ground on a papery sail—August 14.

Toxicodendron, poison ivy and poison sumac

Anacardiaceae: Cashew family

This genus contains about 10 species of deciduous shrubs and vines distributed in North America and eastern Asia. There are 5 species in the United States, and 3 in Minnesota. (*Toxicodendron* is from the Greek for poison tree.)

The sap contains a toxic oily compound (3–*n*-pentadecyl-catechol) that is carried in specialized resin ducts in the phloem of the plant and is found in the leaves, flowers, stems, and roots of all *Toxicodendron* species (Klingman et al. 1983). If any portion of the plant is bruised or broken, the poison may exude onto the surface, which is how people typically come in contact with it. It is initially a clear liquid, but it turns into a black gummy substance in a few hours and can remain toxic for an indefinite period, reportedly for several hundred years (Klingman et al. 1983).

Contact may be direct between plant and bare skin, or the poison may travel on the fur of a dog, camping equipment, clothing, or other intermediary. The compound is not volatile, so it is not normally transmitted through the air, although it can be carried as droplets on particles of ash in the smoke of burning plants. Such particles are sometimes inhaled, causing serious problems, or they can settle on surfaces and be picked up from there.

Sensitivity to poisoning can vary from individual to individual and can change over time. Very few individuals are immune, and those that appear so could easily lose their immunity unexpectedly. The poison is absorbed by the skin almost immediately, although symptoms may not appear for 12 to 24 hours or in some cases several days. Washing the exposed skin with soap and cold water (warm water speeds absorption through the skin) probably will not prevent symptoms from appearing unless done within 1 to 3 minutes after exposure (Klingman et al. 1983), but washing can remove residual poison and prevent it from being spread. The fluid in the blisters does not contain the poison and cannot spread the rash. A number of animal species regularly eat the fruit and leaves with no apparent harmful effects; in fact, it appears that only humans are susceptible.

Key to the Genus Toxicodendron *in Minnesota*

---

1. Leaflets 9–13 ....*T. vernix*
1. Leaflets 3.
    2. Tall branching shrub often > 2 m tall, or vines climbing with aerial roots; petioles moderately to densely hairy; leaflets ovate, usually more than 1.5 times as long as wide (leaflet length/width > 1.5) .... *T. radicans* subsp. *negundo*
    2. Low shrubs with few if any branches and usually < 1 m tall, not producing aerial roots; petioles glabrous or sparsely hairy; leaflets broadly ovate, usually less than 1.5 times as long as wide (leaflet length/width < 1.5) .... *T. rydbergii*

Common poison ivy

Tall rhizomatous and much branching **shrubs** to 3 m tall and 3 cm dbh; or **vines** climbing by aerial roots to heights of 20 m and diameters of 6 cm. **Bark** gray, slightly rough. **Branchlets** brown to gray-brown; moderately to sparsely hairy the 1st year, usually glabrate the 2nd year. **Leaves** compound, alternate, deciduous. **Petioles** 5–16 cm long, moderately to somewhat densely hairy. **Leaflets** 3; the lateral leaflets on petiolules 1–7 mm long, the terminal leaflet on petiolule 2–4 cm long; ovate; 8–18 cm long, 5–11 cm wide; base broadly rounded to obtusely angled or nearly truncate, often asymmetrical; apex acuminate; margins irregular and coarsely crenate, toothed or lobed, often on one side only, or sometimes entire, ciliate; upper surface dark green, with sparse or scattered appressed hairs; lower surface pale green, hairy, especially along main veins. **Inflorescence** a ± ascending panicle borne from leaf axils on 1st-year branchlets. **Flowers** functionally unisexual, each plant bearing either male flowers or female flowers; 5-merous; sepals 0.5–1.5 mm long; petals whitish, 1.5–3 mm long; stamens not exceeding the petals; style 3-lobed; **anthesis** early to late June; insect-pollinated. **Fruit** a roughly spherical drupe; whitish to pale yellowish green; 4–5 mm in diameter; maturing late August to late September, often held through winter; animal-dispersed. (*radicans*: rooting, putting forth aerial roots; *negundo*: in reference to the similarity of the leaves to those of boxelder, *Acer negundo* L.)

Identification

Common poison ivy exhibits two distinct growth forms: that of a climbing vine and that of a free-standing shrub. The vine climbs not with tendrils or by twining but with aerial roots that attach firmly to its host, much like Virginia creeper (*Parthenocissus quinquefolia*). The shrub form typically develops a single, self-supporting stem as tall as 10 ft (3 m), with a branched, open crown. This form can look similar to poison sumac (*Toxicodendron vernix*) or the true sumacs (*Rhus typhina* or *R. glabra*). Among all these look-alikes, only common poison ivy has 3 leaflets; the others have 5 or more. Although there are other plants in the forest with 3 leaflets, the rhyme "leaflets three, let it be" is worth remembering.

Distinguishing common poison ivy from western poison ivy (*T. rydbergii*) can be difficult. But western poison ivy is typically a much smaller shrub or even a

subshrub. It rarely gets more than about waist high and produces only short, stubby branches if any at all, and it never becomes a vine or produces aerial roots. Also, the leaves of common poison ivy tend to be larger and proportionately narrower and somewhat hairier on the upper surface; even the petioles are generally hairier. Furthermore, the inflorescence is usually larger and has more flowers and yet produces smaller fruits.

Natural History

Common poison ivy occurs primarily in hardwood forests on the floodplain of the Mississippi River downstream of Hastings. It is occasionally found in upland forests at some elevation above the floodplain but never far from the river. It has also been found at one location on the floodplain of the St. Croix River near Stillwater. The known sites are in mature, stable forests, not ruderal habitats. In this sense it does not seem to behave as a "weed" in Minnesota as it is reported to do in other parts of its range (Gillis 1971).

Although it is locally abundant at several sites, "common" poison ivy is not widespread or common in Minnesota. In fact, it is quite rare in the state as a whole, so it is unlikely to be casually encountered. Yet it is every bit as toxic as the more common and widespread western poison ivy, and it should be avoided.

Each fruit is a spherical drupe less than 1/4" (4–5 mm) across—August 25.

Male flowers look similar to female; these are female—June 21.

Using aerial roots to climb a silver maple.

Each leaf has 3 leaflets with irregular margins.

Toxicodendron rydbergii (Small) Green

Western poison ivy
[*Rhus radicans* L. var. *rydbergii* (Small) Rehd.]

Midsize rhizomatous or stoloniferous **shrubs** to 2 m tall and 2 cm diameter; lacking aerial roots; little if at all branching. **Bark** gray, smooth. **Branchlets** brown; moderately to sparsely hairy the 1st year, usually glabrate the 2nd year. **Leaves** compound, alternate, deciduous. **Petioles** 7–27 cm long; sparsely hairy to glabrous. **Leaflets** 3; the lateral leaflets on petiolules 1–5 mm long, the terminal leaflet on petiolule 2.5–4 cm long; ovate to broadly ovate or suborbicular; 8–13 cm long, 4–9.5 cm wide; base broadly rounded to obtusely angled, often asymmetrical; apex acuminate; margins irregularly and coarsely crenate or toothed, often on distal half or one margin only, or sometimes margins entire, ciliate; upper surface dark green, with scattered appressed hairs or ± glabrous; lower surface pale green, usually hairy especially along main veins. **Inflorescence** a loosely erect panicle borne from leaf axils on 1st-year branchlets. **Flowers** functionally unisexual, each plant bearing either male flowers or female flowers; 5-merous; sepals 0.5–1.5 mm long; petals whitish, 1.5–3 mm long; stamens not exceeding the petals; style 3-lobed; **anthesis** early to late June; insect-pollinated. **Fruit** a roughly spherical drupe; whitish to pale yellowish green; 4.5–6 mm in diameter; maturing late August to late September, often held over winter and into the following spring; animal-dispersed. (*rydbergii*: named in honor of American botanist Per Axel Rydberg, 1860–1931)

Identification

Western poison ivy is a smallish, nonclimbing shrub usually about knee high, with a single stem and only a few stubby branches or no branches at all. The leaves can be relatively large but always with three leaflets. Virginia creeper (*Parthenocissus quinquefolia*) and woodbine (*P. vitacea*) are superficially similar but have 5 leaflets instead of 3. Jack-in-the-pulpit (*Arisaema triphyllum*) and the trilliums (*Trillium* spp.) do have 3 leaflets, but they have nonwoody stems. It may be enough to keep in mind that western poison ivy has a short woody stem and 3 leaflets.

Natural History

Western poison ivy occurs essentially statewide and is common everywhere except the northern tier of counties. Although it is primarily a forest species, it is adapted to a remarkably wide range of ecological conditions. It occurs in the interior of mature hardwood forests but also in young successional forests, forest ecotones, and brushy thickets. It is also found in native prairies (where fire has been suppressed), sand dunes, talus, rock fields, and floodplains. Conditions range from dry to moist, and from weakly acidic to basic (calcareous); soils include sand, silt, clay, and loam. It seems to be absent only from permanently wet habitats.

Western poison ivy often forms rhizomatous colonies, sometimes 20 ft (6 m) or more across. The rhizomes spread horizontally just beneath the soil surface or sometimes at the surface. They grow quickly and can spread aggressively, especially in damaged habitats where community structure has been compromised and species diversity reduced. This is certainly the case on roadsides, ditch banks, utility rights-of-way, and old fields. It is also notoriously adept at encroaching into mowed lawns from adjacent woods.

These male flowers are ready to release their pollen—June 18.

Fruits are often held over winter into the following spring—August 23.

Dense patches of western poison ivy are common in the open.

Flowers from a female plant—June 2.

Poison ivy 🌿 **631**

Toxicodendron vernix (L.) Kuntze

Poison sumac
[*Rhus vernix* L.]

Tall **shrubs** to 4.5 m tall and 5 cm dbh. **Bark** light gray, smooth or somewhat rough. **Branchlets** brown, glabrous. **Leaves** pinnately compound, alternate, deciduous. **Petioles** 2–9 cm long, essentially glabrous. **Leaflets** 9–13; the lateral leaflets sessile or nearly so, the terminal leaflet on a petiolule 1–3 cm long; elliptical to oblong or obovate; 6–14 cm long, 2.5–6 cm wide; base acutely tapered; apex short acuminate; margins entire; upper surface dark green; glabrous or with a few scattered stiff hairs, especially near margins; lower surface pale green, essentially glabrous. **Inflorescence** a loosely erect or ascending (drooping in fruit) panicle borne from leaf axils on 1st-year branchlets. **Flowers** functionally unisexual, each plant bearing either male flowers or female flowers; 5-merous; sepals 0.5–1.5 mm long; petals whitish, 1.5–2.5 mm long; stamens exceeding the petals; style 3-lobed; **anthesis** early to late June, insect-pollinated. **Fruit** a roughly spherical drupe; whitish to pale yellowish or greenish; 4–5 mm in diameter; maturing late August to late September, often held through winter; animal-dispersed. (*vernix*: varnish; mistakenly thought by Linnaeus to be a related Asian species that is a true source of lacquer)

Identification

Poison sumac is a tall shrub with stout branches and thick, coarse twigs. Closest in appearance would be the true sumacs (*Rhus hirta* and *R. glabra*), which have long, pinnately compound leaves like poison sumac and roughly the same growth form. But the leaflets of poison sumac have entire margins, while those of the true sumacs are coarsely serrate. Wherever you find poison sumac, you will probably find black ash (*Fraxinus nigra*), which has a similar pinnately compound leaf, but the leaves (not just the leaflets) are opposite, while those of poison sumac are alternate. It might also be helpful to remember that poison sumac grows only in swamps, and it is relatively rare in Minnesota. Caution is essential around poison sumac; the leaves and twigs are at least as toxic as those of poison ivy (*T. rydbergii* and *T. radicans* subsp. *negundo*).

Natural History

Poison sumac is rather uncommon in Minnesota, and it is largely restricted to sites in and around the Anoka Sand Plain in the east-central counties. It occurs only in wetlands, particularly marshy lakeshores, wet meadows, and swamps. These habitats are often dominated by cattails (*Typha* spp.), but may also have scattered willows (*Salix* spp.), tamarack (*Larix laricina*), black ash (*Fraxinus nigra*), bog birch (*Betula pumila*), or speckled alder (*Alnus incana* subsp. *rugosa*). Soils are usually sandy or peaty and saturated all year; pH ranges from weakly to moderately acidic.

These habitats are typically located in isolated basins where there may be local flooding in the spring. This type of flooding is from snow that melts within the immediate watershed and is different from the type of flooding that occurs along major rivers, where strong currents typically cause scouring and leave sediments behind.

Poison sumac is fast growing and short-lived, probably on the order of 10 to 15 years, and it reproduces only by seeds, which are spread in the droppings of birds. Yet, it is not aggressive and does not often invade ruderal habitats such as roadsides, ditches, or old fields; to the contrary, it is typically found in relatively stable native habitats.

An 8' (2.5 m) tall specimen from Anoka County.

Flowers from a male shrub—June 25.

Each leaf has 9–13 smooth-margined leaflets.

Unisexual flowers appear in June; these are female.

Bark is light gray, and somewhat rough.

Fruits in large, drooping clusters (panicles) in late summer.

Poison sumac   **633**

Tsuga, eastern hemlock

Pinaceae: Pine family

The hemlocks make up a genus of about 10 to 15 species of evergreen trees, primarily in temperate regions of Asia and North America. There are 4 species in North America, and 1 in Minnesota. (*Tsuga* is the Japanese name for the native hemlocks of Japan.)

Tsuga canadensis (L.) Carr.

Eastern hemlock

Large **trees**, to 30 m tall and 60 cm dbh (estimated potential for Minnesota). **Bark** gray or brownish; scaly when young, developing ridges and furrows with age. **Branchlets** slender, initially greenish or yellowish and hairy; becoming brown or gray-brown and glabrous by the 3rd or 4th year. **Leaves** linear or tapered; petiolate; spirally arranged but often twisted at the petiole so to appear 2-ranked; evergreen, persisting about 3 years; ± flat, straight; 7–13 mm long, 1.5–2 mm wide; borne on a persistent peglike base; apex rounded to nearly truncate; margins spinulose, especially on distal portion; upper surface slightly grooved; lower surface with protruding midrib, and faint rows of stomata. Trees monoecious with separate male and female **cones** (strobili) on the same tree. **Male (pollen) cones** subglobose, about 1 cm long at maturity; borne in leaf axils on 2nd-year branchlets; pollen shed in May or early June. **Female (seed) cones** pendent; ellipsoidal before opening, ovoid after opening; 1–2 cm long; on short stalks 1–4 mm long; borne at the tips of 2nd-year branchlets; maturing in autumn of the 1st year, shedding seeds through winter and falling from the tree soon after; wind-pollinated. **Seeds** 1.5–3 mm long, with wings 3–6 mm long; wind- and gravity-dispersed. (*canadensis*: of Canada)

Identification

Eastern hemlock is a large forest tree, with horizontal or somewhat drooping branches and soft, evergreen leaves. It has a roughly conical shape, similar to other conifers, but the leader often has a peculiar leaning or drooping aspect, and it may look curiously bare. It is superficially similar to the spruces (*Picea* spp.) and balsam fir (*Abies balsamea*), but differs by the size and shape of the needles and how they attach to the twig (see key) and by having bark with ridges and furrows.

Natural History

In Minnesota, eastern hemlock is usually scattered in mixed hardwood-conifer forests with yellow birch (*Betula alleghaniensis*), northern white cedar (*Thuja occidentalis*), white pine (*Pinus strobus*), or white spruce (*Picea glauca*), typically on moist, well-drained soils in cool, sheltered valleys and ravines. It is a long-lived late-successional species, very tolerant of shade but vulnerable to drought, windthrow, and especially deer predation (Mladendoff 1993). The continental climate of Minnesota, especially the cold, dry autumns, could be another limiting factor (Calcote 1986).

Eastern hemlock is one of Minnesota's rarest and most imperiled trees. It was rare even before the era of unrestrained logging and slash fires changed the composition of Minnesota's forests, and it has fared poorly since (Coffin and Pfannmuller 1988). The largest reported stand of eastern hemlock in Minnesota was situated on 280 acres in St. Louis County near the town of Paupore. At one time this stand had nearly 5,000 hemlock trees of all sizes (Lawson 1942). In 1912, about 8,000 hemlock ties were cut from this stand, and in an effort to protect the remaining trees a state park was proposed for the site. Tragically, the Moose Lake–Cloquet fire of 1918 intervened, destroying all but a few individual trees; eventually they all died.

Currently, the number of known sites is around 10, with a total of perhaps 50 mature trees. The largest site consists of 14 mature trees and fewer than 50 juveniles and seedlings. Other sites may have only a single tree, rarely more than 4 or 5, with little if any reproduction. Eastern hemlock currently receives no legal protection in Minnesota, and its future is not bright.

Female strobili appear singly at tips of branchlets—June 6.

Male strobili develop in leaf axils near tip—June 6.

Mature bark is ridged and furrowed—this trunk is 17" (43 cm) dbh.

Seed cones are less than an inch (1–2 cm) long—September 5.

Eastern hemlock **637**

Ulmus, the elms

Ulmaceae: Elm family

The elms constitute a genus of 20 to 40 species of deciduous trees and shrubs distributed in the temperate regions of the Northern Hemisphere, with 10 species in the United States and 3 in Minnesota (plus 1 naturalized species). (*Ulmus* is the classical Latin name for the elm.)

The history of elms in Minnesota is now dominated by the story of Dutch elm disease, one of the most devastating plant diseases known. It is a fungal disease of the vascular system caused by the pathogen *Ophiostoma ulmi* (Buis.) Nannf. The fungus invades the vessels in the outer ring of the xylem and blocks the flow of sap from the roots to the branches. The affected branch ultimately dies from lack of water.

The first symptom is a yellowing of the leaves on a single branch, usually in the upper part of the crown. Soon the yellow leaves turn brown and die, and the symptoms spread to the rest of the tree, branch by branch, until the entire tree dies, usually within a year or two. The infected branches can be diagnosed by a brown discoloration in the outer xylem, just beneath the bark.

The disease was first recognized in northwestern Europe in about 1918 and from there spread throughout Europe with devastating effects (Gibbs 1978). All of the native European elms are susceptible, but the losses were particularly great among wych elm (*U. glabra* Hudson), small-leaved elm (*U. minor* Miller), and English elm (*U. procera* Salisb.).

The disease reached the East Coast of North America in the late 1920s in a shipment of elm logs from Europe (Gibbs 1978). It turned out that the American elms were even more susceptible than the European elms, and the disease spread westward. The first Minnesota case was found in St. Paul in 1961, and by the mid-1980s the disease had spread throughout the state.

The fungus is carried from infected trees to healthy trees by the native elm bark beetle (*Hylurgopinus rufipes* [Eichhoff]) and the introduced European elm bark beetle (*Scolytus multistriatus* [Marsham]). The disease can also spread through root grafts, which occur naturally whenever elms grow closely together. There is no effective cure for the disease once it has progressed beyond the early stages. It does little if any good to simply remove the individual branches as they show symptoms. There are systemic chemicals currently available that may prevent infection when injected into the roots of healthy trees, but the treatment is expensive and must be repeated every 3 years. The only practical way to protect healthy trees is to remove diseased trees as soon as the disease is detected.

Control of Dutch elm disease has worked, to a limited extent, in metropolitan areas where removal of diseased trees has been a priority. But American elm was a codominant species in native forests throughout southern and central Minnesota, where control is impractical. As a result, statewide losses of mature canopy trees in native habitats have exceeded 90 percent. Losses of red elm and rock elm have also been great. Since American elm is a prolific seed producer, the few remaining mature trees still produce large numbers of seedlings, but few survive to become large trees. The disease does not abate, so remaining healthy trees will continue to be at risk.

A few clones of disease-resistant American elm trees, and elm hybrids, have recently been propagated and are beginning to appear in commercial nurseries (Sherald et al. 1994). This may restore elms to boulevards and parks, but it will not return elms to their native forests.

Key to the Genus Ulmus in Minnesota

1. Leaf blades < 7 cm long and < 4 cm wide, lower surface usually hairy only in axils of lateral veins; fruit (samara) glabrous .... *U. pumila*
1. The larger leaf blades ≥ 7 cm long and 4 cm wide, lower surface evenly and continuously hairy, or at least hairs not confined to axils of lateral veins; fruits hairy to some extent, either on margins (as cilia) or on the flat surfaces, or both.
    2. Twigs developing thick, corky ridges after 4–6 years; leaf bases nearly symmetrical; flowers in an elongate drooping raceme 2–5 cm long; fruits evenly hairy over surfaces and margins .... *U. thomasii*
    2. Twigs not developing corky ridges; leaf bases strongly asymmetrical; flowers in tight clusters (fascicles) ≤ 3 cm long; fruits either hairy only on margins or hairy only on the central portion that covers the seed but not evenly hairy over the entire surface.
        3. Most leaves with at least 3 lateral veins per side that fork evenly 1/2 to 3/4 of the way to the leaf margin; both lower and upper surface of leaves rough to the touch; fruits hairy on the flat central portion that covers the seed but not on the margins; flowers on pedicels 1 mm long or less .... *U. rubra*
        3. Most leaves with lateral veins that remain unforked their entire length, or occasionally with 1 or 2 veins in the lower half of the leaf that fork evenly; lower surface of leaves soft to the touch, the upper surface only sometimes rough; fruits hairy only on the margins (ciliate), glabrous elsewhere; flowers on pedicels 5–20 mm long .... *U. americana*

Ulmus americana L.

American elm

Large **trees**, to 37 m tall and 117 cm dbh. 1st-year **branchlets** hairy or occasionally glabrous or glabrate. **Bark** of mature trees thick, ashy gray, with narrow interlacing ridges and deep irregularly shaped furrows. **Leaves** simple, alternate, deciduous. **Petioles** 4–10 mm long, hairy to glabrate or occasionally glabrous. **Leaf blades** elliptical or occasionally somewhat obovate; 8–15 cm long, 4–9 cm wide; base rounded or tapered, strongly asymmetrical; apex abruptly acuminate; margins double serrate; lateral veins not forking, or occasionally 1 or a few veins in the basal half of the blade forking; upper surface dark green, ± glabrous and smooth to the touch, or with scattered stiff hairs and rough; lower surface pale green, with ± soft wavy hairs, usually soft to the touch. **Flowers** bisexual; borne in loose fascicles of 5–15 from leaf axils on branchlets of the previous year; pedicels somewhat drooping, 5–20 mm long, glabrous, jointed above the middle; sepals 6–9, irregularly rounded, 0.5–1.5 mm long, ciliate; petals absent; stamens 6–9; styles 2; **anthesis** early April to early mid-May, before the leaves appear; wind-pollinated. **Fruit** a flat 1-seeded samara; broadly elliptical to nearly circular, 8–13 mm long; margins densely ciliate; surfaces glabrous; maturing early mid-May to early mid-June; wind-dispersed. (*americana*: of America)

Identification

American elm is familiar to most people in Minnesota. It is a tall tree, commonly over 100 ft (30 m) in height, with a broad crown and slender twigs. The bark is ashy gray in color, but it may also have broad, pale brown streaks caused by a harmless bacterium. The leaf base is noticeably asymmetrical; one side is attached lower on the petiole than the other side, and the two halves are usually different shapes.

Natural History

Prior to the arrival of Dutch elm disease in the 1960s, American elm was one of the most common tree species in the hardwood forests of southeastern and central Minnesota, especially in the late-successional forest type called the "Big Woods." It was typically codominant with sugar maple (*Acer saccharum*), red oak (*Quercus rubra*), and basswood (*Tilia americana*). Tragically, nearly all the dominant elms have since died.

American elm is moderately tolerant of shade, so saplings survive well in a forest understory until a canopy gap opens, then they grow quickly to fill the gap. But it cannot compete directly with sugar maple, which is even more tolerant of shade and can survive even longer in the understory.

The natural habitats of American elm also include floodplain forests and hardwood swamps, where it is sustained by a remarkable root system that tolerates spring flooding and moderate levels of sedimentation. This has allowed it to extend its range along forested river corridors westward into the prairie region. It grows in just about any type of mineral soil but does best in deep, moist, calcareous loam.

American elm flowers in April, well before the leaves appear. The fruits develop and mature in as little as 30 days and are released just as the leaves are reaching full size. Each fruit consists of a single large seed surrounded by a broad, papery wing and can be carried on the wind for a quarter of a mile (406 meters) or more (*fide* Harlow et al. 1991). Seeds germinate within a few days and grow rapidly. It is an aggressive colonizer, and fast-growing seedlings and saplings are still common in old fields, roadsides, and vacant lots in spite of Dutch elm disease.

Flowers cover the branches before the leaves appear—
April 10.

Note the fringe of hairs around each
samara (winged fruit)—May 10.

Stiff, serrate leaves with asymmetrical bases—
up to 6" (15 cm) long.

Mature bark has narrow, interlacing
ridges—this trunk is 21" (53 cm) dbh.

Elms 🍃 **641**

Ulmus pumila L.

Siberian elm

Large, nonnative, naturalized **trees**, to 27 m tall and 94 cm dbh. 1st-year **branchlets** hairy or sparsely hairy. **Bark** of mature trees thick, gray, with interlacing flat-topped ridges and deep irregularly shaped furrows. **Leaves** simple, alternate, deciduous. **Petioles** 2–7 mm long, hairy. **Leaf blades** elliptical or occasionally ovate to lanceolate; 2–6 cm long, 1–3 cm wide; base tapered or blunt, or occasionally somewhat rounded, slightly asymmetrical; apex acute to acuminate; margins serrate or double serrate; lateral veins sometimes forking; upper surface dark green, glabrous and smooth to the touch, or with short, stiff, erect hairs and rough; lower surface pale green, with tufts of hairs in axils of lateral veins otherwise usually glabrous, ± smooth to the touch. **Flowers** bisexual; borne in dense fascicles of 5–15 from leaf axils on branchlets of the previous year; pedicels to 1 mm long, or essentially lacking; sepals 4–5, generally rounded, 0.5–1.5 mm long, lacking cilia; petals absent; stamens 4–5; styles 2; **anthesis** early April to early May, before the leaves appear; wind-pollinated. **Fruit** a flat 1-seeded samara; ± circular, 1–1.6 cm long; margins not ciliate; surfaces glabrous; maturing early mid-May to early mid-June; wind-dispersed. (*pumila*: dwarf, the reference unclear)

Identification

Siberian elm can become a large tree with a broad, rounded crown and deeply furrowed bark. It differs from the native elms by having smaller leaves, which are usually single serrate rather than double serrate, and by the hairless fruit. Siberian elm is reported to hybridize freely with the native red elm (*U. rubra*) (Sherman-Broyles 1997).

Natural History

Siberian elm is native to northern China and eastern Siberia. It was introduced into North America in the 1860s and was promoted as a street tree and as a windbreak tree for semiarid regions. It was probably brought to Minnesota soon after its arrival in North America, but it was never very popular here. American elm (*U. americana*) was preferred because of its more durable branches. Over time, Siberian elm gained a decidedly negative reputation even though it is hardy throughout the state and is not susceptible to Dutch elm disease. It is rarely planted today, and even existing trees are held in low regard.

There are still a few large specimens of Siberian elm surviving in parks and residential yards in the southern half of the state. There are even a few surviving in elm hedges, which were popular for a brief period. However, most specimens seen today are unwanted volunteers that have managed to find their own way into the landscape via windborne seeds. In fact, Siberian elm has become a common and aggressive invader in open habitats, such as roadsides, old fields, and abandoned urban lots, especially in sandy or loamy soil.

The usual concern with naturalized species is that they may invade wild habitats and outcompete native species, causing the disruption of important ecological processes. We have seen this happen with common buckthorn (*Rhamnus cathartica*) and the imported honeysuckles (*Lonicera* spp.) with devastating results. The situation with Siberian elm does not seem so dire. Although it does invade native grasslands, it is easily controlled with fire or cutting, and fortunately it does not survive in the understory of native forests. For the most part, Siberian elm is considered a nuisance rather than an ecological threat.

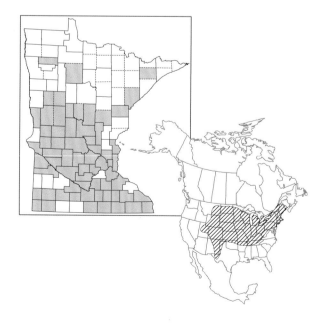

Leaves are small, less than 2.5" (6.5 cm) long.

Flowers are in tight clusters along 2nd-year twigs—April 16.

Samaras (winged fruits) are like other elms but hairless—May 21.

A mature tree in a Hennepin County park.

Furrowed bark is similar to American elm— this trunk is 37" (94 cm) dbh.

Elms

Ulmus rubra Muhl.

Red elm; slippery elm

Large **trees**, to 32 m tall and 90 cm dbh. 1st-year **branchlets** hairy. **Bark** of mature trees moderately thick, gray or brown, with narrow parallel ridges and shallow narrow furrows. **Leaves** simple, alternate, deciduous. **Petioles** 4–10 mm long, hairy. **Leaf blades** elliptical to broadly elliptical or obovate; 9–18 cm long, 5–10 cm wide; base rounded or tapered, asymmetrical; apex abruptly acuminate; margins double serrate; lateral veins mostly forking once before reaching the margins, or sometimes with an equal or slightly greater number of nonforking veins; upper surface dark green, with short, stiff, erect hairs, very rough to the touch; lower surface pale green, with hairs similar to upper surface but somewhat longer and softer and somewhat less rough to the touch. **Flowers** bisexual; borne in dense fascicles of 10–20 from leaf axils on branchlets of the previous year; pedicels to 1 mm long or essentially lacking; sepals 5–8, generally rounded, 0.5–1 mm long, ciliate; petals absent; stamens 5–8; styles 2; **anthesis** late March to late mid-May, before the leaves appear; wind-pollinated. **Fruit** a flat 1-seeded samara; ± circular, 10–20 mm long; margins not ciliate; surfaces hairy over the seed portion but the wing glabrous; maturing late April to late May; wind-dispersed. (*rubra*: red, in reference to the color of the buds)

Identification

Red elm is a tall forest tree with a relatively broad crown and slender twigs. It is superficially similar to American elm (*U. americana*), but there are ways to tell them apart without having the flowers or fruit in hand. To start with, both surfaces of the leaf are sandpapery rough, and at least some of the lateral veins of the leaves will fork evenly about 1/2 or 3/4 of the way to the margin. In the absence of leaves, examine a longitudinal section through the outer bark: American elm shows distinct alternating bands of whitish and pale brown layers 1–2 mm thick. A similar section through bark of red elm shows narrower bands of less contrasting colors that are barely distinct.

Natural History

Although red elm is a large canopy tree, it never seems to get quite as large as American elm (*U. americana*), even when growing in the same forest. And for some reason it is never as common, especially going northward. Habitats of the two elms are similar to a certain extent; both occur in mixed stands with oaks (*Quercus* spp.), basswood (*Tilia americana*), sugar maple (*Acer saccharum*), or black cherry (*Prunus serotina*), yet red elm differs in that it does not grow in swamps and rarely on floodplains, and it does not aggressively colonize ruderal habitats.

Seedlings and saplings of red elm are commonly seen in the understory of mature forests and have the peculiar habit of spreading across the forest floor by the processing of layering. The process begins when a flexible young stem becomes horizontal (decumbent) on the forest floor. How this happens is not clear, but the newly horizontal stem will take root along its length. However, the tips of the branches continue to grow upward until they get about 2 or 3 ft high, then they too may become decumbent. Eventually, a "colony" will develop that may be 10–15 ft (3–5 m) across and consist of several waist-high, upright branches. The colony may exist in this form for many years, perhaps aided by root grafting with the parent tree. When a gap in the canopy opens above the colony, the tallest branch will exert apical dominance and grow rapidly upwards to fill the gap; the other branches will eventually die.

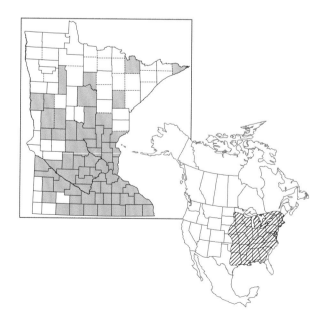

Flowers of red elm are sessile, those of American elm are stalked—April 17.

Samaras (winged fruits) are hairy at the center—May 20.

Note how some lateral veins fork near margin.

Ridges tend to run parallel rather than interlace—this trunk is 17" (44 cm) dbh.

Ulmus thomasii Sarg.

Rock elm; cork elm
[U. *racemosa* Thomas]

Large **trees**, to 30 m tall and 72 cm dbh. 1st-year **branchlets** brown, hairy; developing thick corky ridges after 4–6 years. **Bark** of mature trees thick, gray, with interlacing ridges and deep irregularly shaped furrows. **Leaves** simple, alternate, deciduous. **Petioles** 2–8 mm long, hairy. **Leaf blades** elliptical; 7–15 cm long, 4–9 cm wide; base tapered to blunt or somewhat rounded, nearly symmetrical; apex short-acuminate or occasionally acute; margins double serrate; lateral veins not forking, or occasionally 1 or a few veins in the basal half of the blade irregularly forking; upper surface dark green, glabrous and smooth to the touch, or sometimes with scattered stiff hairs and rough; lower surface pale green, with soft, wavy hairs, and somewhat soft to the touch. **Flowers** bisexual; borne in loose pendulous racemes of 5–13 from leaf axils on branchlets of the previous year; pedicels 2.5–10 mm long, minutely hairy, jointed; sepals 5–8, generally rounded, 0.5–1.5 mm long, ciliate; petals absent; stamens 5–8; styles 2; **anthesis** early April to mid-May, before the leaves appear; wind-pollinated. **Fruit** a flat 1-seeded samara; broadly elliptical to nearly circular, 1.5–2.3 cm long; margins densely ciliate; surfaces evenly hairy; maturing mid-May to early mid-June; wind-dispersed. (*thomasii*: named for David Thomas, 1776–1859)

Identification

Rock elm is a tall, slender tree with relatively short branches and a narrow crown. The trunk typically remains distinct for nearly the full height of the tree, even when grown in the open. The leaves are distinctly elmlike with double-serrate margins and a narrowly pointed tip. But in contrast to American elm (*U. americana*), the base of the leaf is nearly symmetrical. Rock elm is easily told from all other elms by the corky ridges, or wings, that develop on the twigs after 4 to 6 years. They look somewhat like the twigs of bur oak (*Quercus macrocarpa*).

Natural History

Rock elm is relatively widespread in southern and central Minnesota, but it has never been as common as American elm (*U. americana*) or even red elm (*U. rubra*). And like the other native elms, rock elm is clearly susceptible to Dutch elm disease; in fact, it

is now easier to find dead trees than live ones. In another decade or two, rock elm could be nearly gone from Minnesota.

Recent surveys show rock elm to occur primarily in forests on floodplains and terraces of major tributaries of the Mississippi River, such as the Cannon River, Root River, and principally the Minnesota River. It follows the Minnesota River westward into the prairie region, nearly to the western border of the state. In these riverine habitats it typically occurs as a scattered canopy tree with American elm (*U. americana*), hackberry (*Celtis occidentalis*), basswood (*Tilia americana*), or bur oak (*Quercus macrocarpa*). It does well in these habitats because it can survive moderate levels of spring flooding and associated sedimentation. Rock elm has also been found, but less often, in upland habitats away from rivers, primarily in forests dominated by oaks (*Quercus* spp.) and aspens (*Populus* spp.). In this situation, it is usually in sandy or sandy-loam soil and often where the water table is near the surface.

Seedlings and saplings will survive several years suppressed in a moderately shady understory and will respond with rapid growth when a gap opens in the overstory. But without an opening to provide direct sunlight for at least a portion of the day, saplings will decline and eventually die. This inability to tolerate perpetual shade seems to be a characteristic of elms in general.

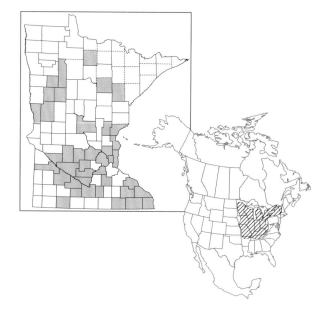

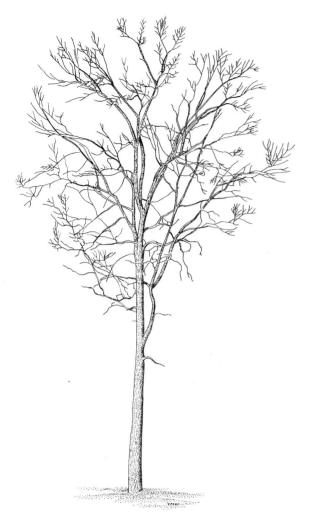

Twigs develop corky ridges after 4–6 years.

Flowers are in loose, pendulous racemes—April 16.

Samaras (winged fruits) are large and covered with hairs—May 28.

Bark of rock elm is coarser than other elms—this trunk is 15" (38 cm) dbh.

Leaves are nearly symmetrical and double serrate.

Elms

Vaccinium, the blueberries and bilberries

Ericaceae: Heath family

Vaccinium is a large and widespread genus with 300 to 400+ species of deciduous and evergreen shrubs and rarely small trees, occurring primarily in temperate climates and in mountainous regions of the tropics. There are about 30 species in the United States, and 5 species in Minnesota. The familiar native cranberries (*Oxycoccus quadripetalus* and *O. macrocarpus*) have often been included in this genus, but their distinctive floral morphology seems to warrant a separate genus. (*Vaccinium* is the classical Latin name for an Old World species in this genus.)

The University of Minnesota has conducted a program to breed cold-hardy blueberries for local fruit production (Luby 1991). Since the 1980s, it has been releasing "half-high" cultivars bred from Minnesota's native sweet lowbush blueberry (*V. angustifolium* Ait.) and the commonly cultivated highbush blueberry of the eastern United States (*V. corymbosum* L.), which is known from wild populations as close to Minnesota as central Wisconsin.

Key to the Genus Vaccinium *in Minnesota*

1. Leaves ± thin, deciduous (present only on the twigs produced during the current year); corolla 5-lobed; berries ripening blue or blackish; lower surface of leaf lacking dark bristlelike glands.
    2. Mature leaves 2.2–5 cm long, the apex tapered to an acute or obtuse point, the upper surface hairy, at least on midvein; flowers borne in racemes of 2–15; branches with "warty" bumps.

3. Leaf margins with sharp gland-tipped serrations, the margins either lacking hairs or with scattered short curved hairs; branches with minute recurved hairs in lines or patches .... *V. angustifolium*

3. Leaf margins entire, with long hairs; branches densely and evenly covered with long ± straight hairs .... *V. myrtilloides*

2. Mature leaves 1–2.8 cm long, the apex usually blunt or rounded, the upper surface glabrous; flowers borne singly or in fascicles of 2; branches not "warty."

4. Leaf margins with gland-tipped serrations, the lower surface glabrous; flowers borne singly from axils of the lowest leaves; pedicels 1–3.5 mm long .... *V. cespitosum*

4. Leaf margins entire, the lower surface minutely hairy especially on the veins; flowers borne singly or in 2s from short leafless branches; pedicels 2–6 mm long .... *V. uliginosum*

1. Leaves thick and leathery, evergreen (persisting on twigs of the previous year as well as the current year); corolla 4-lobed; berries ripening red; lower surface of leaf with dark bristlelike glands (usually visible to the unaided eye as dark flecks) .... *V. vitis-idaea*

Vaccinium angustifolium Ait.

Sweet lowbush blueberry

Low **shrubs**, with 1 or a few upright **stems** to 50 cm tall; forming rhizomatous colonies. **Branches** greenish to brownish; minutely hairy in patches or lines; warty. **Bark** greenish to brownish or reddish brown, rough, eventually splitting. **Leaves** simple, alternate, deciduous; sessile or on petioles to 1 mm long. **Leaf blades** elliptical; 2.2–4 cm long, 0.8–1.8 cm wide; base acute to obtuse; apex acute or occasionally obtuse, with a short blunt mucro; margins with sharp, gland-tipped serrations, glabrous or short-hairy; upper surface dark green, hairy to sparsely hairy on main veins otherwise glabrous; lower surface pale green otherwise similar to upper surface. **Inflorescence** a crowded raceme of 2–15 flowers. **Flowers** 5-merous, bisexual, white or pale pink, 4.5–7 mm long; pedicels 1–3 mm long, glabrous; corolla cylindrical or urn shaped, lobes 0.5–1.5 mm long; style about equaling the corolla, glabrous; **anthesis** mid-May to mid-June, before the leaves are half-grown; insect-pollinated. **Fruit** a globular berry, glaucous blue or occasionally black, 7–10 mm in diameter; maturing late July to early September; animal-dispersed. (*angustifolium*: narrow-leaved)

Identification

There are two native blueberries in Minnesota: sweet lowbush blueberry (*V. angustifolium*) and the similar velvet-leaf blueberry (*V. myrtilloides*). Both are low, bushy shrubs rarely more than knee high with elliptical leaves and crowded clusters of white or pinkish flowers. The best ways to distinguish sweet lowbush blueberry are by its minutely serrate leaf margin (usually visible without magnification) and nearly hairless branches. The fruit of the two blueberries are usually indistinguishable in appearance and taste.
Note: Sweet lowbush blueberry is the blueberry of commerce and is harvested on a small scale from wild stands in Minnesota. In easily accessible sites the harvesting can become intensive and highly competitive.

Natural History

Sweet lowbush blueberry is common in the forested region of Minnesota, especially north of the Twin Cities. It is usually found in areas of dry, sandy soil in the vicinity of pines (*Pinus* spp.), oaks (*Quercus* spp.), or trembling aspen (*Populus tremuloides*). Habitats include dry, open ridgetops, exposed bedrock outcrops, and sandy barrens. Paradoxically, it can also be found in cool *Sphagnum* bogs, where it grows in saturated peat. Soils typically have a pH range of 2.8–6.6, which translates as strongly to weakly acidic (Vander Kloet 1988). Even though sweet lowbush blueberry is basically a forest species, it does not tolerate dense shade; it usually sets fruit only when growing in openings or clearings. It can take this one step further and colonize abandoned agricultural land if soil conditions are right.

Sweet lowbush blueberry thrives only in fire-prone habitats, and although fire may consume the stems, the deep horizontal rhizomes usually survive a fire and resprout vigorously. In fact, well-established colonies often expand significantly as a result of dormant-season fire. This trait is exploited by growers, who typically burn commercial stands every other year to maximize fruit production (Vander Kloet 1988). Stems can also be killed if exposed above the snow during long winters, and a variety of animals browse the branches. Yet under ideal conditions, aerial stems can live 10 to 15 years and individual rhizomes perhaps 20 to 25 years (Hall et al. 1979). The whole colony (clone), which can often be distinguished on the ground and may exceed 33 ft (10 m) in diameter, can reportedly reach an age of 150 years (Hall et al. 1979).

The entire plant is rarely more than knee high.

Flowers are somewhat urn shaped, and white or pale pink—June 21.

This is the wild version of the commercial blueberry—August 4.

Vaccinium cespitosum Michx.

Dwarf bilberry

Low **shrubs**, with 1 or a few upright **stems** to 18 cm tall; forming rhizomatous colonies. **Branches** greenish to brownish; minutely and evenly hairy; not warty. **Bark** greenish to brownish or reddish brown, becoming somewhat flaky. **Leaves** simple, alternate, deciduous; sessile. **Leaf blades** oblanceolate to obovate or occasionally elliptical; 1.6–2.8 cm long, 0.7–1.2 cm wide; base acute or occasionally somewhat acuminate or decurrent; apex obtuse to blunt or occasionally rounded; margins with small, gland-tipped serrations; upper surface dark green, glabrous; lower surface pale green, glabrous. **Flowers** 5-merous, bisexual, white or pale pink, 4.5–6 mm long; borne singly from axils of the lowest leaves; pedicels 1–3.5 mm long, ± glabrous; corolla cylindrical to urn shaped, the lobes 0.5–1 mm long; style about equaling the corolla, glabrous; **anthesis** early June to early July; insect-pollinated. **Fruit** a globular berry, blue and glaucous or occasionally black and somewhat shiny, 5–9 mm in diameter; maturing late mid-July to late August; animal-dispersed. (*cespitosum*: growing in dense clumps)

Identification

Dwarf bilberry is a small, compact shrub, just over ankle high. The native blueberries (*V. angustifolium* and *V. myrtilloides*) are similar, but dwarf bilberry is a much smaller plant; the leaves in particular are much smaller and have a more rounded tip. They are also completely hairless. The flowers are not particularly distinctive, other than they are borne singly from the leaf axils rather than in multiflowered racemes.

Natural History

Dwarf bilberry is widespread in the forested region of northern and central Minnesota, yet it is sporadic and generally uncommon. It is also one of Minnesota's smallest shrubs and is easily overlooked, which may enhance its reputation for being hard to find. The best habitats seem to be openings or clearings in coniferous forests, especially in dry, sandy soils near pines (*Pinus* spp.) or occasionally oaks (*Quercus* spp.) or trembling aspen (*Populus tremuloides*).

It has also been found on sandy or gravelly ridges, rocky talus, cliff tops, bedrock outcrops, and rocky lakeshores. Since many of these habitats are notably hot and dry, the plants may experience periods of seasonal water stress. This does not seem to affect dwarf bilberry's ability to stay green all summer and produce fruit, even though other species may turn brown and go dormant.

Dwarf bilberry occurs exclusively in fire-prone landscapes and apparently depends on periodic fire to maintain the openness of its habitat. This seems risky because the rhizomes are shallow and easily killed by a hot ground fire. Yet, it occurs in habitats with sparse vegetation that may not carry a ground fire, or where a fire might burn quickly or leave unburned patches.

There is no experimental evidence, but observation indicates that if "burned out" of a habitat, it will not aggressively recolonize. If it does return, it can persist for decades if certain characteristics of its habitat are maintained, particularly exposure to direct sunlight for at least a portion of the day, freedom from competing vegetation, and perhaps some protection from ground fires. Under these conditions the growth of rhizomes can eventually result in relatively large, dense mats (clones).

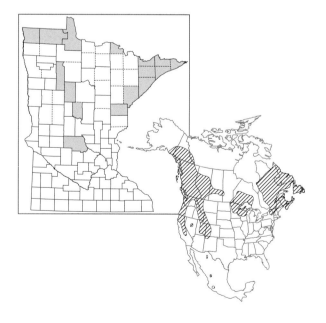

Flowers are only about 1/4" (4.5–6 mm) long—June 21.

Fruits are similar to the blueberries, only slightly smaller—August 22.

Dwarf bilberry is often only ankle high.

Vaccinium myrtilloides Michx.

Velvet-leaf blueberry

Low to midsize **shrubs**, with 1 or a few upright **stems** to 75 cm tall; forming rhizomatous colonies. **Branches** greenish to brownish or reddish brown; densely and evenly long-hairy; warty. **Bark** reddish brown to purplish, minutely roughened, eventually splitting and peeling. **Leaves** simple, alternate, deciduous; sessile or on petioles to 1.5 mm long. **Leaf blades** elliptical; 2.2–5 cm long, 0.9–2 cm wide; base acute to obtuse or rounded; apex acute to obtuse, with a short blunt mucro; margins entire, long-hairy; upper surface dark green, hairy to sparsely hairy especially on main veins; lower surface pale green, hairy especially on main veins. **Inflorescence** a crowded raceme of 2–13 flowers. **Flowers** 5-merous, bisexual, whitish or pale pink, 4–6.5 mm long; pedicels 1–3 mm long, glabrous or sparsely hairy; corolla cylindrical to urn shaped, the lobes 1–2 mm long; style about equaling the corolla, glabrous; **anthesis** mid-May to late June, after the leaves are half-grown; insect-pollinated. **Fruit** a globular berry, blue or occasionally blackish, 6–9 mm in diameter; maturing late July to early September; animal-dispersed. (*myrtilloides*: resembling *myrtillus*, in reference to the European *Vaccinium myrtillus* L.)

Identification

Velvet-leaf blueberry is a low, bushy shrub about knee high, with velvety leaves and clusters of whitish or pinkish flowers. It is often mistaken for the more common sweet lowbush blueberry (*V. angustifolium*); both have sweet edible berries and a nearly identical growth form, and they sometimes occur side by side. But the leaves and young branches of velvet-leaf blueberry are, as its name suggests, uniformly velvety-hairy, and the leaf margins lack serrations.

Natural History

Velvet-leaf blueberry is fairly common in the eastern and central part of the state, especially northward, but it never seems to be as common as sweet lowbush blueberry (*V. angustifolium*). It often grows in sandy or loamy soil in upland forests, especially with pines (*Pinus* spp.), oaks (*Quercus* spp.), or paper birch (*Betula papyrifera*). Surprisingly, it occurs just about as often in swamps and bogs, where it grows in wet

peat with scattered black spruce (*Picea mariana*) or tamarack (*Larix laricina*). The soils, whether mineral or peat, are always acidic and relatively low in nutrients, with published pH values ranging from 3.3 to 5.6 (Vander Kloet and Hall 1981). Where the two blueberry species occur in proximity, sweet lowbush blueberry tends to favor drier, open sites, while velvet-leaf blueberry is more competitive in somewhat shadier, moister or even wet habitats.

Populations of velvet-leaf blueberry can consist of scattered individuals or discernable colonies. Colonies develop from a network of relatively deep horizontal rhizomes, and although the aboveground stems are easily consumed by fire, the rhizomes generally survive and are stimulated to resprout vigorously. In fact, aboveground growth is most abundant in the years following a fire. The stems are heavily browsed by a variety of animals and can be winter-killed if not covered by snow (Vander Kloet and Hall 1981).

The berries of velvet-leaf blueberry vary in taste and are sometimes described as sour. But they are more often considered equal in flavor to those of sweet lowbush blueberry. Most berry pickers do not distinguish between the two species.

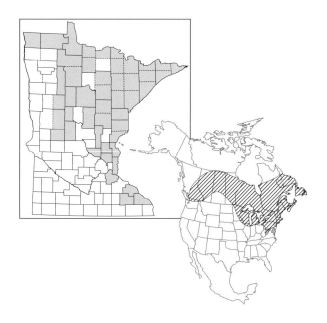

Flowers appear between mid-May and late June.

A large individual may reach 30" (75 cm) in height.

Leaves and twigs are covered with soft, "velvety" hairs—August 15.

Vaccinium uliginosum L.

Bilberry

Low **shrubs**, with 1 or a few upright or decumbent **stems** to 30 cm tall; clonal. **Branchlets** of the year brown to greenish brown, minutely hairy; 2nd-year branchlets brown to reddish brown, minutely hairy or glabrate, not warty. **Bark** ± smooth, gray to brown or reddish brown. **Leaves** simple, alternate, deciduous; sessile or on short hairy petioles to 1 mm long. **Leaf blades** elliptical to broadly elliptical or obovate, sometimes nearly circular; 10–22 mm long, 7–17 mm wide; base tapered or occasionally rounded; apex obtusely tapered to rounded, with a small stout apiculus; margins entire, flat; upper surface dark green, glabrous; lower surface pale green, minutely hairy especially on veins. **Flowers** 4- or 5-merous (5-merous in Minnesota), bisexual, white or pink, 4–6 mm long, borne singly or in fascicles of 2; pedicels 2–6 mm long, glabrous; corolla short-cylindrical to urn shaped, the lobes 1–1.5 mm long; style about equaling the corolla or a little shorter, glabrous; **anthesis** early mid-June to early mid-July; insect-pollinated. **Fruit** a globose berry, blue and glaucous or occasionally blackish and shiny, 6–8 mm in diameter; maturing mid-August to early mid-September; animal-dispersed. (*uliginosum*: growing in marshes)

Identification

Bilberry is a low-growing, stiffly branched deciduous shrub with small, roundish leaves. It could easily be mistaken for the common bear-berry (*Arctostaphylos uva-ursi*), but bilberry leaves are thin and deciduous, while those of bear-berry are thick and evergreen. *Note:* This is a polymorphic species with populations in arctic and alpine regions throughout the northern hemisphere. A number of varieties and subspecies have been proposed based largely on leaf pubescence, growth form, and fruit characteristics (Young 1970). The Minnesota population does not closely conform to any of the published subspecific taxa, and it is uncertain how it should be treated.

Natural History

Bilberry is apparently very rare in Minnesota; it has been known to occur at only two sites. Both are bedrock outcrops along the shore of Lake Superior in Cook County. One of the two has not been relocated since 1937 in spite of several attempts to do so and

may now be gone. The remaining site is about 9 miles (14.5 km) away in crevices on a rhyolite outcrop that projects prominently into Lake Superior. It was discovered there in 1891, but no description of the population was recorded at the time. Recently (2002) it was determined to consist of only 11 discontinuous patches, probably clones, covering a combined area of about 20 square ft (2 square m).

These numbers seem precariously low, but they may not represent an actual decline. The biology of the species indicates that it could maintain such a small population for an indefinite period. This is because bilberry can reproduce vegetatively rather than rely on the periodic and chancier recruitment of seedlings. The exact method of vegetative reproduction is not clear; it may be by the process of layering or the production of invasive rhizomes. Either way, the result is long-lived clones.

Bilberry is reportedly more common along the shore farther east in Ontario and in bog habitats farther north (Soper and Heimburger 1982). Apparently all of the reported habitats receive direct sunlight for most of the day, are relatively nutrient poor, and have pH values from 3.5 to 6.2, which means strongly acidic to weakly acidic (Vander Kloet 1988).

Flowers are similar to those of the blueberries—June 19.

Note the roundish, reticulate-veined leaves and blue berry—August 11.

Bilberry is a spreading, mat-forming shrub.

Vaccinium vitis-idaea L.

Mountain cranberry; lingonberry

Low **shrubs**, with 1 or a few upright, ascending or decumbent **stems** to 20 cm tall; forming colonies by rhizomatous growth and layering. **Branches** brownish to reddish brown, minutely hairy. **Leaves** simple, alternate, evergreen, persisting up to 4 years. **Petioles** 1–2.5 mm long, minutely hairy. **Leaf blades** thick and leathery, obovate; 1–2 cm long, 4–8 mm wide; base acutely or obtusely tapered; apex rounded, often slightly emarginate with a small tooth in the notch; margins entire, revolute; upper surface dark green and shiny, glabrous or minutely hairy on midvein; lower surface pale green, dull, with dark bristlelike glands (usually visible without magnification). **Inflorescence** a short terminal raceme of 3–10 flowers. **Flowers** 4-merous, bisexual, white or pink, 4.5–6.5 mm long; pedicels 0.5–3 mm long, minutely hairy; corolla bell shaped to nearly spherical, the lobes 1.5–3 mm long; style usually exserted somewhat beyond the corolla; **anthesis** early mid-June to early mid-July; insect-pollinated. **Fruit** a globose berry, dark red, 7–10 mm in diameter; maturing mid-August to early mid-September, often persisting over winter; animal-dispersed. (*vitis-idaea*: grape of Mount Ida)

Identification

Mountain cranberry is an ankle-high "bog" shrub with thick, shiny, evergreen leaves and usually only 2 or 3 short branches. It is superficially similar to some other heath shrubs, especially the true cranberries (*Oxycoccus macrocarpus* and *O. quadripetalus*), but it grows upright instead of vinelike and has glands on the underside of the leaf that look like scattered black flecks (may require a hand lens).
Note: This is a wide-ranging circumboreal plant known in Europe (and Newfoundland) as lingonberry. The plants that occur in North America and northern Asia differ slightly from those in Europe and are sometimes treated as a geographically isolated subspecies (subsp. *minus* (Lodd.) Hult.) or variety (var. *minus* Lodd.)

Natural History

Mountain cranberry is somewhat sporadic but not uncommon in bogs across the northern part of the state. It is typically found growing in *Sphagnum* moss where there are scattered or thin stands of black spruce (*Picea mariana*), northern white cedar

(*Thuja occidentalis*), or tamarack (*Larix laricina*). Although associated with forests, it usually avoids deep shade. It is also found in lichen communities on dry bedrock exposures, especially along the shore of Lake Superior. All of these habitats are acidic, nutrient poor, and usually in direct sunlight.

The general landscape in northern Minnesota is prone to periodic wildfires, but the ground flora in bogs usually escapes catastrophic fires and is not typically subject to prolonged flooding or drought. So in a sense bogs can be considered late-successional or climax communities, and the establishment of mountain cranberry seedlings in such a stable habitat is apparently uncommon. But once mountain cranberry becomes established, it persists well and spreads clonally by shallow rhizomes that send up shoots some distance from the parent plant, and by decumbent stems that may take root. Given time, these clones can become very dense and almost carpetlike, although not large in extent.

The berries are commercially harvested in the Scandinavian countries and in a few areas of Canada, mostly Newfoundland (Hendrickson 1997). There is no local tradition of harvesting mountain cranberries in Minnesota, although they are sporadically harvested as a novelty or for home use. However, for a brief period in history huge quantities of the berries were imported into Minnesota to satisfy the demands of recent Norwegian immigrants (Fernald and Kinsey 1943).

The leaves are evergreen, thick and leathery—June 18.

Fruits ripen dark red, and are sometimes called "lingonberries"—August 22.

Viburnum, the viburnums

Adoxaceae: Moschatel family

The viburnums make up a genus of 200 to 250 species. It includes both deciduous and evergreen shrubs and small trees, distributed in Europe, Asia, North America, and South America. The United States has about 15 native species, and Minnesota has 4 native and 1 naturalized species. (*Viburnum* is the classical Latin name for the Eurasian wayfaring tree, *V. lantana* L.)

The naturalized species is the guilder-rose, or European high-bush cranberry (*V. opulus*). There are other nonnative viburnums that are commonly cultivated in Minnesota but have not become naturalized, including the wayfaring tree (*V. lantana* L.) and southern arrowwood (*V. dentatum* L.).

Key to the Genus *Viburnum in Minnesota*

1. Leaves 3-lobed; petioles with prominent glands near the summit or at the base of the blade.
    2. Inflorescences 2–3 cm across, with < 50 flowers, borne at the tips of short 2-leaved shoots; flowers all alike (fertile), with small inconspicuous corollas; stamens not projecting beyond the corolla (included); stipules generally absent; lateral lobes of leaf blades with tips pointing forward .... *V. edule*
    2. Inflorescence 5–13 cm across, with > 100 flowers, borne at the tips of relatively long 4-leaved shoots; flowers of 2 types: an outer ring of sterile flowers with large conspicuous corollas, and an inner cluster of fertile flowers with small inconspicuous corollas; stamens projecting well beyond the corolla (exserted); stipules present; lateral lobes of leaf blades with tips often curved outward.

3. Glands at summit of petiole 2–4, usually stalked or columnar, ± circular in cross section, and with a flat top 0.3–0.7 mm across; the channel in the upper surface of the petiole with relatively long coarse hairs, at least near the summit .... *V. trilobum*

3. Glands at summit of petiole 2–8, sessile, elliptical in cross section, and with a distinctly concave top 0.8–1.5 mm across; the channel in the upper surface of the petiole glabrous or with scattered short fine hairs .... *V. opulus*

1. Leaves not lobed; petioles and leaf bases lacking glands.

4. Leaf margins finely serrate with > 25 teeth per side, lateral veins anastomosing before reaching the margin, lower surface glabrous; petioles 1.5–3 cm long, margins conspicuously flattened; stipules absent; inflorescences 5–10 cm across, sessile; flowers > 100 .... *V. lentago*

4. Leaf margins coarsely serrate with < 15 teeth per side, lateral veins remaining distinct to the margin, lower surface hairy at least in axils of larger veins; petioles 3–12 mm long, margins not flattened; stipules present; inflorescences 2–6 cm across, borne on a peduncle 0.3–5 cm long; flowers < 100 .... *V. rafinesquianum*

Viburnum edule (Michx.) Raf.

Squashberry

Midsize **shrubs**, with single or multiple upright or sprawling **stems** to 2 m tall and 4 cm basal diameter; clonal. 2nd-year **branchlets** pale gray-brown to yellow-brown, often black-dotted; glabrous. **Bark** gray to brown; rough. **Leaves** simple, opposite, deciduous. **Petioles** 0.5–2 cm long; glabrous or sparsely hairy, often gland-dotted; with 1 or more pair of projecting glands at the summit of the petiole or more often at the base of the blade; stipules generally absent. **Leaf blades** broadly ovate to broadly elliptical, or nearly orbicular; shallowly 3-lobed, or the uppermost leaves sometimes unlobed; 5–8 cm long, 5–8 cm wide; base rounded to cordate, or nearly truncate; apex of lobes acutely or obtusely tapered; margins coarsely serrate; upper surface dark green, essentially glabrous; lower surface pale green, hairy along the larger veins especially in the axils, often glandular. **Inflorescence** a round-topped lateral cyme 1.4–3 cm across; borne on short, 2-leaved shoots from lateral buds on 2nd-year branchlets; with 15–50 flowers; peduncle 2–3.5 cm long. **Flowers** bisexual, 5-merous, whitish; sepals ovate to deltate, about 0.5 mm long; petals obovate to broadly elliptical, 1–2.5 mm long; stamens included, filaments 0.5–1.5 mm long; **anthesis** mid-June to early mid-July; insect-pollinated. **Fruit** a single-seeded drupe, ± globose, 7–12 mm in diameter, ripening dark red, shiny; maturing late July to late August, sometimes persisting through winter; animal-dispersed. (*edule*: edible)

Identification

This is the smallest of the native viburnums, often only waist high, and usually with just a few weak stems that may sprawl or arch to the ground. Because of the leaf shape, it is most likely to be confused with high-bush cranberry (*V. trilobum*). But squashberry is a smaller shrub, and the leaves are generally more rounded in outline and have shallower lobes; the later leaves may have no lobes at all. Also, the leaf margins are lined with a continuous row of serrations, often as many as 50 to 75. Compared to high-bush cranberry, the inflorescence is smaller and lacks the ring of enlarged showy flowers around the edge, and the branchlet that bears the inflorescence has only 2 leaves instead of 4. The leaves also look something like those of mountain maple (*Acer spicatum*),

thimbleberry (*Rubus parviflorus*), and the currants (*Ribes* spp.).

Natural History

Squashberry is the most northerly of all the viburnums, ranging from near the Arctic Circle, south through the boreal regions of Alaska and Canada, just reaching the northeast corner of Minnesota. It is associated most strongly with spruce-fir (*Picea-Abies*) forests, but it is not a strong competitor in shady habitats and does not normally inhabit forest interiors. Instead it behaves more as an opportunist, exploiting edge or transitional habitats where there is less competition for sunlight.

Squashberry is apparently most common along the shore of Lake Superior in Cook County, especially at the margin of the woods that line the shore. Away from the lake it occurs on cliffs, talus, gravelly or rocky lakeshores and riverbanks, and in brushy thickets and open-canopy woodlands.

It is clonal in the sense that it sometimes forms small colonies by vegetative means, possibly by root suckering or layering. But it does not spread aggressively, even where it might seem to have plenty of room. Individual stems are relatively short-lived; even entire colonies seem somewhat transient or ephemeral.

Flowers are fewer and smaller than in other viburnums—June 15.

Early leaves are 3-lobed, but later leaves are unlobed.

Each fruit is a red, single-seeded drupe—August 28.

Viburnum lentago L.

Nannyberry

Tall **shrubs** or small trees, with single or multiple upright **stems** to 8 m tall and 15 cm dbh; clonal by root suckers. 2nd-year **branchlets** brown to reddish brown or gray-brown; glabrous. **Bark** gray-brown; rough, becoming shallowly furrowed or scaly in age. **Leaves** simple, opposite, deciduous. **Petioles** 1.5–3 cm long; glabrous or somewhat ciliate in the spring, often minutely scurfy; margins irregularly winged or undulating; glands absent; stipules absent. **Leaf blades** ovate to elliptical or broadly elliptical, occasionally nearly circular; 5–10 cm long, 3.5–6 cm wide; base obtusely tapered or rounded; apex abruptly acuminate; margins finely serrate; upper surface dark green, glabrous; lower surface slightly paler than upper, glabrous or often scurfy. **Inflorescence** a round-topped terminal cyme, 5–10 cm across; borne at the tips of 1st-year branchlets; with a few to several hundred flowers; sessile. **Flowers** bisexual, 5-merous, pale yellow to creamy white; sepals ovate, about 0.7 mm long; petals ovate to elliptical, 1.5–3 mm long; stamens exserted, filaments 2.5–5.5 mm long; **anthesis** mid-May to early June; insect-pollinated. **Fruit** a single-seeded drupe, ellipsoidal, somewhat flattened, 8–15 mm long, ripening blue-black; maturing late August to late September, often persisting through winter; animal-dispersed. (*lentago*: an old name of the wayfaring tree *V. lantana* L.)

Identification

Nannyberry is a large, coarse shrub or sometimes a small, irregularly formed tree. In either form it is the largest of the native viburnums, often reaching heights of 20 ft (6 m) and stem diameters of 3 inches (8 cm). The leaves are most likely to be confused with those of choke-cherry (*Prunus virginiana*) or American wild plum (*P. americana*), but the margin of the petiole is thin and undulating, almost winglike.

Natural History

Nannyberry is typically a large, understory shrub in mesic or moist hardwood forests, usually with oaks (*Quercus* spp.), trembling aspen (*Populus tremuloides*), basswood (*Tilia americana*), or a variety of other canopy species. It is also found on lakeshores, riverbanks, floodplains, and pond margins, usually in fine- or coarse-textured mineral soils but sometimes in shallow peat. It occurs statewide, but it is more common in the south.

The range of nannyberry extends from the forests into the prairie region, where it grows in brushy coulees or thickets, either in single-species clones or in multiple-species shrub communities with species of similar size, such as American wild plum (*Prunus americana*), fireberry hawthorn (*Crataegus chrysocarpa*), and choke-cherry (*Prunus virginiana*). The interior of these thickets is usually unaffected by grass fires because the shade prevents a buildup of fuel. But if stems of nannyberry are killed, they resprout from surviving root crowns and from adventitious buds on shallow roots. If the entire plant is killed it readily reinvades via seeds carried in the droppings of birds. In this way it also colonizes old fields, abandoned pastures, and roadsides.

If unimpeded, these nannyberry thickets can eventually cover a rather large area and persist for decades. In one study, an open-grown patch of nannyberry 50 by 50 ft (15 by 15 m) maintained its integrity and resisted tree invasion for at least 50 years (Niering et al. 1986). By way of contrast, forest-grown nannyberry is a modest shrub, usually much smaller than open-grown plants, and with only a few stems. It will rarely if ever form thickets under stable forest conditions.

Note the large inflorescences and rather droopy leaves—May 27.

Margins of petioles are flattened, almost winglike.

Multiple stems are typical, some can reach 26'
(8 m) in height.

Fruits don't ripen until September.

A typical edge-grown specimen 13' (4 m) tall—Anoka County.

Viburnum opulus L.

Guelder-rose, European high-bush cranberry

Tall, nonnative, naturalized **shrubs**, with single or multiple upright **stems** to 6 m tall and 6 cm dbh; occasionally clonal by layering or tip-rooting. 2nd-year **branchlets** brown to grayish, often black-dotted; glabrous. **Bark** brown to gray; smooth or somewhat rough. **Leaves** simple, opposite, deciduous. **Petioles** 1–3 cm long; glabrous or with scattered hairs near distal end; with 2–8 sessile glands near the distal end, the glands concave and elliptical, 0.8–1.5 mm across; stipules 1–5 mm long, linear. **Leaf blades** 3-lobed; 3.5–8 cm long, 3.5–8 cm wide; base obtusely tapered to rounded or nearly truncate; apex of lobes acuminate; margins irregularly and coarsely serrate; upper surface dark green, glabrous or glabrate; lower surface pale green, moderately to densely hairy especially along main veins; palmately veined. **Inflorescence** a flat-topped lateral cyme 5–13 cm across; borne on 4-leaved shoots from lateral buds at the end of 2nd-year branchlets; with 100+ flowers; peduncle 1.5–5 cm long. **Flowers** bisexual, 5-merous, whitish; outer ring of flowers sterile, with enlarged flat corollas to 2.5 cm across; inner cluster of flowers fertile, with inconspicuous corollas 3–6 mm across; stamens long-exserted, filaments 2–4 mm long; **anthesis** mid-May to late June; insect-pollinated. **Fruit** a single-seeded drupe, subglobose, 6–10 mm in diameter, ripening translucent orange or red; maturing early to late August, often persisting through winter; animal-dispersed. (*opulus*: an old generic name of the viburnums)

Identification

The guilder-rose, or European high-bush cranberry, looks very much like the native American high-bush cranberry (*V. trilobum*) but differs most consistently in the size and shape of the glands at the top of the petiole. The glands of the native species are usually stalked or slenderly columnar, more or less round in cross section and flat-topped. The glands of the European species are generally larger, stouter, and elliptical in cross section. Also, the top of the gland is cratered or cupped and has a prominent rim around the margin, making it look like something like an ear or a car tire. Because of the obvious similarities, the two species are often considered varieties or subspecies of a single species.

Natural History

This species is native to Europe, parts of northern Africa, and western Asia. In Europe it has been cultivated for centuries under the name guelder-rose and was probably introduced into North America during colonial times as a landscaping shrub. It became popular in Minnesota sometime after the middle of the twentieth century and has, unfortunately, been sold as "high-bush cranberry" without any acknowledgment of its European origin. It may even be labeled *V. trilobum* and promoted as a native species. Regrettably, nearly all the "high-bush cranberry" sold by nurseries in Minnesota today are in fact the European *V. opulus*.

Beginning about 1960, guelder-rose started appearing spontaneously in native habitats in southern Minnesota, apparently spread by birds that feed on the fruits. It has now become naturalized in woodlands, forest margins, stream banks, and brushy habitats. It seems to compete more aggressively than the native high-bush cranberry and is better able to withstand habitat disturbances. In the area around the Twin Cities and southward, the European species is now more common than the native species. Although it is not likely that the native species is being physically displaced by the European species, it is clear that the native species is declining because of habitat loss, and the European species is increasing because of its aggressiveness. Another cause for concern is hybridization; it is possible that the native genotype could be altered by introgression from the European genotype.

The outer ring of flowers are sterile, just for show—June 2.

The fruits will persist through winter if not eaten—August 29.

Multiple concave glands just below leaf blade.

Multiple stems; bark is smooth or slightly rough.

A bushy, edge-grown specimen from Winona County—June 2.

Viburnums 🌱 **667**

Viburnum rafinesquianum Schult.

Downy arrow-wood

Tall **shrubs**, with multiple upright **stems** to 3 m tall and 3 cm basal diameter; clonal by root suckers. 2nd-year **branchlets** brown to reddish brown; glabrous. **Bark** gray or brown-gray; smooth or slightly rough. **Leaves** simple, opposite, deciduous. **Petioles** 3–12 mm long; hairy, lacking glands; stipules linear, 3–9 mm long. **Leaf blades** ovate to ovate-lanceolate; 4–8 cm long, 2.5–5.5 cm wide; base rounded or slightly cordate; apex acute to acuminate; margins coarsely serrate; upper surface dark green, moderately to sparsely hairy; lower surface pale green, hairy, at least along the larger veins. **Inflorescence** a round-topped, terminal cyme 2–6 cm across; borne at the tips of first-year branchlets; with 30–100 flowers; peduncles 0.3–5 cm long. **Flowers** bisexual, 5-merous, creamy white; sepals deltate, about 0.5 mm long; petals broadly ovate to broadly elliptical, 1.5–3 mm long; stamens exserted, filaments 1.5–4 mm long; **anthesis** late May to early July; insect-pollinated. **Fruit** a single-seeded drupe, oblong to ellipsoidal, somewhat flattened, 7–12 mm long, ripening black to purple-black; maturing early August to early September; animal-dispersed.
(*rafinesquianum*: named for American naturalist Constantine Samuel Rafinesque-Schmaltz, 1783–1840)

Identification

Downy arrow-wood is a moderately large, bushy shrub, usually 5–7 ft (2 m) tall, distinguished by coarsely serrate leaf margins and short petioles. Based on leaf shape alone, it is easily told from the other native viburnums, but it could be confused with southern arrow-wood (*V. dentatum* L.), which is not native to Minnesota but is occasionally planted here as an ornamental. Southern arrow-wood differs by lacking stipules and having longer petioles.
Note: There are two generally accepted varieties of downy arrow-wood: The leaves of variety *rafinesquianum* are uniformly hairy underneath and have relatively short petioles (average 6 mm). Leaves of variety *affine* (Bush) House are hairy only on the larger veins and have longer petioles (average 10 mm). Although it appears that both varieties occur in Minnesota, they are not always easy to tell apart; the characters are sometimes variable and not always well correlated.

Natural History

Downy arrow-wood is a common understory shrub throughout most of the forested region of Minnesota. It is found under a variety of hardwood and conifer species, especially oaks (*Quercus* spp.), trembling aspen (*Populus tremuloides*), and paper birch (*Betula papyrifera*). It does less well in the deeper shade cast by maples (*Acer* spp.), basswood (*Tilia americana*), and green ash (*Fraxinus pennsylvanica*). It seems to prefer well-drained soils, usually avoiding heavier clay soils.

In a stable forest interior, downy arrow-wood will normally be widely spaced and produce only a few stems each, or it may sometimes form loose colonies. But if the canopy is removed or downy arrow-wood is otherwise freed from competition, it can expand slowly by root suckers, eventually forming dense colonies 10–13 ft (3–4 m) across that consist of numerous, closely spaced stems. This usually happens as the result of logging or grazing within a native woodland where downy arrow-wood was already well established. This could lead to the conclusion that it thrives in degraded habitats, which may be true for a period of time. However, it does not normally venture on its own into degraded habitats, especially not old fields, pastures, or other nonforested habitats.

At peak anthesis on June 9—Washington County.

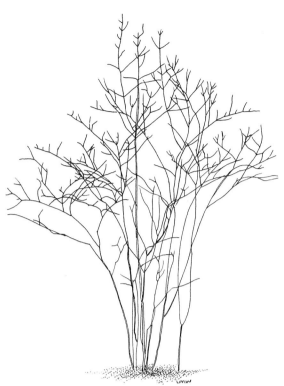

Leaves are coarsely serrated; fruits are slightly flattened—
August 22.

Multiple stems are the rule, usually about 1/2" (1.3 cm) diameter.

Viburnums 🌿 **669**

Viburnum trilobum Marsh.

American high-bush cranberry

[*V. opulus* L. var. *americanum* Ait.; *V. opulus* L. subsp. *trilobum* (Marsh.) R. T. Clausen]

Tall **shrubs**, with multiple upright **stems** to 5 m tall and 6 cm dbh; occasionally clonal by layering or tip-rooting. 2nd-year **branchlets** pale brown to gray-brown, often black-dotted; glabrous. **Bark** brown to gray; smooth or somewhat rough. **Leaves** simple, opposite, deciduous. **Petioles** 1–3.5 cm long; hairy on the upper surface where the petiole and blade join, otherwise glabrous; with 2–4 projecting glands near the distal end, the glands ± flat-topped and circular, 0.3–0.7 mm across; stipules 1–5 mm long, linear. **Leaf blades** 3-lobed; 5–12 cm long, 5–11 cm wide; base obtusely tapered to rounded or nearly truncate; apex of lobes acuminate; margins entire or coarsely serrate; upper surface dark green, sparsely hairy to glabrate; lower surface pale green, sparsely hairy or moderately to densely hairy along main veins. **Inflorescence** a flat-topped lateral cyme 6–13 cm across; borne on 4-leaved shoots from lateral buds at the end of 2nd-year branchlets; with 100+ flowers; peduncle 1.5–5 cm long, turning red in late summer. **Flowers** bisexual, 5-merous, whitish; outer ring of flowers sterile, with enlarged flat corollas to 3 cm across; inner cluster of flowers fertile, with inconspicuous corollas 3–6 mm across; stamens long-exserted, filaments 2–4 mm long; **anthesis** late May to late June; insect-pollinated. **Fruit** a single-seeded drupe, subglobose or short-ellipsoidal, 7–12 mm long, ripening translucent orange or red; maturing early August to early September, often persisting through winter; animal-dispersed. (*trilobum*: three-lobed)

Identification

This is a large, bushy shrub with multiple stems that easily reach 9–12 ft (3–4 m) in height. The inflorescence is a flat-topped cluster of small, fertile flowers surrounded by a ring of much larger, sterile flowers. It is very similar to the guelder-rose, or "European high-bush cranberry" (*V. opulus*), which is commonly cultivated here and frequently escapes into the wild. The surest way to tell the two apart is by the shape and size of the glands at the top of the petiole (see key). The three-lobed leaf could also be mistaken for that of a maple (*Acer*).
Note: The native highbush cranberry and its European counterpart are similar but distinctly different in a number of characters, although perhaps differing only at the level of subspecies.

Natural History

American high-bush cranberry is common in a variety of upland and lowland forest types, mostly with hardwoods but occasionally with conifers. It may also occur scattered in shrub swamps with willows (*Salix* spp.) or bog birch (*Betula pumila*). Other habitats include tamarack (*Larix laricina*) swamps, marshy lowlands, and seasonally wet areas at the edges of ponds, lakes, or streams. It seems to prefer edges and partial openings, and perhaps low spots in a forest where the canopy is patchy. It can probably be characterized as moderately shade tolerant, relatively fast growing, and short-lived.

In most woody species the tip of the green twig will stop growing in midsummer so it can "harden off" in preparation for winter. At the tip of each twig will be a single terminal bud that will begin growing the next spring in the same direction as before, a growth pattern termed monopodial. But in this species, the tip does not harden off; it keeps growing until it is frost-killed in fall. It will die without having produced a terminal bud, but it will have produced a pair of lateral buds at each node. The next spring the lateral buds highest on the twig will each produce an inflorescence and a new lateral bud, which becomes the vegetative twig the following year. The lateral buds are always produced in pairs on opposite sides of the stem, which results in true sympodial growth (Donoghue 1981).

Large sterile flowers encircle the smaller fertile flowers—June 25.

Bark is brown or gray, smooth or somewhat rough.

A 7' (2.2 m) specimen at home in a conifer swamp—June 25.

Shiny, translucent fruits are important wildlife food— September 5.

Leaves have 3 pointed lobes.

A pair of slender, round-topped glands below the leaf blade.

Viburnums   **671**

Vitis, the grapes

Vitaceae: Grape family

The grapes constitute a genus of about 80 species of deciduous woody vines that climb with tendrils. They are widely distributed in temperate and warm regions of the Northern Hemisphere, with 17 species native to the United States and 2 native to Minnesota. (*Vitis* is the classical Latin name for the grape vine.)

Key to the Genus Vitis in Minnesota

1. Lower surface of leaf silvery or grayish, markedly paler than the upper surface, and with scattered tufts or strands of reddish cobwebby hairs; nodes glaucous (especially noticeable on new growth); teeth on leaf margins broadly rounded, more than twice as broad as high, and lacking cilia on margin .... *V. aestivalis*
1. Lower surface of leaf green, only slightly paler than the upper surface, often with tufts of whitish hairs in axils of veins but lacking reddish cobwebby hairs; nodes not glaucous; teeth sharply pointed, less than twice as broad as high, with cilia on margin .... *V. riparia*

Vitis aestivalis Michx. var. *bicolor* Deam

Summer grape

High-climbing or sprawling **vines**, with tendril-bearing **stems** to 20 m tall and 20 cm dbh. 1st-year **branchlets** reddish or reddish brown, glabrous, glaucous at the nodes; 2nd-year branchlets greenish brown, glabrous. **Bark** of mature stems brown or reddish brown, exfoliating in thin strips or shreds. **Tendrils** 10–20 cm long, bifurcate, arising opposite a leaf, becoming woody and persisting. **Leaves** simple, alternate, deciduous. **Petioles** 5–15 cm long, glabrous or somewhat hairy on upper surface, often reddish; stipules 1.5–2.5 mm long, persistent until midsummer. **Leaf blades** 3–5 lobed; 10–25 cm long, 10–25 cm wide; base cordate; apex acute to short acuminate or occasionally somewhat rounded; margins round-toothed, nonciliate; upper surface dark green, glabrous to glabrate; lower surface silver-gray to green-gray, glaucous, hairy on veins and in axils of veins, and also with scattered tufts of reddish cobwebby hairs. **Inflorescence** a narrowly triangular or elongate panicle 5–15 cm long, arising opposite a leaf. **Flowers** 5-merous, unisexual, greenish; pedicels glabrous, 2.5–5.5 mm long; calyx minute, reduced to a collar at the base of the flower; petals 1.5–2.5 mm long, remaining united at the apex while separating at the base and falling off as a unit at anthesis; stamens 5 or 6; **anthesis** mid-June to early July; insect-pollinated. **Fruit** a blue-black, glaucous berry, globose 7–9 mm in diameter; maturing mid-July to early September; animal-dispersed. (*aestivalis*: of the summer)

Identification

Summer grape is a climbing or sprawling vine with large, blunt-toothed leaves. It looks something like riverbank grape (*V. riparia*) except the undersides of the leaves are conspicuously whitened in comparison to the dark green upper surface.

Note: Three varieties of summer grape have been described from the eastern United States, differing mostly in the size of the fruit, degree of pubescence, and other minor characters (Moore 1991). The Minnesota plants have been identified as var. *bicolor* Deam [var. *argentifolia* (Munson) Fern.], which is a widespread northern form with small, sour-tasting fruit.

Natural History

Summer grape is restricted to habitats in the southeastern corner of the state where the terrain is defined by deep valleys and tall bluffs. Relatively little is known about the species in this region, except it seems to favor oak forests, especially forest margins where there is more sunlight. It also occurs in brushy habitats and in pioneering stands of young forest trees, but it is absent from floodplains, where the more common riverbank grape (*V. riparia*) is often so abundant.

In a forest interior, summer grape may manage to climb into the canopies of the tallest trees. But under these conditions its overall presence and effect on the forest community are limited by the intense competition for light. The situation is different in highly disturbed habitats where competition for light has been reduced, like after a logging operation or a major storm. Under such conditions an established population of summer grape can grow rampantly, clambering over shrubs and tree saplings. In extreme cases the weight of the vines is enough to deform the branches of a host, and the large closely spaced leaves can smother shrubs and saplings. It is also possible that the tendrils may cause some minor damage by girdling small twigs of the host (Lutz 1943). However, potential damage caused to the host should not be overemphasized; summer grape is an uncommon and benign member of the natural forest community to which it is well adapted.

Plants are unisexual; these flowers are female—June 30.

Released from competition, vines can form a smothering mat.

Vines are tough and durable, and can easily climb 65' (20 m).

*Fruits are less than 3/8 " (10 mm) across, and sour-tasting—
August 29.*

These flowers are from a male vine—June 26.

Vitis riparia Michx.

Riverbank grape

High-climbing or sprawling **vines**, with tendril-bearing **stems** to 25 m tall and 20 cm dbh. 1st-year **branchlets** usually glabrous or with tufts of cobwebby hairs at nodes, not glaucous. **Bark** of mature stems brown, exfoliating in strips or shreds. **Tendrils** 5–15 cm long, bifurcate, arising opposite a leaf from 2st-year branchlets, becoming woody and persisting. **Leaves** simple, alternate, deciduous. **Petioles** 2–7 cm long, variously hairy or glabrate; stipules 3–5 mm long, persistent until midsummer. **Leaf blades** 3-lobed; 6–14 cm long, 6–15 cm wide; base cordate; apex acute to acuminate; margins sharply and deeply serrate, ciliate; upper surface dark green, minutely hairy on main veins otherwise glabrous or glabrate; lower surface somewhat paler than upper surface but not glaucous, hairy on main veins and in axils of veins. **Inflorescence** a ± cylindrical or narrowly triangular panicle 3–10 cm long, arising opposite a leaf on 1st-year branchlets. **Flowers** 5-merous, unisexual or occasionally bisexual, greenish; pedicels glabrous, 2–4.5 mm long; calyx minute, reduced to a collar at the base of the flower; petals 1–2 mm long, remaining united at the apex while separating at the base and falling off as a unit at anthesis; stamens 5; **anthesis** late May to late June; insect-pollinated. **Fruit** a blue-black, glaucous berry, spherical, 8–12 mm in diameter; maturing late July to early September; animal-dispersed. (*riparia*: of riverbanks)

Identification

Riverbank grape is a high-climbing or sprawling vine with sharply serrate, 3-lobed leaves and strong, woody tendrils. In most of Minnesota there is nothing similar to confuse it with, but the less common summer grape (*V. aestivalis*) is found in the southeast and looks similar. But the leaves of summer grape are generally larger, with rounded teeth and a conspicuously "whitened" undersurface.

Natural History

Riverbank grape is common throughout most of Minnesota, especially in the forested region. It is common in a variety of edge habitats, ecotones, and brushy thickets, most notably along lakeshores and riverbanks. It is also common on floodplains, where it is highly tolerant of seasonal flooding and sedimentation. It even does well in dry habitats including sand dunes and rocky bluffs. Although it does not normally occur on actual prairies, its range does extend into the prairie region, where it occurs principally in riverine forests and brushy thickets.

It is by nature a climbing vine, and it occasionally climbs to heights of 70–80 ft (21–25 m), yet it never seems to quite reach the tops of large trees, and it causes no significant damage. In fact, in a mature, stable forest it usually has only a minimal presence and rarely acts aggressively. But the seeds are widely distributed by birds, often to ruderal habitats such as old fields, fencerows, rock piles, and roadsides, where the seeds germinate easily and grow quickly. As a pioneer in such early-successional communities, it competes aggressively with grasses and shrubs, even to the point of creating a smothering mass of vines.

This same aggressive tendency is exhibited when a well-established forest population is released from the suppressing effect of a dense overstory, which might happen as a result of logging. It may then grow rapidly and sprawl over the tops of saplings destined for the canopy and inhibit their growth or deform their branches. It may actually affect the course of forest succession, although on a small scale, and is perhaps the only vine in Minnesota capable of doing so.

Petals are shed before the flowers peak—June 13.

Note the large, sharply pointed serrations.

Clusters of fruits look and taste distinctly grapelike—August 21.

Riverbank grape can become aggressive along a forest edge.

Bark exfoliates in narrow strips or shreds.

Zanthoxylum, prickly ash

Rutaceae: Rue family

Prickly ash belongs to a genus of about 200 species of deciduous and evergreen shrubs and small trees, mainly in tropical and subtropical regions of Central and South America, Africa, and Asia, with 7 species in the continental United States, and 1 in Minnesota. (*Zanthoxylum* is from the Greek *xanthos*, yellow, and *xylon*, wood.)

Zanthoxylum americanum P. Mill.

Prickly ash

Tall **shrubs** or occasionally small **trees**, with single upright **stems** to 6 m tall and 6 cm dbh; forming colonies by root suckering. **Branches** weakly ascending to spreading, stout, with paired spines about 1 cm long at nodes. 1st-year **branchlets** brown to reddish brown, sparsely hairy or glabrate. **Bark** of mature stems gray to brown, often with light blotches; smooth or somewhat rough. **Leaves** pinnately compound, alternate, deciduous. **Petioles** 2–4 cm long, hairy. **Leaf blades** 7–20 cm long. **Leaflets** 5–13; subsessile; ovate to elliptical or occasionally oblong; 4–7 cm long, 2–3.5 cm wide; base tapered or rounded; apex acute or acuminate; margins shallowly crenulate, with a small gland at each notch; upper surface dark green, sparsely hairy to glabrate; lower surface pale green, hairy. **Flowers** unisexual, with separate male flowers and female flowers on different plants; 5-merous, small, greenish; in axillary clusters of 2–12; peduncles 1–4 mm long; sepals absent; petals 2–3 mm long, greenish and reddish, with a tuft of crinkly reddish hairs at apex; stamens 5; pistils 3–5, hairy or glabrous; **anthesis** late April to late May; insect-pollinated. **Fruit** a red, warty pod, roughly spherical, 4–6 mm long; borne in dense clusters close to the branchlet; with a strong citrus fragrance but bitter and numbing; splitting to release a single black, glossy seed about 4 mm long; maturing late July to mid-September; animal- and gravity-dispersed. (*americanum*: of America)

Identification

Prickly ash is indeed a tall, prickly shrub, but it bears no reasonable likeness to a true ash (genus *Fraxinus* in the family Oleaceae). But it could easily be mistaken for a sapling of black locust (*Robinia pseudoacacia*). Both have sharp spines and compound leaves, but prickly ash has fewer leaflets (usually fewer than 10), and the leaflets have pointed tips. And since prickly ash is in the same family as citrus, the fruits have a strong fragrance of orange or lemon. They also have a powerful numbing effect and have supposedly been used to relieve toothaches.

Natural History

Prickly ash is fairly common in the understory of hardwood forests throughout southern and central Minnesota. It is especially common on floodplains, where it shows a high tolerance for spring flooding and accompanying sedimentation. It also occurs on slopes and level terrain above floodplains, typically with oaks (*Quercus* spp.), basswood (*Tilia americana*), elms (*Ulmus* spp.), or green ash (*Fraxinus pennsylvanica*). It also has a talent for finding habitat in abandoned fields, clearings, utility rights-of-way, rock piles, and any challenging habitat that rewards aggressiveness and tenacity.

It generally prefers nonacidic, loamy, sandy or alluvial soils and does well in full or partial shade. It is also tolerant of heat and drought and seems to be little bothered by browsing mammals or insects. However, it does not tolerate fire. While it might survive a "cool" fire, an intense fire will kill the long, shallow roots.

These roots can become quite invasive and will sprout suckers (new shoots) unless inhibited by competition. Suckers can even form dense thickets, especially in grazed woodlands, where cattle wisely avoid it. Plants in these thickets tend to hold their lower branches, even in dense shade, and are covered with sharp spines about 1/2 inch (1.3 cm) long. By any standard, prickly ash thickets qualify as truly impenetrable. Yet they are rarely great in extent, and although they may persist for 30+ years, they do not seem to hinder forest succession or influence the overall diversity of a forest community.

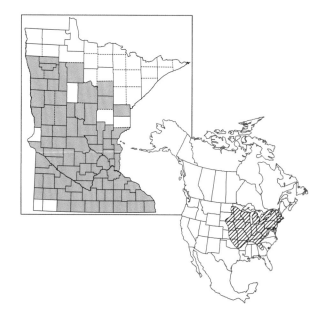

The yellow anthers identify these as male flowers—May 16.

Look for a pair of stout, sharp spines at each node.

Each pod contained a single, black, shiny seed (empty now)—August 23.

Note green styles protruding from these female flowers—May 20.

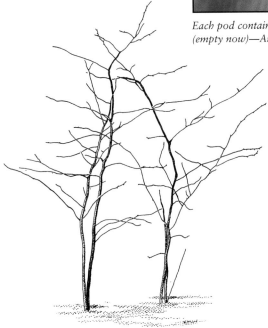

Each leaf has 5–13 leaflets.

Glossary

achene   a small, dry, indehiscent fruit with a single seed

aciculate   needle shaped; very slender and with a sharp tip, roundish in cross section

acidic   having a pH less than 7.0

acorn   the fruit of oaks (genus *Quercus*); a single large seed with a woody, cuplike base

acuminate   contracted to a narrow point; the sides concave (see page 690)

acute   tapering evenly to a point; the sides straight or somewhat convex and forming an angle less than 90 degrees (see page 690)

adnate   fusion of unlike parts or organs, as stamens to a corolla

adventitious   a structure or organ developing in an unusual or abnormal location, such as a root originating from a stem

aerial   existing or growing in the air rather than in the ground or water

alluvial   of or relating to a stream or river

anther   the portion of the stamen that contains the pollen, usually attached to a filament

anthesis   the period of time when the flower is fully developed and functional

apex (*pl.* apices)   the tip of an organ or structure

apiculate   ending abruptly in a short, pointed tip (see page 690)

apomixes   a form of asexual reproduction in which viable seeds are produced without fertilization, the resulting progeny being genetically identical to the parent plant

appressed   lying close and flat against a surface

arching   curving; forming an arc

aril   a fleshy outgrowth of a seed, typically covering or enveloping the seed

ascendate   an inflorescence with a cluster of only 1 to 3(5) flowers growing in a strongly upward direction. All the pedicels will be approximately the same length, and the axial or central flower will open first.

ascending   growing obliquely upward

attenuate   tapered gradually to a long, narrow point (see page 690)

auricle   an ear-shaped appendage or lobe (see page 690)

awn   a bristlelike appendage

axil   the angle formed between any two attached organs, such as a leaf and stem; typically the point of the upper angle

axis   the longitudinal central supporting structure around which various organs are borne, as a stem bearing leaves

bark   the outermost layers of a woody stem or branch, including all living and nonliving tissue external to the cambium

basal   positioned at or arising from the base of a structure or organ

basic   having a pH greater than 7.0; alkaline

berry   a fleshy fruit lacking a pit or core, with several or many immersed seeds, such as a grape (genus *Vitis*) or blueberry (genus *Vaccinium*)

biennial   living 2 years, as in the stems (canes) of *Rubus*, which normally live 2 years, then die

bipinnate   twice pinnate

bisexual   a flower with both male and female reproductive organs

blade   the expanded portion of a leaf

bog   a plant community/habitat type occurring on deep, saturated peat and isolated from the influence of groundwater; characteristically acidic and nutrient poor

boreal   of or relating to the north. Used in an ecological context to describe the climatic region between the temperate (to the south) and the arctic (to the north)

bract   a modified or reduced leaf, typically at the base of a flower or within an inflorescence

bracteole   a bractlet

bractlet   a secondary or smaller bract

branch   a division of the stem

branchlet   a small branch; the ultimate division of a branch

bristle   a stiff hair or hairlike structure; not as hard or strong as a prickle

calcareous   containing calcium (in the form of calcium carbonate); having a pH greater than 7.0

callous   a hardened or thickened area

calyx   a collective term for all of the sepals of a flower; the outer perianth of the flower

cambium   a layer of cells between the wood and the bark, giving rise to elements of both

cane   the long, slender stems of certain shrubs, especially the blackberries and raspberries (genus *Rubus*)

canescent   a dense covering of short, fine, gray or white hairs

canopy   the uppermost layer of tree branches in a forest; the combined crowns of all the trees in the tallest height class

capitate   headlike or head shaped

capsule   a dry, dehiscent fruit derived from a compound ovary of two or more carpels

carpel   a simple pistil, or one member of a compound pistil

catkin   a pendent inflorescence consisting of a spike or raceme of apetalous, unisexual flowers, such as in the willows (*Salix*) and birches (*Betula*)

caudate   with a tail-like appendage, as in the long, drawn-out tip of a leaf (see page 690)

caudex   a short, thick, woody stem, usually terminating at or near ground level, giving rise to a nonwoody aerial stem or stems

cauline   on or of the stem, as leaves arising from the stem

ciliate   with a marginal fringe of hairs

cilium (*pl.* cilia)   a fine hair or hairlike structure

circumboreal   occurring throughout the boreal region in a more or less continuous ring around the Earth

circumpolar   occurring throughout the Arctic region in a more or less continuous ring around the North Pole

claw   the long, narrowed base of some petals or sepals

climax   the final successional stage of a plant community, characterized by relative stability in species composition, dominance, and community structure

clone   an individual or group of individuals originating from a single parent by asexual reproduction

closed-canopy forest   a forest of trees so closely spaced that their crowns touch

compound   a structure or organ composed of two or more similar parts united into a whole, as a compound leaf made up of separate leaflets

cone   a dense cluster of sporophylls arranged spirally on an axis and borne at the tip of a stem; a strobilus; essentially the fruit of certain gymnosperms

conifer   a species of tree or shrub characterized by bearing cones or strobili, as in many gymnosperms, e.g., pines (*Pinus*) and spruces (*Picea*)

conspecific   being of the same species

cordate   heart shaped, with the notch at the base (see page 690)

corolla   a collective term for all of the petals of a flower; the inner perianth of a flower

corymb   a flat-topped or round-topped inflorescence in which the outer flowers open first

corymbose   having flowers in a corymb

creeping   a stem or branch growing along the surface of the ground and producing roots, usually at the nodes

crenate   with rounded teeth along a margin (see page 690)

crenulate   with very small, rounded teeth along a margin

crown   the portion of a tree bearing the leaves; the upper portion of a tree

cucullate   hooded or hood shaped

cylindrical   the shape of a cylinder; a solid body longitudinally elongate and round in cross section

cyme   a flat-topped or round-topped inflorescence where the lower pedicels are longer than the upper, and in which the central flowers open first

cymule   a small cyme or a division of a cyme

dbh   diameter at breast height; the diameter of a tree trunk at 4 1/2 feet (138 cm) above the ground; the standard measurement of tree trunk diameter used in forestry and ecology

deciduous   not persisting; falling off, as the leaves of a tree in autumn

decumbent   stems or branches reclining on the surface of the ground with tips ascending

decurrent   extending along a stem downward from a leaf attachment or along a petiole downward from the blade (see page 690)

deltate   with the shape of the Greek letter delta; an equilateral triangle (see page 689)

dentate   toothed along a margin, the teeth directed outward rather than forward. (see page 690)

dichotomous   branched or forked into two more or less equal divisions

dioecious   with unisexual flowers; male flowers and female flowers borne separately and on different plants

diploid   with two complete sets of chromosomes in each cell

disjunct   a portion of a species geographical range that is separate and discontinuous from the main portion

distal   toward the tip or the end of a structure, opposite the end of attachment

divergent   diverging or spreading; inclining away from each other

drupe   a fleshy or pulpy fruit with a stony endocarp enclosing the usually solitary seed

drupelet   a small drupe, as in the individual segments of a blackberry (*Rubus*) fruit

ecosystem   a biological system comprising a natural community of plants and animals (or mosaic of interrelated communities) and the energy/nutrient cycles necessary to sustain it

ecotone   the transition zone between two plant communities

edaphic   relating to the soil

eglandular   without glands

ellipsoidal   a solid body, elliptical in long section and circular in cross section

elliptical   in the shape of an ellipse; a plane, symmetrical form broadest at the middle and narrower at the two equal curved ends (see page 689)

emergent   rising out of standing water

endemic   occurring naturally only in a specific geographic area or habitat type

entire   a margin that is not toothed, notched, lobed, or otherwise discontinuous (see page 690)

epidermis   the outermost layer of cells of a nonwoody structure or organ

evergreen   having green leaves through the winter

exfoliate   to peel off in flakes or strips, as in the outer bark of some trees

exserted   projecting beyond the surrounding parts, as stamens from a corolla

fascicle   a tight cluster or bundle

fen   a type of wetland strongly influenced by groundwater and occurring on saturated peat; generally pH circumneutral or calcareous and comparatively nutrient rich

filament   the part of the stamen that supports the anther; often thin and threadlike

filiform   threadlike

floodplain   level land along a stream or river that may be submerged by floodwaters

floricane   flowering cane; specifically the second year of the biennial stem (cane) of a raspberry or blackberry (*Rubus*) that produces flowers

foliaceous   leaflike in color and texture

follicle   a dry, dehiscent fruit composed of a single carpel and opening along a single side

forest   a natural community characterized by a closed canopy of trees

fruit   a ripened ovary; the seed-bearing portion of a plant

glabrate   becoming glabrous; almost glabrous

glabrous   hairless

gland   an appendage, protuberance, or other structure that produces a sticky, greasy, or viscous substance

glaucous   covered with a cloudy, whitish or bluish, waxy coating

globose   globe shaped; spherical

hardwood   a general and nonspecific term for broad-leaved trees, as in oaks, maples, ashes, and so on

hastate   arrowhead shaped, but with the basal lobes pointing outward rather than backward (see page 690)

herbaceous   a plant with no persistent woody stem; nonwoody

hypanthium   a ring or cup around the ovary, usually formed from the union of the basal parts of the calyx, corolla, and androecium; often the part of the flower to which the petals and sepals seem to be attached

included   not projecting beyond the surrounding parts, as stamens contained within a corolla

indehiscent   a body, such as a fruit, not opening at maturity along any specific lines, valves, or pores but rather bursting or breaking irregularly

inflorescence   the flowering portion of the plant, in particular the arrangement of flowers on an axis

infructescence   the inflorescence in fruit

internode   the portion of a stem that occurs between any two nodes

invasive   tending to be aggressive or to encroach; able to become established quickly and spread rapidly in a new habitat, especially in a geographic area to which it is not native

involucre   a whorl of bracts subtending a flower or an inflorescence

laciniate   divided into narrow, irregular lobes or segments

lanceolate   shaped like the head of a lance; broadest below the middle and gradually tapered to a pointed apex; much longer than wide (see page 689)

lateral   located at or arising from the side

layering   the process by which an aerial stem or branch comes into contact with the ground and produces roots

leaflet   a single division of a compound leaf

leaf scar   the scar remaining on a twig after the leaf falls

legume   a dry, podlike fruit formed from a single carpel and usually opening along two lines of dehiscence; the fruit of plants in the family Fabaceae

lenticel   a slightly raised, somewhat corky or warty area on the surface of a young stem or branch, often lens shaped

lignified   having become woody

linear   long and narrow with parallel sides; resembling a line (see page 689)

loam   a type of soil consisting of varying portions of minerals (sand, silt, or clay) and organic material

lobe   a division or segment of an organ such as a leaf; larger than a tooth but may have a tooth at its apex or margin, or more often rounded (see page 690)

marcescent   withering but persistent, as in the leaves of some oaks that turn brown and wither in the autumn but are held on the twig until spring

marsh   a type of emergent wetland developing on mineral soil or shallow muck, in stagnant or slowly moving water. Relatively nutrient rich and typically dominated by narrow-leaved plant species such as cattails (*Typha*) and bulrushes (*Scirpus*)

meadow   a treeless habitat dominated by sedges and/or broad-leaved herbaceous plants

-merous (*suffix*)   referring to the number of parts of a set. A 5-merous flower has 5 petals and 5 sepals

mesic   soil conditions between wet and dry; moist

monoecious   with unisexual flowers, the separate male and female flowers borne on the same plant

monotypic   including a single representative; a genus containing a single species, or a habitat with a single species

morphology   the form and structure of a plant

mucronate   tipped with a short, sharp, slender point (see page 690)

muskeg   a plant community occurring on deep, saturated peat in very acidic, low-nutrient conditions; typically dominated by *Sphagnum* moss, sedges (Cyperaceae), and various shrubs of the family

Ericaceae, especially those of the genera *Chamaedaphne*, *Kalmia*, and *Andromeda*

native originating or occurring naturally in a certain place; indigenous

naturalized plants introduced from elsewhere but now established in the wild and reproducing as if native

nectary a structure that produces nectar, usually associated with a flower

node a place on a stem where a leaf originates, usually seen as a hard swelling or enlargement

nut a relatively large, dry, indehiscent fruit with a hard wall and usually a single seed

nutlet a small nut

oblanceolate inversely lanceolate, with the attachment at the narrow end

oblate spheroidal and flattened at the poles

oblong a symmetric plane figure two to four times longer than wide, widest at the midpoint with margins essentially parallel and ends equally curved (see page 689)

obovate inversely ovate, with the attachment at the narrow end (see page 689)

obtrullate inversely trullate

obtuse tapering evenly to a point; the sides straight or somewhat convex and forming an angle greater than 90 degrees (see page 690)

old-growth forest a forest in which the trees have attained a great age

open-canopy forest a forest of widely spaced trees, their individual crowns separated by some distance (not touching)

orbicular circular (see page 689)

ovary the expanded basal portion of the pistil that contains the ovules (immature seeds)

ovate a plane, symmetrical figure with the widest axis below the middle and with the margins evenly curved; egg shaped in outline and attached at the broad end (see page 689)

overstory the uppermost layer of tree branches in a forest; the canopy

ovoid ovate but in three dimensions (a solid form); egg shaped

Paleozoic Plateau the portion of southeastern Minnesota thought to be ice-free during the Wisconsin glaciation. It is a thickly forested region characterized by deep stream valleys and high ridges

palmate with three or more lobes, leaflets or veins arising from a common point, like fingers from the palm of a hand (see page 690)

panicle a branched inflorescence with pedicelled flowers, such as a branched raceme or corymb

peat soil composed entirely of partially decomposed plant material

pedicel the stalk of an individual flower in an inflorescence

peduncle the stalk of a solitary flower or the stalk of an inflorescence

peltate shieldlike; a flat structure, such as a leaf, with a stalk attached to the lower surface rather than to the base or margin

perfoliate a leaf with the margins entirely surrounding the stem so the stem appears to pass through the leaf (see page 690)

perianth all of the sepals and petals of a flower in whatever number or form

petal an individual segment or member of the corolla

petaloid petal-like in appearance

petiole the stalk of a leaf

petiolule the stalk of a leaflet in a compound leaf

pH the logarithm of the reciprocal of the hydrogen ions in solution, represented on a scale of 1 to 14 with 7 being neutral, numbers greater than 7 being basic or alkaline, and numbers less than 7 being acidic

phenology the study of timing and sequence of recurring stages or processes in the life history of a plant

pinnate a compound leaf with leaflets arranged on opposite sides of an elongate axis (see page 690)

pinnatifid pinnately lobed or cleft half the distance or more to the midvein but not reaching the midvein

pistil the female reproductive organ of a flower, typically consisting of a stigma, style, and ovary

pith the spongy parenchymatous tissue at the center of some stems and roots

placenta the portion of the ovary bearing the immature seed(s)

plumose feathery; with hairs or fine bristles on both sides of a central axis, as a plume

pod any dry, dehiscent fruit, especially a legume

pollen the mass of developing male gametophytes produced in the anther of an angiosperm or the microsporangium of a gymnosperm

polyploid with three or more complete sets of chromosomes in each cell, indicative of hybridization

pome a fleshy fruit derived from a compound, inferior ovary with seeds in a stiff core, as in an apple or pear

prickle a small, stiff, and usually slender, sharp outgrowth of the epidermis, generally harder and stronger than a bristle

primocane literally prime cane; the first year of the biennial stem (cane) of a raspberry or blackberry (*Rubus*). The same cane produces flowers the second year and is referred to as a floricane.

prostrate lying flat on the ground

proximal toward the base or the end of the structure to which it is attached

pubescent bearing hairs of any kind

punctate dotted with pits or translucent, sunken glands

pustulate with small blisters or pustules, often at the base of a hair

raceme   an unbranched, elongate inflorescence with pedicellate flowers maturing from the bottom upward

rachis   the main axis of a structure; the axis to which the individual leaflets of a compound leaf are attached

receptacle   the portion of the pedicel or peduncle to which the flower parts are attached

recurved   curved backward or downward

reflexed   bent abruptly backward or downward

reticulate   netlike; in the form of a network; net-veined

revolute   with the margins rolled backward toward the underside

rhizome   an underground stem usually producing roots and/or aerial shoots at the nodes

rhombic   a symmetrical, plane figure in the shape of a diamond (see page 689)

root crown   the specific portion of a root or root system that produces aerial stems

root sucker   an aerial stem arising from an adventitious bud on a root rather than from an established root crown or a rhizome

sac   a bag-shaped compartment, as the cavity of an anther

samara   an indehiscent winged fruit

savanna   a natural community with widely scattered trees or small groves of trees in a prairie setting

scale   any thin, flat, membranous structure

scurfy   covered with small, exfoliating scales or scaly incrustations

sedimentation   the deposition of silt or fine-textured materials suspended in water, usually a result of flooding, erosion, or stream action

sepal   an individual segment or member of the calyx

serrate   sawlike; toothed along the margin, the teeth sharp and pointing forward (see page 690)

serrulate   finely or minutely serrate

sessile   attached directly by the base; without a stalk of any kind

shoot   a young stem or branch

shrub   a woody plant with multiple bushy stems or a single stem not exceeding 16.25 feet (5 m) in height at maturity

sinus   the cleft or recess between two lobes

sp. (*pl.* spp.)   species; typically following a genus name to indicate an unknown or unspecified species within that genus

spatulate   shaped like a spatula; with a rounded apex gradually tapered to the base (see page 689)

spherical   shaped like a sphere; a three-dimensional structure round in outline

spine   a stiff, slender, sharp-pointed structure arising from below the epidermis, representing a modified leaf or stipule

sporangium   a spore-bearing case or sac

sporophyll   a sporangium-bearing leaf usually modified in shape and structure, as in the cones of gymnosperms

stamen   the male reproductive organ of a flower, consisting of an anther and a filament

staminode   a modified stamen that has no anther and is therefore sterile

stellate   star shaped, as in hairs with several to many branches radiating from the base

stem   the portion of the plant axis bearing nodes, leaves, and buds; if found belowground, it is called a rhizome

stigma   the portion of the pistil that is receptive to pollen, usually supported by the style

stipe   the stalk of a structure, especially the stalk of a pistil or ovary

stipitate   borne on a stipe

stipule   an appendage found at the base of the petiole of some plant species

stolon   a runner; an aboveground, horizontal stem rooting at the tip or nodes and giving rise to new shoots

stomate (*pl.* stomata)   a pore or mouthlike opening in the epidermis that allows gaseous exchange, usually surrounded by two guard cells and often located on the lower surface of leaves

stone   the hard, woody endocarp enclosing the seed of a drupe

strobilus (*pl.* strobili)   a dense cluster of sporophylls on an axis; a cone

style   the portion of the pistil connecting the stigma to the ovary

subsp.   standard abbreviation of subspecies; a taxonomic rank between species and variety; sometimes abbreviated ssp.

subtend   to be immediately below

subulate   awl shaped; short, narrowly tapered, and sharply pointed (see page 689)

succession   the ecological process by which one forest type is gradually succeeded by another, moving successively toward a self-perpetuating climax type

swale   a low, wet area or depression

swamp   a type of tree- or shrub-dominated wetland occurring on peat soil with moderate to strong groundwater influence

syncarp   a multiple fruit; an aggregate fruit as in the genus *Morus*

tapered   narrowed toward a point, the sides straight

taxonomy   the classification of plants or animals according to natural relationships

temperate   the climatic region immediately south of the boreal region, marked by a moderate climate with warm summers and cold/cool winters

tendril   a slender, twining organ by which a climbing plant (vine) grasps its support

terminal   at the tip or apex

ternate   in threes, as a leaf divided into three leaflets

tetraploid   with four complete sets of chromosomes in each cell

thorn   a stiff, woody structure with a sharp point; a modified stem

tomentose   with a dense covering of short, matted or tangled, woolly hairs

trailing   prostrate but not rooting

tree   a large, woody plant, usually with a single stem or trunk, reaching a minimum height of 16.25 feet (5 m) at maturity

trifoliate   with three leaflets

triploid   with three complete sets of chromosomes in each cell

trullate   a symmetrical, plane figure with the widest axis below the middle, with straight sides and attached at the broad end; ovate but with sides straight; trowel shaped (see page 689)

truncate   with the apex or base transversely straight or nearly so, as if cut off (see page 690)

tubular   with the form of a tube

twining   wrapping around or encircling, as a vine around a support

umbel   a flat-topped or convex inflorescence with the pedicels arising from a more or less common point, like the struts of an umbrella

understory   the area beneath the canopy of a forest; shrubs and small trees growing beneath a canopy of larger trees

unisexual   a flower with either male or female reproductive organs but not both

valve   one of the segments of a dehiscent fruit, separating from other such segments at maturity

variety (*abr.* var.)   the taxonomic rank below subspecies

vein   a vascular bundle, especially if visible externally, as in leaves

vine   a type of plant in which the stem is not self-supporting but instead climbs or trails on some exogenous support

whorl   a ringlike arrangement of three or more similar parts radiating from a common point, such as three or more leaves arising from a single node

xeric   dry, desertlike

xylem   the water conducting tissue of vascular plants

Leaf Shapes and Margins

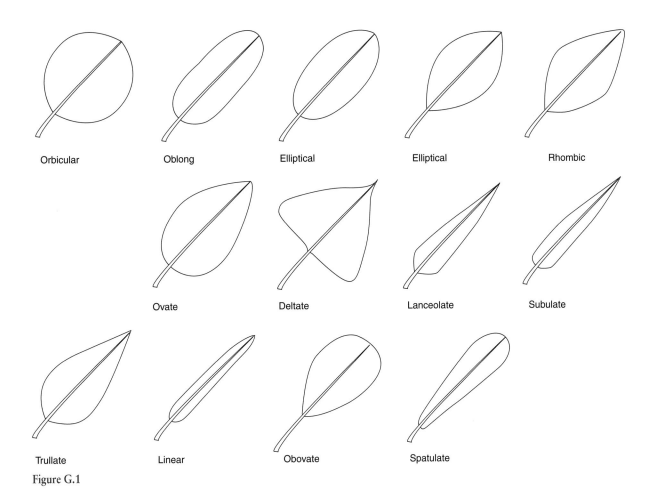

Orbicular   Oblong   Elliptical   Elliptical   Rhombic

Ovate   Deltate   Lanceolate   Subulate

Trullate   Linear   Obovate   Spatulate

Figure G.1

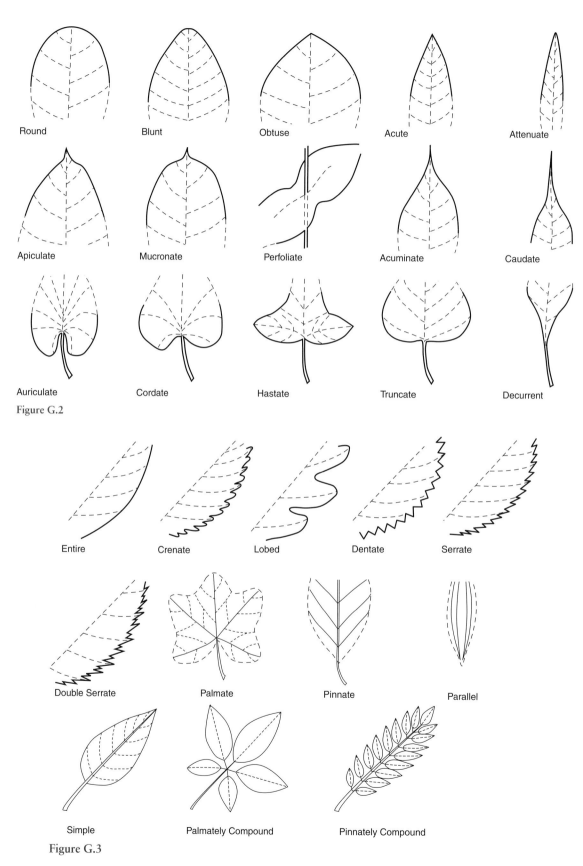

Round   Blunt   Obtuse   Acute   Attenuate

Apiculate   Mucronate   Perfoliate   Acuminate   Caudate

Auriculate   Cordate   Hastate   Truncate   Decurrent

Figure G.2

Entire   Crenate   Lobed   Dentate   Serrate

Double Serrate   Palmate   Pinnate   Parallel

Simple   Palmately Compound   Pinnately Compound

Figure G.3

Bibliography

Ågren, J. 1988. Sexual differences in biomass and nutrient allocation in the dioecious *Rubus chamaemorus. Ecology* 69: 962–73.

Ahlgren, C. E. 1959. Some effects of fire on forest reproduction in northeastern Minnesota. *Journal of Forestry* 57: 194–200.

Ahlgren, C. E. 1970. *Some effects of prescribed burning on jack pine reproduction in northeastern Minnesota.* University of Minnesota, Agricultural Experiment Station, Misc. publ. 94.

Ahlgren, C. E. 1976. Regeneration of red and white pine following wildfire and logging in northeastern Minnesota. *Journal of Forestry* 74: 135–40.

Ahlgren, C. E., and I. Ahlgren. 2001. *Lob trees in the wilderness.* Minneapolis: University of Minnesota Press.

Anderson, G. J. 1976. The pollination biology of *Tilia. American Journal of Botany* 63: 1203–12.

Anderson, M. L., and A. W. Bailey. 1979. Effects of fire on a *Symphoricarpos occidentalis* shrub community in central Alberta. Canadian Journal of Botany 57: 2819–23.

Anderson, R. C., and L. E. Brown. 1980. Influence of a prescribed burn on colonizing black locust. In *Proceedings, Central Hardwoods Forestry Conference III,* ed. H. E. Garrett and G. S. Cox, 330–36. Columbia: University of Missouri.

Anderson, W. A. 1944. The oldest Iowa tree. *Proceedings of the Iowa Academy of Science* 45: 73–74.

Argus, G. W. 1986. The genus Salix (Salicaceae) in the southeastern United States. *Systematic Botany Monographs* 9: 1–170.

Argus, G. W. 1997. Infrageneric classification of *Salix* (Salicaceae) in the New World. *Systematic Botany Monographs* 52: 1–121.

Backlund, A., and N. Pyck. 1998. *Diervillaceae* and *Linnaeaceae,* two new families of caprifolioids. *Taxon* 47: 657–61.

Bailey, L. H. 1944. Species batorum. The genus *Rubus* in North America. VIII. *Alleghenienses. Gentes Herbarum* 5: 507–88.

Barlow, C. 2001. Ghost stories from the Ice Age. *Natural History* 110: 62–67.

Barnes, B. V. 1966. The clonal growth habit of American aspens. *Ecology* 47: 439–47.

Barnes, B. V., B. P. Dancik, and T. L. Sharik. 1974. Natural hybridization of yellow birch and paper birch. *Forest Science* 20: 215–21.

Barnes, B. V., and K. S. Pregitzer. 1985. Occurrence of hybrids between bigtooth and trembling aspen in Michigan. *Canadian Journal of Botany* 63: 1888–90.

Barnes, B. V., and W. H. Wagner, Jr. 1981. *Michigan trees.* Ann Arbor: University of Michigan Press.

Barnes, W. J., and G. Cottam. 1974. Some autecological studies of the *Lonicera* ×*bella* complex. *Ecology* 55: 40–50.

Bond, G. 1967. Fixation of nitrogen by higher plants other than legumes. *Annual Review of Plant Physiology* 18: 107–26.

Borell, A. E. 1962. *Russian-olive for wildlife and other conservation uses.* Leaflet no. 517. Washington, D.C.: U.S. Department of Agriculture.

Brady, T. 2003. The mystery of a map and a man. *Minnesota Conservation Volunteer.* January–February: 21–31.

Bray, J. R. 1956. Gap phase replacement in a maple-basswood forest. *Ecology* 37: 598–600.

Bray, J. R. 1960. A note on hybridization between *Quercus macrocarpa* Michx. and *Quercus bicolor* Willd. in Wisconsin. *Canadian Journal of Botany* 38: 701–4.

Buckman, R. E. 1964. Effects of prescribed burning on hazel in Minnesota. *Ecology* 45: 626–29.

Buell, M. F., and W. A. Niering. 1957. Fir-spruce-birch forests in northern Minnesota. *Ecology* 38: 602–9.

Burns, R. M., and B. H. Honkala, tech. coords. 1990. *Silvics of North America: 2. Hardwoods.* Agriculture Handbook 654. Washington, D.C.: USDA, Forest Service.

Butters, F. K., and E. C. Abbe. 1953. A floristic study of Cook County, northeastern Minnesota. *Rhodora* 55: 21–55; 63–101; 116–54; 161–201.

Calcote, R. R. 1986. "Hemlock in Minnesota: 1200 years as a rare species." MS thesis, University of Minnesota.

Campbell, C. S., C. W. Greene, and T. A. Dickinson. 1991. Reproductive biology in subfam. Maloideae (Rosaceae). *Systematic Botany* 16: 333–49.

Canham, C. D. 1985. Suppression and release during canopy recruitment in *Acer saccharum. Bulletin of the Torrey Botanical Club* 112: 134–45.

Catling, P. M., S. M. McKay-Kuja, and G. Mitrow. 1999. Rank and typification in North American dwarf cherries, and a key to the taxa. *Taxon* 48: 483–88.

Catling, P. M., and Z. S. Porebski. 1994. The history of invasion and current status of glossy buckthorn,

Rhamnus frangula, in southern Ontario. *Canadian Field-Naturalist* 108: 305–10.

Chambers, K. L. 1993. *Thuja*. In *Flora of North America*, vol. 2, ed. Flora of North America Editorial Committee. New York: Oxford University Press.

Clausen, K. E. 1962. Introgressive hybridization between two Minnesota birches. *Silvae Genetica* 11: 142–50.

Clay, K. 1983. Myrmecochory in the trailing arbutus (*Epigaea repens* L.) *Bulletin of the Torrey Botanical Club* 110: 166–69.

Clay, K., and N. C. Ellstrand. 1981. Stylar polymorphism in *Epigaea repens*, a dioecious species. *Bulletin of the Torrey Botanical Club* 108: 305–10.

Clements, F. E., C. O. Rosendahl, and F. K. Butters. 1912. Minnesota Trees and Shrubs. *Report of the Botanical Survey IX*. Minneapolis: University of Minnesota.

Coffin, B., and L. Pfannmuller, eds. 1988. *Minnesota's endangered flora and fauna*. Minneapolis: University of Minnesota Press.

Cooper, D. T., and D. F. Van Haverbeke. 1990. *Populus deltoides*. In *Silvics of North America: 2. Hardwoods*, R. M. Burns and B. H. Honkala, tech. coords., 530–42. Agriculture Handbook 654. Washington, D.C.: USDA, Forest Service.

Cooper, W. S. 1935. *The history of the upper Mississippi River in Late Wisconsin and postglacial time*. Minneapolis: University of Minnesota Press.

Dalton, D. A., and A. W. Naylor. 1975. Studies on nitrogen fixation by *Alnus crispa*. *American Journal of Botany* 62: 76–80.

Daly, G. T. 1966. Nitrogen fixation by nodulated *Alnus rugosa*. *Canadian Journal of Botany* 44: 1607–21.

Dancik, B. P., and B. V. Barnes. 1972. Natural variation and hybridization of yellow birch and bog birch in southeast Michigan. *Silvae Genetica* 21: 1–9.

Daubenmire, R. F. 1936. The "Big Woods" of Minnesota: Its structure and relation to climate, fire, and soils. *Ecological Monographs* 6: 233–68.

Davidson, C. G., and L. M. Lenz. 1989. Experimental taxonomy of *Potentilla fruticosa*. *Canadian Journal of Botany* 67: 3520–28.

Davis, H. A., A. M. Fuller, and T. Davis. 1968a. Contributions toward the revision of the *Eubati* of eastern North America. II. *Setosi*. *Castanea* 33: 50–76.

Davis, H. A., A. M. Fuller, and T. Davis. 1968b. Contributions toward the revision of the *Eubati* of eastern North America. III. *Flagellares*. *Castanea* 33: 206–41.

Davis, H. A., A. M. Fuller, and T. Davis. 1969a. Contributions towards the revision of the *Eubati* of eastern North America. IV. *Castanea* 34: 157–79.

Davis, H. A., A. M. Fuller, and T. Davis. 1969b. Contributions towards the revision of the *Eubati* of eastern North America. V. *Arguti*. *Castanea* 34: 235–66.

Davis, H. A., A. M. Fuller, and T. Davis. 1982. Some comments on *Rubus*. *Castanea* 47: 216–19.

Del Tredici, P. 1977. The buried seeds of *Comptonia peregrina*, the sweet fern. *Bulletin of the Torrey Botanical Club* 104: 270–75.

De Steven, D. 1983. Reproductive consequences of insect seed predation in *Hamamelis virginiana*. *Ecology* 64: 89–98.

Dickinson, M. B., F. E. Putz, and C. D. Canham. 1993. Canopy gap closure in thickets of the clonal shrub, *Cornus racemosa*. *Bulletin of the Torrey Botanical Club* 120: 439–44.

Dickinson, T. A., S. Belaoussoff, R. M. Love, and M. Muniyamma. 1996. North American black-fruited hawthorns (*Crataegus* sect. *Douglasii* Loud.): 1. Variation in floral construction, breeding system correlates and their possible evolutionary significance. *Folia Geobotanica Phytotaxonomica* 31: 355–71.

Dickson, E. E., S. Kresovich, and N. F. Weeden. 1991. Isozymes in North American *Malus* (Rosaceae): Hybridization and species differentiation. *Systematic Botany* 16: 363–75.

Donoghue, M. 1981. Growth patterns in woody plants with examples from the genus *Viburnum*. *Arnoldia* 41: 2–23.

Dorn, R. D. 1975. A systematic study of *Salix* section *Cordatae* in North America. *Canadian Journal of Botany* 53: 1491–1522.

Duncan, D. P., and A. C. Hodson. 1958. Influence of the forest tent caterpillar upon forests of Minnesota. *Forest Science* 4: 71–93.

Dziuk, P. M. 1998. Buckthorn and its control. Minnesota Department of Agriculture, Pest Management Unit, Fact Sheet.

Eck, P. 1990. *The American Cranberry*. New Brunswick, N.J.: Rutgers University Press.

Eckenwalder, J. E. 1977. North American cottonwoods (*Populus*, Salicaceae) of sections Abaso and Aigeiros. *Journal of the Arnold Arboretum* 58: 193–208.

Eilers, L. J., and D. M. Roosa. 1994. The vascular plants of Iowa. Iowa City: University of Iowa Press.

Elkington, T. T. 1969. Cytotaxonomic variation in *Potentilla fruticosa* L. *New Phytologist* 68: 151–60.

Eriksson, O. 1992. Population structure and dynamics of the clonal dwarf-shrub *Linnaea borealis*. *Journal of Vegetation Science* 3: 61–68.

Evans, J. E. 1983. A literature review of management practices for multiflora rose (*Rosa multiflora*). *Natural Areas Journal* 3: 6–15.

Farrar, D. R. 2001. Exotic and invasive woody plant species in Iowa. *Journal of the Iowa Academy of Science* 108: 154–57.

Fassett, N. C. 1941. Mass collections: *Rubus odoratus* and *R. parviflorus*. *Annals of the Missouri Botanical Garden* 28: 299–374.

Fassett, N. C. 1942. Mass collections: *Diervilla lonicera*. *Bulletin of the Torrey Botanical Club* 69: 317–22.

Fernald, M. L., and A. C. Kinsey. 1943. *Edible wild plants of eastern North America*. Cornwall-on-Hudson, N.Y.: Idlewild Press.

Flint, F. F. 1957. Megasporogenesis and megagametogenesis in *Hamamelis virginiana* L. *Virginia Journal of Science* 8: 185–89.

Fulling, E. H. 1953. American witch hazel: History, nomenclature, and modern utilization. *Economic Botany* 7: 359–81.

Furlow, J. J. 1979. The systematics of the American species of *Alnus* (Betulaceae). *Rhodora* 81: 1–121, 151–248.

Furlow, J. J. 1987. The *Carpinus caroliniana* complex in North America. II. Systematics. *Systematic Botany* 12: 416–34.

Gaut, P. C., and J. N. Roberts. 1984. *Hamamelis* seed germination. *Plant Propagation* 34: 334–42.

Gauthier, S., Y. Bergeron, and J. P. Simon. 1993. Cone serotiny in jack pine: Ontogenetic, positional, and environmental effects. *Canadian Journal of Forest Research* 23: 394–401.

Gibbs, J. N. 1978. Intercontinental epidemiology of Dutch elm disease. *Annual Review of Phytopathology* 16: 287–307.

Giddings, J. L. 1962. Development of tree ring dating as an archeological aid. In *Tree growth*, ed. T. T. Kozlowski, 119–32. New York: Ronald Press.

Gilbert, E. F. 1966. Structure and development of sumac clones. *American Midland Naturalist* 75: 432–45.

Gill, C. J. 1970. The flooding tolerance of woody species: A review. *Forestry Abstracts* 31: 671–88.

Gillis, W. T. 1971. The systematics and ecology of poison-ivy and the poison-oaks (Toxicodendron, Anacardiaceae). *Rhodora* 73: 72–159; 161–237; 370–443; 465–540.

Gleason, H. A., and A. Cronquist. 1991. *Manual of vascular plants of northeastern United States and adjacent Canada*. Bronx, N.Y.: New York Botanical Garden.

Godman, R. M., and L. W. Krefting. 1960. Factors important to yellow birch establishment in Upper Michigan. *Ecology* 41: 18–28.

Grant, V. 1981. *Plant speciation*, 2nd ed. New York: Columbia University Press.

Graves, W. R. 2004. Confirmation that *Dirca* spp. (Thymelaeaceae) reproduces from rhizomes. *Rhodora* 106: 291–94.

Green, P. S. 1966. Identification of the species and hybrids in the *Lonicera tatarica* complex. *Journal of the Arnold Arboretum* 47: 75–88.

Green, S. B. 1898. *Forestry in Minnesota*. Delano, Minn.: Eagle Printing Co.

Grigal, D. F., and L. F. Ohmann. 1975. Classification, description, and dynamics of upland plant communities within a Minnesota wilderness area. *Ecological Monographs* 45: 389–407.

Grigson, G. 1955. *The Englishman's Flora*. Phoenix House, London.

Hale, C. M. 1996. "Comparison of structural and compositional characteristics and coarse woody debris dynamics in old growth versus mature hardwood forests of Minnesota, USA." MS thesis, University of Minnesota, St. Paul.

Hall, I. V., L. E. Aalders, and C. F. Everett. 1976. The biology of Canadian weeds 16. *Comptonia peregrina* (L.) Coult. *Canadian Journal of Plant Science* 56: 147–56.

Hall, I. V., L. E. Aalders, N. L. Nickerson, and S. P. Vander Kloet. 1979. The biological flora of Canada. 1. *Vaccinium angustifolium* Ait., sweet lowbush blueberry. *Canadian Field-Naturalist* 93: 415–30.

Hamer, D. 1996. Buffaloberry [*Shepherdia canadensis* (L.) Nutt.] fruit production in fire-successional bear feeding sites. *Journal of Range Management* 49: 520–29.

Hardig, T. M., S. J. Brunsfeld, R. S. Fritz, M. Morgan, and C. M. Orians. 2000. Morphological and molecular evidence for hybridization and introgression in a willow (*Salix*) hybrid zone. *Molecular Ecology* 9: 9–24.

Hardin, J. W., and L. L. Phillips. 1985. Hybridization in eastern North American *Rhus* (Anacardiaceae). *Association of Southeastern Biologists Bulletin* 32: 99–106.

Harlow, W. M., E. S. Harrar, J. W. Hardin, and F. M. White. 1991. *Textbook of Dendrology*, 7th ed. New York: McGraw-Hill.

Harper, K. A. 1995. Effect of expanding clones of *Gaylussacia baccata* (black huckleberry) on species composition in sandplain grassland on Nantucket Island, Massachusetts. *Bulletin of the Torrey Botanical Club* 122: 124–33.

Haugen, D. E., and M. E. Mielke. 2002. *Minnesota forest resources*. Resource Bulletin NC-205. St. Paul, Minn.: USDA Forest Service.

Hawksworth, F. G., and D. Weins. 1972. *Biology and classification of dwarf mistletoes (Arceuthobium)*. Handbook No. 401. Washington, D.C.: USDA.

Heidorn, R. 1991. Vegetation management guideline: Exotic buckthorns: Common buckthorn (*Rhamnus cathartica* L.), glossy buckthorn (*Rhamnus frangula* L.), Dahurian buckthorn (*Rhamnus davurica* Pall.). *Natural Areas Journal* 11: 216–17.

Heinselman, M. L. 1970. Landscape evolution, peatland types, and the environment in the Lake Agassiz

Peatlands Natural Area, Minnesota. *Ecological Monographs* 40: 235–61.

Heinselman, M. L. 1973. Fire in the virgin forests of the Boundary Waters Canoe Area, Minnesota. *Quaternary Research* 3: 329–82.

Hendrickson, P. A. 1997. The wild lingonberry (*Vaccinium vitis-idaea* L. var. *minus* Lodd.) industry in North America. *Acta Horticulturae* 446: 47–48.

Hepting, G. H. 1971. *Diseases of forest and shade trees of the United States*. Agriculture Handbook Number 386. USDA, Forest Service.

Hicks, D. J., and D. L. Hustin. 1989. Response of *Hamamelis virginiana* L. to canopy gaps in a Pennsylvania oak forest. *American Midland Naturalist* 121: 200–204.

Hils, M. H. 1993. *Taxus*. In *Flora of North America*, vol. 2, ed. Flora of North America Editorial Committee. New York: Oxford University Press.

Hodgdon, A. R., and F. Steele. 1966. *Rubus* subgenus *Eubatus* in New England: A conspectus. *Rhodora* 68: 474–513.

Holman, K. 1987. Stop oak wilt! *Minnesota Horticulturist* 115: 102–3.

Holmgren, P. K., N. H. Holmgren, and L. C. Bernett. 1990. *Index Herbariorum Part I: The Herbaria of the World*, 8th edition. Bronx, N.Y.: New York Botanical Garden.

Hornfeldt, C. S., and J. E. Collins. 1990. Toxicity of nightshade berries. *Clinical Toxicology* 28: 185–92.

Hultén, E. 1968. *Flora of Alaska and neighboring territories*. Stanford, Calif.: Stanford University Press.

Hultén, E. 1970. *The Circumpolar Plants. II. Dicotyledons*. Band 13. Nr. 1.

Hultén, E. 1971. *The Circumpolar Plants. II. Dicotyledons*. Fjärde Serien. Band 13. Nr 1. Uppsala, Sweden: Almquist and Wiksells.

Isely, D. 1998. *Native and naturalized leguminosae (Fabaceae) of the United States*. Provo, Utah: Brigham Young University.

Isely, D., and F. J. Peabody. 1984. *Robinia* (Leguminosae: Papilionoidea). *Castanea* 49: 187–202.

Johnson, A. G., and S. S. Pauley. 1967. Rare native trees of Minnesota. *Minnesota Science* 23: 27–31.

Johnson, A. M. 1927. The bitternut hickory, *Carya cordiformis*, in northern Minnesota. *American Journal of Botany* 14: 49–51.

Kartesz, J. T., and K. N. Gandhi. 1994. Nomenclatural notes for the North American Flora. XIII. *Phytologia* 76: 441–57.

Katovich, S., and R. Haack. 1991. *Gypsy moth in the northern hardwood forest*. Northern Hardwood Notes 7.10. St. Paul, Minn.: USDA, Forest Service, North Central Forest Experiment Station.

Kelly, P. E., E. R. Cook, and D. W. Larson. 1994. A 1,397-year tree-ring chronology of *Thuja occidentalis*

from cliff faces of the Niagara Escarpment, southern Ontario, Canada. *Canadian Journal of Forest Research* 24: 1049–57.

Klingman, D. L., D. E. Davis, E. L. Knake, W. B. McHenry, J. A. Meade, and R. E. Stewart. 1983. *Poison ivy, poison oak, and poison sumac: Identification, poisoning, and control*. Washington, D.C.: U.S. Department of Agriculture.

Knopf, F. L., and T. E. Olson. 1984. Naturalization of Russian-olive: Implications for Rocky Mountain wildlife. *Wildlife Society Bulletin* 12: 289–98.

Koevenig, J. L. 1976. Effect of climate, soil physiography, and seed germination on the distribution of river birch (*Betula nigra*). *Rhodora* 78: 420–37.

Korpelainen, H. 1994. Sex ratios and resource allocation among sexually reproducing plants of *Rubus chamaemorus*. *Annals of Botany* 74: 627–32.

Kron, K. A., and W. S. Judd. 1990. Phylogenetic relationships within the Rhodoreae (Ericaceae) with specific comments on the placement of *Ledum*. *Systematic Botany* 15: 57–68.

Lakela, O. 1954. The occurrence of *Rubus chamaemorus* in Minnesota. *Rhodora* 56: 272–73.

Lakela, O. 1965. *A flora of northeastern Minnesota*. Minneapolis: University of Minnesota Press.

Larson, D. W. 1997. Dendroecological potential of *Juniperus virginiana* L. growing on cliffs in western Virginia. *Banisteria* 10: 13–18.

Lawson, E. L. 1942. What happened to the hemlock? *Conservation Volunteer* Jan.: 64–66.

Leatherberry, E. C., I. S. Spencer Jr., T. L. Schmidt, and M. R. Carroll. 1995. An analysis of Minnesota's Fifth Forest Resources Inventory, 1990. *Resources Bulletin NC-165*. St. Paul, Minn.: USDA, Forest Service, North Central Forest Experiment Station.

Lee, K. C., and R. W. Campbell. 1969. Nature and occurrence of juglone in *Juglans nigra* L. *Hortscience* 4: 297–98.

Lei, T. T., and M. J. Lechowicz. 1990. Shade adaptation and shade tolerance in saplings of 3 *Acer* species from eastern North America. *Oecologia* 84: 224–28.

Lewis, W. H. 1959. A monograph of the genus *Rosa* in North America. I. *R. acicularis*. *Brittonia* 10: 1–24.

Lewis, W. H. 1962. Monograph of *Rosa* in North America. IV. *R. ×dulcissima*. *Brittonia* 14: 65–71.

Little. E. L. 1971. *Atlas of United States trees: Vol. 1. Conifers and important hardwoods*. Misc. publ. 1146. Washington, D.C.: USDA, Forest Service.

Little, E. L. 1977. *Atlas of United States trees. 4. Minor eastern hardwoods*. Misc. Publ. No. 1342. Washington, D.C.: USDA, Forest Service.

Little, E. L., Jr., and S. S. Pauley. 1958. A natural hybrid between black and white spruce in Minnesota. *American Midland Naturalist* 60: 202–11.

Looman, J. 1984. The biological flora of Canada. 4. *Shepherdia argentea* (Pursh) Nutt. *Canadian Field-Naturalist* 98: 231–44.

Löve, A. 1954. Cytotaxonomic remarks on some American species of circumpolar taxa. *Svensk Botanisk Tidskrift* 48: 211–32.

Löve, D. 1960. The red-fruited crowberries in North America. *Rhodora* 62: 265–92.

Lovell, J. H., and H. B. Lovell. 1934. The pollination of *Kalmia angustifolia*. *Rhodora* 36: 25–28.

Luby, J. J. 1991. Breeding cold-hardy fruit crops in Minnesota. *HortScience* 26: 507–12.

Luken, J. D., and J. W. Thieret. 1995. Amur honeysuckle (*Lonicera maackii*; Caprifoliaceae): Its ascent, decline, and fall. *Sida* 16: 479–503.

Lutz, H. J. 1943. Injuries to trees caused by *Celastrus* and *Vitis*. *Bulletin of the Torrey Botanical Club* 70: 436–39.

Lutz, H. J. 1958. Observations on "diamond willow" with particular reference to its occurrence in Alaska. *American Midland Naturalist* 60: 176–85.

Maeglin, R. R., and L. F. Ohmann. 1973. Boxelder (*Acer negundo*): A review and commentary. *Bulletin of the Torrey Botanical Club* 100: 357–63.

Mangaly, J. K. 1968. A cytotaxonomic study of the herbaceous species of *Smilax*: Section *Coprosmanthus*. *Rhodora* 70: 55–82; 247–73.

Marion, C., and G. Houle. 1996. No differential consequences of reproduction according to sex in *Juniperus communis* var. *depressa* (Cupressaceae). *American Journal of Botany* 83: 480–88.

Marks, P. L. 1974. The role of pin cherry (*Prunus pensylvanica* L.) in the maintenance of stability in northern hardwood ecosystems. *Ecological Monographs* 44: 73–88.

Marschner, F. J. 1974. The original vegetation of Minnesota (map scale 1: 500,000). St. Paul, MN: USDA Forest Service, North Central Forest Experiment Station.

Martin, A. C., H. S. Zim, and A. L. Nelson. 1951. *American wildlife plants*. New York: McGraw-Hill.

Matlack, G. R., D. J. Gibson, and R. E. Good. 1993. Regeneration of the shrub *Gaylussacia baccata* and associated species after low-intensity fire in an Atlantic coastal plain forest. *American Journal of Botany* 80: 119–26.

McAndrews, J. H. 1965. Postglacial history of prairie, savanna, and forest in northwestern Minnesota. *Memoirs of the Torrey Botanical Club* 22: 1–68.

McKay, S. M. 1973. "A biosystematic study of the genus" *Amelanchier* in Ontario. MS thesis, University of Toronto.

McLeod, K. W., and J. K. McPherson. 1973. Factors limiting the distribution of *Salix nigra*. *Bulletin of the Torrey Botanical Club* 100: 102–10.

Meikle, R. D. 1984. *Willows and poplars of Great Britain and Ireland*. London: Botanical Society of the British Isles.

Meyer, F. G. 1997. Hamamelidaceae. In *Flora of North America*, vol. 3, ed. Flora of North America Editorial Committee. New York: Oxford University Press.

Miller, D. R., J. W. Kimmey, and M. E. Fowler. 1959. *White pine blister rust*. Forest Pest Leaflet 36, USDA, Forest Service.

Mills, E. L., J. H. Leach, J. T. Carlton, and C. L. Secor. 1994. Exotic species and the integrity of the Great Lakes. *BioScience* 44: 666–76.

Minnesota Department of Conservation. 1932–52. Biennial Reports.

Minnesota Department of Natural Resources. 1993. *Minnesota forest health report: 1992*. St. Paul: Minnesota Department of Natural Resources, Division of Forestry.

Minnesota Department of Natural Resources. 2003. *Field guide to the native plant communities of Minnesota: The Laurentian Mixed Forest Province*. St. Paul: Minnesota Department of Natural Resources, Ecological Land Classification Program, Minnesota County Biological Survey, and Natural Heritage and Nongame Research Program.

Mirick, S., and J. A. Quinn. 1981. Some observations on the reproductive biology of *Gaultheria procumbens* (Ericaceae). *American Journal of Botany* 68: 1298–305.

Mladendoff, D. J. 1993. Eastern hemlock regeneration and deer browsing in the northern Great Lakes region: A reexamination and model simulation. *Conservation Biology* 7: 889–900.

Moe, S., and H. Pellett. 1986. Breeding of cold hardy azaleas in the land of the Northern Lights. *Journal of the American Rhododendron Society* 40: 158–61.

Moore, D. M., J. B. Harborne, and C. A. Williams. 1970. Chemotaxonomy, variation and geographical distribution of the Empetraceae. *Botany Journal of the Linnean Society* 63: 277–93.

Moore, M. O. 1991. Classification and systematics of eastern North American *Vitis* L. (Vitaceae) north of Mexico. *Sida* 14: 339–67.

Moriarty, J. J. 1998. The trouble with backyard buckthorn. *Minnesota Volunteer* 61: 43–49.

Morley, T. 1969. *Spring flora of Minnesota*. Minneapolis: University of Minnesota Press.

Muniyamma, M., and J. B. Phipps. 1979a. Cytological proof of apomixis in *Crataegus* (Rosaceae). *American Journal of Botany* 66: 149–55.

Muniyamma, M., and J. B. Phipps. 1979b. Meiosis and polyploidy in Ontario species of *Crataegus* in relation to their systematics. *Canadian Journal of Genetics and Cytology* 21: 231–41.

Muniyamma, M., and J. B. Phipps. 1984. Studies in *Crataegus*. XI. Further cytological evidence for the occurrence of apomixis in North American hawthorns. *Canadian Journal of Botany* 62: 2316–24.

Muniyamma, M., and J. B. Phipps. 1985. Studies in *Crataegus*. XII. Cytological evidence for sexuality in some diploid and tetraploid species of North American hawthorns. *Canadian Journal of Botany* 63: 1319–24.

Musselman, L. J. 1968. Asexual reproduction in the burning bush, *Euonymus atropurpureus*. *Michigan Botanist* 7: 60–61.

Nielsen, E. L. 1939. A taxonomic study of the genus *Amelanchier* in Minnesota. *American Midland Naturalist* 22: 160–206.

Niering, W. A., G. D. Dreyer, F. E. Egler, and J. P. Anderson Jr. 1986. Stability of a *Viburnum lentago* shrub community after 30 years. *Bulletin of the Torrey Botanical Club* 113: 23–27.

Nixon, K. C. 1997. *Quercus*. In *Flora of North America*, vol. 3, ed. Flora of North America Editorial Committee, 445–506. New York: Oxford University Press.

Ohman, L. F., H. O. Batzer, R. R. Buech, D. C. Lothner, D. A. Perala, S. L. Schipper Jr., and E. S. Verry. 1978. *Some harvest options and their consequences for the aspen, birch, and associated conifer forest types of the Lake States*. USDA Forest Service, General Technical Report NC-48.

Ohman, L. F., and R. R. Ream. 1971. Wilderness ecology: Virgin plant communities of the Boundary Waters Canoe Area. St. Paul: North Central Forest Experiment Station.

Ojakangas, R. W., and C. L. Matsch. 1982. *Minnesota's geology*. Minneapolis: University of Minnesota Press.

Ostry, M.E., M. E. Mielke, and R. L. Anderson. 1996. How to identify butternut canker and manage butternut trees. HT-70. St. Paul, Minn.: USDA Forest Service, North Central Forest Experiment Station.

Ownbey, G. B., and T. Morley. 1991. *Vascular plants of Minnesota: A checklist and atlas*. Minneapolis: University of Minnesota Press.

Packer, J. G., and K. E. Denford. 1974. A contribution to the taxonomy of *Arctostaphylos uva-ursi*. *Canadian Journal of Botany* 52: 743–53.

Parker, J. 1969. Further studies of drought resistance in woody plants. *Botanical Review* 35: 317–71.

Pellett, H., and F. De Vos. 1978. *Northern Lights, new winter hardy azalea hybrids*. Misc. Report, Minnesota Agricultural Experiment Station 155.

Pelton, J. 1953. Studies on the life-history of *Symphoricarpos occidentalis* Hook. in Minnesota. *Ecological Monographs* 23: 17–39.

Petraborg, W. H. 1969. Regeneration of white cedar in northern swamps. *Journal of the Minnesota Academy of Science* 36: 20–22.

Phipps, J. B., and M. Muniyamma. 1980. A taxonomic revision of *Crataegus* (Rosaceae) in Ontario. *Canadian Journal of Botany* 58: 1621–99.

Phipps, J. B., R. J. O'Kennon, and R. W. Lance. 2003. *Hawthorns and medlars*. Portland, Ore.: Timber Press.

Phipps, J. B., K. R. Robertson, P. G. Smith, and J. R. Rohrer. 1990. A checklist of the subfamily Maloideae (Rosaceae). *Canadian Journal of Botany* 68: 2209–69.

Pokorny, J. 1999. *How to identify, prevent, and control oak wilt*. NA-FR-01–99. USDA, Forest Service.

Pooler, M. R., R. L. Dix, and J. Feely. 2002. Interspecific hybridizations between the native bittersweet, *Celastrus scandens*, and the introduced invasive species, *C. orbiculatus*. *Southeastern Naturalist* 1: 69–76.

Post, T. W., E. McCloskey, and K. F. Klick. 1989. Two-year study of fire effects on *Rhamnus frangula* L. *Natural Areas Journal* 9: 175–76.

Pringle, J. S. 1971. Taxonomy and distribution of *Clematis*, sect. *Atragene* (Ranunculaceae), in North America. *Brittonia* 23: 361–93.

Pringle, J. S. 1997. *Clematis*. In *Flora of North America*, vol. 3, ed. Flora of North America Editorial Committee. New York: Oxford University Press.

Putz, F. E., and H. A. Mooney, eds. 1991. *The Biology of Vines*. New York: Cambridge University Press.

Randall, J. M., and J. Marinelli, eds. 1996. *Invasive plants: Weeds of the global garden*. Brooklyn, N.Y.: Brooklyn Botanic Garden.

Reader, R. J. 1977. Bog ericad flowers: Self-incompatibility and relative attractiveness to bees. *Canadian Journal of Botany* 55: 2279–87.

Records, P. C. 1913. *Tree planting for shelter in Minnesota*. Forest Service Bulletin No. 1; Minnesota Forestry Board.

Rehder, A. 1940. *Manual of cultivated trees and shrubs hardy in North America*. New York: MacMillan.

Renlund, D. W. 1971. *Forest pest conditions in Wisconsin*. Wisconsin Department of Natural Resources Annual Report for 1971.

Ritter, L. B. 1941. *White pine blister rust control in Minnesota*. USDA, Educational Pamphlet No. 4.

Rodriguez-Barrueco, C. 1968. The occurrence of nitrogen-fixing root nodules on nonleguminous plants. *Botanical Journal of the Linnean Society* 62: 77–84.

Roe, E. I. 1957. *Silvical characteristics of tamarack*. Lake States Forest Experiment Station, Station Paper No. 52.

Rohrer, J. R. 2000. The sand cherry in Wisconsin and neighboring states. *Michigan Botanist* 39: 59–69.

Rosatti, T. J. 1987. Field and garden studies of *Arctostaphylos uva-ursi* (Ericaceae) in North America. *Systematic Botany* 12: 67–77.

Rosendahl, C. O. 1955. *Trees and shrubs of the Upper Midwest*. Minneapolis: University of Minnesota Press.

Rydberg, P. A. 1898. *Sibbaldiopsis. Memoirs from the Department of Botany of Columbia University* 2:187.

Schoen, D. J. 1977. Floral biology of *Diervilla lonicera* (Caprifoliaceae). *Bulletin of the Torrey Botanical Club* 104: 234–40.

Shafroth, P. B., M. L. Scott, J. M. Friedman, and R. D. Laven. 1994. Establishment, sex structure and breeding system of an exotic riparian willow, *Salix ×rubens. American Midland Naturalist* 132: 159–72.

Sherald, J. L., F. S. Santamour Jr., R. K. Hajela, N. Hajela, and M. B. Sticklen. 1994. A Dutch elm disease resistant triploid elm. *Canadian Journal of Forest Research* 24: 647–653.

Sherman-Broyles, S. L. 1997. *Ulmus.* In *Flora of North America*, vol. 3, ed. Flora of North America Editorial Committee. New York: Oxford University Press.

Sinnott, Q. P. 1985. A revision of *Ribes* L. subg. *Grossularia* (Mill.) Pers. sect. *Grossularia* (Mill.) Nutt. (*Grossulariaceae*) in North America. *Rhodora* 87: 189–286.

Skene, K. R., J. I. Sprent, J. A. Raven, and L. Herdman. 2000. Biological flora of the British Isles: *Myrica gale* L. *Journal of Ecology* 88: 1079–94.

Smith, P. G., and J. B. Phipps. 1988a. Studies in *Crataegus* (Rosaceae, Maloideae), XIX. Breeding behavior in Ontario *Crataegus* series *Rotundifoliae. Canadian Journal of Botany* 66: 1914–23.

Smith, P. G., and J. B. Phipps. 1988b. Studies in *Crataegus* (Rosaceae, Maloideae), XV. Patterns of morphometric variation in *Crataegus* series *Rotundifoliae* in Ontario. *Systematic Botany* 13: 97–106.

Soper, J. H., and M. L. Heimburger. 1982. *Shrubs of Ontario.* Toronto: Royal Ontario Museum.

Soper, J. H., and E. G. Voss. 1964. Black crowberry in the Lake Superior Region. *Michigan Botanist* 3: 35–38.

Sork, V. L., and J. Bramble. 1993. Ecology of mast-fruiting in three species of North American deciduous oaks. *Ecology* 74: 528–41.

Stearns, F. 1951. The composition of the sugar maple-hemlock-yellow birch association in northern Wisconsin. *Ecology* 32: 245–65.

Stone, D. E. 1997. Juglandaceae. In *Flora of North America*, vol. 3, ed. Flora of North America Editorial Committee. New York: Oxford University Press.

Tappeiner, J. C. 1971. Invasion and development of beaked hazel in red pine stands in northern Minnesota. *Ecology* 52: 514–19.

Tester, J. R. 1995. *Minnesota's natural heritage: An ecological perspective.* Minneapolis: University of Minnesota Press.

Tester, J. R. 1996. Effects of fire frequency on plant species in oak savanna in east-central Minnesota. *Bulletin of the Torrey Botanical Club* 123: 303–8.

Tietmeyer, A., and P. Bristol. 2002. Potential invasibility of crabapple species and cultivars in the Chicago Region. *Malus.* 16:3–11.

U.S. Surveyor General. 1847–1908. *Field notes: Township and exterior subdivision lines.* Minnesota State Archives, 57.J.5.9B–57.J.8.8F. St. Paul: Minnesota Historical Society.

Upham, W. 1884. Catalogue of the flora of Minnesota. Part VI of the annual report of progress for the year 1883. The Geological and Natural History Survey of Minnesota.

Upham, W. 1969. *Minnesota geographic names.* St. Paul: Minnesota Historical Society.

Vander Kloet, S. P. 1983. The taxonomy of *Vaccinium* § *Oxycoccus. Rhodora* 85: 1–43.

Vander Kloet, S. P. 1988. The genus *Vaccinium* in North America. Research Branch, Agriculture Canada, Publication 1828.

Vander Kloet, S. P., and I. V. Hall. 1981. The biological flora of Canada. 2. *Vaccinium myrtilloides* Michx., velvet-leaf blueberry. *Canadian Field-naturalist* 95: 329–45.

Viereck, L. A. 1970. Forest succession and soil development adjacent to the Chena River in interior Alaska. *Arctic and Alpine Research* 2: 1–26.

Vincent, A. B. 1965. Black spruce: A review of its silvics, ecology, and silviculture. Ottawa: Ministry of Forestry.

Voss, E. G. 1983. Errata (letter to the editor). *Castanea* 48: 57–58.

Voss, E. G. 1985. *Michigan flora.* 3 vols. Bulletin 59. Bloomfield Hills, Mich.: Cranbrook Institute of Science.

Weaver, J. E. 1954. *North American prairie.* Lincoln, Neb.: Johnson Publishing Company.

Weaver, J. E., and J. Kramer. 1932. Root system of *Quercus macrocarpa* in relation to the invasion of prairie. *Botanical Gazette* 94: 51–85.

Webb, S. L., et al. 2000. The myth of the resilient forest: Case study of the invasive Norway maple (*Acer platanoides*). *Rhodora* 102: 332–54.

Wetter, M. A., T. S. Cochrane, M. R. Black, H. H. Iltis, and P. E. Berry. 2001. Checklist of the vascular plants of Wisconsin. Technical Bulletin No. 192. Wisconsin Department of Natural Resources.

Wheeler, W. A. 1899. Field book on file in the library of the herbarium of the University of Minnesota, St. Paul.

Whitney, G. G. 1982. The productivity and carbohydrate economy of a developing stand of *Rubus idaeus. Canadian Journal of Botany* 60: 2697–703.

Widrlechner, M. P. 1998. The genus *Rubus* L. in Iowa. *Castanea* 63: 415–65.

Wilbur, R. L. 1964. A revision of the dwarf species of *Amorpha* (Leguminosae). *Journal of the Elisha Mitchell Scientific Society* 80: 51–65.

Wilson, J. S. 1964. Variation of three taxonomic complexes of the genus *Cornus* in eastern United States. *Transactions of the Kansas Academy of Science* 67: 747–817.

Winchell, N. H. 1875. Notes on the Big Woods. *Minnesota State Horticultural Society* 3: 47–50.

Winchell, N. H. 1876. *The geological and natural history survey of Minnesota*. The fourth annual report for the year 1875. St. Paul, Minn.: Pioneer-Press Company.

Wood, C. E., Jr. 1961. The genera of Ericaceae in the southeastern United States. *Journal of the Arnold Arboretum* 42: 58–60.

Woods, K. D. 1993. Effects of invasion by *Lonicera tatarica* L. on herbs and tree seedlings in four New England forests. *American Midland Naturalist* 130: 62–74.

Wovcha, D. S., B. C. Delaney, G. E. Nordquist. 1995. *Minnesota's St. Croix River valley and Anoka Sandplain: A guide to native habitats*. Minneapolis: University of Minnesota Press.

Wright, H. A., and A. W. Bailey. 1982. *Fire Ecology, United States and Southern Canada*. New York: John Wiley and Sons.

Wright, H. E., Jr. 1972. Quaternary history of Minnesota. In *Geology of Minnesota: A centennial volume*, ed. P. K. Sims and G. B. Morey, eds., 515–47. St. Paul: Minnesota Geological Survey, University of Minnesota.

Young, J. A., and C. G. Young, 1992. *Seeds of woody plants in North America*. Portland, Ore.: Dioscorides Press.

Young, L. J. 1934. The growth of *Ostrya virginiana*. *Michigan Academy of Science, Arts, and Letters* 19: 341–44.

Young, S. B. 1970. On the taxonomy and distribution of *Vaccinium uliginosum*. *Rhodora* 72: 439–59.

Index

Welby R. Smith is a botanist for the Division of Ecological Services at the Minnesota Department of Natural Resources. He is the author of *Orchids of Minnesota* and a contributor to *Minnesota's Endangered Flora and Fauna*, both published by the University of Minnesota Press.